TINKLING CYMBALS
AND SOUNDING BRASS

The Collected Works of Hugh Nibley

Volumes published to date:

Old Testament and Related Studies

Enoch the Prophet

The World and the Prophets

Mormonism and Early Christianity

Lehi in the Desert/The World of the Jaredites/There Were Jaredites

An Approach to the Book of Mormon

Since Cumorah

The Prophetic Book of Mormon

Approaching Zion

The Ancient State

Tinkling Cymbals and Sounding Brass

The Collected Works of Hugh Nibley: Volume 11
Joseph Smith and the Restored Gospel

TINKLING CYMBALS AND SOUNDING BRASS
The Art of Telling Tales about Joseph Smith and Brigham Young

Hugh Nibley

Edited by
David J. Whittaker

Deseret Book Company
Salt Lake City, Utah
and
Foundation for Ancient Research and Mormon Studies
Provo, Utah

Library of Congress Cataloging-in-Publication Data

Nibley, Hugh, 1910–
   Tinkling cymbals and sounding brass : the art of telling tales about Joseph Smith and Brigham Young / Hugh Nibley ; edited by David Whittaker.
     p. cm. — (The collected works of Hugh Nibley ; v. 11)
   Includes index.
   ISBN 0-87579-516-1
   1. Mormon Church—Apologetic works. 2. Church of Jesus Christ of Latter-day Saints—Apologetic works. 3. Mormon Church—Controversial literature—History and criticism. 4. Church of Jesus Christ of Latter-day Saints—Controversial literature—History and criticism. I. Whittaker, David J. II. Title. III. Series: Nibley, Hugh, 1910–   Works. 1986 ; v. 11.
BX8635.5.N54   1991
289.3—dc20   91-11539
                                             CIP

Printed in the United States of America

10   9   8   7   6   5   4   3   2   1

Contents

v

Foreword:
Responding to the Critics

Even before the Church was organized in April 1830, Joseph Smith's prophetic claims were ridiculed and dismissed. Such attacks were frequent and harsh in the earliest days of the Church, and they have not abated since. At the same time, responding to critics is also a long-standing Latter-day Saint tradition. To be properly understood, the essays in this volume of the *Collected Works of Hugh Nibley* must be viewed in the context of that tradition.

When the first anti-Mormon pamphlets and books began to appear, the Mormon response was to send missionaries to preach and testify as individuals in an effort to counter the falsehoods being circulated against them.[1] Such an approach was appropriate as long as missionaries remained in the rural hamlets and small villages of New England, but when proselyting efforts entered the larger cities, oral responses were no longer sufficient to counter the mass-marketing techniques of tract societies or the accounts appearing in newspapers with large circulations available to urban and cosmopolitan audiences. Thus, Mormon missionaries were forced by changing circumstances to use the written word to defend themselves and explain their message. The Church was eight years old when the first specific reply to an anti-Mormon attack was published by Parley P. Pratt in New York City.[2]

Thereafter, these works were regularly issued by the Latter-day Saint press. Pratt authored a number of replies

to attacks that had been published in England during the
early years of the British Mission, and many of his tracts
established the arguments and patterns that subsequent
Latter-day Saint writers, including his brother Orson, followed.[3] He finally concluded that he had responded to all
the serious issues and thereafter refused to dignify these
works further by additional rejoinders,[4] but critics continued to repeat the same old charges, most of which focused
on Joseph Smith's character or on the Book of Mormon.

This critical literature circulated throughout the British
Empire in the nineteenth century, and Mormon missionaries met it in South Africa, India, and Australia, as well
as in the United States.[5] While many of these tracts were
produced for local consumption, they all reprinted or repeated the early arguments that often circulated in garbled
form. Extant missionary journals express dismay that such
rubbish was so readily accepted by the public. Most came
to feel, like Brigham Young, that it was best to ignore the
malicious stories constantly circulating about him. He explained his approach in a letter to Jefferson Davis:

> I am often made aware of the utter uselessness, and
> folly of seeking to vindicate my character, from such foul
> aspersions as are occasionally raised against me; for the
> simple fact, that although, the foul aspersion can be
> bruited far and wide, held to the fluttering breeze by
> every press, and rolled as a sweet morsel under every
> tongue, yet when the vile slander is fairly refuted, and
> truth appears in the most incontestable manner, it is
> permitted to lie quietly upon the shelf to slumber the
> sleep of death, or if by chance, it should get published
> in some obscure nook or corner of this great Republic,
> be most religiously suppressed, as though in fear that
> the truth should be known and believed.[6]

But as a sagacious leader, Brigham Young also knew
that public attacks on the institution could and did affect
its missionary work and its ability to accomplish its divine

mission. He therefore encouraged efforts to spread and explain the gospel; however, he did little to correct the developing negative image of the Church, especially following the public announcement of plural marriage in August 1852. The establishment of Mormon publications in strategic locations throughout the United States during this period seems to reflect President Young's concerns about the public perceptions of the Church's doctrines,[7] but they did little to counter the growing use of the negative stereotypes used by the critics in their discussions of the Mormons.[8] From our contemporary perspective President Young's approach allowed the critical images to go unchallenged and therefore to become more acceptable explanations in the popular prints. In 1877 President Young, in a letter to a missionary son, summarized his general approach to these matters:

> If, when declaring the word of truth, you are attacked by the wicked, do not condescend to argue with them, much less to retaliate. Do not attempt to "repay them in their own coin," to use an old English adage; such is below the dignity of your calling. Recrimination proves no truth; it enlightens no man's mind, but it is one of the weapons used by the adversary to produce hatred and malice in the hearts of mankind, and should never be indulged in by a Latter-day Saint. When you may be assailed, heed it not, bear your testimony to the great work the Lord is doing on the earth, proclaim the truth in meekness, and if they will not listen, leave them to their own folly. We are not called to cavil with the world. Some of my brethren have felt as though I ought to answer all the falsehoods that have been put in circulation during the last few months against the Latter-day Saints, and which have swept over this nation like a flood. I have said to them, "Brethren, I have lived on this earth longer than most of you, and have perhaps a little more experience. When you get to be as old as I am you will learn to trust in God. This is His work, and

He will take care of it. If He does not, we cannot." And
in this faith I am already fully justified, as our enemies
have gone to such lengths that their stories are dese-
crated [discredited], they have missed the mark they shot
at, and have not accomplished the end for which they
set out. Without our help God has made them the instruments of manifesting their own folly and wickedness. So will it always be if we put our trust in Him.[9]

During this same time, George Q. Cannon came to see
the importance of effective public relations, a lesson that
he eventually drew upon in the editorials he authored in
a number of eastern newspapers, as well as through
George Q. Cannon and Sons, his own publishing house.[10]
But even Cannon's approach became more focused on internal consumption and thus concentrated on educating
the youth of the Church rather than correcting the unfavorable perceptions that were gaining a national audience
during this period. When he sold his establishment to the
Church, it was renamed the Deseret Book Company. It
remains a publishing arm of the Church.

The intense anti-polygamy crusade of the late nineteenth century also encouraged Church defensive efforts
further, as a positive public image seemed even more important in the era of aggressive anti-Mormon agitation and
yellow journalism. As the subject of many dime novels in
the late nineteenth and early twentieth centuries, Mormonism was seldom treated fairly or seriously. Themes of
sensuality, vengeance, and even murder ran through the
various novels and even in the more serious histories produced during this period. Authors learned that a racy Mormon theme would sell. In fact, so pervasive were the images they created that they continue to shape the public
image of the Church and its members.[11] The acquiring of
Church historic sites, the establishment of Church Bureaus
of Information, and the instituting of the Mormon Tabernacle Choir were early twentieth-century efforts to allow
Mormons to tell their own story to a broader audience.[12]

Mormon defenders such as B. H. Roberts authored various replies and histories in this period, seeking to explain Mormonism to a generation that had been saturated with the negative reports.[13] The advent of the motion picture era increased the opportunities for both the Church and its critics to expand their respective activities.[14]

In spite of the seeming "respectability" that has come to the Church in the twentieth century, anti-Mormon literature has increased in size and virulence. Well over 200 book-length attacks have appeared since 1945, and there is little evidence this flood will abate, in spite of a number of competent responses to such arguments and authors.[15]

The religious claims of Joseph Smith are such that it is almost impossible to be entirely neutral about them, whatever the pretense of the author. A review of the criticism and invective issued during the Prophet's lifetime suggests that almost every charge, moral and otherwise, that could be made against him was made while he was yet alive. If we add the name of Brigham Young to the list, very few attacks that have been made on the Church and its leaders were not in print by 1877, the year President Young died. Thus the foundational evidence and arguments against the Joseph Smith story were a product of the first generation of critics. This fact lies at the heart of Hugh Nibley's analysis of anti-Mormon literature, most of which has been gathered into this volume.[16]

Trained in history and interested in classical rhetoric, Hugh Nibley brings a broad perspective to his study of the early writings critical of the Latter-day Saint movement. His knowledge of language and history has given him a particular advantage in studying texts. First, his approach is historical. He shows that in the nineteenth century, the core anti-Mormon writing suffered from geographical distance (few authors came to see for themselves), and that in the twentieth century it has suffered from historical distance (few authors have consulted the available original sources). Secondly, he shows how distorted even the Mormon accounts of their own origins become in the jumbled and confused works of the critics. Third, he shows that most anti-Mormon writing suffers from a ghastly inbreeding and that much of what continues to pass for good history is just a rehash of the old arguments. Finally, he sees that the heart of much of this critical work has not focused on the topics and subjects of Latter-day Saint history but rather is aimed at the claim to modern revelation which most anti-Mormon authors simply reject out of hand.

In his treatments of the flaws of the works of those critical of the Church, Hugh Nibley's sense of humor, combined with a biting satire, is often evident.[17] Because of this, he has been dismissed by some as flippant. His style can be a problem if the reader does not penetrate to the heart of the issues at hand. Satire in the hands of someone like Hugh Nibley, weary as he is with the poor logic and the uncritical acceptance of the undependable sources upon which so many anti-Mormon works are built, can reveal that the anti-Mormon emperor is not after all, wearing any clothes. And since the cool, dispassionate approach taken by Latter-day Saints such as the Pratt brothers, George Q. Cannon, B. H. Roberts, Francis Kirkham, and others for over a century had not been heeded, Nibley opted to invoke some of the critics' own rhetorical standbys, such as ridicule and caricature. His essay "How to Write an Anti-Mormon Book" is an especially useful summary of the whole genre, and it illustrates well Nibley's own approach to these attacks.[18]

While Nibley has been somewhat concerned with anti-Mormon literature throughout his career, the majority of his work on the subject was done between 1959 and 1963. Acting in part under assignment, and preferring that his time could be devoted to other projects, his responses to anti-Mormon literature sometimes manifest considerable impatience. But he did devote extensive attention to the critical literature, and his efforts are worth reading, even though he made no claims to be an expert in American or Mormon history. He is best understood as a counter-puncher. He did not start the fight and he will not finish it, but his efforts buy time for others to enter the arena by showing that the opponent has serious flaws in style and content. The critic, in fact, seems to have rigged the fight, or at least refuses to fight fairly.

Nibley's first work in this vein was a response to Fawn Brodie's widely touted biography of Joseph Smith, *No Man Knows My History*, published in 1945.[19] Nibley's response was *No Ma'am, That's Not History*. It appeared the same year, was reissued in 1959, and has been available in pamphlet format since. In 1959 his series " 'Mixed Voices': A Study of Book of Mormon Criticism" was serialized in the *Improvement Era*. In 1961, from July to November, "Censoring the Joseph Smith Story," in which Nibley takes on such anti-Mormon writers as Henry Caswall, John C. Bennett, and J. B. Turner, appeared in the *Improvement Era*. In 1961 *The Myth Makers* appeared, in which Nibley presents "the case of the World *versus* Joseph Smith," with a host of anti-Mormon witnesses whose testimonies become a hopeless mass of contradictions and absurdities. *Sounding Brass* followed in 1963, focusing on the story and anti-Mormon writings of Ann Eliza Webb Dee Young Denning, divorced wife of Brigham Young. As early as 1965, Nibley had turned his attention to the criticisms of the book of Abraham, some of which he included in the early instalments of his series "A New Look at the Pearl of Great Price," published in 1968 in the *Improvement Era*.[20] In 1974, he again reflected on Fawn Brodie's work on Joseph Smith, pointing out that her subsequent biographies, especially her book on Thomas Jefferson, share the same flaws that her work on Joseph Smith exhibits.

Because the main thrust of Nibley's work is to analyze the published criticism of the Church, he does not focus on the manuscript sources of Latter-day Saint history. Most of the collections of the Church Archives were uncatalogued or unavailable when he was doing his work on early Mormon history. In his work, Nibley provides an analysis of printed literature; his work is primarily intellectual history that examines the larger picture rather than the minute details. He focuses on ideas rather than on biography or just historical facts. Thus, although his general campaign is potent and persuasive, readers thirty years later should not be surprised to discover that, with the subsequent professionalization of the Church library and archives, the study of Mormon history has progressed on a variety of details discussed in Nibley's works. For example, recent work has been done on the now available accounts of Joseph Smith's First Vision,[21] as well as on money digging[22] and his 1826 trial,[23] and the earliest treatments of his religious claims.[24] His discussion of the use of the "Danite" theme by anti-Mormon writers was right on target, and he early drew attention to the negative portrayal of Mormons in the various graphic cartoons that appeared in these early works.[25] Such new research has strengthened Nibley's arguments in many cases; it has corrected him in others.

One of the consequences of Nibley's work on anti-Mormon writing was to deepen his own understanding of Brigham Young. Nibley has broadened our understanding and appreciation of President Young in a variety of subsequently published essays on such topics as the environment, consecration, Zion, education, and dealing with the "enemy." Nibley has thus invited us to take a closer look at Brigham Young's ideas, and not just his colonizing or politics.[26]

Much of Nibley's own work has focused on the sacred texts of the Latter-day Saints. Only indirectly, and usually by assignment, has he analyzed the critical literature. Even in his works in which he is essentially evaluating anti-Mormon arguments, he invites critics to take more seriously the basic claims of Joseph Smith. He has tried to remove from the road the fog that has obscured the view for students of Mormon history. He functions as a classical apologist in the highest sense (that is, as one who responds, clarifies, or defends) as he explains and vindicates the life and teachings of the prophets.[27] Nibley's own loyalty to the gospel message allows him to separate the chaff from the wheat. He knows the scriptures; he knows that Joseph's name would be known for good and evil, but he has clearly chosen to be numbered among those who sought counsel from the Prophet. He has little patience with those who write to persuade others to dismiss either the prophets or their divine messages.

Many people have assisted with this volume. I am particularly glad to acknowledge their invaluable work, especially in checking citations and performing various other necessary editorial labors. They include Glen Cooper, Lyle Fletcher, Fran Hafen, Andrew Hedges, Alan Goff, Michael Lyon, Tyler Moulton, Phyllis Nibley, Don Norton, William Quist, Shirley Ricks, Stephen Ricks, James Tredway, John W. Welch, and Natalie Whiting. Jack Lyon of Deseret Book has been very helpful as this volume has progressed to a finished product.

David J. Whittaker

Notes

1. This was the counsel of D&C 71 and 73, specifically on the impact of the Ezra Booth letters that appeared in the *Ohio Star* [Ravenna] (October–December 1831). Even after the publishing in 1834 of E. D. Howe's *Mormonism Unvailed*, which reprinted the Booth letters, no printed reply was issued by the Latter-day Saints. Mormons did move to establish several newspapers, but no pamphlet literature appeared this early. Only when Howe's volume was reprinted in 1840 with the title *History of Mormonism; Or, a faithful account of that singular imposition and delusion, with sketches of the char-*

acters of its propagators . . . (Painesville, Ohio) did Latter-day Saint authors respond more directly in print. On Booth and his letters, see Max Parkin, "The Nature and Cause of Internal and External Conflict of the Mormons in Ohio between 1830 and 1838," Master's thesis, Brigham Young University, 1966, 101–20; and Dennis Rowley, "The Ezra Booth Letters," *Dialogue: A Journal of Mormon Thought* 16 (Fall 1983): 133–37.

2. *Mormonism Unveiled: Zion's Watchman unmasked, and its editor, Mr. L. R. Sunderland exposed: Truth vindicated: the devil mad, and priestcraft in danger!* (New York: Printed for the publisher, 1838). In 1835 Parley had published an account of the rough treatment he received at the hands of an anti-Mormon mob: *A Short Account of a Shameful Outrage, committed by a part of the Town of Mentor . . . April 7th [Kirtland?, 1835?].*

3. His replies include *Plain Facts, Showing the falsehood and folly of the Rev. C. S. Bush* (Manchester: Thomas, 1840); *A Reply to Mr. Thomas Taylor's 'Complete Failure,' &c. and Mr. Richard Livesey's 'Mormonism Exposed'* (Manchester: Thomas, 1840); and *An Answer to Mr. William Hewitt's Tract against the Latter-day Saints* (Manchester: Thomas, 1840). On the larger influence of Pratt see Peter Crawley, "Parley P. Pratt: Father of Mormon Pamphleteering," *Dialogue* 15 (Autumn 1982): 13–26.

4. See his editorial comments in *LDS Millennial Star* 1 (April 1841): 312.

5. An overview is presented in David J. Whittaker, "Early Mormon Pamphleteering" Ph.D. diss., Brigham Young University, 1982, 236–320.

6. Brigham Young to Jefferson Davis, 8 September 1855, MS in Brigham Young Collection, Historical Department, The Church of Jesus Christ of Latter-day Saints, Salt Lake City, Utah. This letter was originally called to my attention by Dean C. Jessee.

7. See the summary in Brigham H. Roberts, *A Comprehensive History of the Church of Jesus Christ of Latter-day Saints, Century I,* 6 vols. (Salt Lake City: Deseret News Press, 1930), 4:55–68.

8. See the perceptive comments of Leonard J. Arrington, "Mormonism: Views from Without and Within," *BYU Studies* 14 (Winter 1974): 140–53, esp. 148–50.

9. Brigham Young to Lorenzo D. Young, 15 June 1877, in Dean C. Jessee, ed., *Letters of Brigham Young to His Sons* (Salt Lake City: Deseret Book for the Historical Department, The Church of Jesus Christ of Latter-day Saints, 1974), 290–91. Cf. Joseph Smith's comments in December 1833: *Teachings of the Prophet Joseph Smith,* com-

piled by Joseph Fielding Smith (Salt Lake City: Deseret Book, 1939), 43. See also Hugh Nibley, "Brigham Young and the Enemy," in *The Young Democrat* (Provo: BYU Democrats, [1970]).

10. George Q. Cannon bridged the first- and second-generation Mormon publishers. He learned the printing business from John Taylor; he honed these skills further under Parley P. Pratt, and he was further guided through the maze of the non-Mormon Eastern printing establishment by Thomas L. Kane. He also received regular counsel from Brigham Young.

11. Recent studies include Jon Haupt and Leonard J. Arrington, "The Missouri and Illinois Mormons in Ante-Bellum Fiction," *Dialogue* 5 (Spring 1970): 37–50; and Arrington and Haupt, "Intolerable Zion: The Image of Mormonism in Nineteenth Century American Literature," *Western Humanities Review* 22 (Summer 1968): 243–60. Even the most superficial look at popular books on Mormons today will reveal that the same themes continue to be used.

12. See the overview in B. H. Roberts, *A Comprehensive History of the Church*, 6:422–31; and in Thomas G. Alexander, *Mormonism in Transition, A History of the Latter-day Saints, 1890–1930* (Urbana: University of Illinois Press, 1986), 239–57.

13. On Roberts's work see Davis Bitton, "B. H. Roberts as Historian," *Dialogue* 3 (Winter 1968): 25–44; Truman G. Madsen, "B. H. Roberts after Fifty Years: Still Witnessing for the Book of Mormon," *Ensign* 13 (December 1983): 10–19; and John W. Welch, "B. H. Roberts: Seeker after Truth," *Ensign* 16 (March 1986): 56–62.

14. See Richard A Nelson, "A History of Latter-day Saint Screen Portrayals in the Anti-Mormon Film Era, 1905–1936," Master's thesis, Brigham Young University, 1975.

15. See, for example, Richard Lloyd Anderson, "Joseph Smith's New York Reputation Reappraised," *BYU Studies* 10 (Spring 1970): 283–314; Dean C. Jessee, "The Reliability of Joseph Smith's History," *Journal of Mormon History* 3 (1976): 23–46; Lester Bush, Jr., "The Spaulding Theory Then and Now," *Dialogue* 10 (Autumn 1977): 40–69; A Latter-day Saint Historian, *Jerald and Sandra Tanner's Distorted View of Mormonism: A Response to 'Mormonism—Shadow or Reality?'* (Salt Lake City: n.p., 1977); Craig Foster, "British Anti-Mormon Pamphleteering, 1837–1860," Master's thesis, Brigham Young University, 1989; and Gilbert W. Scharffs, *The Truth about "The Godmakers"* (Salt Lake City: Publisher's Press, 1986).

16. The main exception is the series "Mixed Voices: A Study in Book of Mormon Criticism," *Improvement Era* 62 (1959), which appears in *CWHN* 8:127–206.

17. The first piece of satire published by a Mormon author was Parley Pratt's *An Epistle of Demetrius, Junior, The Silversmith . . .* (Manchester, England, 1840). It compared the actions of certain English clergy to the mob activity of the Ephesian silversmith in Acts 19 when his income from making idols was threatened by Paul's missionary work.

18. It was first published in the *1962 Seminar on Joseph Smith* (Provo: Extension Publications, Brigham Young University, 1962), 30–41, and later included in *Sounding Brass*; reprinted in this volume on pages 407–727.

19. A useful discussion of the various responses to Brodie's biography is Newell G. Bringhurst, "Applause, Attack, and Ambivalence — Varied Responses to Fawn M. Brodie's 'No Man Knows My History'," *Utah Historical Quarterly* 57 (Winter 1989): 46–63. Marvin S. Hill has written two article-length critiques of her work on Joseph Smith: "Brodie Revisited: A Reappraisal," *Dialogue* 7 (Winter 1972): 72–85; and "Secular or Sectarian History? A Critique of *No Man Knows My History*," *Church History* 43 (March 1974):78–96.

20. See especially *Improvement Era* 71 (January–October 1968). In BYU Education Week lectures in Oakland, California, in 1965, he also discussed these matters.

21. Recent study on Joseph Smith's First Vision include Paul R. Cheesman, "An Analysis of the Accounts Relating Joseph Smith's Early Visions," Master's thesis, Brigham Young University, 1965; Dean C. Jessee, "The Early Accounts of Joseph Smith's First Vision," *BYU Studies* 9 (Spring 1969): 275–94; Milton V. Backman, Jr., *Joseph Smith's First Vision: Confirming Evidences and Contemporary Accounts*, 2nd ed. (Salt Lake City: Bookcraft, 1980); and Marvin S. Hill, "The First Vision Controversy: A Critique and Reconciliation," *Dialogue* 15 (Summer 1982): 31–46.

22. On money digging see Ronald W. Walker, "The Persisting Idea of American Treasure Hunting," *BYU Studies* 24 (Fall 1984): 427–59; and Alan Taylor, "Rediscovering the Context of Joseph Smith's Treasure Seeking," *Dialogue* 19 (Winter 1986): 18–28.

23. Useful research on the 1826 trial includes Marvin S. Hill, "Joseph Smith and the 1826 Trial: New Evidence and New Difficulties," *BYU Studies* 12 (Winter 1972): 223–33; and Gordon A. Madsen, "Joseph Smith's 1826 Trial: The Legal Setting," *BYU Studies* 30 (Spring 1990): 91–108.

24. A particularly valuable study of the earliest treatments of Joseph Smith and his religious claims in the public prints is Walter A. Norton, "Comparative Images: Mormonism and Contemporary

Religions as Seen by Village Newspapermen in Western New York and Northeastern Ohio, 1820–1833," Ph.D. diss., Brigham Young University, 1991. Norton shows how the critical perceptions of Joseph Smith were very early established in the local newspapers. And he shows further how, owing to Federal legislation that allowed free carriage of exchange newspapers between newspaper offices throughout the country, the various newspapers were thus encouraged to reprint material appearing in each others' prints, thus allowing the negative reports to spread far and wide.

25. See Rebecca F. Cornwall and Leonard J. Arrington, "Perpetuation of a Myth: Mormon Danites in Five Western Novels, 1840–1890," *BYU Studies* 23 (Winter 1983): 147–65; David J. Whittaker, "The Book of Daniel in Early Mormon Thought," in John M. Lundquist and Stephen D. Ricks, eds., *By Study and Also By Faith: Essays in Honor of Hugh W. Nibley*, 2 vols. (Salt Lake City: Deseret Book and F.A.R.M.S., 1990), 1:155–201; and Gary L. Bunker and Davis Bitton, *The Mormon Graphic Image, 1834–1914* (Salt Lake City: University of Utah Press, 1983).

26. These essays will appear in a future volume of the *Collected Works of Hugh Nibley*.

27. See especially Hugh W. Nibley, *The World and the Prophets*, vol. 3 of the *Collected Works of Hugh Nibley* (Salt Lake City: Deseret Book and F.A.R.M.S., 1987).

No, Ma'am, That's Not History

*A Brief Review of Mrs. Brodie's Reluctant
Vindication of a Prophet She Seeks to Expose*

1

No, Ma'am, That's Not History

A Brief Review of Mrs. Brodie's Reluctant
Vindication of a Prophet She Seeks to Expose

Preface

When the writer first read Mrs. Brodie's book thirteen years ago he was struck by the brazen inconsistencies that swarm in its pages, and so wrote this hasty review. At that time he had no means of knowing that inconsistency was the least of the author's vices, and assumed with other reviewers that when she cited a work in her footnotes, she had actually read it, that when she quoted she was quoting correctly, and that she was familiar with the works in her bibliography. Only when other investigations led the reviewer to the same sources in ensuing years did the extent of Mrs. Brodie's irresponsibility become apparent. While a large book could (and probably should) be devoted to this remarkable monument of biographical mendacity,[1] more than a decade of research abetted by correspondence with Mrs. Brodie's defenders has failed to discredit a single observation made in our 1946 review, which is printed here with only a few typographical errors corrected.[2]

What Brought This On

People are still trying to explain Joseph Smith. That is as it should be, for no man who claims as much as he did should go unchallenged. Joseph Smith's own story is by

---

This was originally published in pamphlet form in Salt Lake City by Bookcraft in 1946 and was subsequently reissued with minor changes at various times.

3

no means the only possible explanation of his career; for everything in the universe there are as many explanations at hand as the mind is willing to devise. Only one rule must be observed; it is the old "law of parsimony"—of all explanations of a thing, the one which is the simplest, i.e., the freest from contradiction, requiring the fewest qualifications and the least elaboration of explanation, must be given preference to the exclusion of all others.

The latest explanation of Joseph Smith is Mrs. Brodie's.[3] It is not animated by violent hatred. That fact is reassuring but, strangely enough, irrelevant. The average man is as free from prejudice as Thadamanthus when it comes to tensor analysis or the interpretation of Sumerian texts— but that does not qualify him to speak on either subject, and if Mrs. Brodie preserved the calm of a Nestor we would still have to judge her explanation strictly on its own merits, and not assume that she must be telling the truth because she is not mad at anybody.

Brodie takes an awful beating from the law of parsimony. Far simpler and more to the point are the thumping biographies of an earlier day, which simply announced that the man Joseph Smith was a complete scamp, and there an end—simple and direct. With that same admirable simplicity and directness, these authors ran headlong into a brick wall of contradictions, and that was their undoing. Altogether too much is known about Joseph Smith to let the "total depravity" theory get by. So Mrs. Brodie will qualify it by introducing into the picture an element which she thinks solves everything: Joseph Smith was a complete imposter, the new light teaches, but he *meant well*. He was just an easy-going rustic with irresponsible ways and an overactive imagination. That takes care of everything.

But as soon as we get down to cases, the new and humane interpretation of the Prophet, far from improving things, makes everything much worse. Brodie's Joseph Smith is a more plausible character than the consummate fiend of the earlier school in that his type is much more likely to be met with on the street any Tuesday afternoon. But he is actually much *less* plausible as the man who accomplished what Joseph Smith did. Some kind of an inspired super-devil might have gotten away with some of the things he did, but no blundering, dreaming, un-disciplined, shallow and opportunistic fakir could have left behind what Joseph Smith did, both in men's hearts and on paper.

Brodie's task is to fit the recorded words and acts of one Joseph Smith to her idea of a well-meaning but not too reliable oaf. To do this the words and acts in question must be changed around a bit: there must be a good deal of critical interpretation and explaining in the light of the answer she wants to get. All this is pardonable if it does not go too far. But how far does it go? That is the all-important question which can be answered only by con-sulting the book itself.

After a glance at those learned pages we shall be able to point out a real and solid contribution which Mrs. Brodie has made to the advancement of knowledge. It is in view of that contribution that we are moved to discuss a work that might otherwise have been gravely misunderstood. We believe in giving credit where credit is due—but not elsewhere—and for that reason take the pains to point out a few interesting aspects of Mrs. Brodie's celebrated bi-ography.

A Little Discourse on Method

Mrs. Brodie begins her study with the observation that though there is no lack of documents for the history of Joseph Smith, these documents are "fiercely contradic-tory."[4] In that case, it is necessary for a writer to pick and choose his evidence. Now, by the simple process of picking and choosing one's evidence, one may prove absolutely anything. For which reason it is important to ask what principle Mrs. Brodie follows in making her choice.

This is not hard to discover. Our guide first makes up her mind about Joseph Smith and then proceeds to accept any and all evidence, from whatever source, that supports her theory.[5] The uncritical acceptance of evidence from all sources gives her work at first glance an air of great impartiality. At the same time she rejects any and all evidence, from whatever source, that refutes her settled ideas.

Thus she flatly rejects the sworn affidavit of fifty-one of Joseph's neighbors because their testimony does not suit her idea of the Prophet's character.[6] We would applaud such strong-mindedness were it not that on the very next page she accepts the stories of the same witnesses regarding "seer stones, ghosts, magic incantations, and nocturnal excavations."[7] Now scandal stories thrive notoriously well in rural settings, while the judgment of one's neighbors regarding one's general character over a number of years is far less likely to run into the fantastic. Yet Brodie can reject the character witnesses as prejudiced while accepting the weirdest extravagances of their local gossip.

In the same spirit, John C. Bennett and Joseph H. Jackson, who are "unreliable witnesses, to say the least,"[8] become reliable sources whenever their testimony supports Brodie, and hopelessly prejudiced when it does not.

"The press accounts" (there is only one such "account") of the charlatan [Luman] Walters "stated significantly that when he left the neighborhood, his mantle fell upon young Joseph Smith."[9] What is "significant" about it? What is meant by the vague figure of speech more than that one scamp was succeeded by another? Even Obadiah Dogberry [a.k.a. Abner Cole] does not do more than insinuate that Joseph was one of Walter's audience of yokels. Why should his bitter enemies not come out and say he was Walter's disciple if he was—why nothing but an extremely noncommittal hint and a veiled figure of speech if they had anything at all to go by? Yet this is the whole evidence for one of Brodie's proudest discoveries. For her it is an absolute certainty upon which she repeatedly insists,[10] that Walters was Joseph's most particular teacher.

"No two of Joseph's neighbors had the same version of the story" of the plates, we are told.[11] What does one do in that case? One simply accepts or rejects the stories according to one's own fancy. This is fun until one runs up against flatly contradictory evidence that cannot be sidestepped or ignored. Regarding the claims that no one ever saw anything but an empty box, Brodie sagely observes: "It is difficult to reconcile this explanation with the fact that these witnesses, and later Emma and William Smith, emphasized the size, weight, and metallic texture of the plates."[12] Yes, how *do* you reconcile them? Here is Brodie's method: "Exactly how Joseph Smith persuaded so many of the reality of the golden plates is neither so important nor so baffling as the effect of this success on Joseph himself."[13] Whereupon she drops the question for good. There may be ten thousand things more important and baffling than the problem of disproving the plates, but that fact has no bearing on the problem and can hardly pass for a solution in a book "where honesty and integrity presumably should count for something."[14] She is simply side-stepping the issue, and the law of parsimony screams bloody murder: It must have an explanation of those plates, but such is not forthcoming from our oracle.

"The Hebraic origin of the Indians [is an idea which] seems . . . to have come chiefly from a popular book by Ethan Smith" entitled *View of the Hebrews*.[15] Though this possibility quickly becomes a dead certainty for Brodie, "it may never be proved that Joseph saw *View of the Hebrews* before writing the Book of Mormon."[16] Since there is nothing in his own words to give him away, that, for Brodie, is proof that he was careful to cover up his traces. What proves the stealing of the Book of Mormon from Ethan

Smith is the presence of "striking parallelisms" between the two.[17] This brings up a very important aspect of the Brodie method, namely, the use of parallels as an argument. It has become the favorite device of non-Mormon writers. Oriental literature bristles with parallels to the Book of Mormon that are far more full and striking than anything that can be found in the West.

There are "outside" parallels for every event in the Old and New Testaments, yet that does not prove anything. Of recent years, literary studies have shown parallels not to be the exception but the rule in the world of creative writing, and it is well known that great inventions and scientific discoveries have a way of appearing at about the same time in separate places. A scholar by the name of Karl Joel has recently amassed a huge amount of material on the subject,[18] and though we need not accept his conclusion that the same sort of thing that is happening in one place at a given time will be found to be happening all over the world at the moment (!), still his vast volumes present a great wealth of undeniable parallels. The fact that two theories or books present parallelisms, no matter how striking, may imply a common source, but it certainly does not in itself prove that the one is derived from the other. We know (thanks to Brodie) that there was a great and widespread interest in the Indian problem in Joseph's day, and we also know that these people of that day had a way of referring everything to the Bible; in that case it is hard to see how anyone could have avoided the Indian-Hebrew tie-up.

Mrs. Brodie sees parallels everywhere. To cite a few of her howlers, there is the case of a herdsman who kills a number of rustlers with a sword. Now herdsmen have been fighting with rustlers since the dawn of time, but for Brodie this is simply a direct steal from the story of David and Goliath. Again, the barges of the Jaredites "contained everything which the settlers might need on the new continent,"[19] like any Chinese junk, Viking ship, or the *Mayflower* itself; in fact, ships have a way of carrying with them whatever the personnel will need. Brodie, however, knows that the whole thing is a dishonest adaptation of Noah's ark. Certain fortifications of earth and timbers mentioned in the Book of Mormon resemble those in western New York—also, we add, in Russia, England, Africa, France, China, and everywhere else. Such structures are universally common to a certain type of warlike culture. At one place in the Book of Mormon, atheism is denounced; since there were atheists on the frontier, Brodie knows that the whole idea is simply an adaptation of the local scene.[20] The fact that atheism has been an issue in sundry civilizations since the world began means nothing to our author; she chooses her parallels as she chooses her evidence—where it suits her.

Sidney Rigdon once in an article "openly quoted" from Thomas Dick's *Philosophy of a Future State*.[21] That to Brodie *proves* that Joseph Smith "had recently been reading" the book.[22] Dick mentions the old familiar doctrine that the stars may be inhabited by intelligent *progressive* beings. So Brodie knows that all the Prophet's "later teachings [on the subject] came directly from Dick."[23] He could not very well have gotten his *earlier* teachings from Dick, though his later teachings are simply a continuation of them. Yet as soon as a work appears that resembles what he is doing, Brodie immediately pounces upon it as the Prophet's only source. If she would show how the doctrine of progress was stolen from Dick, the lady should not have been at such pains to show that progressivism had been a basic part of its background from the first.

A useful form of parallel is the "identical anecdote." To prove Joseph Smith's dishonesty in operating the bank, "several apostates at different times related an identical anecdote" about money-boxes.[24] Now, identical anecdotes can be assumed to indicate a common source, but no more:

they say nothing as to the nature of that source or its reliability. For Mrs. Brodie the fact that they are identical proves not that they are commonly derived, but that they are actually true! What kind of history is that? The greatest possible wealth of "identical anecdotes" attests the orgies in the temple, and yet Brodie does not hesitate to scout the lot as absolutely worthless, identical or not. How infinitely weaker is the "whispered talk"[25] which attests the activities of the Danites? Yet Mrs. Brodie accepts it, forsooth, because it is "fragmentary [to say the least], but consistent."[26] The stories once current about the nocturnal orgies of the early Christians and the child-eating rites of the Jews were not too fragmentary and were remarkably consistent — only they weren't true.

"Bald parallels of Masonic oaths"[27] the lady finds particularly crude. How did he dare it? Why didn't he disguise it?[28] The answer is that to those who know both, the resemblance is not striking at all; it is not nearly so striking as the resemblance between the church Joseph Smith founded and the other churches, and yet even though the Mormon Church and these institutions present one parallel after another, they are really totally different in form and meaning.

Speaking of parallels, however, one cannot pass by one of the most remarkable studies in religious parallels ever written. The name of the most learned man who ever made a study of the Mormons, and one of the best-informed men who ever lived, does not appear in Mrs. Brodie's pages. At the end of the last century, the great tradition of European scholarship in the grand style culminated in the person of Eduard Meyer. If he did not have the stature of some earlier scholars, it is certain that he was in a position to survey and assimilate more of the learning of the past than any human being before or since his day. To his famous rotunda at the University of Berlin flowed, as it has never flowed since, all the learning of the ages for his examination and exploitation. No other man ever combined the learning both of the East and the classical world in a work of such high and lasting authority as Meyer's *Geschichte des Altertums*—the ultimate and, in fact, the last general history of antiquity to be the work of a single mind.[29]

This man had a particular interest in ancient religions, and it occurred to him that in Mormonism he might study at first hand how a real religion gets started. So impressed was he by the possibilities of such a study that he packed up and went to Utah in 1904, to devote a year of his priceless time to studying the Mormons. Few churches have had the good fortune to be examined at first hand by a man of such vast learning and complete impartiality. For in keeping with the high *Wissenschaft* of his day, Meyer himself professed no religion. He was neither partial nor hostile to the Mormons, who as far as his feelings were concerned might have been beings on another planet or a heap of ants.

Meyer's entire *Ursprung und Geschichte der Mormonen* is a study in parallels, comparing the new religion with revealed religions of the past.[30] While grandly contemptuous of Joseph Smith's low coefficient of *Kultur*, the great savant illustrates at length the "exact identity" of his Church both in "atmosphere" and sundry particulars with that of the early Christians. A "striking and irrefutable" parallelism supports Mormon claims to revelation; "with perfect right" they identify themselves with the apostolic church of old. The similarity extends to the faults as well as the virtues of the Prophet and his followers—they may be matched "at every point" by the faults and virtues of the ancient prophets and the ancient church. We shall have occasion to refer to Eduard Meyer a number of times below, not because he was favorably disposed (he is in fact far less sympathetic than Brodie), but because with his infinitely greater knowledge he reaches such totally different conclusions. He is a necessary "control" in testing our author.

Incidentally, the faithful need not be too utterly crushed by Brodie's erudite announcement that the word "Nauvoo" is purely a figment of Smith's imagination,[31] since no less an Orientalist than Meyer himself is naive enough to be taken in by the Prophet's ruse. He observes that the word is a plain transliteration of the Hebrew *nava*, which is feminine (the proper gender for place names) and happens to mean "the beautiful."[32] Mrs. Brodie can put her stuffed mourning-dove back into its box now: her philology is of the same brand as her history.

Evolution at Any Price

Of all Mrs. Brodie's preconceived ideas, the most fundamental is her certainty that Joseph Smith did not receive revelations. That sudden and dazzling enlightenment which is the essence of religious experience of the highest sort is unthinkable in his case. All his own statements on the subject are to be discarded out of hand. To Brodie "there are few men, however, who have written so much and told so little about themselves."[33] Which is simply to say that though Joseph Smith tells a great deal about himself, Brodie chooses not to believe it.

Instead, she will cling to the theory that all the Prophet's thought and action were the result of a slow and gradual evolution. This is an easy mechanical rule-of-thumb that may be employed to make any thesis sound very scientific. The first objection to it Brodie ignores entirely; namely, the well-known fact that great religious conviction is usually born of sudden insight. Other religious leaders may have their moments of inspiration, but in Joseph's case everything is slow and gradual.

Barring this objection, how does Mrs. Brodie support her evolutionary theory? To begin with, there was no "first vision." True, such visions "were common in the folklore of the area"[34] and Joseph was the most imaginative youth in the world; still, *he* had no such vision—not even a false one! The proof is that the newspapers say nothing about it. The argument of silence is always a suspicious one, yet how much more suspicious when we are told that "there are no detailed descriptions of the revivals in Palmyra and Manchester . . . when they were at their wildest?"[35] If the press ignores the revivals at their wildest, why should it not ignore a mere episode of the movement? Joseph Smith specifically says it was the ministers who united to persecute him—it was persecution from the pulpit (*not*, as Brodie insinuates, a sort of militant mob movement). But, says Brodie, these same newspapers "in later years gave him plenty of unpleasant publicity."[36] In later years he was an important public figure with a large following—their silence at this time merely proves his own statement that he was "an obscure boy"[37] (JS-H 1:23) and anything but news.

If Joseph Smith claimed to have had a vision in 1820, the newspapers "took no notice of Joseph's vision at the time it was supposed to have occurred" *or at any other time.*[38] Therefore we can only conclude that no such claim was made, either in 1820 or at any other time. The last clause nullifies the whole argument, for if the silence of the newspapers is proof of anything, then Joseph Smith never at any time claimed to have had the vision, which Brodie knows is false.

However, she hastens to corroborate the silence of the press with the testimony of Obadiah Dogberry: "It is well known that Joe Smith never pretended to have any communion with angels until a long period after the *pretended* finding of his book."[39] Even if Dogberry were a reliable witness (which he definitely is not), we can only ask, "well known" to whom? Why, indeed, to the thousands of people to whom the Prophet never mentioned his visions. A million people in London and Paris could have sworn affidavits that Joseph Smith never told them a thing about the angel; the entire city of Peking and large areas of the Central Sudan could honestly report that they had never been informed of Moroni's visit. That Joseph Smith should not noisily divulge the great and sacred things he had been ordered to keep secret does not seem possible to Brodie. If the first vision was so "soul-shattering,"[40] how, she asks triumphantly, could it have "passed totally unnoticed in Joseph's home town?"[41] It never occurs to her that there are things, especially if they are of a transcendent and "soul-shattering" nature, which one does not run off to report to the press and the neighbors.[42] Joseph reported his vision only to his family and to a minister he thought he could trust. It was the minister who caused the trouble.

What was the first vision, then? A remembered dream, says Brodie, "created some time after 1834,"[43] for "dream images came easily to this youth"[44]—in 1834, that is, but not in 1820!

As a final clincher to her argument of silence against the first vision, our author points out that in 1820 Joseph was not religious at all: "he reflected the irreligion and cynicism of his father,"[45] he was merely a "likable ne'er-do-well,"[46] "immune to religious influence of any sort."[47] Later on, after the first vision has been thus debunked and forgotten, in order to prove something else, Brodie flatly refutes all these judgments as worthless: "It is clear that he was keenly alert to the theological differences dividing the sects and was genuinely interested in the controversies."[48] Now it is *his* version she is accepting, and that in the teeth of all testimony to the contrary. If that much of his story turns out to be true against positive testimony, what about the rest of the story? There is no contemporary mention of Joseph's religious propensities, and yet those propensities are real, Brodie decides; the same sources fail to mention his most intimate and hidden religious experience—therefore such an experience never occurred, Brodie decides!

The next major issue is the Book of Mormon. "For a long time," we are told, "Joseph was *extremely reluctant* to talk about the plates."[49] Extremely reluctant indeed; why didn't he simply let the matter drop? Because "once the masquerade had begun, there was no point at which he could call a halt."[50] Why not? Everyone would have been glad to forget the business. If his own family believed implicitly in the plates they never saw, they certainly would believe in any explanation he might give for their disappearance: they willingly accepted his story later that the angel had taken the plates back. And was Joseph of the super-resourceful imagination, devious, cunning, agile and "utterly opportunistic" in the matter of the Book of Mormon, the one to be at a loss for explanations? Why did he hang on to the plates that no one could see, that only made trouble, that he hated to talk about? Surely he of all persons could think of a better game than that. And at the time, remember, he had absolutely no conception of the Book of Mormon-to-be, according to Brodie.[51]

The writing of the first one hundred and sixteen pages was "painfully slow, . . . [for] Joseph had yet to learn how to write,"[52] a long and difficult process at best. Yet less than a year later we find him tossing off a 275,000–word manuscript in three months! This feat simply proves to Brodie that Joseph Smith's stupidity has been deliberately exaggerated: he was really rather smart. Only she resolutely refuses to face the problem she has raised: Here was a man of twenty-two giving free rein to a "completely undisciplined imagination,"[53] an imagination that "spilled over like a spring freshet"[54] in a riot of intense color and luxuriant detail, a wild, unbridled fancy that was not to be "canalized by any discipline";[55] the man sits behind a curtain and dictates to a semiliterate peasant on the other side ("none of Joseph's secretaries knew the rudiments of punctuation").[56] He simply dictates: He takes no notes and holds no conferences, for he must impress his secretaries and not appeal to them for aid — once a sentence is spoken "revision was therefore unthinkable,"[57] says Brodie. What a hilarious document this will turn out to be! What an impossible tangle of oriental vagaries, what threads and tatters of half-baked narrative losing themselves in contradictory masses, what an exuberance of undisciplined fancies flying off at wild tangents! What a wealth of irrelevant sermonizing at unexpected moments (as in the Koran), what a collection of bizarre conceits and whopping contradictions it must be! Surely all one needs to do is to cite a page of the stuff — any page — to expose the whole business; a few of these obviously faked passages will do the trick far more simply and effectively than the laborious chapters Mrs. Brodie devotes to it. Why the laborious chapters? Because the inevitable flaws of a book produced in the manner Brodie describes strangely fail to appear! Instead of an opium dream, we find an exceedingly sober document, that never flies off at tangents, never loses the thread of the narrative (which is often quite complicated), is totally lacking in oriental color, in which the sermons are confined to special sections, and which, strangest of all, never runs into contradictions. Joseph might get away with his "outrageous lying"[58] in little matters, but what outrageous liar can carry the game to half the length of the Old Testament without giving himself away hundreds of times? Brodie doesn't say.

Early in her book the lady prepares us for the Book of Mormon by making much of Joseph's gaudy imagination, and especially of his skill in holding everybody spellbound for hours by his exotic and colorful tales. Why, then, is the Book of Mormon, his best effort, simply "chloroform in print,"[59] lacking all the qualities for which the author was remarkable? Why does the language, with its strained and remarkably Semitic structure, in no way resemble his own vigorous and extravagant prose?

To prove that the Book of Mormon was the product of gradual evolution, Mrs. Brodie maintains with great insistence that until the first one hundred and sixteen pages were finished it was not a religious book at all but "merely an ingenious speculation,"[60] "a mere money-making history of the Indians";[61] as to the plates themselves " 'no *divine* interposition had been *dreamed* of.' "[62] Yet all along these plates had been "too sacred to be seen,"[63] nay, according to Brodie, Joseph maintained that the very sight of them would strike one dead![64] And it never occurred to him for a moment that such a singularly holy document might have even the slightest religious significance!

To demonstrate how the book evolved, Brodie observes that it improves in style and story as it goes along. That is *her* version: to others the first part of the book is by far the most interesting. Anyway, as he was finishing it up, the Prophet, being worried about the scientific aspects of what he had produced, decided, according to Mrs. Brodie, to add another book (Ether) to it. In this book, designed specifically to correct the unscientific tone of the rest, he was far more careless than ever before, mentioning all sorts of domestic beasts "when it was known even in his own day [and very well to a man of his sly researches] that Columbus had found the land devoid of these species."[65]

In criticizing the Book of Mormon or any of the other writings of Joseph Smith, it is necessary first of all to find out what these writings say. The theories and doctrines which Mrs. Brodie exposes are not found in these books, but are picked up from various people's ideas about them. The Book of Mormon has suffered particularly from a glib jumping at conclusions by its attackers. The book describes the doings of "a lonesome and a solemn people" (Jacob 7:26) who do not claim for a moment to be the sole inhabitants of the hemisphere. When Brodie talks of Moundbuilders and Mongolians,[66] she is not talking about the Book of Mormon at all; she is setting up a straw man for her "science" to "disembowel."[67]

Having finished the Book of Mormon, Joseph Smith "was rapidly acquiring the language and even the accent of sincere faith."[68] He had no sincere faith, you understand; what he had been through in the past had been merely drill to improve his "accent." Next "he slipped into" the role of Prophet "with ease, without the inner turmoil that preceded the spiritual fervor of so many of the great religious figures of the past."[69] The fact that Joseph is the only prophet, true or false, who never once gave evidence of doubting his calling, closely engaged the attention of the great Eduard Meyer, to whom the explanation is obvious: the Prophet had a vision — a real vision — right at the outset of his career.[70] If we do not accept that interpretation, we must follow Mrs. Brodie's psychological gymnastics. Joseph Smith was a deceiver, she decides, and "the casual reader will be shocked by his deceptions . . . in the field of religion, where honesty and integrity presumably should count for something."[71] He had no honesty or integrity; instead he had a "highly compensated" but "very real sincerity";[72] however, he had no real faith. And so, now you know: "What Joseph had created," our authority tells us, "was essentially an evangelical socialism, which made up in moral strength what it lacked in grandeur."[73] So, you see, the "completely undisciplined imagination,"[74] devoid of honesty and integrity[75] and lacking, moreover, "the diligence . . . [and] the constancy to master reality"[76] produces an organization noted for its lasting stability and characterized by great moral strength! What kind of reasoning is that? If there is anything which should mark a brainchild of Brodie's Joseph, it would be a tendency to grandeur and a lack of moral strength: just the opposite is found to be the case.

Next, in the process of Joseph's evolution an amazing

thing happens: he performs a miraculous healing. "Joseph must have been overwhelmed by this miracle," says our shrewd informant, "for he had *no idea* how common were such occurrences."[77] No idea! And that after Brodie has been at pains to tell us how he had grown up in a world of "faith healers and circuit-rider evangelists"[78] and camp-meeting miracles. Miracles of this sort had been his everyday fare from infancy, and yet in 1830 he has no idea that faith cures are common occurrences. His performance is not half as overwhelming as Brodie's discovery.

Shortly after this, Joseph founds the Church and "with an insight rare among the prophets of his own generation, he did not make a complete break with the past. He continued the story, he did not present a new cosmology."[79] In her summing up, however, our author takes the Prophet severely to task for his "insight" and speaks bitter words: "Within the dogma of the Church there is no new Sermon on the Mount [why should there be? — the old one is good enough], no *new* saga of redemption."[80] Joseph Smith, according to her, should have brought a *new* saga of redemption; she is actually disgusted with the man because he makes no attempt, absolutely none, to displace Jesus Christ! She is equally disgusted when at this time he speaks through revelation, depending on God rather than standing squarely on his own feet.[81] This to her can only mean that he is still "troubled by a sense of inadequacy."[82]

This sort of forced and predetermined reasoning makes one wonder, but no more so than her observations on the coined word *telestial* and the idea of a third degree of glory as that of the stars.[83] It is almost unbelievable that anyone presuming to write on religion should not be perfectly familiar with this very well-established and ancient doctrine — it is regular old stock-in-trade in ancient times, though the sources were not accessible to Joseph Smith. They were accessible to Brodie, if she is competent to judge of religious matters; and, true or false, the doctrine is anything but the fantastic aberration she makes it out to be.

At the end of 1832, we find Joseph Smith at last "taking himself very seriously as a prophet."[84] And that *after* the Book of Mormon and the revelations and visions founding the Church! He is moreover *"beginning* to grasp *something* of the tremendous potentiality of his power."[85] That *after* his repeated descriptions of himself as the key character in the dispensation of the fulness of times. Yet, at the end of 1833 he is "racked with a sense of impotence and irresolution,"[86] without substantial "certainty of the divinity of his mission."[87] It will be seen that Brodie's argument throughout the whole period rests ultimately on nothing but her own insight into the inner, nay the unconscious, mind of the Prophet.

Keeping to the evolution-at-any-price method, Brodie notes that in 1834, "little by little Joseph came to understand how basic were the animosities between his people and the old settlers,"[88] for of course it would never occur to him that there might be a basic animosity between his "small and peculiar people" and what he had repeatedly described as the doomed and wicked world of the last days. It was only with the troubles of Zion's Camp, we are told, that he was shocked by a "first-hand acquaintance with the ferocity of anti-Mormonism."[89] The affair in Ohio, where he had been the special victim of concentrated and deadly mob fury, and the awful times in Missouri, could not possibly have made an impression on him, for, don't you see, all this is a matter of slow and gradual evolution.

Now comes a "subtle change in his public attitude toward learning."[90] "Flinging aside his cloak of omniscience"[91] (not a very subtle gesture), he no longer "exulted in his lack of learning."[92] How a pretension to omniscience can go hand in hand with pretensions to gross ignorance is not clear — especially since the omniscience was of a very tangible sort, dealing with all kinds of ancient language and scientific truth. "Now he was *at last* pursuing knowledge the hard way," and Brodie applauds.[93] But in doing so she raises (and ignores) a very tough question. The hard research necessary to have produced the Book of Mormon, even as a work of pure fiction, must have been colossal; and if there were *no* such research, then its production was at least a hundred times harder. Remembering all those details without notes; preserving an even tone and regular flow, and that, without any revision or rewriting, or shuffling of notes; the mere writing of a big book—that takes *hard* thinking. It is a book, moreover, that "shows elaborate design, its narrative is spun coherently, and it demonstrates throughout a unity of purpose,"[94] according to Brodie—to have produced it with all the notes and aids and reference books in the world would have taken *hard* work. Yet our guide insists that Joseph Smith never studied "the hard way" until 1833. If this is so, how did he produce the Book of Mormon? Yet he no sooner suffers this change of heart than the Prophet basely reverts again "into accustomed paths and [dictates] a translation by direct inspiration from heaven."[95] The fact that he is not keeping the rule and evolving according to schedule disgusts our researcher.

Then in 1836, being a man with "a hard core of common sense"[96] and a "shrewd understanding"[97] and moreover a complete and very resourceful opportunist, and much worried about the scientific risks his Book of Mormon was running, Joseph Smith proceeds to lay himself wide open to the ridicule of scholars by a number of very daring Egyptian interpretations.[98] The only way to judge these is to present the documents to Egyptian scholars who have no knowledge of their history in America and compare their judgments with each other and with the Prophet's. This has never been done. If we are to believe the latest authoritative utterance on the subject,[99] the dogmatic certitude of another day may well yield to the humble acknowledgment that the real meaning of many Egyptian texts still eludes us. At any rate it is anything but the open-and-shut proposition that Brodie, the glib English major, makes it out to be.

In the affairs of the bank, the Saints were "robbed, abused and insulted" by the Prophet.[100] Only, strangely, they were not aware of the fact or seemed actually to enjoy it. It is not odd that "the gentiles shook their heads in wonder" at this strange contradiction.[101] It is odd, too, that only *after* this merciless exploitation "slowly something of the ruthlessness and cynicism of the frontier began to seep into his own thinking."[102] There is no trace of cynicism in his acts or his writings, you understand—it is only in his *thinking*.

In 1842, after years of temple building, Joseph Smith suddenly becomes a Mason and steals all their rites.[103] Yet the temples do not change their design or their meaning. The founding of an endowment house and a temple at the same time, in 1841, shows, as Meyer observes, that the essence of the temple rites was well established before then.[104] In founding the rites "it is doubtful whether Joseph sensed the truly staggering implications of his endowment system."[105] More than five years before, Elijah himself had brought the keys to this work "lest the whole earth be smitten with a curse," but Joseph failed to realize that it was really a big thing (D&C 110:15). Repeatedly our guide refuses to give Joseph Smith credit for knowing what he was about, in spite of his own emphatic declarations on the subject; she knows that he is really undergoing a slow evolution, stumbling blindly forward from one surprise to the next.

Thus she can give us the glib assurance that "Joseph laid no great emphasis on the temple ordinances,"[106] even though the one consuming interest of his life was temple building. He was simply interested in the "pomp and spectacle"[107] of the temple. Then where are the candles and drapes, the bells, incense, jewels and glass and gold; where the chants and processions, the scarlet and purple; in short, all the legitimate Oriental fixtures of other cults? Where are the old-accepted and sure-fire properties of "pomp and spectacle," Christian and pagan, in every age? Why are the temples so austere? Where is the "intense color and luxuriant detail"[108] he loved? It is simply another case of the facts stating one thing and Brodie stating another, basing her assertions on her own imponderable knowledge of Joseph's inmost mental processes.

As he approaches the end of his career, "it [is] now easy for him to believe . . . that God had willed [his success]."[109] After what he has been through it is about time. Yes, "Joseph was coming to look upon himself as the key figure in the setting up of a great religious kingdom."[110] And what, pray, did he think he was doing all those years during which he was receiving revelations by the dozen, writing the Book of Mormon, building temples, establishing the Church, and whatnot? Was that all just a game with no idea behind it?

Next an Episcopal divine claims that Joseph Smith said a Greek Psalter was really Egyptian.[111] In the speech in which he gives himself away, Joseph is quoted as saying things such as, "Them characters is like the letters that was engraved on the golden plates." Now Joseph Smith in 1842 never made that remark. The description of the grotesque illiterate is a false one, not merely "exaggerating the imperfections of Joseph's grammar"[112] as Brodie claims, but exaggerating to a degree which amounts to pure fabrication. The language is invented (whole volumes of Joseph's own words have survived from this period); the character is totally out of keeping with the Prophet's fine style and grand manner in 1842: it is the picture and the language of another person that the Reverend Caswall does not scruple to invent. Yet this book, published in England, is the only evidence for the story. Since inventing stories about Joseph Smith was a popular parlor game with respectable people, and since Brother Caswall is not overscrupulous, and *is* certainly overeager, what value is to be placed on the story at all? It needs corroboration, and Brodie finds such in a most wonderful manner.

When sometime after this most dubiously attested event a really clever trap is set, Joseph does *not* walk into it. That, for Brodie, proves the Caswall story, for why was Joseph so devilishly clever unless he "had been made cautious by the Greek psalter trick?"[113] This is known as playing with loaded dice—it usually gets a D-minus on a term paper.

Next comes the problem of polygamy. "Paul had said that in heaven there would be no marriage or giving in marriage, but Joseph taught that this would not apply to his Saints"[114] (cf. Matthew 22:29–30; Mark 12:25; Luke 20:35). Quite the contrary, it is the literal acceptance of this very doctrine that makes the endowment work on this earth so urgent. It is remarks like the above that betray a complete misunderstanding or willful distortion of the most elementary aspects of Mormonism. They also betray something else: Mrs. Brodie deals lightly with holy writ, for it is not Paul but Jesus to whom the remark is attributed by no fewer than three gospels. To explain the loyalty of sensible women to the institution, Brodie can think of no better line than her old chestnut: the doctrine somehow had great "magnetism."[115] In her treatment of the subject her sources are extremely weak. In any city in the United States almost any day of the year young women may be found making vivid, full, circumstantial, and sincere accusations against attackers that are found upon investigation to be nothing more than the objects of their own overwrought desires and imaginings. This does not mean that such accusations are necessarily false, but it does mean that they call for corroboration. And what better corroboration than the words of John C. Bennett, whom Brodie willingly condemns as untrustworthy—but only after his words have sunk in.

In the matter of Joseph Smith's wives, Mrs. Brodie feels free to pick and choose at will: some of the marriages were entirely spiritual, she freely admits—not all—but some. And by pure inference she can tell us just which were and which were not.[116] She never explains why, with his passionate desire for progeny, he had so few children.

By the end of 1843, to fit the evolutionary scheme of things, "Joseph was now fully intoxicated with power and drunk with visions of empire and apocalyptic glory";[117] he "by now had become a law unto himself, [with] . . . utter incapacity for contentment with a moderate success."[118] Yet this maniac "suffered from no illusions about his chances of winning the supreme political post in the nation";[119] his campaign utterances are models of acumen and common sense—"What other voice in all the madness was so sane?" asks Don C. Seitz in his study of the campaign of 1844.[120] Yet Brodie passes by the speeches and writings of the campaign in perfect silence—they would destroy her smooth curve of evolution.

Still more wonderful, at this time his idea of the kingdom of God on earth becomes "subtly transformed from a *mere symbol* to a thing of substance."[121] Many years before, Brodie entitled her chapter on the affairs of Kirtland "My Kingdom Is of This World";[122] now she decides that from the beginning the whole thing has been "a mere symbol" without substance.

When Joseph Smith says that the power of truth alone will bring all nations under the gospel, Brodie is good enough to correct him: "This was only partly true. The Legion now numbered almost four thousand men."[123] So the leader who had often ordered his own men to desist from conflict and readily admitted defeat when outnumbered, who on the same page is described as realizing that he cannot cope with the violence on the local frontier and will have to emigrate, and who suffered no illusions in things political, this same man believes he can subject all nations with a band of "almost four thousand men"!

For evolution had made him drunk with pride: "Almost never in these days did Joseph step outside himself and look with surprise and humility upon what he had become."[124] How *does* she know? How can she check up on such a deeply subjective matter? By pure intuition, to be sure. Thus she and she alone can tell us that Joseph's remark, "No man knows my history,"[125] was delivered "in a wanton moment of self-searching said with a kind of wonder."[126] Who said so? The reader who has plunked down four dollars has a right to expect something better than proof that is always found to rest on nothing but the woman's instincts.

When the *Expositor* wrote, "We will not acknowledge any man as king or lawgiver to the church,"[127] it was repeating a hackneyed Fourth of July phrase. Yet Brodie sees in this "an unmistakable allusion to Joseph's kingship,"[128] for which virtually no other evidence exists. If he actually was acclaimed king, why doesn't the *Expositor* say so? Why does it attack his kingship by a perfectly familiar figure of speech and then say no more?

The culmination of Joseph's megalomania finds him without courage, "empty of conviction when he needed it most."[129] Again we search for the little birdie that tells little Brodie these things. "He stood proudly before his men, betraying nothing of the tumult and anxiety racking him within."[130] Since he betrayed nothing by look, word, or gesture of his inner feelings, we take the liberty to report that he was really thinking of a fishing trip made on his seventh birthday; there is no evidence for this, but of course his thoughts were *perfectly* concealed, you know. Is this history? To present as facts what a man might have or could have or even possibly would have been thinking on an occasion when, far from revealing his thoughts, he covers them up, is a good game; but a book built up of alternate layers of psychological speculation and haphazard sources that only support them if accepted with a certain peculiar interpretation—such a book is not history.

In all her account of the evolution of things, Brodie never once mentions the true name of the Church, though great importance has always been placed upon it by the Mormons. For if she lets out that the Church received its long title by revelation in 1838, her picture of endless and dubious gropings suffers an eclipse. The name describes a very specific thing and implies an unvarying and uncompromising program. It is the undeviating and unshakable firmness of the Prophet in following a single line that Meyer, our learned control, finds "so astounding," and that makes the survival of the Church in his opinion "well-nigh incomprehensible" in view of its rigid and inflexible stand. For him the whole significance of Mormonism in world history lies in the fact that it is one of a few "revealed religions" (*Offenbarungsreligion*), like primitive Christianity and Islam, and is not essentially the product of evolution or study.[131] Brodie has missed this basic point entirely. She does not even seem to be aware of the fact that there are such religions, and that they have nothing in common with the run-of-the-mill cults of the sectarians and scholastics.

When Brodie Holds Her Peace

Once you have explained Joseph Smith by the safe conventional rules-of-thumb (1) that he was neither as good nor as bad as he has been painted, and (2) that his whole career followed a perfectly natural course of evolution, you still have to explain his success. This Mrs. Brodie attempts to do by demonstrating (1) that Joseph Smith had a great personal "magnetic" appeal,[132] (2) that his teaching was a product of New England and "smelled of the frontier,"[133] (3) that it was pleasingly materialistic and emphasized worldly prosperity,[134] and (4) that it was a "potpourri" of everything.[135]

The first three of these arguments break down completely in consideration of the fact that the Church derived its numbers and its strength largely from European converts who had never set eyes on Joseph Smith, who were far removed from the Yankee tradition, and to whom the frontier was a foreign and a hostile thing (incidentally, the Church was never very popular in New England, and it was detested on the frontier). Moreover, the materialistic appeal was all against joining the Church in their case. Brodie must rest her whole case here on the economic urge, and she becomes frankly deceptive in speaking of "phenomenal conversions among the poverty-ridden English workers."[136] She assumes they were poverty-ridden because George A. Smith describes great poverty in England, yet the one source she cites specifically states, "its converts are not made from the lowest ranks [but] are mechanics and tradesmen who have saved a little money."[137] The economic appeal, even in the Church paper, was that offered by America, not the Church. These people all paid their own way: it was quite possible for them to go to America without complicating matters and ruining their economic outlook by becoming Mormons.

But why argue? The proof lies to hand—and Brodie has passed it by in tiptoe silence. We refer to the journals and reminiscences of the converts themselves. These were not written for publication and are often very frank; the writers have not the slightest reason for concealing their interests and motives, and if they did not know their own strong minds, it is not likely that anyone else ever will. Almost without exception they tell the same story: joining the Church meant loss of economic security and social status, one became a pariah of the worst sort; there were impassioned scenes in the family and brickbats in the streets. The prospect in America was not brilliant—they looked forward only to hardships and privations in the new land. If one wanted to go to America to improve one's fortune, there were certainly better ways of doing it than making enemies of all the world. Of all this, not a word in Brodie—only the insinuation that the people joined up to get rich.

If the personality, American background, and materialism of Joseph Smith do not explain his success, it must lie in the secret of the "theology";[138] namely, that it was "a patchwork of ideas and rituals drawn from every quarter."[139] To her this is a mark of degeneracy, and she neglects to mention Joseph Smith's frequent declaration that he gladly accepts truth from any and all sources—for it must appear that Brodie has made a great discovery.

Now there is no such thing as a completely original religion, and every religion, including Christianity, is full of things that may be found elsewhere. If Joseph Smith thought of the sky as being blue, so did the ancient Chinese. It is no condemnation of the teachings of Jesus that, as Justin Martyr demonstrates at great length, they may also be found in the philosophers.[140] But the mere throwing together of a "potpourri" of everything does not make a doctrine. In this regard we must point to another remarkable, perhaps the most remarkable, feature of Mormonism, which our authority has completely neglected to mention.

Experience has shown that no religious body, from the smallest country congregation to the church of Rome itself, can subsist for long without finding itself under the necessity of interpreting the scriptures. The result is the "History of Dogma." But the Mormons have no History of Dogma. There has never been a Mormon scholar. Learned men in various fields have been Mormons, but there are no experts on matters of doctrine; there has never been a council or synod to alter or even discuss any matter of doctrine.

If Joseph Smith were to walk into a conference of the Mormon Church today he would find himself completely at home; and if he were to address the congregation they would never for a moment detect anything the least bit strange, unfamiliar, or old-fashioned in his teaching. Yet for all this incredible doctrinal stability, the Mormons have been of all people the least disposed to fight change — no one insists more emphatically on their passion for progress than Brodie herself. Moreover, the Saints have always had more than their share of crackpots, and these have always been given a hearing. Yet of all churches in the world, only this one has not found it necessary to readjust any part of its doctrine in the last hundred years.

If we are to believe Mrs. Brodie, it was the shrewdness and agility of Joseph's "highly compensated . . . sincerity,"[141] plus a great "magnetic"[142] appeal, that induced people to swallow his doctrine as he held them spellbound from the pulpit; and when "his magnetic presence"[143] left the pulpit even for a moment, it "left a void that they had found intolerable."[144] What, then, would be the first result of his death? Doctrinal chaos, of course. Why didn't the whole thing explode? Was it because Joseph Smith had left a legacy of written revelation? But every page of scripture is just so much more grist for controversy. Were people indifferent to matters of doctrine? Not when they would go forth by the thousands as unpaid preachers. The fact that everyone has a share in Church work, though it makes for loyalty, should only lead to doctrinal confusion. Let it be borne in mind that the Mormons regard the heavens as still open, and every man and woman eligible to receive inspiration. How does Brodie explain the fact that the doctrine she claims was the haphazard outgrowth of complete opportunism remains the most stable on earth? She doesn't.

What Eduard Meyer sees in the Mormon doctrine is before everything else *Konsequenz* (consistency; to use his own words, that doctrine is "absolutely literal, sober, and logical"; *verstandesgemäss*). Moreover, says Meyer, the scientific aspects of the dogma, "in full agreement with the later discoveries of science," may well be a cause of considerable gratification to believers.[145] These impressive aspects of doctrine mean nothing to the glib and superficial mind of the modern English major, the copy-desk mind with its inevitable leaning towards journalism, and its buoyant faith in accomplishing all things by the mere manipulation of words. Brodie's silences are an eloquent commentary on the shallow thinking of the times.[146]

The Art of Insinuation as Illustrated by a Few Succinct Examples from a Highly Reliable Source

In 1835, Joseph Smith reports having given a brief sketch of his early life, including the first vision, to Erastus Holmes. Brodie objects: "But Joseph admittedly did not begin writing his history until 1838."[147] We are to assume that the report must be a mistake. Only Joseph Smith is talking about a brief informal sketch, while Brodie is talking about the formal Church history, an entirely different thing. She insinuates that they are the same thing and that the Prophet is lying.[148]

The Moundbuilders actually resemble the Book of Mormon people not at all.[149] Who said they did? The Book of Mormon tells of a people ages removed from the Moundbuilders and very far away. Yet Brodie insinuates that because the Moundbuilders (of all people) do not resemble the Nephites, the Book of Mormon is a fraud.

One of Brodie's favorite insinuations is that Joseph Smith was a charlatan because he constantly used the language of the King James Bible, including whole passages from the ancient scriptures, in modern revelations.[150] That is the equivalent of accusing an author of stealing words from the dictionary. Jesus and the disciples constantly spoke the language of the prophets, not in the original, but in the religious idiom of their own time and place. Just so, the prophets themselves quote from the Psalms and the Mosaic Law. Now the religious idiom of the West was the language of the King James Bible; that was and still is the standard of "formal" English for great occasions. If Joseph Smith had been living in Germany he would not have used the King James Version at all—he would have spoken Luther's German, but that would not prove him a hoax and a plagiarist. Of course Brodie knows this, but she repeatedly insinuates that the use of Bible language by Joseph Smith implies fraud.

"Foot-washing was practiced regularly on the Western Reserve."[151] So what? What if it was practiced in Tierra del Fuego? Anyone can read about it in the New Testament.

Confronted with the testimony of the eight witnesses, the lady neatly turns it aside with a witticism of Mark Twain regarding the prominence of the Whitmer family in the list.[152] But if all the eight had been named John Jones, the document still remains to be explained.

Brodie tells a perfectly fictitious story of an attempt by Joseph Smith to walk on the water, but dismisses it with the remark, "Baseless though this story may be, it is none the less symbolic."[153] The reader is told that though no justification exists for believing the story, Joseph Smith must always have been doing silly things like that, and that makes it "symbolic." Why bother with mere symbols? Why not give the concrete examples? Can she do no better than to cite a tale that is *known to be false* simply because it symbolizes her idea of Joseph Smith?

"Very early the young prophet learned to use persecution as a means of identifying himself with the great martyrs."[154] Now the first thing any Christian thinks of upon being persecuted for his religion, the thing in fact which the Bible enjoins us to think of, is the assurance, "blessed are ye, . . . for so persecuted they the prophets which were before you" (Matthew 5:11–12). Yet in Joseph

Smith's case this natural and Christian reaction is evidence to Brodie of a singular vanity and shallowness.

The case of Grandison Newell against the Prophet is given at length: then "when the court convened . . . it was clear that he had no case."[155] In the meantime, however, we are left with the impression that Joseph Smith *was* somewhat of a rascal.[156] In the same way, John C. Bennett's lurid description of the "Danites and 'Angels' " appears at length.[157] Later it turns out that Bennett is an "unreliable [witness], to say the least,"[158] but meantime it has all sunk in and the reader is left with a definite impression that the charges may well be true. This is a favorite trick of Brodie's, giving worthless but quite damning evidence at length just for effect, and then refuting or qualifying the testimonies in a single brief sentence.

The Brodie evolutionary theory rests heavily on the word "now." If it is written, "he now refused to beat his wife," or "he now ate eggs for breakfast," one naturally assumes that the subject formerly did beat his wife in the one case, and in the other, that he formerly did *not* eat eggs for breakfast. That is what the words insinuate, but it is not what they say: actually the man may never have beaten his wife and always had eggs for breakfast. Mrs. Brodie introduces every selected key event in the life of Joseph Smith with a "now" of this sort, making it appear in each case that the thing was occurring for the first time; for this she has no proof, of course, but the little "now" enables her to build up his career step by step the way she wants it.

Super-Psychology

Mrs. Brodie applauds the honesty of Josiah Quincy's conclusion: "If the reader does not know just what to make of Joseph Smith, I cannot help him out of the difficulty. I myself stand helpless before the puzzle."[159] But not Brodie! On no other evidence than Quincy's own, she tells us what he should have seen but failed to. When Quincy reports that Joseph Smith joked with him about the ridiculous figure he must sometimes cut in the eyes of unbelievers, he simply notes that the Prophet has the sense to acknowledge the humor of the situation (a risk no false prophet would take). This interpretation will never do for Brodie; let Josiah look again: is it not plain that Joseph is expressing a "[mood] of uncertainty and doubt?"[160] Likewise when he says, "I do not think there have been many good men on the earth since the days of Adam. . . . I do not want you to think I am very righteous, for I am not,"[161] he is not just speaking plain truths, he is confessing that he has grave doubts as to his calling.[162]

In dealing with Emma, our author allows free rein to her woman's intuition. One day Joseph was bantering his wife while she was setting the table; Parley Pratt was present, and everybody was jolly.[163] Pratt asks Joseph why he does not eat alone like Napoleon, and Emma observes that he is greater than Napoleon, whereupon Joseph congratulates her on the wisest utterance of her lifetime. It is all very merry and typical—Brodie often points out that Joseph Smith was a great hand for joking about everything—yet she does not hesitate to see in this episode a clear revelation "of the prophet's vanity."[164]

When Joseph Smith faced Emma for the last time, "he knew that she thought him a coward."[165] So Brodie knows that Emma knew that Joseph knew what Emma thought! Is this *history*? There might be some merit in this sort of thing if, like the invented speeches of the Greek historian, it took some skill to produce. But, if anything, it is hard for the historian to avoid the pitfalls of such cheap and easy psychology. The business of the historian is to tell what happened, not what someone might have been thinking about what was happening.[166] Does it take any skill or knowledge at all to write that "the Book of Mormon must have been a source of secret worry,"[167] or "Mormon ritual doubtless had its roots in the same unconscious drives that led the prophet into polygamy,"[168] or to appeal continually to a secret imponderable quality known as "magnetism?"[169]

At the end of the book in which she has leaned so heavily on the categorical "must have," our author displays an equal virtuosity with the categorical "would have." She tells us without a moment's hesitation just what would have happened if the Prophet had not been killed: the Saints "would have" followed him West, he "would have" lost some converts, his empire "would" have been more colorful than Brigham Young's; Emma "would have" followed him, and the Gentiles "would not have" been able to rejoice in her second marriage.[170] This is history in the Brodie tradition. The young woman who can tell us with perfect confidence just what *must* have happened and what *would* have happened is not one to be stopped by un-cooperative documents and recalcitrant sources; and she is most at home when there are no documents at all.

A Solid Contribution

If anyone has a right to reject Joseph Smith's own story, it is also anybody's right to ask the skeptic for a more plausible version of what happened. Such a version Fawn Brodie has bravely attempted to produce. She tells the plausible enough story of a guy named Joe, who walks and talks and laughs and looks just like Joseph Smith. Only there the resemblance ends. We know a butcher who looks just like the great Johann Sebastian Bach, and he walks and talks and eats and breathes—the very things that Bach did—only there is one slight difference: the butcher can't write music. Brodie's Joseph is a real enough character—all the details are there, except one: he can't do the things Joseph Smith did—the only things about Joseph Smith, incidentally, that really interest us.

Brodie's Joseph is decidedly *not* the man who produced the Book of Mormon; for the former is wildly imaginative, undisciplined, lazy, and short-sighted, while the Book of Mormon is the work (even if you take it as fiction) of an exceedingly sober, self-controlled, incredibly industrious, and well-organized brain.

Brodie's Joseph picks up ideas like a thieving magpie, throws them together haphazardly, and sells them from the pulpit. He is therefore *not* the man whose teachings are so well-knit and perfectly logical that they have never had to undergo the slightest change or alteration during a century in which every other church in Christendom has continually revamped its doctrines.

Brodie's Joseph is the man who works by personal magnetism and dispenses his far-fetched and jumbled ideas by rhetorical legerdemain. This is *not* the Joseph who won his following among the artisans and farmers of Great Britain, Scandinavia, and Switzerland—a finely disciplined, hard-headed, and Bible-bred generation which was looking for light but not interested in vaudeville or voodoo.

Brodie's Joseph appealed to the Yankee and the frontier minds. The real Joseph was suspected by the one and hated by the other and enjoyed his great success in distant lands and on the islands of the sea. Incidentally, no effort of the imagination can fit these islanders, or Europeans, for that matter, into the contemporary American scene.

Brodie's Joseph announces, "My kingdom is of this world." The real Joseph describes this world as one whose "substance is that of an idol, which waxeth old and shall perish in Babylon, even Babylon the great" (D&C 1:16), and he tells how "the hour is not yet, but is nigh at hand, when peace shall be taken from the earth, and the devil shall have power over his own dominion" (D&C 1:35). Joseph Smith's message was before everything one of warning, of clear specific warnings against the very things that are transpiring in our day. No man ever sized up "this world" better than he.

Brodie's Joseph is not the man who organized the

Church. That man always knew exactly what he was doing. Brodie's Joseph never does. That man, from the first, sent out messengers with messages so crystal clear, so specific, and so unequivocal that they either convinced on the spot or excited paroxysms of rage. There was nothing hazy in what these men had to say, nor in the church they represented. Brodie's Joseph lives and dies in a fog.

Brodie's Joseph never had the plates. The Joseph the witnesses talk about *did* have them; and as long as Mrs. Brodie refuses to face the witnesses, her Joseph cannot turn the real one out of doors.

Brodie's Joseph, rioting with his fifty wives, is not the man whose conception of marriage so completely escapes her. Emma Smith and Eliza Snow were not acquainted with the oversexed rake that Mrs. Brodie knows so well.

Brodie's Joseph, the crazy fool who is "simply drunk" with dreams of power and personal glory, has nothing in common with the Joseph Smith whose pronouncements in the campaign of 1844 (still there for all to read) are models of wisdom and statesmanship that have excited the unqualified admiration of experts. Brodie as good as tells us that the Joseph Smith that Josiah Quincy saw and admired is not the Joseph *she* has in mind.

So we could go on, distinguishing between the two Josephs. That is just a way of answering the question we set at the beginning: does Mrs. Brodie go too far? "Too far" is putting it mildly. The book is nothing but a mass of strained interpretations and limiting explanations, mostly in terms of a highly intimate and intuitive psychology. It would take more than the impressive padding of an appendix to support so much manipulating, unless the new and wonderful documents thus brought to light should turn out to be not merely rare but actually to have something to say.[171] Like a buyer of first editions, Mrs. Brodie is dazzled enough by the mere rarity of her finds to overlook the fact that they tell us absolutely nothing that was not known before.

Still and all, the good woman's contribution is a real one. She has set about to answer the question: "How can you explain Joseph Smith if you reject his own story?" The result is surprising: time and again the discriminating reader asks in wonderment, "Can't the dear woman do better than *this*?" Must it always be "would have" and "must have" and fourth-dimensional psychology and "Mormonism Unvailed" and reading between the lines of vindictive but ambiguous newspaper articles? If we ever had doubts about the real Joseph Smith, Brodie's struggles have dispelled them. The question is no longer "How can the world explain Joseph Smith?" but "Can the world explain him at all?" And Brodie gives us the answer: It can't. It thinks Brodie has done the trick and hails her with a prize: Nothing could more clearly reveal its own sad lack of resources or its pathetic eagerness to find *some* sort of explanation for Joseph Smith than this acclaim of such a poor effort to make seminar rhetoric sound like history.

All his life, Augustine, the father of medieval and modern Christianity, wrestled mightily with the problem of working out a doctrine that would satisfy both reason and faith. Both Grabmann and Gilson bear witness to the inadequacy of his solution, the former noting the saint's failure to answer any of the basic questions which it is ostensibly the purpose of the gospel to answer,[172] and the latter pointing out the "undefined" and "vulnerable" nature of the answers he does give.[173] It remained for later ages to try to hammer out a complete and convincing statement of doctrine, and they have had no easy time of it. A long line of canons and decrees attests alike the determination and the failure of the learned divines to give the Christian doctrine a definitive and final form, from which we conclude that it is one thing for the sweating revivalist to fling out his ecstatic pronouncements as they come to him in hot and frenzied disorder, and a very different thing to give logical and consistent form to those ideas.

The gospel as the Mormons know it sprang full-grown from the words of Joseph Smith. It has never been worked over or touched up in any way and is free of revisions and alterations. Joseph Smith took the same elements that have proven so recalcitrant and so hopelessly conflicting in the hands of the churchmen and threw them together, with an awful lot of other stuff (to follow Brodie) into a single wildly chaotic mess. And lo and behold, everything fell into line of its own accord; all the haphazard elements in the bewildering heap fitted together perfectly to form a doctrine so commanding that not even a hint of rhetorical paradox is needed to support it, and no "Gregorian compromise" with a pleasure-loving world has been necessary to assure its vigorous growth.

The merciless logic of the Mormon doctrine made its strictly amateur missionaries from the outset the bane of the learned cloth throughout the world. What a piece of luck for Joseph! How her chuckle-headed, pipe-dreaming, glory-mongering hero ever produced a doctrine more wholly logical than anything done by a St. Thomas or a Calvin and at the same time as vivid and intimate as the faith of the Primitive Church is one of the more important issues our Sibyl has avoided. Certainly her Joseph is not up to the task, and until a more likely candidate than the Brodie mannequin turns up, we will just have to accept Joseph Smith's own story of what happened.

Notes

1. See for example, nn. 111 and 166 below.

2. This preface appeared in Hugh W. Nibley, *No Ma'am, That's Not History*, 3rd ed. (Salt Lake City: Bookcraft, 1960), 5.

3. Fawn M. Brodie, *No Man Knows My History* (New York: Knopf, 1945). A second revised and enlarged edition was published by Knopf in 1971. Through page 404, these editions are very similar, and page numbers may refer to either edition, except where otherwise noted.

4. Ibid., viii.

5. [Cf. Fawn M. Brodie's 1975 statement: "I was convinced before I ever began writing the book that Joseph Smith was not a true prophet," in "Biography of Fawn McKay Brodie," interview with Shirley E. Stephenson, 30 November 1975, Oral History Collection, Fullerton State University, Fullerton, CA, p. 10.]

6. Ibid., 18.

7. Ibid., 19.

8. Ibid., 331.

9. Ibid., 19.

10. Ibid., 31.

11. Ibid., 37.

12. Ibid., 80.

13. Ibid.

14. Ibid., 84.

15. Ibid., 46.

16. Ibid., 47.

17. Ibid.

18. Karl Joel, *Wandlungen der Weltanschauung: Eine Philosophiegeschichte als Geschichtsphilosophie*, 2 vols. (Tübingen: Mohr, 1928–34).

19. Brodie, *No Man Knows My History*, 71.

20. Ibid., 70.

21. Thomas Dick, *The Philosophy of a Future State* (Brookfield, MA: Merriam, 1829). [Cf. *Latter-Day Saints' Messenger and Advocate* 2 (December 1836): 423–25; 3 (February 1837): 461–63; and 3 (March 1837): 468–69; cf. also Edward T. Jones, "The Theology of Thomas Dick and Its Possible Relationship to That of Joseph Smith," Master's thesis, Brigham Young University, 1969.]

22. Brodie, *No Man Knows My History*, 171.

23. Ibid., 172.

24. Ibid., 196.

25. Ibid., 213.

26. Ibid., 214.

27. Ibid., 65.

28. Ibid., 281.

29. Eduard Meyer, *Geschichte des Altertums*, 2nd ed., 3 vols. in 5 parts (Stuttgart: Cotta, 1909–37).

30. Eduard Meyer, *Ursprung und Geschichte der Mormonen* (Halle: Neimeyer, 1912), 142, n. 2; English translation by Heinz F. Rahde and Eugene Seaich, in *The Origin and History of the Mormons* (Salt Lake City: University of Utah, 1961), 102, n. 3.

31. Brodie, *No Man Knows My History*, 256. This has been deleted from the second edition.

32. Meyer, *Ursprung und Geschichte der Mormonen*, 2; Rahde and Seaich, *Origin and History of the Mormons*, 3.

33. Brodie, *No Man Knows My History*, vii.

34. Ibid., 22.

35. Ibid., 14.

36. Ibid., 23.

37. *HC* 1:7.

38. Brodie, *No Man Knows My History*, 23. What has been emphasized in the first edition has been deleted from the second edition.

39. Ibid.

40. Ibid., 24.

41. Ibid., 25.

42. [Cf. Hugh W. Nibley, *Since Cumorah* (Salt Lake City: Deseret Book, 1967), 96–126; reprinted in *CWHN* 7:84–110.]

43. Brodie, *No Man Knows My History*, 25. This quotation is from the first edition; the second edition says "after 1830."

44. Ibid.

45. Ibid., 16. This becomes "religious independence of his father" in the second edition.

46. Ibid.

47. Ibid., 24. This was deleted from the second edition.

48. Ibid., 26.

49. Ibid., 38 (emphasis added).

50. Ibid., 41.

51. Ibid , 49.

52. Ibid., 53.

53. Ibid., 84.

54. Ibid., 27.

55. Ibid.

56. Ibid., 53–54.

57. Ibid., 53.

58. Ibid., 27.

59. Ibid., 63; Mark Twain, *Roughing It* (Avon, CT: Heritage, 1972), 82.

60. Brodie, *No Man Knows My History*, 55.

61. Ibid., 83.

62. Ibid., 38. The author quotes the Palmyra *Reflector*.

63. Ibid., 42.

64. Ibid., 37, 41, 53.

65. Ibid., 72.

66. Ibid., 34–36.

67. Ibid., 99.

68. Ibid., 80.

69. Ibid., 84.

70. Meyer, *Ursprung und Geschichte der Mormonen*, 16–18, 81–83.

71. Brodie, *No Man Knows My History*, 84.

72. Ibid., 85.

73. Ibid., 100.

74. Ibid., 84.

75. Ibid.

76. Ibid., 69.

77. Ibid., 86 (emphasis added).

78. Ibid., 14.

79. Ibid., 91.

80. Ibid., 403 (emphasis added).

81. Ibid., 91–92.

82. Ibid., 87.

83. Ibid., 118.

84. Ibid., 123.

85. Ibid., 128 (emphasis added).

86. Ibid., 138.

87. Ibid.

88. Ibid., 140.

89. Ibid., 159.

90. Ibid., 168.

91. Ibid., 169.

92. Ibid., 168.

93. Ibid., 169 (emphasis added).

94. Ibid., 69.

95. Ibid., 171.

96. Ibid., 107.

97. Ibid.

98. Ibid., 174.

99. Hermann Kees, *Ägypten* (Munich: Beck, 1933), 282; [cf. Hugh W. Nibley's series of articles, "A Look at the Pearl of Great Price," *Ensign* (1968–70).]

100. Brodie, *No Man Knows My History*, 210.

101. Ibid.

102. Ibid., 211.

103. Ibid., 280.

104. Meyer, *Ursprung und Geschichte der Mormonen*, 166–67; cf. Rahde and Seaich, *Origin and History of the Mormons*, 121–22.

105. Brodie, *No Man Knows My History*, 282–83.

106. Ibid., 283.
107. Ibid.
108. Ibid., 275.
109. Ibid., 285.
110. Ibid., 286.
111. This writer has pointed out that the Reverend Caswall published not only one but no fewer than six conflicting versions of his famous interview with Joseph Smith. It is a moot question whether it is more reprehensible for a biographer to be ignorant of such a vital and readily accessible fact as this, or to conceal it if he knows of it. Mrs. Brodie cites as her source for the story Caswall's earliest version, that of 1842, while the tale she actually tells is the elaborately revamped version of 1851, to which she adds important touches of her own not to be found in any of Caswall's accounts. A little of her vaunted "primary research" could have shown Mrs. Brodie that while Caswall's Psalter trick was carefully prepared in advance, the interview with the Prophet never took place. Cf. Henry Caswall, *The City of the Mormons; or, Three Days at Nauvoo in 1842* (London: Rivingtons, 1842), Henry Caswall, *America, and the American Church* (London: Mozleys, 1851), 358–59. Cf. also Hugh W. Nibley, *The Myth Makers* (Salt Lake City: Bookcraft, 1961), 194–287, reprinted in this volume, pages 103–406.
112. Brodie, *No Man Knows My History*, 290.
113. Ibid., 291.
114. Ibid., 299.
115. Ibid., 304.
116. Ibid., 338.
117. Ibid., 354.
118. Ibid., 356.
119. Ibid., 362.
120. Don C. Seitz, *Uncommon Americans* (Indianapolis: Bobbs-Merrill, 1925), 13.
121. Brodie, *No Man Knows My History*, 356 (emphasis added).
122. Ibid., 181.
123. Ibid., 357.
124. Ibid., 366.
125. Ibid.
126. Ibid.
127. Ibid., 375, citing Nauvoo *Expositor*, 7 June 1844.
128. Ibid.
129. Ibid., 376.
130. Ibid., 378.

131. Meyer, *Ursprung und Geschichte der Mormonen*, 1; cf. Rahde and Seaich, *Origin and History of the Mormons*, 1.

132. Cf. Brodie, *No Man Knows My History*, 73, 86, 210.

133. Ibid., 187.

134. Ibid., 402.

135. Ibid., 70.

136. Ibid., 212.

137. Ibid., 264–65.

138. Ibid., 403.

139. Ibid.

140. Justin Martyr, *Apology* II, 8, in *PG* 6:457; cf. ibid., I, 59, in *PG* 6:416; and Justin Martyr, *Cohortatio ad Graecos* 32, in *PG* 6:300.

141. Brodie, *No Man Knows My History*, 85.

142. Ibid., 73.

143. Ibid., 210.

144. Ibid.

145. Meyer, *Ursprung und Geschichte der Mormonen*, 156–58; cf. Rahde and Seaich, *Origin and History of the Mormons*, 113–15.

146. Since Mrs. Brodie's book appeared, a number of studies by non-Mormon writers (Whitney R. Cross, *The Burned-over District* [Ithaca, NY: Cornell, 1950]; David B. Davis, "The New England Origins of Mormonism," *New England Quarterly* 26 [June 1953]: 147–68; and W. H. G. Armytage, "Liverpool, Gateway to Zion," *Pacific Northwest Quarterly* 48 [April 1957]: 39– 44, for example) have shown that Mormonism was definitely not a product either of the American Frontier or of the revival meeting. Thus, two of Mrs. Brodie's basic assumptions, on which she counts heavily to explain her peculiar view of Joseph Smith and his work, have been discredited. See Hugh W. Nibley, "What Frontier, What Camp Meeting?" *IE* 62 (August 1959): 590–91; reprinted in *CWHN* 8:182–92.

147. Brodie, *No Man Knows My History*, 24. This is in the first edition only.

148. Ibid. This was deleted from the second edition. See footnote in first edition marked with an asterisk.

149. Ibid., 36.

150. [Cf. Hugh W. Nibley, "Literary Style Used in Book of Mormon Insured Accurate Translation," in *The Prophetic Book of Mormon*, vol. 8 in *The Collected Works of Hugh Nibley* (Salt Lake City: Deseret Book and F.A.R.M.S., 1989), 212–18.]

151. Brodie, *No Man Knows My History*, 176.

152. Ibid., 79; Twain, *Roughing It*, 84.

153. Brodie, *No Man Knows My History*, 84.

154. Ibid., 88.

155. Ibid., 203.

156. [Cf. Marvin S. Hill, C. Keith Rooker, and Larry T. Wimmer, *The Kirtland Economy Revisited* (Provo, UT: Brigham Young University, 1977), 51. The authors present a detailed quantitative analysis of the Kirtland Safety Society issue which is critical of Brodie's conclusions; cf. 3, 16, 24, 59, 69.]

157. Brodie, *No Man Knows My History*, 315.

158. Ibid., 331.

159. Ibid., 294: Josiah Quincy, "Joseph Smith at Nauvoo," in *Figures from the Past* (Boston: Roberts Brothers, 1892), 400.

160. Brodie, *No Man Knows My History*, 295.

161. *HC* 5:401.

162. Brodie, *No Man Knows My History*, 296.

163. It was not Parley P. Pratt; of course, it was W. W. Phelps. Cf. *HC* 6:165–66.

164. Brodie, *No Man Knows My History*, 326.

165. Ibid., 384.

166. Note on mind-reading: The eminent American biographer Douglas S. Freeman is reported to have said that he knew where General Lee was and what he was doing "every minute of the Civil War," but that he "wouldn't dare presume what he was thinking" at any time. Mrs. Brodie's principles of research are the exact reverse: though ever so vague as to where the Prophet is or what he is doing, she is never at a loss to tell us exactly what is going on in his mind. "For the popular, novelized biography full of glib insights into the inner man," says Freeman's reviewer, "Freeman has nothing but contempt"; see review of Douglas S. Freeman, see heading *George Washington* in "The Virginians," *Time* 52 (18 October 1948): 108. To this day it remains unclear whether Mrs. Brodie intended a serious biography or a novel.

167. Brodie, *No Man Knows My History*, 275.

168. Ibid., 279.

169. Ibid., 73, 86, 210.

170. Ibid., 398–99.

171. Careful search reveals that Mrs. Brodie has not made a single new documentary find!

172. Martin Grabmann, *Geschichte der scholastischen Methode*, 2 vols. (Graz: Akademische Druck- und Verlagsanstalt, 1957).

173. Etienne Gilson, "The Future of Augustinian Metaphysics," in *A Gilson Reader* (Garden City, NY: Hanover, 1957), 85, 90.

A Note on F. M. Brodie

A Note on F. M. Brodie

Almost thirty years ago, Mrs. F. M. Brodie wrote what purported to be a biography of the Prophet Joseph Smith. It was instantly proclaimed to be the one definitive, authoritative book on Joseph Smith and the Mormons. Reviewers vied in heaping praises on it. Schools and libraries accepted it as the true and official account of Mormonism. Ministers and priests went into ecstasies about it and invariably placed it in the hands of any of their flock who wondered about the Mormons.

Mrs. Brodie went on to produce other biographies, receiving mostly favorable but not enthusiastic reviews, but nothing like the attention and acclaim accorded the Joseph Smith epic.

Then she wrote a long biography of Thomas Jefferson, and promptly the roof fell in. "Two vast things" wrote an eminent reviewer, "make this book a prodigy—the author's industry, and her ignorance. . . . She regularly treats us to sub-freshman absurdity. . . . Error on this scale, and in this detail, does not come easily. There is a skill involved. And much nerve. . . . As usual, Ms. Brodie has her facts wrong, even before she loads them with unsustainable surmise."[1] Can this be the same Mrs. B. who wrote about Joseph Smith; is it her vaunted scholarship of which we now read, "the same appetites can be more

---

These brief comments on reviews of Fawn Brodie's Thomas Jefferson: An Intimate History *(New York: Norton, 1974) were written around 1974 and presented as a talk.*

49

readily gratified by those Hollywood fan magazines, with their wealth of unfounded conjecture on the sex lives of others, from which Ms. Brodie has borrowed her scholarly methods"?[2]

It is the same Brodie. With one important difference. Now, at last, she is writing about a man whose life and character is the close concern of many students and some eminent scholars.

When she writes about Richard Burton, who is going to bother to check up on her? Does it really make that much difference just what kind of a man he was? Is it anybody's intimate personal concern? Even when she writes about Thaddeus Stevens she is on safe grounds—few are they who love or remember him, or care about him at this distance.

She could proceed with the most slapdash methods on such neutral ground, having once established her status by her first mighty opus, which was a *sure thing*. For in that she ran not the slightest danger of offending anybody but the Mormons; she told everybody exactly what they *wanted* to hear about Joseph Smith. Her huge bibliography was accepted at its face value, and awarded her prize after prize.

Those of us who presumed to point out her foibles are still denounced as "flippant." But it needs no profound learning to detect crude and persistent cheating—and that was obvious.

It took this venture into the biography of a man who really interests people, and who is really liked by them, to show the Brodie method for what it is. "One can only be so intricately wrong by deep study and long effort, enough to make Ms. Brodie the fasting hermit and very saint of ignorance. The result has an eerie perfection, as if all the world's greatest builders had agreed to rear, with infinite skill, the world's ugliest building."[3]

Exactly the same charges which we brought against the

Brodie method in 1946, with scandalized hushings from the intellectuals, are now brought against her later and with riper effort by the most respected scholars. As her students at the University of Utah reported, the lady was all out to "get" Joseph Smith, and her motivation was betrayed on many occasions. But with nothing against Thomas Jefferson, she gives him exactly the same treatment. Her manipulating and tangling of evidence, which we once compared to a nest of garter snakes, is now as vividly described in Mr. Wills' illustration of what he calls "the garbled mess she has made of things."[4]

He comments, as we did, on her gross ignorance of the larger background of the subject she was treating, on her manipulation of words ("she constantly finds double meanings"),[5] and on her obsession with sex ("Ms. Brodie delights in the small titillation of finding sexual references wherever possible").[6]

Were we flippant? No more than this: "It seems a shame to deprive her of such innocent fun; but the game becomes tedious to anyone who has not got her endless appetite for it [sex]."[7] "Guilt, torment, and conflict are interlineated through all his writings to make his soul quiver in tune with la Brodie's. Yet there is no scrap of evidence for this passion."[8] It was just the same with Joseph Smith — "la Brodie" could look right into his soul with her Freudian intuition: "Ms. Brodie proves that the attempt to construct one [picture of Jefferson] more to the liking of today's romantic daydreamers involves heroic feats of misunderstanding and constant labor at ignorance."[9]

No one listened when we protested the unfairness of Mrs. B.'s sly and constant insinuations. But now Mr. W. writes: "Typical of Ms. Brodie's hint-and-run method [flippant again] [is] to ask a rhetorical question, and then proceed on the assumption that it has been settled in her favor, making the first surmise a basis for second and third ones, in a towering rickety structure of unsupported conjecture."[10] We called this the "House-That-Jack-Built" method, a great favorite of all anti-Mormon writers.[11]

Notes

1. Gary Wills, "Uncle Thomas's Cabin," *New York Review of Books* 21 (18 April 1974): 26–27.
2. Ibid., 28.
3. Ibid., 26.
4. Ibid.
5. Ibid.
6. Ibid.
7. Ibid.
8. Ibid., 27.
9. Ibid., 28.
10. Ibid., 26.
11. Hugh W. Nibley, *Sounding Brass* (Salt Lake City: Bookcraft, 1961), 81–85; reprinted in this volume, pages 407–727.

Censoring the
Joseph Smith Story

Censoring the
Joseph Smith Story

The Problem

Joseph Smith's "official" account of his first vision and the visits of the angel Moroni was written in 1838 and first published in the *Times and Seasons* in 1842. Since the writing took place from eleven to eighteen years after the events described, anti-Mormon writers were quick to exploit the time-lag as a welcome chink in the Mormon armor. "Why," they asked, "did Smith wait so long to make his official statement?" And they insisted that the only possible answer was that the stories of the first vision and the golden plates were invented in retrospect—they were pure fabrications.

In 1842 J. B. Turner declared that the story of Moroni was a product of the year 1834, "when the history was first interlarded with prophetic declarations of the angel, which had already been fulfilled, the whole story new vamped, stereotyped, and given to the world for the edification of the Saints, in the columns of the *Messenger and Advocate*."[1] John C. Bennett took up the cry, citing as proof a report of one of Joseph Smith's former neighbors to the

This originally appeared as a series of articles in the Improvement Era: *"Part I: The Problem," 64 (July 1961): 490–92, 522, 524, 526, 528; "Part II: Suppressing the First Vision Story after 1842," 64 (August 1961): 577–79, 605–9; "Part III," 64 (October 1961): 724–25, 736, 738, 740; and "Conclusion," 64 (November 1961): 812–13, 865–69.*

effect that in the years before the publication of the Book of Mormon, Joseph Smith, Sr., had said nothing to *him* about its being a religious book—"He gave me no intimation, at that time, that the book was to be of a religious character, or that it had anything to do with revelation. He declared it to be a speculation."[2] In the following years Henry Caswall, following Turner, declared the story of the first vision to be a "blasphemous tale substituted for the former inventions of the same description," the former inventions being "various and contradictory stories respecting the angel and the golden plates, the narrative being altered to suit his successive exigencies."[3]

Invariably these reports turn out upon examination to be not the declarations of Joseph Smith or his followers at all, but remarks attributed to them at second and third hand by former neighbors: "various and contradictory" they certainly are, but the contradictions are among the statements made by the "witnesses" and not by the accused.

But critics love to speculate. In 1844 a *History of Illinois*, after giving a very garbled version of the first story, commented: "Whether the above reflections passed through the mind of a lad of fifteen, uneducated, and exhibiting, as yet, no evidence of precocious genius; or whether they are the reflections of maturer life, or the emanations of other and brighter intellects than his own, our readers will judge for themselves."[4]

It was literary intuition that convinced the eminent W. J. Conybeare, writing in the *Edinburgh Review* in 1854, that Joseph Smith's report that he was commanded to join no church and told that "all existing Christian sects [were] in error . . . was no doubt an afterthought. At the time, he probably only proclaimed that his 'deliverance from the enemy' had been effected by a supernatural appearance."[5] And why was it "no doubt" an afterthought? And by what authority does Conybeare put the words of "deliverance from the enemy" in quotation marks, as if they were the actual words of Joseph Smith, which they are not? The same writer assures us, speaking of the Book of Mormon: "At first he only claims to have miraculously discovered a sacred record, but does not himself pretend to inspiration." The proof of this he finds in sections 9, 13, and 14 of the Doctrine and Covenants: since these passages refer to *future* revelation, Conybeare assumes that there cannot have been any *earlier* revelations before them.[6]

To prove that Joseph Smith was guilty of "changing the story about his alleged golden plates . . . as a means of making him a prophet," the much-quoted Mr. Linn produced a letter received by James T. Cobb of Salt Lake City "under date of April 23, 1879, from Hiel and Joseph Lewis, sons of the Rev. Nathaniel Lewis, of Harmony, Pennsylvania, and relatives of Joseph's father-in-law, in which they gave the story of the finding of the plates as told in their hearing by Joe to their father, when he was translating them. This statement, in effect, was that he dreamed of an iron box containing gold plates . . . 'he saw a man standing over the spot who, to him, appeared like a Spaniard, having a long beard down over his breast, with his throat cut from ear to ear and the blood streaming down, who told him that he could not get it alone.' (He then narrated how he got the box in company with Emma.) 'In all this narrative there was not one word about visions of God, or of angels, or heavenly revelations; all his information was by that dream and that bleeding ghost. The heavenly visions and messages of angels, etc., contained in the Mormon books were afterthoughts, revised to order.' "[7] The learned Linn makes no effort whatever to test the reliability of this report, reaching him as it does at third-hand from parties who claimed that it is "in effect" the memory of a dream that they overheard Joseph Smith telling to somebody else more than fifty years before; he accepts it without question as the one true and authentic account of the origin of the Book of Mormon.

A very little research would have shown Mr. Linn that his Reverend Nathaniel Lewis is none other than Elder Nathaniel C. Lewis, who in 1834 swore an affidavit that he knew Joseph Smith to be "an imposter . . . and [a] liar," though he admits that his behavior was unobjectionable. He rests his case on Joseph Smith's connection with the Book of Mormon, claiming that the Prophet actually asked *him* "whether he should proceed to translate the Book of Plates . . . or not," explaining that "God had commanded him to translate it, but he was afraid of the people."[8]

Since Joseph proceeded with the translation, Mr. Lewis must have advised him to do so. Or did he? Did Joseph Smith, having God's instructions, as he thought, really ask his hostile neighbor what to do? Though it is Lewis's purpose in writing this document to discredit the Book of Mormon, *he* knows nothing of the damning Spanish dream story which was supposedly addressed to *him* and overheard by his two sons, who suddenly remembered it fifty years later. The Lewis boys insist that "there was not one word about visions of God or angels," etc., in Joseph's story at the time "when he was translating." Yet their father's own story, written forty-six years earlier, is that at that time or earlier—when Joseph was still hesitating as to "whether he should proceed to translate or not"—he not only claimed to have the plates, but also insisted that *God* had commanded him to translate them. All this simply confirms what the Prophet himself says in the preface to the first edition of the Book of Mormon, namely that there actually were all kinds of wild stories circulating about the as-yet-unpublished book.

According to D. H. C. Bartlett, writing in 1911, "the foregoing account of the origin of the Book [of Mormon] accepted by orthodox Mormons, . . . written by Smith, under the inspiration of Rigdon, some eleven years later when in Nauvoo, was clearly an afterthought." What makes this so clear is again the Lewis letter, showing that "Smith at that time had no thought of God, angels, or divine revelations. He was simply a magical dreamer, beholding the ghost of a murdered Spaniard."[9] "It is well for us to remember," writes the Rev. John Quincy Adams in 1916, "that the story of these experiences and of the great discovery [of the Book of Mormon] was not written before 1838, when it was prepared under the direction of Sidney Rigdon, or by him. Others say positively that the story was revised from time to time, always gaining in its miraculous and mysterious character."[10] Never mind who the "others" were—they were positive. "We cannot trust his narrative," J. H. Snowden wrote of the Prophet in 1926, "especially as his *history of himself* was written in 1838, eighteen years after the first vision, during which interval he had plenty of both time and reasons for letting his imagination elaborate and embellish if not invent his story."[11]

Finally, Mrs. Brodie, the present-ranking authority on the subject, accepts the old theory that the Book of Mormon as originally conceived was "merely an ingenious speculation," "a mere money-making history of the Indians" (who, incidentally, are never mentioned in the Book of Mormon), in the production of which "no divine interposition was dreamed of."[12] As to the first vision, according to the same author, there is in all Mormon and anti-Mormon writings of every kind and type not so much as a hint of it before the year 1840: " 'Between 1820 and 1840 Joseph's friends were writing long panegyrics; his enemies were defaming him in an unceasing stream of affidavits and pamphlets, . . . but no one in this long period even intimated that he had heard the story of the two gods. At least no such intimation has survived in print or manuscript.' "[13] Joseph's own description of the first vision was not published until 1842, twenty-two years after the memorable event.

Characteristically, Mrs. Brodie labors to stretch the gap to its maximum width. We intend to show here that the gap is really a very narrow one and can be quite easily explained. But first let us consider the common argument that the existence of earlier and widely differing accounts of Smith's youthful doings is proof in itself that his own story is a late fabrication, the earlier tales being nearer the truth, no matter how wildly they conflict.

"Owing to the many reports which have been put in circulation by evil-disposed and designing persons," Joseph Smith begins his story, "I have been induced to write this history."[14] Since the very purpose of publishing this account is to refute a great number of stories already in circulation, it is comical to see the zeal with which anti-Mormon writers pounce upon every faintest indication that such stories did exist as a refutation of Joseph and as absolute proof that his story, since it came later, must have been an afterthought.

But the usual object of official statements is to correct already prevailing errors. It was for that reason that Luke undertook the writing of his gospel: *Because* "many have taken in hand to set forth . . . those things . . . which they who were eye-witnesses from the beginning handed down to us, I have thought it proper, knowing what really happened from the first, to write you an accurate and full account in chronological order, my good friend Theophilus" (Luke 1:1–4; author's translation). Luke wants to set the record straight once and for all; his is *not* the first story to be told, but that does not mean that it is borrowed from earlier tales. Nor does the mere fact that an official account is published at a given time prove that it was invented at that time. Note further that the stories which Luke intends to supersede are not necessarily anti-Christian stories (though many such were in circulation), but tales told by believers with the best intention in the world.

The devoted followers of religious leaders are not noted for restraint and objectivity in the things they tell about their adored leaders; and the least reliable class of all are former believers who have turned against a leader. The only authority for what John says is John, and the only acceptable authority for Joseph Smith's story is Joseph Smith, not the Whitmers or Willard Chase or Pomeroy Tucker. Some critics, for example, seem to think that if they can show that a friend or enemy of Joseph Smith reports him as saying that he was visited by Nephi, they have caught the Prophet in a fraud.[15] It has, moreover, long been an axiom with anti-Mormon writers that if Joseph Smith's enemies tell wildly conflicting stories about him, that does not prove that *they* are lying, but that *he* deceived and tricked them all!

The Reticence of the Saints

But, one may ask, why should Joseph Smith have waited so long to tell his story officially? From his own explanation it is apparent that he would not have told it publicly at all had he not been "induced" to do so by all the scandalous stories that were circulating. It was a rule among those possessing the gospel in ancient times that the greater teachings be not publicly divulged.[16] Even at the risk of serious misunderstanding and persecution, the early Christians and the Jewish sectaries before them would not reveal the secrets of their religion to the world.[17] The constant charge against the Mormons from the beginning, and especially against Joseph Smith, was that they clothed their affairs and doings in secrecy.[18]

The injunction to secrecy is more than a desire to mystify; it is fundamental to all eschatological thinking: "To you it is given to know the secrets of the kingdom of heaven," Christ told a few elect disciples behind locked doors, "but to them it is *not* given" (Matthew 7:6–8). Eduard Meyer drew a parallel between Joseph Smith's first vision and the New Testament accounts of the Transfiguration and Paul's vision.[19] These instances all furnish interesting commentaries on the subject of secrecy.

Consider for a moment the Transfiguration. Jesus chose three special apostles, Peter, James, and John, to go with him to a remote spot, "where they were alone" (Mark 9:2), to pray, and "while he was praying the appearance of his face changed and his raiment became white and brilliant as lightning" (Luke 9:28). Then a cloud came and overshadowed them: and they were sore afraid, but a voice came out of the cloud, saying, "This is my beloved Son; in whom I am well pleased; hear him" (Luke 9:34–35); or "This is my chosen (or elect) Son: hear him" (Mark 9:7); or "This is my beloved Son: hear him" (Luke 9:35).

When the apostles came to themselves, Jesus raised them to their feet (Matthew 17:6–8), and gave them strict instructions "that they should tell no man what things they had seen, till the Son of man were risen from the dead" (Mark 9:9). Accordingly "they kept it close, and told no man in those days any of those things which they had seen" (Luke 9:36).

Now the Transfiguration was the greatest of all manifestations of the Father and the Son. Yet John, the most searching of the gospels, makes no mention of it; none of the apostolic Fathers ever refers to it; there is no hint of it in any of the Apologists; even the vast literature of debate on the nature of the Godhead contains hardly a note of it. Aside from the three synoptic gospels which tell the story with variations, nobody seems to know anything about it. What could such a strange silence possibly mean, save that the fathers and doctors of the Church have never heard of the Transfiguration, for if they had, they surely would be talking of it all the time.

Or take the Gospel of Luke, which begins and ends

with wonderful manifestations: First of all an angel appears to Zacharias in the temple and introduces himself: "I am Gabriel, that stand in the presence of God; and I have been sent to converse with you and to preach the gospel to you" (Luke 1:19). The conversation, full of scriptural citations, must have lasted a very long time, since we are told that the multitude outside grew restless with waiting and wondered what could possibly have happened to Zacharias. Yet Luke records only a few short sentences of the angel; and this great visitation—the one opening the Dispensation of the Meridian of Time—is mentioned nowhere else in the New Testament!

Again, at the end of his gospel Luke tells of a great sermon delivered by the Lord after his resurrection when, "beginning at Moses and all the prophets, he expounded unto them in all the scriptures the things concerning himself" (Luke 24:27). Yet Luke gives us only the two opening sentences of that all-enlightening discourse, and nobody else mentions it.

These instances illustrate the important point that silence in the record is not a proof of ignorance or lack of interest by the writers; the holiest things were not meant for general distribution: "If I have told you earthly things, and ye believe not," said the Lord, "how shall ye believe if I tell you of heavenly things?" (John 3:12). Those to whom "the mysteries of the Kingdom" have been imparted have always been bound to secrecy, and the more wonderful the information, the more carefully guarded it was.[20] The pearls are not to be thrown about promiscuously: such things are given *only* to those who ask for them sincerely; the door is open only to those who knock at it; the treasures are found only by those who seek for them (Matthew 7:6–8).

The writer's great-grandfather, a Jew, one day after he had given Joseph Smith a lesson in German and Hebrew in 1844 asked him about certain particulars of the first vision. In reply he was told some remarkable things, which he wrote down in his journal that very day. But in the ensuing forty years of his life, during which he had many children and grandchildren and preached many sermons, Brother Neibaur seems never once to have referred to the wonderful things the Prophet told him—it was quite by accident that the writer discovered them in his journal. Why was the talkative old man so close-lipped on the one thing that could have made him famous? Because it was a sacred and privileged communication; it was never published to the world and never should be.

The Book of Mormon Sets the Tone

Now let us turn briefly to the theory that the Book of Mormon was strictly a secular document, that Joseph Smith "when he was translating it" had no idea whatever "about visions of God, or of angels, or heavenly revelations," those being added to his story in 1838 or 1834. The refutation of this absurd claim is simple, but it requires doing something that critics of Joseph Smith are invincibly opposed to doing, namely reading the Book of Mormon. If that is too much to ask, let them read only the first five pages: On page one of the first edition there is a summary: *"The Lord warns Lehi to depart out of the land of Jerusalem, because he prophesieth unto the people concerning their iniquity."* We also read of "many prophets, prophesying unto the people." On page two, a "pillar of fire" appears to Lehi in the desert, and after hearing and seeing many wonderful things he returns to his house at Jerusalem and is promptly "carried away in a vision, even . . . that he saw one descending out of the midst of Heaven, and he beheld that his lustre was above that of the sun at noon-day; . . . and the first came and stood before my father, and gave unto him a Book, and bade him that he should read." Again, marvelous manifestations follow, and on the next page the Lord speaks to Lehi in a dream. On page four, Nephi "did cry unto the Lord; and behold he did visit me." And on the fifth page, "the Lord spake unto me"—a prophecy follows, and then "I, Nephi, returned from speaking with the Lord, to the tent of my father."

Now all this belongs to the strictly historical part of the Book of Mormon; the really religious parts are yet to come. And yet this book, copyrighted before the middle of 1829, is supposed to have been written by a man who had not the remotest idea "about visions of God, or of angels, or heavenly revelations." The book swarms with wonders and marvels, and the earliest stories about Joseph Smith — the local newspaper reports from 1829 and the affidavits of 1833 — charge him with pushing the miraculous and mysterious to the extreme.

How, then, could Joseph Smith's own story have "gained in the miraculous and mysterious" through the years until its official culmination in 1838? His own visions and visitations are not more marvelous than those reported throughout the Book of Mormon, which, in fact, they closely resemble. What, then, is all this nonsense about Joseph Smith getting all these ideas later? Or Brodie's idea that he only converted it into a religious book at the last moment?

There is nothing extraneous or afterthought about the religious element in the Book of Mormon, to remove the religious parts of which would be equivalent to removing the rice from a rice pudding—there is really nothing else to it.

The author knew perfectly well that this could not be a popular book. If any reader is naive enough to think that those words (and there are many others like them) were merely inserted for effect, let him study the newspaper announcements appearing *before* the publication of the Book of Mormon to see what excellent reason Joseph Smith had for knowing how the public would receive his efforts to set up, of all things, another word of God right beside the Bible. Those who charge Joseph Smith with writing the Book of Mormon as a publicity stunt do not hesitate to accept the affidavit of Nathaniel Lewis, who says that Smith was worried as to "whether he should proceed to translate the Book of Plates . . . or not. He said that God had commanded him to translate it, but he was afraid of the people."[21] And this was his idea of a *popular* book? Every page of the Book of Mormon proclaims its status as scripture; to say that there was a time when "no divine interpretation was dreamed of"[22] is to talk about another book entirely; there is nothing accidental, capricious, or makeshift about the Book of Mormon, whose religious element is solidly built into every sentence.

But now it is time to consider how the critics have dealt with the first vision story since the publication of the official statement in 1842. This is a most enlightening history.

Suppressing the First Vision Story after 1842

In 1842 J. Turner gave the following resumé of Joseph Smith's story of the first vision: Joseph Smith was, "as he states, in disgust with all the sects, and almost in despair of ever coming to the knowledge of the truth, amid so many contradictory and conflicting claims. He resorted to prayer for 'a full manifestation of divine approbation,' and 'for the assurance that he was accepted of him.' This occurred sometime in the winter of 1823."[23] This is the whole story as Turner tells it; the first part is obviously taken, as he avers, from Joseph Smith's own story, but the other parts, actually put in quotation marks as if they were Smith's own words, are not found in that story at all. Turner has reedited the story until there is virtually nothing left of it.

In the following year an ambitious study in the *Dublin University Magazine* describes the first vision thus: "Into this cloud of glory, Smith," says the narrative, "was received, and he met within it two angelic personages, who exactly resembled each other; they informed him that all his sins were forgiven."[24] Here again there can be no doubt that the story is told from the original, but those all-important words, which Joseph Smith puts in italics, which identify the heavenly visitors, and which give the account of the vision its unique status, are completely omitted. That the omission is studied and deliberate appears from the statement of the editor that "every part of this tale is an obvious plagiarism from Mohammed's account of the first revelation made to him in the cave of Hira." For "every part of this tale" has certainly not been reported, the most obvious parallel of all, the very words with which the Father introduced the Son on the Mount of Transfiguration, being deleted. Why should young Smith have gone to Mohammed when the Bible, as Eduard Meyer points out, presents much closer and much more readily available material for plagiarism?

In 1851 the *American Whig Review* reported: "Occasionally he was heard advancing contradictory statements concerning the discovery made by himself of certain gold plates, and declaring the existence of a connection between himself and the spirit world. These various stories gradually assumed form, and in after times, the story told . . . was as follows." Then comes Joseph Smith's account of the revivals and his perplexity, and then, "one day, as he retired to a grove for purposes of prayer and meditation, an angel from heaven appeared, . . . prophesying that he should be the founder of a sect destined to be greater than all others, and to embrace all mankind as its members. He was directed to search on the summit of the hill Camora [sic]," and told "he was to be married to a woman described to him, and whom he should know as soon as they might meet; and was to prepare himself for the labor of translation by diligent study of the Coptic. In 1827 he might return and claim the book."[25] The thing to note is that this wild hodge-podge is confidently put forth as the final, official Mormon version of what happened, after that version had been in circulation for at least thirteen years.

In the following year (1852), Gunnison's famous work on the Mormons appeared, in which the story of Joseph Smith is told from the beginning "according to his autobiography"; and yet the first vision is nowhere mentioned, the appearance of Moroni being put forth as the first manifestation seen by Joseph: "Judging from what he says in his autobiography," writes Gunnison, ". . . his prayers were answered by a heavenly vision," whereupon the author proceeds to tell of Moroni's visit.[26]

The *Edinburgh Review* of 1854 takes the prize with this: "Young Joseph amused himself by . . . fixing the attention of his pious friends upon himself, by an 'experience' more wonderful than any of theirs. . . . 'I saw,' says he, 'a pillar of light above the brightness of the sun, which descended gradually upon me.' " Joseph Smith's own story is then given right up to the words "standing above me in the air," where—it abruptly breaks off with the comment, "He goes on in his 'Autobiography' (from which we quote) to say, that these heavenly messengers declared all existing Christian sects in error, and forbade him to join any of them."[27] Again the all-important part has been skipped, our critic checking himself in the nick of time. This article was printed again with some changes in 1863, but with still no indication of who the heavenly beings might be.

And here is the complete story as told by J. Reynolds in 1855: "Smith became interested for the salvation of his soul, and prayed fervidly in a grove near his father's house in Palmyra, and at last the darkness gave way and the light descended from Heaven until the whole country was illuminated with a dazzling brilliancy that was indescribable."[28] That, as we said, is the whole story.

One of the most famous anti-Mormon books was John Hyde's *Mormonism*, which goes so far as to report that

"Smith pretends to receive his first vision while praying in the woods. He asserts that God the Father and Jesus Christ came to him from the heavens." Hyde specifies the time as April 1820. Yet having admitted so much, Hyde covers it up later in his book when he writes: "Joseph Smith, born in 1805, sees an angel in 1820, who tells him his sins are forgiven. In 1823 he sees another angel."[29] This is an interesting example of how a critic will refute himself to discredit Joseph Smith's story.

One of the first and most important anti-Mormon books to appear in a foreign language was Olshausen's *Geschichte der Mormonen*, 1856, which recounts: "As Joseph Smith completed his sixteenth year of life (1822), he began to think about the salvation of his soul. He frequently went to a retired spot in the forest [to pray]. . . . After he had prayed fervently and often, and thereby removed the powers of darkness by which he was possessed, he saw one day 'a bright and glorious light.' . . . His spirit was carried away and he saw two bright figures."[30] But like the others, Olshausen gives never a hint as to who the bright figures might be.

In what pretended to be a very sophisticated and objective study, J. deRadius wrote in 1864: "Whether from insanity or sheer hypocrisy, the lad professed to have been favored, while in prayer, with a miraculous vision. 'A pillar of light above the brightness of the sun gradually descended upon me,' he says, 'and I saw two personages whose brightness and glory defy all description standing above me in the air.' They assured him that his sins were forgiven, . . . [and that] all existing churches were alike in error. His vanity led him to proclaim his vision, and the persecution which he says he met with . . . made him only the more obstinate."[31]

Then in 1867 came Pomeroy Tucker's immortal work in which the first vision is described thus:

About this time [1827] Smith had a remarkable vision. He pretended that, while engaged in secret prayer, alone in the wilderness, an "angel of the Lord" appeared to him, with the glad tidings that "all his sins had been forgiven," and proclaiming further that "all the religious denominations were believing in false doctrines, and consequently that none of them were accepted of God as of His Church and Kingdom"; also he had received a promise that the true doctrine of the fulness of the gospel should at some future time be revealed to him. Following this, soon came another angel (or possibly the same one), revealing to him that he was himself "the favored instrument of the new revelation."[32]

The distortions and omissions, as well as the typical Tucker embellishments, are quite apparent; characteristic is the lavish use of quotation marks, making it appear that Tucker remembers the very words of Joseph Smith, forty years later.

An official history of Ohio, in 1875, assures us that "Joe Smith's story is as follows: 'He says that in the year 1820, as he in a retired place was earnestly engaged in prayer, two angels appeared to him. They informed him that God had forgiven all his sins, and . . . that all the then religious denominations were in error; that the Indians were the descendants of the lost tribes; that they had brought with them to the country inspired writings; that these writings were safely deposited in a secret place, and that he was selected by God to receive them, and translate them into the English tongue."[33] *He* says all that . . . ?

And listen to the once highly touted Mrs. Dickinson:

> In 1821 there was a revival in the Methodist, Baptist, and Presbyterian churches at Palmyra, and some of the Smith family declared they were "converted." . . . Joe asserted his partiality for the Methodists, but ultimately declared he could not decide which was right. He said that . . . he gave himself up to prayer for days, "ago-nizing," that the truth might be made known to him

among all the conflicting opinions that he heard among these different sects; that suddenly his chamber became illuminated, an angel appeared and conversed with him, instructed him in the ways of righteousness, and informed him that there was *no true Church on earth.* He was further told that his prayers were heard, that he was "dearly beloved of the Lord, and should be commissioned a priest after the order of Melchisedec — organizing a church of the faithful persons in that line to receive the Lord, in the Millennium. In a second visit the angel informed him "that the truth should spring out of the earth."[34]

It would be hard to do a more careful job of garbling the first vision story.

R. W. Beers's version is remarkable for the fulness of detail with which it leads up to — nothing: "Joseph, in his own account of his early life, says that he 'became somewhat partial to the Methodist sect,' but he was not able to decide which was right. In his bewilderment he gave himself up to prayer for days that the truth might be made known to him among all the conflicting opinions that he heard among these different sects; and finally a heavenly messenger bade him not to join any sect. And three years afterward, in September 22, 1823," etc.[35]

In the same year W. Messaros wrote: "In 1820, young Smith pretended to be converted at a Methodist revival and was received into the Church. The next month he claimed that he saw a vision of the Saviour and several Apostles, who informed him that his sins were forgiven, and that he had been chosen to preach a new gospel on earth, holier than any that had been hitherto taught. Before six months had elapsed, he was worse than ever, swearing, drinking, and comporting himself with his accustomed vileness. But this did not frighten away his celestial visitors."[36]

Though frankly hostile, C. F. Ward's *Mormonism Ex-*

posed is no more inaccurate than the others: "In the spring of the year 1820 (at this time, be it remembered Smith was a lad of 15 years of age) an angel appeared to him (so he alleges) and forbade him to join himself to any church or sect, as they were all wrong. I leave it to you to reflect upon the tremendous improbability of this yarn for a beginning."[37] But did *he* ever allege that? And though Thomas Gregg in his anti-Mormon "classic" promises to include "the more important portions" of "Joseph Smith's statement," he omits the part of the first vision which Smith puts in italics—obviously one of the less important portions.[38]

"This is the fabricated story published to the world by this imposter." M. W. Montgomery declares in 1890: "Smith claimed that the Lord visited him in visions at frequent intervals and told him that the golden plates contained the fulness of the Gospel dispensation."[39] A fabricated story indeed!

The twentieth century was ushered in by T. W. Young's remarkable work, which tells us that when Joseph Smith was fifteen years old no church would receive him as a member, since he "pretended to have revelations and visions, and to have received visits from John the Baptist, and the apostles Peter, James, and John. It is hardly to be expected that any sensible church would receive such a questionable character. His pretended revelations and incredible experiences made him the butt of the community. . . . He finally left home to escape ridicule." Four years later, according to this high authority, Smith returned to Palmyra and was visited there by Moroni.[40]

In 1911 two writers played an identical trick with the first vision story. G. Townsend told Joseph Smith's version down to "standing above me in the air," and continued as follows: "One of them spoke unto me. . . . When I came to myself again I found myself lying on my back looking up into heaven. Three years later he had two similar experiences."[41] And D. H. C. Bartlett uses the useful little dots to the same effect: "Thick darkness gathered round me, and it seemed to me for a time as if I were doomed to sudden destruction. . . . When I came to myself again, I found myself lying on my back, looking up into heaven."[42] Is it pure coincidence that the dot technique should be thus twice employed in a single year? Anti-Mormon writings have a way of following a changing pattern through the years.

The Reverend J. Q. Adams published an influential little anti-Mormon book in 1916. In it he tells of the revivals, which took place according to him in 1821: "At this time, Joe gave himself up to prayer, so he said, for many days 'agonizing' to know the truth. [Shades of Mrs. Dickinson! Did he really say 'agonizing'?] Suddenly his chamber was illuminated and an angel appeared and told him that there was no true church on earth. It is easy to prophesy now. The angel assured him that his prayers were heard, and 'he was the dearly beloved of the Lord, and should be commissioned a Priest after the order of Melchizedek, organizing a church of faithful persons in that line to receive the Lord in the Millennium.' In a second visit he was further told 'that the truth should spring out of the earth'; and then, or at a later time, that the earth was the hill Cumorah, near his home."[43] Mr. Adams lifts from Mrs. Dickinson as freely as Mrs. Brodie later does from him ("It was easy to prophesy now"), and yet he insists that this mishmash "in brief sums up a long story as told by Joe and later Mormon authorities." And then the Rev. Adams makes a significant comment: "A decent reverence for the Holy God ought to forbid the repetition of these stories, such, as for example, that the Father appeared in human form and introduced his Son Jesus Christ, to Joseph Smith. But reverence has never been a Mormon characteristic."[44] This is an enlightening statement of policy: Decent, reverent people should on principle *never mention* the story of the first vision.

This is bad enough, but what shall we say of a master's thesis written in 1929 on Joseph Smith and his work, which can report: "After a series of visions in which two angels appear and converse with him, a being 'surrounded with a light like that of day . . . ' materialized. Smith was directed by this apparition whom he afterwards says is Mormon, to a stone box of 'golden plates' "?[45]

For artful dodging, the doctor's dissertation of George Arbaugh surpasses the mere master's thesis of Miss Pancoast by as much as the glory of the doctorate surpasses that of the Magister Artium. Here we have a Ph.D. thesis from the University of Chicago, reprinted as late as 1950, devoted *entirely*, as the title proclaims, to the subject of *Revelation in Mormonism*, and the first vision is only mentioned in *one* sentence, where it is diligently buried: "How different was the official account worked out at Nauvoo, containing artificial visions and pious platitudes and generous Scripture quotations! Riley amazingly assumed the historicity of the official story. Meyer recognized that the vision in which Father and Son appear is borrowed from the transfiguration of Christ, but he mistakenly supposed that Riley's interpretation was, in general, sound."[46]

And that, if you please, is the only mention in Arbaugh's whole book on Mormon revelation of the first vision, one of the most important revelations of all. If Riley's position is so "amazing," and if a scholar of Eduard Meyer's eminence accepts it, why doesn't Arbaugh tell us just what is wrong with it? That should be the proper business of his thesis, and yet he will not even touch it. Nor will he consider Meyer's very good reasons for accepting 1820 as the date for the first vision, whatever might have happened. For Eduard Meyer, who knew perhaps more about the history of religions than any other man of our century, was convinced that the first vision furnished a reliable key to Joseph Smith's career: without the first vision nothing Smith does makes sense; with it, everything he does makes very good sense.[47]

In 1957 Arbaugh returned to the fray with an impartial little book called *Gods, Sex, and Saints: The Mormon Story,* in which he has this to say of the first vision: "In 1820, according to divine plan, two gods, the Father (Adam) and Jesus, appeared to Joseph Smith near his home in New York. They revealed to him the Nephite scriptures which in time were restored to him by Moroni."[48] The gratuitous touches about Adam and the Nephite scriptures are Mr. Arbaugh's own invention; he cannot simply repeat the story without disfiguring it with gross inaccuracies. Why is that? Does he suspect that the original story makes very good sense, so that the ordinary reader cannot be trusted with it? Arbaugh's irresponsibility is apparent in the opening blast of his new book: "About 1830, in the state of New York, a new sect was founded by Joseph Smith."[49] Can't he do better than guess the year?

In its original form, the present study was burdened by quotations from more than fifty important anti-Mormon writings, all of which were guilty of deliberately disfiguring the first vision story. To save space this monotonous cat alog has been cut in half, so that we have presented above only twenty-five of the list, and herewith consign to the decent obscurity of a footnote the other sources, which the reader may consult at his leisure.[50] All of them will be found busily censoring Joseph Smith's story by calculated distortion and omission, and invariably by deleting the all-important words which identify the heavenly visitors. The writers from whose works we have just quoted are by no means obscure or minor figures in the field; in fact, we know of no really important anti-Mormon writer who is not mentioned in this article — if we have overlooked some (which is quite possible), the fact still remains that the above twenty-five include the really big names in anti-

Mormon literature, i.e., it is a genuinely representative list. All of these writers were acquainted with the official history of the first vision, and most of them explicitly assert that they are simply reporting that history; yet not one of them mentions the key episode of the story as the Mormons told it, the words underlined in the original, so that nobody could possibly miss them, the words that identify the Father and the Son.

There are indeed anti-Mormon books that report the crucial part of Joseph Smith's story, but they are the exception that proves the rule. A government publication dealing with the history of religious denominations in the United States for the year 1844 actually printed Joseph Smith's own story *without comment*,[51] but the reader will search many a day without finding another book that can pass such a test for honesty. At least this writer has still to discover one. In 1861 the *Edinburgh Review* broke down and quoted the key lines from Joseph Smith's story: "Scarcely had he uttered this prayer, when his tongue, he says, became paralyzed and he fell into a state of profound depression. . . . One of them, calling him by name said, pointing to his companion — 'This is my well-beloved Son: Hearken to him.' " At last the all-important words are out (though inaccurately reported), but their effect must be instantly expunged by the acid of editorial comment: "This alleged vision is an excellent sample of the poverty of invention and impudent audacity by which all the visions or revelations of the prophet were characterized."[52] If it is such an excellent example, why don't anti-Mormon writers welcome it instead of avoiding it? Because there is nothing they can say to disprove it, though some of them try hard, as when Mrs. Brodie, after quoting Joseph Smith's story at length, hastens to add: "Lesser visions than this were common in the folklore of the area" (so what? we dare say people even had dreams), and follows this up with a typical insinuation: "Oddly, however, the Palmyra newspapers, which in later years gave him plenty of unpleasant publicity, took no notice of Joseph's vision at the time it was supposed to have occurred."[53] We are to understand that there is something very odd about that newspaper silence, something very suspicious. Only Mrs. Brodie has overplayed her hand, for it is she who tells us that "in later years" when the newspapers "gave him plenty of unpleasant publicity" *and when they certainly knew all about the first vision,* they *still* did not mention it — either "at the time it was supposed to have occurred" *or at any other time.* Thus her argument of silence is worthless as proving ignorance on the part of the newspapers, for they preserved the same silence at a time when they definitely knew Joseph Smith's story.

Stimulated by the reading of this article in manuscript, Dr. Milton V. Backman, Jr., of Brigham Young University undertook a search through all available histories of the United States and of religion in America, and discovered that all writers who mention the first vision *without a single exception* have distorted Joseph Smith's account, even while they profess to be following it.[54] It would be hard to match such thorough and wholesale abuse of a document in the whole history of historiography.

Mrs. Brodie, it will be recalled, rests her impeachment of the first vision story on the silence of the record between 1820 and 1840. But the argument of silence is, if anything, even less significant before 1840 than after. For if fifty-odd "standard works" on the history of Mormonism can all omit the key to that history even after that history has been formally published to the world, what are the chances of finding anything like a coherent account of that supremely unpopular and much mishandled story in the much scantier literature of the earlier period, *before* there was any official Mormon version to act as a source, a check, or a control? One might argue that it is inconceivable that anti-Mormon writers, eager to convict Joseph Smith of blasphemy and boundless impudence, would pass by such a juicy item as the first vision story in silence. Yet we have just seen that fifty of them did just that; though they claimed to be quoting Joseph Smith's own story, none of them "even intimated," to quote Mrs. Brodie, "that he had heard the story of the two gods." All of which shows that ignorance of an event is not the only reason for silence concerning it. Policy and prejudice play a dominant role in religious history, and especially in anti-Mormon history.

But, it may be argued, the suppression of the story after 1840 was not *total*. Neither was it before 1840. Let us consider some of the "implications" that turn up in the earlier literature which have somehow—but not surprisingly—quite escaped the notice of Mrs. Brodie, in spite of her predilection for implications. We must warn the reader that the stories we are about to quote are a mess—but no more so than those we have already quoted. It has been standard procedure among anti-Mormon writers to attribute all this confusion to Joseph Smith himself, who is charged with having told a great many conflicting stories, by way of explaining why the stories told against him by his enemies never agree. To this charge the fifty writers just cited provide an adequate refutation: No two of them tell the same story, even after Joseph Smith is long dead and when they all claim to be following a single original. Who is responsible for that? Not Joseph Smith and the Mormons, certainly.

It will be recalled that Joseph Smith was, as he puts it, "induced" to write his story "owing to the many reports which have been put in circulation by evil-disposed and designing persons." Did he merely imagine such things? He did not. On November 30, 1830, the Painesville *Telegraph* reported: "To record the thousand tales which are in circulation respecting the book and its propagators, would be an endless task, and probably lead to the promulgation of a hundred times more than was founded in truth."[55] The editor is well aware of what a swarm of stories about Joseph Smith are going around, and how easily they depart from the truth. Did Joseph Smith and the Mormons make up all those shockers—about themselves? We have examined a great number of those stories, which we compared in a recent study,[56] and found that they all turn on a few stock themes: There are the digging stories, the peep stones, appearances of angels and devils, crooked business deals and speculations, the mysterious plates, and, not least of all, the first vision story.

Let us see how Mrs. Brodie tries to build up a case against Joseph Smith by implication. It was in 1834 "shortly after *Mormonism Unvailed* appeared" that Joseph Smith published the "first sketch of his early years," which "took the form of an apology for his youthful indiscretions."[57] This statement is misleading: an apology is an explanation or justification of actions which are explicitly admitted; but Joseph Smith's "apology" flatly denies Howe's charges that make him "the vilest wretch on earth," and insists that his "imperfections" are nothing worse than "a light, and too often, vain mind, exhibiting a foolish and trifling conversation."[58] In issuing this denial, Joseph Smith tells no story whatever; this is *not* a "first sketch of his early years" or of anything else, but simply a refutation of charges of gross misconduct. But by pretending that it is a history, Mrs. Brodie can announce that it "differed surprisingly" from the "official autobiography" of 1838 or 1842.[59] Of course it did; they are two totally different types of documents, but there is not the slightest conflict between them; they are photographs of the same man, just as Lincoln's jokes and his Gettysburg address, though they "differed surprisingly," are different photographs of the same man.

But if Joseph Smith invented all his heavenly visitors in reply to Mr. E. D. Howe, one is at a loss to explain how all those religious manifestations got into Howe's book in the first place; for example, Howe quotes Ezra Booth as reporting in 1831: "Smith describes an angel, as having the appearance of 'a tall, slim, well-built, handsome man, with a bright pillar upon his head.' "[60] Now, what we would like to know is how Joseph Smith could have been going around in 1831 giving intimate firsthand descriptions of angels—pillar of light and all—if he first invented his angelic interviews in 1838? Howe is not one to report the first vision; he declares his extreme reluctance to report any of Joseph Smith's supernatural tales[61] and insists that "no one but the vilest wretch on earth, disregarding all that is sacred, would ever dare to have profaned the sacred oracles of truth to such base purposes. . . . We are left without weapons to combat the credulous Mormon believer."[62] Yet on the other hand he resents Joseph's reticence and accuses him of "mystifying everything." From which it is quite plain that Howe was denied access to a good deal of information, and that he was angered and frustrated. As a result his record is a monument of confusion, contradiction, and invective.

Take, for example, Peter Ingersoll's story of how, when he was "once ploughing near the house of Joseph Smith, Sr.," he was returning to work through the field when the elder Smith stopped him and gave him a lecture on seer stones, gazed at one in his own hat, and "being very much exhausted, said in a faint voice, 'If you knew what I had seen, you would believe.' " This, according to Ingersoll, took place sometime between 1822 and "about 1830."[63] One wonders just how reliable this story is. Is Ingersoll making up the story or just mixing it up? Could this be a garbled version of what happened to Joseph Smith the day after Moroni's first visit—working in the field, going back to the house, fainting, the appearance of a vision, a conversation with the elder Smith in the field, Father Smith's declaration of belief? It is all there, only with Peter Ingersoll, one of the greatest storytellers of them all, in the leading role.[64]

The man who claimed to have known Joseph best, to have been in fact his intimate associate "from his twelfth to his twentieth year," reported in 1867:

> About this time [1827] Smith had a remarkable vision. He pretended that, while engaged in secret prayer, alone in the wilderness, an "angel of the Lord" appeared to him, with the glad tidings that "all his sins had been forgiven," and proclaiming further that "all religious denominations were believing in false doctrines, and consequently that none of them were acceptable of God as of His Church and Kingdom"; also he had received a "promise that the true doctrine and the fullness of the gospel should at some future time be revealed to him." Following this, soon came another angel (or possibly the same one), revealing to him that he was himself to be "the favored instrument of the new revelation. . . . " In the fall of the same year Smith had yet a more miraculous and astonishing vision than any preceding one.[65]

Mr. Tucker does not bother to tell us what the most marvelous vision of all might have been, but instead he reports that Joseph then "announced to his family, friends and the bigoted persons who adhered to his supernaturalism," that he would go and get the plates. These visions, according to Tucker, were "repeatedly quoted by his credulous friends at the time."[66]

Now if Tucker is anything like the reliable firsthand source that the critics take him to be, it would be hard to deny that the story of the first vision was being told and retold in 1827: the usual distortions are there, but it is plain enough what is being distorted. At the very least it is certain that Tucker lived in Palmyra in the early 1820s (he moved to Canandaigua in 1822 or 1823 and stayed there four years), and he does seem to have the strong impression that stories of Joseph Smith's visions were current at that time.

A closer check is provided by an article in the Rochester

Advertiser and Telegraph for August 31, 1829: "In the fall of 1827," it says,

> a person by the name of Joseph Smith, of Manchester, Ontario county, reported that he had been visited in a dream by the spirit of the Almighty and informed that in a certain hill in that town was deposited this golden Bible. . . . As he states, . . . after penetrating "mother earth" a short distance the bible was found. . . . [It was] nicely wrapped up and excluded from the "vulgar gaze of poor wicked mortals."[67]

Here we find the usual freedom of invention, including the flowery editorial terms "mother earth" and "vulgar gaze of poor and wicked mortals" explicitly attributed to Joseph Smith himself two years before, though no sources are given. Again we see that the supernatural element in the Book of Mormon story is full blown in 1827 or at least in 1829 — no need for Joseph Smith to wait until 1838 to invent it. The piece is just as thoroughly mixed up as the others we have cited, and an interesting note emerges in the confusion: it is not an angel who visits the young Joseph Smith but "the spirit of the Almighty," and that not in any abstract or mystic sense, but as a conveyor of specific information. If Joseph Smith was not talking to angels in 1827, it would seem from this scrambled account that he was talking to someone much higher up. Where could that *rumor* have started?

Just two weeks later (September 16, 1829) the Palmyra *Reflector* reported: "The Book of Mormon is expected to be ready for delivery in the course of one year. Great and marvelous things will 'come to pass' about these days."[68] Again the Book of Mormon is surrounded with an aura of the supernatural even before its publication. Then eight months later (May 15, 1830), the Rochester *Gem* announced: "The translator, if we take his word for it, has been directed by an angel in this business. . . . [This] is in point of blasphemy and imposition, the very summit."[69]

So the stories of the angel were *not* invented years later, after all. But why wasn't it an angel in the Rochester *Advertiser* account of the previous year, where "the spirit of the Almighty" was the visitor? Obviously, the earlier report has mixed up the story of Moroni with the first vision. That was a common blunder, as we have seen, in later years as well.

A few weeks after the appearance of the Book of Mormon, Obadiah Dogberry published a satire on Joseph Smith in the Palmyra *Reflector*;[70] it is the *Book of Pukei*, and we quote from chapter 2. First the contents of the chapter are given: "1. The idle and slothful reverence the prophet. 2. The prophet reveals to them the first appearance of the Spirit. 3. The admonition and promises. 4. Description of the Spirit."

Then beginning with verse 2:

> And the Prophet answered and said . . . lo! yesternight stood before me in the wilderness of Manchester, the *spirit*. . . . And he said unto me, "Joseph, thou son of Joseph, hold up thine head; . . . hold up thine face and let the *light* of mine countenance shine upon thee. . . . I am the spirit that walketh in darkness, and will shew thee great signs and wonders." And I looked, and behold a little old man stood before me, clad, as I supposed, in Egyptian raiment, except his Indian blanket and moccasins — his beard of silver white, *hung* far below his knees. On his head was an old-fashioned military half cocked hat such as was worn in the days of the patriarch Moses — his speech was sweeter than *molasses*, and his words were the reformed Egyptian. And again he said unto me, "Joseph thou who has been surnamed the *ignoramus*, knowest thou not, that great signs and wonders are to be done by thine hands?"[71]

The broad, heavy Yankee humor is apparent enough, and it would be hard to explain such expressions as "reformed Egyptian" as coming from any but an official

source. But what about the rest of the satire? Note the table
of contents: "2. The prophet reveals to them *the first appearance of the Spirit*. 3. The admonition and promises. 4.
Description of the Spirit." The *first* appearance of the Spirit
is then depicted as taking place "in the wilderness of
Manchester," where the Spirit addresses Joseph by name,
introduces himself, and promises great things to come,
including a work to be done by Smith himself. In the burlesque description of "the Spirit," special mention is made
of the *light* of his countenance and the extreme whiteness
of his beard. With the coming of this light, Smith is told,
"hold up thine head," as if before he had been cast down.

Now is Mr. Dogberry simply making all this up or is
he satirizing? The humor of his heavy-handed discourse
is anything but intrinsic; his long, laborious spoofing of
the Book of Mormon (from which we have quoted only a
few lines) is only effective if the reader recognizes each
point as a takeoff on Joseph Smith, who is represented as
having told his followers, "the idle and slothful" — and no
one else! — of that "first appearance of the Spirit" which
took place "in the wilderness of Manchester."

Just a week after the Painesville *Telegraph* had deplored
"the thousand tales which are in circulation respecting the
book and its propagators," that journal (December 7, 1830)
added to the confusion with yet another tale:

> Friends and advocates of this wonderful book state
> that Mr. Oliver Cowdery has his commission directly
> from the God of Heaven, and that he has his credentials,
> written and signed by the hand of Jesus Christ, with
> whom he has personally conversed, and as such, said
> Cowdery claims that he and his associates are the only
> persons on earth who are qualified to administer in his
> name.[72]

The source of this story is not given; we are not even
told whether the "friends and advocates" in question were
Mormons or merely sympathizers, or whether the report

came at first, second, or third hand from personal friends of Cowdery. It is simply another of those "thousands of tales" going around in 1830; but the elements of the story are familiar — a personal face-to-face conversation with Jesus Christ, as a result of which it can be confidently announced that there was no authorized church on the earth at that time.

Another version of the story puts Sidney Rigdon in the leading role. One Alexander Majors claimed to recall that "an elder by the name of Rigdon preached in the courthouse one Sunday in 1832, in which he said he had been to the third heaven, and had talked face to face with God Almighty. The preachers in the community the next day went en masse to call upon him. He repeated what he had said the day before."[73]

Yet according to the same Majors, Joseph Smith's story anticipated Rigdon's by a good two years, for in 1830

> five Mormon elders made their appearance in the county and commenced preaching, stating . . . that they were chosen by the priesthood which had been organized by the Prophet Joseph Smith, who had met an angel and received a revelation from God. In that day and age it was regarded as blasphemous or sacrilegious for anyone to claim that they had met angels and received from them new revelations, and the religious portion of the community, especially, was very much incensed and aroused at the audacity of any person claiming such interviews from the invisible world.[74]

From this it would appear that at an early date people were much angered and excited by Joseph Smith's claims to heavenly visitations; note that a distinction is made between the angel's visit and "a revelation (i.e., a particular revelation) from God."

Since Oliver Cowdery and Sidney Rigdon were understandably confused with Joseph Smith in the stories that were going around, it is not surprising that Martin

Harris had the same distinction. The indefatigable E. D. Howe was able to get an affidavit from one testifying that Martin Harris "frequently declares that he has conversed with Jesus Christ, Angels and the Devil. . . . He says he wrote a considerable part of the book, — as Smith dictated and at one time the presence of the Lord was so great that a screen was hung up between him and the Prophet."[75] One could not ask for a more obvious juggling of hearsay reports. We are told that the man claimed actually to have conversed with the Lord, and yet in his most wonderful experience he did not see Christ at all, but merely sensed "the presence of the Lord," from which he was shielded by a screen — only the screen was not between him and the Lord at all, but "between him and the Prophet." That would make Joseph Smith the one who was really in "the presence of the Lord," and not Harris. It is quite plain that somebody is confusing the story of the first vision with the well-known accounts of the translating of the plates.

An exceedingly wild story was attributed to Martin Harris by the *Weekly Visitor* in 1841, a story which Harris was reported to have told back in 1827 — what memories these people have! According to this, after a futile attempt to get the plates,

> Joe went alone in silence home and was met on the way by an angel in the woods: "He spoke in a voice of thunder, and forked lightning shot through the trees and ran along upon the ground. The terror of the Divine messenger's appearance instantly struck Smith to the earth, and he felt his whole frame convulsed with agony." . . . The angel upbraided him and disappeared. "Smith went home trembling and full of terror. . . . Another Divine communication was made to him, authorizing him to go alone and bring the chest and deposit it secretly under the hearth of his dwelling."[76]

Again the suggestive and misleading quotes, again the garbled stories; this is another example of how thoroughly corrupted the first vision story can get, but the familiar elements are there: Joseph Smith alone in the silent woods, the light in the treetops, the young man struck to the ground and overcome so that "he felt his whole frame convulsed with agony," the awesome appearance of "the Divine messenger," who gives him instructions, the specification that the vision about the plates came later as well as the useful information that this story is being told at the third hand after a lapse of many years. The authority for this story is an editor of the *Episcopal Recorder* of Philadelphia, who describes in detail how Harris told the tale to him "early in the autumn of 1827."[77] A very unflattering retelling of the first vision story—what else could one expect?—but at least an early one.

On October 12, 1832, one J. B. Pixley wrote a worried letter to the editor of the *Christian Watchman*, in which he deplored the coming of the Mormons to Missouri. What particularly annoyed this correspondent was that the invaders had not changed any of the crazy ideas they had back in Ohio and New York: Their creed, he wrote, "appears to have undergone but little change. . . . The Mormons *still* prefer to talk with angels, visit the third heaven, and converse with Christ face to face. They pretend to have discovered where the Ark of the Covenant, Aaron's Rod, the Pot of Manna, etc., etc., now remain hid." Again the free invention—the Ark, the Rod, and the Pot are a unique contribution of the writer; but along with that go the now familiar motifs of angelic visitation and face-to-face conversation with Christ.

Pixley's complaint is confirmed in the reports of a great mass meeting that was held at Independence, Missouri, on July 20, 1833. There was a report:

> The committee fears that . . . they [the Mormons] will soon have all the offices in the county in their hands; and that the lives and property of other citizens would be insecure, under the administration of men who are

so ignorant and superstitious as to believe that they have been the subjects of miraculous and supernatural cures; hold converse with God and his angels, and possess and exercise the gifts of divination, and of unknown tongues.

The *Missouri Intelligencer and Boone's Lick Advertiser* of August 10, 1833, reports it thus:

What would be the fate of our lives and property, in the hands of jurors and witnesses, who would not blush to declare and would not upon occasion hesitate to swear, that they have wrought miracles and supernatural cures; have converse with God and His angels; and possess and exercise the gift of divination and of unknown tongues . . . may be better imagined than described.

"Of their pretended revelations from Heaven," an editor comments, "their personal intercourse with God and his angels — the maladies they pretend to heal, by the laying on of hands, and the contemptible gibberish with which they habitually profane the Sabbath, and which they dignify by the appellation of 'unkown tongues,' we have nothing to say."[78] Alexander Majors claims to have had a conversation with Joseph Smith in Missouri at this time: "I told him frankly [Majors reports] that it [the trouble with the mobs] grew out of the fact that they claimed to have seen an angel, and to have received a new revelation from God. . . . He then scouted at the idea that people would receive such treatment as they did merely because they claimed to have seen angels and talked with God and claimed to have a new revelation."[79] Whether Majors is gilding the lily or not, it is clear that the one thing that most enraged the Missourians when the Mormons first came to Missouri in the early 1830s was the Mormon claim that somebody had "seen angels *and* talked with God."

This writer has made no systematic search of "intimations" of the first vision story in early Mormon and anti-

Mormon writings. What we have presented here is simply what we have turned up on short notice among a lot of old notes which we gathered years ago with a wholly different project in view; but it is quite enough to refute the claim that not a single intimation that anyone ever heard the first vision story is to be found anywhere between 1820 and 1840. What the present state of the evidence most strongly suggests is that Joseph Smith did tell his story to some of his followers at an early date, that the story got abroad, as such things will, and in the process of being handed around inevitably became contaminated and corrupted beyond recognition, until at last Joseph Smith was obliged to issue a public statement. He did this reluctantly, confining his report to bare essentials. Throughout his life Joseph Smith was never eager to tell the story of his first vision. This is a thing which the publicity-minded writers of anti-Mormon books seem quite incapable of comprehending; hungry for "success" and attention themselves, they find it simply inconceivable that Joseph Smith or any of the prophets should have "kept it close, and told no man of any of those things which they had seen" (Luke 9:36). For them, the complete proof that Joseph Smith had no first vision is that he did not advertise it.

They're Still at It

We should not conclude without referring the reader to a mimeographed sheet which was widely circulated in the mail in Utah during the third week of February of the present year (1961), and which brings our little study conveniently up to date.[80] The writing begins with a pompous and resounding declaration: "It has recently been discovered that the teaching that God the Father and his Son Jesus Christ appeared to Joseph Smith in 1820 was not a part of early church doctrine until after the death of Brigham Young." This gives us a new terminal date for our story—1877! The proof of this sensational claim is as

follows: "Brigham Young said, *'The Lord did not come. . . .
But He did send His angel to this same obscure person, Joseph
Smith, Jun., . . . and informed him that he should not join any
of the religious sects of the day, for they were all wrong."*[81]

What Brigham Young *did* say at the place indicated
was:

> But as it was in the days of our Savior, so it was in
> the advent of this new dispensation. . . . The Lord did
> not come with the armies of heaven, in power and glory,
> nor send His messengers panoplied with aught else than
> the truth of heaven, to communicate to the meek, the
> lowly, the youth of humble origin, the sincere inquirer
> after the knowledge of God. But he did send his angel
> to this same obscure person, Joseph Smith, Jun., who
> afterwards became a Prophet, Seer, and Revelator, and
> informed him that he should not join any of the religious
> sects of the day, for they were all wrong.[82]

By suppressing most of the first sentence, which explains that as in ancient times the Lord did not come himself nor send his messengers *in visible splendor,* our critics
make the sentences appear to say that he did not come at
all. And by further juggling, it is made to appear that the
Lord sent an angel instead of coming himself, and that it
was the angel who told Joseph Smith that all the religious
sects were wrong. Actually the statement "the Lord did
not come" is promptly followed by the fuller specification
"nor send His messengers," which our critics have carefully
omitted, since that makes it perfectly clear that Brigham
Young is denying neither class of heavenly manifestation,
but simply stating that they did not happen *in a particular
way;* for in the next sentence he goes on to specify that
God "did send his angel to this same obscure person,"
and God (not "who"!) "informed him that he should not
join any of the religious sects." God both instructed Joseph
Smith and sent his angel—but he did not do either in visible
splendor.

Next our discoverers quote a passage from Orson Hyde: "Some one may say 'If this work of the last days be true, *why did not the Savior come himself* and communicate this intelligence to the world?' *Because to the angels was committed the power* of reaping the earth, and it was committed to *none else.*"[83]

Again they have pulled the same stunt, underlining the words that would make it appear that Jesus does not come at all, while what the author actually says is that he did not come "to the world," which is exactly the point that Brigham Young was making: Jesus Christ did not make a public appearance in glory; he did not personally circulate among men, but sent his angels for the reaping and the gathering. The preaching of the gospel and the reaping of the harvest, of which Brother Hyde is speaking, is one aspect of the work of this dispensation, under the direction of the angels; the visit of the Father and the Son is another and totally different aspect; there is no conflict whatever between the two great events, but Orson Hyde is speaking only of the preaching and the gathering, and what he says is perfectly correct.

Having with great fanfare fired off these two duds, the experts now bring their atomic cannon into play. The Great Discovery is a quotation from the *History of Joseph Smith* as published in the *Deseret News* of May 29, 1852:

> This afternoon, Erastus Holmes, of Newbury, Ohio, called on me to inquire about the establishment of the church, and to be instructed in doctrine more perfectly. I gave him a brief relation of my experience while in my juvenile years, say from six years old up to the time I received the *first visitation of angels,* which was when I was about *fourteen years old;* also the revelations that I received *afterwards* concerning the Book of Mormon, and a short account of the rise and progress of the church up to this date.

The discoverers of this passage have been at pains to

underline the parts of it which make it clear that the
Prophet *is* speaking of the first vision and nothing else.
They have *not*, however, taken pains to point out that the
date of this interview is Saturday, October 17, 1835 — which
makes a hash of the prevailing Party Line that Joseph Smith
invented all his vision stories in Nauvoo some years later.
This date of 1835 leads desperate contrivers to cry forgery,
surmising that the date was slyly interpolated into the
Deseret News account. But here we have an excellent control, for if the editors of the paper were free to invent stories
and dates to suit their fancy, it is hardly conceivable that
they would run the risk of a misunderstanding by using
the ambiguous term "angels" when for many years it had
been uniformly taught by the Church that the two visitors
were the Father and the Son. The peculiarity of the language vouches for the authenticity of the story.

Nor have our searchers bothered to note that exactly
one week previous to his interview with Holmes, Joseph
Smith had another visitor, as reported in the *Deseret News*
just two weeks before the above item appeared:

> I was this morning introduced to a man from the
> east. After hearing my name, he remarked that I was
> nothing but a man, indicating by this expression, that
> he had supposed that a person to whom the Lord should
> see fit to reveal his will, must be something more than
> a man. . . . And indeed, such is the darkness and ig-
> norance of this generation, that they look upon it as
> incredible that a man should have any intercourse with
> his Maker.[84]

Since all Christians have always believed that a man
can have intercourse with his Maker through prayer, meditation, or mystical experiences, it must have been something very different to which the Prophet and his visitor
were alluding. As we have noted, Joseph Smith did not
choose to discuss these matters; indeed, he told Erastus
Holmes very briefly of his "juvenile years . . . *up to* the

time I received the first visitation of angels," resuming again with "the revelations that I received afterwards concerning the Book of Mormon." This could mean, and seems to imply, that he actually skipped the part about his first vision.

But to return to our shrewd discoverers. "This statement of Joseph Smith," they triumphantly announce, "refutes the teaching that the Father and the Son appeared to him in the first vision of 1820." Refutes it? Does he say that the Father and Son did *not* appear to him? That would be a refutation. Does he say who the angels were, or how many? If our experts had taken the trouble to consult a good dictionary, they would have made another startling discovery, namely that an angel is "1. A ministering spirit or divine messenger. . . . 2. *Any* messenger of God, as a prophet, or preacher. . . . 4. A messenger generally."[85] The word *angel* in English has "acquired a special meaning, particularly in the singular, as the designation of a supernatural bearer of a divine revelation. The transition was then easy to the sense of a generic name for the beings of the heavenly world."[86] That is to say, *any* heavenly being is properly an angel. Messrs. Schaff and Herzog spare us the trouble of a long excursion into the *Patrologia* by admitting, though reluctantly, that it was "assumed by the Greek Fathers, the older Lutheran dogmaticians, and Hengstenberg" that Jesus Christ, the Logos, was an angel, and that in the Bible "the distinction between the angel and Yahweh does not hinder from making the angel speak as of Yahweh or from speaking of the angel as Yahweh"; that is to say, Jehovah himself in his capacity of a messenger to men is an angel, just as, in the same capacity but in an evil sense, "Satan . . . is reckoned among the angels."[87] Even Elohim, when he visits the earth, has been called an angel (Psalm 8:5).[88] Not to labor the point, it is perfectly correct usage to refer to *any* heavenly visitor as an angel. So when Joseph Smith, reviewing the past in "a brief relation" to a stranger, passes over the first vision as his "first visitation of angels," he is being both correct and evasive. Remember that this was some years before he was finally "induced" to come out with a public statement about the first vision; but all the time the story is there.

Since these articles began to appear in the *Improvement Era*, the writer has been drenched by a steady drizzle of letters from people who seem to make an avocation of searching for anything that might be interpreted as an inconsistency in the record. There is something comical in these laborious attempts to prove a negative and override living revelation by exploiting—while ignoring—the first principle of textual criticism. That principle (only too well known to the conscientious genealogist) is, that *no* written record of any length is free of serious errors. The reader of a written document, the greatest living authority on documents has said, never perceives more than a shadow of reality.

The sources of Latter-day Saint church history, like all human chronicles, bristle with errors; the only way of approximating certitude is to check them against one another. If among a hundred fairly consistent reports of the first vision story three or four differ radically, that is simply to be expected; their existence does not discredit the consensus. And where such intimate and personal things as unique revelations to individuals are concerned it would be very strange indeed if wild aberrations and wide discrepancies did not appear in the reports. We know the policy of the early leaders regarding the reporting of revelations. A favorite theme of Brigham Young's was the tangible, personal nature of God, which he *never* illustrates by any mention of the first vision. Why not? He has explained at length:

> That man who cannot know things without telling any other living being upon the earth, who cannot keep

his secrets and those that God reveals to him, never can receive the voice of his Lord. . . . Should you receive a vision of revelation from the Almighty . . . you should shut it up and seal it as close, and lock it as tight as heaven is to you, and make it as secret as the grave. The Lord has no confidence in those who reveal secrets, for he cannot safely reveal Himself to such persons. . . . If a person understands God . . . and the Lord reveals anything to that individual no matter what, unless he gives permission to disclose it, it is locked up in eternal silence.[89]

The youthful and impulsive Joseph Smith was sometimes lax in this regard, and we all know how terribly he suffered for it in the case of the 116 pages. When he told a minister of the first vision, it only made trouble. Did he later deliberately disguise important revelations to keep them from the world? The code names occasionally used in the Doctrine and Covenants to designate persons and things show that (speaking by revelation) he did. If William Smith and Oliver Cowdery give confusing accounts of the first vision, we must remember that the Prophet knew from the first that those men were not to be trusted with too much information. The vanity and ambition of Cowdery were rebuked as early as 1829 (D&C 9), and George Albert Smith, Sr., commenting on "the conduct of William Smith in the days of Joseph and afterwards," describes it as a campaign "to annihilate and destroy the principles which the Prophet taught to the nations of the earth."[90] Were such men to be trusted with a full account of the first vision before it was officially given to the world?

Constantly beset by the designing and overcurious, Joseph Smith was often obliged to put his questioners off, just as the Lord himself did. Whether it was the sly schoolmen ever striving to catch him in a contradiction or his earnest disciples seeking to know the mysteries, Jesus would put them off, sometimes with a flat rebuke, sometimes with half-answers, but most often with words of hidden meaning: "He who has ears to hear, let him hear!" As a result, people were constantly puzzled and offended by what he taught them—his disciples wrangled, and the public rioted. The trouble was, as Brigham Young often points out, that Christ was speaking of the things of eternity to people wholly in thrall to the things of this world. It was utterly impossible to understand the Son without the spirit of revelation from the Father. Once one has that spirit, the truth of things is made clear no matter how deplorable the state of the documents may be; without it, all the "scholarship" in the world is of no avail to determine what really happened.

Notes

1. J. B. Turner, *Mormonism in All Ages, or the Rise, Progress, and Causes of Mormonism* (New York: Platt and Peters, 1842), 17.

2. John C. Bennett, *The History of the Saints; or, an Exposé of Joe Smith and Mormonism* (Boston: Leland and Whiting, 1842), 79.

3. Henry Caswall, *The Prophet of the Nineteenth Century; or, the Rise, Progress, and Present State of Mormons or Latter-Day Saints* (London: Rivingtons, 1843), 72, 77.

4. Henry Brown, *History of Illinois* (New York: Winchester and New World, 844), 387.

5. W. J. Conybeare, "Mormonism," *Edinburgh Review* 202 (April 1854): 322.

6. W. J. Conybeare, *Essays Ecclesiastical and Social* (London: Longem, Brown, 1853), 289.

7. William A. Linn, *The Story of the Mormons from the Date of Their Origin to the Year 1901* (New York: Macmillan, 1923), 28–29.

8. E. D. Howe, *Mormonism Unvailed: Or a Faithful Account of That Singular Imposition and Delusion* (Painesville, OH: Howe, 1834), 266–67.

9. Reverend D. H. C. Bartlett, *The Mormons, or Latter-Day Saints, Whence Came They?* (Liverpool: Thompson, 1911), 8.

10. John Q. Adams, *The Birth of Mormonism* (Boston: Gorham, 1916), 20–21.

11. J. H. Snowden, *The Truth about Mormonism* (New York: Doran, 1926), 52.

12. Fawn M. Brodie, *No Man Knows My History* (New York: Knopf, 1947), 55, 83, 38.

13. Ibid., 405.

14. *HC* 1:1.

15. L. Petersen, *Problems in Mormon Text* (Salt Lake City: Peterson, 1957), 4–5, labors this point most strangely. He cites as evidence the *Millennial Star* for August 1842 and the 1851 edition of the Pearl of Great Price—the first printed in England, far away from Joseph Smith, and the second edition years after his death; for them Joseph Smith cannot be held responsible nor for a Reorganite history published in 1902. Petersen's prize exhibit is the statement of a *nephew* of David Whitmer, who avers that he had heard his *grandmother* say that the angel had shown *her* (!) the plates, the angel being "Brother Nephi." [On the Nephi-Moroni matter, see Dean C. Jessee, ed., *The Papers of Joseph Smith* (Salt Lake City: Deseret Book, 1989), note on 277.] That Mr. Peterson should have to search so far among literally thousands of retellings of the story of Moroni to find this inevitable slip is actually a vindication of the original. Teachers of the Book of Mormon know well how often the proper names in the book are confused by students in writing papers and exams; the names Mormon, Nephi, Lehi, and Moroni especially are mixed with great frequency. This writer has made the mistake more than once.

16. This principle is stated by Tertullian, *De Praescriptionibus* 25–26, in *PL* 2:43–46; Origen, *Contra Celsum* I, 17, in *PG* 11:651–56; Clement of Alexandria, *Stromatum* I, in *PG* 8:704. Cf. Matthew 7:6–8; 11.25–27, 13:9–17; 16:20; 19:11; 21:3, etc. Cf. also Hugh W. Nibley, *Since Cumorah* (Salt Lake City: Deseret Book, 1967), 96–126; reprinted in *CWHN* 7:84–110.

17. This is well brought out in Minucius Felix, *Octavius* 9–10, in *PL* 3:270–76.

18. David Marks, *Life of David Marks* (Limerick, Main: Office of the Morning Star, 1831), 341–42.

19. Eduard Meyer, *Ursprung und Geschichte der Mormonen* (Halle: Niemeyer, 1912), 279–81.

20. To the sources given above in n. 16 one might add the interesting (and very ancient) discussion in *Clementine Recognitions* II, 4; III, 1,34, in *PG* 1:1250, 1281, 1297–98.

21. Howe, *Mormonism Unvailed,* 266.

22. Brodie, *No Man Knows My History,* 55, 83, 38.

23. Turner, *Mormonism in All Ages,* 14.

24. Editorial, "Mormonism; or, New Mohammedanism in England and America," *Dublin University Magazine* (March 1843): 285.

25. "The Yankee Mahomet," *American Whig Review* (June 1851): 557.

26. J. W. Gunnison, *The Mormons or Latter-day Saints* (Philadelphia: Lippincott, 1856), 26, 91.

27. Conybeare, "Mormonism," 322.

28. John Reynolds, *My Own Times, Embracing Also, the History of My Life* (Illinois: John Reynolds, 1855), 565.

29. John Hyde, *Mormonism, Its Leaders and Designs* (New York: Fetridge, 1857), 199, 240.

30. Theodor Olshausen, *Geschichte der Mormonen* (Göttingen: Vandenhoeck and Ruprecht, 1856), 11.

31. J. S. C. de Radius, *Historical Account of Every Sect of the Christian Religion*, 2nd ed. (London: Blower, 1864), 112.

32. Pomeroy Tucker, *Origin, Rise, and Progress of Mormonism* (New York: Appleton, 1867), 28.

33. John S. C. Abbott, *History of the State of Ohio* (Detroit: Northwestern, 1875), 698.

34. E. E. Dickinson, *New Light on Mormonism* (New York: Funk and Wagnalls, 1885), 32–33.

35. R. W. Beers, *The Mormon Puzzle and How to Solve It* (New York: Funk and Wagnalls, 1887), 28.

36. Waldo Messaros, *The Road to Heaven* (Philadelphia: Globe Bible, 1888), 584.

37. C. Fenwick Ward, *Mormonism Exposed: The Origin of Mormonism — Fiction and Fraud* [The Second of a Series of Lectures] (Manchester: Taylor, Garnett, Evans, 1898), 34.

38. Thomas Gregg, *The Prophet of Palmyra* (New York: Alden, 1890), 12.

39. M. W. Montgomery, *The Mormon Delusion* (Boston and Chicago: Congregational Sunday School and Publishing Society, 1890), 17–18.

40. Thomas W. Young, *Mormonism: Its Origin, Doctrines and Dangers* (Ann Arbor, MI: Wahr, 1900), 12.

41. George Townsend, *The Conversion of Mormonism* (Hartford: Church Mission, 1911), 15.

42. Bartlett, *Mormons, or Latter-day Saints*, 6.

43. Adams, *Birth of Mormonism*, 19.

44. Ibid., 19–20.

45. Eva L. Pancoast, "Mormons at Kirtland," Master's thesis, Western Reserve University, 1929, 4.

46. George B. Arbaugh, *Revelation in Mormonism: Its Character and Changing Forms* (Chicago: University of Chicago, 1932), 34–35.

47. Meyer, *Ursprung und Geschichte der Mormonen*, 28–33; cf. 16–17.

48. George B. Arbaugh, *Gods, Sex, and Saints: The Mormon Story* (Rock Island, IL: Augustana, 1957), 24.

49. Ibid., 9.

50. We give them in chronological order: I. Daniel Rupp, ed., *An Original History of the Religious Denominations at Present Existing in the United States* (Philadelphia: Humphreys, 1844), cited by C. F. Potter, *The Story of Religion as Told in the Lives of Its Leaders* (New York: Simon and Schuster, 1929), 528; E. Hickman, *Mormonism Sifted* (London: Jarrold and Sons, 1850), 3; *Tracts on Mormonism*, No. 2 (London: Wertheim and Macintosh, 1850), 3, 5; Emerson Davis, *The Half Century* (Boston: Tappan and Whittemore, 1851), 394; *Census of Great Britain 1851, Religious Worship* (London: Eyre and Spottiswoodey, 1853), cvi; Samuel M. Smucker, ed., *The Religious, Social, and Political History of the Mormons, or Latter-day Saints, from Their Origin to the Present Time* (London: Miller, Orton, and Mulligan, 1851), 20, and in many subsequent editions; Abel Stevens, ed., "Nauvoo and Deseret," *National Magazine* 4 (June 1854): 482; Reverend Emilius Guers, *Irvingism and Mormonism Tested by Scripture* (London: Nisbet, 1854), 52; B. G. Ferris, *Utah and the Mormons: The History, Government, Doctrines, Customs, and Prospects of the Latter-day Saints* (New York: Harper and Bros., 1857), 57; *Is Mormonism True or Not?* (London: Religious Tract Society, 1855), 11. *The Lamps of the Temple: Crayon Sketches of the Men of the Modern Pulpit* (London: Snow, 1856), 179, 490–92; S. M. Smucker, *Religious, Social and Political History of the Mormons or Latter-day Saints* (New York: Miller, Orton, and Mulligan, 1856), 20, 32; John Timbs, *English Eccentrics and Eccentricities* (London: Bentley, 1866), 228; N. W. Green, *Mormonism: Its Rise, Progress, and Present Condition* (Hartford: Belnap and Bliss, 1870), 412; J. H. Beadle, *Life in Utah; or, the Mysteries and Crimes of Mormonism; the History of Mormonism* (Toronto: Hovey, 1873), 23; W. Lang, *History of Seneca County* (Springfield, OH: Transcript Printing, 1880), 649; George Wotherspoon, *Mormonism; Or the Faith of the Latter-day Saints: Its History and Moral* (London: Sunday Lecture Society, 1886); Thomas E. Hill, *Hill's Album of Biography and Art* (Chicago: Hill Standard, 1888), 32–33; *Knowledge, A Weekly Magazine* 1/9 (2 August 1890): 176; O. F. Berry, *The Mormon Settlement in Illinois*, in *Transactions of the Illinois State Historical Society*, 1906, no. 7, p. 88; J. D. McMillan, "An Outline of Mormon History," *Gospel of the Kingdom* 5/8 (August 1913): 113; Harry M. Beardsley, *Joseph Smith and His Modern Empire* (Boston: Houghton Mifflin, 1931), 83–84; "Mar-

rying Mormons: The Strange Case of American Polygamy," *M.D. Magazine* 3 (June 1959): 111–15.

51. Rupp, *Religious Denominations in the United States*, 404–10.

52. *Edinburgh Review* (October 1861): 202. "This alleged vision is an excellent sample of the poverty of invention and impudent audacity by which all the visions or revelations of the prophet were characterized."

53. Brodie, *No Man Knows My History*, 22–23.

54. [Milton V. Backman, Jr., *Joseph Smith's First Vision*, 2nd ed. (Salt Lake City: Bookcraft, 1980.)]

55. Quoted in Francis W. Kirkham, *A New Witness for Christ in America*, 2 vols. (Salt Lake City: Utah Printing, 1959), 2:43.

56. Hugh Nibley, *The Myth Makers* (Salt Lake City: Bookcraft, 1961), reprinted in this volume, pages 103–406.

57. Brodie, *No Man Knows My History*, 17.

58. Joseph Smith, Jr., letter to Oliver Cowdery, in *Latter-Day Saints' Messenger and Advocate* 1 (December 1834): 40.

59. Brodie, *No Man Knows My History*, 21.

60. Howe, *Mormonism Unvailed*, 187.

61. Ibid., 75–76.

62. Ibid., 74.

63. Ibid., 232–33.

64. Ibid., 233–34.

65. Tucker, *Origin, Rise, and Progress of Mormonism*, 28–29.

66. Ibid., 29.

67. Cited in Kirkham, *New Witness for Christ in America*, 2:31.

68. Ibid., 29–30.

69. Ibid., 47.

70. [Cf. Russell R. Rich, "The Dogberry Papers and the Book of Mormon," *BYU Studies* 10 (Spring 1970): 315–20.]

71. Ibid., 53.

72. Ibid., 45.

73. Alexander Majors, *Seventy Years on the Frontier* (Denver: Western Miner and Financier, 1893), 44–45.

74. Ibid., 43–44.

75. Howe, *Mormonism Unvailed*, 14.

76. "Mormon Superstition—The Mormonites—No I," *Visitor or Monthly Instructor* (1941): 63.

77. John A. Clark, *Gleanings by the Way* (Philadelphia: Simon, 1842), 222.

78. Howe, *Mormonism Unvailed*, 140.

79. Majors, *Seventy Years on the Frontier*, 50–51.

80. A mimeographed sheet circulated by Mr. and Mrs. Jerald Tanner (319 No. 5th West, Salt Lake City), is called "Joseph Smith Speaks on the First Vision," and can be located in the Brigham Young University Library.

81. *JD* 2:171.

82. Ibid.

83. Ibid., 6:335.

84. *Deseret News,* 15 May 1852.

85. James A. H. Murray, ed., *A New English Dictionary on Historical Principles,* 10 vols. (Oxford: Clarendon, 1897), 1:323.

86. Samuel Macauley Jackson, ed., *Schaff-Herzog Encyclopedia of Religious Knowledge,* 15 vols. (Grand Rapids, MI: Baker, 1977), 1:174–76.

87. Ibid., 175–76.

88. Most commentators interpret the Elohim of Genesis 32:28–30 as "the angel." See for example, Adam Clarke, *Clarke's Commentary,* 3 vols. (Nashville: Abingdon, 1810), 1:203.

89. *JD* 4:287–88.

90. Ibid., 5:101–2.

The Myth Makers

Part 1

The Crime of Being a Prophet

i. Everybody knew him when . . .

> *Scene:* The assembly hall of a public school in Palmyra, New York, at the turn of the century. There is a low platform at one end of the hall. At the center table sits the Chairman; at the table to his left the Clerk is taking notes amid a heap of documents; at the table on the right sits Eber D. Howe with bulging dossiers. The hall is full of people. The Chairman looks like a combination of Aristophanes, Rabelais, and Rhadamanthus.

Too many witnesses

Chairman: Let us have a little order, please. This is the time and place fixed by stipulation for the deposition of a number of witnesses in the case of the World *versus* Joseph Smith, for the purpose of examining parties of record without being bound by the answers.

We want it understood that this is not a formal trial. This is merely an inquiry into some phases of the evidence that has been brought against Mr. Smith, who will not be present.

Eber D. Howe (who has made no effort to conceal his disgust): As counsel for these good people here I object to the whole procedure. The witnesses have already given their sworn affidavits—

The Myth Makers *was originally published in Salt Lake City by Bookcraft in 1961.*

Chairman: —and we will do no more than to ask them to repeat those affidavits. We have instructed the Clerk to put their original statements in quotation marks.

Howe: But why is the defendant not present? We can't have a trial without him.

Chairman: No one should know that better than you, sir! It was you and all these people here who have insisted on trying and condemning Smith *in absentia* through the years. Actually it is your claims rather than Smith's that we are examining at this time. Now, we want this to be a very informal investigation. Anyone who has anything relevant to say is invited to speak up at any time. All we really want to find out is what you people actually knew about Joseph Smith, since your testimony has convicted him of fraud in the eyes of the world. I warn you that I may be a little rough on some of the witnesses, but I have been directed to get to the bottom of this thing. In 1875 a Jesuit writer sought to discredit the work of Smith by appealing to "a published statement by sixty-two contemporary residents of Palmyra."[1] Are the sixty-two present?

John C. Bennett (looking very much like Napoleon): It was fifty-one, your honor. Fifty-one reputable citizens of Palmyra, plus eleven prominent citizens of Manchester, make sixty-two in all.[2]

Chairman: The clerk has the record here. How many was it, clerk?

Clerk: According to some sixty-four, according to others seventy or seventy-four. There seems to be some disagreement.

Lu B. Cake: What difference does it make how many? What is important is that they all said the same thing. "Sixty-four sworn reputables to one reprobate. Now do you believe Joe?"[3]

Chairman: That will do. We are here to let the witnesses speak for themselves. Will the clerk please read the primary document—the one signed by sixty-two male residents of Palmyra on 3 November 1833?

Clerk (reads): "We, the undersigned have been acquainted with the Smith family, for a number of years, while they resided near this place, and we have no hesitation in saying that we consider them destitute of that moral character, which ought to entitle them to the confidence of any community. They were particularly famous for visionary projects, spent much of their time in digging for money which they pretended was hid in the earth. . . . Joseph Smith, Sen., and his son Joseph, were in particular, considered entirely destitute of *moral character, and addicted to vicious habits.*"[4]

Bennett: It was the fifty-one who said that. Now let him read the testimony of the other eleven.

Clerk (reads): Eleven prominent citizens of Manchester signed the following: "We the undersigned, being personally acquainted with the family of Joseph Smith, Sen., with whom the celebrated Gold Bible, so called, originated, state:—That they were not only a lazy, indolent set of men, but were also intemperate, and their word was not to be depended upon; and that we are truly glad to dispense with their society."[5]

Chairman: Are there any others?

Parley Chase: Parley Chase speaking. My affidavit was taken separately a month after the others. What I said was that "I was acquainted with the family of Joseph Smith, Sr., both before and since they became Mormons. . . . They were lazy, intemperate, and worthless men, very much addicted to lying. In this they frequently boasted of their skill."[6]

Chairman: "Frequently"? A liar's "skill," sir, consists in *not* being recognized as a liar. Skillful liars don't boast about it. Your own technique is defective. Next witness.

John Hyde: Mr. Stafford here can tell you how "Joseph Smith, Sen., was a noted drunkard, that most of his family followed his example, especially Joseph Smith, Jun., the Prophet, who was very much addicted to intemperance," and that "he got drunk in my father's field, and that when drunk would talk about his religion."[7]

Chairman: Let him speak for himself, Mr. Hyde. You say, Mr. Stafford, that Smith would get drunk in your father's field and in that condition would talk about his religion?

B. Stafford: Though Mr. Hyde put my words in quotes, that is not the way I said it. What I said was that "he one day while at work in my father's field, got quite drunk on a composition of cider, molasses and water [and] . . . fell to scuffling with one of the workmen, who tore his shirt nearly off from him."[8]

Chairman: That is quite a different story from Mr. Hyde's, who on your testimony has Smith making a regular practice of getting drunk in the Stafford field and giving sermons in that situation.

Hyde: I didn't say he always gave his drunken sermons in the field.

Chairman: No, you merely implied it, so that others could take it up from there. Mr. Weil, I believe you have something to say about Joseph Smith's discourses in the horizontal.

Robert Richards: Indeed I have. While I was on my way to California in the 1840s, I visited Montrose, Iowa, where "looking over a fence I saw Joseph Smith himself lying alone on the grass, with a whiskey bottle by his side, and decidedly far gone in a state of intoxication. He was talking and laughing, and evidently congratulating himself, in a soliloquy, on the success of his devices. 'I am a prophet,' he said, 'a profitable profit.' "[9]

Chairman: That will do for now; we shall hear the rest later. You see, gentlemen, how these things grow. Who is next?

Willard Chase: I am Willard Chase. "I have regarded

Joseph Smith Jr. from the time I first became acquainted with him . . . as a man whose word could not be depended upon. . . . After they [the Smith family] became thorough Mormons, their conduct was more disgraceful than before."[10]

H. Harris: I appended my testimony to Chase's: "The character of Joseph Smith, Jun., for truth and veracity was such that I would not believe him under oath."[11]

Howe: Before we hear from the others I would like to introduce the testimony of a man of impeccable character and cultivated mind, President Fairchild of Michigan College. President Fairchild, would you please tell us your story?

President Fairchild: "It was in August, 1850, that I found myself spending a week in the immediate vicinity of Palmyra and Manchester. Three men were mentioned to me who had been intimately acquainted with Joseph Smith from the age of ten years to twenty-five and upwards. The testimony of these men was given under no stress of any kind. It was clear, decided, unequivocal testimony in which they all agreed."[12]

Chairman: Since the three men are here in person, and all present have been duly sworn, we would like to hear from them personally what they told Dr. Fairchild.

Man No. 1: "Joseph Smith was simply a notorious liar."

Man No. 2: "We never knew another person so utterly devoid of conscience as he was."

Man No. 3: "The thing for which Joseph was most notorious was his vulgar speech and his low life of unspeakable lewdness."[13]

Cake: Think of it! "Seventy reputable men who knew, stated under oath that this Smith family was ignorant; that the males were drunkards, blasphemers, liars, thieves; who put in their time digging for hidden treasures of the Captain Kidd kind, and defrauding their neighbours. Reputable citizens aver under oath that these Smiths were a low, wicked household and *Joe was the worst of the lot.*"[14]

Hyde: That about sums up the case. May I call the attention of our worthy Chairman (who as an outsider seems to be somewhat prejudiced in favor of the accused) to the fact that this evidence is irrefutable: "Here are positive statements by men who knew Smith *well*; who had known him *long*; who had no motive to exaggerate. . . . No attempt has been made to meet them."[15]

Cake: May I underline that last point. "The Smiths never controverted these affidavits, which is a silent plea of guilty. *They left,* which is equivalent to—no defense."[16]

Chairman: They left?

Cake: Yes, they moved right out of Palmyra, bag and baggage.

Hyde: "The Smiths never could, and did not, oppose to these affidavits anything but a bare denial, but *moved out of that part of the country.*" "No attempt has been made to meet them, only to cry persecution and *run away.* . . . To run away is to tacitly admit, if not the direct charge, certainly their inability to refute it."[17]

Chairman: And by leaving they in effect pled guilty to the charges?

Cake: That is what we said.

Chairman: When did they leave?

Cake: Let me see. I think it was some time early in 1831.

Chairman: So they left Palmyra in 1831 because they could not face up to "these affidavits" which were made in 1833? I don't think further comment on that is necessary. Let's see how reliable these witnesses are. Mr. Hyde's statement goes to the root of the matter. If you will recall, he made three unqualified claims: (1) that the affidavit swearers had known Smith *well* and *long,* (2) that they made *positive* statements about him, and (3) that they had no motive to exaggerate. As to the first point, the most specific claims were made by Dr. Fairchild's three witnesses. Will they please come forward? It was stated that you three were "intimately acquainted with Joseph Smith from the age of ten years to twenty-five." Will the clerk please confirm that?

Clerk (reads): ". . . from the age of ten years to twenty-five and upwards."

Chairman: So you all knew the defendant intimately for at least fifteen years?

Three Men: That is right.

Chairman: How could you be acquainted with him when he was "twenty-five and upwards" when he left Palmyra for the last time at the age of twenty-five?

Howe: A mere quibble!

Chairman: Not when absolute accuracy is the point in question. Since he is posing as the discoverer of perfect and unshakable testimony, Dr. Fairchild at least should have taken the pains to check his facts. But the point we wish to emphasize here is that these men knew Smith very intimately for at least fifteen years. Now why would these three honest and reputable men, and for that matter all the "prominent residents" of Palmyra and Manchester who knew Smith so long and so well, have persisted in associating with this monster for so many long years?

Man No. 2: "Monster" is putting it a bit strong, sir.

Chairman: Your actual words were, "notorious liar, . . . utterly devoid of conscience, . . . low life of unspeakable lewdness." Is that strong enough for your boon companion?

Three Men: He wasn't a boon companion. We just knew him.

Chairman: Already you are weakening your priceless testimony. The term Dr. Fairchild used was "intimately associated." Did you at any time share in Smith's "low life of unspeakable lewdness?"

Three Men (horrified): Of course not!

Howe: I object to these insinuations that blacken the character of my clients.

Chairman: Exactly. If they were really Smith's cronies, they must have been pretty low-life themselves. And if they were not his cronies, how could they have discovered the vices they know so much about?

Intimate strangers

Howe: I will tell you how: *Everybody* knew about those vices. You heard all the witnesses say that Smith was *notorious* for them.

Chairman: Indeed I did hear them say it, and it immediately made me very suspicious. The worth of all these testimonies lies entirely in the fact that the witnesses are supposed to have known the accused personally and intimately—that they are in a position to give concrete and specific information not known to the general public. Yet every last one of them is careful to specify that what he knows about Smith is "notorious" *general* knowledge. Even so, I wonder just how notorious these things were. Take Mr. Harris's notorious "Gold Bible Company," for example. Mr. Harris, what did you say about it in 1833?

Harris: I said that "a while before the gold plates were found . . . Joseph Smith, Jun., Martin Harris and others" were "familiarly known by the name of the 'Gold Bible Company.' "[18]

Chairman: You see, they were so well known as to be given a familiar, popular moniker. Yet of all the witnesses of the time, racking their brains to remember every scandal, *only* Mr. Harris remembers this notorious Company. So when I read that the sixty-two signers confine their testimony exclusively to characteristics for which Smith was "particularly famous," I wonder the more. In all those years of intimate association with Smith did these three or any of the others ever see him commit any specific crime? I notice that the most eloquent witnesses of all, Messrs.

Stafford, Ingersoll, and Chase, confine their testimony not to what they saw Smith do, but to what they claim *other* people *told* them about him, and to secret private conversations between themselves and Smith. The utter viciousness and depravity of the Smith family to which all testify must have expressed itself from time to time in overt acts odious to society and punishable by law. Why was no legal action ever taken against them? Why are none of those acts ever reported? Can it be that our witnesses are holding back from feelings of modesty? Were they in any way reluctant to testify, President Fairchild?

Fairchild: Indeed they were not. They volunteered their testimony frankly, as I said before, and "it was clear, decided, unequivocal testimony in which they all agreed."[19]

Chairman: Thank you. Well, it is plain that these men had no intention either of shielding Smith or denying their own association with him.

Howe: Have you considered, sir, that there might have been some youthful peccadillos which the witnesses might not wish to be made public?

Chairman: Youthful peccadillos at twenty-five and upwards? We are not talking about youthful peccadillos but gross immorality. Here three men rush forward, eager to tell all — after fifteen years of intimate association with the most notorious scoundrel alive! We wait with bated breath for their report — what stories they can tell! And what do we get? The monotonous repetition of familiar generalities as they lamely fall back on what *they* insist are matters of common knowledge. This brings us to Mr. Hyde's second point, which is that the witnesses all make *positive* statements. Positive statements about what? About Smith's "notorious" traits of character. Consider again what these three say about Smith. Will the clerk read from their testimony?

Clerk (reads): "We the undersigned have been acquainted with the Smith family for a number of years, while they resided near this place, and we have no hesitation in saying that we consider them destitute of that moral character which ought to—"

Chairman: Thank you, that will do. The key to the whole thing, you will observe, is "we consider"—the Smiths were not what these people thought they "ought to" be. Much has been made of the claim that "no attempt was made to meet" the charges. Only there were no charges—only opinions. If you swear that in your opinion I am a scoundrel, you have said nothing at all, and I could only deny it by saying you were another. But if you say I robbed a bank on the 13th then we would have something to go on. Read the testimony of the third witness.

Clerk (reads): "The thing for which Joseph was most notorious was his vulgar speech and his low life of unspeakable lewdness."

Chairman: Here we have the sort of thing that promises to be most intimate and personal—yet even here our witness sticks to things "for which Joseph was most notorious," i.e., charges that could not and in the public's mind need not be examined or proved. He is playing it safe. But what did our sixty-two star witnesses say Smith was "most notorious" for?

Clerk (reads): The sixty-two testified "that they were *particularly famous* for visionary projects."

Chairman: And what did Mr. Stafford swear to?

Clerk (reads): "Joseph Smith, Sen., was a *noted drunkard,* that most of his family followed his example, especially Joseph Smith, Jr., the Prophet."

Chairman: Apparently some of these witnesses who knew Smith so long and so well (as Mr. Hyde assures us they did) overlooked his most conspicuous trait—his drunkenness, while others failed to comment on his gross licentiousness, and still others failed to make any mention of his visionary propensities, though the sixty-two claimed that the Smiths were "particularly famous" for *them.* When certain parties diligently trying to recall all the worst traits of the so-well-known Smith fail even to mention characteristics described as "most notorious" and "particularly famous" by others, a person cannot but wonder just how well those people really knew Smith.

Infallible in-laws

Howe: But here we have members of the family to testify! I think Mrs. Abigail Harris has something to tell us.

Abigail Harris: Yes, I have plenty to tell! One night I was at the Martin Harris house and Joseph Smith, Sr., and his wife were there; we talked "until about 11 o'clock" about Joseph Smith and his golden Bible.[20]

Chairman: Was Joseph Smith, Jr., present?

A. Harris: No. He was away in Pennsylvania.

Chairman: Yet your *entire affidavit* is taken up with what you heard during that one visit to the Harrises, when Joseph Smith was nowhere around. Now the fact that you are introduced as an inside witness speaks well for the defendant.

Howe: What do you mean, "speaks well"?

Chairman: I mean that whether or not Mrs. Harris has rightly remembered after a lapse of five years what was said in an evening of gossip, all she has to report of Smith's evil doings through all those years of family association is what she remembers of that one night's chin-fest. It is perfectly plain that the lady had never seen or even heard of Smith doing anything really bad. Her silence, taken with her willingness to tell the worst, is most eloquent in Smith's favor.

Howe: Here's something that isn't in his favor! Mrs. Harris, tell us what you heard Martin Harris say to his wife that time at your house.

A. Harris: It was in "the second month following." Mrs. Harris "observed, that she wished her husband would quit them [the Mormonites], as she believed it was all false and

a delusion. To which I heard Mr. Harris reply: '*What if it
is a lie; if you will let me alone I will make money out of it!*' I
was both an eye and an ear witness . . . and I give it to
the world for the good of mankind."[21]

Chairman: Thank you for telling us your motive for
embellishing this important report, Mrs. Harris.

A. Harris: Motive? Embellishing?

Chairman: Yes. Five years after the event you tell this
story "for the good of mankind," and in doing so you slip
in a damning confession by Martin Harris: "What if it is a
lie." It is that remark that makes your tale what you intend
it shall be—a weapon against the Mormons. But what did
Mrs. Martin Harris herself report? What is your version,
Mrs. Harris?

Lucy Harris: "One day, while at Peter Harris' house I
told him he had better leave the company of the Smiths,
as their religion was false; to which he replied if you would
let me alone, I could make money by it."[22]

Chairman: Are you sure that is what your husband said?

L. Harris: I should know, he said it to me!

Chairman: Yet though both you and Abigail Harris
swear that you are quoting the man's very words, your
speeches are not the same . . .

Howe: Oh sir, a mere quibble!

Chairman: They are the same except where that all-
important "*What if it is a lie*" comes in. That, you will notice,
is underscored by Mr. Howe, yet Mr. Harris' wife failed
to mention it entirely. I am sure she would be the last
person in the world to overlook the outright admission by
her husband that Smith was a fraud—she could have taxed
him with that the rest of his days. I think it is plain enough
that Mrs. Abigail Harris in her zeal "for the good of mankind" has displayed an adequate motive for adding those
six little words which have been heavily exploited by anti-
Mormon writers. From all accounts, Mrs. Harris, you had

some terrible tiffs with your husband. Were his words on the occasion in question calm and considered?

L. Harris: What difference does it make? "It is vain for the Mormons to deny these facts; for they are all well known to most of his former neighbors."[23]

Chairman: Mrs. Harris, the "facts" contained in your testimony I find to consist exclusively of very private remarks exchanged between you and your husband. How could *all* of them be "well known" to most of the neighbors? Were the neighbors invited in?

L. Harris: It wasn't our neighbors, but Smith's neighbors—"most of *his* former neighbors."

Chairman: So you appeal to Smith's neighbors to confirm "these facts," namely, what passed secretly between you and your husband?

Howe: We can get a lot closer than that. Smith's own father-in-law has something to say about his character. Could you ask for more reliable evidence than that?

Chairman: To be frank, Mr. Howe, the answer is yes— I *can* think of more reliable character references than one's in-laws, though I realize that Mr. Hale because of his daughter is generally regarded as the star witness for the case against Joseph Smith. Mr. Isaac Hale, what can you tell us about Joseph Smith's character?

Isaac Hale: He was "very saucy and insolent to his father."[24]

Chairman: Indeed, that seems to be a rather common vice in young people—it hardly suggests unspeakable depravity. But Joseph Smith was always very close to his father, and you are the only person to report any signs of disrespect. Sauciness and insolence in the young are not usually regarded as criminal. You knew both Smith and his father well?

Hale: "Smith, and his father, with several other 'money-diggers' boarded at my house while they were employed in digging for a mine."[25]

Chairman: Was it their mine?

Hale: No, they were merely employed by others.

Chairman: Well, every mine is a speculation, and every owner hopes to make money; I hardly see how that makes out the Smiths to be money-diggers. They were digging for hire, not for gold.

Howe: So what?

Chairman: So it is evident that Mr. Hale is stretching a point to make Smith look as bad as possible. I notice that you don't accuse Smith outright of being a money-digger, gentlemen, but put the words in quotes. Your successors were not so careful. Did they stay long at your place, Mr. Hale?

Hale: No, "they soon after dispersed. This took place about the 17th of November, 1825; and one of the company gave me his note for $12.68 for his board, which is still unpaid."

Chairman: Was it one of the Smiths who did that?

Hale: No. If that was the case I would have said so. Joseph Smith came back soon after and asked to marry my daughter.

Chairman: Before we get to that, may I observe that the peevish and gratuitous little note about the deadbeat gives an unpleasant color to your account, some of which of course rubs off on Smith. It indicates a desire on your part, sir, to put Smith in the worst possible light. Why?

Hale: He ran off with my daughter.

Chairman: Why wouldn't you let him marry your daughter? Why did you refuse?

Hale: I "gave my reasons for so doing; some of which were, that he was a stranger, and followed a business I could not approve."

Chairman: Is that all?

Hale: I said those were only *some* of the reasons.

Chairman: And plainly the worst you could think of. But is it a crime for one to be a stranger? Many people don't approve of the mining business—but that was not Smith's business at all; he was merely in the employ of others, who paid him wages. I will admit that that is not a very promising outlook to a man with ambitions for his daughter, but I find nothing criminal about it.

Hale: But consider this. "Not long after this, he returned, and while I was absent from home, carried off my daughter, into the state of New York, where they were married without my approbation or consent."

Chairman: That must have rankled, but where is the crime? Did your daughter protest?

Hale: No. She wrote me soon after, asking for her property, which I let her have.

Chairman: How old was she at the time?

Hale: Let's see, Emma was born on 10 July 1804, and this took place in November 1825. That would make her twenty-one.

Chairman: So she was of age, and all that was required was *her* consent. Smith at the time was not yet twenty, incidentally, and from all accounts Emma was a very strong-minded lady. I mention this because many authors play this episode up as a shocking case of bride-stealing. It was nothing of the sort. Didn't the couple soon come back to your house?

Hale: Oh yes, they lived there a while, though I wouldn't let Smith keep the gold plates in the house. "I . . . informed him that if there was anything in my house of that description, which I could not be allowed to see, he must take it away; if he did not I was determined to see it. After that, the Plates were said to be hid in the woods."[26]

Chairman: So you won't let anybody stay at your place who won't let you examine his personal effects, including his mail. You seem to be a rather bossy and possessive person, sir.

Howe: Just a minute, here! It is Smith's character we are examining, not Mr. Hale's.

Chairman: Well, Mr. Hale, what about Smith's character? So far we have learned that he sassed his father, married your daughter, and worked for a mining company. Haven't you anything worse than that?

Hale: Well, a short time after, when Smith was living in another house, I dropped in and got a look at a paper which Smith and Harris "were comparing, and some of the words were 'my servant seeketh a greater witness, but no greater witness can be given him.' " There was also something said about " 'three that were to see the thing' — meaning, I supposed, the Book of Plates. . . . I enquired whose words they were, and was informed by Joseph or Emma (I rather think it was the former), that they were the words of Jesus Christ. I told them, that I considered the whole of it a delusion, and advised them to abandon it."[27]

Chairman: So you vaguely recall "something said" about "some of the words" on a paper, whose meaning you merely surmised — "supposed" — at the time, and were told by Joseph *or* Emma — you don't remember which, but "rather think" it was Joseph, that they were the words of Christ. It is too bad you were never cross-examined, sir. But even if you were clearly and correctly remembering things nine years after the event, instead of groping and guessing as you are, where is the crime in all this? Is this all you have to say about the monster?

Hale: "I conscientiously believe from the facts I have detailed . . . that the whole 'Book of Mormon' (so called) is a silly fabrication of falsehood and wickedness, got up for speculation, and with a design to dupe the credulous and unwary — and in order that its fabricators may live upon the spoils of those who swallow the deception."[28]

Chairman: So you don't judge the book on its own merits, but solely from the "facts you have detailed." But we have seen what those facts are, and they prove nothing except that you were a disgruntled and angry father. Your testimony, however, has been heavily exploited for one thing—your positive knowledge of the profit motive involved. But as you have so well expressed it, that is merely your conscientious opinion—an opinion of the witness and nothing more. But I assure you, sir, that anyone who reads the Book of Mormon as far as the second chapter of the first edition (chapter 6 of the standard edition) will find serious reason for doubting your profit motive. For at the beginning of that chapter we find, "Wherefore the things which are pleasing unto the world, I do not write, but the things which are pleasing unto God and unto them which are not of the world." You see, the author knew he was not writing a popular book. In a society which recognized only *one* Word of God, the author of the new revelation invariably chose the most dangerous, the most unpopular, and the most laborious imaginable way of making money. Now to get back to the other affidavits—their remarkable unanimity disturbs me.

The open conspiracy

Howe: What do you mean, sir, "disturbs"? It is the very unanimity of the affidavits that offers their most striking confirmation.

Thomas Gregg: Exactly. "With great unanimity" all these people report that Smith was "indolent, ignorant, untruthful, and superstitious."[29]

Famous Editor: As the editor of the most intellectual American magazine of the mid-nineteenth century I wish to confirm Mr. Gregg's position: "There is the most satisfactory evidence—that of his enemies—to show that from an early period he [Smith] was regarded as a visionary and a fanatic."[30]

Chairman: So our affidavit-swearers were no friends of the Prophet?

Editor: Of course not. I said they were his enemies, didn't I?

Chairman: But Mr. Hyde's third point was that all these witnesses "had no motive to exaggerate." Mr. Hyde, if all these people were Smith's enemies, wouldn't they have a very good motive to exaggerate? And you, Mr. Gregg, have discovered a most remarkably useful principle of psychology — that while one's friends are always, as friends, biased in one's favor, one's enemies, since they are not friends, are free of bias. With equal skill and cunning you parade a specious unanimity of opinion regarding Smith: having declared it your policy to discount all testimony in the defendant's favor, you then triumphantly point to the marvelous unanimity of the testimony that is left. All the testimony admitted tells the same story for the simple reason that you will not admit any that does not. Who collected these affidavits?

Howe: Mr. Hurlburt, Mr. Bennett, and I did nearly all of the work, I believe.

Chairman: And did Joseph Smith ever have more openly avowed enemies than you three?

Howe: But we did not sign the affidavits. We merely gathered them.

Chairman: Rather, you wrote them and asked people to sign them.

Hyde: What difference does that make? The so-called three witnesses of the Book of Mormon all signed the same statement.[31]

Chairman: But they claimed to have been together when they witnessed the phenomena described. The claim made for your seventy-odd witnesses is that they are testifying to knowledge acquired individually and separately. The value of these affidavits lies in the claim that each testified independently and that there was absolutely no collusion among them. The fact that we find many signatures on one document shows that we are not dealing with independent testimonies at all. Instead of testifying separately, the witnesses simply say "yes" to suggestive and leading statements. Did any of the affidavit swearers ever go back on their testimony, by the way?

Clerk: When nine of them were interviewed years later, some of them spoke very well of Smith, and had nothing bad whatever to say about him.[32]

C. A. Shook: But can't you see that such denials, since they are not unanimous, leave Smith's reputation just about where it was before?[33]

Chairman: No, sir, I do not see it.

Shook: But surely in a case of a few against many . . .

Chairman: This is not a case of a few against many, but of unanimous as against far from unanimous.

Howe: Well, against the eleven witnesses to the Book of Mormon, we place the respectable host which are here offered, we claim that "no credit ought to be given to those witnesses [of the Book of Mormon]."[34]

Chairman: But your mighty band have nothing to testify to at all about the Book of Mormon. The eleven said they saw and felt the plates, while your "respectable host" aver that they were aware of certain indications that Smith was a rascal, in which case he cannot have been a prophet, in which case no angel would visit him, in which case there would be no plates, in which case Smith invented the story.[35] We are not interested in syllogisms. No, sir, there are altogether *too many witnesses*. Will anyone here who has a close personal friend raise his hand—I mean a friend who is so dear and intimate as to know one's real thoughts and give a true picture of one's character? (Almost all raise their hands.) Splendid. Now think hard. How many have *two* such friends? Still impressive. Now think very carefully: is there anyone here who can boast *twenty* such intimate personal friends?

Howe: We see plainly enough what you are getting at. But these persons do not claim ever to have been Smith's *friends.* They only say they knew him well for a long time. You know how it is in a small town — everybody knows everybody else pretty well.

Chairman: The affidavit signers are regularly designated as "prominent residents," as if that title gave more weight to their testimonies. Wouldn't you say that everyone is prominent in a small town?

Howe: No. Not in the sense of being leading citizens.

Chairman: Then Joseph Smith was not prominent?

Howe: Of course not. He was an utterly contemptible nobody.

Chairman: Then how did all the prominent people get to know him so well? Did he seek them out, or did they seek him? If three or four or maybe even five people had said about Joseph Smith what all this cloud of witnesses swore to, their testimony might have borne some weight. But when we get up into the fifties and sixties and seventies — isn't it just possible that some of those did not really know Joseph Smith very well after all?

Howe: Well, you know how it is in a small town — everybody sees a lot of everybody else.

Chairman: Yes, and everybody talks a good deal about everybody else; and people learn to keep pretty much to themselves. Knowing people is a very different thing. I believe your American literature is full of comment on the devastating gossip of the small town — especially of the rural New England town. Now, according to many reports, the Smiths kept pretty much out of circulation — shunning and shunned by all.

Howe: Yes, indeed. "He spent his days and nights among the rugged fastnesses of the forest, went and came stealthily, wrapping his movements in a mystery. . . . Vicious and vulgar, he was shunned by the boys of his own age, while the girls fled in terror from the 'Money-Digger.' "[36]

Chairman: Then when and where did all this intimate contact occur?

Howe: You know what we mean. For example, when Joe was a boy he used to come once a week to the printing office to pick up the newspaper for his father.

Chairman: And how did he act on those occasions?

Howe: He was very shy, and the boys who worked in the shop used to have fun with him — you know, throw inkballs at him and things like that.[37]

Chairman: So you saw him in the printing shop once a week . . .

Howe: Yes, and at the store, and at the mill where he worked sometimes.

Chairman: Such were the occasions on which all these people got to know Smith so intimately. Now on these occasions in which Smith appeared in public, just what acts of "unspeakable lewdness" did the shy and awkward fellow commit?

Howe: Well, now of course you are speaking of very private affairs . . .

Chairman: On the contrary, those who report these things say Joe was *notorious* for them. Since all of these people claim to have been close neighbors and intimate acquaintances of Smith for years, I think we have a right to demand some specific instances of criminal behavior on his part, preferably such instances as were witnessed by more than one person. According to testimony given, Joseph Smith's misdemeanors were matters of perpetual public display. What, then, were some of the things he did in the sight of any of these good people to acquire his tremendous reputation for wickedness? As late as the year 1955 the world has been assured that "these accounts are not idle gossip or empty accusations; they are simply a matter of cold hard facts. Joseph Smith was a notoriously immoral man."[38] So naturally we are exceedingly curious to be shown just one cold, hard fact, but so far none of the so-called witnesses has given us any satisfaction.

Howe: You must bear in mind, sir, that Smith was very cunning and adroit. Of course he would not let himself get caught at anything.

N. C. Lewis: Exactly. When I made my deposition I had admittedly never seen him do anything reprehensible — but why not? I will tell you: "From my standing in the Methodist Episcopal Church, I suppose he was careful how he conducted or expressed himself before me," so of course I would see nothing wrong.[39]

Chairman: But the fact that you saw nothing wrong did not prevent or discourage you from signing an affidavit against Smith?

N. C. Lewis: Of course not! I signed an affidavit stating that he was "an imposter, hypocrite and liar."[40]

Chairman: How did you know he was, since he never did anything wrong, to your observation?

Howe: A character witness need not describe overt actions. These people are all giving a uniform and unbiased account of Smith's character in the community. As Mr. Hyde put it, "they had no motive to exaggerate."

Chairman: Unbiased? Will Miss Nancy Towle please come forward? Miss Towle, your activities as a traveling evangelist took place between the years of 1818 and 1831, did they not?

Nancy Towle: That is correct.

Chairman: Did you ever visit western New York during those years?

Towle: I did indeed. I preached on the Geneva Road, near Manchester.[41]

Chairman: And did you ever meet with any opposition in those parts?

Towle: I most certainly did. I was vilely treated.

Chairman: And what would you say was the main source of the opposition?

Towle: Corrupt and "rotten-hearted" ministers.[42]

Chairman: But what motive could they possibly have had for opposing you? Didn't you preach the same religion they did?

Towle: Certainly I preached the gospel. But you, my good man, obviously do not understand the workings of the human heart—*jealousy* is a most powerful motive; nor do you seem to be aware how very limited are the views of "unregenerate men!!"[43] In matters of religion "the world abounds with priestcraft and superstition!"[44] That has made me the "butt of envy to all the combined powers of earth and hell, during my stay below."[45]

Chairman: Now take the case of Joseph Smith. Would you say his claims were primarily religious ones?

Towle: They were utterly abominable. They were blasphemous. When I visited Joseph Smith and his people in Kirtland, Ohio, in 1831, "I viewed the whole, with the utmost indignation and disgust."[46]

Chairman: And just what was it that you saw and heard to fill you with indignation and disgust?

Towle: Well, as I said in my book, I was only in Kirtland one day, and while there was treated with great kindness and courtesy, and it is only fair to say that during that time "I saw nothing indecorous; nor had I, any apprehension, of any thing of the kind."[47]

Chairman: Then I must ask you again—whence the loathing and disgust?

Towle: Young man, don't you realize that this Smith person was misleading "so many men of skill [of whom] . . . many, had actually intended, forsaking all for Christ, [by his] 'cunningly devised fables'?" Need I say more?[48]

Chairman: Thank you, Miss Towle. I think Miss Towle and Mr. Lewis have given us a pretty good idea of the real charges that all these witnesses are bringing against Joseph Smith. Miss Towle has exploded the popular argument that all who were not actually supporting Smith were innocent of any bias, prejudice, or motive for exaggeration. Why was Miss Towle herself so meanly handled by the same ministers who attacked Smith? And why does she boil with indignation when she mentions Smith's name? Combine the ambition and jealousy of small souls with the sanctions of religion and you have the most powerful motivation for persecution and chicanery, however the guilty parties may protest their freedom from bias and their Christian motives.

Weak memories and weak heads

Howe: May I call the Chairman's attention to the fact that he is overlooking a good deal of the concrete evidence which he says is lacking. Here is a "seceder from the delusion" who can prove Smith a fraud. He was at a meeting once and heard him speak in tongues.

Chairman: Your name, sir?

James H. Hunt: He prefers not to tell his name. But listen to his story.

Seceder: I was present at a meeting in an upper room in Kirtland, where were assembled from fifteen to twenty elders and high priests.

Chairman: When was this?

Seceder: On a certain occasion, Joseph Smith gave a sermon and "next arose, and passing round the room, laying his hand upon each one, spoke as follows, as near as the narrator can recollect: — 'Ak man oh son oh man ah ne commene en holle goste en haben en glai hosanne hosanne en holle goste en esac milkea jeremiah, ezekiel, Nephi, Lehi, St. John,' &c., &c."[49]

Chairman: What does the double *et cetera* stand for?

Seceder: Well, it was things like that.

Chairman: And why didn't you capitalize *jeremiah* and *ezekiel* as you did *Nephi* and *Lehi*?

Hunt (indignantly): The question is absurd. The man didn't *speak* in capitals!

Chairman: Why did our witness capitalize the other names, then? He is the one who claims a knack for detecting when Smith spoke in capitals or lower case. You assume, sir, that if you put in an *etc., etc.,* any reader will be able to carry on the speech at will?

Seceder: Well, you get the idea.

Chairman: And once one has the general idea, one is free to compose what one will, and attribute it to Joseph Smith as his actual words — or deeds?

Seceder: It is not as bad as that.

Chairman: Are these Smith's actual words?

Seceder: As nearly as I can remember.

Howe: This is only one of many such experiences. "This gibberish was for several months practiced almost daily" at that time in Kirtland.[50]

Chairman: Indeed. Could you describe some other such events?

Hunt: No! Please don't! "We will not dwell upon this part of our history. A particular recital of such scenes of fanaticism gives too much pain to the intelligent mind, and excites a contempt for our species."[51]

Chairman: Then the reason you people do not give specific details is that the whole business offends your sensibilities? You are afraid of exciting too much contempt?

Hunt: That is correct.

Chairman: Then why did you write your book at all, Mr. Hunt?

Hunt: "It has been our purpose to set Mormonism in such a light before those whose reason cannot perceive the truth, that they may nevertheless see its inherent grossness, and look upon it with utter contempt."[52]

Chairman: Yet you expect to achieve that end by *avoiding* unpleasant details? I think it is plain enough, sir, that you are by no means lacking in the will to publish the worst things about the Mormons, and the worse the better. I believe that the delicacy with which you avoid a recital of particulars is dictated only by the fact that you have none to recite.

Hunt: But we were just considering such particulars, sir, when *you* changed the subject!

Chairman: Forgive me. When did this meeting take place, by the way?

Seceder: Early in 1833.

Chairman: And when did you report it to Mr. Howe?

Seceder: In December of that year.

Chairman: And for a year you remembered Smith's nonsense-syllables to the letter?

Howe: As near as the narrator can recollect.

Chairman: Let us test his recollection again. The clerk has taken the words down — now would the witness mind repeating them again?

Seceder: Well, it was almost a year, and there were lots of other meetings, I can hardly be sure . . .

Chairman: Not a year, sir; three minutes! It has been barely three minutes since you recited those words.

Hunt: This is hardly fair. You are confusing the witness.

Chairman: If he is a genius with a phenomenal memory, a little thing like that should not disturb him.

Hunt: He makes no claim to be a genius.

Chairman: Very well, then, let us spare his feelings, and ask *you*, Mr. Hunt, or Mr. Howe, or anyone else in the room — or for that matter, let us ask the reader of this report — to repeat those words we all heard a few minutes ago without looking at them. Bear in mind that our witness, who claims to be no mnemonic wizard, heard those words just once, and yet from that one hearing he can repeat them almost a year later. Will anyone offer to repeat the thirty nonsense syllables that the witness uttered a few minutes ago?

Howe: But can't you see that the witness is only referring to the general *kind* of speech uttered — the sort of thing that went on?

Chairman: I see it only too clearly. Everybody knows the *kind* of nonsense Joe Smith would utter, so everybody can fill in that "&c., &c." And now it is plain enough that that is all the witness himself is doing. Either he is making up the speech attributed to Smith, or else he is remembering it. It is clear that he does not remember it, though he maintains that they are Smith's actual words . . .

Howe: "As near as the narrator can recollect." Please remember that!

Chairman: That is the whole point, in fact. If you are going to exploit this man's memory as a deadly weapon, you can hardly ask us to excuse him in case his memory breaks down! It was his idea to tell the story that way, and the strength of his testimony is no more nor less than the strength of his memory. Have you nothing better than this?

Howe: Here we have some sayings of Smith that are worse than nonsense syllables! Mr. McKune, tell the people here what you reported in 1834 under oath.

H. McKune: Joseph Smith said that "he was nearly equal to Jesus Christ; that he was a prophet sent by God to bring in the Jews."[53]

Levi Lewis: That's right. He told me that "he was as good as Jesus Christ."[54]

Sophia Lewis: I heard him say it another time. Once when he was having an argument with the Reverend J. B. Roach, I heard Smith call Mr. Roach "a d — —d fool. Smith also said in the same conversation that he (Smith) was as good as Jesus Christ."[55]

Eminent Editor: As editor of the *American Whig Review*, I can affirm that Joseph Smith "was *often* heard during his life to declare himself *far* superior to our Savior."[56]

Chairman: And when did you first affirm that, sir?

E. Editor: In 1851.

Chairman: Well, you see how these things grow. First Mr. McKune in 1834 says that Smith claimed he was "*nearly equal*" to Jesus; then the Lewises improved on that—each of them heard Smith say he was "*as good as* Jesus Christ"; finally in 1851 it is remembered that he "was *often* heard . . . to declare himself *far superior* to our Savior." In 1833 Smith's nearest neighbors remember nothing of this great blasphemy, which by 1851 is numbered among his habitual daily vices.

Howe: What do you mean, none of his neighbors remembered? We have just heard three separate and independent testimonies?

Chairman: Were they separate and independent? Mr. McKune, didn't you and the Lewises go together to make your depositions before the justice?

McKune: Yes. But you will notice that we testified to three separate experiences.

Chairman: Indeed I did notice it, and it struck me as very significant. Here the *only* witnesses to a thing Smith is supposed to have done many times are a husband and wife and a close friend of theirs, all testifying together. Isn't it odd that of all the witnesses, Smith told only the companions McKune and Lewis — separately — that he was as good as Christ, and that it was Mrs. Lewis who just happened to be listening when he said it to the Reverend Roach, from whom we have no report? Isn't it fairly probable that the three cooked the story up among themselves before they went to the magistrate? Any others?

Howe: Here is a man who can tell you a thing or two.

Wm. Bryant: I knew the Smiths.

Chairman: You seem rather old, sir; how long ago did you know them?

Bryant: Well, let's see. This affidavit was taken in 1880 — that's more than fifty years after I saw any of them.[57]

Chairman: But you remember them?

Bryant: As I was saying, I knew the Smiths, but did not associate with them, for they were too low to associate with.

Chairman: You were apparently more fastidious than

your respectable and prominent fellow-citizens. What was wrong with the Smiths?

Bryant: "There was no truth in them. Their aim was to get in where they could get property. They broke up homes in that way. Smith had no regular business. He had frequent revelations."[58]

Chairman: Though you didn't associate with those people, you seem to have known a good deal about the more intimate aspects of their activity. Whose were some of the homes they broke up? The victims must have been your neighbors, too. How does it happen that in fifty years none of them has come forward to testify? Whose homes did the Smiths break up?

Howe: I will not have my witness badgered in this way!

Mrs. William Bryant: Please cease molesting my husband, sir. "For the last few years his mind has been somewhat impaired."[59]

Chairman: Yet it was in that state that he made his affidavit against the Smiths.

Processed gossip: the laundry legend

Howe: If you must have particulars, here is Mrs. Eaton. She can tell you all about the Smiths.

Chairman: Can you, Mrs. Eaton?

Mrs. Dr. Horace Eaton: Indeed I can. My speech on the early life of Joseph Smith has become a classic. Let me say at the outset that "as far as Mormonism was connected with its reputed founder, Joseph Smith, always called 'Joe Smith,' it had its origin in the brain and heart of an ignorant, deceitful mother."[60]

Chairman: Indeed, that fact seems to have escaped the early witnesses to the crimes of the Smiths. Perhaps they were just being gallant. When did you make your report on the Smiths, Mrs. Eaton?

Eaton: My celebrated and much-quoted address was

first delivered 27 May 1881, before an important religious body.

Chairman: You delivered the speech on other occasions?

Eaton: I traveled about the country giving *authoritative* lectures on the Mormons. I was billed as Mrs. Dr. Horace Eaton of Palmyra — the fact that I actually came from Palmyra puts my authority, you will agree, beyond question.

Chairman: Very interesting. How well did you know the Smiths?

Eaton: Well, I never knew them personally. I first moved to Palmyra in 1850.

Chairman: That was twenty years after the Smiths had departed. Where did you get your information about them?

Eaton: From talks with neighbors, who of course knew and remembered the Smiths very well.

Chairman: So your famous report was issued in 1881, that is, thirty years after you had settled in Palmyra and long after anyone who had known the Smiths as an adult was dead. Even so, you do not name a single one of your valued informants. In your report you specialize on the *early* period of the Smith's residence in Palmyra, that is, at least thirty years before you went there and a good sixty-four years before your report — and you were paraded and advertised as one (at last) who could give an intimate, *firsthand* report of the doings of the Smith family! Tell us, please, how the Smiths used to operate.

Eaton: "Mrs. Smith used to go to the houses of the village and do family washings. But if the articles were left to dry upon the lines and not secured by their owners before midnight, the washer was often the winner — and in these nocturnal depredations she was assisted by her boys, who favored in like manner poultry yards and grain bins."[61]

Chairman: At long last we have the Smiths charged with specific crimes. But do you think it is clever to steal clothing one has been paid to wash? How can you steal a thing which the owner knows is in your possession?

Eaton: You can say it has been stolen.

Chairman: Do you have to go out after midnight with your boys and steal them? Can't you say they were stolen — that they simply aren't there — without having to go through the motions of stealing them yourself? What could Mrs. Smith do with the clothes she stole? The owners would recognize them if anybody wore them. Can you make more selling old clothes than washing them? And what would happen to the laundry business if customers regularly failed to get back their clothes?

Eaton: Regularly?

Chairman: Yes. You said that Mrs. Smith "used to" do this, and that she was "often the winner." She must have made a regular practice of hanging up clothes by day and stealing the same clothes by night. Isn't the woman who washes the clothes expected to be responsible for them and to take them off the line personally when they are dry? Apparently everyone was on to Mrs. Smith and her trick, but went on contributing steadily to her growing collection of used clothing; while she continued to wash and wash without getting paid for it.

Howe: Oh, your honor, now you are deliberately attempting to make my client look ridiculous.

Chairman: Not at all. It is, I admit, a monstrously ridiculous situation; but that which she herself has depicted as such furnishes proof of malicious slander.

Rev. J. E. Mahaffey: I think I can clear up this business. What happened was this: "Mrs. Smith did washing by the day, but her employers soon learned that it was not safe for the clothes to remain out after dark. Young Joseph assisted generally and soon had a reputation of being adept at robbing henroosts and orchards. Indeed the reputation of the Smith family is said to have been of the worst kind. 'They avoided honest labor, were intemperate, untruthful and suspected of sheep-stealing and other nefarious practices.' From all accounts they were the terror and torment of the neighborhood."[62]

Chairman: From your language, sir, it is obvious either that you have borrowed from Mrs. Eaton (directly or indirectly) or she has borrowed from you. When did you make this declaration?

Mahaffey: In 1902, and naturally I used Mrs. Eaton's material.

Chairman: And you have made changes in it. Who authorized you, for example, to change "poultry yards and grain bins" to "hen-roosts and orchards," and to read "she was assisted by her boys" as meaning "young Joseph assisted generally?"

Mahaffey: No fundamental changes: If the first statements are true the others must be.

Chairman: And so you take the liberty to improve on your source. You say her employers *soon* learned of Mrs. Smith's tricks, where Mrs. Eaton says "the washer was often the winner." Mrs. Eaton puts midnight as the deadline for getting in the clothes, but you, with better logic, say they could not remain out after dark.

Mahaffey: Thank you for the compliment. I have made a few rational emendations — to make the thing more plausible, you know.

Chairman: In other words, you feel free to correct the obvious inconsistencies and absurdities that prove Mrs. Eaton's story a piece of vicious gossip, so that it can pass muster as reliable testimony. That, I may observe here, is an extremely common practice among the biographers of Joseph Smith. Yet even when you get through, what do you tell us, Mr. Mahaffey? That Smith "had a *reputation* of being adept at robbing hen-roosts," that the *reputation* of the Smiths was of the worst kind, that they were *suspected* of sheep-stealing. Now, I will not ask you to prove that there were any grounds for such a reputation and such suspicions — Mr. Tucker can tell us about that — but I would like to know whether you have discovered a scrap of evidence to show that the Smiths had such a reputation *before* they were Mormons. I know that the affidavits claim to refer to that earlier period, but they were all given in retrospect. If the Smiths really had been "the terror and torment of the neighborhood" for many years before the Book of Mormon, there should certainly be some evidence of it. How well known were the Smiths before 1830?

Tricks with the calendar

Hunt: I can answer that! "The Smith family . . . emigrated from . . . Vermont, about the year 1820, when the Prophet was, as is supposed, about sixteen years of age. From their peculiar habits of life . . . they became *known to a vast number of persons* in that portion of the country, and without a single exception, as I am informed, every person knowing them united in representing the general character of the family as unprincipled, idle, ignorant, and superstitious."[63]

Chairman: Thank you, sir. So "a vast number of persons" knew the Smiths so well before 1830 that they could later swear oaths as to their character — though apparently they did not get close enough to Joseph to distinguish a ten-year-old from a sixteen-year-old. But where is the earlier evidence?

T. B. H. Stenhouse: I think I can answer that. "After Joseph's announcement of his prophetic mission, the neighbors of his parents who were opposed to his claims remembered, with wonderful facility, that the Smith family had always been 'dreamers and visionary persons,' and applied these terms in their most offensive meaning."[64]

Chairman: If I recall, the same sort of thing happened when the Spaulding story came out. During the years before, no one ever so much as mentioned a hint of the Rigdon-Spaulding-Pratt-Cowdery-Harris-Smith, etc., plot;

but as soon as the Spaulding theory was proposed, everybody suddenly remembered strange visits by mysterious strangers, and, as Mrs. Fawn M. Brodie so nicely puts it, "Through the years the 'Spaulding theory' collected supporting affidavits as a ship does barnacles."[65] That stirs familiar echoes. One noted affidavit-collector of antiquity was Celsus, who ran down some scandalous stories about Jesus' family. Will Celsus please come forward?

Celsus: I must say I am here under protest. This is not my show—I belong in the second century.

Chairman: And we are not asking you to leave that century. Tell us where you got your affidavits about the scandalous youth of Jesus.

Celsus: The Jewish doctors sent people out to the village to gather them.

Chairman: Years after the death of Christ.

Celsus: What difference does that make? The neighbors all remembered the clever, ambitious boy who was ashamed of his low parentage and overawed the yokels with the magic tricks he had picked up in Egypt, and how he gave out those wild reports about being the son of God and the rest.

Chairman: And did they remember anything about his disciples?

Celsus: Of course. "He gathered some ten or eleven notorious men about him, publicans and sailors of the most vicious type, and with these he tramped up and down the country, eking out a miserable existence by questionable means."[66]

Chairman: Such as raiding hen-coops? Note the parallels, ladies and gentlemen: Our informant is not even sure of the number of the apostles—where facts are concerned all is characteristically vague—but the charges are the very same as those against Smith. But what I want you particularly to note is that our authority insists that the apostles were notorious for their wicked ways *before* Jesus ever chose them. This is the old trick of building up a case in retrospect. Do you remember what happened after Tom Sawyer found the treasure? "Wherever Tom and Huck appeared they were courted, admired, stared at. The boys were not able to remember that their remarks had possessed weight before; but now their sayings were treasured and repeated; everything they did seemed somehow to be regarded as remarkable. . . . Moreover, their past history was raked up and discovered to bear marks of conspicuous originality. The village paper published biographical sketches of the boys."[67] You see, it works both ways, gentlemen, and Joseph Smith's case is perhaps unique, since from being as obscure a person as ever lived he became in a matter of months one of the most talked-about men in the world. Then, of course "a vast number of persons" suddenly remembered everything the Smiths ever did—though how they could get away with crimes like theirs for a week, let alone for decades, no one has bothered to explain.

Howe: It is all very well to talk of inventing evidence in retrospect, but we have positive proof that Joseph Smith was a public menace *before* he ever claimed to have had a vision.

Chairman: That is just the sort of thing we are looking for. By all means, sir, produce this evidence.

Howe: You must have it here. It is the invaluable Bainbridge Court Record of 26 March 1826.

Chairman: Will the clerk please read that record?

Clerk (after much searching and fumbling among his papers): I'm sorry, sir, we don't seem to have such a document.

Howe: What do you mean, you don't have it? Why man, that is the most important if not the only existing piece of evidence to Joseph Smith's early character and activities. You *must* have it!

Clerk (after much searching): This is all we have, your honor. This is not a court record but a printed article from a religious encyclopedia. The item is reprinted in that encyclopedia in 1889 and 1891, but in subsequent editions thereafter it does not appear.[68]

Howe: But Mrs. Brodie specifically says that the document was "first unearthed in southern New York by Daniel S. Tuttle."[69]

John Quincy Adams: Mrs. *who* said it? That's what I wrote in 1916!

Eminent Critic: You must be mistaken, sir. Mrs. Brodie's work is the last word in "primary scholarship,"[70] and this is one of her finest discoveries.

Chairman: Let me see what Mrs. Brodie and Mr. Adams have written, clerk. This is what Adams said in 1916:

> An interesting record of one of these visits was unearthed a few years ago by Bishop Daniel S. Tuttle in the records of a justice's court in Bainbridge, Chenango County. The story is told and documents quoted in the article on Mormonism in the *Schaff-Herzog Encyclopedia of Religious Knowledge.*[71]

And this is how Mrs. Brodie announces her great discovery in 1947 and after:

> The earliest and most important account of Joseph Smith's money-digging is the following court record, first unearthed in southern New York by Daniel S. Tuttle, Episcopal Bishop of Salt Lake City, and published in the article on "Mormonism" in the *New Schaff-Herzog Encyclopedia of Religious Knowledge.* The trial was before a justice of the peace in Bainbridge, Chenango County, New York.[72]

I find these two statements substantially the same. Does Mrs. Brodie anywhere mention the Adams book in her writing?

Clerk: Adams is nowhere mentioned. His book is not even listed in Mrs. Brodie's extensive bibliography.

Chairman: In view of the obvious resemblance between

the two passages, that may be significant. Of course, the later one is not a literal quotation, but it seems to bear just those marks of retouching which one would expect in case of borrowing; it is to be noted that while nothing essential has been added to the later text, neither has anything essential been omitted. And then there are hints, like that interesting word "unearthed," a little bit unusual, vague, yet colorful—a clue, I would say. That would seem to me to be a link between the two writings. But let us get back to the court record. It was stated that the vital document was actually found "in the records of the justice's court." In that case, it should be easy to produce today. Where is it?

Clerk: If it please the court, a communication just received from the present clerk of the court in question informs us that no court records were ever kept in Chenango County before the year 1850, and that there is no knowledge of the destruction of any records of that court.[73]

Chairman: Well, that seems to settle it. The 1826 record was somebody's invention.[74] We shall look further into this matter. But first, is there anyone else who can give personal testimony?

The total oaf

Peter Cartwright: I can. I was personally acquainted with Joe Smith.

Chairman: Your name?

Cartwright: I am Peter Cartwright, the Frontier Preacher. "On a certain occasion I fell in with Joe Smith, and was formally and officially introduced to him in Springfield, then our county town. We soon fell into a free conversation on the subject of religion, and Mormonism in particular. I found him a very illiterate and impudent desperado in morals, but, at the same time, he had a vast fund of low cunning."[75]

Chairman: How's that again—"a vast fund of low cunning"?

Cartwright: That's what I said.

Chairman: Are you trying to tell the investigators that a man who displayed a vast cunning also revealed himself as an impudent desperado in the course of a formal conversation carried on with a total stranger in the presence of witnesses at a county seat? What kind of clowning could he have done to advertise his utter moral depravity to the world? And how could such abandoned behavior possibly be accompanied by the smallest iota of sense, let alone "vast cunning"? It seems that Smith was determined at any price to wreck his chances in Springfield. Did he go up to you and start talking wildly?

Cartwright: No, it was a civilized enough conversation, formal and official, as I said.

Chairman: Yet in the course of that conversation, carried on in an atmosphere of formality, Smith demonstrated in your presence that he "was an impudent desperado in morals." How?

Cartwright: He didn't say very much. I did nearly all the talking. He tried to flatter me, and "upon the whole, he did pretty well for clumsy Joe."[76]

Chairman: Cunning but clumsy. In a few words he contrived to make it clear to you that he was an impudent desperado in morals. And you call that doing pretty well. He must have staged quite a pantomime. Since you have given the whole conversation at length, why don't you report any of the things Smith said or did to advertise his depravity?

Cartwright: Now you are being facetious, sir. I had other dealings with Smith's people. One old Mormon woman wanted to speak at one of my meetings, but I gave *her* a sermon, believe me. Her husband tried to interfere.

Chairman: How did he interfere?

Cartwright: He said I could not speak to his wife that

way, but we threw them out. My actual words were, "Now start, and don't show your face here again, nor one of the Mormons. If you do, you will get Lynch's Law."[77]

Chairman: Isn't lynching rather harsh treatment for people whose only offense is that they wanted to speak at your meeting? I believe it was common practice at religious revivals to allow many persons to speak.

Cartwright: With Mormons it's different. "They should be considered and treated as outlaws in every country and clime."[78]

Chairman: I am afraid the American Constitution would not allow that here.

Cartwright: No law applies to them: "Any man or set of men that would be mean enough to stoop so low as to connive at the abominations of these reckless Mormons, surely ought to be considered unworthy of public office, honor, or confidence."[79]

Chairman: So you would disfranchise not only the Mormons but any who tolerate them?

Cartwright: That's it.

Chairman: Yet we search your book in vain for any account of what might be by any stretch of the imagination called an abomination; and you are supposed to have lived close to Joseph Smith and the Mormons. Have we any other witnesses?

J. Hendrix: I knew Joseph Smith. "Everyone knew him as Joe Smith. He was the most ragged, lazy fellow in the place, and that is saying a good deal."[80]

Chairman: What do you mean, "saying a good deal"?

Hendrix: I mean of course, that to be the most ragged and lazy fellow in *that* place was an achievement!

Chairman: Then lots of fellows were ragged and lazy?

Howe (caustically): Our esteemed chairman begins to get the idea.

Chairman: But do you? In a community where the ragged and lazy abound it can hardly be a crime for a boy to

be ragged and lazy. Yet by far the commonest charge
against Joseph Smith is that he was lazy and slovenly—a
common charge against Jesus Christ also, by the way. Now
what is so bad about being lazy?

Hendrix: Isn't that a foolish question?

Chairman: Not at all. Have you practiced your oboe
today?

Hendrix: What do you mean, practiced my oboe? I have
no oboe.

Chairman: Then you are lazy. You have never learned
to play the oboe. You have never even *tried!* Lots of times,
perhaps even today, you have done little or nothing at all,
while you *could* have been practicing the oboe.

Hendrix: I have plenty of other things to do besides
practicing an oboe, sir.

Chairman: So the fact that you do not play the oboe
does not prove that you are lazy?

Hendrix: Of course not. You judge a man's industry
not by what he *doesn't* do but by what he does. There are
millions of things that *you* don't do, for that matter!

Chairman: At last you see my point. Everybody says
Joseph Smith was lazy because of the things he didn't do,
but what about the things he did do? What good does it
do to say that you, with your tiny routine of daily busy-
work, think another man is lazy if that man happens to
accomplish more than ten ordinary men in a short lifetime?
Joseph Smith's activities are a matter of record and they
are phenomenal. You might as well claim that Horowitz
doesn't know how to play the piano to a man who owns
a library of Horowitz recordings, or that Van Gogh couldn't
paint to the owner of an original Van Gogh, or that Demp-
sey couldn't fight to a man who had fought him, as to
maintain that Joseph Smith was a lazy loafer to the historian
who gets dizzy merely trying to follow him through a few
short years of his tremendous activity. I think this constantly reiterated unfailing charge that Joseph Smith was

a raggle-taggle, down-at-the-heels, sloppy, lazy, good-for-nothing supplies the best possible test for the honesty and reliability of his critics. Some of them reach almost awesome heights of mendacity and effrontery when, like Mrs. Brodie, they solemnly inform us that Joseph Smith, the laziest man on earth, produced in a short time, by his own efforts, the colossally complex and difficult Book of Mormon.

Howe: But you can't just brush public opinion aside.

A quick check-up

Chairman: Which is just what you do when you discount all but one segment of that opinion. Did anyone, by the way, ever check up on all this public opinion about Smith?

An Editor: When I was working for a St. Louis newspaper I attempted to test public opinion about the Mormons.

Chairman: Sort of a Gallup poll?

Editor: The nearest we could get to it in those days. "What do you think of the Mormons? I asked. I had scarcely spoken before my ears were saluted from all quarters, from high and low, rich and poor. . . . They would rob and plunder, . . . [and] after they had stripped the poor stranger of his all, they confined him in a kind of dungeon, underneath the Temple, where he was fed on bread and water, until death put a period to his sufferings."[81]

Howe: There's public opinion, for you! Unanimous—no "segment" about it!

Chairman: Could all, or any, of those people have had firsthand experience of what they declared so emphatically?

Editor: It was obvious that they had not, but I was not satisfied with mere rumors—I went to Nauvoo to see for myself.

Chairman: Excellent. And what did you find?

Editor: I can only repeat what I wrote at the time: "Joseph Smith the Mormon prophet, is a singular character; he lives at the 'Nauvoo House' which is, I understand, intended to become a home for the stranger and traveler; and I think, from my own personal observation, that it will be deserving of the name. The Prophet is a kind, cheerful sociable companion. I believe he has the good-will of the community at large, and that he is ever ready to stand by and defend them in any extremity."[82]

J. C. O'Hanlon: I can confirm that report.

Howe: Who are you, sir?

O'Hanlon: I was a Roman Catholic priest and missionary in Missouri. Though I came west after Smith's time, I was soon "made aware of the fact . . . that during the lifetime of their prophet Joe Smith, Catholic bishops and priests were courteously received and hospitably entertained by him, whenever they had occasion to visit his growing city of Nauvoo; and they often spoke in praise of his personal kindness and generosity."[83]

Lily Dougall: That reminds me. When I was gathering material for my writings about Joseph Smith in and around Kirtland —

Howe: May we ask this lady to identify herself before she proceeds?

Dougall: I am Lily Dougall, sir, and if you suspect that I am prejudiced I'll have you know that my stories about Joseph Smith are as scandalous as anything *you* ever wrote! But as I was saying, "I visited a sweet-faced old lady — not, however, of the Mormon persuasion — who as a child had climbed on the prophet's knee. 'My mother always said,' she told us, 'that if she had to die and leave young children, she would rather have left them to Joseph Smith than to anyone else in the world: he was always kind.' "[84]

Howe: Then how could *you* write such scandalous things about Smith, madam?

Dougall: My stuff was fiction — and it sold well.

Howe: I can give you an editor who tells a very different story. Here, Mr. Editor, tell us about Joe Smith.

Editor No. 2: "It was asserted that he inculcated the legality of perjury and other crimes. . . . It was reported that an establishment existed in Nauvoo for the manufacture of counterfeit money, and that a set of outlaws was maintained for the purpose of putting it in circulation. Statements were circulated to the effect that a reward was offered for the destruction of the *Warsaw Signal* . . . and that the Mormons . . . threatened all persons who offered to assist the constable in the execution of the law, with the destruction of their property and the murder of their families. There were rumors that an alliance had been made with the Western Indians, that in case of war—"[85]

Chairman: I think we have heard enough: "It was asserted . . . it was reported . . . statements were circulated . . . there were rumors . . . " What is the date of this man's report?

Howe: 1879.

Chairman: Haven't we something more contemporary?

Mr. Flagg: Way back in 1838 I made an inquiry something like that of the first editor, but without results. Everybody had strong feelings about the Mormons, but when it came to facts that was a different story: "no one with whom I met could, for the life of him, give a subsequent expose of *Mormonism,* though often requested."[86]

Chairman: Did anyone else follow the example of our first editor and visit Nauvoo?

The Man from Quincy: Yes. I was one of a party from Quincy, Illinois, that went to look into matters there. "We had supposed from the stories and statements we had read of 'Jo Smith,' (as he was termed in the papers) to find him a very illiterate, uncouth sort of man; but from a conversation, we acknowledge an agreeable disappointment. In conversation he appeared intelligent and candid, and divested of all malicious thought and feeling towards his relentless persecutors."[87]

Chairman: This is interesting. Public opinion had prepared you, as you describe it, to find one sort of Joseph Smith, while the real Joseph Smith gave you quite a surprise. There was no such surprise in store for Mr. Cartwright. I think we have here irrefutable proof of extreme prejudice.

Howe: Yet the same Quincy newspaper that gave this favorable report some years later charged the Mormons with a specific crime, the shooting of Boggs!

Chairman: What does the newspaper report say? Will the clerk please read it?

Clerk (reads): "A man was suspected, and is probably arrested before this. There are several rumors in circulation in regard to the horrid affair. One of which throws the crime upon the Mormons."[88]

Howe: There you have it. Many books charge this crime to the Mormons.

Chairman: On such flimsy evidence? That was but one of many rumors — an inevitable one, I might add. What crimes were they not charged with?

Howe: But there is more to it than that. Read on, clerk!

Clerk (reads): "Smith . . . , the Mormon Prophet, as we understand, prophesied a year or so ago, his death by violent means. Hence, there is plenty of foundation for rumor."[89]

Chairman: So instead of proving him a true prophet, the prophecy made him a tactless assassin. That little sophism was often used against the Christians in ancient times: since they prophesied evil, whenever evil came — in fulfillment of the prophecy — they, of course, were to blame for it. "Plenty of foundation," indeed! Before we recess let us hear the reports of any others who have tried to get to the bottom of all the mere talk and rumor about Smith.

Let's hear from these three who have raised their hands. Don't I know you, sir?

John Greenleaf Whittier: Yes, we have met elsewhere. I am John Greenleaf Whittier, once considered something of a poet. I was visited by some Mormon missionaries in the 1840s and made something of a study of Joseph Smith and his background. My conclusion was that "the reports circulated against them [the Mormons, that is] by their unprincipled enemies in the west are in the main destitute of foundation."[90]

Chairman: Thank you. And the next gentleman?

Editor: I was the editor of the *American Whig Review* when we undertook a rather ambitious investigation into the early life of Smith. Our finding was that "the knowledge of his early life which has been given to the world is limited; for all that seems to have been desired by those who made researches or gave testimony concerning him, was either to establish the bad character of the Smith family, or to show the real origin of the Book of Mormon."[91]

Chairman: And after all these years that still holds true of the critics today. Our next witness seems rather reluctant. Come on up, sir. What have you to report?

F. B. Greene: Not very much. We of the Illinois State Historical Society set out to solve the riddle of Joseph Smith, but the documents wouldn't take us through. We found that after 1865 "the life of the prophet . . . has furnished material for a flood of literature, which has failed to a great extent in establishing the truth or falsity of the story as told by Smith and his followers."[92]

Chairman: So it seems that our cloud of witnesses have not succeeded in their purpose.

Howe: We are not through yet. Far from it. Since our really powerful testimony is to come, I move we take a recess before hearing from the next witness.

Notes for Part 1, Scene i

1. John S. C. Abbott, *The History of the State of Ohio* (Detroit: New World, 1875), 180.

2. John C. Bennett, *The History of the Saints; Or, An Exposé of Joe Smith and Mormonism* (Boston: Leland and Whiting, 1842), 79–80.

3. Lu B. Cake, *Peepstone Joe and the Peck Manuscript* (New York: Cake, 1899), 20.

4. Eber D. Howe, *Mormonism Unvailed; Or, a Faithful Account of That Singular Imposition and Delusion* (Painesville, OH: the author, 1834), 261–62.

5. Ibid., 262.

6. Ibid., 248.

7. John Hyde, *Mormonism, Its Leaders and Designs* (New York: Fetridge, 1857), 246.

8. Howe, *Mormonism Unvailed*, 250–51.

9. Robert Richards, *The California Crusoe* (London: Parker, 1854), 84.

10. Howe, *Mormonism Unvailed*, 247.

11. Ibid., 251.

12. D. H. C. Bartlett, *The Mormons or Latter-day Saints, Whence Came They?* (Liverpool: Thompson, 1911), 5–6.

13. Ibid., 6.

14. Cake, *Peepstone Joe and the Peck Manuscript*, 9.

15. Hyde, *Mormonism, Its Leaders and Designs*, 246.

16. Cake, *Peepstone Joe and the Peck Manuscript*, 20 (emphasis added).

17. Hyde, *Mormonism, Its Leaders and Designs*, 243, 247.

18. Howe, *Mormonism Unvailed*, 251.

19. Bartlett, *Mormons or Latter-day Saints*, 6.

20. Howe, *Mormonism Unvailed*, 253–54.

21. Ibid., 254; Bennett, *History of the Saints*, 75.

22. Howe, *Mormonism Unvailed*, 256.

23. Ibid.; Bennett, *History of the Saints*, 76.

24. Ibid., 263.

25. Ibid.

26. Ibid., 264.

27. Ibid., 265.

28. Ibid., 265–66.

29. Thomas Gregg, *The Prophet of Palmyra* (New York: Alden, 1890), 9.

30. "Mormons," *Knowledge, A Weekly Magazine* 1/9 (2 August 1890): 175–76.

31. Hyde, *Mormonism, Its Leaders and Designs*, 250.

32. Charles A. Shook, *The True Origin of Mormon Polygamy* (Mendota, IL: W.A.C.P. Association, 1910), 28–40.

33. Ibid.

34. Howe, *Mormonism Unvailed*, 95–98.

35. Ibid., 231.

36. Orvilla S. Belisle, *Mormonism Unveiled: A History of Mormonism from Its Rise to the Present Time* (London: Clark, 1855), 18.

37. Ruth Kauffman and Reginald W. Kauffman, *The Latter-Day Saints: A Study of the Mormons in the Light of Economic Conditions* (London: Williams and Norgate, 1912), 23.

38. Walter R. Martin, *The Rise of the Cults (An Introductory Guide to the Non-Christian Cults)* (Grand Rapids, MI: Zondervan, 1955), 50.

39. Bennett, *History of the Saints*, 83; Howe, *Mormonism Unvailed*, 266.

40. Howe, *Mormonism Unvailed*, 267; Bennett, *History of the Saints*, 83.

41. Nancy Towle, *Vicissitudes Illustrated, in the Experience of Nancy Towle, in Europe and America* (Charleston: Burges, 1832), 164.

42. Ibid., 185.

43. Ibid., 229.

44. Ibid., 16.

45. Ibid., 17; cf. 33, 57, 170–71, 185, 212, etc.

46. Towle, *Vicissitudes Illustrated*, 142.

47. Ibid.

48. Ibid., 143.

49. James H. Hunt, *Mormonism* (St. Louis: Ustick and Davies, 1844), 125.

50. Ibid., 121–25.

51. Ibid., 125.

52. Ibid., iv.

53. Bennett, *History of the Saints*, 84; Howe, *Mormonism Unvailed*, 268.

54. Howe, *Mormonism Unvailed*, 268.

55. Ibid., 269.

56. "The Yankee Mahomet," *American Whig Review* 7 (June 1851): 559 (emphasis added).

57. Shook, *True Origin of Mormon Polygamy*, 25.

58. Ibid.

59. Shook, *True Origin of Mormon Polygamy*, 29.

60. Ibid., 23; Mrs. Dr. Horace Eaton, "Speech Delivered May 27, 1881," in *Handbook of Mormonism* (Salt Lake City: Handbook, 1882), 1.

61. Shook, *True Origin of Mormon Polygamy*, 23–24; Eaton, "Speech," in *Handbook on Mormonism*, 1.

62. J. E. Mahaffey, *Found at Last! 'Positive Proof' That Mormonism Is a Fraud and the Book of Mormon a Fable* (Augusta, GA: Chronicle Job Office, 1902), 6.

63. Hunt, *Mormonism*, 5.

64. T. B. H. Stenhouse, *The Rocky Mountain Saints: A Full and Complete History of the Mormons* (New York: Appleton, 1873), 14.

65. Fawn M. Brodie, *No Man Knows My History* (New York: Knopf, 1947), 68.

66. Origen, *Contra Celsum* I, 1, 7, in *PG* 11:652, 668; cf. Hugh W. Nibley, "Early Accounts of Jesus' Childhood," *Instructor* 100 (January 1965): 35–37; reprinted in *CWHN* 4:1–9.

67. Samuel L. Clemens, *The Adventures of Tom Sawyer* (New York: Saalfield, 1931), 305.

68. Francis Kirkham, *A New Witness for Christ in America: The Book of Mormon*, 2 vols. (Salt Lake City: Utah Printing, 1951), 1:386; 2:480.

69. Brodie, *No Man Knows My History*, 427.

70. Dale L. Morgan, "The 'Peculiar People,' " *Saturday Review* 40 (28 December 1957): 9.

71. John Quincy Adams, *The Birth of Mormonism* (Boston: Gorham, 1916), 17–18.

72. Brodie, *No Man Knows My History*, 427.

73. Kirkham, *A New Witness for Christ in America*, 1:389; 2:482.

74. [Useful research on the 1826 trial includes Marvin S. Hill, "Joseph Smith and the 1826 Trial: New Evidence and New Difficulties," *BYU Studies* 12 (Winter 1972): 223–33; and Gordon A. Madsen, "Joseph Smith's 1826 Trial: The Legal Setting," *BYU Studies* 30 (Spring 1990): 91–108.]

75. W. P. Strickland, *The Autobiography of Peter Cartwright: The Backwoods Preacher* (New York: Carlton and Porter, 1856), 341–42.

76. Ibid., 342.

77. Ibid., 345.

78. Ibid., 346.

79. Ibid.

80. Bartlett, *Mormons or Latter-day Saints*, 5.

81. Charles McKay, *The Mormons; Or, Latter-Day Saints, with Memoirs of the Life and Death of Joseph Smith, the "American Mahomet"* (London: Office of the National Illustrated Library, 1852), 127.

82. Ibid., 129.

83. J. C. O'Hanlon, *Life and Scenery in Missouri* (Dublin: Duffy, 1890), 122.

84. Lily Dougall, *The Mormon Prophet* (London: Richards, 1899), viii–ix.

85. *History of Tazewell County, Illinois* (Chicago: Chapman, 1879), 107.

86. Edmund Flagg, *The Far West*, 2 vols. (New York: Harper and Brothers, 1838), 2:84.

87. *Missouri Republican*, 3 May 1839.

88. See subheading, "Assassination of Ex Governor Boggs of Missouri," *Quincy Whig*, 21 May 1842.

89. Ibid.

90. William and Mary Howitt, eds., *Howitt's Journal* (London: Lovett, 1847), 158.

91. "Yankee Mahomet," 556.

92. Evarts B. Greene and Charles M. Thompson, eds., *Illinois State Historical Society Publications Governors' Letter-books, 1840–1853*, 2 vols. (Springfield, IL: Illinois State Historical Library, 1911), lxxviii.

ii. *Come now, Mr. Tucker!*

Scene: Same as Scene i.

Le chevalier sans peur et sans reproche

Chairman: Mr. Pattengill has requested and been granted permission to address us. Mr. Pattengill.

Mr. C. N. Pattengill: I have been asked by Mr. Howe to speak a few words on the singular qualifications of the next witness, Mr. Pomeroy Tucker of Palmyra, New York. He is the one and only real authority on the early life of Joseph Smith. His book "is a standard work on the rise and early progress of Mormonism. The only authentic one on that subject, and its value will increase as time takes the world farther from the origin of the delusion." In short, "no man, probably, was so well qualified as himself to give a veritable account of that imposition, especially in its incipient stages."[1]

Chairman: Very pretty. And what makes Mr. Tucker so peculiarly qualified in the field indicated?

Pattengill: "From the office of the Wayne *Sentinel* the first Mormon Bible was issued."[2]

Chairman: And you think printers are authorities on the books they print?

Pattengill: Tucker had the searching, objective mind of an editor. "Had he drawn somewhat on his imagination, he might perhaps have made a book that would have been more popular, but it would have been less valuable."[3]

Chairman: So Mr. Tucker does not ever draw on his imagination — even "somewhat"?

Walter R. Martin: Not in the least. "Witness his unprejudiced testimony. . . . It should be noted that this is contemporary evidence, not the product of flowery Mormon historians who distorted the true character of Smith."[4]

Chairman: And what is the date of Mr. Tucker's "contemporary evidence"?

Pattengill: His immortal book first appeared in the year 1867.

Chairman: Did you know Smith as late as 1867, Mr. Tucker?

Pomeroy Tucker: Of course not. He was dead then. I distinctly remember him "from the age of twelve to twenty years."[5]

Chairman: That would be between 1818 and 1826 about, whereas your report is dated 1867. And you call that "contemporary evidence" — Mr. Martin — a mere gap of forty to fifty years?

Pattengill: I submit that Mr. Tucker's memory was an unusually good one; his absolute refusal to draw on his imagination makes his report completely trustworthy.

Chairman: May I see the book, clerk? I find here a rather interesting frontispiece; who put it in the book?

Pattengill: The publisher, I suppose.

Chairman: Since Mr. Tucker is himself a publisher, isn't it pretty certain that this picture, the only illustration in the book, was put there with Mr. Tucker's knowledge and consent?

Pattengill: It could hardly be otherwise. After it appeared in Mr. Tucker's book the picture was often reproduced.[6]

Eber D. Howe (with impatience): What's all the fuss about? It is Mr. Tucker's book, isn't it—the first edition? Of course the frontispiece is his.

Chairman: Thank you. Now, it is maintained that the peculiar value of this book is that its author never allows himself to draw upon his imagination. But what do I see here? The engraving shows Smith on a hillside, on his knees, facing a small, nearly nude female figure floating in the air in a semiprone position with upraised arms and very long white wings. On the ground around Smith a host of tiny devils, little men about eight inches high with horns and forked tails, seem to be dancing and cavorting about. Aren't the unearthly beings depicted here by Mr. Tucker's arranging just a little bit fanciful?

Howe: What if they are? Every engraver takes some artistic license with his subjects.

Chairman: The engraver made the picture, but the engraver did not write the caption under it. It is to this that I would draw your attention, for it says that this fantastic drawing actually depicts *"Smith's* account of taking the 'golden Bible' from Mormon Hill." But how did Smith describe angels?

Howe: "Smith describes an angel as having the appearance of 'a tall, slim, well-built, handsome man.' "[7]

Chairman: Thank you. No one denies that the story of the angel Moroni was told and retold from 1830 on, while others of Smith's persuasion also reported seeing angels. Whether such reports were reliable or not, the fact is that those people always described angels in the same terms. Did Joseph Smith or any of his followers ever state at any time that the angel Moroni, a mighty warrior of the Book of Mormon, was a little woman, as shown in this picture? Or was he ever described as a nude figure? Or was he ever said to have wings—as angels were supposed to have in conventional Christian imagining? Did Smith or any Mormon ever describe Satan as an imp with horns and a tail?

SMITH'S ACCOUNT OF TAKING THE "GOLDEN BIBLE" FROM MORMON HILL.

Howe: Well, as I say, the engraver obviously took some liberties . . .

Chairman: And somebody obviously took still greater liberties in attributing that engraver's fancies to Joseph Smith. I would say that this oft-reprinted frontispiece shows that Mr. Tucker, the author of this book, not only drew "somewhat on his imagination" but relied heavily on it to score a point against Smith. Now Mr. Tucker, I would like to ask you, first of all, just how well you knew Joseph Smith.

Tucker: Very well indeed: "he is distinctly remembered by me . . . from the age of twelve to twenty years."

Chairman: One can remember a person distinctly without ever having known him at all; many people distinctly remember seeing the President of the United States. The years indicated would run from 1818 to 1826, then?

Tucker: Yes. Smith was twelve in 1818. I was four years older, having been born in August 1802.

Chairman: Did you live in Palmyra between 1818 and 1826?

Tucker: I lived there during that period.

Chairman: All of it?

Howe: Quibbling again!

Chairman: Mr. Pattengill can tell us whether we are quibbling. Mr. Pattengill, didn't Mr. Tucker leave Palmyra early in his career?

Pattengill: Well, yes, there was a time. Before he was twenty-one he moved to Canandaigua.

Chairman: That would have been in the year 1822 or 1823. How far is Canandaigua from Palmyra?

Pattengill: About thirty miles away.

Chairman: And how long did Mr. Tucker stay in Canandaigua after he left Palmyra?

Pattengill: "Nearly four years."[8]

Chairman: Now, Mr. Tucker emphatically stated—

Clerk (reads): "I distinctly remember him from the age of twelve to twenty years."

Chairman: Mr. Tucker, were you referring to your age or his age?

Tucker: His age, of course. That is clear enough if you read the rest of the description.

Chairman: So you claim to be giving a firsthand account of Joseph Smith between 1818 and 1826, and yet you left Palmyra at the latest in the middle of 1823. In other words, for *at least* three and a half of the eight years during which you say you knew Smith so well, you were not in Palmyra at all.

Howe: Mr. Tucker could have kept in touch with affairs in Palmyra while he was away.

Chairman: What kind of affairs interested him?

Pattengill: I can answer that, if Mr. Tucker is too modest to do so. From early youth Mr. Tucker was extremely ambitious to succeed; even at seventeen "he determined to excel as a writer as well as a compositor." Of course he sought only the best society and in Canandaigua "was thrown into the constant society of those who were foremost in political affairs."[9]

Chairman: And Smith was an important figure in Palmyra from the age of twelve to twenty years?

Tucker: Don't make me laugh, sir. "From the age of twelve to twenty years he is distinctly remembered as a dull-eyed, flaxen haired, prevaricating boy — noted only for his indolent and vagabondish character."[10]

Chairman: So during all the time you knew him, Smith was noted for one thing *only* — being a lazy tramp. Was he much of a public figure?

Tucker: On the contrary, "taciturnity was among his characteristic idiosyncrasies, and he seldom spoke to anyone outside of his immediate associates. . . . He nevertheless evidenced the rapid development of a thinking, plodding, evil-brewing mental composition — largely given to inventions of low cunning, schemes of mischief and deception, and false and mysterious pretensions. He . . . was never known to laugh."[11]

Chairman: From what you say, Mr. Tucker, it is clear that you not only remember Joseph Smith distinctly, but that you knew him very well indeed — perhaps better than anyone else. It is plain that Smith was exceedingly hard to get acquainted with and that he was devilishly secretive, but even if he had been frank and open, the intimate knowledge you profess of his mental composition could only come from the closest association. Now, what was it that induced you, a very hard-working and ambitious young man, to spend your time with a perfectly worthless vagabond four and a half years your junior? You were no child when you first met Smith.

Tucker: You don't have to be a man's close friend to observe his character.

Chairman: According to you, you had to get close to Smith to observe him at all, since he wouldn't even speak to anyone "outside of his associates." And to say immediately what any man "largely" devoted his time and energy to, and what things he "was never known" to do, requires spending a good deal of time with him—unless, of course, your famous firsthand report is only hearsay. Did you think associating with Smith could contribute to your career? Did you perhaps find him an interesting person—even in a bad way?

Tucker: Of course not. As I told you, he was "noted only for his indolent and vagabondish character." He was "a dull-eyed, flaxen-haired, prevaricating boy" who never spoke to anybody and "was never known to laugh."

Chairman: That answers my question. It would be hard to imagine duller company. What did he do all day?

Tucker: The Smiths spent their time "hunting and fishing, trapping muskrats, digging out woodchucks from their holes, and idly lounging around the stores and shops in the village."[12]

Chairman: And where were you all that time? I must insist on this, sir, because you claim to be telling all from personal observation. If you were hard at work all the time, as your panegyrist Mr. Pattengill assures us you were, then you were far from the picturesque scenes you are describing, and your testimony is no better than that of the other affidavit-swearers—who, incidentally, paint a very different picture of Smith—bad, but very different.

The homey touch

Tucker: Oh, Joe came to town, all right. He used to go around selling cakes that his mother had baked. It was quite amusing: "The boys of those bygone times used to delight in obtaining the valuable goods intrusted to Joseph's clerkship in exchange for worthless pewter imitation two-shilling pieces."[13]

Chairman: Didn't you say Smith was pretty sharp at some things? Read it, clerk.

Clerk (reads): "He nevertheless evidenced the rapid development of a thinking, plodding, evil-brewing mental disposition—largely given to inventions of low cunning."

Chairman: A pretty shrewd operator, I take it, as sharp as he was crooked.

Tucker: He was cunning, all right.

Chairman: And also, he spent a good deal of time "lounging around the stores and shops in the village." Money didn't interest him, I take it.

Tucker: Joe the money-digger? Don't make me laugh.[14]

Chairman: Yet Joe the money-digger was the only boy in the village who couldn't tell a real coin from a "worthless pewter imitation." That was the point of the joke, as I recall.

Tucker: Well, that was when they first came to Palmyra . . . he was very young.

Chairman: On the contrary, by your own testimony he must have been at least twelve years old. But apparently his greedy family didn't know real money when they saw it, either.

Tucker: What do you mean?

Chairman: As you so romantically recalled it, "the boys of those bygone times used to delight in" "buying good cakes for worthless tokens. They made a practice of it—a habitual source of merriment."

O. Turner: That is right!

Chairman: Who are you, sir?

Turner: The author of an early study on the settlement of western New York. "The young people of the town considered him not quite full-witted and, with the cruelty of youth, made him the butt of their practical jokes."[15]

Chairman: Mr. Tucker, are we to believe that Mrs. Smith continued to bake cakes day after day while her unsuspecting son continued to sell them for pewter coins? The story does have the homey touch that biographers love as a mark of guileless candor—but it is phonier than the pewter two-shilling pieces. If it is true, then it was the Smiths who were the gullible victims, with all the "schemes of mischief and deception" on the other side. Were they that innocent?

The dragon's lair

Tucker: "In unbelief, theory, and practice, the Smith family, all as one, so far as they held any definable position upon the subject of religion—basing this conclusion upon all the early avowals and other evidences remembered, as well as upon the subsequent developments extant—were unqualified atheists."[16]

Chairman: That puts it on the line: A formidable store of things both heard and seen, "evidences remembered" by you, authorized you to brand *all* the Smiths *unqualified* atheists both in theory and *practice*. We couldn't ask for a plainer or more unequivocal statement. But where does that leave Smith's other neighbors, that host of prominent and respectable residents who knew him so well? None of their eager affidavits ever mentions this blatantly paraded atheism! Indeed the famous sixty-two (to cite but one group) said the Smiths were "particularly famous for visionary projects." Atheists don't have visions. How did all the neighbors, bent on telling the worst, happen to overlook the Smiths' atheism?

Howe: A person can be an atheist and conceal the fact.

Chairman: But no gross, unqualified atheist can display his convictions in all his "avowals" *and* acts for fifteen years without having his close associates come to suspect that he may not be an orthodox believer. You seem to have been a very privileged character, Mr. Tucker, to be taken so much more into the confidences of the Smiths than anyone else was. What was your interest in them — did they show signs of future greatness?

Howe: I can answer that. "With the exception of their natural and peculiar habits of life, there is nothing in the character of the Smith family worthy of being recorded, previous to the time of their plot to impose upon the world by a pretended discovery of a new Bible."[17]

Chairman: Then I must ask again, how did it happen that an ambitious and eminently respectable young man like you, Mr. Tucker, fully occupied with your busy career and high political connections, had time and inclination to cultivate the miserable Smiths, who didn't even live in town, and to follow the backwoods odysseys of worthless Joe with such keen personal interest that forty years later you alone can recall conversations word for word and vividly remember "all the early avowals" of the Smiths on religion?

Howe: Mr. Tucker was a newspaperman. It was his business to know about people.

Chairman: And did Mr. Tucker shadow everybody in and around Palmyra as faithfully as he did the most uninteresting boy in the place? Could he have written an intimate biography of every other boy in Palmyra? If he found the Smiths so uniquely interesting, why are they never mentioned in his paper?

Tucker: They are, after 1830.

Chairman: That is just the point. After 1830 "vast numbers of people" suddenly become authorities on the Smiths. But how do you prove your case? The clerk will read your remarks about the foundations of your testimony.

Clerk (reads): "The Smith family, . . . basing this conclusion upon all the early avowals and other evidences remembered, as well as upon the subsequent developments extant—were unqualified atheists."

Chairman: Just what are the "subsequent developments extant" that prove the Smiths to be atheists?

Tucker: "Can their mockeries of Christianity, their persistent blasphemies, be accounted for upon any other hypothesis?"[18]

Chairman: Well, the cat is out of the bag again. What gives unique value to your book, Mr. Tucker, is that it rests upon your personal testimony of the Smiths. If you know from personal experience that the Smiths were atheists, what need to try to prove it by dragging in "subsequent developments" with which you were *not* acquainted? You say the Smiths were unqualified atheists in practice—to what practices do you refer? You say you base this conclusion on "evidences remembered"—why don't you tell us the evidences, if you remember them?

Tucker: As I said, "their mockeries of Christianity, their persistent blasphemies . . . "

Chairman: Are you a Christian, Mr. Tucker?

Tucker: Well, I never belonged to any church or "made a public profession of religion," but towards the end of my life I did discuss things with clergymen.[19]

Chairman: But that was long after you knew Smith. What in his behavior would you, who were not a confessing Christian, say made a mockery of Christianity?

Tucker: Everybody knows the answer to that: I specifically stated that these were "subsequent developments."

Chairman: And you also indirectly admitted that Smith's atheism was a hypothesis, based on a conclusion of your own, which you can only prove by referring to the behavior of the Smiths *after* you knew them. Don't you know that a court is not interested in a "conclusion" of the witness, and that you are not supposed to be testifying to any "hypothesis" but to fact? You should confine your testimony to the Smiths as you knew them, and not lamely appeal to "subsequent developments" to prove your conclusion.

Tucker: But the Smiths never changed; we know that.

Chairman: In that case, how did gloomy Joe, who, according to you, "was never known to laugh," become the "merry prophet" that so many other witnesses describe? Lots of people believed that your atheist was an exceedingly devout and religious man.

Tucker: I know that. They were his dupes and gulls.

Chairman: Nevertheless, their conviction means that your charges of mockery and blasphemy are purely a matter of opinion. Even though you may hold the majority opinion, there are large numbers of intelligent people who view Smith's teachings in a totally different light. It is a very suspicious thing when a witness who is supposed to be giving impartial and objective testimony to things seen and heard tries to shore up that testimony with theological arguments and beseeching appeals to public opinion and hearsay. Now, we have only time here to deal with the Book of Mormon; can you give us anything specific on that head?

The wonder-cave

Tucker: I certainly can. "The work of translation" on the Book of Mormon was carried out "in the recess of a dark artificial cave, which Smith had caused to be dug in the east side of the forest-hill near his residence, now owned by Mr. Amos Miner."[20]

Howe: There you have it! You asked for particulars, now you are getting them. The witness knows the very name of the man who owned the land!

Chairman: Yes, tricks like that do give the impression

of intimate knowledge. But Mr. Tucker is merely giving us the name of the man who owned the land when he wrote his book in 1867 — actually it has nothing to do with the story. It is not a contemporary or very relevant fact. So the Book of Mormon was translated in a cave, Mr. Tucker?

Tucker: That is correct, "a dark artificial cave. At least such was one account given out by the Mormon fraternity."[21]

Chairman: What, again? Already backing out?

Tucker: What do you mean?

Chairman: That you are trying to pass the buck. Is it you or the Mormons who are telling about this cave?

Tucker: Naturally my reports, being inside information, come from them. They told "another version that the prophet continued . . . at his house, and only went into the cave to pay his spiritual devotions and seek the continued favor of Divine Wisdom."[22]

Chairman: By either account, the Mormons must have thought it a very holy place. Why do they never mention it? Why have they never sought to locate its remains? Was it secret?

Tucker: Not at all. Our local "men and boys" passing by used to see Smith at work in the cave translating the Book of Mormon.[23]

Chairman: Then there were plenty of non-Mormons who witnessed the cave business?

Tucker: That is what I reported.

Chairman: Then why don't you follow their reports instead of those of the Mormons, whom you obviously distrust? The clerk will please read your words.

Clerk (reads): "At least such was one account given out by the Mormon fraternity."

Chairman: Why bother with such dubious stuff, when you have a host of men and boys from the town who can tell you all about it? Confine yourself for the present to their accounts.

Tucker: According to them, "Joseph Smith's stays in the cave varied from fifteen minutes to an hour or over — the entrance meanwhile being guarded by one or more of his disciples. This ceremony scarcely attracted the curiosity of outsiders."

Chairman: Frankly, it is hard for me to imagine any "ceremony" more perfectly calculated to excite the wildest curiosity than mysterious comings and goings at a theatrical grotto placed under armed guard. What was the cave like?

Tucker: "This excavation was at the time said to be 160 feet in extent, though that is probably an exaggeration."[24]

Chairman: That is a pretty large cave, isn't it? It would require a great deal of hard work of somebody, and you said Smith caused it to be dug. The lazy Smiths really got things done, and there must have been a huge dump of tailings. Why did they need to make it so very deep?

Tucker: I didn't say it was that deep. I only said it "was at the time said to be" that deep, and that that was "probably an exaggeration."

Chairman: Are you sure it was an exaggeration?

Tucker: I said it was *probably* an exaggeration.

Chairman: Then it may have been an exaggeration, but you are not sure. Why didn't you go out and measure it yourself?

Tucker: That was impossible. Not only was there an armed guard placed at the cave, but it was closed by "a substantial door of two-inch plank, secured by a corresponding lock."[25]

Chairman: These Smiths seem to have been immensely industrious and resourceful to run a show like that — which is totally out of keeping with their character as you have depicted it. But it is your behavior that amazes me.

Tucker: How so?

Chairman: Here this Smith, whose nefarious career has always attracted your most penetrating scrutiny, is at last doing something really spectacular, only two miles from your house (you said the cave was "near his residence"), and you are the editor of the local newspaper; yet from the nature of your report it is very clear that you neither walked out to inspect the cave yourself nor sent anyone else to. Didn't you think it would make a pretty good news story? You are willing to allow that the whole story of the translating in the cave may be a Mormon myth. But don't you know? Didn't you make any effort to find out? What kind of a newspaper man are you? Why did you never question Smith about it, since you claim he confided so much in you?

Tucker: I said the place was guarded.

Chairman: But you were Smith's old buddy; why didn't you ask him about it? And by whose permission was the cave guarded, anyway? Smith didn't own the land. Why wasn't he ordered off? You make a point of naming the later owner: if the owner of the land is so important to you, why don't you get in touch with him? You are completely vague and noncommittal about the dimensions and even the existence of this cave. Now, the Mormons deserted the place for good in 1830, just a few months at most after it had been used for the "ceremony" of translating the Book of Mormon. There was no guard *then*, and the sturdy door of two-inch plank, open or shut, would have most irresistibly invited inspection. Yet you ask us to believe that all the people of Palmyra, and you, their ever-inquiring editor, were so utterly devoid of normal human curiosity, at a time when the Book of Mormon was exciting the wildest speculation everywhere, that you did not even bother to take a short walk with a candle and tape measure after the Mormons had left, to see what was really out there. And in all the ensuing forty years during which you continued to live in Palmyra and discuss the

Mormons[26] you never so much as took an after-dinner stroll to look at the wonderful cave, nor did you ever delegate anyone to make a study of the fateful place, nor did you even interview anybody who had done so! You tax our credulity, sir.

Tucker: Well, as I said, the whole thing "scarcely attracted the curiosity of outsiders."

Chairman: The story of the origin of the Book of Mormon attracted the curiosity of the nation, yet the melodramatic properties of the most secret cave where it was made interested nobody! What kind of a story is that? Don't you see, sir, that the probability of your story can be checked at a dozen points and collapses at every one?

Tucker: You can't check it now. "From the lapse of time and natural causes the cave has been closed for years, very little mark of its former existence remaining to be seen."[27]

Clerk: If you will excuse the interruption, sir. Mrs. Dickinson here has given a later account of the cave.

Mrs. Ellen E. Dickinson: In 1885 I reported, "Just beyond the well . . . is shown a cave, or excavation, that was used by Smith and his close followers while engaged in deciphering the golden plates. It was originally boarded."[28]

Chairman: This is interesting. In 1867 Mr. Tucker says there was nothing left of the cave — "Very little mark of its former existence remaining," while almost twenty years later Mrs. Dickinson says it was still one of the sights. Did *you* ever see the cave, Mr. Tucker?

The wide-eyed innocents

Howe: I protest this badgering of the witness. Let him tell what he knows about the crimes of the Smiths!

Chairman: What about their crimes, Mr. Tucker?

Tucker: Many things were stolen and people began to guard their sheepfolds and suspect the Smiths.[29]

Chairman: With everybody suspecting them and watching them, the Smiths must have been at a terrible disadvantage. They lived, it would seem, in a goldfish bowl of public attention, yet, stupid and tactless as they were, nobody ever caught them at anything! Did they steal sheep, Mr. Tucker?

Tucker: "It is but common fairness to accompany this fact . . ."

Chairman: Which fact, Mr. Tucker?

Tucker: The fact that they were suspected.

Chairman: Thank you. You gave the impression that the fact in question was not that they were suspected but that they stole. Proceed.

Tucker: ". . . though it is but common fairness to accompany this fact by the statement, that it is not within the remembrance of the writer . . . if the popular inferences in this matter were ever sustained by judicial investigation."[30]

Chairman: Through the years, then, "popular inferences" burdened the Smiths with all kinds of crimes that could never be proven. If they were the stupid criminals that you make them out to be, the Smiths would certainly have been caught a hundred times over. All we have here is slander.

Tucker: Not a bit of it! "The whole idea of an attempt to harm Smith *in any* way . . . is purely a Mormon invention."[31]

Turner: That is correct. It was perfectly absurd for Smith to complain, as he often did, that he was persecuted for his opinions.[32]

Howe: He pretended he was being persecuted, simply because people wouldn't believe his wild stories. That's why he left Palmyra.[33]

Willard Chase: Yes. "His neighbors having become disgusted with his foolish stories, he determined to go back to Pennsylvania, to avoid what he called persecution."

Chairman: And when was that, sir?

Chase: At the end of September in the year 1827.[34]

Chairman: But according to you, Smith had been telling his foolish stories in Palmyra since early 1820, and in 1830 you and your fellows in Palmyra were still having intimate dealings with him. How long did it take you good people to discover that Smith's stories were foolish? Did Smith's opinions deserve censure, Mr. Tucker?

Tucker: "His interpretations of scriptural passages," when he was a child, "were always original and unique, and his deductions and conclusions often disgustingly blasphemous, according to the common apprehensions of Christian people."[35]

Chairman: "Original and unique" exegesis is hardly the business of adolescents noted only for indolence and dullness. And are you, Mr. Tucker, as a shrewd observer of human nature, so unaware of the normal reactions of "Christian people" to opinions which they consider "disgustingly blasphemous"? Persecution takes many forms. Are we to understand that this Joe Smith, whose mere memory inspires *your* impassioned invective a quarter of a century after his death, was never the object of severe treatment while he was alive?

Tucker: As I have said, "the whole idea of an attempt to harm Smith *in any way* . . . is purely a Mormon invention."

Chairman: And your own book is written only as a kindness to your old bosom friend? Come, now, Mr. Tucker! Don't you believe that spreading unsubstantiated criminal charges against a man constitutes an "attempt to harm" him? You have said that the Smiths were suspected of stealing many things, you have charged them "one and all" with the grossest atheism, and described young Joseph as brewing and executing one evil plot against society after another — and you meant him no harm by telling such stories?

Tucker: They were the truth.

Chairman: Then what kind of a community was Palmyra, and what kind of a man were you, to allow such monstrous goings-on to continue year after year without so much as raising a finger of protest? The Smiths, we are told, were the terror and torment of the neighborhood, "a pest to society," says Mr. Chase;[36] theft, fraud, and "unspeakable lewdness" were the order of the day, but never an arrest or trial. Those who give the most lurid reports claim to have their knowledge from the most intimate and prolonged personal association with the Smiths: a day or a week of such association would disgust and sicken any normal person, yet these eminently respectable people, including yourself, go on month after month and year after year receiving and encouraging the confidences of Smith and his family.

Howe: Encouraging their confidences?

Chairman: Would Smith have continued to air his vices and expose his intrigues through the years to these intimates if they had showed any tendency to upbraid or discourage him? You all knew what he was up to—but none of you ever did anything about it. As his most intimate associate and public-spirited man, were you, Mr. Tucker, not under any obligation to society to check and expose his awful deeds? Why did you wait until the culprit was dead twenty-three years to expose him? Don't you know that makes you virtually an accessory to his crimes?

Howe: Oh, lots of people knew what Joe was up to. Joseph Capron here can tell you.

Joseph Capron: Joe Smith "would often . . . urge them [his neighbors] to embark in the money digging business" with him.[37]

Chairman: And you call that being secretive. Did any join up?

Capron: Yes, indeed. "Some of them were influenced by curiosity, others were sanguine in their expectations of immediate gain."[38]

Chairman: This is worse than I thought. Specifically,

did any of our affidavit-swearers participate in Joe's activities?

Howe: Yes. Peter Ingersoll helped Joseph Smith, Sr., practice dowsing, and William Stafford and Willard Chase both assisted Smith in digging operations accompanied by magical rites.[39]

Chase and William Stafford: It was just out of curiosity![40]

Chairman: Whatever their excuse, the fact is that all three of the witnesses just named claim to have enjoyed the intimate confidences of Joseph Smith from 1820 to 1830, a thing which would have been utterly impossible unless they had given him sympathy and encouragement--such intimacy cannot be wholly unilateral. So I ask again, Mr. Tucker, since you knew Smith so long and so well in all his wickedness, why you never took steps to put an end to it.

Pattengill: Mr. Tucker had no *personal* prejudice against Smith, sir. What motive could he possibly have for such?

Chairman: You yourself supplied the motive, sir, when you told how at seventeen Mr. Tucker was determined to make his mark in the world, to shine as a writer and publisher; driven by fierce ambition, at the age of twenty-one he was an editor and at twenty-three he owned his own newspaper.[41] Cultivating the society of important people, he never stopped pushing himself, and in the end, what was his sole claim to fame? That he had known Joe Smith! Can you imagine anything more perfectly calculated to excite the jealous rage of a boundlessly ambitious, self-centered man—a frustrated prodigy, bachelor, and freethinker, whose whole life and religion was his own career—than to see a nobody from the farm give Palmyra the only celebrity it ever had? Let me sum up a few points:

Twenty-three years after the death of Joseph Smith and thirty-seven years after Smith had left Palmyra, a citizen of that town brings out a book telling most intimately of the mind and doings of Smith at the time of the writing of the Book of Mormon. (1) Now, since the author of the book is an editor by profession, I find it very strange that he should have waited so long to tell the public what it had been clamoring to hear for decades. (2) He prefaces his book with a purely fanciful drawing depicting an angel and devils as neither Smith nor his followers ever described them, yet he labels the picture "Smith's account of the finding of the golden plates." Here is a plain fabrication. (3) Then he describes young Smith as a totally uninteresting tramp whose every characteristic disgusts him — and yet goes on to depict himself, an ambitious and important young man, as spending his days observing Smith's every move and receiving all his secret confidences. (4) He describes the Smith family as cynical and cunning, but makes them the simple dupes of a pewter-coin joke that could not have fooled the village idiot. (5) He describes them also as outspoken atheists constantly parading their atheism in public; yet none of the public in question, when requested to think of all the bad things they could about the Smiths, ever mentioned their atheism — far from it, superstition was their charge. (6) While Tucker was intimate with the Smiths for some fourteen years, he tells none of the countless firsthand experiences that he should have had with them, but instead offers as proof of their villainy their *subsequent* behavior, which he did *not* observe. (7) Tucker tells of a wonderful cave, but can give no certain information about it, though he lived very near to it for forty-two years. (8) True, he insists that nobody was particularly interested in the mysterious doings at the cave, but that only makes me more suspicious, since the whole country was then talking about Smith and his gold plates, and it is inconceivable that he, who took the pains to write a whole book about Joseph Smith, simply wasn't interested enough in the cave to look it over himself or have somebody else do it. (9) He has the lazy Smiths running a full-scale Army Command Post at the cave, with extensive digging and construction work, changes of guard and all the rest, on land that did not belong to them, but with never a word of protest from anybody. (10) In fact, he insists that no one opposed Smith's operations at any time or had the slightest intention of harming him, even while he reports the most vicious slanders and adds his own against the Smiths. (11) He describes Joseph Smith as brewing and executing one evil plot after another, while he, a public-spirited man and witness to all this depravity, raised no word of protest until forty years after. (12) Finally, we have seen in the career of Tucker and his unguarded expressions of passion what we think is ample indication of a motive and will to malign the Smiths. It would be instructive to examine Mr. Tucker's book page by page, but we have had time here only to consider the parts dealing with the Book of Mormon, and I think we have heard enough to form a pretty fair opinion of his trustworthiness.

This court is adjourned until tomorrow morning at ten o'clock.

Notes for Part 1, Scene ii

1. C. N. Pattengill, *Light in the Valley: Memorial Sermon Delivered at the Funeral of Pomeroy Tucker* (Troy, NY: Times Steam, 1870), 8–9.

2. Ibid., 8.

3. Ibid.

4. Walter R. Martin, *The Rise of the Cults (An Introductory Guide to the Non-Christian Cults)* (Grand Rapids, MI: Zondervan, 1955), 49.

5. Pomeroy Tucker, *Origin, Rise, and Progress of Mormonism* (New York: Appleton, 1867), 16.

6. R. W. Beers, *The Mormon Puzzle and How to Solve It* (New York: Funk and Wagnalls, 1887), 25–26, uses it as evidence.

7. Eber D. Howe, *Mormonism Unvailed; Or, a Faithful Account of That Singular Imposition and Delusion* (Painesville, OH: the author, 1840), 187.

8. Pattengill, *Light in the Valley*, 5.

9. Ibid., 4, 37.

10. Tucker, *Origin, Rise, and Progress of Mormonism*, 16.

11. Ibid., 16–17.

12. Ibid., 14.

13. Ibid.

14. Ibid., 23–30.

15. Ruth Kauffman and Reginald W. Kauffman, *The Latter-Day Saints: A Study of the Mormons in the Light of Economic Conditions* (London: Williams and Norgate, 1912), 23, citing Orsamus Turner, *History of the Pioneer Settlement of Phelps and Gorham's Purchase and Morris' Reserve* (Rochester, NY: Alling, 1851), 213–14.

16. Tucker, *Origin, Rise, and Progress of Mormonism*, 18.

17. Howe, *Mormonism Unvailed*, 11.

18. Tucker, *Origin, Rise, and Progress of Mormonism*, 18.

19. Pattengill, *Light in the Valley*, 9.

20. Tucker, *Origin, Rise, and Progress of Mormonism*, 48–49.

21. Ibid.

22. Ibid., 49.

23. Ibid.

24. Ibid.

25. Ibid.

26. Pattengill, *Light in the Valley*, 42–43.

27. Tucker, *Origin, Rise, and Progress of Mormonism*, 49.

28. Ellen E. Dickinson, *New Light on Mormonism*, with an introduction by Thurlow Weed (New York: Funk and Wagnalls, 1885), 247.

29. Tucker, *Origin, Rise, and Progress of Mormonism*, 15.

30. Ibid.

31. Ibid., 119 (emphasis added).

32. J. B. Turner, *Mormonism in All Ages* (New York: Platt and Peters, 1842), 302.

33. Howe, *Mormonism Unvailed*, 246.

34. Ibid., 245.

35. Tucker, *Origin, Rise, and Progress of Mormonism*, 17.

36. Howe, *Mormonism Unvailed*, 247.

37. Ibid., 259.

38. Ibid.

39. Ibid., 234, 238–39.

40. Ibid., 238.

41. Pattengill, *Light in the Valley*, 4–6.

iii. Portrait of a Prophet

Scene: The same. The hall is empty save for the presence of the Chairman and his Clerk, who is gathering papers together preparatory to departure. It is obviously late at night.

" . . . in the mind's eye, Horatio"

Chairman: Before you go, Mr. Beckmesser, there are some things I would like to talk over with you. Since this is not a trial but only an investigation, I would like to get your reaction to Mr. Tucker's portrait of the youthful Smith. A sulky, taciturn, evil-minded brat gains a loyal and devoted following simply by telling wild and wonderful stories—how does it strike you?

Clerk: A bit odd, sir. But then, didn't a mischievous boy in East Side New York have a million people in a high state of religious excitement a few years back by announcing that the Virgin had appeared to him in a back lot?

Chairman: Yes, I recall the case. But how long did that kid's glory last—five days? A week, maybe? That only shows what a different sort of thing we are up against here. By the way, have you got that material for a portrait of Smith?

Clerk: You mean all those intimate descriptions of what he looked like? Yes sir, I collected them as you asked. Here they are.

Chairman: Do they present a uniform picture of the man? I mean, did Smith make a consistent impression on people?

Clerk: If you mean, do they all think he is a scoundrel, the answer is yes; otherwise, their books would not be classified as anti-Mormon. His friends praise him, his enemies hate him, but aside from hating him they don't seem to be able to agree on a thing. Here is one, for example, who writes: "I can see him now in my mind's eye, with his torn and patched trousers held to his form by a pair of suspenders made out of sheeting, with his calico shirt as dirty and black as the earth, and his uncombed hair sticking through the holes in his old battered hat."[1]

Chairman: Very picturesque. The "mind's eye," indeed. Is this the child Joseph Smith?

Clerk: By no means, sir. This is supposed to describe the man when "he was about twenty-five years old" — that would be after the publication of the Book of Mormon and the founding of the Church.[2]

Chairman: But does anybody take this seriously?

Clerk: Mr. Linn accepts it as an accurate portrait. Here is a homey touch that gives it an air of simple honesty: "Joe had a jovial, easy, don't-care way about him that made him warm friends. He was a good talker, and would have made a fine stump-speaker with training."[3]

Chairman: A sloppy tramp with the gift of gab.

Clerk: So it seems, sir. But here is another eyewitness description from the same period: "He was always well dressed, generally in black with a white necktie. He looked like a Reverend. . . . Joseph was no orator. He said what he wanted to say in a very blundering sort of way."[4] So now he's a well-dressed gent who can't talk at all. And that is typical. Mr. Tucker said taciturnity was one of Smith's most conspicuous characteristics, and here another witness says, "Joseph did not talk much in society, his talk was not very fluent, . . . he was by no means interesting in company."[5] Stephen S. Harding, one-time governor of Utah Territory, who claims to have known Smith personally in Palmyra, says, "Young Joe was hard to be approached. He was very taciturn, and sat most of the time as silent as the Sphinx."[6]

Chairman: Silent Smith, eh?

Clerk: That is what some say, but others say the opposite: "very voluble in speech, having great self-confidence,"[7] "endowed with the requisite cunning and volubility."[8]

Chairman: But isn't that the later Smith?

Clerk: No, sir, this is the boy of Palmyra, who used to attend "revival meetings praying and exhorting with great

exhuberance of words,"⁹ "used to help us solve some por-
tentous question of moral or political ethics in our juvenile
debating club . . . and subsequently . . . was a very pass-
able exhorter in evening meetings."¹⁰ Here is another: "At
times he would be very active in a religious revival, praying
and exhorting with unusual fervor, in that exuberance of
words which he had wonderfully at his command."¹¹ It is
rather puzzling—blundering, stammering, taciturn Sphinx
with a wonderful exuberance of words. "His address is
easy," wrote Mr. Howe himself of this stammerer, "rather
fascinating and winning, of a mild and sober deportment,"
though at times inclined to jest and be exceedingly merry.¹²
This is the boy whom Mr. Tucker says "was never known
to laugh." And while Mr. Tucker also assures us from the
most intimate experience that everything Joe and his family
did proclaimed their sordid atheism, the other neighbors
report him as zealously active in religious circles.

  Chairman: So somebody is lying.

  Clerk: At least they can't all be right. You remember
Mr. Tucker said Joseph Smith was of a "plodding, evil-
brewing mental composition," that "he seldom spoke to
anyone outside of his intimate associates," and above all,
that he "was never known to laugh."¹³ And Mrs. Eaton,
taking the cue, says "he rarely smiled or laughed. 'His
looks and thoughts were always downward bent.' "¹⁴ Yet
one high authority says he had "a deep vein of humor that
ran through all he said and did,"¹⁵ and Charles Dickens
declares that "the exact adjective for Joe's religion is—
jolly!"¹⁶ The poet Whittier speaks of Smith's "rude, bold,
good-humoured face,"¹⁷ and even some of the most damning witnesses tell us "Joe had a jovial, easy, don't-care way
about him,"¹⁸ and that "he used to laugh from the crown
of his head to the soles of his feet, it shook every bit of
flesh in him."¹⁹ Also, while Mr. Hendrix assures us that
he made "warm friends," other neighbors say "he was
shunned by the boys of his own age" and that he was "an

awkward [and] unpopular lad."[20] Here is a nice impasse: Chase, Ingersoll, and Stafford, who knew him so well, describe him as a brawler, who frequently got drunk, and "when intoxicated was very quarrelsome,"[21] while Tucker and Harding, who knew him just as well, assure us that Smith "was noted as never having had a fight or quarrel with any other person."[22] Whom are we to believe?

Chairman: It might be easier to check up on his physical appearance. What do they say to that?

Clerk: He is described by eyewitnesses in 1830 as being "tall and slender—*thin favored*."[23] Mr. Dogberry calls him "spindle shanked";[24] here is a remarkable description by Harding, who "describes him as having been a tall, long-legged and tow-headed youth, who seldom smiled, hardly ever worked and never fought, but who was hard on truth and bird's nests."[25]

Chairman: At least we know that Smith was tall and skinny.

Clerk: But do we? Thurlow Weed's description of Smith from that time is of "a stout, round, smooth-faced young man."[26] Tall he may have been, but how he could have been "thin-favored" and stout and round at the same time is not so obvious. And just two years later another eyewitness who claims to have known Smith very well says he is "a man of mean and insignificant appearance, between forty and fifty years of age."[27] Later on we are told that "the gait of this person was heavy and slouching, his hands were large and thick, his eyes grey and unsteady in their gaze."[28] A year after this was published, another opus describes the prophet as "a tall, elegant-looking man with dark piercing eyes, and features, which if not handsome, were imposing."[29] Another calls him "a man of commanding appearance, tall and well-proportioned." "A noble-looking fellow," says another, "a Mahomet every inch of him."[30] Josiah Quincy says "he was a hearty, athletic fellow, with blue eyes standing prominently out upon his

light complexion. . . . *'A fine-looking man'* is what the pas-
ser-by would instinctively have murmured."[31] Another visitor says Smith had dark hair and eyes and a "strong rugged
outline of face" with features exactly like those of Oliver
Cromwell.[32] Charles Francis Adams described him as "a
middle-aged man with a shrewd but rather ordinary
expression of countenance."[33]

Chairman: So far we have shifty grey eyes, prominent
blue eyes, and dark piercing eyes.

Clerk: Yes, and while one illustrious visitor says he
could not see Smith's eyes since the man refused to look
people in the face,[34] others speak of his "penetrating eagle
eyes."[35] Some think Smith's huge, fat, enormous awkward
hands worthy of special mention,[36] while others comment
on the remarkably *small* size of his hands.[37] One says that
he had "a Herculean frame and a commanding appearance,"[38] another that he was sloppy and slouching, "very
lank and loose in his appearance and movements."[39]

Chairman: A portrait artist would have a wonderful time
depicting him from these honest firsthand descriptions.
How do you account for the discrepancies?

Clerk: I think the report of the celebrated Mr. Conybeare, the foremost literary critic of the midnineteenth century, can help us out there. His classical description of
Joseph Smith's appearance is warranted solely by the con-
templation of a small wood engraving of the prophet, the
work of neither a sympathetic nor a skillful hand. This has
been reproduced in numerous anti-Mormon books as the
official non-Mormon portrait of Smith. As he views the
small and clumsy drawing, Mr. Conybeare gives forth:

> It is inexplicable how anyone who had ever looked
> at Joseph's portrait [it was not really a portrait, of course,
> since Smith did not pose for it], could imagine him to
> have been by possibility an honest man. Never did we
> see a face on which the hand of heaven had more legibly
> written rascal. That self-complacent simper, that sensual

Joseph Smith (from a sketch by M. Didier). (Charles Mackay, *The Mormons: Or Latter-day Saints,* 3rd ed. [London: Vizetelly, 1852], 160.)

mouth, that leer of vulgar cunning, tell us at one glance the character of their owner.[40]

Chairman: Dear me, all this from a crude woodcut the size of a postage-stamp! Our artist must have been a supreme caricaturist.

Half-witted superman

Clerk: Not at all. If you will look at the picture you will see that it is a perfectly ordinary performance—typical of the nineteenth-century school of engraving at which Robert Louis Stevenson poked fun in his *Moral Emblems.* All that consummate viciousness is simply what Mr. Conybeare reads into it. Yet a Dutch scholar has taken Conybeare's interpretation of this grotesque little vignette as solid psychological evidence for the character of Smith.[41] You get the same sort of thing when you deal with Joseph Smith's intelligence and knowledge. Here we read of "a natural genius, strong inventive powers of mind, a deep study, and an unusually correct estimate of the human passions and feelings,"[42] "a fertile immagination,"[43] "an omnivorous reader of the 'buckets of blood' literature,"[44] "highly original and imaginative, . . . an audacious and original mind,"[45] "a retentive memory; a correct knowledge of human nature,"[46] "a strong mind (says Quincy) utterly unenlightened by the teachings of history,"[47] and "a great shrewdness and worldly wisdom, . . . boundless energy and intrepidity of character, of most fearless audacity."[48] "Great powers of reasoning were his natural gift, . . . and a deep vein of humor ran through all he said and did."[49] "Joseph was the calf that sucked three cows. He acquired knowledge very rapidly. . . . He soon out-grew his teachers."[50] "His own autobiography shows him well studied at an early period in the nice shades and differences of modern sectarian creeds, and . . . well-read in the history of Mohammed and other religious imposters."[51] "The skill with which he carried out his imposture, . . . his eloquence, rude but powerful—his letters, clever and sarcastic—the manifold character and boldness of his designs—his courage in enterprise—his perseverance despite great obstacles—his conception and partial execution of the temple of Nauvoo—these and other things mark him as a man of more than ordinary calibre."[52]

Chairman: A sort of superman. And on the other hand?

Clerk: On the other hand, the same Smith in 1830 is "that *spindle shanked* ignoramus, *Joe Smith.* This fellow appears to possess the *quintessence* of impudence . . . having but little expression of countenance other than that of dullness; his mental powers appear to be extremely limited."[53] One of the earliest says, "I thought the man either crazed or a very shallow imposter."[54] "His knowledge was slight and his judgment weak."[55] "He was lounging, idle (not to say vicious), and possessed of less than ordinary intellect. The author's own recollections of him are distinct ones."[56]

"He was as self-indulgent as he was ignorant,"[57] "a dissolute, unprincipled young rake, and notorious only for his general wickedness."[58] "Jo from a boy appeared dull and utterly destitute of genius."[59] "His untutored and feeble intellect had not yet [in 1830] grasped at anything beyond mere toying with mysterious things."[60] "We can discover in his career no proof of conspicuous ability. . . . His chief, if not his only talent, was his gigantic impudence."[61] He was never "noted for much else than ignorance and stupidity, to which might be added . . . a fondness for everything marvelous."[62] "Joseph was unkempt and immoderately lazy. He could read, though not without difficulty, wrote a very imperfect hand, and had a limited understanding of elementary arithmetic."[63] "Ignorant and ill-prepared, as he confessedly was for such a work, he made no special effort to qualify himself."[64] "He had neither the diligence nor the constancy to master reality,"[65] a "completely undisciplined imagination"[66] not to be "canalized by any discipline."[67] He was not liked. The young people of the town considered him not quite full-witted, and with the cruelty of youth, made him the butt for their practical jokes.[68]

Chairman: So it was the village idiot who wrote the Book of Mormon. This brings up a little question of motive. Surely there are easier ways of fooling people than by composing a large and complex book which, as the book itself foretells, simply invites persecution. How do these people explain the colossally exhausting and dangerous task of writing, publishing, and spreading it abroad as the enterprise of the laziest man on earth?

Clerk: There are two schools of thought. One holds that Smith was sincerely religious, the other that he was not; the latter is the larger faction by about one hundred to one. We are to believe that he undertook the writing of the Book of Mormon out of sheer impudence, "his only talent." According to Mrs. Brodie this silly, sneaky, shallow, prevaricating boy dictated the whole Book of Mormon as a sort of practical joke on his parents "to carry out the fun." This is her idea of fun. Here are some other verdicts: "That he was a religious enthusiast we cannot grant. . . . One principle . . . actuated him through life, and that was—selfishness, . . . [which makes his religion] one of the most unfounded and abominable systems that ever sprung from the depths of human or Satanic depravity."[69] His Book of Mormon is "but a wicked, silly, filthy romance, founded in ignorance, nay, the quintessence of ignorance, even the ignorance of Joseph Smith, got up for speculation, in order to gull the American Indians, and dupe the English!"[70] "You have not even the poor merit of either talent or originality," wrote Professor Turner to Joseph Smith. "You have at once outraged and disgraced human nature itself."[71] "If there is one fact in American history that can be regarded as definitely established it is that the engaging Joe Smith was a deliberate charlatan."[72] "The camel-driver of Medina was probably a sincere fanatic, whereas the seer of Palmyra was almost certainly a cunning imposter."[73] His "only object at that time was to play upon the credulous, earn applause from the debased, and extort money from the simple, under the plea of a divine mission."[74] "He was one of those indolent and illiterate young men . . . who hope to shun honest labor, and who have imbibed the pernicious doctrine embraced in the phrase: 'The world owes me a living.' "[75] "Colossal egotist, ribald wit, handsome giant, ruthless enemy, loudmouthed braggart, . . . religious charlatan, great administrator, master politician, cheap exhibitionist."[76] "Smith was a bank-note forger, . . . shifty, illiterate and credulous,"[77] "the greedy speculator without conscience, and without shame."[78] "Their leaders are evidently atrocious imposters, who have deceived a great many weak-minded but well-meaning persons, by holding out to them the promise of great temporal advantage."[79] Joseph Smith's "own character gives no shred of prestige for his pretentious claims. Yet, most individual Mormons are sturdy, sincere, honorable, and fine citizens."[80] Mormonism grew from "the pure rascality of the Mormon prophet," "an uneducated youth, without wealth or social standing; indeed, without a prestige of common morality (for the founder of Mormonism is said to have been a dissolute, unprincipled young rake, and notorious only for his general wickedness)."[81] "I have yet to find anybody, or any book, not Mormon, that has a single good word to say of Joseph Smith."[82] For Mrs. Brodie, Joseph Smith was "utterly opportunistic." Mr. Conybeare calls him "a profligate and sordid knave, . . . making the voice of heaven pander to his own avarice and lust."[83] And so on and so on; you get the idea: Smith was the last word in depravity, but he wanted power and money, and that explains everything. His success can be attributed either to audacity or cunning or both.

Chairman: So I ask myself, Why would a cunning and ambitious rogue too lazy to do any work invariably choose the hardest, the most dangerous, and the least rewarding ways of getting what he wanted—especially since he is supposed to have had an uncanny insight into the foibles of human nature? Or is he?

Clerk: He is, all right. Mr. Howe himself says Smith has "a natural genius, strong inventive powers of mind, a deep study, and an unusually correct estimate of the human passions and feelings."[84] He knew his public—no doubt about it. And so he proceeded to make and keep himself the most unpopular man of the century.

Chairman: Does that strike you as being believable?

Clerk: Historians admit the inconsistency, but they won't discuss it. Here is one who admits that it is "marvelously strange that . . . a dissolute, unprincipled young rake . . . should excite a revolutionary movement in the religious world . . . and that, too, in an age of refinement and scientific intelligence."[85] By admitting that this is "mar-

velously strange," this author seems to think he has relieved himself of any further responsibility of explaining
the paradox. Mrs. Brodie has her own characteristic solution of the problem. She explains away all her whopping
contradictions by what she calls "the unusual plasticity of
Joseph's mind."[86] By having him sufficiently plastic you
can have one man take any form you want to.

Chairman: But again the word simply *describes* the phenomenon—it does not *explain* a thing. Does a biographer
or a portrait painter, when his picture fails to resemble
anything human, have a right to introduce new and unex-
ampled dimensions into his art, and attribute the weird
results not to his own creativity but to the "unusual plasticity" of his subject? Here we have a young man producing
large and difficult books by his own efforts, converting
thousands of deeply religious people to a willingness to
give their lives for what he teaches, leading great migrations, founding many cities and societies—structures of
solid and enduring quality—and all the time enduring persecution and opposition of great persistence and ferocity.
And this young man is not only a complete cynic but
incredibly tactless and silly; he is in fact the most unprincipled, irresponsible, shallow, undisciplined, lazy young
man alive. Does it make sense to you?

Clerk: I would feel much better about it if there were
some historical parallels to match this, but I know of none.
In real life, lazy loafers do not write big books, opportunistic charlatans do not risk their lives in hard and exhausting projects when by changing their tune they could become rich and respectable, and ambitious men with keen
insight into human nature don't insist on doing and saying
just the things that are bound to offend the most people
the most. Here is one authority who confesses that "a mere
imposter . . . would have been broken down under such
a tempest of opposition and hate as Smith's preaching

excited. Smith must have been at least in part honest in his delusion."[87]

Chairman: Now *there* is a generous concession—he "must have been at least *in part* honest." That explains everything; he's going to have his cake and eat it. But is anyone going to tell us in which "part" he is honest? Where was Smith's real genius?

Clerk: I think Mrs. Brodie answers that in a passage that takes all the prizes. She assures us that "the facility with which profound theological arguments were handled is evidence of the unusual plasticity of Joseph's mind. But this facility was entirely verbal. The essence of the great spiritual and moral truths with which he dealt so agilely did not penetrate into his consciousness. . . . He knew these truths intimately as a bright child knows his catechism, but his use of them was utterly opportunistic."[88]

Chairman: A remarkably revealing statement. It was Theodore Schroder, the rabid anti-Mormon, who once observed that psychological studies of Joseph Smith only reveal the minds of those who make them and leave Smith untouched. Mrs. Brodie might as well have discoursed on the qualities of silent music, invisible etchings, or odorless perfume as to talk of dealing in "great spiritual and moral truths" without grasping anything of their "essence"— without such a grasp there is simply nothing to talk about; how on earth can one know things "intimately" or at all unless they do somehow penetrate into one's consciousness? They exist nowhere else. Since "Mrs. Brodie's intense atheism . . . actually determines . . . the content of her book,"[89] it would be interesting to know what are the "profound spiritual truths" which *she* grasps so well and which so completely escaped Joseph Smith.

Clerk: Here are some more descriptions: "A shrewd schemer whose ethical sense was poorly developed," "an ever-inventive and fertile genius" who succeeded because he had no scruples whatever. It beats me how such a clever man bent on deception could be so clumsy at the same time. Josiah Canning laughs at Smith's "school-boy tact,"[90] and Peter Cartwright calls him "clumsy Joe."[91] Kidder is amazed that a "miserable plagiarist . . . had . . . the unaccountable stupidity" to include extensive Bible passages in the Book of Mormon, which was designed to fool a public that knew the Bible better than any other book.[92] A classic example of his shrewdness is the oft-repeated story of how the youthful Smith went around town singing the song of his hero Captain Kidd, whose autobiography he eagerly and often perused. "He chanted it at play, quoted it over and over at the village store until it became indelibly associated with him in the minds of the people of Manchester and Palmyra,"[93] who incidentally never mention the fact in the early period. Not a very sly way to begin a life of religious deception.

Chairman: To say the least. Yet that Captain Kidd story is a great favorite with twentieth-century writers on Mormonism. I wonder where they got it.

Clerk: I think I have a pretty good idea. In 1830 a Rochester newspaper recalled that back in 1815 there had been considerable interest among "a certain class" of people in western New York in searching for Captain Kidd's treasure. The article makes it clear that there is no necessary connection between this mania and any of Joseph Smith's activities.[94] Taking up from here, Mr. Howe reports that the Smiths went around "pretending to believe that the earth was filled with hidden treasures, buried there by Kidd or the Spaniards."[95] From there on it is easy: Joseph Smith soon emerges as the unique disciple of the terrible pirate. It is fascinating to see how Smith's critics can turn anything and nothing into direct evidence against him. But we are going to look into the treasure-digging stories in the morning. They should be good.

Notes for Part 1, Scene iii

1. From an interview with Daniel Hendrix in the *New York Times,* 15 July 1898.

2. Ibid.

3. Ibid.

4. W. Wyl, *Mormon Portraits; Or, the Truth about the Mormon Leaders* (Salt Lake City: Tribune, 1886), 25, 27.

5. Ibid., 26.

6. Thomas Gregg, *The Prophet of Palmyra* (New York: Alden, 1890), 38.

7. W. Lang, *History of Seneca County* (Springfield, OH: Transcript, 1880), 649.

8. John S. C. Abbott, *The History of the State of Ohio* (Detroit: Northwestern, 1875), 697.

9. Lang, *History of Seneca County*, 649.

10. George W. Cowles, *Landmarks of Wayne County, New York* (Syracuse, NY: Mason, 1895), 78.

11. Abbott, *History of the State of Ohio*, 697.

12. Eber D. Howe, *Mormonism Unvailed; Or, a Faithful Account of That Singular Imposition and Delusion* (Painesville, OH: the author, 1834), 13.

13. Pomeroy Tucker, *Origin, Rise, and Progress of Mormonism* (New York: Appleton, 1867), 16–17.

14. Mrs. Dr. Horace Eaton, "Speech Delivered May 27, 1881," in *Handbook on Mormonism* (Salt Lake City: Handbook, 1882), 1.

15. "The Yankee Mahomet," *American Whig Review* 17 (June 1851): 556.

16. Charles Dickens, "In the Name of the Prophet—Smith!" *Household Words* 69 (19 July 1851): 387.

17. William and Mary Howitt, eds., *Howitt's Journal* (London: Lovett, 1847), 158.

18. From an interview with Daniel Hendrix in the *New York Times*, 15 July 1898.

19. Wyl, *Mormon Portraits*, 26.

20. Ruth Kauffman and Reginald W. Kauffman, *The Latter-Day Saints: A Study of the Mormons in the Light of Economic Conditions* (London: Williams and Norgate, 1912), 23.

21. John C. Bennett, *The History of the Saints; Or, An Exposé of Joe Smith and Mormonism* (Boston: Leland and Whiting, 1842), 72.

22. Gregg, *Prophet of Palmyra*, 39.

23. Francis Kirkham, *A New Witness for Christ in America: The Book of Mormon*, 2 vols. (Salt Lake City: Utah, 1951), 2:68.

24. Ibid., 56.

25. Charles A. Shook, *The True Origin of Mormon Polygamy* (Cincinnati: Standard, 1914), 17.

26. Thurlow Weed, *Autobiography*, 2 vols. (Boston: Houghton and Mifflin, 1884), 1:358.

27. E. S. Abdy, *Journal of a Residence and Tour in the United States of North America from April 1833 to October 1834* (London: Murray, 1835), 324–25.

28. Robert Richards, *The Californian Crusoe* (London: Parker, 1854), 60.

29. Maria Ward, *The Mormon Wife* (Hartford, CT: Hartford, 1872), 19.

30. Wyl, *Mormon Portraits*, 28.

31. Josiah Quincy, *Figures of the Past from the Leaves of Old Journals* (Boston: Roberts Brothers, 1883), 380–81.

32. Edwin de Leon, *Thirty Years of My Life on Three Continents*, 2 vols. (London: Ward and Downey, 1890), 1:56.

33. Henry Adams, "Charles Francis Adams Visits the Mormons in 1844," *Proceedings of Massachusetts Historical Society* 68 (October 1944–May 1947): 21.

34. Henry Caswall, *The Prophet of the 19th Century; Or, the Rise, Progress, and Present State of Mormons or Latter-Day Saints* (London: Rivington, 1843), 223.

35. M. H. A. van der Valk, *De Profeet der Mormonen, Joseph Smith Jr.* (Kampen: Kok, 1921), 28.

36. Caswall, *Prophet of the 19th Century*, 223; Henry Brown, *History of Illinois* (Chicago: Brown, 1844), 401.

37. John Quincy Adams, *The Birth of Mormonism* (Boston: Gorham, 1916), 101.

38. "Yankee Mahomet," 556.

39. Wyl, *Mormon Portraits*, 26.

40. W. J. Conybeare, "Mormonism," *Edinburgh Review* 202 (April 1854): 338.

41. Van der Valk, *Profeet der Mormonen*, 28.

42. James H. Hunt, *Mormonism* (St. Louis: Ustick and Davies, 1844), 7.

43. Fawn M. Brodie, *No Man Knows My History* (New York: Knopf, 1947), 26.

44. George Seibel, *The Mormon Saints* (Pittsburgh: Lessing, 1919), 15.

45. Brodie, *No Man Knows My History*, 48–49.

46. "Yankee Mahomet," 556.

47. Ibid., 399.

48. *The Lamps of the Temple* (London: Snow, Paternoster Row, 1856), 477.

49. "Yankee Mahomet," 556.

50. Wyl, *Mormon Portraits*, 25.

51. Benjamin G. Ferris, *Utah and the Mormons* (New York: Harper and Bros., 1856), 66.

52. T. W. P. Taylder, *Mormon's Own Book or Mormonism* (London: Partridge/Patternoster Row, 1847), li.

53. Kirkham, *New Witness for Christ in America*, 2:56, 68.

54. Weed, *Autobiography*, 1:359.

55. Samuel M. Jackson, ed., *The New Schaff-Herzog Encyclopedia of Religious Knowledge*, 15 vols. (Grand Rapids: Baker, 1977), 8:13.

56. Orsamus Turner, *History of the Pioneer Settlement of Phelps and Gorham's Purchase and Morris' Reserve* (Rochester, NY: Alling, 1851), 213.

57. George Townsend, *The Conversion of Mormonism* (Hartford, CT: Church Mission, 1911), 21.

58. *History of Caldwell and Livingston Counties, Missouri* (St. Louis: National Historical Company, 1886), 106.

59. John A. Clark, *Gleanings by the Way* (Philadelphia: Simon, 1842), 225.

60. Gregg, *Prophet of Palmyra*, 4.

61. Conybeare, "Mormonism," 338.

62. Kirkham, *New Witness for Christ in America*, 2:68.

63. Jackson, ed., *New Schaff-Herzog Encyclopedia of Religious Knowledge*, 8:12.

64. Gregg, *Prophet of Palmyra*, 20.

65. Brodie, *No Man Knows My History*, 69.

66. Ibid., 84.

67. Ibid., 27.

68. Kauffman and Kauffman, *Latter-Day Saints*, 23.

69. Taylder, *Mormon's Own Book*, li–lii.

70. J. Theobald, *Mormonism Harpooned* (London: Horsell, 1855), 24.

71. J. B. Turner, *Mormonism in All Ages* (New York: Platt and Peters, 1842), 301.

72. Earnest S. Bates, *American Faith* (New York: Norton, 1940), 346.

73. W. S. Simpson, *Mormonism* (London: Pigott, 1853), 6.

74. Orvilla S. Belisle, *Mormonism Unveiled: A History of Mormonism from Its Rise to the Present Time* (London: Clark, 1855), 37.

75. Gregg, *Prophet of Palmyra*, 4.

76. Sidney Bell, *Wives of the Prophet* (New York: Macaulay, 1935), introduction.

77. Horton Davies, *Christian Deviations* (London: SCM, 1954), 80.

78. Jules Remy, *A Journey to Great-Salt-Lake City*, 2 vols. (London: Jeffs, 1861), 1:xxxi.

79. *History of Caldwell and Livingston Counties, Missouri*, 106.

80. Phillips E. Osgood, *Religion without Magic* (Boston: Beacon, 1954), 79.

81. *History of Caldwell and Livingston Counties, Missouri*, 106.

82. T. W. Young, *Mormonism: Its Origin, Doctrines, and Dangers* (Ann Arbor, MI: Wahr, 1900), 16–17.

83. Conybeare, "Mormonism," 336–37.

84. Howe, *Mormonism Unvailed*, 12.

85. *History of Caldwell and Livingston Counties, Missouri*, 106.

86. Brodie, *No Man Knows My History*, 70.

87. "Mormons," *Knowledge, A Weekly Magazine* 1/9 (2 August 1890): 176.

88. Brodie, *No Man Knows My History*, 70.

89. "Appraisal of the So-Called Brodie Book," *Deseret News, Church News*, 11 May 1946, 6.

90. Josiah D. Canning, *Poems* (Greenfield, MA: Phelps and Ingersoll, 1838), 107.

91. W. P. Strickland, ed., *The Autobiography of Peter Cartwright the Frontier Preacher* (New York: Carlton and Porter, 1856), 342.

92. Daniel P. Kidder, *Mormonism and the Mormons* (New York: Carlton and Porter, 1842), 255.

93. Harry M. Beardsley, *Joseph Smith and His Mormon Empire* (Boston: Riverside, 1931), 17–18; Seibel, *The Mormon Saints*, 15–16; R. W. Beers, *The Mormon Puzzle and How to Solve It* (New York: Funk and Wagnalls, 1887), 27; Ellen E. Dickinson, *New Light on Mormonism*, with an introduction by Thurlow Weed (New York: Funk and Wagnalls, 1885), 29.

94. Kirkham, *New Witness for Christ in America*, 2:48–49.

95. Howe, *Mormonism Unvailed*, 11.

Part 2

Digging in the Dark

i. The man who was never there

> *Scene:* The same. Ten o'clock the next morning.

Dig for that crazy, mixed-up kid!

Clerk: The meeting will come to order.

Chairman: As we all know, the commonest, most uniform, and most damning charge against Joseph Smith is that he was a money-digger. This morning we want to look into that accusation. Let us first hear from those who assisted Smith in his treasure-digging operations. Will the diggers please come forward? (A long wait. Nobody moves.) Come, come; the charge is that Smith for some years was head of a band of diggers; there must be someone here who took part in those notorious activities. Did they all just vanish?

Pomeroy Tucker: No, sir. In 1867 I could still report that "several of the individuals participating in this, . . . and many others well remembering the stories of the time, are yet living witnesses of these follies."[1]

Chairman: So "several" of the diggers were still in town forty-seven years after the operation, and "many . . . living witnesses" were still around. But how can you call them witnesses to an activity they never witnessed?

Tucker: What do you mean?

Chairman: You call them "living witnesses," but to what? Will the clerk please read Mr. Tucker's first statement?

193

Clerk (reads): "And many others well remembering the stories of the time, are yet living witnesses."

Chairman: So all they can report is what they remember, forty-seven years after, not of the events, but of the *stories* "of the time." You, Mr. Tucker, claim to have been the most intimate associate of Smith during his digging period. How long did that period last?

Tucker: For at least seven years.[2]

Chairman: And do you in your book ever so much as hint at ever having witnessed any phase of those operations?

Tucker: I tell all about the digging in my book.

Chairman: But as an eye-witness to *any* of it?

Tucker: No. I got all my information from Smith himself. I report what I have "recollected from his own accounts."

Chairman: Exactly. In seven or eight years of secret conversations Smith told you everything. But in all that time you never *saw* a thing! Who were these diggers?

W. Stafford: The Smiths "had around them constantly a worthless gang, whose employment was to dig money nights."[3]

Chairman: Did you ever join in the digging yourself?

W. Stafford: Well, yes. Of course, all of Smith's wild tales "I regarded as visionary. However, being prompted by curiosity, I at length accepted of their invitations, to join them in their nocturnal excursions."[4]

Chairman: So that made you one of the "worthless gang."

W. Stafford: I resent that, sir! I was merely a curious spectator.

Chairman: Were these digging activities secret?

W. Stafford: Indeed they were. Once when I came by accident upon Joseph Smith, Sr., and two other men with hoes and shovels in the woods, "on seeing me they ran like wild men to get out of sight."[5]

Chairman: Yet they constantly invited you to witness their indiscretions. Did they invite others?

J. Capron: Yes, all the time. Smith "would often tell his neighbors of his wonderful discoveries, and urge them to embark in the money digging business."

Chairman: And did they accept?

Capron: They did: "A gang was soon assembled. . . . Some of them were influenced by curiosity, others were sanguine in their expectations of immediate gain."[6]

P. Ingersoll: "I had frequent invitations to join the company, but always declined."[7]

Chairman: But didn't you say something earlier about helping Smith, Sr., in such a project?

Ingersoll: Oh yes. I just did it for a joke. "The old man, finding that all his efforts to make me a money-digger had proved abortive, at length ceased his importunities."[8]

Chairman: Now Mr. W. Stafford has told us that the Smiths "had about them constantly a worthless gang" of diggers. And Mr. Capron gives us to understand that this gang was recruited among the neighbors, some of whom even admit their complicity. Not very nice neighbors, I would say.

Eber D. Howe: Oh, they weren't the regular gang. That was Joe's "phalanx," regularly designated as the "money-diggers."[9]

Chairman: And did they believe that Joe could lead them to treasures?

Tucker: Absolutely! It is amazing what complete trust they had in him.[10]

Chairman: Did the Smiths themselves believe there was treasure there?

Howe: The affidavits make that clear enough. Old Smith, Sr., was especially infatuated by the idea.

Ingersoll: Once he said to me, "You notice, said he, the large stones on the top of the ground . . . They are, in fact, most of them chests of money raised by the heat of the sun."[11]

Chairman: If he believed all these treasures were on *top* of the ground, why was the old man always urging you to help him *dig?*

Ingersoll: Ask him.

Chairman: I don't need to. There is one thing that everybody knows about treasure-hunters, and that is that they are desperately determined not to share their secrets.

Howe: Well, our witnesses say that the Smiths were very mysterious and secretive about the business.

Chairman: And also that they not only invited but constantly importuned all the neighbors to join in with them, welcoming them even as idle spectators. That was a necessary fiction to account for the presence of witnesses, but it won't do. Gangs of professional diggers who are sure they have their fingers on the loot don't go around inviting others to learn their secrets and share their swag. It just won't wash, as the saying goes. Who is the earliest witness to all this? You sir, what is your name?

Obadiah Dogberry: Dogberry, editor of the Palmyra *Reflector.*

Chairman: What can you tell us about this digging?

Dogberry: It certainly "did not originate by any means with Smith [Sr.]" At that time "the *MANIA* of money-digging soon began rapidly to diffuse itself through many parts of this country; men and women without distinction of age or sex became marvelous wise in the occult sciences, many dreamed, and others saw visions disclosing . . . rich and shining treasures."[12]

Chairman: You are not just describing Smith, Sr.'s, activities?

Dogberry: No. As I say, everybody everywhere had the *mania.*

J. B. Turner: Smith, Jr., simply followed the trend.

"While he condemned all else as the work of the devil," he accepted "the stone mania" in his followers.[13]

Chairman: What is the "stone mania"?

Dogberry: "Mineral rods and balls . . . were supposed to be infallible guides to these sources of wealth — '*peep stones*' or pebbles, taken promiscuously from the brook or field, were placed in a hat or other situation excluded from the light, when some *wizard* or *witch* . . . applied their eyes, and . . . declared they saw all wonders of nature, including of course, ample stores of silver and gold."[14]

Chairman: Treasure-hunting and visions seem to go hand in hand.

Earnest S. Bates: Yes, Smith, Sr. "was much addicted to the popular frontier sport of digging for buried treasure and was also given to religious visions."[15]

Chairman: So there was nothing unusual at the time in being a money-digger and even a visionary, after all. And yet these things were held as crimes against the Smiths?

Rev. Henry Caswall: The Smiths "spent much of their time in digging for money, which they pretended had been hidden in the earth during the revolutionary war. . . . Their whole object appears to have been to live without work, upon the industry of others."[16]

Chairman: They merely *pretended* there was buried treasure? How could they know whether there was or not, so as to be able to pretend?

Mrs. Cooley: I have often heard my relative, "Jeremiah Lyke, . . . say that Joe Smith, whom he knew well, was a lazy, shiftless fellow, hunting and fishing day times, and at night pretending to dig for treasures in that hill" in front of his house.[17]

Chairman: Apparently this lazy, shiftless fellow found no time for anything as tiring as sleep, and "to wrap his movements in a mystery," to quote Mr. Howe, he did his digging right in front of his own house. Now you say, according to your relative who knew Smith very well, that he only *pretended* to dig for treasures. Why did he pretend to do a disreputable thing like that if he did not actually do it?

Tucker: Oh, he did it, all right. "The fame of Smith's money-digging performances had been sounded far and near. The newspapers had heralded and ridiculed them. The pit-hole memorials of his treasure explorations were numerous."[18]

Chairman: Strange that none of the newspaper notices have ever turned up. It was you, sir, who stated that Smith's great cave near Palmyra, his greatest digging of all, "scarcely attracted the curiosity of outsiders," yet now you tell us that the newspapers even "heralded" his minor diggings. What are we to believe?

Mrs. Dr. Horace Eaton: I can explain that. "Little or no attention was paid to the performances of Smith near his home."[19]

Chairman: Then how did his digging make him so famous?

Tucker: Famous is hardly the word, sir.

Chairman: You said his fame went far and wide, and George Arbaugh, following W. D. Purple, tells that it was because Joseph Smith's fame had spread so that Josiah Stowell hired him to dig for money.[20]

Eaton: Well, it's true that "lovers of the marvelous" came from far away, and "visited the several excavations and wondered."[21]

Chairman: You mean that a few holes in the ground, which, according to all reports, never yielded a thing, actually brought sight-seers, "lovers of the marvelous" to your part of the country? What was marvelous about the holes?

Howe: It wasn't the holes themselves, but the idea of the treasure hunters.

Chairman: But Mr. Dogberry has told us that everybody was digging away all over the country before Smith ever got started. What could be less interesting than just another hole dug by just another treasure-hunter? And why would Joseph Smith get fame and a title for doing what everyone else was doing—only more secretly?

John Quincy Adams: It must have been the immense scope of his operations that distinguished him from the others.

Chairman: Mrs. Eaton mentioned only "the several excavations" near Palmyra, which did not sound like very much. Were there more?

Adams: Were there? "Acres of ground near Palmyra, and elsewhere, were dug over."[22]

George B. Arbaugh: "In 1822 . . . under Jo's direction fourteen men dug a great hole on the farm of Joseph McKune, which fifty years later was used as a swimming pool. . . . It seems that he superintended many similar diggings."[23]

Chairman: Dear me. In less than forty years "the lapse of time and natural causes" had completely obliterated Mr. Tucker's 165–foot cave and Smith's last digging; the original dimensions of these other digs must have been tremendous. Do you realize, sir, how much digging with picks and shovels it takes to make just *one* swimming pool? And what the chances are of keeping such an operation secret while you are doing it and after? And can you imagine the most lazy, shiftless man on earth, at the age of sixteen "superintending many similar diggings"? Oliver Cowdery has commented on this. Will the clerk please read Cowdery's Eighth Letter?

Clerk (reads): They say "that he was always notorious for his idleness," yet he has "been accused of digging down all, or nearly so, the mountains of Susquehannah, or causing others to do it by some art of necromancy."[24]

James H. Hunt: The indolent character of Smith is not incompatible with the accomplishment: indeed, it explains it. "Being withal too lazy to make a living by honest industry, their minds [the Smiths', that is] seemed entirely directed towards discovering where these treasures were concealed. . . . Our hero . . . gather[ed] a horde of idle, credulous young men to perform the labor of digging. . . . In the course of time numerous excavations were made."[25]

Chairman: And all that work was done by idle young men at the behest of a lazy kid who was "shunned by the boys of his own age"? What was the secret of his irresistible appeal?

Howe: It was money. He promised them wealth.

Chairman: And did he ever deliver?

Cooley: I can answer that. "Jeremiah Lyke [the one who knew Smith so well] . . . never for a moment thought that they ever found any treasure."[26]

Gen. John Eaton: That is right. Joe "found people who could be fooled; considerable digging was done under his direction, but he never discovered any treasures."[27]

Hunt: "In the course of time numerous excavations were made, but, unfortunately, they never dug deep enough to find the object of their search."[28]

C. Sheridan Jones: I must disagree with these witnesses. "The turning point in Smith's career" came when,

> learning from a strolling Indian of a place where treasure was said to be buried, Smith had gone out to dig for it. On the way he met with another party of diggers, intent on the same object, and a dispute arose as to the *locus* of the treasure. Now Smith's father had claimed to be a "diviner," . . . and young Joe claimed now—perhaps not for the first time—to have inherited the power. He boldly located the treasure, and challenged his rival to test his belief as to where it lay. By a coincidence, one of the most fruitful in his life, it turned out that he was right. The treasure, a few gold coins, was found at the spot he indicated, and Joe Smith became a force! [From that moment the] ragged, ill-clad young man was a per-

son to be reckoned with, and everywhere his services were in request.[29]

Chairman: A very remarkable story, sir, not the least remarkable thing about it being that you are apparently the only person who has ever heard of it. How does it happen that none of the earlier "witnesses" knows anything about this sensational and vastly publicized discovery that made Smith a real figure in the world? And what is this "perhaps not for the first time"? Don't you know whether this was Smith's first treasure-locating exploit or not? Here Smith is supposed to have been digging for years, yet you describe this as his first find.

J. S. C. Abbott: It was certainly not his first find. Smith "had *seer stones,* in which the illiterate had faith. He had already exhumed from the Indian mounds many mysterious antiquities, not a few of which, it was conjectured, were of his own manufacture."[30]

Chairman: So lazy Joe not only dug everywhere, but toiled away at forging antiquities—what a worker! And you say that this was before the great and sensational find which Mr. Jones reports?

Editor of the American Whig Review: Since "his *childhood* was spent following the occupation of a money-digger, . . . we find Smith, in his early youth, following his father, pickaxe on shoulder, digging eagerly into whatever might seem an Indian tomb . . . and subsisting by the plunder of henroosts, or upon whatever else fortune might throw in his way."[31]

E. C. Blackman: And it was "a straggling Indian" who told Joe of the buried treasure that Mr. Jones referred to. Only he didn't find anything. He "dug a great hole which can still be seen."[32]

Chairman: Another of his many swimming pools. Jones says the treasure was "found at the spot indicated," but if he had any divination at all, or if anyone believed he had, why would it be necessary to dig over the area of a swimming pool? Smith is supposed to have put his finger on the spot, isn't that so, Mr. Tucker? I believed you have described what you claim to be Smith's first digging.

Tucker: In a "dead hour of night . . . the work of digging began at his signal, . . . the magician meanwhile indicating, by some sort of wand in his hand, the *exact spot* where the spade was to be crowded into the earth."[33]

Chairman: Thank you. Here we have them digging over the area of a swimming pool after the *exact spot* has been indicated. Hunt says it was because they never went *deep* enough that the diggers never found anything—why didn't they dig more deeply and less widely? It is all too absurd. Your youthful Joseph must have been a phenomenally industrious boy.

Chorus of Voices: Oh, *he* didn't do the digging!

Chairman: But Mr. Abbott said *he* had exhumed lots of stuff from Indian mounds, and the *American Whig Review* said *he* followed his father with his pickaxe and dug eagerly, and Mrs. Blackman said *he* dug a great hole that can still be seen. Let's get this straight: did Joe dig or didn't he?

Hunt: He did not. "We cannot learn that the Prophet ever entered those excavations, to perform any portion of the labor, his business being to point out the locations of the treasures, which he pretended to do by looking at a stone placed in his hat."[34]

Howe: Mr. Hunt's statement is correct because it is stolen from me. What I wrote was that Smith "soon collected about him a gang of idle, credulous young men to perform the labor of digging. . . . In the process of time many pits were dug in the neighborhood. . . . But we do not learn that the young impostor ever entered these excavations for the purpose of assisting his sturdy dupes in their labors."[35]

Chairman: In other words, there is actually no evidence

that Smith ever dug for treasure at all! But if I find it hard to believe that the lazy and shiftless Joe should have excavated many acres in and around Palmyra and dug many excavations similar to the swimming pool on the McKune farm, I find it just as hard to believe that he could have induced a number of "idle, credulous young men" to do the same. How did it happen?

The mighty band

John C. Bennett: The Smiths "kept around them, constantly, a gang of worthless fellows who dug for money at nights, and were idle in the daytime. . . . It was a mystery to their neighbors how they got their living."[36]

Chairman: So Joe inherited the gang from his family?

S. B. Emmons: Not at all! "*He* had the address to collect about him a gang of idle and credulous young men, whom he employed in digging for hidden treasures."[37]

Chairman: At least you agree on one thing: Joseph Smith "employed" these men to dig for him, and it was he who organized the gang, which he "collected about him." What did he pay them with?

Mrs. Eaton: He hired them "with cider and strong drink."[38]

Mrs. Ellen Dickinson: No, it wasn't that; they were after treasure. Joe "became the head of a band that slept during the day and wandered in the night-time to such places as they were directed to by their leader to dig for hidden treasures. Joe laid down certain laws to his 'phalanx' in their operations."[39]

Chairman: When was this?

Dickinson: It was well before 1819. There were fourteen in the band.[40]

Chairman: So Joe at the age of twelve rules his band with an iron hand and makes them work their heads off—for cider?

Lu B. Cake: Mrs. Dickinson is mistaken. "He first organized a society at the house of Joe Knight, on the South side of the river, near the Lobdell House, in Broome County. Excavations were made in various places for treasures, and rocks containing iron pyrites were drilled for gold." That was "somewhere about 1828 or 1829."[41]

Chairman: That, you say, was his first society. What about the gang of fourteen?

R. C. Doud: In 1822 I was employed, with thirteen others, by Oliver Harper, to dig for gold under Joe's directions. [42]

Chairman: So it was not Joe at all, but Mr. Harper, who hired the fourteen, and there was no "phalanx" at all. Did any others hire Joe?

Isaac Hale: "I first became acquainted with Joseph Smith, Jun., in November, 1825. He was at that time in the employ of a set of men who were called 'money-diggers'; and his occupation was that of seeing."[43]

Chairman: So it seems that the "money-diggers" employed Smith, and not the other way around. Now Mr. Doud says the others were digging "under Joe's directions." How did he direct them, Mr. Doud?

Doud: I don't know. Smith "was not present at the time."[44]

Chairman: So Joseph Smith, only it wasn't Joseph Smith, organized a gang, only it wasn't a gang, to dig for treasure, only it wasn't treasure, under his direction, only he didn't direct it. Perhaps Mr. Tucker, Smith's closest associate, can enlighten us.

Tucker: Smith claimed to spy out treasures in the ground. "Of course but few persons were sufficiently stolid to listen to these silly *pretentions*. . . . Yet he *may* have had believers."[45]

Chairman: So Mr. Howe's band of idle and credulous young men now fades to a mere conjecture. When would Smith have got these helpers?

Tucker: It was not until 1820 that he finally got people

to help him dig on "the then forest hill, a short distance from his father's house."

Chairman: Then 1820 was his first digging, Mr. Tucker?

Tucker: Yes. "This was the inauguration of the impostor's money-digging performance, . . . [the] first trial," though as has been said, Joe didn't dig—he merely located the treasure.[46]

Rev. J. E. Mahaffey: But he had already been doing that for years!

Chairman: How do you know that, Mr. Mahaffey?

Mahaffey: Because "his name appears in the criminal records of 1817. An old man testifies that Smith was about this time employed to locate wells and look for gold with his 'divining rods' of witch-hazel and his 'seerstone' in that community. He was put in the Onondago County jail for 'vagrancy and debt.' "[47]

Chairman: But people went right on hiring the eleven-year-old criminal. It occurs to me that "sturdy dupes" and "indolent young men" no matter how "credulous" do *not* let a fourteen-year-old or twelve-year-old kid make fools of them night after night while they go on with their back-breaking toil. They want results. What did they do when the treasure failed to materialize? Does anyone remember?

Hale: I do. "When they had arrived in digging to near the place where he had stated an immense treasure would be found, he said the enchantment was so powerful that he could not see. They then became discouraged, and soon after dispersed." That was on November 17, 1825.[48]

Chairman: That, at least, is a natural and understandable reaction—nobody likes to go on digging for nothing: "They then became discouraged, and soon after dispersed." But how long did these pointless operations continue? What kept them going?

Howe: "Whenever the diggers became dissatisfied at not finding the object of their desires, his inventive and fertile genius would generally contrive a story to satisfy them. For instance, he would tell them that the treasure was removed by a spirit just before they came to it, or that it sunk down deeper into the earth."[49]

Chairman: And that satisfied them, after all their toil — those lazy young men?

Howe: I said it *generally* satisfied them.

Chairman: But if Smith was to stay in business — and keep his health! — he would have to satisfy them *every* time. "Whenever" means always but "generally" means sometimes. Which was it?

Mrs. Eaton: Smith always gave them the same explanation: Someone "always broke the spell by speaking — the riches were spirited away to another quarter, and the digging must be resumed another night. Thus matters went on for seven or eight years."[50]

Chairman: You mean the idle, credulous young men took this beating for seven or eight *years*?

Tucker: That is right: "The imposture was renewed and repeated at frequent intervals from 1820 to 1827."[51]

Chairman: And in all that time they went right on digging, though they never found a thing. And what kind of people were these?

Dickinson: " 'The diggers,' as they were called, consisted of a band of genuine vagabonds, with Joe as their leader."[52]

Chairman: One does not give orders to "genuine vagabonds" or get them to do a lot of hard work by "satisfying" them over and over again with the same lame, repetitious explanation. You expect us to be as credulous as they.

Tucker: "It certainly evidences extraordinary talent or subtlety, that for so long a period he could maintain the potency of his art over numbers of beings in the form of manhood, acknowledging their faith in his supernatural powers."[53]

Chairman: Yet this is the identical Smith, Mr. Tucker, whom *you* "distinctly remembered" between the ages of twelve and twenty as being "noted *only* for his indolent and vagabondish character." And now you want to attribute "extraordinary talent or subtlety" to him! It is hardly extraordinary, sir, that of the "numbers of beings" who for seven or eight years dug vigorously all about the landscape, neither you nor anyone else has ever given a single name, though the rascals must all have been as well known to you as Smith himself; it is indeed extraordinary that in seven or eight years of digging up "acres of ground around Palmyra and elsewhere" Smith never got arrested for trespassing on anyone's property, though he made holes as big as swimming tanks, and was never sued for damages; it is most extraordinary that of the hundreds of people he bilked out of their money in his digging projects, not one ever came forward either to sue him or complain of his practices. What did Smith have to gain by all of this?

J. D. Kingsbury: "He could see where there was lost treasure and guide people to find chests of gold. In this way he picked up many a penny, and he learned the credulity of man." This was before his vision at fifteen.[54]

Jones: "Joe did well on his 'peek stone.' . . . He raised money to enable him to dig for larger treasure. And if his failures were many and his successes few, still his reputation grew and he prospered."[55]

Chairman: Then he did have some success in locating stuff?

Tucker: Of course not! "It is . . . needless to add that no genuine discoveries of stolen property were made in this manner, and that the entire proceeds derived from the speculation went into Joe's pocket."[56]

Chairman: Why is it "needless to add"?

Tucker: Naturally, he never found anything.

Chairman: Then how did he stay in business through the years? How could his reputation grow if it was only a reputation for failure? What kind of customers did he have?

Dr. Harry M. Beardsley: "Gullible customers, seeking to

recover lost articles, locate stray calves, etc., . . . contributed appreciable to the family exchequer. True, these customers found no chests of gold. . . . But there was always some plausible reason why the magic failed. The moon was not in the right phase, Joe explained."[57]

Chairman: So through the years what people paid for in making their substantial contributions to the family exchequer was not the finding of objects by Smith but a routine explanation of why he never found anything. Even Mr. Tucker has testified that the *only* action ever taken against Smith was one suit to obtain payment of a small debt (though he gave no evidence); yet now we are asked to believe that he openly, systematically, notoriously took people's money in a confidence racket which over the years never returned a penny to the victims — and got away with it! How did he do it?

Tucker: "Individuals were impelled, in their donations in this business, by the motive of ridding themselves of Smith's importunities." In this way he secured "a handsome surplus."[58]

Chairman: So they paid him to tell them where to dig for treasure, just to get rid of him and his "importunities" — this unsocial boy whose one outstanding trait, according to you, was his "taciturnity," — who hid out in the woods and only spoke to his closest associates? How did he "importune" people to distraction — with sign-language? You say his power over his gang was extraordinary, but what was his secret with the general public, to *compel* them ("impelled" is a feeble attempt to dodge the issue) not only to tolerate a fraud, but actually to contribute their hard-earned money to support it? From all you have said, sir, you and your fellow citizens were either Smith's puppets or accessories to his crimes. Now if Smith pocketed all the proceeds from these operations, how did his gang stay alive — and satisfied?

Mrs. Eaton: They got *cider* for their work! "All who could be hired with cider or strong drink were organized into a digging phalanx."[59]

Tucker: Yes, he paid them with money and whiskey.[60]

Chairman: Then they were simply hired workers. They were neither idle nor credulous, since they worked hard not for promises but for pay. I believe some solid citizens are supposed to have paid a good deal.

Orvilla S. Belisle: That is right. Mr. Stowell "swallowed with avidity his [Smith's] monstrosities," and gave him "several large sums of money" to dig for treasure for him.[61]

Caswall: He told Stowell "that he had discovered a cave on the banks of Black River in New York in which he had found a bar of gold as thick as his leg, and about three or four feet long, . . . that if Stowell would convey him with his wife to Manchester, he would get a chisel and mallet and accompany him to the cave. . . . The old Dutchman gladly acceded to this arrangement."[62]

Mahaffey: You see how "he fooled the credulous and superstitious and eked out a precarious subsistence."[63]

Chairman: A "precarious subsistence" hardly sounds like Mr. Tucker's "handsome surplus." But since the credulous and superstitious were willing to pay, why were the operations conducted at night?

Digging techniques

Adams: Because "midnight, with a full moon, was the most desirable time" to dig for treasure.[64]

Jones: "Certain weird ceremonies were invariably connected with the money-digging operations. Midnight and a full moon were held to be essential, and Good Friday was the best date. Joe Smith would direct operations with a wand, sternly enjoining silence, and the simple neighbors would stand around with chattering teeth, afraid to utter a word lest it should break the spell."[65]

Belisle: "Many a night between the witching hours of twelve and one, when there was neither moon, nor stars to spy upon them, had they stolen out to unearth the hidden treasure; but as often they averred, the gnomes that guarded it thwarted them, and they were forced to do as they always had, resort to their wits."[66]

Chairman: Was that the gang, or the Smith family?

Howe: It began with the family: "One night, when darkness had closed over the earth, and ghosts and spirits are supposed to leave their nooks, the elder Smith, followed by Joseph and Hyrum, wended their way . . . to a spot [where] . . . tradition said that, during the Revolutionary war, the British paymaster, while at New York had been robbed of three kegs of gold. . . . All through that night, the next, and many other nights, incantations were made, spirits called, but they refused to give any sign of their presence or reveal the spot of the precious deposit. As months went on, and even years, Joseph Smith, Sr., relinquished the sceptre to the more hopeful hands of his son."[67]

Chairman: And how did you find out about these ultra secret operations? They were very secret, weren't they?

Howe: We have agreed on that—"wrapped in secrecy."

Chairman: Yet according to Mr. Jones the operations were open to the public, with "the simple neighbors" standing around "with chattering teeth," in the light of the full moon, which we are also assured was "essential" to success, though Mrs. Belisle assures us that they dug "when there was neither moon, nor stars to spy upon them." Whom are we supposed to believe? We are told that certain weird ceremonies were "invariably connected with the money-digging operations," requiring among other things a full moon or, according to some, the dark of the moon. What were the ceremonies?

David Stafford: "Joseph Sen. first made a circle. . . . He then stuck in the ground a row of witch-hazel sticks. . . . He next stuck a steel rod in the centre of the circles.

. . . After we had dug . . . [he] went to the house to inquire of young Joseph the cause of our disappointment."[68]

Chairman: Then Smith, Jr., was not on the scene?

Howe: As has been stated by me and others, there is *no* evidence that Smith, Jr., ever participated in the digging.

Chairman: Yet we have been told that he "would direct operations with a wand, sternly enjoining silence." Now it seems we can find not a single eyewitness who ever saw Joseph Smith at one of these diggings. These circles were essential?

American Whig Review: Yes. In their treasure digging they would form a *circle of stones*. The neighbor that described this "sagely concludes, 'that the business brought them more mutton than gold.' "[69]

The sheep story

Chairman: Why more mutton than gold?

George Seibel: Because once "one easy-going and superstitious farmer furnished a sheep for a blood offering."[70]

American Whig Review: That's right. There is a report that "once a black sheep was sacrificed to the evil spirit guarding the treasure, and when this too failed, the Smiths went home and ate the sheep."[71]

W. Stafford: So "the only time they ever made money-digging a profitable business" was when the Smiths ate the sheep. I furnished the sheep.[72]

Chairman: You, Sir?

W. Stafford: Yes. "To gratify my curiosity, I let them have a large fat sheep. . . . This, I believe, is the only time they ever made money-digging a profitable business."[73]

Chairman: If I remember correctly, Mr. Stafford, you accepted an invitation to join the "worthless gang," as you called them, in another of "their nocturnal excursions." Was this before or after you gave them the sheep?

W. Stafford: It was before.

Chairman: Was the first expedition successful?

W. Stafford: It was a complete fiasco, with a mystic circle, witch-hazel wands and all the rest, but no treasure.

Chairman: Just what did Smith, Jr., do on that occasion?

W. Stafford: I didn't see him. He stayed in the house.[74]

Chairman: Dear me. And what did Smith do on the second excursion?

W. Stafford: I don't know. I wasn't there.

Chairman: Is it possible! Why did you go the first time?

W. Stafford: I was "prompted by curiosity."

Chairman: And why did you give the Smiths "a large, fat sheep"?

W. Stafford: "To gratify my curiosity," as I said.

Chairman: So having satisfied yourself the first time that the whole thing was a fraud, you were still dubious enough to pay a high price for more of the same? And having paid a fabulous fee for a ringside seat at the second performance (wouldn't a small, skinny sheep have done just as well?), you failed to attend, in spite of urging!

W. Stafford: Oh, I knew it was a fraud. I just wanted to see what would happen — "to gratify my curiosity."

Chairman: And did they gratify your curiosity?

W. Stafford: "They afterwards informed me, that the sheep was killed pursuant to commandment; but as there was some mistake in the process, it did not have the desired effect."

Chairman: So *they told* you what happened after it was all over, and you were willing to pay a fat sheep for the routine explanation. Your story is fantastic, sir. It is a famous story for which you are the only witness, and it turns out that you are not a witness at all. You are a rustic yarn-spinner.

Cake: But there wasn't just one sheep. There were many. Before this, when Smith was drilling iron pyrites for gold, "previous to digging in *any* place a sheep was killed and the blood sprinkled upon the spot. Lot 62 was the seat of one of these mining operations."[75]

Chairman: So now it would seem that sheep were not killed just once but always, and that in the course, not of treasure hunting, but of perfectly legitimate mining operations.

Dickinson: "When Joe wanted fresh meat for his family he gave out that it would be necessary to insure the success of the 'diggers,' as these worthies were called, by having a black sheep killed, as a sacrificial offering before going to work."[76]

Chairman: Now our single sheep has grown into a regular meat supply.

J. H. Kennedy: No, that is wrong. Only one story of that character has been placed on record.[77]

D. Stafford: You are mistaken, sir. "At different times I have seen them come from the woods early in the morning, bringing meat which looked like mutton. I went into the woods one morning very early . . . and found Joseph Smith, Sen, in company with two other men, with . . . meat that looked like mutton. On seeing me they ran like wild men to get out of sight."[78]

Chairman: You are not consistent, sir. You say you saw this "at different times," and then clearly imply that you saw it just once, and by accident.

Blackman: It wasn't always mutton. When he was digging for Mr. Harper, Smith said he would have to have a perfectly white dog, though some say it was a black dog, since it was substituted for a black ram. But then he said a white sheep would do as well, and when the treasure failed to turn up, he said it was because a white sheep had been offered instead of a white dog.[79]

Chairman: So, being in the mutton business, Smith would not accept a white sheep for a black sheep, but insisted on a white dog—or a black dog, Mr. Tucker?

Tucker: There was only one sheep, and its flesh was eaten by the starving Smiths, for "meat was a rarity at his father's home."[80]

Emily M. Austin: When Smith was digging on Old Uncle Joe Knight's farm, "he told them there was a charm on some of the pots of money, and if some animal was killed and the blood sprinkled around the place, then they could get it. So they killed a dog . . . but again money was scarce in those diggings. Still, they dug and dug, but never came to the precious treasure. . . . And now they were obliged to give up in despair, and Joseph went back again to his father's, in Palmyra."[81]

Chairman: And this is the sort of thing that put his talents in such demand?

Dickinson: Yes. He would have the black sheep killed when his family wanted meat, "as a sacrificial offering before going to work. This state of affairs continued for some time, and his reputation extended to the adjacent counties, which he often visited."[82]

Chairman: And the Knight exploit was typical?

Austin: "While I was visiting my sister, we . . . walked out to see the places where they had dug for money, and laughed to think of the absurdity . . . in such a thought or action."[83]

Chairman: I am laughing too, but not at Smith.

Sidney Bell (indignantly, tears streaming down his face): It is no laughing matter, sir! *You* may find these stories very contradictory, and say there is not a scrap of evidence to prove them, but there was one piece of evidence which was grim enough, even if "but one evidence of the dark deeds of the night remained — the lifeless body of a little black dog."[84]

Chairman: How do you know it was little?

Bell: Haven't you any feelings at all, man? Haven't you any imagination?

Chairman: I have enough to see how you people have been playing with this legend as you pass it around. Now, is there any agreement among you tale-tellers as to how Smith got started in the peeping and digging business?

How it all began, or something

Kennedy: "The first venture made by young Smith in the line of mystification was as a 'Water Witch,' . . . gaining reputation thereby: and meeting with many failures, of which all mention was discreetly omitted by himself and [his] followers. . . . From locating subterranean veins of water he advanced to the discovery of hidden riches." In September 1819 he started looking for treasures with a peepstone.[85]

Mahaffey: No, it couldn't have been 1819, "as his name appears in the criminal records of 1817. An old man testifies that Smith was about this time employed to locate wells and look for gold with his 'divining rods' of witch hazel and his 'seer-stone.' "[86]

Tucker: You are both wrong! I have given a full account of his very first digging, which I had from Smith himself, and which took place in 1820.[87]

Willard Chase: Wrong! It was not until 1822 or after that "Joe began to aver that with his stone he could discover treasure, and see all things both above and beneath the earth."

Chairman: So now it is not only water and treasure beneath the earth but "*all* things both above and beneath the earth." Just how far did his claims go?

Seibel: "Many people paid [Smith] money for the exercise of his clairvoyant gifts," and when they failed, as they always did, "Joe had ever an ingenious explanation for the failure, and nearly always managed to placate the wrath of his disappointed dupes."[88]

Blackman: He "was in the habit of 'blessing' his neighbors' crops for a small consideration" — with disastrous results to the crops.[89]

Chairman: So his hard-headed Yankee neighbors went right on paying him good money to ruin their crops, just as they paid him to find all those treasures which he never found? I find all this a bit far-fetched. What of those whom he did not placate? I must remind you again that people do not like being made dupes of, yet the neighbors testify that no action of any kind was ever taken against this much-publicized menace, operating with impunity in many counties. It has been said that Smith began as a "water witch" with a witch-hazel rod; is that so?

W. Stafford: There is a misunderstanding here. The family used witch-hazel sticks, to detect and drive away evil spirits, when digging for money.[90]

Chairman: So it was not water but money after all, and it was a family affair?

Caswall: Yes. "When the worthless family engaged in their nocturnal excursions for money-digging," Joseph was always their conductor.[91]

Chairman: If Joseph was always in charge, what of all the tales about Smith, Sr., running the show?

American Whig Review: The father trained the son, who was "constantly revelling amid the wildest fictions which the avarice-stimulated imagination of his parents could fabricate."[92]

Caswall: It was his father who trained him, as Mr. Linn will confirm.[93]

Dickinson: No, it was his mother; "very early Mrs. Smith instructed her son Joseph to set up a claim for miraculous powers, which he willingly adopted."[94]

M. W. Montgomery: You are both wrong! "Even this 'peep-stone' humbug was an idea borrowed from a fortune-telling old woman who lived not many miles distant."[95]

William Alexander Linn: Wrong again! Joe picked up "crystal-gazing" in Pennsylvania.[96]

Chairman: Mr. Tucker does not think so.

Linn: "Tucker was evidently ignorant both of Joe's previous experience with 'crystal-gazing' in Pennsylvania and of crystal-gazing itself."[97]

Chairman: Who told you about this previous experience in Pennsylvania? After all, since Mr. Tucker is intimately acquainted with all of Smith's activities from the time he was twelve years old, there could hardly have been much "previous experience"!

Linn: The key to the digging is Mr. Blackman.

Blackman: I was merely quoting Mr. J. B. Buck.

J. B. Buck: I never said I saw Joe dig. I only said he was in Pennsylvania "soon after my marriage, which was in 1818, some years before he took to 'peeping' and before diggings were commenced under his direction. These were ideas he gained later."[98]

Chairman: So all Mr. Linn's prize witness can say is that Joe did *not* peep or dig when he knew him. It was only "some years" after 1818 that he gained those ideas, that is, not before 1821 at the earliest. When *did* Smith, Jr., learn about money-digging, Mr. Linn?

Linn: "The Elder Smith . . . was known as a money-digger while a resident of Vermont."[99]

Chairman: Then how can you insist that "these ideas were gained later" if Smith was exposed to them from childhood?

Linn: Sir, may I remind you that to this day my book is hailed as the most "scientific" work in existence on the life of Joseph Smith. It explains everything. Please pay attention:

> (1) The Elder Smith was known as a money-digger while a resident of Vermont.
>
> (2) Of course that subject was a matter of conversation in his family, and
>
> (3) his sons were of a character to share in his belief. . . .
>
> (4) The son Joseph . . . professed to have his father's gifts, and
>
> (5) . . . soon added to his accomplishments the power to locate hidden riches.

(6) It can easily be imagined how interested any member of the Smith family would have been in an exhibition like that of a 'crystal-gazer,' and we are able to trace very consecutively Joe's first introduction to the practice, and the use he made of the hint thus given.[100]

Chairman: To what hint do you refer?

Linn: To the hint picked up in Pennsylvania.

Chairman: Yet according to your only witness it took him several years to react to the hint — though the so-called witness was nowhere around when he did. Allow me a brief commentary on the scientific objectivity of your report, point by point:

(1) First you merely state that Smith, Sr., *"was known as a money-digger"* in Vermont, though you do not say by whom, when, and how that was known and reported;

(2) then you say the family discussed the business — and your evidence for that is simply a casual *"of course"*;

(3) next you say the Smith boys went along, not because there is any evidence that they did, but because in your estimation they *"were of a character"* to do it;

(4) then you say that Joseph Smith, Jr., *"professed* to have his father's gifts" — when and where did he ever make such a profession? and

(5) that he "soon *added"* to it "the power to locate hidden riches." But what gift did he profess, if the treasure-finding was an *added* gift?

(6) Further, there is no evidence that the Smiths ever took to crystal-gazing, and your only proof for it is that "it can easily be *imagined"*;

7) finally, you claim "to trace very consecutively Joe's first introduction to the practice" to a *"hint"* he received when he was eleven years old in Pennsylvania. But a hint is only a possible source, never a proven one.

Linn: He reacted to the hint, didn't he?

Chairman: But not until "some years" later, according to your informant. And how was he to know what particular hint Smith was reacting to far away and years later? But do you actually think this is a "scientific" presentation of evidence?

Beardsley: I consider myself quite as scholarly as Mr. Linn. Let *me* tell you what happened.

> On the outskirts of a little village in New York State in the year James Monroe became President of the United States for the second time, a barefoot boy waded along a gravelly creek, looking for "lucky stones" when he should have been hoeing corn. Wearying of the search, he threw himself face downwards in the grass in the shade of a maple tree, pulled a precious 'lucky stone' from his pocket, and placed it in the crown of his battered old felt hat.

That's how it all began.[101]

Chairman: Dr. Beardsley, did you ever read the story of Susannah and the elders? If you will recall, two vile old men accused the chaste Susannah of immoral practices which they claimed to have witnessed together in a garden. The youthful Daniel proved them both liars by asking each separately, "Under what kind of a tree and where in the garden did you behold her?" The one promptly answered, "It was under a *schinon* [a mastich tree]," and the other just as emphatically declared, "It was under a *prinon* [an evergreen-oak tree]." Now tell me, doctor, how do you know it was a maple tree under which the boy reclined, and who was there to report it?

Beardsley: That is, after all, a very trivial point.

Chairman: Not when your authority and Smith's reputation depend on it. Is there anything at all in your little story that is not fanciful?

Beardsley: Certainly there is. The peepstone and the hat. Those are realities. All the books tell about them.

Chairman: Then let us hear about the peepstone. How did Smith get it?

J. Smith, peepstones for all occasions

F. Lapham: According to Joseph Smith, Sr., "his son Joseph, . . . when he was about fourteen years of age, happened to be where a man was looking into a dark stone and telling people therefrom where to dig for money and other things. Joseph requested the privilege of looking into the stone, which he did by putting his face into the hat where the stone was. It proved to be not the right stone for him; but he could see some things, and among them he saw the stone, and where it was, in which he could see whatever he wished to see. . . . The place where he saw the stone was not far from their house, and under pretense of digging a well, they found water and the stone at a depth of twenty or twenty-two feet. After this, Joseph spent about two years looking into this stone, telling fortunes, where to find lost things and where to dig for money and other treasures."[102]

Chairman: But a number of other witnesses have already told us that Smith was in the peeping business years before that. Aren't you a bit late?

Chase: Lapham doesn't put the date too late, he puts it much too early! It wasn't until 1822 that they dug the well, and there was no "pretense" about it! I was digging it myself—in fact there was no one in the well but myself when the stone was found. "After digging about 20 feet below the surface . . . we discovered a singularly appearing stone which excited my curiosity."[103]

Chairman: There is no doubt but that this is the same well—the "20 feet" line proves that—but you say it was you who dug the well, not the Smiths, that you discovered the stone, and that yours was the first curiosity attracted by it. What did you do with it?

Chase: Smith asked to see it, "put it into his hat and then his face into the top of the hat." He borrowed it from me and "began to publish abroad what wonders he could discover by looking in it. . . . He had it in his possession about two years."[104]

Chairman: That disposes of Mr. Lapham's story. But there seem to be some objections. Mr. Tucker?

Tucker: "Joseph Jr." was at the well-digging "as an idle looker-on"; it was Joseph Sr., Alvin, and Hyrum Smith who were doing the digging; when they dug up the stone the "lounger manifested a special fancy for this geological curiosity; and he carried it home with him, though this act of plunder was against the strenuous protestations of Mr. Chase's children, who claimed to be its rightful owners."[105]

Mrs. Eaton: That's *almost* right. "At the age of 15 while watching his father digging a well, Joe espied a stone of curious shape. . . . 'This little stone was the acorn of the Mormon oak.' "

Chairman: Is that the way it happened, Mr. Chase?

Chase: No! What happened was that "the next morning he came to see me, and wished to obtain the stone, alleging that he could see in it; I told him I did not wish to part with it, on account of its being a curiosity, but would lend it." After that "he made so much disturbance, that I ordered the stone to be returned to me again. He had it in his possession about two years."[106]

Chairman: Did you get it back at the end of that time?

American Whig Review: Certainly not! "Smith could never be prevailed upon to give it up." This very stone was "used in the translation of the Book of Mormon."[107]

Tucker: That's right. After he took it from the children, "Joseph kept this stone, and *ever afterward* refused its restoration to the claimants."[108]

Chairman: What kind of a stone was it?

George W. Cowles: I can answer that. It was "such a pebble as might any day be picked up on the shore of Lake Ontario — the common hornblende."[109]

Chairman: So any kind of stone would do for this peeping business?

Ingersoll: Just about. Once after a conversation with Joseph Smith, Sr., in the fields, in which he urged me to become a money-digger, "on my return I picked up a small stone and was carelessly tossing it from one hand to the other. Said he (looking very earnestly), what are you going to do with that stone? Throw it at the birds, I replied. No, said the old man, it is of great worth; and upon this I gave it to him."[110]

Chairman: What did he do with it?

Ingersoll: He put it into his hat, and after "sundry manoeuvres . . . took down his hat, and being very much exhausted, said in a faint voice, 'If you knew what I had seen, you would believe.' His son Alvin then went through the same performance, which was equally disgusting."

Chairman: Did you ever try to get the stone back?

Ingersoll: Of course not. It was just an ordinary stone.

Chairman: And we have heard that Mr. Chase's stone was also just an ordinary stone. Why was he so eager to get *his* stone back? Could Smith really see things in the stone, Mr. Chase?

Chase: Don't be absurd. It was all a hoax.

Chairman: Then why were you so extremely eager to get possession of this perfectly ordinary stone, *which you or Smith could have duplicated with ease any day?* Why did Hyrum and Joseph have fits when you asked them for it? If we are to believe our witnesses, they have drawers full of stones — and every one phony. Why all the excitement about one stone?

Chase: "It excited my curiosity." I asked for it back the first time because "he made so much disturbance, that I ordered the stone to be returned to me again. He had it in his possession about two years."

Chairman: Couldn't he have caused just as much disturbance with any other stone, since he was only faking? If it was such a menace, why did you lend it to him again and again? If not, why was he so anxious to have it?

Tucker: Can't you see? It was Mr. Chase's *children* who clamored for the stone. Joe Smith, "an idle looker-on and lounger" at the well-digging, "manifested a special fancy for this geological curiosity; and he carried it home with him, though the act of plunder was against the strenuous protestations of Mr. Chase's children, who claimed to be its rightful owners."[111]

Chairman: And where was Mr. Chase? Was he going to let a fifteen-year-old kid walk off with his property while his children howled in protest? Mr. Chase tells us that *he* found the stone while digging *his* well on *his* property, and that it excited *his* curiosity, and two years later, when *he* "ordered the stone to be returned," Smith gave it back to *him*. I think it rather obvious why Mr. Tucker told a totally different story fifty years after the event: it had to be the Chase *children* who got excited about the stone, because of the patent absurdity of having Chase, a grown man, get all worked up about a thing which he declared worthless, and which could be duplicated without any trouble.

Dickinson: I think if we study the matter we can give a more cautious and rational explanation of the whole thing. Let us put it this way: "While he [Smith] was watching the digging of a well, or himself digging it, he found, or pretended to find, a . . . stone."[112]

Chairman: That is the safe, conservative school, followed by some of Smith's latest biographers. Let me tell *you* a story: "While I was walking to work last week or today, or lying in my bed, I saw or heard, or my friend saw, a horse or a dog running or lying down in the street, or in a field." Notice with what exemplary caution I avoid the pitfalls of positive statement. Doesn't it give my story an air of modest objectivity? But can you tell me what happened? Did Smith find the stone or didn't he?

Dickinson: I don't think he did. "It has been said that this little stone . . . had been in the possession of Mrs. Smith's family for generations, and that she merely presented it to Joseph when he was old enough to work miracles with it: and that he hid it in the earth to find again when it was convenient."[113]

Chairman: You realize, of course, that what you say makes a hash of Mr. Chase's Revised Standard Version? Mr. Linn says that Smith first looked into a second-class peepstone in which he saw not any treasures, but another peepstone, which was the one he finally used. Did he use more than one stone?

J. Stowell: He must have, for when he was tried for fraud, he displayed in court a stone "about the size of a small hen's egg, in the shape of a high *instepped* shoe. It was composed of layers of different colors passing diagonally through it."[114]

Arbaugh: That "must have been the Chase stone, since it resembled 'a child's foot in shape' and was opaque"; it "was clearly not the Belcher stone."[115]

Chairman: What is this Belcher stone?

Blackman: Oh, don't you know? That was "the stone he afterwards used."

Chairman: After what?

Buck: After he took to peeping; that is, after I knew him in 1818. "The stone which he afterwards used was then in the possession of Jack Belcher, of Gibson, who obtained it while at Salina, New York, engaged in drawing salt. Belcher bought it because it was said to be 'a seeing stone.' I have often seen it."[116]

Chairman: In Smith's possession?

Buck: No. I told you I only knew Smith "some years before he took to 'peeping,' and *before* the diggings were commenced under his direction. . . . These were ideas he gained later."

Chairman: How do you know that Smith ever used that particular stone?

Buck: As I said, "I have often seen it. It was a green

stone, with brown, irregular spots on it. It was a little larger than a goose's egg, and about the same thickness."

Chairman: Your description shows that Mr. Arbaugh is right. That cannot possibly be the stone that the other witnesses described. Also, there is no doubt that you saw the stone. But since that was years before Smith got interested in stones, I don't see how you connect it up with him since you last saw him use it.

Cowles: What do you mean, years before? Haven't we been told that his father practiced peeping already in Vermont, and that the Chase stone had been in the family for a long time?

Mahaffey: That is right: "It had been in the family for generations."

Chairman: Then how could Mr. Chase claim that he personally dug it up in 1822?

Dickinson: The contradiction vanishes if we realize that Smith planted the stone there.[117]

Chairman: Why? Is a stone any more wonderful that is found by digging a well than if it has been in the family for years? Smith, we are told, was much too lazy to do any digging himself—he was only a lounging onlooker— yet the men had to dig down twenty feet before they came to it. A nice bit of stone-planting by Smith, so that Chase could lay legal claim to *his* precious stone! All this rationalizing and explaining is obviously meant to reconcile conflicting reports that discredit each other at every step.

Cowles: Oh, there were earlier stones, all right. "Long before the Gold Bible demonstration, the Smith family had with some sinister object in view, whispered another fraud in the ears of the credulous. They pretended that in digging for money, at Mormon Hill, they came across 'a chest, three feet by two in size, covered with a dark-colored stone.' In the center of the stone was a white spot about the size of a sixpence. Enlarging, the spot increased to the size of a 24–pound shot, and then exploded with a terrible noise. The chest vanished and all was utter darkness."[118]

Chairman: If I were giving prizes, Mr. Cowles, you should certainly get something for that one. There were no witnesses to the phenomenon?

Cowles: Of course not; the Smiths only "pretended" that it happened.

Chairman: And why would they pretend such a thing?

Cowles: "With some sinister object in view."

Chairman: You can't even guess what the object might have been yet you know it was "sinister." And to achieve it, they claimed there was something there which really wasn't there, and then, boom! It really *wasn't* there—and so they tell their story and prove their case. Are you sure there were any stones at all?

O. Turner: Yes, there were the stone spectacles. Actually they were the only stones Smith ever used.[119]

Chairman: How do you know that, sir?

Turner: I was very intimately acquainted with the Smith family at Palmyra, where I grew up with Joseph Smith, Jr. I know all about his money digging and treasure hunting, and have given a lengthy deposition on the subject, but I know nothing of any stone except "a pair of large spectacles" found with the gold plates. "The stones or glass set in frames were opaque to all but the prophet." These were the only peepstones he ever used.[120]

Chairman: More contradictions. Some important witnesses have stated that the Chase stone was actually identical with what Smith called the Urim and Thummim, is that not correct?

American Whig Review: That is correct. Chase tried to get the stone back, "but Smith could never be prevailed upon to give it up. It was afterwards used in the translation of the Book of Mormon and styled the mysterious Urim and Thummim."[121]

Howe: Imagine it! Two of the sixteen stones that belonged to the brother of Jared! We are asked to believe that "two of these stones were sealed up with the plates, according to a prediction before Abraham was born. How, and in what manner they became set in the 'two rims of a bow,' and fell into the hands of the Nephites, has not been explained, nor what has become of the remaining 14 molten stones, is likewise hidden in mystery."[122]

Thomas Gregg: One impeccable witness says they were "two small stones of a chocolate color, nearly egg-shaped and perfectly smooth, but not transparent . . . which were given him with the plates."[123]

Chairman: Then they cannot have been the stones mentioned by Mr. Howe, which were perfectly transparent. It is marvelous, sir, how you, the most-quoted authority on these matters should blithely identify any stone that comes along with Smith's peepstone.

Howe: Does it make so much difference? The main idea is that Smith had an obsession for magic stones. Any stone would do, as Mr. Ingersoll's testimony shows. Mrs. Brodie has discovered clear evidence of Smith's stone mania in the Book of Mormon itself.

Chairman: Indeed, and what is the evidence?

Howe: Here it is (reads): "Joseph's preoccupation with magic stones crept into the narrative . . . " and here is the proof: God "had given the Nephites . . . *two crystals* with spindles inside which directed the sailing of their ships."[124] There you have it—*two crystals*, Urim and Thummim!

Chairman: But what the Book of Mormon says is that the compass was given to *Lehi*, not Nephi, and that it consisted of a "round ball of curious workmanship; and it was of fine *brass*. And within the ball were two spindles" (1 Nephi 16:10). For Mrs. Brodie a bronze sphere becomes without the slightest effort "two crystals with spindles inside." Now this is most instructive: in the middle of the twentieth century an expert pretending to high scholarly objectivity sits at her desk and unwittingly turns out a *brand-new original peepstone story,* as if there were not enough already. Having glanced at the text only long enough to sustain the trend of her own wishful thinking, she gives us *two new crystals,* bred of an airy word. After that performance, can anyone maintain that any of the peepstone stories are not or cannot be pure fabrication? Another point: Didn't you say, Mr. Howe, that the Book of Mormon was discovered by peeping in the first place?

Howe: I said that "the mineral-rod necromancy of Joseph Smith, Jun., searching after Robert Kidd's money . . . found the plates of Nephi."[125]

Chairman: Then by peeping and dowsing the plates were discovered?

Arbaugh: It was search for buried treasure that gave Joseph Smith the idea of the "Golden Bible."[126]

Emmons: You will recall, sir, that Smith led "a gang of idle and credulous young men, whom he employed in digging for hidden treasures. It is pretended that, in one of the excavations they made, the mysterious plates from which the Golden Bible was copied were found. Such briefly is the origin of the Mormon faith."[127]

Howe: By this gang "many pits were dug in the neighborhood, which were afterwards pointed out as the place from whence the plates were excavated."[128]

Walter R. Martin: Smith "was engaged for the most part of his youth in seeking Captain Kidd's treasure and in gazing through 'peep stones.' "[129]

Hunt: Let a real old-timer get in a word, here! "In the course of time numerous excavations were made, but unfortunately, they never dug deep enough to find the object of their search. However, the good resulting from their labors overbalances their misfortunes, as Joe has since informed us that here the golden plates were found, containing the important facts upon which the salvation of the world depends."[130]

Chairman: So it is very clear that Smith found the gold

plates while he was digging for treasure. It is equally clear that he never dug without *first* using his peepstone.

Rev. John A. Clark: That is correct! "Long before the idea of a *Golden Bible* entered into their minds, in their excursions for money-digging . . . Jo used to be usually their guide, putting into his hat a peculiar stone he had through which he looked to decide where they should begin to dig."[131]

Chairman: So we know that Smith always used a stone when digging. Some of the best and oldest witnesses insist that he only had *one* peepstone, and with that stone he discovered the buried plates, and *with* the plates were found buried — guess what? The wonderful stone! Where did he get the stone? He found it with the plates. How did he find the plates? By looking in the stone! You see, gentlemen, how silly this all is. Now let's talk a little about that hat. Did Smith always use a hat in peeping?

. . . and that hat!

Hale: "The manner in which he pretended to read and interpret, was the same as when he looked for the money-diggers. With the stone in his hat, and his hat over his face, while the Book of Plates were at the same time hid in the woods!"[132]

Chairman: Why hid in the woods?

Hale: Because, as I explained yesterday, I would not allow the plates in my house. So they took them and hid them in the woods.

Chairman: But you were describing the translation as it took place at Smith's house, *not* at your house. Did they still have to keep the plates in the woods? This I am afraid is another example of the vagueness of your testimony and the eagerness with which you seize upon every opportunity to make Smith look ridiculous. Such things can backfire. But let's get back to the beginning. Smith always used a hat?

Beardsley: He did. When our history opens we see Joe, the "barefoot boy" looking at "a precious 'lucky stone' . . . placed . . . in the crown of his battered old felt hat."[133]

Daniel Hendrix: That hat! "I can see him now . . . with his uncombed hair sticking through the holes in his old battered hat."[134]

Chairman: Why did he put the stone in his hat?

Tucker: Because in his peeping for treasures his "discoveries finally became too dazzling for his eyes in daylight, and he had to shade his vision by looking at the stone in his hat."[135]

Chairman: Indeed. I thought everybody knew that eyes are better accustomed to strong light in the daylight than at any other time, and that the one way to make an object brighter is to look at it in the dark. If you have ever driven a car, Mr. Tucker, you would know that oncoming headlights that are painfully bright at night are hardly noticed in the daytime. You have got it just backwards. How did the stone and hat operate?

Kennedy: "With a bandage over his eyes he would fall upon his knees and bury his face in the depths of an old white hat, where the stone was . . . hidden."[136]

Chairman: How could he hope to see anything with a bandage over his eyes?

Kennedy: Don't you see? It was necessary to shut out every bit of light.

Chairman: But Mr. Hendrix, an eyewitness, tells us Joe's hat was full of holes.

Howe: It may have been another hat.

Chairman: No. Joe, it seems, was famous for a particular hat. An old hat.

Bennett: That's right. He was called the *"Holy Old White Hat Prophet."*[137]

Chairman: And when did Smith start using the white hat?

Dickinson: From the very beginning. From the time

when Mrs. Smith presented her son with the family peep-stone—"from that time on Joseph Smith fooled the credulous residents of the sparsely settled vicinity with the 'peeker' in his white stove-pipe hat."[138]

Blackman: That is right. "He would sit for hours looking into his hat at the round colored stone."[139]

Chairman: Do I understand that it was a stovepipe hat?

Mahaffey: That is correct. "In these ways, decked in his white stove-pipe hat, he fooled the credulous and superstitious and eked out a precarious subsistence."[140]

Chairman: But we have been told most emphatically that it was a "battered old felt hat." Stove-pipe hats are not made of felt. The picture of a notoriously ragged and dirty teenager going about the country "decked out" in a white stove-pipe hat is a comical one, I will admit, but how could he keep it white all those years?

Howe: All those years?

Chairman: Yes, the old stove-pipe hat that Smith wore and used at the beginning of his peeping career was still in use at the time of translating the Book of Mormon, I believe.

Montgomery: True enough. While translating "Joseph kept his face in 'the old white hat.' "[141]

Chairman: You see, it was old at that time—he had not got him a new white hat. And later in Nauvoo, as General Bennett has told us, Smith was the "Old White Hat" Prophet.[142] Now, Smith began treasure-peeping, some have told us, as early as when he was eleven or twelve years old, an amusing figure in the old white stove-pipe hat. In the year before his death we find him going about in the same old "white stove-pipe hat."[143] Apparently his head never grew and the hat never lost its whiteness—which always caused comment—and being already ancient when he got it, never went out of style: it is invariably described as "old." The white hat is an interesting "control" for the reliability of a lot of stories about Joseph Smith.

There is another such key, I believe, in the frequent and significant references to *boxes* in the stories of the Book of Mormon. To expedite matters let us hear from our witnesses in chronological order. Mr. Ingersoll, most writers give you priority in this matter. What is your story?

The sand-box epic

Ingersoll: Joseph Smith said to me: "As I was passing, yesterday across the woods after a heavy shower of rain, I found in a hollow, some beautiful white sand, that had been washed by the water. I took off my frock, and tied up several quarts of it, and then went home. On my entering the house I found the family at the table eating dinner. They were all anxious to know the contents of my frock. At that moment, I happened to think of what I had heard about a history found in Canada, called 'the Golden Bible'; so I very gravely told them it was the Golden Bible. To my surprise, they were credulous enough to believe what I said. Accordingly I told them that I had received a commandment to let no one see it; for, says I, no man can see it with the naked eye and live. . . . 'Now,' said Joe, 'I have got the d—d fools fixed, and will carry out the fun.' "[144]

Chairman: When was this?

Ingersoll: In 1825, Joe at the time was being urged "to resume his old practice of looking in the stone. He seemed much perplexed as to the course he should pursue. In this dilemma, he made me his confidant, and told me what daily transpired in the family of Smiths."[145]

Chairman: But at that time, Joe had barely begun his peeping. It was convenient that he made you his confidant instead of his family, with whom, until now, we have been told he worked most closely. Why did he turn to you for comfort and guidance in his perplexity?

Dr. Fairfield: He had other confidants.

Chairman: The dictionary says a confidant is "a confidential or bosom friend," — one who is by nature a unique friend, and certainly from his words Mr. Ingersoll claims to have been such a friend: "in his dilemma, he made me his confidant." There could be no others.

Fairfield: But there were! I talked to two of them. Here they are.

Witnesses Numbers Two and Three (together): "One day he told us that his 'Daddy' and 'Mammy' were very ignorant and superstitious and that he was going to play a trick on them. He said he would fill a little box with sand and set it on the hearth in the spare room. . . . He said that no one but himself could see one of the plates and live. . . . This trick was played several years before the finding of the Book of Mormon."[146]

Chairman: But this trick is quite different from that reported by Mr. Ingersoll; yet I need only point out the element of premeditation in the two stories, and such details as the sand and the box to show that they are meant to be the same tale.

Dickinson: What really happened was that "in 1826 Joe Smith returned to Palmyra, and began to act his role [he had been spending his time until then with Pratt and Rigdon]. . . . At dinner-time, one day, he told his family that in crossing through a grove he found a book in some white sand."[147]

Chairman: So it was his family he told about the white sand. From then on, he pretended to have the plates?

Ingersoll: Yes. He immediately got to work on Martin Harris. "I there met that damn fool Martin Harris," he said to me, "and told him that I had a command to ask the first *honest man* I met for fifty dollars in money, and he would let me have it."[148]

Chairman: Apparently Smith called everyone who supported him a damn fool, and made "confidential or bosom friends" of those who loathed him.

Jonathan Lapham: He and "Martin Harris, and others,

used to meet together in private, awhile before the gold plates were found, and were familiarly known by the name of 'The Gold-Bible Company.' "[149]

Chairman: So here we have a Gold-Bible Company going full-blast *before* Smith ever claimed to have found any plates, though the Gold-Bible idea did not pop into his head until the day he pretended to have found them: and here we have Smith "several years before *finding* the Book of Mormon" claiming to possess the plates from which the Book of Mormon was translated; and here we have Smith using a peepstone for years before that identical stone was discovered buried with the plates. But how about the box? Witness Number One said it all began when Smith found some beautiful white sand, quite unexpectedly, and hid it in his coat. Witnesses Two and Three said he planned ahead of time to fill a little box with sand and then tell his family about the book. Number Four said he told them right off that he had discovered a book in some white sand.

Ingersoll: He put the sand in a box later. "He told me that he actually went to Willard Chase to get him to make a chest."[150]

Caswall: Smith made the box himself after Chase refused to make it. Then "he put the sand in a pillow-case and then into the box."[151]

Chairman: Why did Chase refuse to make the box?

Caswall: He did not want to be party to a fraud.[152]

Chairman: So he knew it was a fraud. Joe was telling everybody in town about the trick — except his family.

Montgomery: But not for long! "The Smith family joined in the hoax and declared their firm belief in the story. They seemed to expect that their love for notoriety and for unearned money was about to be gratified from this stupid fraud. And they were not mistaken."[153]

Chairman: "Stupid fraud" is putting it mildly, since insiders and outsiders alike were all in on the secret. So the "little box" was the one with the plates in it?

Bennett: It had a predecessor. Abigail Harris told Mr. Howe who told me that Mrs. Smith had told her that Joseph Smith had told her that "Joseph had also discovered by looking through his stone, the vessel in which the gold was melted . . . and also the machine in which they [the plates] were rolled."[154]

Chairman: Thank you for your valuable firsthand testimony. Mr. Chase, what about that box?

Chase: Smith told me "that on the 22d of September, he arose early in the morning, and took a one horse wagon, of some one that had stayed over night at their house, without leave or license; and, together with his wife, repaired to the hill which contained the book. . . . He then took the book out of the ground and hid it in a tree top, and returned home. He then went to the town of Macedon to work. After about ten days, it having been suggested that some one had got his book, . . . he . . . went home . . . found it safe, took off his frock, wrapt it round it, put it under his arm and ran all the way home, a distance of about two miles. . . . A few days afterwards, he told one of my neighbors that he had not got any such book, nor never had such an one; but that he had told the story to deceive the d—d fool (meaning me) to get him to make a chest."[155]

Chairman: And he couldn't simply have ordered a chest without telling your neighbor that wild story? If he didn't have the book, why did he want to have the chest?

Chase: Obviously, to fool people with.

Chairman: But he told other people that he had no book, and that he told the story to you *only* to get you to make a chest—that was as far as his interest in the deception went. He told you he had a book so you would make him a chest. Why a chest? To put the nonexistent book in, of course!

Chase: To make people *think* there was a book in it.

Chairman: After telling the neighbors that he only

wanted *you* to think so? But this is too ridiculous. Incidentally, the frock and the d—d fool motif seems to be falling into a sort of pattern. But I believe the plates were already in a box.

W. S. Simpson: Yes, but they were taken out of it. It was a wonderful box. Smith said "the chest in which they [the plates] were preserved was exhibited to him, but shortly moved, and glided away out of his sight. 'Joe Smith,' however, and his father who had accompanied him, succeeded in obtaining another view of its dimensions; but then, as the account blasphemously relates, 'the thunders of the Almighty shook the spot, . . . lightning swept along over the side of the hill, and burnt around the spot' where Joseph had been excavating; 'and again, with a rumbling noise, the chest moved out of their sight.' "[156]

Tucker: "Smith told a frightful story of the display of celestial pyrotechnics on the exposure to his view of the sacred book." That was when at the appointed hour "the prophet, assuming his practiced air of mystery, took in his hand his money-digging spade and a large napkin, and went off in silence and alone in the solitude of the forest, and after an absence of some three hours, returned, apparently with his sacred charge concealed within the folds of the napkin."[157]

Chairman: If I may be allowed a comment, it has been agreed that Smith, the lazy lout, never did any excavating himself—now you have him with his trusty spade; also you have him going alone, while our other witness said his father was with him.

Chase: No, it wasn't his father at all; it was his wife.[158]

Chairman: And still another version of the cloth wrapping. What about the box?

Hale: I was shown a box . . . which had to all appearances, been used as a glass box, of the common[-sized] window glass."[159]

Chairman: So it wasn't necessary to make a box after all: they just used a glass box.

Abbott: But Joseph Smith also displayed along with the plates the original chest in which the plates came.

Chairman: Really now, after all we have heard of wrapping up and trying to get a box made for the book?

Abbott: Absolutely. He "also showed a very highly polished marble box, which he said had contained the plates, and which in that case, must have miraculously retained its lustre for countless centuries."[160]

Chairman: Then Smith had the original chest all along?

Dickinson: Indeed. "To his adherents Smith said he had been shown the box . . . and had tried many times to open it, but was struck back by an invisible blow coming from Satan."[161]

Adams: "There is a story—quite generally believed, but of course it cannot be true!—that a party of Palmyrans were taken into the room, or at least obtained entrance into it, and were shown a box within which rested the precious plates decently covered with a cloth. They were not satisfied, and with speech more vigorous than reverent, raised the cloth, and, behold, nothing but a brick was seen! Either Moroni had substituted the brick for the plates while they were talking, or else had anticipated their visit. Both explanations are given."[162]

Chairman: By whom?

Tucker: By no one! Mr. Adams has taken the story from my account: "An anecdote touching this subject used to be related by William T. Hussey and Azel Vandruver. They were notorious wags, and very intimately acquainted with Smith."

Chairman: Naturally. Proceed.

Tucker: Well, Hussey said, " 'Egad! I'll see the critter, live or die!' and stripping off the cover, a large tile-brick was exhibited. But Smith's fertile imagination was equal to the emergency." He said it was a trick; "and 'treating' with the customary whiskey hospitalities, the affair ended in good nature."[163]

Chairman: And this is your dark, taciturn, unsocial Smith of 1825? What had happened to the sand?

Cowles: Smith's mysterious boxes were even earlier than that. His peepstone was "carefully wrapped in cotton and kept in a mysterious box."[164]

Chairman: Now even the peepstone has to have its mysterious box.

G. Townsend: It was Joseph Smith, Sr.'s, dream about "the Magic Box discovered in a wilderness of 'dead and fallen timber' [that] suggested the finding of the Golden Bible; that of the Fruit Trees is incorporated in the Book of Mormon."[165]

Chairman: But we have already been told that it was a story from Canada that suggested it. What about this dream of Joseph Smith, Sr.?

Townsend: You can read it in 1 Nephi 8.[166]

Chairman (turning to the chapter): I find nothing here about a magic box, and no dream of Joseph Smith, Sr.

Townsend: How can you be so naive? Lucy Smith herself told of her husband dreaming of a wilderness of dead and fallen timber.

Chairman: But no such dream is mentioned in the Book of Mormon. Because Joseph Smith, Sr., has one dream, and Lehi has another, are we to assume as proven that dream number two is simply a copy of number one?

Hunt: The Book of Mormon itself proves that it was written by a money digger—just read page 126 of the first edition! Here Jacob says explicitly: "Providence hath smiled upon you most pleasingly, that you have obtained many riches." That absolutely proves the money-digging charges!

Chairman: Well, I will admit that the proof is as good as any we have had so far.

Cowles: "Long before the Gold Bible demonstration, the

Smith Family . . . pretended that in digging for money, at Mormon Hill, they came across 'a chest, three feet by two in size, covered with dark-colored stone.' " I have already told about that stone and how it exploded and vanished.[167]

Chairman: Just like the chest that vanished in a clap of thunder in another and totally different version.

Preston T. Wilkins: The Mormons were crazy about chests. "At the time of the Mormon excitement and while on a visit to a Mormon family" in Broome County, I "learned that there was a chest of Mormon Bibles in the barn, that it was guarded by an angel, and that it would be utterly impossible for anyone to steal one of them." So I "prepared a key that would unlock the chest, and taking one of their Bibles carried it home in the evening and placed it over the front door. . . . The Mormons declared that an angel had brought the book, and . . . would never acknowledge that one of their books was missing."[168]

Chairman: Aren't you confusing the original gold plates with an ordinary printed edition, sir?

W. Wyl: I know where all this talk about sand and window-glasses came from.

Chairman: Indeed, sir, do you know anything about sand and window-glass boxes?

Wyl: Yes. When Smith was pretending to run a bank in Kirtland in 1837, "in the bank they kept eight or nine window-glass boxes, which seemed to be full of silver; but the initiate knew very well that they were *full of sand*, only the top being covered with 50–cent pieces."[169]

Chairman: So the old motifs still crop up. That might explain something.

Clark: Only it is all wrong. It wasn't eight or nine boxes of sand at all: "he had some one or two-hundred boxes made, and gathered all the lead and shot that the village had or that part of it that he controlled, and filled the boxes with lead, shot, &c, and marked them $1000 each. Then, when they went to examine the vault, he had one box on a table partly filled for them to see, . . . and they saw that it was silver, and they hefted a number and Smith told them that they contained specie."[170]

Chairman: The "hefting" is another familiar note. Why did he bother to fill all two hundred boxes with lead and shot, if only a few were to be hefted?

Ingersoll: A correction, please: "The prophet . . . filled one box with dollars, and about 200 others with iron and stone. Having called together his creditors, Smith pointed out to them the 200 boxes all marked '1000 dollars,' and showed them the one which contained the silver. The trick answered for a time."[171]

Chairman: There seems to be some disagreement as to the real contents of the boxes.

O. H. Olney: There were all sorts of stuff in the boxes: "They got hold of a quantity of boxes, And nearly filled them with sand, Lead, old iron, stone, and combustibles, And covered it up with clean coin. That darkened the deception beneath, That showed they were not to be run, By the men of the world. But the skim on the top soon disappeared."[172]

Alexander Campbell: But just the same they continued selling bogus money—and also stones and sand for bogus.[173]

Reed Peck: "While the 'money fever' raged in Kirtland the leaders of the Church and others were more or less engaged in purchasing and circulating 'bogus' money, or counterfeit coin."[174]

Chairman: "More or less"? Who are you, sir?

Peck: I was one of Smith's neighbors in Palmyra.

Chairman: But you are testifying to what happened years after in Kirtland. Did you know Smith in Kirtland?

Campbell: It was afterwards that they counterfeited. "It appears that counterfeiting has been the principal part of the business [in Nauvoo] for some years, and that it has been carried on by the heads of the Church. The amount counterfeited has been immense, and the execution has been so nice, as in many cases to prevent its being detected. The Prophet, Joe Smith, used to work at the business with his own hands."[175]

Chairman: If the stuff can't be detected as such, how can you call it counterfeit? And how can *you* tell the source of this counterfeit money that is so nicely executed as to prevent detection? Do you, or does anyone else, possess or remember having possessed any of that clever counterfeit which you say was circulated in "immense" quantities as "the *principal* part of the business at Nauvoo for some years?" Don't you know that large-scale counterfeiting even for a month or two cannot possibly be concealed, and if the source is known invites immediate disaster? What you say is patently absurd, sir, but you are not the only one. How casually you drop the charge of counterfeiting against Joseph Smith — working "at the business with his own hands," forsooth! Have you or do you even pretend to offer one iota of evidence to support that terrible charge? You should all be ashamed of yourselves!

Howe: That does it! The time has come to call upon our star witnesses. Bishop Tuttle, will you . . .

Chairman: Just a moment please. Before these stars come out, does anyone else have anything to say about boxes?

D. H. C. Bartlett: Yes indeed! Smith's original Book of Mormon story was about an iron box, a dream he had of "an iron box, containing gold plates which he was to translate into a book over which stood a Spaniard having a long beard with his throat cut from ear to ear. . . . Smith at that time had no thought of God, angels, or divine revelations. He was simply the magical dreamer, beholding the ghost of a murdered Spaniard."[176]

Linn: Hear, hear! That is just what I said: "In all this narrative there was not one word about visions of God, or of angels." They were all "afterthoughts revised to order."[177]

Chairman: And what is the source of this narrative you both tell?

Bartlett: It was the Lewis boys. They wrote it in a letter.

Chairman: What is the date of the letter?

Bartlett: 23 April 1879.

Chairman: And those men both remember Smith telling them a dream before 1827 — fifty-two years before?

Linn: It wasn't told to them; it was told to their father, the Rev. Nathaniel Lewis.

Chairman: But that man, I believe, gave Mr. Howe one of his longest affidavits — in 1833, not 1879 — and he knew nothing about the Spanish chest.

Bartlett: It didn't have to be so long before. After all, that stuff about heavenly visions leading to the Book of Mormon was first "written by Smith . . . some eleven years later when in Nauvoo."[178]

Adams: That's right. "It is well for us to remember also that the story of these experiences and of the great discovery was not written before 1838."[179]

Chairman: So you men all agree that the heavenly element in Smith's story of the Book of Mormon was a late interpolation . . .

Adams: "Others say positively that the story was revised from time to time, always gaining in its miraculous and mysterious character."[180]

Chairman: In that case, how does it happen the affidavit swearers back in 1833 all accuse Smith of pushing the miraculous and the mysterious to their absolute limits from childhood? Why should this talented liar begin with a dream that anybody might have, when as a little child he was already imitating the exploits of Captain Kidd?

Linn: Well, it's "the heavenly visions and messages of angels" that are introduced late — 1838 at the earliest.

Chairman: Mr. Linn, when was the Book of Mormon published?

Linn: In 1830.

Chairman: And in case you gentlemen don't know it, the Book of Mormon is full of "heavenly visions and messages of angels" from the beginning to the end. If you would read a little of it you would see that it could not possibly have been written with "no thought of God, angels, or divine revelations," to quote Mr. Bartlett. It is a religious book and nothing else, from cover to cover. Just a novel to make money, forsooth! Tell that to Mrs. Brodie — she believes you.

The Tuttle-tale

Howe: That brings us back to our star witnesses. When I was so rudely interrupted, I was about to call on Bishop Tuttle and Mr. Purple. These are the gentlemen whose evidence, as Mrs. Brodie assures us, proves "beyond any doubt" the tales of Smith's early peeping.[181] Could we hear from Mr. Tuttle first?

Chairman: Bishop Tuttle, did you know Joseph Smith?

Tuttle: Of course not. Smith lived before my day.

Chairman: Did you "unearth in southern New York" the original court record of a trial of Smith in 1826, as Mr. Adams (in 1916) and Mrs. Brodie (in 1947) say you did?

Tuttle: I did not. "The [manuscript] was given me by Miss Emily Pearsall, who . . . was a woman helper in our mission and lived in my family, and died [there]."[182]

Chairman: When and where did she give you the manuscript?

Tuttle: In Salt Lake City, in 1871. "Miss Pearsall tore the leaves out of the record found in her father's house and brought them to me."

Chairman: Who was her father?

Tuttle: "Her father or uncle was a Justice of the Peace

in Bainbridge, Chenango Co., New York, in [Joseph] Smith's time, and before him Smith was tried."

Chairman: Before whom?

Tuttle: "Her father or uncle."[183]

Chairman: Which one?

Tuttle: She didn't say.

Chairman: Then it's plain she didn't know. Where is the document? Don't you want to present it as Exhibit A?

Tuttle: I do not have it. I "presented the original manuscript pages of the trial to the *Utah Christian Advocate,* which published them in January 1886."

Chairman: Published what? Will you say that again.

Tuttle: I am quoting Mrs. Brodie: the *Utah Christian Advocate* published *"them"* — that is, "the original manuscript pages of the trial."[184]

Chairman: But that is absurd. You can't publish *original manuscript pages.* You might publish a copy or even a photograph of them, but you cannot *publish* a unique document. Don't you mean that they published the *contents* of the manuscript?

Tuttle: Of course.

Chairman: Ah, that is something entirely different! Having seen the purported contents of the court record in print, we must determine whether they were correctly copied or not. That is no minor issue when Mrs. Brodie herself can turn a bronze sphere into two crystals just by sloppy note-taking. As soon as the document was published, in Utah, the Mormons had the duty and right to challenge the original manuscript. Where is it? What happened when it was "published" in 1886?

Tuttle (quoting Brodie): "At this point the manuscript seems to have disappeared."[185]

Chairman: Most convenient. No one has seen the document since 1886. How did you know it was genuine?

Tuttle: "Miss Pearsall tore the leaves out of the record found in her father's house and brought them to me."

Chairman: So you didn't see her tear them?

Tuttle: No. As I said, she *brought* them to me.

Chairman: Did she ask her father about them?

Tuttle: Obviously not. Her father was not available for consultation—she did not even know whether he or her uncle had been the justice. After all, the trial had taken place forty-five years before.

Chairman: Why didn't she bring you the whole book?

Howe: Obviously because it did not belong to her; it was an official document.

Chairman: Is it any worse to walk off with an official document than to disfigure it by tearing pages out of it? The former offense could well be an oversight, the latter never. Why wasn't the official document returned to the official archives where the Bishop and Miss Pearsall could have called the world's attention to it and made their case stick? Was it because there were no such archives and no such records before 1850?

Howe: Let us admit that it was foolish to tear the book. But people often do foolish things on impulse.

Chairman: We are not speaking of impulse, sir, but of very long and deliberate calculation, not only on Miss Pearsall's part but on Bishop Tuttle's part as well. For at least eighteen years he exploited this document. Miss Pearsall gave it to him in 1871: why didn't he, a high church dignitary and expert on the Mormons (he even wrote encyclopedia articles about them)—why didn't he publish it *at once?* Why did he arrange to have another person, who did not even give his name, publish it years later in a foreign country? Did he have some doubts about the manuscript?

Tuttle: But I did expose it to the world!

Chairman: Yes, ten years after "C.M." published it in England! Now, you are an intelligent man, sir. Between the time of your first coming into possession of the document and its first publication you had plenty of time to study it. You knew its immense value as a weapon against Joseph Smith *if* its authenticity could be established. And the *only* way to establish authenticity was to get hold of the record book from which the pages had been purportedly torn. After all, you had only Miss Pearsall's word for it that the book ever existed. Why didn't you immediately send her back to find the book or make every effort to get hold of it? Why didn't you "unearth" it, as they later said you did?

Howe: Bishop Tuttle may have done just that. He may have looked for it.

Chairman: In which case his researches were vain. The book never materialized. The authenticity of the record still rests *entirely* on the confidential testimony of Miss Pearsall to the Bishop. And who was Miss Pearsall? A zealous old maid, apparently: "a woman helper in our mission," who lived right in the Tuttle home and would do anything to assist her superior. The picture I get is that of a gossipy old housekeeper. Now, Bishop Tuttle, *if* this court record is authentic it is the most damning evidence in existence against Joseph Smith. Why, then, was it not republished in your article in the *Schaff-Herzog Encyclopedia of Religious Knowledge* after 1891?

Howe: Why don't you ask the editors?

Chairman: Because they would have to have the author's approval. But to come closer to home, in 1906 Bishop Tuttle published his *Reminiscences of a Missionary Bishop* in which he blasts the Mormons as hotly as ever. Now bear in mind that he is the key witness to the existence of the Bainbridge court record, and that that record is the most devastating blow to Smith ever delivered, yet in the final summary of his life's experiences he never mentions the story of the court record—his one claim to immortal fame and the gratitude of the human race *if it were true!*

So what is the evidence that proves to Mrs. Brodie "beyond any doubt" that Smith was a peeping rascal? In

1873 a certain A, who does not give his name, says that a certain B (Bishop Tuttle), told him that a certain C ("a woman helper [who] . . . lived in my family, and died there"—a euphemism, we suspect, for old-maid house-keeper) told *him* that some pieces of paper she gave him had been torn by her from a court record which she found in her father's house. She knew enough to recognize the value and authority of a *court record* when she saw one— and yet it was she who proceeded to destroy that authority by forcibly detaching the incriminating pages from the authentic binding that alone gave them authority! In the end, we have only Miss Pearsall's word, through Tuttle, that that document, the court record, ever existed, while the pages supposedly torn from it disappeared promptly after their publication in Utah, though completely in possession and control of the non-Mormons. No wonder Bishop Tuttle thought twice and dropped the whole business.

Some Purple patches

Howe: But that is not all. Here is a man who, as Mrs. Brodie says, "was an eye-witness to the trial, and took notes." I give you Mr. W. D. Purple.[186]

Chairman: When did you write your report of the Smith trial, Mr. Purple?

W. D. Purple: My report was published in 1877.

Chairman: Rather a suspicious year, I would say.

Howe: Why "suspicious"?

Chairman: For two reasons. In the first place, that is just a few years after 1873, when the Pearsall court record was first published both in England and America. That means that Mr. Purple could very well have heard of it from that source. If not (and this is our second point), why did he wait fifty-one years to report his sensational information?

Purple: But I didn't wait fifty-one years. Through the

years I gave "public and private rehearsals" of the events described.[187]

Chairman: And were these "public rehearsals" given near the place where the events occurred?

Purple: They were given "in this County."[188]

Chairman: Then how does it happen that the affidavit-collectors and scandal-seekers know nothing of you or your story?

Howe: Perhaps they didn't get around to Mr. Purple.

Chairman: They didn't have to. "Public rehearsals" means that Mr. Purple's story got around widely enough, even if *he* didn't. There should have been many people in and around Palmyra who remembered those public recitations when the affidavits were taken—but there were none; there should have been eager souls to refer the investigators to Mr. Purple or at the very least have repeated bits of his story, whether they knew the source or not. Yet no bits or fragments of that all-important tale, which Mr. Purple says he circulated so widely and so long, are found floating about anywhere from 1830 to 1877! Doesn't that strike you as odd? Why do Mr. Purple's juicy tidbits never turn up in the local gossip of half a century?

Howe: Purple and the others might not have seen the significance of the thing at the time. It may well have been the article of 1873 that brought its true importance to their attention.

Chairman: But that is just the point. Purple *did* realize the importance of his information at the time, for he not only gave "public and private rehearsals [of it] . . . in later years," but actually took full and complete notes at the trial.[189] That claim to have taken notes is another very suspicious circumstance.

Howe: I would say just the opposite. It is the one thing that places Mr. Purple's testimony "beyond any doubt."

Chairman: And that is just what it was intended to do. Anyone can see that without those notes the Purple testimony is the object of the very serious doubts and misgivings that naturally attach to a tale for which the only authority is an old man's memory more than fifty years after the event. Suspicion increases when one considers the great length and detail of that story. Mr. Purple simply *had* to add that touch about taking notes, but it is plainly nothing but a trick to disarm criticism.

Howe: How can you prove that, sir?

Chairman: Very easily, by the fact that Purple made no use of the notes in writing up his 1877 report. If he didn't use them, why bother to mention them, unless it was to give the impression of high reliability?

Howe: How do you know he didn't use them?

Chairman: Mr. Purple, you entitle your opus on the Smith trial "Historical Reminiscences." You were simply remembering all those things, I take it?

Purple: As I wrote, "The scenes and incidents of that early day are vividly engraven upon his [the writer's] memory, by reason of his having written them when they occurred, and by reason of his public and private rehearsals of them in later years."[190]

Chairman: There we have it. He states most explicitly that the taking of notes at the time and the repetitions of the story later served to make the whole thing "vividly engraven upon his *memory*." If he had the original notes, that would settle everything, and he would not need to convince us that his memory was adequate. Indeed the whole advantage to having notes is that one does not have to trust one's memory at all. So when Mrs. Brodie tells us simply that "Purple was an eye-witness to the trial, and took notes," she is up to her old tricks, since the casual reader would naturally assume that Purple's report was based on those notes; she is doing exactly what Purple himself has done — creating by implication an impression of high reliability in testimony which actually has every mark of being spurious. So we are back on the old familiar ground: Smith is shown to be a rascal not on the testimony of any prosecution witnesses, but by pouring out his soul in a gratuitous and foolish confession, for which the only authority is the word of one man who claims to have remembered it all years afterwards. If we are to get any farther with this evidence we must consider its internal consistency and inherent probability. It will not be necessary to have Mr. Purple repeat his long account at length; we will simply ask him a few questions referring to his written report. Mr. Purple, Mr. Josiah Stowell was not a child at the time Smith was working for him, or was he?

Purple: Of course not. "He had at that time grown-up sons and daughters to share his prosperity and the honors of his name."[191]

Chairman: Irresponsible fools do not achieve honor and prosperity. What kind of a man was he?

Purple: "Mr. Stowell was a man of much force of character, of indomitable will. . . . He was a very industrious, exemplary man."[192]

Chairman: Mr. Stowell had an established reputation and considerable wealth?

Purple: Yes.

Chairman: How did the trial turn out?

Purple: "It is hardly necessary to say that, as the testimony of Deacon Stowell could not be impeached, the prisoner was discharged."[193]

Chairman: So Stowell's prestige overrode everything. And this Stowell hired Smith?

Purple: Yes.

Chairman: Did Smith come to Stowell looking for work, or did Stowell seek him out? How did the two come together?

Purple: "Mr. Stowell, while at Lanesboro, heard of the fame of . . . Joseph, who . . . had become a famous seer of lost or hidden treasures. . . . [Stowell] harnessed his team, and filled his wagon . . . and started for the residence of the Smith family. In due time he arrived at the humble log cabin, . . . and found the sought for treasure in the person of Joseph Smith Jr. . . . He, with the magic stone, was at once transferred from his humble abode to the more pretentious mansion of Deacon Stowell."[194]

Chairman: So Smith went to live with the Stowell family after Mr. Stowell had sought him out and taken him into his employment. Did Stowell hire other men?

Purple: Of course. A Mr. Thomas said in court that "he and another man . . . always attended the Deacon and Smith in their nocturnal labors."[195]

Chairman: Would you say Smith was Mr. Stowell's favorite employee?

Purple: Yes. "The youthful seer had unlimited control over the illusions of" Stowell.[196]

Chairman: Did Stowell pay him well?

Purple: It wasn't a matter of mere pay. Things reached the point where, according to Mr. Stowell's sons, Smith "as they believed, was eating up their substance, and depriving them of their anticipated patrimony."

Chairman: This state of things had been going on for some time at the time of the trial?

Purple: Yes. The Stowell boys stood it for some time but at length "they made up their minds that 'patience had ceased to be a virtue.' "[197]

Chairman: How long had Smith been working for Stowell at the time?

Purple: It must have been several months at least, since Mr. Stowell went to fetch Smith in 1825 and the trial took place in March of 1826.

Chairman: And Mr. Stowell's sons had about all they could stand?

Purple: Yes, "in February, 1826, the sons of Mr. Stowell, who lived with their father, were greatly incensed against Mr. Smith."[198]

Chairman: It was high time to get rid of him?

Purple: It was. They "resolved to rid themselves and their family from this incubus, who, as they believed, was eating up their substance."[199]

Chairman: Did old Mr. Stowell stand up for Smith at the trial?

Purple: Absolutely. He swore that he not only believed all Smith had told him, but, he said, "I positively know it to be true."[200]

Chairman: Did he admit employing Smith, having him live at his house, and the rest?

Purple: Certainly. Mr. Stowell "confirmed all that is said above in relation to himself," that is, he confirmed everything I have said about his relationships with Smith.[201]

Chairman: Did Smith continue on at Stowell's after the trial?

Purple: Yes, after "the prisoner was discharged, and in a few weeks he left the town."[202]

Chairman: So Smith was living on the bounty of Stowell before, during, and after the trial, precisely as Mr. Stowell's own "grown up sons" were—that, in fact, was the very thing those men objected to. Now, what was the charge they brought against Smith to get rid of him?

Purple: "They caused the arrest of Smith as a vagrant, without visible means of livelihood."[203]

Chairman: And that was the grounds of arrest?

Purple: Yes. "The affidavits of the sons were read and Mr. Smith was fully examined by the court."[204] I have given a long and detailed account of the trial.

Chairman: But isn't that all rather preposterous, since you have just stated that Smith was very securely and profitably employed at that very time? How could you accuse him of being "a vagrant, without visible means of support" if Mr. Stowell, a rich man, was paying him excellent wages and stoutly endorsing his honesty? I notice that you have not so much as hinted that the prosecution presented any evidence whatsoever to support their case, or that the defense did what they *must* have done if there ever was such a trial. Why were not Mr. Thomas and the other man who worked with Stowell and Smith arrested for being vagrants "without visible means" of livelihood? And why were not Mr. Stowell's grown sons arrested as vagrants "without visible means of support"?

Purple: The question is absurd. I have said that his sons "shared his prosperity" and "lived with their father."

Chairman: But that is exactly what Smith was doing — the very thing that angered the brothers, according to you. How old was Smith at the time?

Purple: He was "a lad of some eighteen years of age . . ."[205]

Chairman: So if the rich and respected Mr. Stowell wanted to hire Smith, that was his business. If he wanted to support him in style without doing any work at all (and Mr. Smith was still a minor), that was still Stowell's business. In either case, you should see that there was absolutely no case against Smith; on the contrary, he was in a perfect position to sue for false arrest. All the elder Stowell or Joseph Smith himself had to do to quash the whole thing would be to point out that Smith had a job. Mr. Purple says "the affidavits of the sons were read, and Mr. Smith was fully examined by the court." Since the affidavits were that Smith was a vagrant without visible means of support, how could such an examination fail to reveal that he had a very good job? Though the charge is vagrancy, not one mention is made in Purple's story of Smith's being a vagrant!

Purple: Not a vagrant at the time, maybe. But Smith told how he had wandered over the country far and wide looking for a seer stone "when he was a lad."[206]

Chairman: You can't arrest a man for having had no visible means of support years ago, when he was a mere child — not if he has a good job today. Now according to you, Mr. Purple, Smith was not convicted. You cite no evidence against him save the stories that he and his loyal employer, Mr. Stowell, told in court. All either man had to do to have the case dismissed was to show that Smith was employed. But instead of that, each of them gets up and tells long, lurid, and scandalous tales about himself! What a trial! How do you describe the testimonies of the two, Mr. Purple?

Purple: "What a picture for the pencil of a Hogarth! . . . It could have been done only by the hallucination of diseased minds, that drew all their philosophy from the Arabian Nights and other kindred literature of that period!"[207]

Chairman: And you call that Stowell's unimpeachable testimony?

Purple: I called it that?

Chairman: The clerk will read what you said of the outcome of the trial.

Clerk (reads): "As the testimony of Deacon Stowell could not be impeached, that prisoner was discharged."

Chairman: That is enough. But even that is not as preposterous as having the shrewd Mr. Stowell and the sly and canny Smith exhibit themselves as obsessed with "the hallucination of diseased minds," when all in the world either of them had to do was to show that Smith had a job. Now, Mr. Purple's account of the trial differs substantially from that of Miss Pearsall's missing document. That means that they cannot both be telling the truth, but both *can* be lying. In both cases the testimony is half a century overdue.

Star witness

Howe: Well, sir, prepare for a shock. Here is a witness who told all about the trial of 1826 in 1831 ! Here is Mr. "A. W. B." who in that year wrote a letter to the *Evangelical Magazine,* and that letter proves that the trial did take place.

Chairman: To whom was your letter addressed, Mr. A. W. B.?

A. W. Benton: To a "correspondent in Ohio, where [as I explained], perhaps, the truth concerning him [Jos. Smith] may be hard to come at."[208]

Chairman: The paper, apparently, had a wide circulation, and though you would not sign your name you were willing to pose as something of an authority on Smith.

Benton: Not "pose," sir. I lived right in Bainbridge, Chenango County, where the trial took place. Let me tell you about it. "For several years preceding the appearance of his book, he was about the country in the character of a glass-looker; pretending, by means of a certain stone, or glass, which he put in a hat, to be able to discover lost goods, hidden treasures, mines of gold and silver, &c. Although he constantly failed in his pretentions, still he had his dupes who put implicit confidence in all his words."[209]

Chairman: Why do you think he did all that?

Benton: "So that he might secure to himself," as I explained, "the scandalous honor of being the founder of a new sect, which might rival, perhaps, the Wilkinsonians, or the French Prophets of the 17th century."[210]

Chairman: There seems to be some commotion here. What seems to be the trouble, Mr. Dogberry?

Dogberry: I would like to ask Mr. Benton when he wrote all this to the paper?

Benton: It was on 9 April 1831.

Dogberry: I *thought* it sounded awfully familiar. I wrote all that stuff in the Palmyra *Reflector* two and three months earlier, and the Painesville *Telegraph* took it up a couple of *weeks later;* but that stuff about the Wilkinsonians had already appeared in the Rochester *Gem* in May of 1830.

Howe: But the part about the trial isn't there. That is what interests us! Tell us about the trial, Mr. Benton.

Benton: "In this town, a wealthy farmer, named Josiah

Stowell, together with others, spent large sums of money in digging for hidden money, which this Smith pretended he could see, and told them where to dig; but they never found their treasure. At length the public, becoming wearied with the base imposition which he was palming upon the credulity of the ignorant, for the purpose of sponging his living from their earnings, had him arrested as a disorderly person, tried and condemned before a court of Justice. But, considering his youth (he being then a minor), and thinking he might reform his conduct, he was designedly allowed to escape."[211]

Chairman: But according to Mr. Purple he did not escape, but *was acquitted and* went right on living at Stowell's for "a few weeks."

Benton: Well, "from this time he absented himself from this place, returning only privately, and holding clandestine intercourse with his credulous dupes, for two or three years."[212]

Chairman: By your references to "this town" and "this place" it is plain, sir, that you lived on the spot. And now you tell us that Joseph Smith continued to operate there for *two or three years?*

Benton: Privately, I said — secretly, just with his dupes.

Chairman: But that is exactly what he was doing before! He was in a business in which, as you describe it, his communications with his wealthy employers could only have been very private and confidential at any time. You say "the public" became "wearied" of the spectacle of this youngster imposing on the ignorant and "sponging" off the rich. Since when does the public have such a tender conscience for the ignorant? Your expression, sir, is lifted right out of Dogberry. And who are the ignorant? "Josiah Stowell, together with others" — rich, respected, successful Squire Stowell. Was it the responsibility of his poor neighbors to see to it that he suffered no financial loss? But no, the public was not *worried* about what was going on, they were just "wearied" by it. So they "arrested him as a *disorderly* person." What could that have to do with his "clandestine" swindling?

Benton: Well, it was all that digging that was going on.

Chairman: But that wasn't Smith's doing; it was Stowell and the others who "spent large sums of money in digging." Smith was merely their hired help, and the whole responsibility was theirs, not only for digging but for contributing to the delinquency of a minor. This is the silliest thing I ever heard of.

Howe: However silly, it *does* mention a trial—the trial of 1826.

Chairman: What was the date of the trial, Mr. Benton?

Benton: In 1831 I wrote that it was "four or five years ago."

Howe: But that wasn't the only trial! Tell them about the 1830 trial, Mr. Benton, the one you attended in person.

Benton: I didn't say I attended it in person, though I lived in the town. In the summer of 1830 Smith "was again arraigned before a bar of Justice . . . to answer a charge of misdemeanor. . . . During the trial it was shown that the Book of Mormon was brought to light by the same magic power by which he pretended to tell fortunes, discover hidden treasures, &c."[213]

Chairman: Most interesting. I have never heard of Joseph Smith *himself* ever stating that he had that power. Just how was it shown?

Benton: "Oliver Cowdery, one of the three witnesses to the book, testified under oath, that said Smith found with the plates, from which he translated his book, two transparent stones, resembling glass, set in silver bows. That by looking through these, he was able to read in English, the reformed Egyptian characters, which were engraved on the plates."[214]

Chairman: Well?

Howe: Well what?

Chairman: That is exactly what Smith himself always said. We know all about *those* stones. Where do the peep-stones come in?

Benton: Don't you see? The "two transparent stones [were] undoubtedly of the same properties, and the gift of the same spirit as the one in which he looked to find his neighbor's goods."[215]

Chairman: That is only your conclusion, sir, as that "undoubtedly" makes clear.

Benton: But "it is reported, and probably true, that he commenced his juggling by stealing and hiding property belonging to his neighbors, and when inquiry was made, he would look in his stone."[216]

Chairman: The fact that you must appeal to an unidentified and unverified rumor now makes it perfectly clear that nothing was said about any peepstones in the court. Did anyone else testify?

Benton: Yes, Josiah Stowell, Joseph Knight, and Newell Knight did, but their testimony "needs no comment" since they stoutly supported Smith. But we have Smith's "own confession, that he was a vile, dishonest imposter."[217]

Chairman: Now we are getting somewhere. Those were his words in court?

Benton: Not exactly. What he said when asked whether he could see this money or not was "To be candid, between you and me, I cannot, any more than you or any body else; but any way to get a living."[218]

Chairman: And he confessed that in court?

Benton: No. He said it once to Addison Austin when he "was in company with said Smith alone." Austin reported it in court.[219]

Chairman: Don't you know that such a report cannot be used as evidence? And do you really believe the ignorant farmboy used such urbane language? I am glad you have mentioned this trial of 1830, Mr. Benton, but if you had been wiser you would never have brought it up.

Benton: Why so?

Chairman: Because while it produced nothing whatever to incriminate Smith, it supplies the clue to the whole mythical trial of 1826. Consider. The *only* mention of peep-stones in this 1830 story is what you yourself supplied in your own comments and reflections, made in 1831. Though the *seerstones* were actually described in the court by the Mormons, yet there was no discussion or mention of any *other* stones—which you, sir, would have been the last person on earth to overlook had there been such. Then in the spring of the following year the accounts of the seer-stones widely circulated by the Mormons suggested to Mr. Dogberry what he thought to be a significant parallel, which he pointed out in a purely speculative and half-serious way in a series of articles in the Palmyra *Reflector*. Such information, "hard to come at" in Ohio, as you put it, was readily available to you, sir, where you lived. So I find it significant that a few weeks after these articles appear you write a letter to a correspondent in distant Ohio in which you show both by the things you say and the way you say them that you have most certainly read Mr. Dogberry's articles: you also show that you know a good deal about a trial of Joseph Smith, less than a year before, at which nothing damning was brought out—by the way, you never reported how that trial turned out. Or did you? Did you perhaps use it in the story you told of another trial, a wishful-thinking trial which took place in a safely vague and distant time four or five years before?

Howe: Are you insinuating, sir, that Mr. Benton *invented* the trial of 1826?

Chairman: Let me call your attention to a few peculiar facts, sir. In the first place the two trials, in 1826 and 1830, are so much alike that even the experts confuse them. In both cases the charges are vague and unconvincing, the accused is not found guilty, the only solid evidence for the prosecution is all given freely by the defense; in both cases

Stowell is a star witness and puts on the same foolish defense of Smith. Notice further that Addison Austin has Smith making a damning confession to him in secret "at the very same time that Stowell was digging for money," yet still no mention of peepstones or of any trial of 1826! Now, I am wondering if Mr. Benton did not transfer this confession, freely embellished, to the trial of "four or five years ago"; if he did not combine the trial motif, which he had at firsthand, with the peepstone motif, which he got from Dogberry, in an imaginary trial for which he cannot or dare not even give the year. If there really was an earlier peepstone trial, why did not Mr. Benton himself, or anybody else for that matter, bring it to the attention of the prosecutor in 1830? Why did nobody in 1830 remember a case the recollection of which (Mr. Purple assures us fifty years later) was to electrify the countryside for years? Cowdery himself in 1830 actually brought up the issue of the seerstones in the court, and yet even that did not suggest to anybody Smith's supposedly notorious career in peeping. It is only a year *later* that Benton, having read Dogberry's surmise, sees in Cowdery's speech a clue connecting Smith with the old peepstone mania. Even in Purple's and Pearson's accounts of the trial of 1826 nobody shows up to tell about Smith's peeping and digging — instead he and Stowell must tell it all themselves, confessing to crimes of which no one had accused them, and baring all their secret past and present as they regale the court with their Arabian Nights tales.

Howe: But even though they don't agree at all, the Pearson and Purple stories show at least that there was a trial in 1826, and now Benton's evidence corroborates them.

Chairman: It only corroborates them if it is an *independent* witness. But I doubt that very much. I think all these stories are connected. The reports of Pearson and Purple both rest on documents purportedly written right in the court, but upon examination they turn out to be sham documents — the one is a page never openly exhibited, taken from a document never proven to have existed, while the other consists of notes taken in the court but *not* available to their writer at the time we are supposed to assume he was using them in preparing his long and detailed report fifty years later. Now, since Mr. Benton's letter was printed in a very popular sectarian journal that circulated far beyond the bounds of New York State (Mr. Benton's own correspondent is in Ohio), his story must have been spread abroad: and there is no reason why it cannot have been the ultimate source of the stories of Pearson and Purple. The wide disagreements between those two documents prove that at least one of them is corrupt, while their inherent absurdities show that both are — at best they do not have their information at firsthand, as they pretend. What they have in common they share with Benton's tale, and that is the scandal-story of how Joseph Smith, when he was still a minor, imposed on the rich Mr. Stowell, was hauled into court — and acquitted. But in view (1) of the improbability of the Stowell trial occurring twice, (2) of Benton's failure to get a peepstone into the trial of 1830 (which he could not take, since it was less than a year away), and (3) of the close resemblance of his peepstone commentary to that of Dogberry and the Rochester *Gem*, we are inclined to regard Benton's story of the 1826 trial as fiction. Please remember that the two earlier peepstone essays were both *admittedly guesses*, purely theoretical reconstructions. So that part, at least, of Benton's story is made up. But without the reality of the peepstones, the whole legend of the 1826 trial collapses. The 1830 trial was real; the 1826 trial, unattested in any source but his for fifty years, was a product of Benton's own wishful thinking. By now it should be clear to all of us that people are not above such invention. The tall story was not unknown to early rural America, I am told, and I can believe it.

Howe: But as Mrs. Brodie herself observes, one must face not only "the reality but . . . the implications of this document."[220]

Chairman: I agree that Mrs. Brodie specializes in implications. But what *are* the implications of a fifty-year gap and drastic disagreements? Just consider these digging stories. It all began in Vermont, in Pennsylvania, in Broome County, in Chenango County, in Palmyra, in 1817, in 1819, 1820, 1822, 1828, 1829; the Smiths "kept around them constantly" a gang of diggers; Joseph "may have had believers," "he laid down laws to his phalanx," he hired them, they hired him; full moon was the best time for digging, or was it the dark of the moon? Smith himself dug, he never dug; he found stuff, he never found anything; he sacrificed one black sheep, a whole flock of them, a white dog, a black dog. What are we to make of all this?

And the stones! It was a *glass* Smith looked into,[221] a "dark glass,"[222] a "dark colored stone,"[223] "a white, glass-like . . . opaque" stone,[224] "a curious piece of quartz,"[225] "a transparent stone,"[226] "a glassy stone,"[227] "a green stone with brown irregular spots on it,"[228] a "peculiar shape resembling that of a child's foot[229] which must have resembled the stone foot of Buddha at Bangkok, Siam,"[230] Or it had colored stripes running through it diagonally,[231] "two small stones of chocolate color,"[232] "two large bright diamonds,"[233] a couple of prisms,[234] a little longer than a goose's egg,[235] "a stone of peculiar quality [luminous],"[236] a "stone of singular appearance,"[237] "a curious stone,"[238] a perfectly ordinary pebble,[239] a piece of "common hornblende;"[240] we have been informed that the stone was nothing less than the Urim and Thummim found buried with the plates, we have been told by the most intimately close observers that Smith never had or used more than one stone, yet the same observers describe different stones.

"... but their witness agreed not together," or who's lying?

Howe: Hold on here! We admitted from the first that the testimonies were full of contradictions, but can't you see the implications of that—that merely proves that the *Smiths* were lying! "We show by the witnesses, that *they* told contradictory stories, from time to time, in relation to their finding of the plates, and other circumstances attending it, which go clearly to show that none of them had the fear of God before their eyes."[241]

Chorus of Voices from the Audience: Hear! Hear!

W. Stafford: "Respecting the manner of receiving and translating the Book of Mormon, their statements were always discordant. The elder Joseph would say that he had seen the plates, and that he knew them to be gold, at other times he would say that they looked like gold; and at other times he would say he had not seen the plates at all."[242]

Hunt: "Various verbal accounts, all contradictory, false, and inconsistent, . . . were given out by the Smith family."[243]

Bennett: If all these stories about the Smiths conflict, the reason for that is obvious: it is because *"their* statements were always discordant."[244]

Clark: "The statements of the originators of this imposture varied. . . . At first it was a Gold Bible—then golden plates engraved—then metallic plates stereotyped or embossed with golden letters."[245]

Parley Chase: "In regard to their Gold Bible speculation, they scarcely ever told two stories alike."[246]

H. C. Sheldon: I think we must agree, gentlemen, that "the different stories which Smith himself told about the plates of the Book of Mormon impeach his honesty and veracity in the matter."[247]

Chairman: Thank you, gentlemen. I think we are agreed that the wide discrepancies among the stories about Smith are an indication of skulduggery, impeaching somebody's "honesty and veracity in the matter." But whose? The claim is that the various witnesses tell conflicting stories only because the Smiths told *them* conflicting stories. Is that right?

John Hyde, Jr.: Exactly. In my book I cited eight conflicting testimonies against Smith. These stories were all by his enemies, it is true, yet what do those conflicts prove? That "either they are perjurers, or Smith is an impostor. . . . Either they are *all* perjurers [I wrote], or they *all* tell the truth. The above [the eight] are but a selection from many. . . . They must be believed; Smith did contradict himself, and should therefore be rejected."[248]

Chairman: That is a remarkable line of reasoning, sir. Why must your conflicting witnesses be believed?

Hyde: Because, as I pointed out, "they are perfectly disinterested."[249]

Chairman: Can you say that seriously in view of what we have heard from them?

Hyde: Yes. Because *"had they been disposed to assist in the imposture, they could have made a great deal."*[250]

Chairman: Are you trying to tell us that the Book of Mormon was ever a profitable business in Palmyra? I think you will agree that since the prosecution has placed the whole responsibility for the conflicting stories on the shoulders of the Smiths, it is up to them to show that said stories actually did originate with the Smiths. How early do these contradictions begin? Do we have any witnesses from 1830?

Editor of the Painesville Telegraph: When the Book of Mormon was just six months old I wrote that "to record the thousand tales which are in circulation respecting the book and its propagators would be an endless task and probably lead to the promulgation of a hundred times more than was founded in truth."[251]

Chairman: Well, we have heard that the Mormons circulated a lot of conflicting stories, but did all these thousand tales come from them?

Editor of Painesville Telegraph: Of course not. Everybody was speculating on the subject—there was no law limiting wild stories to Mormons. As I said at the time, my own contribution on the subject would only add to the misunderstanding.[252]

Chairman: So we can be sure that at least some of the stories did not originate with the Smiths. But what about the others, those that are actually attributed to them? Is there any firsthand evidence incriminating the Smiths?

Benton: Indeed there is, and from Joe Smith himself. "We have his own confession, that he was a vile, dishonest impostor."[253]

Chairman: That's plain enough. And where may we find this vital confession?

Benton: Addison Austin testified that once when "he . . . was in company with said Smith alone," Smith told him, when asked whether he could really see money with his peepstone, "To be candid, between you and me, I cannot, any more than you or any body else; but any way to get a living."[254]

Chairman: Here we go again. I asked for *Smith's* confession, and you want to give me Mr. Austin's report of a secret conversation with Smith which of course can never be checked up on; and you call that "his own confession!" The really damning evidence of Chase, Ingersoll, Tucker, Stafford, and the rest all goes back to the same secret, private conversations. Smith is always brutally frank when he talks to these people—but there is never anyone else present. Mr. Howe sneers that the only Mormon reply to these tales was a categorical denial. What other reply is possible? Mr. Tucker can give us a good demonstration of what we are up against. Mr. Tucker, you gave, I believe, a full firsthand account of Joseph Smith's first digging venture?

Tucker: That is right, "and the description given of this first trial and of its results is as near exactitude as can at this time be recollected from his own accounts."[255]

Chairman: From whose accounts?

Tucker: From the impostor Smith's. "Such," I wrote, "was Joe's explanation."[256]

Chairman: So it is from him and him alone that you have the story. You did not witness the operation at all. You simply heard it all in a confidential confession by Smith. You wouldn't touch the Smiths with a forty-foot pole, to hear you tell it, yet they were always baring their souls to you. And you weren't the only one. Here is Mr. Harris, who can tell us what he and the community always thought of the Smiths. Mr. Harris?

Henry Harris: They were always regarded "as a *lying* and indolent set of men and no confidence could be placed in them."[257]

Chairman: So that was *his* opinion of Smith. Yet *after* the Book of Mormon was published, Smith in a private confidential discourse to Lapham told him a wild story about the plates that could only discredit everything else he had said about them.[258] Why to Lapham? Why to him alone? What good could possibly come of a secret, damning admission to a man who had always hated him? Here are Messrs. Chase, Ingersoll, and Stafford, whose testimonies consist almost entirely of what Joseph Smith *Senior*, told them each in private. Willard Chase can spin out the old man's long account *verbatim* from memory six and a half years later. And after a long and unpleasant affair about the peepstone in which Chase seeks to thwart the activities of the Smiths, who in turn heap threats and abuse on him, we suddenly find Smith confiding in Chase alone and telling him privately the true story of the gold-plate hoax.[259]

Chase: But "I might proceed . . . by relating one transaction after another, which would all tend to set them in the same light . . . viz: as a pest to society."[260]

Chairman: So you *might* give us some concrete testimony, Mr. Chase, but all you *do* give is the wild stories which you say your detested enemy insisted on confiding to your hostile ear.

Howe: "Detested enemy?" "Hostile ear?" Mr. Chase and Mr. Smith may have been good friends once.

Chairman: Not if we believe Mr. Chase's original testimony. Will the Clerk please read it?

Clerk (reads): "I have regarded Joseph Smith, Jun., from the time I first became acquainted with him, . . . as a man whose word could not be depended upon."[261]

Chairman: That will do. So, Mr. Chase, from the time you first met Smith until you swore your affidavit you had only one opinion of him. And are we to suppose that Smith, with his uncanny insight into human nature, was not aware that you were hardly the man for him to confess to? Then there is your co-swearer, Mr. Ingersoll, who hates Smith as much as you do and whose testimony is the most lurid of all. What does Smith do when he is tempted to resume digging against his better judgment? Does he consult with his family or any of the "many warm friends" he has in Palmyra? Not a bit of it. How was it, Mr. Ingersoll?

Ingersoll: "In this dilemma, he made me his confidant and told me what daily transpired in the family of Smiths."[262]

Chairman: So during the most crucial days of the coming forth of the Book of Mormon, Smith sought out and daily confided in one man alone—his mortal enemy Peter Ingersoll, who had been displaying his contempt for the Smiths ever since 1820. What a complete fool this Smith must have been, to let the cat out of the bag any time he could confide in an enemy, while consistently referring to his loyal supporters as d—d fools! Why did the ancient law insist on things being established "in the mouths of two or three witnesses"? Not as a check on the accused but as a direct test of the witnesses themselves. If their stories disagree it is the *witnesses* that must be suspect. But now we have an interesting theory of evidence, that when the witnesses for the prosecution all tell conflicting stories, that proves not that they are lying but that the accused is a rascal for giving so many false impressions.

Hyde: But Smith has "contradicted himself in his own words, but still more extensively in the statements he has made to his companions and neighbors; many of these testified to such contradictions."[263]

Chairman: What you are saying, Mr. Hyde, is that it is not the words of Smith but those of his "companions and neighbors" that are full of contradictions. You must realize that it is not enough for a person to say that the Mormons told him this or that, to prove that they actually did so. Here, for example, is a book printed as late as 1957, in which the baseless story of the Spaulding manuscript is told at length under the heading: "This is the Mormon Story of It."[264] As if the Mormons had ever propounded or accepted the Spaulding theory! It is the easiest thing in the world when public opinion is on one's side, to pick up and repeat any absurd twaddle that is going around, and when questioned as to its authenticity, simply shrug one's shoulders and say, "Well, that's the way the Mormons tell it!" No other group on earth has done more journal writing and record keeping than the Mormons, upon whom a meticulous recording of events is imposed as a duty (cf. D&C 128). In all the mountains of material they have turned out there should be masses of evidence for these wild and conflicting stories if the Mormons were the authors of them.

Howe: Oh, but there is, plenty of it!

Chairman: In that case, why is it necessary to use any of this third- and fourth-hand hearsay at all? Why not convict Smith out of his own voluminous writings? If he is the absolute ninny these "witnesses" make him out to be his own recorded words are more than ample to prove it.

Howe: Well, as Mrs. Brodie says, "there are few men . . . who have written so much and told so little about themselves."[265] He deliberately made himself mysterious, he "was well skilled in legerdemain. . . . He doubtless had become acquainted with mystifying everything."[266]

Chairman: Yet in all the stories about Smith we never hear of his legerdemain. A supreme exhibitionist, he never on any recorded occasion yielded to the natural temptation to display his sleight-of-hand. But he was mysterious, very mysterious. We have heard a lot of that.

E. G. Ferris: Yes, "he affected great mystery in his movements, . . . traveled about the country, appearing and disappearing in a mysterious manner." Many witnesses mention it.[267]

Chairman: Of course. When you say a man's doings are mysterious, you are simply admitting that *you* don't know what he is up to. It is a regular practice of writers on Joseph Smith to palm off their extreme ignorance about his life as useful information about the man himself. Latin, I am told, is a most mysterious language to those who can't read it. But is the mystery in the language or in the lazy student? Is the mystery of Joseph Smith, the enigmatic quality which Mrs. Brodie finds so conspicuous, in him or in his biographers? Of course, if you don't believe his story, then in view of his actual proven accomplishments, the whole thing becomes a whopping mystery.

Hunt: We must bear in mind that the Smiths covered up their contradictions. "The various verbal accounts, all contradictory, false, and inconsistent, which were given out by the Smith family," are contained in the affidavits and go back to an early time. "Since the publication of their bible, they have been less contradictory in their statements respecting it."[268]

Chairman: So they started to watch themselves in 1830?

Howe: Mr. Hunt is simply paraphrasing (without acknowledgment, as usual) what I wrote in 1834: "Since the publication of the book they have been generally more uniform in their relations respecting it."[269]

Turner: No, it wasn't until 1834 that they started exercising caution. Things were "related and varied to suit the exigencies of the case, until the year 1834, when . . . the whole story [was] new vamped, stereotyped, and given to the world."[270]

Chairman: So the Mormons went on all that time trying to convince the world that their story was true, yet apparently blithely unaware that it would not do to tell a thousand conflicting versions!

Kelly and Birney, Inc.: "The testimony relative to the actual origin of the Book of Mormon is conflicting, due to the Prophet's telling various stories before selecting one and deciding to stick to it."[271]

W. E. Biederwolf: "There are irreconcilable discrepancies between Joe Smith's earlier and later accounts of how the plates were discovered to him."[272]

Chairman: Where do we find the "earlier" accounts?

Biederwolf: "Willard Chase on affidavit swore that Joe told him he discovered the plates by means of his peepstone. Peter Ingersoll testified."[273]

Chairman: One moment, sir. Those are not Smith's affidavits you are referring to, they are the statements of Chase and Ingersoll, and there are "irreconcilable discrepancies" between *them.* But what are Smith's "later accounts" to which you refer?

Biederwolf: "The final version as set forth in Joe's biography written in 1838."[274]

Chairman: So Smith is a liar for not telling the same stories about himself that his enemies do. He certainly would have been a suicidal fool to repeat *those* stories — and an even greater fool to have told them to his enemies in the first place. Do you really believe he went about telling such damning things about himself to anybody, friend or foe? Now, some have said that Smith decided to stick to one story as early as 1827, others say Smith and the Mormons followed a consistent account only after 1830, others after 1834, 1838, or 1842. But while all admit that the Mormon story does become more or less consistent after this or that date, the stories of the anti-Mormons about them do *not* show any tendency to become less exotic and contradictory down through the years to the present time. Do you know what that means? It means that these wild contradictions are the critics' very own; they are not due to Mormon fabrication at all, it is the others who are lying.

Clark: But how about all those conflicting Mormon stories about the plates? "The statements of the originators of this imposture varied. . . . At first it was a Gold Bible — then golden plates engraved — then metallic plates stereotyped."[275]

Chairman: Indeed, I know of no Mormon source that mentions stereotyping, and I fail to see any necessary contradiction between a Gold Bible and golden plates, since a Bible can be written on any type of writing surface. From whom do you have your information?

Clark: From "several gentlemen in Palmyra" reporting what Harris and others told them.[276]

Chairman: Well, here we go again! Are these "gentlemen in Palmyra" the "originators of the imposture?"

Clark: Of course not.

Chairman: But it is *their* "statements" you are citing, while confidently labeling them "statements of the originators." What you have actually given us is a written report of other written reports (Mr. Howe's) of statements made orally by certain anti-Mormons regarding what *they said* "Harris and others" (*not* the Smiths) told them. Do you follow?

Howe: But you cannot rule out "the various verbal accounts, all contradictory, vague, and inconsistent, which were given out by the Smith family respecting the finding of certain gold or brazen plates."[277]

Chairman: Did the Smiths sign these statements?

Howe: No. I specifically said they were "*verbal ac-*counts."

Chairman: Then actually we have no check on them at all.

Howe: Fortunately they have been written down.

Chairman: Then they are not *verbal* accounts, but *written* accounts. Granted that the Smiths didn't write them, who did? You and Mr. Hurlbut. From whose dictation — the Smiths? No. What you wrote down were the "various verbal accounts" given out *not* "by the Smith family" at all, but by their gossipy neighbors years after they had moved away.

Dogberry: Leaving Smith out of it, there still "appears to be a great discrepancy, in the stories told by the famous three witnesses to the Gold Bible."[278]

Chairman: And in what does this discrepancy consist?

Dogberry: "Whitmer's description of the Book of Mormon, differs entirely from that given by Harris."[279]

Chairman: Entirely? Didn't both men say the plates were gold, that they were on rings, that they were written in strange characters?

Howe: I think I gave a more accurate estimate of the situation when I wrote, "this account is sometimes partly contradicted by Harris."[280]

Chairman: "Sometimes" and "partly" is certainly a comedown from "entirely." What is this *entire* disagreement, Mr. Dogberry?

Dogberry: Well, Whitmer says "that the leaves were divided . . . so that the front might be opened . . . while the back part remained stationary and immovable, . . . a *sealed book.* . . . On opening that portion of the book which was not secured by the *seals,* he discovered . . . divers and wonderful characters."[281]

Chairman: So, according to Whitmer, the back part of the plates was sealed by being soldered so as to form a single block. And what does Harris say that is entirely contrary to this?

Dogberry: "Harris . . . gives the lie to a very important part of Whitmer's relation, and declares that the leaves or pages of the book are not cut, and a part of them sealed, but that it opens like any other book, from the edge to the back, the rings operating in the place of common binding."[282]

Chairman: Does Harris specifically state that Whitmer was lying or mistaken?

Dogberry: No, he does not say he was lying, he "*gives the lie*" to his report by a different description of his own.

Chairman: Does he specifically say that the book is *not* cut into two parts or three or four, or that no part of it is sealed?

Dogberry: No, he gives the lie when he says that it opens like any other book.

Chairman: But Whitmer also gives us to understand that it opens like any other book.

Dogberry: Only the part that was not sealed.

Chairman: Harris chose not to talk about the part that was sealed, because it was sealed and secret. He was specifically asked to testify about the plates from which the Book of Mormon was translated. The two descriptions agree perfectly as far as they go, and the one man talks about something that the other discreetly omits. Ask any two people to describe a book to you, and I guarantee that their descriptions will not be identical—the one party will surely mention something important that the other omits. But that does *not* mean that he is giving the other the lie. Even Mr. Howe saw that. Haven't you a better case of conflicting reports?

Dogberry: Yes, there is one other. "In the first place, . . . Smith and Harris gave out, that no mortal save Joe could look upon it [the book] and live." Yet a short time after, we have three witnesses looking on it and living![283]

Chairman: Where did Smith ever make that statement about no one seeing the book and staying alive?

Tucker: It was when he came in that day with the sand in his coat.[284]

Chairman: And Smith himself tells that story in his own writings?

Tucker: No. Peter Ingersoll is the authority for it.[285]

Chairman: And is he any more reliable than Willard Chase, who tells a very different story?

D. P. Kidder: The conflicting stories of those two only show that "as is usual, in such cases of fibbing, his [Smith's] stories were contradictory."[286]

Chairman: Then *no matter who made them up,* the stories were not true?

Kidder: Of course not.

Chairman: How then can they be used to incriminate Joseph Smith? Here he is telling all these awful things about himself, which show that he is a terrible sinner but they are not true! His crime is not that he *did* wicked things, but made up a lot of sensational crime stories (all false) with himself as the hero. And this brings up a fatal objection to the theory that the "various verbal accounts" reported by the affidavit swearers, "all contradictory, false, and inconsistent," were actually "given out by the Smith family." The most contradictory and inconsistent of them could not possibly have been given out by the Smiths.

Howe: Why not?

Chairman: First, consider that almost any of these stories standing alone makes Smith look pretty bad. Is it likely that Smith or his followers would go around telling such things against themselves? Did Smith spread abroad tales of his own "unspeakable lewdness?" Did his family tell how they were suspected of sheep-stealing? Was it they who claimed to have dug up acres of ground around Palmyra? Did Smith announce to the world that he used to forge Indian relics? Did he say he made a "handsome profit" by bilking his gang? Or that people paid him to get rid of his importunities? Or that he stole the Chase stone? Mr. Kennedy, you said something interesting about how the Smith crowd covered up his early fiascos. Do you remember it?

Kennedy: I said Smith gained a reputation, but met with many failures, "of which all mention was discreetly omitted by himself and his followers."[287]

Chairman: This nice bit of double-talk (do Smith and his followers ever mention their *successes* in the business?) tells us that the scandalous information regarding Smith's operations does *not*, as is charged, come from the Smiths, and indeed as we have just noted, it would be absurd to expect it to do so. Consider the most lurid digging stories. They all rest on what the neighbors claim they actually saw independently of what the tactless Smiths might have reported; yet no tales are more contradictory, wild, improbable, and inconsistent than they. Did Mr. Tucker and Mr. Dickinson get their description of the cave from the Smiths? Not a bit of it, yet they give totally different accounts. Did Joseph Smith tell one party that he was notorious for his drunkenness and another that he was a forger? Did he insist that he was an atheist or describe his own fervid preaching at the revivals? Did he tell one person that he was always scrapping and another that he never had a fight? Who told all those stories about the sheep sacrifices — the Smiths? No one pretends it, yet where can you find wilder contradictions? Take the descriptions of the youthful Joseph Smith: they are as contradictory as anything you can find — but did Joseph Smith supply the clashing details, or did the Mormons invent them? Not for a moment — they go back to the neighbors who knew Smith so well and recount what *they* maintain were their own experiences, yet they are in complete disagreement. Plainly in these cases there is an awful lot of lying going on that cannot possibly be laid to the charge of the Mormons.

W. Graham: But these people only *seem* to disagree; "these conflicting stories only *appear* to be at variance as to the origin of the much-discussed plates."[288]

Chairman: And if they appear to be at variance, it is only because they are. If not, why have such pains been taken to attribute their variations to the Smiths? Why should contradictory statements be damning when the Smiths make them and only apparent contradictions when their enemies make them? We have been told by Mr. Sheldon that "the different stories which Smith himself told about the plates of the Book of Mormon impeach his honesty and veracity in the matter." Now, if it can be shown that the people who report those stories, and who are the only authority for them, frequently tell different tales on their own authority in situations in which the Smiths cannot possibly be implicated, does not that impeach their honor?

Our experts on Joseph Smith would have no difficulty at all condemning Jesus. They could have been of real assistance to the high priest when he was embarrassed because his witnesses contradicted each other—"their witness agreed not together" (Mark 14: 56, 59). The Sanhedrin could have used the useful theory that such disagreement was proof positive that Jesus had been deceiving all those people. And to what did the diligent perjurers bear witness? It was the old story: "We heard him say . . . " "Once he told me . . . " (Mark 14:58; Matthew 26:61). In vain the Lord pointed out that he did not make secret disclosures to individuals (John 18:20–21). They convicted him in the end for claiming he was the Messiah (Matthew 26:65; Mark 14:63)—which was legally no crime at all.

Howe: Hold on a minute here! Badly garbled though these accounts may be, they still must have had an original. They may be widely ranging variations on a theme—but somebody or something furnished the theme in the first place. Say what you will, there *must* be something behind all this, and it must concern Joseph Smith!

Chairman: I am inclined to agree with you there, Mr. Howe. I think we should look more closely into the earliest digging stories. The court will take a ten-minute recess.

Notes for Part 2, Scene i

1. Pomeroy Tucker, *Origin, Rise, and Progress of Mormonism* (New York: Appleton, 1867), 22.

2. Ibid.

3. Eber D. Howe, *Mormonism Unvailed; Or, a Faithful Account of That Singular Imposition and Delusion* (Painesville, OH: the author, 1834), 239.

4. Ibid., 238.

5. Ibid., 249–50.

6. Ibid., 259.

7. Ibid., 232.

8. Ibid., 234.

9. Ibid., 263.

10. Tucker, *Origin, Rise, and Progress of Mormonism*, 22–23.

11. Howe, *Mormonism Unvailed*, 233.

12. Francis Kirkham, *A New Witness for Ch: in America: The Book of Mormon*, 2 vols. (Salt Lake City: Utah Printing, 1951), 2:69.

13. J. B. Turner, *Mormonism in All Ages* (New York: Platt and Peters, 1842), 29.

14. Kirkham, *New Witness for Christ in America*, 2:69.

15. Earnest S. Bates, *American Faith* (New York: Norton, 1940), 345.

16. Henry Caswall, *The Prophet of the 19th Century; Or, the Rise, Progress, and Present State of Mormons or Latter-Day Saints* (London: Rivingtons, 1843), 28–29.

17. T. W. Young, *Mormonism: Its Origin, Doctrines, and Dangers* (Ann Arbor, MI: Wahr, 1900), 16.

18. Tucker, *Origin, Rise, and Progress of Mormonism*, 27.

19. Mrs. Dr. Horace Eaton, "Speech Delivered May 27, 1881," in *Handbook on Mormonism* (Salt Lake City: Handbook, 1882), 2.

20. George B. Arbaugh, *Revelation in Mormonism* (Chicago: University of Chicago Press, 1932), 28.

21. Eaton, "Speech," in *Handbook of Mormonism*, 2.

22. John Quincy Adams, *The Birth of Mormonism* (Boston: Gorham, 1916), 16.

23. Arbaugh, *Revelation in Mormonism*, 27.

24. Oliver Cowdery, letter to W. W. Phelps, in *Latter-Day Saints' Messenger and Advocate* 2 (October 1835): 200–201.

25. James H. Hunt, *Mormonism* (St. Louis: Ustick and Davies, 1844), 5–6.

26. Young, *Mormonism: Its Origin, Doctrines, and Dangers,* 16.

27. John Eaton, *The Mormons of Today* (Washington, D.C.: Eaton, 1897), 5.

28. Hunt, *Mormonism*, 6.

29. C. Sheridan Jones, *The Truth about the Mormons: Secrets of Salt Lake City* (London: Rider, 1920), 10–11.

30. J. S. C. Abbott, *The History of the State of Ohio* (Detroit: New World, 1875), 697–98.

31. "The Yankee Mahomet," *American Whig Review* 7 (June 1851): 555–56.

32. Emily C. Blackman, *History of Susquehannah County* (Philadelphia: Claxton, Remsen, and Haffelfinger, 1873), 579–80.

33. Tucker, *Origin, Rise, and Progress of Mormonism,* 21 (emphasis added).

34. Hunt, *Mormonism,* 6.

35. Howe, *Mormonism Unvailed,* 12.

36. John C. Bennett, *The History of the Saints; Or, An Exposé of Joe Smith and Mormonism* (Boston: Leland and Whiting, 1842), 72.

37. S. B. Emmons, *The Spirit Land* (Philadelphia: Potter, 1857), 101.

38. Eaton, "Speech," in *Handbook of Mormonism,* 2.

39. Ibid., 31.

40. Ellen E. Dickinson, *New Light on Mormonism* (New York: Funk and Wagnalls, 1885), 30.

41. Lu B. Cake, *Peepstone Joe and the Peck Manuscript* (New York: Cake, 1899), 13–14.

42. Blackman, *History of Susquehannah County,* 580.

43. Howe, *Mormonism Unvailed,* 262–63.

44. Blackman, *History of Susquehannah County,* 580.

45. Tucker, *Origin, Rise, and Progress of Mormonism,* 21 (emphasis added).

46. Ibid., 21–22.

47. J. E. Mahaffey, *Found at Last! 'Positive Proof' That Mormonism Is a Fraud and the Book of Mormon a Fable* (Augusta, GA: Chronicle Job Office, 1902), 14.

48. Howe, *Mormonism Unvailed,* 262.

49. Ibid., 12.

50. Eaton, "Speech," in *Handbook of Mormonism*, 2.

51. Tucker, *Origin, Rise, and Progress of Mormonism*, 22.

52. Dickinson, *New Light on Mormonism*, 247.

53. Tucker, *Origin, Rise, and Progress of Mormonism*, 22–23.

54. John D. Kingsbury, *Mormonism: Whence It Came, What It Is, Whither It Tends* (New York and Salt Lake City: Congregational Home Missionary Society, n.d.), 5.

55. Jones, *Truth about the Mormons*, 11.

56. Tucker, *Origin, Rise, and Progress of Mormonism*, 20.

57. Harry M. Beardsley, *Joseph Smith and His Mormon Empire* (Boston: Houghton Mifflin, 1831), 18.

58. Tucker, *Origin, Rise, and Progress of Mormonism*, 23.

59. Eaton, "Speech," in *Handbook of Mormonism*, 2.

60. Tucker, *Origin, Rise, and Progress of Mormonism*, 23.

61. Orvilla S. Belisle, *Mormonism Unveiled: A History of Mormonism from Its Rise to the Present Time* (London: Clark, 1855), 20.

62. Caswall, *Prophet of the 19th Century*, 33.

63. Mahaffey, *Found at Last!*, 6.

64. Adams, *Birth of Mormonism*, 17.

65. Jones, *Truth about the Mormons*, 11.

66. Belisle, *Mormonism Unveiled*, 16.

67. Ibid., 17–18.

68. Howe, *Mormonism Unvailed*, 238–39.

69. "Yankee Mahomet," 557.

70. George Seibel, *The Mormon Saints* (Pittsburgh: Lessing, 1919), 16–17.

71. Howe, *Mormonism Unvailed*, 239.

72. Ibid.

73. Ibid.

74. Ibid.

75. Cake, *Peepstone Joe and the Peck Manuscript*, 14 (emphasis added).

76. Dickinson, *New Light on Mormonism*, 31.

77. J. H. Kennedy, *Early Days of Mormonism, Palmyra, Kirtland, and Nauvoo* (New York: Scribner, 1888), 31.

78. Kennedy, *Early Days of Mormonism*, 31; Bennett, *History of the Saints*, 72.

79. Blackman, *History of Susquehannah County*, 580.

80. Tucker, *Origin, Rise, and Progress of Mormonism*, 24–25.

81. Emily M. Austin, *Mormonism; Or, Life among the Mormons, Being an Autobiographical Sketch* (Madison, WI: Cantwell, 1882), 32–33.

82. Dickinson, *New Light on Mormonism*, 31.

83. Austin, *Mormonism; Or, Life among the Mormons*, 32.

84. Sidney Bell, *Wives of the Prophet* (London: Rich and Cowen, 1936), 6.

85. Kennedy, *Early Days of Mormonism*, 19.

86. Mahaffey, *Found at Last!*, 14.

87. Tucker, *Origin, Rise, and Progress of Mormonism*, 22.

88. Seibel, *Mormon Saints*, 16–17.

89. Blackman, *History of Susquehannah County*, 580.

90. Howe, *Mormonism Unvailed*, 238.

91. Caswall, *Prophet of the 19th Century*, 29.

92. "Yankee Mahomet," 556.

93. William A. Linn, *The Story of the Mormons, from the Date of Their Origin to the Year 1901* (New York: Macmillan, 1902), 15.

94. Dickinson, *New Light on Mormonism*, 30.

95. M. W. Montgomery, *The Mormon Delusion* (Boston: Congregational Sunday School and Publishing Society, 1890), 16.

96. Linn, *Story of the Mormons*, 21.

97. Ibid.

98. Blackman, *History of Susquehannah County*, 577.

99. Linn, *Story of the Mormons*, 15.

100. Ibid., 18.

101. Beardsley, *Joseph Smith and His Mormon Empire*, 3.

102. Linn, *Story of the Mormons*, 19–20.

103. Howe, *Mormonism Unvailed*, 240–41.

104. Ibid.

105. Tucker, *Origin, Rise, and Progress of Mormonism*, 19.

106. Howe, *Mormonism Unvailed*, 241.

107. "Yankee Mahomet," 557.

108. Tucker, *Origin, Rise, and Progress of Mormonism*, 19 (emphasis added).

109. George W. Cowles, *Landmarks of Wayne County New York* (Syracuse, NY: Mason, 1895), 80.

110. Howe, *Mormonism Unvailed*, 232–33.

111. Tucker, *Origin, Rise, and Progress of Mormonism*, 19.

112. Dickinson, *New Light on Mormonism*, 30.

113. Ibid., 30.

114. Arbaugh, *Revelation in Mormonism*, 28.

115. Ibid.

116. Blackman, *History of Susquehannah County*, 577.

117. Dickinson, *New Light on Mormonism*, 30.

118. Cowles, *Landmarks of Wayne County*, 81.

119. Ibid., 77–80.

120. Ibid., 80.

121. "Yankee Mahomet," 557.

122. Howe, *Mormonism Unvailed,* 90.

123. Thomas Gregg, *The Prophet of Palmyra* (New York: Alden, 1890), 26.

124. Fawn M. Brodie, *No Man Knows My History* (New York: Knopf, 1947), 71 (emphasis added).

125. Howe, *Mormonism Unvailed,* 31–32.

126. Arbaugh, *Revelation in Mormonism,* 26.

127. Emmons, *Spirit Land,* 101.

128. Howe, *Mormonism Unvailed,* 12.

129. Walter R. Martin, *The Rise of the Cults* (Grand Rapids, MI: Zondervan, 1955), 47.

130. Hunt, *Mormonism,* 6.

131. John A. Clark, *Gleanings by the Way* (Philadelphia: Simons, 1842), 225.

132. Howe, *Mormonism Unvailed,* 265.

133. Beardsley, *Joseph Smith and His Mormon Empire,* 3.

134. From an interview with Daniel Hendrix in the *New York Times,* 15 July 1898.

135. Tucker, *Origin, Rise, and Progress of Mormonism,* 20–21.

136. Kennedy, *Early Days of Mormonism,* 20.

137. Bennett, *History of the Saints,* 220–21.

138. Dickinson, *New Light on Mormonism*, 30.

139. Blackman, *History of Susquehannah County,* 580.

140. Mahaffey, *Found at Last!* 6.

141. Montgomery, *Mormon Delusion*, 23.

142. W. Wyl, *Mormon Portraits; Or, the Truth about the Mormon Leaders* (Salt Lake City: Tribune, 1886), 79.

143. R. W. Beers, *The Mormon Puzzle; and How to Solve It* (Chicago: Funk and Wagnalls, 1887), 28.

144. Howe, *Mormonism Unvailed,* 235–36.

145. Ibid., 235.

146. Samuel Fellows and Helen M. Fellows, *The Mormon Menace* (Chicago: Women's Temperance, 1903), 14–16.

147. Dickinson, *New Light on Mormonism*, 34.

148. Howe, *Mormonism Unvailed,* 236; John Bowes, *Mormonism Exposed* (London: Edinburgh, 1849), in Tracts, 8–9.

149. Howe, *Mormonism Unvailed,* 251.

150. Ibid., 236.

151. Caswall, *Prophet of the 19th Century,* 36.

152. Ibid.
153. Montgomery, *Mormon Delusion*, 18–19.
154. Bennett, *History of the Saints*, 74.
155. Howe, *Mormonism Unvailed*, 245–46.
156. W. Sparrow Simpson, *Mormonism: Its History, Doctrines, and Practices* (London: Pigott, 1853), 11.
157. Tucker, *Origin, Rise, and Progress of Mormonism*, 30.
158. Howe, *Mormonism Unvailed*, 245.
159. Ibid., 264.
160. Abbott, *History of the State of Ohio*, 699.
161. Dickinson, *New Light on Mormonism*, 35.
162. Adams, *Birth of Mormonism*, 39.
163. Tucker, *Origin, Rise, and Progress of Mormonism*, 32.
164. Cowles, *Landmarks of Wayne County*, 80.
165. George Townsend, *The Conversion of Mormonism* (Hartford, CT: Church Mission, 1911), 13.
166. Ibid.
167. Cowles, *Landmarks of Wayne County*, 81.
168. Cake, *Peepstone Joe and the Peck Manuscript*, 15.
169. Wyl, *Mormon Portraits*, 36.
170. Clark, *Gleanings by the Way*, 334.
171. *Is Mormonism True or Not?* (London: Religious Tract Society), 5–6.
172. O. H. Olney, *Absurdities of Mormonism* (Hancock Co., IL: n.p., 1843), 4–5.
173. Cf. Alexander Campbell and W. K. Pendleton, eds., "The Mormons—Counterfeiters," *Millennial Harbinger* 3 (March 1846): 180.
174. Cake, *Peepstone Joe and the Peck Manuscript*, 86.
175. Campbell and Pendleton, eds., "The Mormons—Counterfeiters," 180.
176. D. H. C. Bartlett, *The Mormons or, Latter-day Saints, Whence Came They?* (Liverpool: Thompson, 1911), 8.
177. Linn, *Story of the Mormons*, 28–29.
178. Bartlett, *Mormons or, Latter-day Saints, Whence Came They?* 8.
179. Adams, *Birth of Mormonism*, 20.
180. Ibid., 20–21.
181. Brodie, *No Man Knows My History*, 440.
182. *Utah Christian Advocate* 2 (January 1886): 1.
183. Ibid.
184. Brodie, *No Man Knows My History*, 440.
185. Ibid., 141.

186. Ibid., 418.
187. Kirkham, *New Witness for Christ in America,* 1:476.
188. Ibid.
189. Ibid., 1:476, 479.
190. Ibid., 1:476; Brodie, *No Man Knows My History,* 441.
191. Kirkham, *New Witness for Christ in America,* 1:476.
192. Ibid.
193. Ibid., 1:485.
194. Ibid., 1:477–78.
195. Ibid., 1:483.
196. Ibid., 1:479.
197. Ibid.
198. Ibid.
199. Ibid.
200. Ibid., 1:482.
201. Ibid.
202. Ibid., 1:485.
203. Ibid., 1:479.
204. Ibid.
205. Ibid., 2:364.
206. Ibid., 1:480.
207. Ibid., 1:484.
208. A. W. Benton, "Mormonites," *Evangelical Magazine and Gospel Advocate* (9 April 1831): 120.
209. Ibid.
210. Ibid.
211. Ibid.
212. Ibid.
213. Ibid.
214. Ibid.
215. Ibid.
216. Ibid.
217. Ibid.
218. Ibid.
219. Ibid.
220. Brodie, *No Man Knows My History,* 441.
221. Benton, "Mormonites," 120. [Cf. Dennis Rowley, "The Ezra Booth Letters," *Dialogue: A Journal of Mormon Thought* 16 (Autumn 1983): 133–37.]
222. Ezra Booth, cited in Howe, *Mormonism Unvailed,* 187.
223. Orsamus Turner, *History of the Pioneer Settlement of Phelps and Gorham's Purchase and Morris' Reserve* (Rochester, Alling, 1851), 216.

224. Harry M. Beardsley, *Joseph Smith and His Mormon Empire* (Boston: Riverside, 1921), 28.

225. Seibel, *The Mormon Saints*, 16.

226. Belisle, *Mormonism Unveiled*, 20.

227. Benton, "Mormonites," 120; "Oliver Cowdery, one of the three witnesses to the book, testified under oath, that said Smith found with the plates, from which he translated his book, two transparent stones, resembling glass, set in silver bows."

228. Linn, *Story of the Mormons*, 18; Beardsley, *Joseph Smith and His Mormon Empire*, 28.

229. Tucker, *Origin, Rise and Progress of Mormonism*, 19.

230. Beers, *Mormon Puzzle*, 27.

231. I. W. Riley, cited in George B. Arbaugh, *Revelation in Mormonism* (Chicago: University of Chicago Press, 1932), 28.

232. Gregg, *Prophet of Palmyra*, 26.

233. Book review of Caswall, *The City of the Mormons* in *Visitor or Monthly Instructor* (1842), 407: cf. Henry Caswall, *The City of the Mormons, or Three Days at Nauvoo* (London: Rivington, 1842), 27.

234. William E. Biederwolf, *Mormonism under the Searchlight* (Grand Rapids, MI: Eerdman, n.d.), 6.

235. Linn, *Story of the Mormons*, 18.

236. Howe, *Mormonism Unvailed*, 237.

237. Ibid.

238. Tucker, *Origin, Rise, and Progress of Mormonism*, 19.

239. O. Turner, *History of the Pioneer Settlement*, 216.

240. Cowles, *Landmarks of Wayne County*, 80; Turner, *History of the Pioneer Settlement*, 216.

241. Howe, *Mormonism Unvailed*, 232.

242. Ibid., 240.

243. Hunt, *Mormonism*, 12.

244. Bennett, *History of the Saints*, 66 (emphasis added).

245. Clark, *Gleanings by the Way*, 228–29.

246. Howe, *Mormonism Unvailed*, 248.

247. Henry C. Sheldon, *A Fourfold Test of Mormonism* (New York: Abingdon, 1914), 15.

248. John Hyde, *Mormonism, Its Leaders and Designs* (New York: Fetridge, 1857), 243.

249. Ibid.

250. Ibid.

251. Kirkham, *New Witness for Christ in America*, 2:43.

252. Ibid.

253. Benton, "Mormonites," 120.

254. Ibid.

255. Tucker, *Origin, Rise, and Progress of Mormonism,* 22.

256. Ibid.

257. Henry Harris cited in Howe, *Mormonism Unvailed,* 251.

258. Howe, *Mormonism Unvailed,* 252.

259. Ibid., 242–43.

260. Ibid., 247.

261. Ibid.

262. Ibid., 235.

263. John Hyde, *Mormonism, Its Leaders and Designs,* 241.

264. Biederwolf, *Mormonism under the Searchlight,* 5.

265. Brodie, *No Man Knows My History,* vii.

266. Howe, *Mormonism Unvailed,* 43.

267. Benjamin G. Ferris, *Utah and the Mormons, the History, Government, Doctrines, Customs and Prospects of the Latter Day Saints* (New York: Harper, 1856), 53.

268. James H. Hunt, *Mormonism* (St. Louis, MO: Ustick and Davies, 1844), 12.

269. Howe, *Mormonism Unvailed,* 17.

270. J. B. Turner, *Mormonism in All Ages,* 17.

271. Charles Kelly and Hoffman Birney, *Holy Murder: The Story of Porter Rockwell* (New York: Minton, Balch, 1934), 5.

272. Biederwolf, *Mormonism under the Searchlight,* 7.

273. Ibid.

274. Ibid.

275. Clark, *Gleanings by the Way,* 228–29.

276. Ibid.

277. Howe, *Mormonism Unvailed,* 17.

278. Kirkham, *New Witness for Christ in America,* 2:75–76.

279. Ibid.

280. Howe, *Mormonism Unvailed,* 16.

281. Kirkham, *New Witness for Christ in America,* 2:75–76.

282. Ibid.

283. Ibid.

284. Tucker, *Origin, Rise, and Progress of Mormonism,* 22.

285. Howe, *Mormonism Unvailed,* 236–37.

286. Daniel P. Kidder, *Mormonism and the Mormons* (New York: Lane and Tippett, 1844), 23.

287. Kennedy, *Early Days of Mormonism,* 19.

288. Winifred Graham, *The Mormons: A Popular History from Earliest Times to the Present Day* (London: Hurst and Blackett, 1913), 4.

ii. What is behind it

Scene: The same, after a brief recess.

Enter the real diggers

Chairman: During these hearings it has occurred to me, as it has no doubt occurred to many of you, that no matter how wild and contradictory these stories may be, there must be something behind them. Can anyone doubt that there was some sort of digging and some sort of peepstone from which the stories took their rise? We can't accept any of these stories as they stand — there are too many objections to each one: but can we get back to the primordial cell from which they are all derived? The only way to do it is to interview the earliest witnesses we can find. So let us begin with Mr. Obadiah Dogberry. According to you, Mr. Dogberry, the idea of hidden treasures guarded by the spirits was a familiar one in Joseph Smith's part of the world *before* he ever took to digging. Is that correct?

Obadiah Dogberry: It is. "This opinion . . . did not originate by any means with Smith." There was "the *MANIA* of money-digging . . . through many parts of this country" at the time. "Men and women without distinction of age or sex . . . dreamed, and . . . saw visions disclosing to them deep in the bowels of the earth, rich and shining treasures, . . . and although the *SPIRIT* was always able to retain his precious charge, these discomfited as well as deluded beings, would on a succeeding night return to their toil."[1]

Chairman: All this was well before Smith's story of the gold plates. And did these people use peepstones?

Dogberry: They did indeed. *"Peep-stones* or pebbles, taken promiscuously from brook or field" would show these people "all the wonders of nature, including of course, ample stores of silver and gold."[2]

Chairman: And how did these multitudes of people "in

many parts of this country" operate these wonderful *peep-stones?*

Dogberry: The *"peep-stones . . . were placed in a hat* or other situation excluded from the light, when some *wizard* or *witch . . .* applied their eyes."[3]

Chairman: But Mr. Pomeroy Tucker, the learned editor and Mr. Smith's very intimate personal friend, assures us that the practice with the hat was peculiar to Smith, who resorted to it not to make his peepstone look brighter, but to make it look dimmer. The very oddity of Smith and his peepstone techniques has been exploited as a prime explanation of the Book of Mormon. Mr. Lu B. Cake calls his invaluable collection of affidavits, *Peepstone Joe,* as if Smith was the only man who ever peeped; and the most devastating blow dealt to Smith's pretensions has always been the claim that he was known as a money digger. Now we learn that peeping and money digging were everybody's business. Mr. Howe, you said these stories must have a foundation in fact, and now it is apparent that you were right. According to the first mention of the business, the peeping and digging stories do *not* begin with Smith at all, yet his critics, especially in the twentieth century, labor mightily to prove to the world that he and his family were absolutely unique and peculiar in peeping and digging, which queer practices made their doings well known "to vast numbers of people." But I think we can be more specific than this. With everyone around him digging like mad, so to speak, how did young Smith get into the business?

Walters

Dogberry: I can tell you that. It was a man called [Luman] Walters, a sort of conjurer, who "was paid three dollars per day for his services by money diggers in this neighborhood."[4]

Chairman: As a conjurer, he would find the treasures

for them, and they would dig, I take it? That is exactly the business in which Smith was so long engaged, we have been told.

Dogberry: Yes, it was Walters who "first suggested to Smith the idea of finding a book."[5]

Chairman: How did he do that?

Dogberry: He "had procured an old copy of Cicero's *Orations,* in the Latin language, out of which he read long and loud to his credulous hearers, uttering at the same time an unintelligible jargon, which he would afterwards pretend to interpret, and explain, as a record of the former inhabitants of America."[6]

Chairman: Just like Solomon Spaulding, eh? But what proof have you that Smith was ever among his hearers?

Dogberry: I wasn't there, of course, but it stands to reason.

Chairman: How do you know it was Walters who suggested the idea of the Book of Mormon to Joseph Smith?

Dogberry: "There remains but little doubt, in the minds of those at all acquainted with these transactions."[7]

Chairman: It is clear from the way you put it that these people were not witnesses to anything significant: witnesses do not testify to things which are in their minds or matters on which they have "but little doubt"; they either know or they don't know, because they have seen and heard, not because they are "at all acquainted with these transactions." Now tell us, can you name any of these people, or tell how they might have overheard the secret and private conversations between Walters and Smith— whom you earlier describe as Walters' intimate disciple? Can you even give evidence that Smith and Walters ever met?

Dogberry: There are significant coincidences. "Not long previous to the pretended discovery of the 'Book of Mormon,' Walters assembled his nightly band of money diggers in the town of Manchester, at a point designated with his magical book, and . . . absolutely sacrificed a fowl, 'Rooster,' in the presence of his awe-stricken companions, to the foul spirit."[8]

Chairman: And here we have been told all along that it was Smith's very own idea to organize a digging gang. What has all this to do with Joseph Smith?

Dogberry: I told you this happened "not long previous to the pretended discovery of the 'Book of Mormon.' "[9]

Chairman: But according to our most reliable witnesses, Smith could not possibly have learned his art from Walters, since he had already been practicing peeping and digging with his own gang for years! Indeed, by the time he met Walters, according to nearly all our other "witnesses" he would have given up the business—he stopped, they tell us, in 1827, after he had discovered the plates and after seven or eight years of digging. You say repeatedly that the "mantle" of Walters "fell upon the *Prophet* Jo. Smith Jun.," but it should have been the other way around— Joseph was an old hand at all this stuff, according to all the others. He learned it from his father who, we have been assured on high authority, practiced it in Vermont.

Dogberry: "We are not able to determine whether the elder Smith was ever concerned in money-digging transactions previous to his emigration from Vermont."[10]

Chairman: Well then, others tell us it was his mother who taught him the black arts; that the peepstone had been in her family for generations: but others say it was a little old woman who lived down the road; others say Smith first learned divination from a young girl; still others say it was a man in Pennsylvania who introduced Smith to peeping. If Smith learned his art from Walters, who told people where to dig for treasure and, according to you, led "his motley crew of tatterdemalions" on ritual diggings in the woods around Manchester at night, then what happens to all the peepstone stories, which put Joseph Smith in the very same business in 1822 and earlier? He needed

no mantle from you—he had it all down cold! Why did
you say that Walters "absolutely sacrificed a fowl, 'Rooster' " in his digging ritual?

Dogberry: Because he actually did, shocking and incredible as it may seem.

Chairman: Shucks, man, that was *nothing!* Don't you
know that the Smiths had been sacrificing black sheep all
over the place for years? We have been told by more than
one witness that whenever Smith wanted meat for his
family he ordered the sacrifice of a black sheep, and from
those claiming to have been his closest neighbors and observers we have heard how he would sometimes substitute
a white sheep or a white dog or a black dog for his black
sheep. And all this in the years before 1827 and long before
the meeting with Walters which Mr. Dogberry says took
place "not long previous to the pretended discovery of the
'Book of Mormon.' " Now, it has been admitted by the
most hostile witnesses, and denied by none, that there is
no evidence that Joseph Smith himself ever engaged in
digging for treasure, but there *must* be something behind
it all, they tell us. There was: the *tales* of Walters, not his
"mantle" but the *stories* about him, were simply transferred
whole to Smith. Professor Turner speaks of another mantle
falling on Smith.

O. Turner: Yes, it was "the mantle of the prophet which
Mr. and Mrs. Joseph Smith and one Oliver Cowdery had
wove of themselves—every thread of it."[11]

Chairman: That doesn't leave much for Walters, you
see. But when you say as you do, Mr. Dogberry, that the
mantle of Walters fell upon Joseph Smith, you are expressing a truth: the whole fabric of digging-stories about
Walters, even down to small and peculiar details: the stone,
the circle, the sword, the book, the rabble band, the midnight digs, the sacrifices, the ever-disappointing treasure,
the clever explanations—all those things we have been
taught were the peculiar stamp of Smith's genius, now

seem to have belonged to another and much older man, and to have been transferred to Smith not by Walters but by you, Mr. Dogberry.

Dogberry: But the resemblance between the two impostors is much too full and perfect to be a coincidence.

Chairman: True. And therefore Smith must have got his stuff from Walters if the stories about Smith are true. But he denies that those stories are true, and what is worse, ninety percent of them rule Walters out of the picture. The striking resemblance on which you rest your case is not between Walters and Smith, but between Walters and Smith as *you describe him*.

Editor of the Rochester Gem: But Walters was not the only person that Smith resembled most remarkably. In fact his resemblance to Walters may have been just a coincidence after all.

Dogberry: Out of the question, sir!

The other Smith and Mr. Northrop

Gem: Not at all! Let me give you one. Smith's whole "story brings to our mind one of similar nature once played off upon the inhabitants of Rochester and its vicinity, near the close of the last war."[12]

Chairman: Let's get this straight. To what war do you refer?

Gem: The War of 1812, of course. "If we remember aright, it was in the year 1815, that a family of Smiths moved into these parts."

Chairman: By "these parts" you mean "Rochester and its vicinity," and since the final peace treaty was signed just one day after Joseph Smith turned eight, he would have been seven years old "near the close of the last war." I want to get this clear, that the Smiths you are talking about are *not* the family of Joseph Smith.

Gem: That is right. This is simply a case "of similar

nature." Time and place alike make it impossible to confuse them.

Eber D. Howe: Then why all the fuss?

Chairman: Pay close attention, Mr. Howe, and you will see. Proceed, witness.

Gem:

> They had a wonderful son, of about 18 years of age, who, on a certain day, as they said, while in the road, discovered a round stone of the size of a man's fist, the which when he first saw it, presented to him on the one side, all the dazzling splendor of the sun in full blaze — and on the other, the clearness of the moon. He fell down insensible at the sight, and while in the trance produced by the sudden and awful discovery, it was communicated to him that he was to become an oracle — and the keys of mystery were put into his hands, and he saw the unsealing of the book of fate. He told his tale for MONEY. Numbers flocked to him to test his skill, and the first question among a certain class was, if there was any of Kidd's money hid in these parts of the earth. The oracle, after adjusting the stone in his hat, and looking in upon it some time, pronounced that there was.[13]

Chairman: So here we have a young man by the name of Smith peeping for treasure — Captain Kidd's treasure — less than thirty miles from Palmyra. You say there must be something behind the peeping stories — there is, but it has nothing to do with Joseph Smith. I suppose next a band of diggers was organized?

Gem: Of course, how did you guess it? "The question of where, being decided upon, there forthwith emerged a set, armed with 'pick-axe, hoe and spade,' out into the mountains, to dislodge the treasure."[14]

Chairman: Did they ever find it?

Gem: Need you ask? "We shall mention but one man of the money diggers. His name was Northrop. . . . Northrop and his men sallied out upon the hills east of the river, and commenced digging —"

Chairman: By night, of course?

Gem: How did you know? Yes, "the night was chosen for operation—already had two nights been spent in digging, and the third commenced upon, when Northrop with his pick-axe struck the chest! The effect was powerful, and contrary to an explicit rule laid down by himself he exclaimed, 'd—m me, I've found it!' "[15]

Chairman: So he laid down strict rules for his phalanx, just like Joe. Of course this breaking of silence spoiled everything.

Gem: True. "The charm was broken!—the scream of demons,—the chattering of spirits—and hissing of serpents, rent the air, and the treasure moved!"[16]

Chairman: Of course.

Gem: What do you mean, "of course"?

Chairman: Didn't you know? Joseph Smith's treasures always moved away like that when somebody spoke.

Gem: Now you are being facetious.

Chairman: Not at all. I can give you a dozen reports on that. And I suppose the treasure kept moving that way and they never found it.

Gem: You happen to be right.

Chairman: And what happened to young Smith?

Gem: Well, a magistrate came to take his stone away, and the boy said that "he who should take away the inspired stone from him, would suffer immediate death!" But the magistrate "demanded the stone, and ground it to powder." So the Smiths moved away, "the money-diggers joined in the general execration . . . and all turned out to be a hoax!"[17]

Chairman: If all this has nothing to do with Joseph Smith, why do you tell it?

Gem: Because the stories are so much alike: "Now in reference to the two stories, 'put that to that, and they are a noble pair of brothers.' "[18]

The Belcher boy

Chairman: Exactly. They are twins, in fact, identical twins: nay, one is the mirror-image of the other. Here we have a parallel just as close as that between Smith and Walters, but in this case it cannot possibly be maintained that the younger Smith borrowed anything from the older Smith or his diggers or from the Northrop gang: yet the resemblance is too striking to be mere coincidence. How do we account for it, then? One of these Smiths was the real peeper, the other his borrowed reflection. We have seen how clumsily, persistently, and absurdly the experts have attempted to hang a lot of digging stories on Joseph Smith—they don't fit at all. But here we have *other* men to whom these stories *do* apply, and they come *first*, robbing Joseph Smith of all claims to originality. But he makes no such claims!—his friends and followers protest that the digging stories about him are *not* true. *They* never tell such tales. But those who do tell them disagree among themselves and make an awful botch of things. They are trying to dress Joseph Smith in other men's clothes. Here, for example, we have another peepstone story just as good as the others. Mr. Buck, you are credited with the earliest report of Joe's peeping. What was his stone like?

J. B. Buck: The stone he used after he took up peeping was the "green stone, with brown, irregular spots on it." It was somewhat larger than a goose-egg.[19]

Chairman: How did the stone work?

Buck: "When he brought it home and covered it with a hat, Belcher's little boy was one of the first to look into the hat, and as he did so he said he saw a candle." The second time he looked he found his hatchet. "The boy was soon beset by neighbors far and near" to find lost things for them, which he did with great success.[20]

Chairman: And this was before Joseph Smith took to peeping?

Buck: Certainly. "Joe Smith was here lumbering soon after my marriage, which was in 1818, some years before he took to 'peeping'; . . . the stone which he afterwards used was then in the possession of Jack Belcher, of Gibson."[21]

Chairman: Of course you realize that Joe didn't turn thirteen until the last ten days of 1818 — so that makes him a twelve-year-old lumberman, but let it pass. The point is that we have a youngster peeping at a stone in a hat to find lost objects for people before Joseph Smith ever did such a thing. And then later we find Smith using *that very stone* (though we are not told how he got it) to do the same. Here again a story told originally about one boy is transferred to another one — this time consciously so. Mr. Buck's unique data are in conflict with all other versions, he makes no claim ever to have witnessed Joseph Smith's peeping, and does not even suggest the time, place, or manner in which the valuable stone, which was kept and greatly prized in Pennsylvania, changed hands. That is to say, there is *nothing* firsthand about his testimony, and since he is the *only* witness for the story he tells (the cornerstone of Dr. Linn's learned thesis), there is only one thing we can say about it for sure: that the *story* of the peeping Belcher boy was transferred by him from the Belchers to Smith.

Dogberry: Can you prove such a transfer?

Chairman: By direct testimony, of course not — no one is going to admit it. But let us take your own case. One of the most intrinsically absurd aspects of many digging stories about the Smiths is that though they never found anything, their faithful band of lazy loafers continued to dig all over the countryside for years. The picture is preposterous, it cannot be true — but I can tell you where it comes from. What was it you said about the *other* diggers of the time? The clerk will please read it.

Clerk (reads): "And to facilitate those *mighty* mining

operations (money was usually if not always sought after in the night time), divers devices and implements were invented, and although the SPIRIT was always able to retain his precious charge, these . . . deluded beings, would on a succeeding night return to their toil, not in the least doubting that success would eventually attend their labors."[22]

Chairman: There you have the same picture with the Smiths left out, and this time it is plausible. In terms of vast numbers of diggers it is easy to picture the work going on night after night and year after year all over the country, regardless of innumerable disappointments. But that this should apply to but one small household, the lazy Smiths, is quite unthinkable. The earlier and more believable situation has plainly been transferred to a setting in which it simply does not fit. Now, Mr. Dogberry, the number of references you made to "the mantle of Walters the Magician falling upon Joseph, surnamed the prophet" are all found in a writing by you entitled the "Book of Pukei." Is that work to be regarded as a serious piece of historical writing or newspaper reporting?

Dogberry: Mrs. Brodie thinks it is serious — she swears by it.

Chairman: But do you?

Dogberry sows the seed

Dogberry: Of course not! That was only a joke. My serious writing on the subject was in a series of articles entitled "Golden Bible" in the Palmyra *Reflector* for the first three months of 1831.

Chairman: And in those articles you have but one sentence dealing with Smith's relationship to Walters. The clerk will please read it.

Clerk (reads): "There remains but little doubt, in the minds of those at all acquainted with these transactions, that Walters . . . first suggested to Smith the idea of finding a book."[23]

Chairman: That is all you say on this crucial point and, as we have seen, your statement is cautiously noncommittal; you do not vouch for yourself and designate no witnesses, places, or dates. Yet half a year earlier you wrote a long rigmarole on Joseph Smith as Walters' disciple.

Dogberry: As I said, that was a joke. It was a parody.

Chairman: It did not pretend to be factual?

Dogberry: There's many a true word spoken in jest.

Chairman: But I am talking about the charges you did not repeat in your serious articles. You do not claim that any effort was made to be accurate in your "Book of Pukei"?

Dogberry: Read some of it, if you think I was serious!

Chairman: We shall do that. Will the clerk please read?

Clerk (reads): The Book of Pukei, chapter one:

> And it came to pass in the latter days, that wickedness did much abound in the land, and the "idle and slothful said one to another, let us send for Walters the Magician, who has strange books, and deals with familiar spirits, peradventure he will inform us where the *Nephites*, hid their *treasure.* . . . And it came to pass, that when the Idle and Slothful became weary of their night labors, they said one to another, lo! This *imp* of the Devil, hath deceived us, let us no more of him, or peradventure, ourselves, our wives, and our little ones, will become chargeable on the *town.*"[24]
>
> [So Walters the Magician] took his *book,* his rusty sword, and his *magic* stone, and his *stuffed toad,* and all his implements of *witchcraft* and returned to the mountains near Great Sodus Bay, where he holds communion with the Devil, even unto this day. Now the rest of the acts of the magician, how his *mantle* fell upon the *Prophet* Jo. Smith, Jun., and how Jo. made a league with the *spirit,* who afterwards turned out to be an angel, and how he obtained the "Gold Bible" . . . will they not be faithfully recorded in the Book of Pukei?[25]

Later Joseph Smith says:

> Behold! hath not the mantle of Walters the Magician
> fallen upon me . . . for lo! yesternight stood before me
> in the wilderness of Manchester, the *spirit, who,* from
> the beginning, has had in keeping all the treasures, hid-
> den in the bowels of the earth. And he said unto
> me, . . . I am the spirit that walketh in darkness, and
> will shew thee great signs and wonders.[26]
> And I looked, and behold a little old man stood
> before me, clad, as I supposed, in Egyptian raiment,
> except his Indian blanket and moccasins—his beard of
> silver white, *hung* far below his knees. On his head was
> an old fashioned military half cocked hat such as was
> worn in the days of the patriarch Moses—his speech was
> sweeter than *molasses,* and his words were the reformed
> Egyptian.[27]

Chairman: Thank you, that will do. You are quite playful, Mr. Dogberry.

Dogberry: It is jolly, isn't it. Let the clerk read what the
angel says next.

Clerk (reads):

> And again he said unto me, "Joseph, thou who has
> been surnamed the *ignoramus,* Knowest thou not . . .
> that I have been sent unto thee by *Mormon,* . . . who
> was chief among the last ten tribes of Israel? Knowest
> thou not that this same apostle to the Nephites con-
> ducted that *pious* people . . . to these happy shores in
> bark canoes, where . . . God sent the *smallpox* among
> them, which killed two-thirds of them, and turned the
> rest into Indians? Knowest thou not . . . that this same
> Mormon wrote a book on plates of gold . . . concerning
> the aforesaid Nephites and their brethren the Lamanites,
> and their treasures (including a box of gold watches on
> which thou shalt hereafter raise money)?[28]

Chairman: Thank you again. That is enough to show
the type of writing we are dealing with. It is the broadest

satire, the typically heavy-handed Yankee humor of the nineteenth century — or am I wrong? Does anyone want to maintain that this is a serious paraphrase of the Book of Mormon, or that Joseph Smith *himself* would go around telling stories like this on himself? The description of the backwoods angel is obviously meant to be sidesplitting, but do you know, Mr. Dogberry, that some of the most eminent scholars have taken this document in dead earnest?

Dogberry: Impossible!

Chairman: Mrs. Brodie prefers it to your serious writing — she would be lost without it. You recall how your funny angel tells a funny story about the Nephites, including their treasure, a box of gold watches? Well, years later the little old man and the box of watches turn up as a serious part of the Mormon story. Mr. Stafford?

J. Stafford: Joseph Smith, Jr., "at a husking, called on me to become security for a horse, and said he would reward me handsomely, for he had found a box of watches, and they were as large as his fist, and he put one of them to his ear, and he could hear it 'tick forty rods.' . . . He wished to go east with them."[29]

Chairman: If he could hear the thing tick at forty rods, why did he put it to his ear — how would he dare?

John C. Bennett: That would be just a manner of speaking.

Chairman: Still in the tradition of broad American humor. Since your work is the earliest on Smith, Mr. Dogberry, later investigations, honoring its high antiquity, have picked out of the extravaganza whatever suited their theories of Joseph Smith. Mrs. Brodie chooses to believe that Walter's mantle actually did fall on Smith, though you don't say so in your serious attack written *later*; others take the funny touch about the gold watches quite seriously; still others describe the original Moroni as a little old man in a cocked hat! So your fantasy has borne fruit. But let

no one claim hereafter that because there "must be something behind all these stories" that that something is the
true history of Joseph Smith. That is Brodian logic. Now,
since all these full and close parallels between Joseph Smith
and Walters and the Rochester Smith and the Belcher boy
and Northrop cannot be accidental, either Smith's doings
were transferred to those other people, or theirs to him.
Which is it? The first alternative must be rejected out of
hand, since Joseph Smith was much younger than all but
one of the other people, and their stories all come first—
which nobody will deny. Was he their zealous disciple,
then? No, no one claims that Smith ever saw Northrop or
the other Smith or the Belcher boy. For a hundred years
the unanimous charge against Joe Smith was that he was
the author of all this nonsense, a unique and original character. He didn't get it from them, and they didn't get it
from him. And there is not a shred of proof that he got it
from Walters.

    Howe: So we are back where we started.

    Chairman: Not at all. The solution is simple: Smith
didn't get it, period. Here we have two bodies of literature
containing the same strange, fantastic tales. We admit that
this cannot be a mere coincidence: one corpus was inspired
by the other. Which was the original? Of that there can be
no doubt—the stories *not* about Smith are all the older,
they are the original. How then did they all get attached
to Joseph Smith? Did he borrow them? Did his followers
insist on attributing them to him? Not a bit of it! He and
they always *deny* any connection with the great Digging
Cycle. Those who unload the stories on Smith are all his
enemies, and what is more, they have an extremely difficult
time connecting him with those tales in time and place,
while they contradict each other at every step.

    The time has come to sum up our little investigation.
I will be brief. First, as to our witnesses—their quality and
their quantity. The latter was excessive, the former defec-

tive. There were altogether too many witnesses; they were too eager; they all knew Smith so very, very well, though there is not the slightest indication that Smith ever knew *them*. All of which might be forgiven if their stories were not intrinsically absurd and thoroughly conflicting. Mr. Tucker, our prize witness, at no time gave any information that would indicate personal acquaintance with Joseph Smith or even firsthand observation of any act performed by him; whenever his testimony became specific it became absurd; whenever it became rational and confident it became also generalizing and editorial in nature. We were unable to discover any diggers or any victims, living or dead, of Smith's purported treasure-hunting promotions. We were told with the greatest assurance that Smith found treasure and that he found none; that he prospered in the business and that he starved; that he dug in a few places and that he dug everywhere; that he merely pretended to dig; that he first learned peeping from his father, his mother, an old neighbor lady, a man in Pennsylvania; that he learned it from infancy, as an adolescent, and as a disciple of Walters — half-a-dozen specific and conflicting dates being confidently assigned to his acquiring of the black art. We have been told that Smith regularly dug and that he never dug at all; that he had to dig in the full moon and that he preferred the dark of the moon; that his band broke up at the first failures and that they went on for years; that he killed only one sheep and that he slaughtered herds of them; that he had a stone box and a wooden box — at least five different peepstones have been described. And the constant and glaring contradictions between these damning and disgraceful tales have been blithely attributed to conflicting versions circulated by the Smith family themselves!

Finally, when challenged to explain the factual realities which usually hide behind even the wildest rumors, we have not had to part company with the witnesses themselves to discover ample evidence for the efflorescence of strange and exotic tales of treasure digging in early nineteenth-century America among which *every* weird detail of the stories later attached to Joseph Smith is found in full bloom *before* Smith can possibly have been involved. In some cases the actual transfer of a story from an earlier setting to the orbit of the Smith family can be clearly demonstrated. If Joseph Smith is to be condemned, I fear it must be on far better evidence than this. The meeting is dismissed.

Notes for Part 2, Scene ii

1. Francis Kirkham, *A New Witness for Christ in America: The Book of Mormon,* 2 vols. (Salt Lake City: Utah Printing, 1959), 2:69.

2. Ibid.

3. Ibid.

4. Ibid., 2:74.

5. Ibid.

6. Ibid.

7. Ibid.

8. Ibid.

9. Ibid.

10. Ibid., 2:52.

11. Orsamus Turner, *History of the Pioneer Settlement of Phelps and Gorham's Purchase and Morris' Reserve* (Rochester: Alling, 1851), 213.

12. Kirkham, *New Witness of Christ in America,* 2:47.

13. Ibid., 2:47–48.

14. Ibid., 2:48.

15. Ibid.

16. Ibid.

17. Ibid., 2:48–49.

18. Ibid., 2:49.

19. Emily C. Blackman, *History of Susquehannah County, Pennsylvania* (Philadelphia: Claxton, Remsen and Haffelfinger, 1873), 577.

20. Ibid.

21. Ibid.

22. Kirkham, *New Witness for Christ in America,* 2:69.

23. Ibid., 2:74.

24. Ibid., 2:51–52.

25. Ibid., 2:52.

26. Ibid.

27. Ibid.

28. Ibid., 2:53–54.

29. John C. Bennett, *The History of the Saints; Or, An Exposé of Joe Smith and Mormonism* (Boston: Leland and Whiting, 1842), 77–78.

Part 3

The Greek Psalter Mystery
or
Mr. Caswall Meets the Press

Scene: It is the usual TV panel. The participants sit behind large placards designating them as:
The Reverend Henry Caswall
The Moderator
Reporter No. 1—Mr. Ecks
Reporter No. 2—Mr. Wye
Reporter No. 3—Mr. Zee

The Caswall credentials

Moderator: This evening we have as our guest the man whose story of Joseph Smith and the Greek Psalter has been voted the most effective single contribution to anti-Mormon literature; it is, to the best of our knowledge, the only story implicating Smith in a fraud that has never been questioned. We shall ask Mr. Caswall's friend, Mr. W. S. Parrott, to introduce him. Mr. Parrott.

W. S. Parrott: "In our attempt to exhibit Mormonism in its truly diabolical character, it gives us satisfaction to be able to appeal to so high and reliable an authority as the Reverend Henry Caswall, vicar of Figheldean, and Rural Dean of Salisbury."[1] Ladies and gentlemen, I give you the unquestioned, the unchallenged, the undoubted, the one and only Reverend Henry Caswall! (Applause.)

Henry Caswall: Thank you, my friends. "It has come to

304

pass in the course of Divine Providence, that although I am now the pastor of an English congregation, I have become well acquainted with the early history of the 'Latter-day Saints'; and seen and conversed with their 'prophet,' at the head-quarters of their sect in Western America. And, in consequence of the information which I have thus obtained, I do not merely *think* the religion of the 'Latter-day Saints' to be erroneous, but I absolutely *know* that it is founded upon a base and vile imposture."[2]

Reporter 1: You are speaking, then, from firsthand knowledge?

Caswall: Oh, absolutely! I am reporting "what I saw of the 'prophet' myself, and heard from his lips."[3]

Reporter 1: Speaking of reports, Mr. Caswall, here is the latest: "It was from a Lancashire nonconformist pastor, the Reverend Thomas Dent of Billington, near Whalley, that Henry Caswall got much of the material which enabled him to publish in 1843 his well-known book 'The Prophet of the Nineteenth Century.' " I take it from this, sir, that all of your information was not acquired firsthand.[4]

Caswall: Of course not. I used the usual sources. But what gives my work unique authority is the part of it that was acquired firsthand.

Reporter 2: Was *The Prophet of the Nineteenth Century* the only book based on your experience with Joseph Smith?

Caswall: Certainly not. There were others.

Reporter 1: Would you name them for us?

Caswall: Gladly. Let's see — first in 1842 there was my book *The City of the Mormons, or Three Days at Nauvoo,* an enlarged and revised edition of which appeared in the following year; a long report on the same book appeared in the *Weekly Visitor* in 1842; then in 1843 I published *The Prophet of the Nineteenth Century,* which is probably my best-known work. I gave a full account of my visit to Nauvoo in my book *The American Church,* published in 1851, and also in a book entitled *Mormonism and Its Author*, published in the same year. Those were my principal writings.

Parrott: Mr. Caswall is too modest. He forgets that in 1865 he supplied me with a lengthy manuscript on the subject of his visit to Nauvoo, which I printed in my own book, *The Veil Uplifted, or The Religious Conspirators of the Latter-day Saints Exposed.* Do you remember, Mr. Caswall?

Caswall: It was my last major effort.

Moderator: My, that's quite a record. Six printed accounts, at least, of your dealings with Joseph Smith—and all written by you personally?

Caswall: All but the report in the *Weekly Visitor.* That was a review.

Reporter 2: Just how well did you know Joseph Smith, Rev. Caswall?

Caswall: Well enough. He was "a low juggler, without character, without education, without common prudence or decency."[5]

Reporter 2: Others who visited Nauvoo at the time reported very differently.

Caswall: I can only report what I experienced. "But, besides what I saw of the 'prophet' myself, and heard from his lips, I made many inquiries in the neighborhood of Nauvoo, from which I satisfied myself that Joseph Smith was even more wicked than I could have supposed."[6]

Reporter 2: By "*even* more wicked" you mean that you had decided that he was wicked before you ever went to Nauvoo?

Caswall: "It is difficult to imagine a human being more corrupt, or more destitute of redeeming qualities. . . . [There is] little in his character besides unscrupulous audacity, reckless falsehood, low cunning, grovelling vulgarity, daring blasphemy, and grasping selfishness."[7]

Moderator: Excuse me, Mr. Caswall, we are not asking for your opinion just yet; what the gentleman asked, and what we would all like to know, is just how intimately you were acquainted with Joseph Smith.

Caswall: "The task of delineating the prophet's infernal character has been certainly far from agreeable to me."[8]

Reporter 2: Yes, sir, we understand that; but let's put it this way: How many times did you meet Joseph Smith?

Caswall: Once, but that was enough to satisfy myself that he "was even more wicked than I could have supposed."

Reporter 2: That will come later, if you please. How long did you talk with him? An hour? Two hours?

Caswall: I have recorded our conversation with great care, naturally. At present I cannot recall precisely how long it might have taken.

Reporter 2: But from every one of the accounts you have written, sir, it seems to me that your meeting with Smith could not possibly have taken more than ten minutes at the most. That is why I am asking you now. Your name and fame rest on the much-publicized pronouncement that you "have seen and conversed with the prophet"; you have published no less than five books which derive their high authority from that one conversation. Naturally we want to know how close you were to Smith—no offense.

Caswall: None in the least, sir, though I fail to see how you arrive at your limit of ten minutes.

Reporter 2: Very easily. In all your reports of the affair you were introduced to Smith and without any preliminaries you both sat down; you gave him a book and asked him one question; he asked you a short one in reply to which you answered in a single short sentence; then he gave a speech of some fifty-five words and you changed the subject of conversation and asked Smith a short question to which he did not reply, leaving the room immediately and without explanation. That was the last of your one and only meeting with Joseph Smith. It may have lasted ten minutes, but it could all have been over in three.

Even if you dragged it out, it seems from your various accounts that hardly a hundred words could have passed between you. Now what kind of a . . .

Moderator: I am sure the Reverend Caswall will explain all this in the course of our interview. Mr. Zee, we have not heard from you.

Reporter 3: I would like to ask Mr. Caswall where these reports were published.

Caswall: In England, sir.

Reporter 3: All of them?

Caswall: All of them.

Reporter 3: England and America were very far apart indeed in the 1840s. Did the great width of the ocean in those days give you a measure of immunity from criticism by publishing in England?

Moderator: Oh, come now, sir; Mr. Caswall can hardly be asked to take such insinuations seriously. Why do you ask such a question?

Reporter 3: Because the editor of an American journal reviewing Mr. Caswall's book in 1843 raises the point. The English reviewers described Mr. Caswall as an intrepid hero who had "visited 'an utmost corner of the habitable globe — or the haunts of a *megalotherion*,' " an impression which Mr. Caswall's own writings vividly confirm. The American editor feels that our friend's book has grossly misrepresented things; he writes: "If Professor Caswall has, by his book or otherwise, contributed in any measure to confirm the prejudices of the British press against our country and our institutions; if he joins in with the blind and stupid slang of such publications as the article under consideration [that is, the English review of his book], we would counsel him to remain in 'sound, enlightened, and Protestant England.' "[9] This man feels strongly that you have an ax to grind, Mr. Caswall.

Caswall: Well, of course the friends of the Mormons could hardly be expected to applaud my exposures.

Reporter 3: This man I have quoted is no friend of the Mormons, I can assure you—he hates them as much as you do, for he is the editor of the *Methodist Quarterly Review*, from which I have been quoting; he says of the reviewer who praises your work, "By the way, some of the reviewer's statements savor not a little of ignorance of American affairs in general, and of the facts he undertakes to represent."[10]

Moderator: One cannot expect a visitor to a country to be an expert in everything, sir. Perfect knowledge of affairs is too much to hope for.

Reporter 3: But an unprejudiced report of what one actually sees is something else. Our reviewer says that the terms in which Mr. Caswall depicts the American frontier "to an American, sound really ludicrous," which suggested to me that a book written and published in England about Nauvoo might get away with a good deal, especially since the reviewer observes: "We would advise him [Mr. Caswall], that with such narrow and prejudiced views of America . . . he will not long be allowed to teach the youth of the enlightened, enterprising, and chivalrous west. Even a *'divinity'* chair cannot long be occupied by such a 'professor' in any portion of the republic."[11]

Moderator: Obviously the man was wrought up—his patriotism is touched, but he does not object to what Mr. Caswall says about the Mormons, does he?

Reporter 3: He does not accuse him of prejudice towards the Mormons, but only of extreme superficiality in describing their teachings and practices. He specifically takes him to task for presuming to write about the Book of Mormon without having read it. After all, if Mr. Caswall was "narrow and prejudiced" where America in general was concerned and where no religious or moral sentiments were involved, and if he was willing to express his prejudice in distortions that "sound really ludicrous," what are the chances of his giving a cool, impartial account of his arch enemy, Joseph Smith?

Man with a grievance

Caswall: Arch enemy? I admit, what I have said about Smith has not been very flattering, but what gives you the idea that he was my particular enemy?

Reporter 3: Your dramatic account of your soliloquy on the bank of the Mississippi on your first evening in Montrose. Do you remember? You had just arrived at Montrose, across the river from Nauvoo, which you planned to visit for the first time on the following morning. You walked up and down on the shore and gazed at the city across the river, bathed in the golden light of the setting sun. Do you remember the reflections that passed through your mind then?

Caswall: How can I forget them? I said to myself on the eve of my momentous visit to the Mormon headquarters, "Why is Kemper College, the first and only institution of the Church beyond the Mississippi, permitted to languish, while the Mormon temple, and the Mormon university offer their delusive attractions to the rising generation? Why is the venerable Bishop of Illinois permitted to labor almost alone, while the missionaries of Joseph Smith, with a zeal worthy of the true Church, perambulate his diocese and plant their standard in every village?"[12]

Reporter 1: So you viewed Smith and his missionaries as trespassers on your ecclesiastical domain, perambulating your bishop's diocese with impunity?

Caswall: It was worse than that. He was stealing our people. It was the sight of "immense numbers of English Mormons, who passed near Kemper College on their way to the prophet and the temple" that induced me to go there myself;[13] I was animated by "nothing but a sense of duty of exposing imposture."[14]

Reporter 3: Joseph Smith's success with "your people" disturbed you?

Caswall: As I said then, "Oh! how mournful to look around, as I can at present, and to reflect, how many have been enticed away from their homes, dragged across earth and sea, and brought to this unwholesome spot, where, with the loss of substance and of health, they are too often left to perish in wretched poverty and bitter disappointment."[15]

Reporter 1: What is Kemper College, Mr. Caswall?

Caswall: You mean you don't know, sir? I am depressed to hear you ask that. I, sir, was the dean of Kemper College, sent to "these melancholy regions" to establish an institution of higher learning for the training of the clergy.

Reporter 2: Whatever happened to Kemper College?

Caswall: That is a painful question, sir. The promised divinity students never showed up; those students who did come never got around to paying their tuition; the house generously promised by the trustees of the university as a shelter for my family in those remote regions was never built; bickering and mismanagement, for which I was in no way responsible, led from one thing to another. The college came to nothing, while the Mormon university flourished, and I returned to England and the obscurity of a country parish.[16]

Moderator: Hardly obscurity, sir. From there you rocked the world with your books against Joseph Smith.

Reporter 2: Did you hold Smith responsible for the ruin of your career?

Caswall: I resent that question.

Reporter 2: Excuse me, but you specifically contrasted the declining cause of your church with the zeal and success of the Mormon missionaries, and deplored the languishing, as you called it, of Kemper College in face of the "delusive attractions" of the Mormon university. It was

you who suggested a keen sense of rivalry. Did you recommend any steps towards meeting the Mormon threat?

Caswall: Indeed, I suggested that "the appointment of
a self-denying missionary to reside in the immediate vicinity of Nauvoo might in some degree check the rising
heresy," and I also pointed out that "the success of Joseph
Smith appears to warrant a system of emigration and settlement conducted on religious principles."[17]

Reporter 2: Most interesting. You suggested that the
best way to further the cause of your own church in the
new land and the success of your own assignment would
be to copy Joseph Smith's missionary and emigration policies. You actually reported that Smith's success warranted
an imitation of his methods. Plainly you were competitors
in the same business, and he was getting the best of it in
everything. If Joseph Smith was not actually responsible
for the demise of Kemper College and your own life's
hopes, he was guilty of succeeding at every point where
you had failed. We can certainly understand your emotional involvement here, and if, as the Methodist reviewer
pointed out, you allow your prejudices to get the best of
you in describing everything in western America, we can
hardly expect a fair or impartial picture of Joseph Smith.

Caswall: I do not resent the virtues or the successes of
the Mormons, but only their crimes. I found the Mormons
to be good, devout people, "but I believe that the *leaders*
of the Mormon sect have been, from the very first, people
of the worst character; atheists in religion, and utterly corrupt in practice."[18] Smith himself had no virtues; as I said,
"It is difficult to imagine a human being more corrupt, or
more destitute of redeeming qualities."[19]

Reporter 1: Yet you recommended imitating his religious
activities, both in sending out missionaries and in con-
ducting migrations "on religious principles."

Caswall: It was not his religious principles that were
objectionable; when the "furious multitude . . . put the

false prophet to death," it was "not on account of his religion, but for his crimes."[20]

Reporter 3: And you yourself were a witness to those crimes?

Caswall: What I saw of the prophet himself and heard from his own lips "satisfied me that he was even more wicked than I had supposed."

Reporter 2: "*Even* more wicked" means that you approached Smith with the fixed idea that he was very wicked; and you were not dismayed or surprised but "satisfied" to find him so.

Caswall: I have so described him. Even "Sidney Rigdon . . . published a letter in the American papers describing the prophet as one polluted mass of corruption, iniquity, and fraud — a beast and a false prophet."[21]

Reporter 2: Indeed. And in what American papers was that sensational letter published?

Caswall: I cannot tell you now. If I had it I would quote it.[22]

Reporter 1: Why don't you quote it in your book? As a Christian and a clergyman, how can you say such things of one who did you no harm?

Caswall: "Although it is not in general a Christian duty to speak ill of *any* one, especially after he has gone to answer for himself before his Judge, yet in the case of a deceiver, whose lying doctrines are perverting thousands from the right way, the ordinary course of duty is reversed."[23]

Reporter 2: So in the case of Smith alone the normal rule of Christian charity and "the ordinary course of duty" are not only suspended but reversed, so that to speak *ill* of him is a duty. And why? Because of his doctrines — you did not say his *crimes*, but his "doctrines."

Caswall: I said "*lying* doctrines" that "have perverted thousands from the right way."

Reporter 2: But doctrines nonetheless . . .

Caswall: That "have perverted thousands from the right way!"

Reporter 2: From "the right way" as you see it. Smith's crime is that he has found believers of his doctrines.

Reporter 1: How about his followers? You describe them as "respectable" and sincere Christians. Do you think they suffered deservedly at the hands of the mob?

Caswall: I did not call it a mob but a "furious multitude." However, "is it not plain that the persecutions of the Mormons were not persecutions 'for righteousness sake,' but the direct contrary? And when the wrath of an American community was once roused, and the Mormons were driven out of neighborhoods which loathed them, we can scarcely wonder, however we may regret, that the innocent should often have suffered for the guilty."[24]

Reporter 3: Will you not as a minister let God be the judge in these things?

Caswall: "As I am a minister of Christ, bound by my Ordination Vows 'to be ready to drive away from the Church all erroneous and strange doctrines,' it is of course my duty to guard my parishioners and others against being led astray by the false teachings in question."[25]

Reporter 2: There you go again, Mr. Caswall! The real issue is one of "strange doctrines" and "false teachings." You say, sir, that Smith was not murdered for his religious teachings but for his crimes: yet when we ask you what his crimes were, you can only refer us to his religious teachings. Don't you believe in charity towards your enemies?

Caswall: "With the knowledge which I possess on the subject, I should be showing a great want of charity to my countrymen, if I willingly suffered them to think *well* of the 'Latter-day' doctrine. Nor have they any right to call me their Enemy, because I tell them the Truth. . . . [Smith was] a mere cheat and delusion, pernicious to man, and hateful to God."[26]

Reporter 2: "Doctrine" again. I also notice that you speak to Englishmen as one possessing special and firsthand knowledge. You are obviously out to take the fullest advantage of your position, addressing yourself to a public that is in no position to question your "firsthand" report; you have declared it your policy to show no mercy and no quarter where the Mormons are concerned—to do so, you say, would be "to show great want of charity" to your countrymen. You have voiced frustration and rage, singling out Joseph Smith as the special object of your wrath. A fellow minister and anti-Mormon has protested your obvious prejudice and your lamentable tendency to exaggerate. Now the question is: since you are the *only* witness to the story you tell about Joseph Smith, how far is that story to be trusted?

Caswall: As I have just told you, no matter how fiercely I attack this monster, no matter how the Mormons may resent my words, they do not have "any right to call me their Enemy, because I tell them the *Truth*."

Nothing but the truth?

Reporter 1: Since absolute truth is the vindication of your position, Mr. Caswall, it is very important for you not to indulge in any misrepresentation or exaggeration whatever, though, according to your Methodist reviewer, you are prone to those weaknesses. What did you say was the title of your first original report?

Caswall: My first book about my experiences with Joseph Smith was entitled *The City of the Mormons, or Three Days at Nauvoo.*

Reporter 1: Were you three days at Nauvoo?

Moderator: Mr. Ecks, surely nobody questions that part of Mr. Caswall's story.

Reporter 1: I am not questioning it. I am trying to find out what Mr. Caswall means by "Three Days at Nauvoo."

Could you tell us how you spent your first day in Nauvoo, Professor? How many hours did you pass in the town?

Caswall: That was Sunday, 17 April 1842, I crossed the river just in time to attend the Mormon church service there, which began at about half past ten o'clock and lasted almost until two in the afternoon.

Reporter 1: Then what did you do?

Caswall: I had lunch at an inn and returned immediately to Montrose.

Reporter 1: So allowing a full hour for lunch, you were only five hours in Nauvoo at the most on your first day, and the time was all spent in a public religious meeting and in a public eating house. That would hardly give you the time or opportunity to look into the most dark and secret crimes of the Mormons. When did you cross the river to Nauvoo, the next morning?

Caswall: At ten o'clock. I went straight to Joseph Smith's house, but he wasn't home, so I saw some exhibits, conversed with some Mormons, and went back to Montrose again.

Reporter 1: According to one of your accounts you spent the afternoon riding on the prairie around Montrose with an anti-Mormon friend. And what did you do on the third day?

Caswall: That was when I met Joseph Smith. I crossed the river with a Mormon doctor, went directly to Smith's house, and conversed with him there. Then I had a lively religious discussion with some of his followers. It is all recorded in my writings.

Reporter 1: And then?

Caswall: And then I returned again to Montrose and "during the remainder of the day, I employed myself in obtaining testimony from the persons residing in Iowa in reference to the character and conduct of their Mormon neighbors. I have every reason to believe that this testimony is correct, partly because it agrees with what I myself saw in Nauvoo, and partly because of the character and respectability of the witnesses."[27]

Reporter 1: What sort of things did those witnesses report of the Mormons that were so terrible?

Caswall: Well, for one thing, they said that the Mormons preached that they had a right to steal anything they wanted.[28]

Reporter 1: And this astonishing accusation is borne out by what you yourself *saw* in Nauvoo?

Caswall: It is.

Reporter 2: Yet you mention no crimes witnessed in any of your books. You report that the Mormons were not only well behaved but kind and hospitable in their treatment of you. How can such behavior "agree" with the atrocity stories you gathered in Iowa?

Moderator: How did we get on this subject?

Reporter 1: We were testing Mr. Caswall's claim that he used only truth as his weapon, and I pointed out that he entitled his first book *Three Days at Nauvoo*. Now I have done a little figuring and it turns out that of the seventy-two hours Mr. Caswall is supposed to have spent among the Mormons at Nauvoo, at least sixty hours, or five-sixths of the time was spent among the anti-Mormons of Montrose! It was there that he did his real research, which consisted not in seeing with his own eyes but in gathering gossip. I am wondering if his claim of absolute truth will hold up, in view of such things.

Caswall: I resent that, sir. There was far more to it than that. Right among the Mormons "I met with persons at Nauvoo, who were perfectly acquainted with the wickedness of Smith, and did not even pretend to deny it, who yet professed to believe firmly that he was a true prophet."[29]

Reporter 2: That is remarkable indeed, to be "perfectly acquainted" with the man's incredible wickedness and still believe in him. He *was* wicked, you said?

Caswall: I assure you, sir, such were his awful profanations "that nothing but a sense of duty in exposing imposture could have induced me to commit them to paper."[30]

Reporter 3: That's putting it strongly enough, and certainly if you found Mormons in Nauvoo who admitted "the wickedness of Smith," your long trip was worth the trouble. But tell me, Mr. Caswall, why didn't you mention this all-important fact until your last paper on the subject, in 1865?

Caswall: What do you mean?

Reporter 3: In your various books based on your visit to Nauvoo you milked the situation for all it was worth, yet the presence of loyal followers of Smith in Nauvoo who were "perfectly acquainted" with his "wickedness" you did not report until your parting shot in 1865. It was not until twenty-three years after your first report that you remembered the most damning evidence of all.

Caswall: It must have slipped my mind.

Moderator: Come, gentlemen, let us get to Mr. Caswall's story. I hope the Reverend Caswall will understand that these gentlemen of the press are quite frank and searching and won't take offense.

Reporter 2: Before we leave the subject of prejudice I would like to ask Mr. Caswall about one charge he brings against Joseph Smith, or rather three charges; namely, that Smith was an adulterer, a murderer, and a thief. Did you make those accusations, sir?

Caswall: Not three charges, sir, but six.

Reporter 2: These three will do. You said you could prove these things. How do you prove the first one, that Smith was an adulterer?

Caswall: "There is evidence that, early in his career, he was heard to say, that 'adultery was no crime.' "[31]

Reporter 2: You only met Smith at the end of his career, and the same is true of the "neighbors" you interviewed in Iowa, so for all you know the "evidence" from "early in his career" might have been trumped up; even so, you don't say what the evidence was, or how much "is available," and what the evidence is supposed to prove. Not that Smith *practiced* adultery, but simply that "he was heard to say" something about it which any smart-aleck might have said. Have you better "evidence" that Smith was a murderer?

Caswall: I have the best. For on page 218 of Smith's own book, the Doctrine and Covenants, occurs the expression, "thine enemy is in thine hand."[32]

Reporter 2: Well?

Caswall: That proves that Smith was a murderer.

Reporter 1: The expression referred to is, I believe, a biblical one. Doesn't it occur a number of times in the book of Job? The Lord told Satan that Job was "in his hand" — yet that did not mean that Job was to be killed; quite the opposite, Satan was to be held responsible for what happened, and Job was definitely *not* to suffer death.

Moderator: Come, gentlemen, let's not get involved in a theological discussion.

Reporter 1: Not at all. The point is that the passage referred to, taken in or out of context as you will, cannot possibly be construed as evidence of intent to murder, let alone of its commission.

Reporter 2: Come, Mr. Caswall, as you know, what interests us is your personal testimony as to Smith's doings.

Caswall: And it is on that very personal testimony that I rest my charge that he was a thief. Smith actually "said these words, as I am informed by one who heard him."

Reporter 3: Just a moment, sir. Did *you* hear him say the words?

Caswall: The next best thing to it: one of the people I talked with in Montrose, one of Smith's neighbors, told me. And he was actually there and heard him say it!

Moderator: Very well, and what did he hear him say?

Caswall: "He said, . . . 'The world owes me a good living: if I cannot get it otherwise, I will steal it; and catch me at it if you can.' "

Reporter 2: Who told you that?

Caswall: Never mind, it was somebody in Montrose. It makes no difference who said it, since Smith made his remark at a public meeting attended by large numbers of people.

Reporter 1: There were non-Mormons present at the meeting?

Caswall: Of course. My informant was not a Mormon; he was present and heard it.

Reporter 2: Mr. Caswall, you have said that Smith was remarkably successful in his bold and ambitious plans. To what do you attribute his success?

Caswall: To his "low cunning" and to "a genius . . . fertile in its expedients."[33]

Reporter 2: Yet this uncommonly shrewd and cunning man gets up in a big public meeting and, speaking for the record, tells his followers and his enemies alike that he intends to steal. Do you expect us to believe that?

Caswall: But he did steal, "he has not a valid title to a single acre of land around Nauvoo!"[34]

Reporter 2: Who said so?

Caswall: A man who lived near Nauvoo, in a letter he wrote to me personally.[35]

Reporter 2: I suppose that makes it personal testimony. But you don't know, sir, who it is that bestows title to land?

Caswall: Governments do, of course.

Reporter 2: Yes, we will not have to go into that. Now if Smith had no valid title to the land, why did no authorities of county, state, or nation accuse him of trespassing? That is one type of theft that the Mormons could not possibly have gotten away with.

Caswall: Well, actually I did not repeat that charge in my later books. That was in the 1843 edition. In 1851 I wrote that "Smith . . . purchased the site of the new city at a small price (the title being insecure), sold building lots to his followers at a great advance, and realized enormous profits."[36] He was still a thief, you see—he stole from his own followers.

Reporter 2: So you shift your ground from year to year—very convenient. Did Smith *make* his followers buy lots?

Caswall: The same man who wrote me the letter told how "the history of every dupe *reaches Nauvoo in advance,* . . . facts being faithfully reported to the Prophet. He knows how to approach the man when he arrives, and make him an easy prey. So that *all* who join the Mormon community enter upon the the road to beggary and ruin. . . . They desire nothing more of a man than his *money,* and he is then at the mercy of the leader of the Mormon Banditti."[37]

Reporter 2: Yet in the very year you published this letter, you visited Nauvoo and described the people in general as having an "appearance quite respectable, and fully equal to that of the better sort of dissenters . . . in England," while some of the Mormons who talked with you and entertained you were described as looking very prosperous and respectable. Are you trying to tell us now that these people were all ruined beggars?

Caswall: My basic evidence for Smith's thievery is a passage in the Book of Covenants: "It is meet that my servant Joseph should have a house built." That definitely proves that "Smith was a *Covetous Man.*"[38]

Reporter 3: But Mr. Caswall, didn't you expect the trustees of Kemper College to build you a house?

Caswall: We won't go into that. You must also remember that "Smith was a *Profane Swearer.*" I can prove that.

Moderator: Go right ahead, sir, prove it.

Caswall: He told some people who had come from England "that he meant to go on as he had begun, and take his own course, and kill and destroy."[39]

Reporter 1: Who were the people he said that to?

Caswall: Some of his converts who had just arrived from England.[40]

Reporter 2: A most tactful introduction, I must say. But even so I fail to see how that makes him "a profane swearer." Wouldn't it have been much better to use that as evidence that he was a murderer? Why didn't you?

Caswall: You have already objected to hearsay evidence.

Reporter 3: People who intend to kill and destroy in civilized or any other society do not go about announcing the fact to their simple and honest followers. For a clever deceiver Smith seems to have used singularly unguarded language. What could have made him so careless?

The drinking stories

Caswall: Drink, no doubt. "Although a married man and the father of a large family, Joseph Smith is notoriously addicted to several kinds of gross debauchery. He has often been intoxicated; and has sometimes justified his inebriation by asserting, with characteristic invention, 'that it was necessary that he should be seen in that condition to prevent his followers from worshipping him as a God.' "[41]

Reporter 2: You say "often intoxicated." Can you give us a few examples?

Caswall: Certainly. "About the year 1840, at a political meeting in Nauvoo, Joseph became intoxicated, and was led home by his brother Hyrum. On the next Sunday he acknowledged the fact before his assembled congregation."[42]

Reporter 2: You got that story from the Mormons?

Caswall: Of course not. It was told me in Iowa—it was there that I gathered the stories of the prophet's drunkenness.

Reporter 2: In this case your informant was not even

sure of the year in which the interesting event took place. Can't you be more specific?

Caswall: Indeed I can: that is the advantage to doing my research in Montrose, since the Mormons, of course, would not report such things. Let me tell you: "A shop for the sale of ardent spirits having been established at Montrose, a small place opposite Nauvoo, over the river, the 'prophet' was *often* seen intoxicated there by persons who mentioned the fact to me."[43]

Reporter 2: So Smith often got drunk in the small anti-Mormon town of Montrose?

Caswall: Yes.

Reporter 2: And in that state was often seen by the people there?

Caswall: They told me so personally.

Reporter 2: How would Smith behave on those occasions?

Caswall: "While intoxicated at Montrose, . . . he was heard by several persons saying to himself, 'I am a P.R.O.F.I.T. I am a P.R.O.F.I.T.' spelling (or rather misspelling) the word deliberately, and repeating the letters in solemn succession."[44]

Reporter 2: So though this clever Smith "with characteristic invention," as you put it, asserted that he should be seen drunk by his *followers* lest they think him a God, he preferred to do his drinking among his enemies. Was there perhaps a danger that *they* might think him a God?

Caswall: Don't be absurd, sir.

Reporter 2: But what could be more absurd than that a clever man with enormous resources at his disposal, when he gets a taste for liquor, must go to a country store across the river to do his drinking publicly among your anti-Mormon friends? Somehow, Mr. Caswall, your story does not sound too convincing.

Caswall: Actually, sir, it is mild and conservative compared with one eyewitness report.

Reporter 2: Indeed, and what report is that?

Caswall: That of Robert Richards, in *The Californian Crusoe.* You must have it here.

Moderator: We do. This man was a fellow countryman of yours, Mr. Caswall. His book was published in 1854.

Caswall: He tells much the same story I do, if you will take the trouble to read it.

Moderator: Hmm, let's see. Here it is. I will read the passage:

> Having occasion to cross the river to Montrose [it seems he is passing through on his way to California] . . . I happened . . . on leaving the ferry-boat to take a path which conducted me near a shop which had been established for the sale of whiskey. I heard a voice which sounded like that of the prophet, and looking over a fence I saw Joseph Smith himself lying alone on the grass, with a whiskey bottle by his side, and decidedly far gone in a state of intoxication. He was talking and laughing, and evidently congratulating himself, in a soliloquy, on the success of his devices. "I am a prophet," he said, "a profitable profit; a profitable prophet indeed I am. Prophetical profits are good profits, very good profits, capital good profits, I'll be hanged if they ain't. The saints are a pack of fools; but I am a prophet, a profitable prophet, a prophetical, prophesying, profitable prophet. What was Mahomet compared with me? He was a jackass. What was Napoleon? He was a numbskull. What was Alexander? He was a blockhead. I am a greater man than Moses, — hurrah! — I am a greater man than Moses, — hurrah! — hip, hip, hip, hurrah!"[45]

Reporter 2: Mr. Richards heard all that — and remembered it?

Moderator: He says here, "I might have heard much more, but I retreated precipitately, full of horror and consternation."[46]

Caswall: This experience, some years after mine, shows how often Smith went to Montrose to get drunk.

Reporter 1: Giving his "profit" soliloquy on Tuesdays and Thursdays for tourists.

Reporter 2: One would think that his faithful followers would have discouraged such regular behavior. Dear me! Smith not only goes among his enemies to get drunk and deliver his loud and revealing monologue in public, but chooses a back lot near the ferry for his scheduled demonstrations.

Reporter 3: Mr. Caswall, this is even a better story than yours. Do you believe it? Soliloquies are unconvincing even on the stage, but apparently Joseph Smith, one of the busiest and most conspicuous public figures in American life, had the time and inclination at the height of his career to make repeated trips to Montrose to make a spectacle of himself, lying about in vacant lots and crowded country stores and loudly proclaiming to the world that he was a fraud.

Reporter 2: It seems that both you and Mr. Richards found Smith to be exactly the kind of character you expected, Mr. Caswall, and were both filled with exquisite loathing—Mr. Richards "retreated precipitately, full of horror and consternation" when he was right on the verge of getting a priceless earful, while you passed up every chance to know Smith and the Mormons well, refusing repeated invitations to stay with them free of charge, and cutting off your conversation with Joseph Smith when it had hardly begun.

Caswall: I assure you, sir, "only the duty of exposing imposture could have induced me to commit the awful profanations of the man to paper."

Reporter 2: Yet you revel in them. You pounce on the most lurid tales with the least possible proof in the way of evidence and milk them for all they are worth.

Caswall: I beg your pardon, sir!

Reporter 2: Didn't you write this? "We believe that he [Joseph Smith] is constantly sending out emissaries to do deeds of darkness and abomination throughout the land. Many here are afraid to speak out, because they well understand that their lives and property will be in danger."[47]

Caswall: I did write it; and you can see from that why there was so little evidence. Even so, I saw plenty with my own eyes.

Reporter 2: You say in your 1843 book that after attending a meeting in Nauvoo on your first day there, you promptly returned to Montrose, and "during the remainder of the day, I employed myself obtaining testimony from persons residing in Iowa in reference to the character and conduct of their Mormon neighbors."[48] These reports you describe as uniformly horrifying and declared of your own personal knowledge that they were true.[49]

Caswall: Because they agreed "with what I myself saw and heard in Nauvoo."[50]

Reporter 2: That is just it. You had spent a few hours of a quiet Sunday in Nauvoo—at meeting, with the general public invited—yet what you managed to see and hear confirmed beyond doubt all the stories of murder and robbery you picked up in Iowa. It is hard to believe that you came to Nauvoo with an open mind.

Caswall: Well, what should I think? Here at that meeting were "numerous groups of English emigrants, together with many little children, who had been removed from the privileges of their mother Church, and led by their besotted parents into this den of heresy, to imbibe the principles of a delusion worse than paganism."[51]

Reporter 2: And it was in that state of mind that you entered the meeting. No wonder you found what you wanted to in Montrose. And may I again point out that the specific crime—the only crime you could discover—is "heresy."

Caswall: I did not make up the stories.

Reporter 1: Of course you didn't, sir. Such stories were being told everywhere. That has made me rather curious about your informants. Who were the people in Montrose who told you all these things about the Mormons?

Caswall: My principal informant was my kind host in Montrose.

Reporter 1: How did he get on with the Mormons?

Caswall: He hated them with all his soul, while the Mormons on their part "used the most violent language" against my kind entertainer; they "said that he was their bitter enemy and persecutor, that he was as bad as the people in Missouri, and that I should not believe a word that he said." They most earnestly importuned me not to stay at his house.[52]

Reporter 1: And it was at his house and under his direction that you picked up all those stories about Smith's drunkenness and Mormon atrocities?

Caswall: It was.

Reporter 1: So out of the seventy-two hours that made up your famous "Three Days in Nauvoo," at least sixty of them were spent at Montrose with this man and his friends, whom the Mormons considered their worst enemies and unqualified liars.

Caswall: They were prejudiced, the Mormons, that is.

Moderator: Well, gentlemen, we must be getting on, here. Have we made any progress?

Reporter 2: I think we have. I think Mr. Caswall plainly has the will, motive, and trained capacity to exaggerate when he speaks of Joseph Smith.

Caswall: You did not know Smith as I did, sir!

Reporter 2: By a difference of five (or shall we allow ten?) minutes. I don't wish to be captious or insulting, Mr. Caswall, but here is this fiendishly clever Smith, successful as you say, in his great enterprises, his followers convinced that he is a man of God—all depends on his skill as a deceiver to keep up the game. So what does he do? He announces at a public meeting attended by those who believe him to be righteous and those who are seeking occasion against him (your friends from Montrose who told you about it), that the world owes him a good living, that he intends to steal it, and that they are invited to "catch me at it if they can." He tells new converts, just arrived starry-eyed after the long, hard journey from England, "that he meant to go on as he had begun, and take his own course, and kill and destroy." With unlimited resources at his disposal and an all-important reputation to be preserved, this exceedingly sly fellow cannot get drunk in Nauvoo, but must go to a public tavern a mile away to get stewed time after time so that his friends and enemies can enjoy the sight of his colossal indiscretions. I mention these sordid details as a test of Mr. Caswall's impartiality and reliability as a witness.

Moderator: I think we are all agreed that the best thing to do is to begin at the beginning and let Professor Caswall tell the story in his own way. Can you take us back to Kemper College and St. Louis, Mr. Caswall?

The 1842 story

Caswall: Well, there I was in Kemper College, with things going badly and all those vast numbers of Mormons pouring through on their way to Nauvoo with its temple and university—from England, mind you! I talked to one group of them in St. Louis, "and suggested to them the importance of not committing themselves and their property to a person who had long been known in that country as a deceiver." But they would not listen. "From that moment I was determined to visit the stronghold of the new religion, and to obtain, if possible, an interview with the prophet himself." Accordingly, on Friday, 15 April 1842, I took the boat from St. Louis up the river.[53]

Reporter 2: When did you arrive at Montrose?

Caswall: I got off the boat about ten o'clock Sunday

morning, 17 April 1842. I wanted to cross to Nauvoo immediately, but the ferry was not working. But there were some people in a skiff who were just going over to meeting, and they invited me to go with them. They were Mormons going over to Nauvoo to the Sunday meeting.

Reporter 1: Did you talk with them?

Caswall: I tried to convince them, of course, and one man in particular. But I found him "thoroughly wedded to his delusion."

Moderator: I don't believe it will be necessary for Mr. Caswall to describe the Sunday meeting—he has already told us his impression of the respectability of the people he saw there. What we want to hear is of his meeting with Joseph Smith. Was that on the following day, sir?

Caswall: No, sir, it was not. It was on Tuesday, but Monday's experiences were most enlightening. I talked with Smith's mother and leaders of the Church.

Moderator: That should be worth hearing. How did you cross the river next morning?

Caswall: With another boatload of immigrants.

Reporter 1: What sort of people were they?

Caswall: As I have said, "they were very decent-looking people, and by no means of the lowest class."

Reporter 2: Did you argue with them again?

Caswall: I did, but to no avail. "I had laid aside my clerical apparel, and had assumed a dress in which there was little probability of my being recognized as 'a minister of the Gentiles.' In order to test the scholarship of the prophet I had further provided myself with an ancient Greek manuscript of the Psalter written upon parchment, and probably about six-hundred years old."[54]

Reporter 2: Do laymen make a habit of going about arguing religion with ancient Greek parchments under their arm? Your book and your talk were bound to raise questions, with only one possible answer.

Caswall: Oh, they did! The people were curious about me, and they made every effort to discover my identity.

Reporter 2: And you actually think your clever disguise, which consisted of wearing ordinary clothes, while behaving in a most clerical manner, was not penetrated by any of them, even though so many of them had known Church of England ministers all their lives?

Moderator: Please, let Mr. Caswall continue.

Caswall: As soon as I landed I walked up the straggling main street of the town until I came to a respectable-looking store, where I began to converse with the respectable-looking storekeeper. "I mentioned that I had been informed that Mr. Smith possessed some remarkable Egyptian curiosities, which I wished to see. I added that, if Mr. Smith could be induced to show me his treasures, I would show him in return a very wonderful book which had lately come into my possession."

Reporter 1: So you started right in by pushing your "very wonderful book." That must have excited their curiosity.

Caswall: Indeed it did. The storekeeper "begged to be permitted to see the wonderful book" and "I produced to view . . . its mysterious characters. Surprise was depicted on the countenances of all present." They regretted that Smith had gone to Carthage for the day and would not be back until nine o'clock in the evening. They were so excited about the book that they wanted to send a special rider to bring the prophet back to Nauvoo immediately to see it.[55]

Reporter 2: There were others present in the store?

Caswall: There were "many astonished spectators" when "I unfolded it from the many wrappers in which I had enveloped it."

Reporter 2: And your book really made a stir among them?

Caswall: "All expressed the utmost anxiety that I should remain in the City until the prophet's return." They were determined that he should see that book.[56]

Reporter 2: What did you say to their offer to go right away and fetch Smith?

Caswall: "This I declined, and told" them "that my stay in Nauvoo must be very limited. They promised to pay all my expenses, if I would remain; and assured me that they would ferry me over the river as often as I desired it, free of charge; besides furnishing me with a carriage and horses to visit the beautiful prairies in the vicinity."[57]

Reporter 2: What more could you want, man? Here was your golden opportunity to meet Smith face to face and to see "the stronghold of the new religion" as you called it, from the inside. Those, you said, were the two objects of your expedition—and you *refused!* You refused a proffered meeting with Smith and you refused to stay in Nauvoo.

Caswall: I told them that I didn't need Smith to read my book. I said, "I am going to England next week, and doubtless I shall find some learned man in one of the universities who can expound it."[58]

Reporter 2: And with that statement you announced to them that you yourself did not know what the book was— please bear that in mind, sir.

Moderator: Come gentlemen, let us get on with the story. What happened next, Mr. Caswall?

Caswall: "The store-keeper . . . led me to a room behind his store" and there explained some of Smith's Egyptian papyri, which he showed me—the place was Smith's office. After that "a very respectable-looking Mormon asked me to walk over to his house," where we talked about religion for a while. Then I went back to the store, "where the storekeeper expressed his readiness to show me the mummies. Accordingly, he led the way to a small house, the residence of the prophet's mother. On entering the dwelling I was introduced to this eminent personage as a traveler from England, desirous of seeing the wonders of Nauvoo."[59]

Reporter 2: Plainly you had made quite an impression. What did Mrs. Smith do?

Caswall: First she looked at my "wonderful book. She then directed me up a steep flight of stairs into a chamber," where "she showed me a wretched cabinet, in which were four naked mummies."

Reporter 2: What was "wretched" about the cabinet? Was it broken or something?

Caswall: It contained those "most disgusting relics of mortality. One, she said, was a king of Egypt, whom she named."

Reporter 1: Most interesting. And what was the name of the king?

Caswall: I do not remember. Well, Mrs. Smith explained the relics, and "while the old woman was thus delivering herself, I fixed my eyes steadily upon her. She faltered, and seemed unwilling to meet my glance; but gradually recovered her self-possession. The melancholy thought entered my mind, that this poor old creature was not simply a dupe of her son's knavery; but that she had taken an active part in the deception."[60]

Reporter 3: You already knew Joseph Smith was a knave?

Caswall: My remark hardly allows of any other interpretation.

Reporter 3: Yet it was not until then that "the melancholy thought entered your mind," as you say, that his mother also might not be strictly honest. Do you, after what you have said, expect us to believe either that you were surprised by the thought or that it made you melancholy?

Reporter 2: Mr. Caswall, at the time you undertook your investigations in Nauvoo, Mr. Howe's anti-Mormon classic had been off the press for eight years and run into several editions. Indeed, you cite from it extensively in your 1842 report. Permit me to read to you from that work a quotation from the affidavit of one Abigail Harris. Just like you, Miss

Harris had a conversation with Mrs. Smith about her son Joseph while the latter was out of town. In reply for a request for a loan of four or five dollars, to help Joseph out, "I replied," says Abigail, "he might look in his stone and save time and money. The old lady seemed confused and left the room, and thus ended the visit."[61] You depict the old lady's strange discomposure in much the same way. Now I wonder, since you had read Howe's book, whether—

Moderator: Please, gentlemen, let us not engage in personalities and innuendos.

Reporter 3: It would be hard to imagine a more personal remark than that just made by Mr. Caswall about Joseph Smith and his mother. And on what does he base it? His impression that Mrs. Smith "seemed unwilling" to meet his stare. Do you like to be stared at, Mr. Caswall?

Caswall: I was not staring.

Reporter 3: You said that while she was explaining things to you, you fixed your eyes steadily upon her. That describes the rudest kind of a stare. You say she *seemed* unwilling to meet your glance. Do you willingly stare back at people? What did you expect Mrs. Smith to do? To have stared back at you would have been a sure sign (in your book) of unblushing fraud and insolent prevarication. What do you mean when you say the old lady "faltered"? Did she fall down?

Caswall: She hesitated in her speech.

Reporter 3: And because this "poor old creature," as you call her, hesitates or pauses as she points out to you the various objects on display—and who would not falter before such an ill-mannered audience?—you brazenly proclaim that you have discovered proof of criminal conspiracy.

Moderator: Please, Mr. Zee!

Reporter 3: Shall we read Mr. Caswall's statement again?

Moderator: What did you do after viewing the mummies, Reverend Caswall?

Caswall: I requested a copy of the Book of Mormon and she sold me one for a dollar. Then I left the cottage and went to the printing office of the Mormons, where my friend the storekeeper "introduced several dignitaries of the 'Latter-day Church,' and many other Mormons, to whom he begged to exhibit my wonderful book."[62]

Reporter 2: Still the wonderful book. And how did they react to it?

Caswall: "The Mormon authorities . . . formally requested me to sell them the book, for which they were willing to pay a high price."[63]

Reporter 2: What was your reply?

Caswall: "This offer I positively refused, and they next importuned me to lend it to them, so that the prophet might translate it. They promised to give bonds to a considerable amount."

Reporter 1: And you refused even to lend it to them on those conditions?

Caswall: "I was still deaf to their entreaties, and having promised to show the book to their prophet on the ensuing day, I left them and returned to Montrose."[64]

Reporter 2: That was the second time that day you promised to show the book to Smith, wasn't it?

Reporter 3: Really? I missed that. What happened the other time, Mr. Caswall?

Caswall: It was back at the store, when I first arrived that morning. The crowd in the store was "very desirous that I should remain at Nauvoo during the night; but as I had my fears that some of the saints might have a revelation, requiring them to take my book while I slept, I very respectfully declined their pressing invitation."[65]

Reporter 2: They wanted you to show the book to their prophet?

Caswall: Of course. "At length I yielded to their importunities, and promised, that if they would bring me over from Montrose on the following morning, I would exhibit the book to the prophet."⁶⁶

Reporter 2: Isn't it rather odd that you have to be "importuned" to show the book to Smith when, as you have explained, that was your special purpose in acquiring the book in the first place? Isn't it strange that since your whole object in coming to Nauvoo was to bring Smith and the book together, you only "yielded at length" to their importunities?

Reporter 1: I am still puzzled, Mr. Caswall, by your refusal of the Mormons' pressing invitation to stay among them. Here they were offering you complete cooperation in your project of research, and I cannot but ask myself why you didn't make the best of a golden opportunity. I believe you say somewhere that the Mormons begged you to hear their side of the story.

Caswall: Yes. When "I mentioned the name of my hospitable entertainer" in Montrose, the Mormons declared that he was one of their worst enemies, and "again pressed me most earnestly not to return to Montrose; but I continued firm, and expressed my intention of hearing both sides of the question."⁶⁷

Reporter 1: But as you very well know, you can hear the other side of the question at any time and place. You had made a long journey specifically to hear the *Mormon* side, as you claimed — to visit *their* headquarters and meet *their* prophet. Yet you spent five-sixths of your precious time gathering gossip against them.

Caswall: We have already discussed that.

Reporter 2: But it is an issue that comes up again and again in your reports, sir. How about the following day?

Caswall: "The following morning (Tuesday, April 19), a Mormon arrived with his boat, and ferried me over to Nauvoo. A Mormon doctor accompanied me. . . . He argued with me as we were on the passage, and evinced a tolerable share of intelligence and acuteness."[68]

Reporter 2: Which means that you must have done the same. Plainly, sir, you were not advertising yourself to these people as a dunce—or a layman. What next?

Caswall: I proceeded with the doctor along the street, and "as I advanced with my book in my hand, numerous Mormons came forth from their dwellings, begging to be allowed to see its mysterious pages; and by the time I arrived at the prophet's house, they amounted to a perfect crowd. I met Joseph Smith at a short distance from his dwelling, and was regularly introduced to him by the storekeeper."

Reporter 2: At this point in the story, I believe, comes your famous description of the prophet, which has been much quoted. Can you repeat it for us now?

Caswall: Since we are now speaking in the language of my 1842 reports I will confine the description to them, sir: "He is a coarse, plebeian person in aspect, and his countenance exhibits a curious mixture of the knave and the clown. His hands are large and fat, and on one of his fingers he wears a massive gold ring upon which I saw an inscription. . . . I had not an opportunity of observing his eyes, as he appears deficient in that open, straightforward look which characterizes an honest man."[69]

Reporter 2: You stared down the prophet's mother, as I recall, yet you had, you say, "*no opportunity* of observing his eyes." Did Smith keep his back turned to you during your formal introduction?

Caswall: Now, sir, you are being ridiculous.

Reporter 2: But that is the only possible way Smith could have kept you, a close and penetrating observer of eyes (as appears elsewhere in your writings), from observing his own. Did you ever read how Josiah Quincy described Joseph Smith after visiting him at Nauvoo at about the same time you were there?

Caswall: Of course the Mormons would have their own version.

Reporter 2: Quincy was no more a Mormon than you are. This is what he said: "By the door stood a man of commanding appearance, clad in the costume of a journeyman carpenter when about his work. He was a hearty, athletic fellow, with blue eyes standing prominently out upon his light complexion, a long nose, and a retreating forehead. . . . 'A *fine-looking man'* is what a passerby would instinctively have murmured, . . . and one could not resist the impression that capacity and resource were natural to his stalwart person. . . . That kingly faculty which directs, as by intrinsic insight, the feeble or confused souls who are looking for guidance."[70] Quite a contrast to the miserable knave and clown you met, Mr. Caswall.

Caswall: Everyone is welcome to his opinion.

Reporter 1: This gets more peculiar all the time. Mr. Caswall, I think that you will agree with me that there are three things that one does upon being formally introduced to another person: you grasp his hand, look into his eyes, and exchange a few words. Now, I will grant you that the words on such occasions are usually a mere formality, but here you had taken a special trip just to meet this Joseph Smith, yet though you remember and report verbatim every word he spoke to you *after* you handed him the Psalter, you fail to mention that he so much as opened his mouth up until that time.

Moderator: Why should Mr. Caswall bother to report what you yourself describe as mere formalities, Mr. Ecks?

Reporter 1: Because nothing Joseph Smith would have said or done on that momentous occasion could have gone unmarked by Caswall. Smith's followers, according to you, sir, had for two days been in a fever of excitement about the mysterious visitor from England and his wonderful book: they were simply dying to bring you and their prophet together, as you describe it; of course they told him all about you the minute he got to town. But does he ask you the usual questions about yourself, your health, your travels, your impressions of Nauvoo, and the rest, that common curiosity or courtesy demand? Not a bit of it! The prophet is as silent as a clam until he starts his fantastic babbling about your manuscript. That seems strange to me. And to make it even stranger, you say you couldn't get a good look at the eyes of the man you were being "formally introduced" to. If they were "blue eyes standing out prominently," as Quincy describes them, you could not have failed to "observe" them, unless Smith actually kept his back turned to you.

Moderator: He couldn't very well have shaken hands with his back turned!

Reporter 1: Exactly. And that brings us to our third point. Some visitors to Nauvoo from Mr. Caswall's own St. Louis, men just as hostile to the prophet as he, reported their own impression on being introduced to Smith some time later. Among other things, they noted, as reported in the *St. Louis Gazette,* that though Smith's "chest and shoulders are broad and muscular," his hands "are *quite small* for his proportions."[71] But Mr. Caswall in a much quoted and paraphrased statement assures us, "his hands are large and fat" — "huge" hands, Mr. Richards calls them, taking his cue from the Professor.[72] So I naturally begin to wonder, did this man actually hold the prophet's hand and look into his eyes and speak to him?

Moderator: Please, sir, let Mr. Caswall continue.

Caswall: Smith "led the way to his house, accompanied by a host of elders, bishops, preachers and common Mormons. On entering the house, chairs were provided for the prophet and myself, while the curious and gaping crowd remained standing. I handed the book to the prophet, and begged him to explain its contents. He asked me if I had any idea of its meaning. I replied, that I believed it to be a Greek Psalter; but that I should like to hear his opinion." " 'No,' he said, 'it ain't Greek at all; except, perhaps, a few words. What ain't Greek, is Egyptian; and what ain't Egyptian, is Greek. This book is very valuable. *It is a dictionary of Egyptian Hieroglyphics.'* Pointing to the capital letters at the commencement of each verse he said: 'Them figures is Egyptian hieroglyphics; and them which follows, is the interpretation of the hieroglyphics, written in the reformed Egyptian. Them characters is like the letters that was engraved on the golden plates. . . . This book ain't of no use to you; you don't understand it.'"[73]

Reporter 2: Mr. Caswall, fortunately you were not, as we have seen, the only person to visit Nauvoo at this time. As the very active leader of a very active religious movement, Smith, as you know, did a great deal of speaking and writing, and his words have survived in considerable abundance. Nowhere at that time is he found to use the kind of grammar you attribute to him.

Reporter 2: What did you say of his language in 1843?

Caswall: That "the language of the prophet, is gross in the extreme."[74]

Reporter 2: Did you ever hear him preach?

Caswall: No, but my friends in Montrose did.

Reporter 2: And that is doubtless where you got your interesting samplings of his fantastic grammar. But would you not agree with your supporter, Mrs. Brodie, that you are here "exaggerating the imperfections of Joseph's grammar"?[75]

Caswall: There might be some exaggeration.

Reporter 2: Bear in mind, sir, that this quotation just given is the *one and only* piece of evidence accepted to this day as sure proof of the practice of fraud by Joseph Smith, and that you are the *one and only* authority for it. This is no time to be taking liberties! Yet in this crucial sentence you have been guilty not only of exaggeration but of gross and stupid exaggeration: "them which follows," "them characters is like the letters that was engraved on the golden plates." Do you expect anybody who knows anything at all about Joseph Smith to believe that he said those words in 1842? He must have forgotten an awful lot since 1839, when another visitor to Nauvoo reported: "We had supposed . . . to find him a very illiterate, uncouth sort of man; but from a conversation, we acknowledge an agreeable disappointment. In conversation he appears intelligent and candid."[76] And he must have learned an awful lot just after you left Nauvoo, for another visitor from St. Louis reports a short time afterwards: "Far from being clownish [he apparently has your description in mind, Mr. Caswall] . . . in his conversation he is uncommonly shrewd, and exhibits more knowledge of books, sacred and profane, than his personal appearance at first seems to promise."[77] Now, Mr. Caswall, you have heard that Smith was both uncommonly shrewd and well-read, while you found him a complete ignoramus and a fool, babbling about gold plates and reformed Egyptian just as your idea of Joseph Smith, the eyeless one, would be expected to. What happened after he addressed you thus?

Caswall: I replied, "oh, yes . . . "

Reporter 1: Referring to what? Excuse me, I am lost here.

Caswall: Referring to his statement that the book was of no use to me. " 'Oh yes,' I replied, ' . . . I could sell it, and obtain, perhaps, enough to live on for a whole year.' 'But what will you take for it?' said the prophet and his elders. . . . I replied, 'I will not tell you what price I would take: but if you were to offer me this moment nine-hundred dollars in gold for it, you should not have it.' They then repeated their request that I should lend it to them until the prophet should have time to translate it, and promised me the most ample security; but I declined all their proposals. I placed the book in several envelopes, and as I deliberately tied knot after knot, the countenances of many among them gradually sunk unto an expression of great despondency. Having exhibited the book to the prophet,

I requested him in return to show me his papyrus, and to give me his own explanation, . . . hitherto received only at second hand."[78]

Reporter 2: So their faces fell in great despondency because you resolutely refused to sell them a book which their prophet had told them was "very valuable." You wouldn't sell it even for a fabulous sum, you wouldn't even lend it to them; nay, you wouldn't even let them or their prophet look at it another minute. Why wouldn't you sell it?

Caswall: Why should I?

Reporter 2: Because you and your college were in financial straits and could use the money. Because you had but recently acquired the book, as you explained, for the specific purpose of testing Smith's scholarship, and it had now fulfilled that purpose as far as you were willing to let it, you had no sentimental attachment to it (it was a recent acquisition), you could not read it (you said you would find a reader in England), you never made any other use of it thereafter—the mere possession of the book by you could not prove the fraud. On the other hand, if you had sold it to Smith as he begged you to, you would have made a handsome profit and put the prophet on a very hot spot.

Caswall: How do you mean?

Reporter 2: Here all these people were standing around waiting for Smith to do his stuff. They begged you to give him "time to translate it," but you knew and Smith knew that he could never read the book, and that there were people in the world who *could* read it. Therefore, the moment he committed himself before all those sincere and gullible people, your man had really put his foot into it. You had him where you wanted him, and *that* was the time for you to press your advantage. But what did you do? Instead of forcing Smith to go on with his indiscretions while his people were begging you to continue the show, you firmly took the book away from your victim and stuffed it into its wrappings; you came to Smith's rescue just in the nick of time. But if you had sold the book to the prophet in the presence of all those people, he would have to deliver; everybody would know he had it and that he had called it Egyptian; he would have no choice but to exhibit his ignorance before all the world.

Caswall: He had already done so, sir.

Reporter 2: On the contrary, everybody in the room believed him, not you; and your behavior was certainly calculated to confirm their suspicion—for it was you, not Smith, who shied away from any further discussion of the Psalter and changed the subject, firmly and finally, just when everything was supposed to be going your way.

Caswall: Wait for the rest of the story, sir. After I asked to see the papyrus, Smith "proceeded with me to his office, accompanied by the multitude. He produced the glass frames which I had seen on the previous day; but he did not appear very forward to explain the figures. I pointed to a particular hieroglyphic and requested him to expound its meaning. No answer being returned, I looked up, and behold! the prophet had disappeared."

Reporter 3: A supernatural disappearance?

Caswall: Nothing like that. "The Mormons told me he had just stepped out, and would probably soon return. I waited some time but in vain."

Reporter 2: So you waited and waited but Smith never showed up again? Incidentally, that is *just* the way Lucy Smith ran away from Abigail Harris.

Caswall: At length I descended to the street in front of the store. "Here I heard the noise of wheels, and presently I saw the prophet in his wagon, flourishing his whip, and driving away as fast as two fine horses could draw him. As he disappeared from view, enveloped in a cloud of dust, I felt that I had turned over another page in the great book of human nature."[79]

Reporter 1: Mr. Caswall, when Smith said the book was

of no use to you, you replied that it was because you could sell it. You didn't say you could read it.

Caswall: That is so.

Reporter 1: Then if you couldn't read your *own* book, why should Smith be thrown into a panic when you asked him a question about *his* book? He knew nobody could read Egyptian at that day.

Caswall: What do you mean?

Reporter 1: I mean that what upsets Smith is not your Psalter—he had clearly won that round—but a question about his own papyrus to which he knew perfectly well that you did not know the answer; after all, *you* asked *him* the question. Why should Smith, with his celebrated tact and courtesy, to say nothing of his extreme shrewdness and brazen resourcefulness ("characteristic invention" you call it yourself) which was never at a loss, why should Smith be in mortal terror of a deaf old clergyman, and instead of dissembling his feeling have rushed from the room in a panic (with characteristic cunning) to be seen a good while later lashing his horses wildly as he beats a dramatic retreat from the reverend gentleman who has handled him so brilliantly? This story, if I may or may not be excused for saying so, is pure ham, my friends, with the author in the heroic role of the wise, gentle scholar reading the book of human nature without rancor or guile. Pure ham.

Caswall: But I didn't say Smith was running away from me.

Reporter 2: Not in 1842 you didn't. That touch was added in 1843, as were a lot of other things.

Moderator: Before we get to the 1843 accounts, gentlemen, please let Mr. Caswall finish up his 1842 story. You may continue, Mr. Caswall.

Caswall: Well, after Joseph Smith had disappeared in a cloud of dust "the Mormons now surrounded me, and required to know whether I had received satisfaction from the prophet."

Reporter 1: Showing I was right when I said Smith won the first round. From that he evidently won the fight, too.

Caswall: What do you mean, sir?

Reporter 1: That if you made a monkey of Smith, as you later claimed, nobody at the time was aware of it. From what you just said, the Mormons were quite pleased and satisfied that the prophet had come out on top.

Caswall: I soon corrected that illusion. "I replied that the prophet had given me no satisfaction, and that on the contrary, he had proved his own ignorance most effectively."

Reporter 3: What did they reply to that?

Caswall: Nothing. We changed the subject and talked about the Church of England.

Reporter 2: You mean you didn't tell them *how* Smith had proved his ignorance? You not only passed up the chance to pull your clever "Psalter trick" when you were with Smith and before an audience, but actually failed to mention it when others actually asked you how Smith had performed? Well, never mind; we'll come back to it. What did you talk about next?

Caswall: I challenged the Mormons to perform a miracle. "You maintain," said I, "that your prophet is sent to establish a third dispensation. I demand therefore, what signs are given to prove his commission?"[80]

Reporter 1: Don't you know that was the worst thing you could have done from the Mormon point of view? In their eyes, by asking for a sign you had given yourself completely away.

Reporter 2: And don't you know that there never was any Mormon teaching about "a third dispensation"?

Moderator: Let's save the comments and permit Mr. Caswall to tell his story.

Caswall: An "old man replied, that the healing of the

sick, the casting out of devils, and the speaking in un-known tongues, were very frequent in the 'Latter-day Church.' I said that signs of that kind were of a very doubt-ful description, since the imagination possessed great power over the nervous system. I inquired whether Smith had ever walked across the Mississippi, or brought a dead man to life. He replied in the negative."[81]

Reporter 2: By the way, Mr. Caswall, do you know in later years the story was widespread among anti-Mormon writers that Smith actually tried to walk on the Mississippi? It is interesting that in this earliest mention of the water-walking business it is you, the non-Mormon, who suggest and favor such a demonstration, while the Mormons reject such practices.

Caswall: As I say, "he replied in the negative; but said, that among them the blind received their sight, the ears of the deaf were opened. I then observed, 'You perceive that I am rather deaf, and you say that I have no faith. Now can you open my ears so that I may hear your ar-guments more distinctly?' "

Reporter 1: You actually called for a miracle after an-nouncing that you had *no faith?* That's a good one.

Moderator: I must beg you to be silent, sir, until the Reverend Caswall is finished. What happened then, Mr. Caswall?

Caswall: "Immediately the old man stepped forward, and before I was aware of his object, thrust his fingers into my ears, and lifting up his eyes, uttered for about a minute in a loud voice some unintelligible gibberish. 'There,' he said finally, 'the Holy Ghost prompted me to do that, and now you have heard the unknown tongue.' 'But my hear-ing is not improved,' I said. 'That,' he replied, 'is because you have no faith. If ever you believe the Book of Mormon, you will immediately recover perfect hearing, through the gift of the Holy Ghost.' I looked at him somewhat severely and said, 'Take heed, old man, what you say.' "

Reporter 2: That disconcerting gaze again. Mr. Caswall, before you go any farther, may I point out that your story is full of fatal defects. The Mormons practiced healing, but not that way. Who was the old man?

Caswall: I don't know. Just an old man.

Reporter 2: But you have said that many of the leading Mormon dignitaries were in the crowd. Do you mean to say they all stood by and let that old man undertake a fantastic ordinance that, while it no doubt represents the kind of nonsense you would expect the Mormons to engage in, is at odds in every particular with what they have always practiced and preached? If there is anything the Mormons have always deplored it is the idea of asking for signs.

Reporter 1: That is what I meant when I said that was the worst thing you could have done. For any Mormon that would have marked you as a nothing less than hopeless.

Reporter 2: To this you add the emphatic announcement that you have *no faith,* and then challenge them to heal you! And they promptly comply with your request! And how do they comply? With all the high officials standing by, an old man, on his own authority, comes forward alone and "thrusts his fingers in your ears"; and though by your own confession you are "rather deaf" to begin with, even with his fingers thrust in your ears you can tell he is speaking gibberish; and though you soon after give him a rousing sermon on sacrilegious behavior, you patiently put up with that treatment and let him complete the "ordinance," when he tells you that you have heard *"the* unknown tongue!" For you and you alone, sir, Smith and his followers seem to have adopted a most peculiar pattern of behavior, never reported by any other visitors, but exactly like the stereotype of Mormons that you fully expected to find.

Moderator: It is not our business to speculate on what Mr. Caswall may have expected to find in Nauvoo. What happened after the healing fiasco, Mr. Caswall?

Caswall: Some Mormon made a remark to the effect that Mormon preachers did not need the Bible because they were inspired by the Holy Ghost.

Reporter 1: A thing no Mormon ever claimed. To need the Bible and to need nothing but the Bible are two very different things. It seems that Mr. Caswall reduces every Mormon belief and practice to an absurdity, and then claims to have discovered that absurdity brilliantly demonstrated in his few hours in Nauvoo. It is all so marvelously pat.

Moderator: Will you please let Mr. Caswall tell it his way, sir?

Caswall: " 'No,' I said, 'it is not inspiration, it is a Satanic delusion. Your prophet himself has committed himself today, and I will make the fact known to the world. Would you believe a man calling himself a prophet, who should say that black is white?' 'No,' they replied. 'Would you believe him if he said that English is French?' 'Certainly not.' 'But you heard your prophet declare, that this book of mine is a Dictionary of Egyptian hieroglyphics, written in characters like those of the original Book of Mormon. I know it most positively to be the Psalm of David, written in ancient Greek. Now what shall I think of your prophet?' "[82]

Reporter 2: "Now?" After all that, you finally mention the "Psalter trick." These people knew you could not read the book, and they believed Smith rather than you. Now in the street you simply repeat what you have said before to these people and to Smith, and this time they suddenly believe. You burst out with a triumphant *"Now* what do you think?" as if you had introduced some new and sensational proof, yet there is none. You had missed your chance in the upper room. Did the people believe you this time?

Caswall: "They appeared confounded for a while; but

at length the Mormon doctor said, 'Sometimes Mr. Smith speaks as a prophet, and sometimes as a mere man.' "[83]

Reporter 2: They weren't confounded when Smith was consulting the Psalter or when he dashed from the room; they were proud of his performance and asked you if you were duly impressed and were not the least disturbed by your answer. Now you can repeat your old refrain, that the book is a Greek Psalter, and lo! they are confounded. Why? What had changed? You had made it clear that you could not read the book: did they suddenly think you could?

Caswall: But I had also made it far clearer that I knew exactly what my book was. I had repeatedly and emphatically declared before these people and their leaders that the book was a Greek Psalter.

Reporter 2: In that case, how can you possibly expect us to accept your statement that you had "brought along a Greek Psalter to test the prophet's scholarship"? Before you gave him the test, which was to identify the book, you went around telling everybody the answer—you even told Smith the answer before he had a chance to take the test! Remember, you didn't ask him to read the book, which you couldn't read yourself, but simply to tell you what it was—after you had first told *him* what it was! Would he have any reason to doubt you? Did you *expect* him to contradict you?

Caswall: His answer was a surprise.[84]

Reporter 2: Exactly. Yet only if Smith was willing to play into your hands by a completely unpredictable and unforeseeable sequence of perfectly insane statements and actions could there have been any "trick" at all. It was Smith's incalculable behavior that gave you every advantage, yet you, who were supposed in later years to have devised the "trick," never take advantage of it. Instead of closing the trap when he walks into it, you deftly extricate him from it by closing your book. Later, in the street you say, "Your prophet has committed himself today, and I will make it known to the world." Why didn't you call the attention of those present to the event at the time it occurred? Why didn't you press your advantage when you had it, so that there could be no doubt of the issue, instead of closing your book before you or anyone else had a chance to ask Smith a *single question* about its contents? You called the thing off when Smith was definitely on top.

Moderator: Perhaps, Mr. Wye, Caswall didn't want to embarrass the Mormons.

Reporter 2: He had been damning their leader for two days among them, and according to all his reports they never took offense—isn't that right, Mr. Caswall, or shall I quote?

Caswall: No need to quote; they took it all in good part.[85]

Reporter 2: And in your last discussion in the street with them (the one we have been talking about) you even confessed to some fastidiousness about hurting their feelings. Do you recall how they responded to that?

Caswall: " 'Speak out,' said some. 'Go on,' said others. 'If Smith be not a true prophet,' I said, 'you must admit that he is a gross imposter.' 'We must,' they replied."[86]

Reporter 2: They seem to have been a lot more open-minded than you were, sir. *They* could conceive of an alternative possibility; *you* could not. Here they invite you to prove Smith a fraud, making it clear that they will take no offense at whatever you may say—and you have already said plenty! Here was your golden chance to exploit the Psalter trick. You had called them to witness, "Your prophet has committed himself today," and announced your intention to "make it known to the world." But they had witnessed nothing. Had you demonstrated to their complete satisfaction that the book *was* a Greek Psalter? No, you had been saying that all along, but, according to you, you could not make them believe you. Did you demonstrate to their complete satisfaction that Smith could not read the book? You had a golden opportunity to do so, but you resolutely passed it by. And now comes your last chance to score a hit in this farewell speech to the Mormons, when they practically beg you to prove your case against Smith. And what happens? You go into a long theological discussion, *with no mention of the Psalter!* And thus the 1842 version comes to a close.

The 1843 story

Moderator: I am afraid we must hasten on without further discussion to the 1843 accounts.

Reporter 3: You mean we have to go through all this all over again?

Reporter 2: No. That is just the point: we are about to hear a *different* story now!

Caswall: Not different, sir, "Revised and Enlarged." Let me read you the preface to the 1843 edition of *The City of the Mormons, or Three Days at Nauvoo:*

> The following narrative, the result of a few weeks leisure on shipboard, is again presented to the public with a deep sense, on the Author's part, of the iniquity of an imposture, which, under the name of religion, is spreading extensively in America and in Great Britain. Mormonism needs but to be seen in its true light to be hated; and if the following pages, consisting almost exclusively of the personal testimony of the Author, should assist in awakening indignation against a cruel delusion and a preposterous heresy, he will consider himself amply rewarded.

Reporter 1: This seems to support a good deal that was said, but not acknowledged, by Mr. Caswall, regarding his earlier effort. Here he frankly admits that he wants to make Mormonism "hated," to "awaken indignation" against it, that he has been nursing in leisure a "deep sense of iniquity," and that his claim to belief is that his statements "consist *almost exclusively* of his own personal testimony"—though I might add that there is hardly a statement in the book that he did not get from somebody else.

Moderator: Since our panel seems to be out for blood, Mr. Caswall, you can expect them to emphasize and probably exploit the details of your subsequent accounts that are *not* found in the first one. They will probably be very suspicious of these. We will anticipate their zeal, and instead of telling the whole story over again each time, simply examine the salient points in which new elements are introduced. Sometimes the repetitions are significant. Here, for example, in an 1843 version you repeat what you said about "laying aside your clerical apparel," making it clear that you were going incognito, for you say, "I had . . . assumed a dress in which there was little probability of my being recognized as a 'minister of the Gentiles' "—which I think is an important point.[87] Then you repeat that you had got yourself the Greek Psalter with definite purposes in view. Do you recall that, as of 1843?

Caswall: Yes, indeed: "In order to test the scholarship of the prophet, I had further provided myself with an ancient Greek manuscript of the Psalter written upon parchment, and probably about six-hundred years old."[88]

Moderator: Now, would you repeat your story of those interesting little details not found in the earlier versions?

Caswall: Well, I landed in Montrose at 9 o'clock Sunday morning, 17 April, and about an hour later crossed the river in a canoe with thirteen other people, Mormons on their way to meeting. We were just in time for the meeting that began at 10:30. It was held in a grove near the temple. I noted the wholesome nature of the congregation and especially the large number of English people who had come "to listen to the ravings of a false prophet." "The service [if such it may be called] having continued from half past ten o-clock till two finally concluded." I then had lunch at a tavern, where I argued with a "decent and probably intelligent Scotchman."[89]

Reporter 1: What did you argue about?

Caswall: I pointed out "how greatly deficient [the Mormon services] appeared in dignity and spirituality; and contrasted them with the decorous and solemn worship of the Church of England."[90]

Reporter 2: And you thought that by carrying on like that there would be "little probability" of your "being recognized as a 'minister of the Gentiles' "? You must have thought all these respectable and probably intelligent people from the Old Country were extremely naive and gullible not to recognize an Anglican minister out of uniform. Did you stay long in Nauvoo after lunch?

Caswall: No. "From the tavern I proceeded to the landing place and engaged the ferryman to take me over to Montrose."[91]

Reporter 2: Your real mine of information was in Montrose, I take it.

Caswall: Yes, I hastened back to Montrose, where "after the awful proceedings of the morning, I felt happy to be once more among Christians."[92]

Reporter 3: "*Awful* proceedings"?

Caswall: Yes. During the meeting they had actually asked for money, and "the thought arose in my mind, that these earnest appeals for money were designed mainly for the ears of the three hundred green saints who had just arrived."[93]

Reporter 2: So after all, it was the thought in your mind that was awful. Don't you ever ask for money in the Church of England? In some of your writings you are rather exercised on the subject. So you were happy to be among Christians. What kind of a man was your host in Montrose?

Caswall: He was one who possessed "the independence to resist the encroachments of the Mormons, and the ability to expose their designs." For that reason "he has been the object of constant persecution since the settlement of these people in his vicinity."[94]

Reporter 2: And you stayed at this man's house but you would not stay with Mormons; you believed *everything* he told you about them but nothing the Mormons told you about him. Do you call that "hearing both sides of the question"?

Caswall: Oh, I heard the Mormon side. I talked with the ferryman on the way back, and "I afterwards found that his opinion of the characters of his brethren, 'the saints,' was by no means flattering to them. He told a person in Montrose, that it was 'no use to hoist a flag at Nauvoo as a signal to passengers, for it was sure to be stolen.' "[95]

Reporter 2: This is an excellent example of the quality and impartiality of your researches in Nauvoo, Mr. Caswall. You talk with the Mormon ferryman, and announce to the world as a result that you are prepared to give a firsthand report. But the ferryman didn't say that about the flag to you, did he? No. You got it "afterwards" from "a person in Montrose," who told you the ferryman had said it to somebody else. Yet you have the effrontery to announce that your report "consists almost exclusively of personal testimony of the author," such personal testimony being almost exclusively bits of gossip picked up in Montrose.

Moderator: Come, gentlemen, let's not lose our tempers. I notice, Mr. Caswall, you tell almost the same story concerning the second day of your visit in both the 1842 and the "Revised and Enlarged" edition of 1843, except that you insert a long religious discussion with "a very respectable looking Mormon" who invited you to visit his house.[96] It is a wonder to me how you can remember these long conversations word for word. You must have taken careful notes.

Reporter 1: It is even more wonderful, sir, that while

you are always careful to state the hour of the day, the day of the week, the month, and the year, thus giving your report an air of great detail and accuracy, you never once in the whole course of your Nauvoo story designate *anyone* by name save Joseph Smith (who as the star of the piece cannot be omitted) and his mother. Not a single person, Mormon or anti-Mormon, is named or in any way individually designated. You are careful to state that a large crowd of witnesses was present at every crucial event of your stay in Nauvoo, but if the presence of witnesses is to bear any weight we must know who they were. Why do you never name them?

Moderator: Perhaps Mr. Caswall didn't want to get involved in lawsuits.

Reporter 2: He wouldn't need to if he was telling the truth. Mr. Caswall has often commented on the perfect willingness of the Mormons to acknowledge facts when confronted with them; he has even stated that Mormons frankly admitted to him that Joseph Smith made mistakes and practiced deception—but he won't tell us who those Mormons were. He won't even give us the name of his helpful anti-Mormon friends in Montrose! Why not? Since you tell us that *many* of the high dignitaries of the church were your witnesses, Mr. Caswall, it is certain that many of your witnesses kept journals. Couldn't you give us some of their names? Don't you *want* people to check up on your history?

Moderator: That is a serious accusation, sir, and we shall have to return to it. For the present let us continue with the 1843 narrative. So you went back to Montrose, Mr. Caswall?

Caswall: There "after tea my kind host provided me with a horse, and in company with him, I took a delightful ride upon the prairie."[97]

Reporter 3: This is interesting. In 1842 you said the Mormons offered you a horse and carriage to take a ride upon the beautiful prairies, but you refused because you said you were in a hurry. In 1843 you do not mention the Mormon offer, but tell of riding with your Montrose friend—an experience not mentioned in the earlier account.

Moderator: Surely you are not suggesting that Mr. Caswall has transferred the kindness of the Mormons to his friend.

Reporter 3: Not at all, but I am calling attention to the fact that almost all the nice things that Mr. Caswall said about the Mormons in 1842 are *omitted* from the 1843 and subsequent editions—such as this act of hospitality, for example—though the later edition is an *"Enlarged* and *Revised"* one. Also his last report, that of 1865, is by far the *worst*.

Reporter 2: I notice, Mr. Caswall, that this 1843 book is much more anti-Mormon than the earlier one. When you rode out with your host, he told you about the Indians, but when you state that "the Indians have the greatest possible contempt for Joseph Smith, and denominate him a Tshe-wal-lis-ke, which signifies a rascal,"[98] you do so as a matter of personal testimony, whereas actually you are merely stating what your Mormon-hating friend had told you. So it goes. But how is it that you can remember a long and difficult Indian name like that, yet don't remember the name of the Pharaoh whose mummy you saw or the names of the people you met? How is it that you can recite long speeches word for word—whole pages of them—yet do not remember a single word spoken by Joseph Smith until you placed your Psalter in his hands?

Moderator: Perhaps it is not so much a case of remembering, sir, as a judicious selection of material.

Reporter 2: But that makes me even more suspicious. What his Montrose informant said the Indians called Smith is neither here nor there. It is mere gossip. The name of that informant, on the other hand, may be a most useful clue. If Mr. Caswall's story is true, he has nothing to lose and everything to gain by placing in our hands every possible means of checking up on it. Why, then, does he display such skill in leading the reader away from every promising check and control?

Moderator: We must be getting on. Let's go now to the crucial events of the unforgettable third day. You crossed the river in the morning with a Mormon doctor with whom you discussed religion. According to your account it was you who brought up the subject of the Trinity and displayed great literacy.

Caswall: Yes, the doctor "uttered a horrid blasphemy."

Reporter 3: And what is your idea of a horrid blasphemy?

Caswall: He said: "We believe that the Father is God, the Son is God, and the Holy Ghost is God; that makes three at least who are God, and no doubt there are a great many more."[99]

Reporter 2: Don't you believe the first part of his statement?

Caswall: Of course, it is simply the Creed.

Reporter 2: And the doctor was not, apparently, an Episcopalian or a follower of the School of Alexandria. Is that a crime? Don't bother to answer, sir. My point is simply that your quarrel with Smith and his people is a doctrinal one.

Moderator: So you landed with the doctor and walked to Smith's house. As in your 1842 account, the curious people come out to see your wonderful book.

Caswall: Yes. "By the time I arrived at the prophet's house, they amounted to almost a crowd."

Reporter 3: Come again? Would you repeat that, sir?

Caswall: I said, "they amounted almost to a crowd."[100]

Reporter 3: But in 1842 you said that they "amounted to a *perfect* crowd" — now it is "*almost* a crowd." You are revising downward again. Why?

Reporter 2: If Mr. Caswall has toned down his 1843 account, that can only mean that he went too far in 1842.

Caswall: A very minor change, sir. By a "perfect crowd" one can mean "practically a crowd," "almost a crowd," . . .

Reporter 2: Or barely a crowd? I grant you, sir, if this were the only instance of toning down, we could overlook it; but it is only the beginning. In 1842 you said you were "accompanied by a host of elders, bishops, preachers, and common Mormons." How did you know they were bishops? Did they wear miters?

Moderator: They might have been pointed out to Mr. Caswall as such.

Reporter 2: Then why does he omit that part in 1843, when he says he was "accompanied by many elders, preachers, and other Mormon dignitaries"? The "perfect crowd" has become "almost a crowd," the colorful "host" has become a colorless "many," the only specific officials — bishops — have disappeared, but to make up for that the "common Mormons" have vaguely become "dignitaries." You see how Mr. Caswall is increasingly careful not to mention anything *specific*. In 1842 you say of Smith "his hands are large and fat," but in 1843 in your second book you change this to the more plausible and less easily tested remark: "his hands are large and awkward."[101] You may honestly think a man is awkward whether he is or not, but when you say he is fat you have committed yourself. So in *The Prophet of the Nineteenth Century* you again tone down your earlier report. Then Smith and the Mormons wanted you to name a price for your book. Do you remember what you answered, as of 1843? Smith has said, as you will recall, "That book ain't of any use to you."

Caswall: And I replied: "Oh yes, it is of some use; for if I were in want of money, I could sell it for something handsome."[102]

Reporter 2: This is certainly a comedown! In 1842 you

said you answered (you see, I have been unsportingly taking notes): "Oh yes . . . I could sell it, and obtain, perhaps, enough to live on for a whole year." Now, I submit that there is a difference between "something handsome" and "enough to live on for a whole year."

Moderator: I think we can allow some latitude . . .

Reporter 2: Here? Bear in mind, sir, that Mr. Caswall in writing the 1843 edition was making a revised *enlargement* — he had the earlier text before his eyes: every change he made was deliberate. If he was quoting correctly, from his notes or any other source, in 1842, what need to change a single syllable? Note that he always revises the story in the direction of greater plausibility. But no matter how fantastic a story may sound, *if it is true* there is no need to tone it down. But to return to the price of the book. I find here that you told the Mormons in your 1842 story: "I will not tell you what price I would take; but if you were to offer me this moment nine hundred dollars in gold for it, you should not have it." Now, what do you say in 1843? Will you read it?

Caswall: I told them "I would not sell it to them for many hundred dollars."[103] Many hundred, nine hundred — what's the difference? A slight revision.

Reporter 2: A considerable difference, and a not-so-slight revision, sir. In the first book you name a definite offer as below your price: nine hundred dollars in gold — a fabulous sum for a book you had just acquired, and couldn't read, and never made any further use of. Why didn't you take their offers?

Moderator: There's no point in going over that again.

Reporter 2: Excuse me. This time I merely mean to show that Mr. Caswall himself grasped the absurdity of his story when he thought it over, for nothing is said about nine hundred dollars in gold in the 1843 or later versions.

Moderator: Should he go into all those details in every edition?

Reporter 2: He should most certainly repeat them in the second enlarged edition!

Moderator: Let us hear the 1843 story of the Psalter, sir.

Caswall: When an ancient Greek manuscript of the Psalms was exhibited to him as a test of his scholarship, he boldly pronounced it to be a *"Dictionary of Egyptian hieroglyphics."* Pointing to the capital letters at the commencement of each verse, he said, "Them figures is Egyptian hieroglyphics; and them which follows is the interpretation of the hieroglyphics, written in the *reformed Egyptian*. Them characters is like the letters that was engraved on the golden plates." He afterwards proceeded to show his papyri.[104]

Reporter 2: Just a minute, please. In this account you have left out the very crucial fact that first of all *you told Smith* what the book was. You have also omitted his statement "What ain't Greek is Egyptian; and what ain't Egyptian is Greek." In 1842 you said Smith called the Greek capitals Greek, but in 1843 you explicitly state that "pointing to the capital letters, . . . he said, 'Them figures is in *Egyptian hieroglyphics*' " and make no mention of his calling anything Greek. These, I submit, are very material alterations in your story. Then further, you also omit his remark, "This book ain't of no use to you; you don't understand it." And all these significant omissions, mind you, in an enlarged edition!

Caswall: I omitted them in *The Prophet of the Nineteenth Century*, but they are all included in *The City of the Mormons, or Three Days at Nauvoo*, of the same year.

Reporter 2: But the former is by far your most famous and important book. Can't you see that in abridging the story as you have you leave out details that offer important hints as to its truthfulness? The shorter version was given in a book that centers completely about the dominant theme of your personal association with the prophet. Your meeting with him was a very brief one. The book is padded with all sorts of fourth- and fifth-hand information, which shows that you were *not* crowded for space; yet when you chose to delete, you cut out the very heart of your history, the one part of the story that you were qualified to tell at firsthand. Then after Smith's absurd and ungrammatical declaration you say, "He afterwards proceeded to show his papyri." Here again you omit the very suspicious and incongruous statement in your other account that it was *you* who took the damning Psalter away from Smith before he could make another speech about it or before you or anyone else could ask him any questions, and that it was you who changed the subject and asked to see the papyri. Those little omissions are really quite important, sir. They make your story much more plausible.

Moderator: Tell us about the papyri now, if you will.

Caswall: He proceeded, as I said, "to show his papyrus, and to explain the inscriptions; but probably suspecting that the author designed to entrap him, he suddenly left the apartment, leaped into his light wagon, and drove away as fast as possible. The author could not properly avoid expressing his opinion of the prophet to the assembled Mormons; and was engaged for several hours in a sharp controversy with various eminent dignitaries."[105]

Reporter 3: I must agree with Mr. Wye, that this is a very different story from the other one, and that the differences are significant. When someone asked you before whether Smith left the room because he was afraid of you, you pointed out that you made no such claim. But now you do make it, albeit cautiously, using such subjective and moot words as "probable," "suspect," and "design."

Reporter 2: In your 1842 story, Mr. Caswall, you do not say that Smith left the room suddenly—which has now become an important part of the story. You did not see him leave, you were absorbed in looking at the papyrus, so you could not have known whether he left suddenly. Do you know Egyptian?

Caswall: Of course not. It is an "unknown tongue," as Smith's own mother made clear in describing his use of the Urim and Thummim.

Reporter 2: Then Smith had no reason for suspecting that you knew Egyptian. But look where Smith is seized with panic. You ask him the meaning of a hieroglyphic symbol, and then he suspects that you "design to entrap him." This is the first mention of any trick or trap anywhere, yet *it is not the Greek Psalter* at all, but Smith's own familiar papyrus, of which of course you know nothing, that puts the prophet at your mercy. He is so terrified that the stranger who knows no Greek will catch him on a point of hieroglyphics that he rushes from the room, leaps into a wagon, and drives away "as fast as possible." Did you see him leap into the wagon? From your first account that is of course out of the question, yet in this case the reader is bound to take it for granted that you did, since your book is based "almost entirely on the personal testimony of the Author." You said nothing about leaping in the first edition, which paints a very different picture: there you waited long for the prophet's return, and then finally ("at length," as you put it), you gave up waiting and went down to the street, and it was not until you got there that you heard the noise of wheels and then the prophet came in sight furiously lashing his splendid steeds in his superbly tactful effort to escape having to explain the meaning of that hieroglyphic symbol to you. Couldn't he have escaped you by simply stepping into another room or house? Obviously the two stories don't fit at all. What was Smith doing while you waited so long for his return? Was he leaping into a wagon kept three miles away so that he could drive back at breakneck speed to the store for you to see him twenty minutes later? Was he doing a slow leap? If you didn't know where he had gone, why did he need to leave town in total panic and with such a hilarious flourish?

Caswall: "He probably suspected an intention on my part to trap him."

Reporter 2: What a motive for the wily Joe Smith to go completely off his head! You don't *know* that he suspected you, he *"probably"* did; and he knew nothing for sure, he only probably *suspected*; and he did not probably suspect that you had him, but only that you *designed* to; and not that you could expose him, but only probably suspected that you designed to *entrap* him. It is all as vague as that. But there is nothing vague in Smith's behavior—he puts on a four-star display of utter terror in the presence of you and "various eminent dignitaries." That is certainly a story worth telling.

Caswall: It is indeed, sir.

Reporter 2: Then why do you leave it out in all subsequent versions of the Nauvoo story? Why do you never mention it again?

Moderator: Please, gentlemen, we shall get to that in good time. Mr. Caswall, will you tell us what happened next?

Caswall: Well, the 1843 story of the argument that followed is a good deal like that of 1842.

Reporter 1: Is the story of the old man and the healing in it?

Caswall: No, that is left out, but I do include a speech I gave them on their manner of worship. "How miserable were your services last Sunday," I said. "How cold your worship, how unedifying and farcical your preaching. The Holy Ghost was manifestly absent from your assembly, which resembled a Jewish synagogue more than a Christian congregation."[106]

Reporter 2: Indeed. I find it strange that while you are trying to expand this one brief episode of a book you omit picturesque and essential details in one account while putting in their place equally picturesque and essential details omitted from another. I can understand Mr. Caswall's desire for variety in his stories in order to sell as many versions of it as possible; but if his story is to be the testimony that forever damns Joseph Smith, he should be careful to tell just one story. This he does not do.

Moderator: Let us allow Mr. Caswall to proceed. Perhaps those things will explain themselves. Mr. Caswall, did the Mormons ask you in your 1843 version what you thought of Smith's performance?

Caswall: Oh yes, that is there. "The Mormons now surrounded me."

Reporter 2: "Now?" Hadn't they been surrounding you in numbers all the time?

Caswall: " . . . surrounded me, and requested to know whether I had received satisfaction from the prophet's explanation. I replied that the prophet had given me no satisfaction, and that, on the contrary, he had proved his own ignorance most effectually. They wished to know my own religious opinions," and we became involved in a theological discussion.[107]

Reporter 2: But no mention of the Psalter. Here you missed your second chance.

Reporter 3: Mr. Caswall, you seemed to have spoken to the Mormons very boldly.

Caswall: I told them then and there, "I think it likely that most of you are credulous and ignorant, but well-meaning persons, and that the time at least *has* been when you desired to do the will of God. A knot of designing persons, of whom Smith is the center, have imposed upon your credulity and ignorance, and you have been most thoroughly hoaxed by their artful devices. . . . And oh! how gladly would I see you delivered from this awful delusion, and returning to the bosom of that Holy Catholic Church, from which many of you have apostatized."[108]

Reporter 1: I admire your phenomenal memory, sir.

Reporter 3: And I your phenomenal courage — you certainly gave it to them!

Caswall: "As the City Council had passed an ordinance, under which any stranger in Nauvoo speaking disrespectfully of the prophet might be arrested and imprisoned without process, [I] deemed myself happy in leaving Nauvoo unmolested, after plainly declaring to the Mormons that they were dupes of a base and blaspheming imposter."[109]

Reporter 2: Very interesting. Where can I find out about that ordinance?

Caswall: In Mr. John C. Bennett's book.

Reporter 2: Is that where you found out about it?

Caswall: I quoted it as my authority.

Reporter 2: And where did Mr. Bennett get his authority?

Caswall: As you will see here, he quotes from the *Louisville Journal* for 3 August 1842.[110]

Reporter 2: But that news item only appeared four months after your visit to Nauvoo. You aver that it was awareness of that ordinance that made you "happy in leaving Nauvoo unmolested." But there was no such ordinance when you were there; the only ordinance was a fictitious one invented long after your departure. You learned of it from the sources indicated and worked it into your story of 1843 as a personal experience. This little detail supplies a useful clue, if we needed one, to Mr. Caswall's methods, gentlemen.

Moderator: Come now, let's not embarrass our guest.

Reporter 1: Do you remember your parting words to the Mormons of Nauvoo, Mr. Caswall?

Caswall: I have them here: "I have been among you three days; I have expressed my sentiments freely respecting your religion and your prophet, and I heartily thank you that you have listened to me with attention, and that although you have had me altogether in your power, you have not put me under the Mississippi and kept me there."[111] "During the remainder of the day, I employed

myself in obtaining testimony from persons residing in
Iowa in reference to the conduct and character of their
Mormon neighbors. . . . This testimony . . . agrees with
what I myself saw and heard in Nauvoo."[112]

Reporter 2: Those last happen to be the very words with
which Mr. Caswall describes his *first* afternoon in his 1842
versions. Apparently he transposes his own words as
freely as he borrows from others.

Reporter 3: It seems a poor return, sir, for the unfailing
hospitality you enjoyed in Nauvoo, to hasten back to Montrose to continue gathering your stories against those
"credulous and ignorant, but well-meaning persons" who
had treated you so kindly. It is also perfectly apparent from
your farewell address that the Mormons did not resent
your presence among them, no matter how bold and ob-
streperous you were. Yet nowhere do you so much as hint
in any of your accounts that there was ever another Gentile
in Nauvoo beside yourself. I find that very odd.

Reporter 1: And isn't it rather mean of you to tell the
world that you considered yourself happy in leaving Nauvoo unmolested, when all you ever found there was a
desire to be helpful to you?

Reporter 2: And to return the Mormons' courtesy by
thanking them for not drowning you in the Mississippi,
as if that were their custom?

Reporter 3: Didn't the Mormons want you to stay
longer?

Moderator: Please, gentlemen, one at a time!

Caswall: As we ferried back to Montrose for the last
time, the Mormon doctor "said that no man could obtain
salvation, who devoted so little attention to the truth of
God as I had done; and that instead of spending only three
days, I ought to have remained at least three weeks at
Nauvoo."[113]

Reporter 2: Don't you think he was right, in view of all

the books and articles you were going to publish about your famous visit to the Mormons?

Caswall: "I told him that I had seen quite enough to convince any person of ordinary understanding that Smith was an imposter."[114]

Reporter 2: And thereby, sir, you gave yourself away. You showed definitely that your real object in coming to Nauvoo was not to study the Mormons and hear both sides of the question, as you claim, but to "get something" on Smith. You didn't go to convert the Mormons, for you "had laid aside your clerical garb." You were determined specifically, as you say, to get an interview with Smith, and you reached that decision in a moment of anger and frustration. You couldn't hope to learn much about the Mormons in three days of brief conducted tours, and a five-minute conversation with a religious leader is hardly adequate to satisfy a real seeker for knowledge; but the three-day visit and the five-minute talk *were* enough to accomplish your purposes, as you so clearly put it, *"quite enough* to convince any person of ordinary understanding that Smith was an imposter." That was the purpose of your mission, and when that was accomplished you had no more interest in staying another hour in Nauvoo.

Caswall: Now you are talking like the doctor. "It was in vain that I attempted to correct the doctor's false positions; the stream of his heretical eloquence had begun to flow. . . . He said that the truth of Mormonism did not depend on the character of Smith or of any other man."[115]

Reporter 2: And you call that heretical talk?

Moderator: We must not judge the Reverend Caswall too harshly. Remember, he found himself in an awkward position. He had come to expose these people, and naturally had to be on his guard.

Reporter 1: In that case, the bold, heroic speeches must have been brave Ciceronian afterthoughts.

Reporter 3: I have been thinking that myself. Here Mr.

Caswall was obviously too timid to wear clerical garb—though the Mormons were as kind to clergymen as to anyone else, and that certainly would not have hindered his testing of the prophet's scholarship but helped it. He was also plainly too timid to spend a night in Nauvoo—says he was afraid they would steal his book, speaks of the risk he was running among the Mormons, and all that. Yet this same Caswall, *according to him*, gives fiery speeches denouncing Smith and all the Mormon leaders on the streets of Nauvoo and in the presence of those Mormon leaders. You will remember that Cicero used to run away from the opposition and then, at a safe distance, compose the rousing speeches he *would* have given in their presence. I wonder if Mr. Caswall is not doing the same thing? The fact that he does not hesitate to quote the same speeches differently in different books is irrefutable evidence that he does invent things. The question is, how far does he go?

Moderator: I believe Mr. Caswall wanted to tell us about his exposure of the prophet.

Caswall: Yes. After he had driven away and the old man had tried to heal me, I referred again to the false prophet: "Would you believe him if he should say that English is French?" I asked. And when they replied that they could form their own opinions, I answered, "You heard your prophet declare that this book of mine is a Dictionary of Egyptian hieroglyphics, and, farther, that it is written in characters *like those of the original Book of Mormon*. I know it most positively to be the Psalms of David, written in ancient Greek. Now what shall I think of your prophet?"[116]

Reporter 2: Mr. Caswall, why did you italicize the words "like those of the original Book of Mormon"? Was there any possibility that the characters in your book might have been like those on the plates?

Caswall: Don't be absurd, sir; there *were* no plates!

Reporter 2: But there *were* characters. Didn't you know that? For Joseph Smith to say what you have him say—in italics—he would have to be ignorant, as you apparently are, of the fact that all the "dignitaries and high officials" in attendance at your demonstration knew very well what the characters "of the original Book of Mormon" looked like, for Smith had had them copied and widely circulated. Your fatal blunder is to assume that only Smith knew what the characters looked like—a natural assumption for you to make, but one that no Mormon would be guilty of. Then again, if you had read the Book of Mormon you could have spared yourself an even worse blunder. *Had* you read the Book of Mormon?

Caswall: While I was at Montrose I grasped the contents and what it mainly consisted of after I had opened it at half-a-dozen places.

Reporter 2: Well, if you had opened it at a few more you would have known that Joseph Smith would never in the world have claimed to recognize Greek, Egyptian hieroglyphic, and Book of Mormon characters in the same document. The Book of Mormon itself makes it very clear that the script of the people who wrote it was strictly a New World invention, known to no other people on earth, and therefore could not possibly turn up in an *Old* World document containing Greek and hieroglyphic. Though "Reformed Egyptian" was the ultimate origin of the Book of Mormon characters, it had been "altered" beyond recognition by the Nephites. If you had been less eager to incriminate Smith, Mr. Caswall, you might have been more thorough in your researches and avoided falling into your own traps.

Reporter 1: It's getting late. If it is all right with you, I would just as soon get on to Mr. Caswall's next batch of dispatches. When do they occur?

The 1851 story

Moderator: In 1851. I don't think these versions of the Nauvoo story of Mr. Caswall need detain us long. There are a number of points, however, on which our experts of the press might wish to question our celebrated guest. Mr. Ecks?

Reporter 1: I notice that our toning-down process has gone on unabated. For instance the description of Joseph Smith. In 1851 you write: "Smith was a clownish-looking man, but with a decidedly knavish expression. His hands were large and fat, and his manner, though awkward, was energetic; . . . his white hat was enveloped in a piece of black crape."[117] This is the first we have heard of Smith's energetic manner, and the first mention in your writings of his famous white hat. Now, since this is a very abbreviated account, how does it happen to contain details not found in the much fuller accounts written at or near the time? In the ensuing years a number of writings had appeared telling about Smith's fabulous white hat. In 1865 you go so far as to refer to Joseph Smith as "Old Holy White Hat Joe." Yet in your long book accounts of your meeting with Smith published in 1842 and 1843 you make absolutely no mention of the hat, which later becomes Smith's trademark. Isn't this another case of working into your eyewitness picture of Smith bits of information picked up later, like the item about the Nauvoo ordinance?

Reporter 3: As you described your meeting originally, sir, Smith met you "at a short distance from his dwelling," and immediately returned to the house with you. Are we to believe that he put on a hat just to step outside and lead you into the house? I only mention that because you yourself do not mention the hat until 1851.

Moderator: Please, let Mr. Caswall tell his own 1851 story about the interview.

Caswall: Smith "having been previously informed by

his people of my wonderful book, now took it in his hands and asked me if I had any idea of its meaning. I replied that I believed it to be a Greek Psalter, but that I would like to hear his opinion."[118]

Reporter 2: Mr. Caswall, you may recall that we pointed out the absurdity in your other versions of having you start out by telling the prophet what your book was, when your object was to test his scholarship by having him identify it. It is instructive to note that you have now taken steps to rectify the mistake.

Caswall: How?

Reporter 2: By admitting that Smith knew all about the book ahead of time, "having been previously informed by his people" about it. This is a new touch. You had no hesitation in telling him what you thought the book was, because he had already been tipped off "by his people." But in that case, your "test of scholarship" breaks down. So you do not conduct the test at all, but give the whole initiative to Smith: in 1851 he is on to everything ahead of time and takes the initiative from the first; knowing what you have already said about it, he takes the book into his hands and challenges you to tell him "its meaning." The initiative is all with him.

Caswall: You are citing my book *The American Church* of 1851, sir. But if you will only turn to my other book published in the same year, you will find I am true to my original story.

Reporter 1: Then why publish *two* versions?

Reporter 3: Which is the other 1851 book?

Caswall: Mormonism and Its Author.

Reporter 2: I notice that Smith's invisible eyes are not mentioned in these later versions. Another absurdity in the original account has thus been covered up. . . . But what is this? If Mr. Caswall has been leaving things out, he has most certainly made up for it by the introduction in his 1851 stories of sensational new material! In both books!

Moderator: What is this sensational new material?

Reporter 2: Listen to this. "In order to test the 'Prophet's' inspiration in regard to the dead languages, I had brought with me an ancient manuscript of the Greek Psalter, which I still retain as a valuable memorial of the event. Taking this in my hand, I crossed over to Nauvoo on Monday morning, and inquired for the 'Prophet.' "[119]

Caswall: What's wrong with that?

Reporter 2: Heretofore Mr. Caswall has said most explicitly that his purpose in acquiring the Psalter was to test Smith's *scholarship.* Now he is out to test his *inspiration,* a totally different thing. If Smith failed in the 1842 test he would prove himself a poor scholar and an ignoramus; but now if he fails he will demonstrate that he lacks inspiration — that he is a false prophet. Of course the test is silly — inability to read Greek does not prove one a false prophet, yet this is Mr. Caswall's official position as of 1851. It is also a very risky position for a minister of the Gospel to take.

Caswall: How, "risky?"

Reporter 2: Because the wicked seek for such signs. Remember that you suggested having Smith walk on the water or raise the dead to prove his prophetic calling. No true prophet would comply with such a request. When they challenged Jesus to prove that he was a prophet at his trial, he answered not a word, even though they devised a clever trick to put him to the test (Luke 23:64). Now, let Mr. Caswall tell us how he opens the conversation in the other book, *Mormonism and Its Author.* If you will remember, Mr. Caswall, you first mentioned that Smith "seemed very coarse and clownish, and certainly had not the open and straight-forward look which we naturally expect to see in an honest man" — though this time you say nothing about having no opportunity to see his eyes, which in my opinion discredits your first account entirely. What did you say to Smith?

Caswall: "On entering his house, chairs were provided for Joseph and myself, while a good many 'Latter-day Saints' stood round. . . . I then placed the book in his hands, and said, that as I had been told that he was a prophet of God, gifted with the power of understanding unknown tongues, I hoped he would explain its contents. He asked me if I had any idea of its meaning. I replied that I believed it to be the Psalms of David in Greek. 'No,' he said, 'it ain't Greek at all.' . . . He then said, that the letters in the book were 'like the letters that were engraved on the plates of the Golden Book.' "[120]

Reporter 2: You put that last statement of Smith's in quotation marks.

Caswall: Naturally. It was a quotation.

Reporter 2: But in 1842 you quoted Smith as saying: "Them characters is like the letters that was engraved on the golden plates." Now, in 1851 you had access to your other books, from which you quote at length. So you have deliberately changed the text: that last statement of Smith's in your 1851 edition is perfectly grammatical. Why did you take the liberty to correct Smith's grammar after all those years—did you want him to make a better impression? I hardly think so. No, now you are out to prove Smith not an ignoramus, but a false prophet. Of course, the crux of the whole matter is your opening speech to Smith about his being a prophet of God with the power of understanding unknown tongues, etc. That speech establishes the test as a test in inspiration instead of scholarship. *But there is no hint of that all-important speech in any of the earlier versions.* I don't think we need to ask Mr. Caswall to explain: it is as plain as day that he has been thinking it over and shifted his point of attack. Without wishing to embarrass Mr. Caswall further, I would like to ask him to continue, as of 1851, that is.

Caswall: "I might go on to mention a further conversation which I had with Joseph Smith."

Reporter 3: A further conversation? But I thought this was the only one.

Caswall: We conversed further, didn't we?

Reporter 3: But "a further conversation" is something else. At least it definitely gives the impression that this was not your one and only conversation with Smith.

Caswall: I didn't say I had another conversation, I simply said, "I might mention a further conversation."

Reporter 3: "A further conversation" that you *might* mention certainly implies that there is a good deal that you are not telling here, and that you had other conversations with Smith.

Moderator: Implies it, perhaps, Mr. C., but does not state it.

Reporter 3: Insinuation seems to be a fine art in stories about Joseph Smith. What was this further conversation, Mr. Caswall?

Caswall: I do not recount it in my 1851 books. I merely say, "I might go on to mention a further conversation which I had with Joseph Smith; and I might describe how suddenly he took his departure, when he began to suspect that I knew a little more than he at first imagined."[121]

Reporter 2: At the last telling you had said that Smith *"probably* suspected you of a design to entrap him." Now you have changed that to the certainty that Smith was alarmed by your knowledge. Why should that alarm him? Did he think you knew hieroglyphic—but no, *in this story you do not even mention hieroglyphics!* Now the Psalter is everything, and nothing must be allowed to detract from its importance. Well then, he "began to suspect" that you knew "a little more than he at first imagined." How do you know what he at first imagined? Would Smith have any reason to doubt that you knew what was in your own book? But tell us what happens next, please.

Caswall: Well, as I said, Smith took his departure "when he began to suspect that I knew a little more than he at first imagined. I might also state the conversations which I held with some of the Mormons, in Nauvoo, in order to convince them that Smith had proved himself to be a deceiver."[122]

Reporter 1: You might have, but you didn't.

Caswall: In my other book of 1851 I was somewhat more explicit. "The 'Prophet' afterwards exhibited to me the same sheets of papyrus which I had seen on the previous day, and began to give his usual explanation."[123]

Reporter 3: How do you know it was "usual" if you had never heard it before?

Caswall: I had talked to his mother.

Reporter 3: But you say this was "*his* usual explanation."

Reporter 1: And if Smith was on such familiar ground, why should a perfectly natural and routine question from you throw him into a panic?

Reporter 2: Please, gentlemen, let us be fair! Mr. Caswall makes no mention of the prophet's panic in his 1851 books.

Reporter 1: Indeed, I thought that was the most striking and picturesque part of the story. But what about the team of horses, and dashing down the street in a cloud of dust and all that—simply delightful!

Reporter 2: Alas! Not a word of all that in 1851. Indeed, we never hear of the wagon again after 1843.

Reporter 3: Why not, Mr. Caswall? That was easily the best part of the story. Sheer drama. *And in all your later versions you don't even mention it.* If it was true in 1843 and 1842, why do you never tell it again?

Moderator: Perhaps there wasn't room.

Reporter 3: Oh, come now! Through the years Mr. Caswall tells his story again and again—in book-length accounts. He must borrow from everywhere to fill up pages, yet never has room to tell in full of the one brief conversation he had with Joseph Smith—so he leaves out the most entertaining and colorful episode of the whole thing so that he can quote at length from dull letters received from English clergymen and American gossips. That is too much to take, sir. The total disappearance of the wagon story is a most suspicious circumstance — to my mind full proof that it never happened.

Moderator: Let us leave speculation and let Mr. Caswall tell his story.

Caswall: As I said when so rudely interrupted, Smith "began to give his usual explanation. But his suspicions appeared now to be awakened, and he suddenly departed leaving me in the midst of the credulous and fanatical multitude. I then told the bystanders that the book was certainly nothing but a Greek Psalter, and endeavored to make them understand how thoroughly the prophet had committed himself by positively declaring it to be a dictionary of hieroglyphics."[124]

Reporter 2: This, I submit, is a *wholly different story* from the original one.

Moderator: Is there anything there that Mr. Caswall did not say before?

Reporter 2: The same elements are there, but in a new and marvelous combination. In this story Caswall is out to discredit Smith's claim to inspiration, and he is going to do it by the Greek Psalter. So it is necessary for him to take full advantage of the opportunity which he let slip completely in the earlier accounts. *Now* the demonstration must have inspiration as its object and be clearly understood as such — a thing not even mentioned in the first accounts, which are very specific in making scholarship the subject of the test. *Now* the long argument and discussion must take place not in the street but in the room, and pivot about the Greek Psalter. It will not do to have everyone leave the room, as they did before: Caswall must make his point then and there — he is immediately "left in the midst of the fanatical multitude"; there is no place here for the long, quiet wait for Smith's return, the descent to the street, the ridiculous wagon scene, the long theological discussions which only touch on the Psalter incidentally. Caswall immediately pounces on one point alone, proof that Smith "had committed himself by positively declaring" the Greek Psalter to be a dictionary of hieroglyphics.

Moderator: What happened after you exposed Smith then and there in the room?

Caswall: I did not say I exposed him then and there in the room.

Reporter 2: How could you have said it more plainly than this? ". . . he suddenly departed, leaving me in the midst of the credulous and fanatical multitude. I *then* told the bystanders that the book was certainly nothing but a Greek Psalter, . . . " etc. "Then" means "at that time," whereas in your earlier accounts you don't mention the Psalter until later, at another time and place, and you pass up every opportunity to use it in your demonstration.

Reporter 1: You say in 1851 that Smith left the room when "his suspicions appeared to have been awakened," but you don't say suspicions of what.

Moderator: Please let Mr. Caswall continue.

Caswall: "After much fruitless argument, which, however, they took in good part."

Reporter 1: A "credulous and fanatical multitude," as you call them, took your valiant endeavors to prove their prophet a fraud "in good part"? You call that fanaticism?

Moderator: Please, Mr. Ecks, Mr. Caswall has already explained that the people did not believe him.

Caswall: You heard me say it was "*fruitless* argument."

Reporter 2: So you didn't convince them at all.

Caswall: It was fruitless.

Reporter 2: But in 1842 and 1843 you said that the Mormons were quite crestfallen as a result of your discourse, and even admitted that Smith made mistakes like other men, and had been deceived regarding the Psalter. That does not seem like fruitless argument. It is a brilliant victory—which you never mention after 1843! What happened after the fruitless argument which didn't offend the Mormons at all?

Caswall: "One of their number, perceiving my partial deafness, endeavored to work a miracle for my complete restoration. But observing that the touch of his finger and the use of the unknown tongue were in this instance without effect, he assured me that the actual cure was deferred until I should receive Joseph as a true prophet."[125]

Reporter 2: To save embarrassing questions, may I be permitted simply to compare this with Mr. Caswall's earlier account? In 1843 it was Caswall himself who called attention to his deafness and challenged the Mormons to cure it, after telling them he had no faith; in 1851 the initiative is all with them. The silly 1843 gesture of thrusting fingers into both ears has in 1851 become a simple "touch of his finger." We might elaborate on these inventions, but let us hear Mr. Caswall's parting speech.

Caswall: "I felt really grateful to these people for allowing me, when I was completely in their power, to escape so easily with my book, as well as with my life and liberty. Having expressed myself to this effect, I entered the ferryboat."[126]

Reporter 2: Here it is again! Do you forget, sir, that in your 1843 account you did not return to Montrose that last time by the ferry, but in a "small skiff" rowed by the Mormon doctor and two other men using boards, because the oars had been stolen?[127] That was a very picturesque detail. Why do you enter the ferryboat this time, and forget that delightful canoe that went around and around in the current?[128]

The 1865 story

Moderator: Gentlemen, let us remember that we represent the News, and not the Editorial Department. Now let us get on to the final version of Mr. Caswall's story, that published in 1865.

Reporter 1: I notice that the author, W. S. Parrott, gives himself the title of "Voluntary Missionary." What is a Voluntary Missionary? Aren't all missionaries voluntary?

Reporter 2: In this case Mr. Parrott devoted and appointed himself to the profession of traveling about England giving lectures on the Mormons. His mission was to the English, his calling "to exhibit Mormonism in its truly diabolical character." Mr. Caswall's report forms the backbone of his book, *The Veil Uplifted.*

Reporter 1: Would you say that was so, Mr. Caswall?

Caswall: The unique value of my contribution in 1865 is that "I have given my own testimony as to what I myself saw of the false prophet, and heard from his own lips, within his own house."[129]

Reporter 1: Then naturally that is the most important part of your story.

Caswall: Yes. "This testimony helps to destroy the very foundations on which the 'Latter Day' doctrine is built, . . . for if Smith was an imposter, as very plainly appears, then the 'Book of Mormon' is an imposition, and the 'Book of Covenants,' and other 'Latter Day' writings, are a mass of blasphemous rubbish."[130]

Reporter 3: Which leaves no doubt that you, in testifying of your personal experiences with Joseph Smith, are the all-time star witness against the whole "Latter Day" movement.

Reporter 2: So perhaps you will forgive us for seeming hypercritical. After all, sir, it is you who have been Smith's unsparing critic for many long years. Now with an introduction such as Mr. Parrott has given you, we can expect a thoroughly accurate and full account of your brief visit with Smith.

Caswall: Well of course, I can't tell everything.

Reporter 1: This report is economical and to the point.

I see here that you have left out the first two days entirely, Mr. Caswall. Here you concentrate on one episode only — your meeting with Smith. For that reason I think we can expect it to be a particularly full and accurate account. In 1865, how did you describe that momentous meeting?

Caswall: "I met him at a short distance from his own house, in company with a good many of his followers, who were aware that I intended to exhibit a wonderful book to their prophet."

Reporter 2: Excuse me for interrupting already, but this is *not* the story you told earlier. In 1842 you said, "As I advanced, with my book in my hand, numerous Mormons came forth from their dwellings, begging to be allowed to see its mysterious pages; and by the time I arrived at the prophet's house, they amounted to a perfect crowd." In 1843 this perfect crowd had dwindled to "almost a crowd," and finally in 1865 it is not around *you* but around Smith that the crowd gathers, in anticipation of seeing you show the book to him. It is another picture entirely of how the crowd had gathered. You described the prophet as usual?

Caswall: "The appearance of Joseph was very far from saintly; and indeed, conveyed the idea of a knave, much more than of a prophet."[131]

Reporter 2: Every man is entitled to his opinions, sir, but what has happened to the objective evidence that makes your testimony so valuable? Where are the eyes you could not see and the huge fat hands? It is those priceless details for which the world is beholden to you. How do you think a prophet *should* look? Have you ever seen a prophet?

Caswall: Don't be blasphemous, sir. Have a care! "On entering the house, chairs were provided for Joseph and myself, while a good many 'Latter-day Saints' stood around, anxiously expecting to hear their prophet explain the meaning of the book."

Reporter 1: The first part of your quotation is simply a

verbatim repetition of the earlier versions, showing that you used them and cannot plead lapse of memory. But the second part, the anxious expectation, is an added touch. It is apparent, sir, that you are doing everything to play up the one central episode of the Psalter; but it was not always so.

Moderator: Please continue, Mr. Caswall.

Caswall: "I placed the book in his hands, and said, that, as I had been told that he was a prophet of God, gifted with the power of understanding unknown tongues, I hoped he would explain its contents."

Reporter 1: This is the strangest story yet: now its whole issue pivots on the supernatural. You had repeatedly stated earlier that your object was to test his scholarship; then in 1851 you suddenly announced that it was to test his "inspiration." Which was it as of 1865?

Caswall: "As he had given out that God had inspired him with an understanding of unknown tongues, I fixed upon what I considered a very fair method of putting him to the proof."

Reporter 2: So now you are out wholly to test Smith's prophetic inspiration, and you have deliberately devised a test beforehand which in your opinion will do just that. We see now the "Psalter trick" at last full blown, purged of all the dross, irrelevant, confusing, and contradictory details of the earlier stories. Twenty-three years of fixing have at last brought forth a clear, streamlined account that neatly cooks Smith's goose. But is this the truth, the whole truth, and nothing but the truth? If so, what of your other tales? In 1865 you concentrate your whole attack on the Psalter. What about your conversation with Smith?

Caswall: "He asked me if I had any idea of its meaning." And then told me that the letters in the book were "like the letters that were engraved on the plates of the Golden Book!"[132]

Reporter 2: Smith's answer is still in quotes, but what

has happened to his outrageous grammar? And what about your answer to Smith that you believed the book to be a Greek Psalter? That is left out entirely because it would knock in the head your claim that you had "fixed upon a method" of testing his inspiration by asking him to identify the book.

Caswall: The rest of the account is the same as in 1851. "I might go on to mention a further conversation which I had with Joseph Smith; and I might describe how suddenly he took his departure, when he began to suspect that I knew a little more than he at first imagined, . . . etc."[133]

Reporter 2: But after mentioning the conversations (as if there were many of them) you come quickly to the point, I believe.

Caswall: Indeed I do: "But the fact which I desire to be particularly noticed is, that the Founder of Mormonism, the Head of the 'Latter-day Saints,' boldly and confidently pronounced a part of the Holy Bible to be a Dictionary of Egyptian hieroglyphics!"[134]

Reporter 2: As I said—in 1865 you have it all finally worked out. Everything is now subordinated to the Psalter story. In the other versions and as late as 1851 you declared that all your protests to the Mormons on the subject were "fruitless" and that they were convinced that Smith was right. But what do you say in 1865?

Caswall: I told those people, "You heard your prophet declare that this book of mine is a dictionary of Egyptian hieroglyphics, and, farther, that it is written in characters *like those of the original Book of Mormon*. I know it most positively to be the Psalms of David, written in ancient Greek. Now what shall I think of your prophet?"

Reporter 1: This is the crucial speech, all right, and you have put it in quotation marks. Is that what you said?

Caswall: It is.

Reporter 1: Then why is the first part of the speech, the all-important "you heard your prophet declare," etc., that sets the problem up so beautifully, entirely missing in all your other versions?

Reporter 2: What follows is even more important. Mr. Caswall, this is the way you described the reaction to your speech in the 1842 version: "They appeared confounded for a while; but at length the Mormon doctor said, 'Sometimes Mr. Smith speaks as a prophet, and sometimes as a mere man.' . . . I said, 'Whether he spoke as a prophet or as a mere man, he has committed himself.' "[135] That was in 1842. Note here that Caswall wins. Suddenly, without any apparent reason, the Mormons surrender, and admit that Smith was mistaken about the Psalter. That is, of course, the key to the whole business. Yet that all-important incident never appears again in any of Mr. Caswall's other accounts! Why not, if it was true? In 1865, the best Caswall can do is to prove Smith's falseness by a labored syllogism. What was it you said, Mr. Caswall?

Caswall: "Now this certainly goes a great way to prove that Joseph Smith could not have been a prophet of God, nor even a good man. *If he really possessed the power which he claimed,* of reading books in ancient tongues, he would have been likely to know the true Bible even though written in Greek; and since he said that the letters of the book were like those written on the golden plates, it would have been all the easier for him to understand them, because, by his own account, he had translated the writing on those plates by the help of God. But most surely, if he had been a good man, he would have honestly confessed that he did not know the meaning of the book which I showed him; and would not have positively said to me and to the Mormons who were standing by, that the Psalms of David were an Egyptian dictionary. How foolish, then, it is, for any person who knows this fact, to believe this story about the Angel and the Golden Book!"[136]

Reporter 2: Mr. Caswall, this is how you climaxed your demonstration in 1842: "I replied that the prophet had given me no satisfaction, and that on the contrary, he had proved his own ignorance most effectively." Ignorance is the theme, not prophetic inspiration. Now, having shifted your ground, you must go into this long rigmarole to shore up your new position. But it would be impossible for you to deny that it is all invented in retrospect. Did you suddenly remember this long speech for the first time in 1865? Why was all this laborious argument necessary if the Mormons collapsed like a punctured balloon, as in the 1842 version?

Reporter 3: Mr. Caswall, where were the Gentiles all this time?

Caswall: What do you mean?

Reporter 2: That Nauvoo was an open city where the Gentiles like yourself circulated freely among the Mormons, who resented neither your presence nor your preachments. You say your non-Mormon friends were eager and willing to offer you every assistance in prosecuting your researches. Your host in Montrose could spend the afternoon riding with you in the prairies; why couldn't a non-Mormon companion have gone with you as a witness for an hour or two when you went to make your carefully prepared test of the prophet's inspiration?

Caswall: I did not need non-Mormon support. "I met with persons at Nauvoo, who were perfectly acquainted with the wickedness of Smith, and did not pretend to deny it, who yet professed to believe firmly that he was a prophet."[137]

Reporter 2: Now that is a most important point. Yet you do not mention it until twenty-three years after your visit to Nauvoo! If these people were perfectly acquainted with Smith's wickedness, which they *did not even pretend to deny,* why did you waste five-sixths of your precious three days in Nauvoo gathering testimonies among the anti-Mormons of Iowa? The whole thing seems devised in retrospect.

Caswall: There is no retrospect about the Psalter. In my

very first account in 1842 I said that I had provided myself with a Greek Psalter with a specific objective.

Reporter 2: Which was to test the prophet's scholarship, with not a word about inspiration. Oh, I don't deny for a moment that you intended to test the man, and what is more, that you had prepared a trap.

Caswall: But you said I did not mention any trap until 1851.

Reporter 2: Correct. You most certainly did "design to entrap him," as you put it. But you never got the chance — *the original plan was never tried.*

Moderator: You sound like Nero Wolfe, sir. What original plan?

What was the "Psalter trick"?

Reporter 2: Before I tell you that, it must be understood that the "Psalter trick," as described in 1851 and after, was not the original plan. It could not possibly have been.

Reporter 3: Why not?

Reporter 2: Because the success of the whole test depended on Smith's taking everything into his own hands and making a complete fool of himself in a way that could not possibly have been foreseen. In the earlier versions Smith surprises everyone by his unpredictable and unaccountable behavior; the trick is only a trick because *he* insists on turning the tables against himself and dashing down the street in terror. Now, no one could have "fixed upon a method" of making him do that. Mr. Caswall could not possibly have anticipated by any stretch of the imagination the tactless and utterly senseless way in which Smith played into his hands; he might have imagined all sorts of crazy behavior on his part, but not as a reliable reaction to a carefully laid plan. Did he know Smith had a wagon? Did he count on him to use it?

Moderator: Mr. Caswall never claimed that that was part of the trick.

Reporter 2: But without Smith's clowning (Mr. Caswall has taught us the word) there would have been no trick at all.

Reporter 1: But in his early versions Mr. Caswall never refers to a trick, but only to a "test"—a test of Smith's scholarship.

Reporter 2: Exactly. In his first accounts the best he can do is to put Smith to a scholarly test and show him up as an ignoramus. This is what he writes in 1843: "His language is uncouth and ungrammatical, indicating very confused notions respecting syntactical concords. When an ancient Greek manuscript of the Psalms was exhibited to him *as a test of his scholarship,* he boldly pronounced it to be a 'Dictionary of Egyptian hieroglyphics!' "[138] You will note that the object of the Psalter here is to show up Smith's ignorance by testing his scholarship. But in 1865 the talk is all of "unknown tongues." Am I right, Mr. Caswall?

Caswall: I was testing Smith in the light of his own claims: "As he had given out that God had inspired him with an understanding of unknown tongues," I said to him "that, as I had been told that he was a prophet of God, gifted with the power of understanding unknown tongues, I hoped he would explain its contents."[139] Now, if he really possessed the power which he claimed . . .

Reporter 2: But Greek was not an unknown tongue—in those days any minister worth his salt was supposed to be able to read it. You, in fact, had told the Mormons (who told it to Smith) that *anyone* with even a *slight* acquaintance with Greek could read your book easily. Could such a book test anyone in "the power of understanding *unknown* tongues?"

Reporter 3: Had it ever been "given out" by Joseph Smith that he could and would read any ancient document on request? You are testing not what *he* claimed, but what *you* claimed for him. This is akin to your requesting the Mormons to perform a miracle on your ears: it would have

been completely against Smith's teachings and principles
to comply. As I have said before, sir, you are totally unaware of the Mormon concept of spiritual gifts. Smith
claimed no such "power" as you assume he did.

Reporter 2: Mr. Caswall, in 1839 you wrote in your book
America and the American Church: "The Mormonites
. . . consider the study of the Hebrew language to be a
religious duty; and at one of their settlements, in Ohio,
they recently engaged the son of a Jewish rabbi, a distinguished Hebrew teacher, to instruct the whole community."[140] That, sir, plainly shows that Smith did not count
on getting all languages by revelation—and you knew it.
As early as 1831 a non-Mormon newspaper reports: "Mr.
Smith arrived in Kirtland the next day; and being examined
concerning his supernatural gifts by a scholar, who was
capable of testing his knowledge, he confessed he knew
nothing of any language save the king's English."[141] So
you see, someone had already beaten you to it in putting
the prophet's scholarship to the test, and we know exactly
what the man's answer was to that challenge. He had to
translate by the gift and power of God precisely because
he himself knew no language but English. . . . But he
never made a public display of that gift—he knew that gifts
of the Spirit do not operate on such terms. But to return
to Nauvoo. You have told us, Mr. Caswall, that you "fixed
upon a plan" ahead of time, and as part of that plan brought
along a Greek Psalter with the definite object of testing the
prophet's scholarship. But the minute we get a look at that
Psalter it becomes apparent that your "plan to test the
prophet's scholarship" was really a trick "designed to entrap him."

Caswall: What do you mean?

Reporter 2: I mean that after widely announcing that
you were going to give the prophet a *very easy test* by asking
him to read a book so simple "that a slight acquaintance
with Greek would enable any person to decipher its mean-

ing," you were going to confront him with a text in a rare and difficult script that *nobody in America could read!* Let us imagine that a student who has studied Greek all through college comes up for a final examination; a text is placed before him, not in the critical editions that scholars use, but in the odd and illegible script of six hundred years ago, decipherable only to a few experts in paleography. Wouldn't the student rightly object that it was not an examination in Greek at all, but in Greek paleography?

Caswall: In case he couldn't read it, all Smith would have to do was to say so. As I pointed out in 1865, the test he failed to pass was the test of showing himself to be an honest man.

Reporter 2: Exactly. You knew Smith couldn't read the book—if he said he could, he would be trapped; and if he said he could not, then you would have him. You would instantly close your book (as you say you did) and triumphantly announce that Smith "had effectively proven himself an ignoramus" and that you would now "make it known to the world."

Moderator: But if the book was in an illegible script—if it was a trick manuscript—Joseph Smith would only have to point that out.

Reporter 1: Ah! I begin to see a light! One thing that has been puzzling me all along is why Mr. Caswall was so reluctant to let anybody get a good look at his Psalter, especially since he made such capital of it.

Caswall: But I did give them a good look at it—that first day in the store.

Reporter 1: Yes, that first day in the store, where you could be quite certain that nobody knew any Greek, and so nobody would question your statement that the book was simple, straightforward Greek that anybody with "a slight acquaintance" of the language could read. Even then you didn't let the book out of your hands. And after that? Not only did you refuse to sell it for a staggering sum but you wouldn't even let the Mormons take it overnight, though they offered you fabulous security; you refused to stay in Nauvoo overnight, you say, specifically because you feared that the Mormons might get hold of your book. Smith had barely got a look at the book when you took it away from him and hurriedly wrapped and tied it, though the "test" had barely begun, and the Mormons were simply dying to see more of it. You absolutely refused to let the book out of your hands even when there was not the slightest danger of losing it.

Reporter 2: And if you didn't trust the Mormons with it, Mr. Caswall, why didn't you at least trust the Gentiles?

Caswall: Trust the Gentiles?

Reporter 2: Yes. You possessed the book to the end of your life "as a memento," you said, of your visit to Smith. It may have been an interesting memento, but in your hands it was not evidence. Now, if you had sold it to the Mormons, as they begged you to for three days, and got a signed receipt for it from Smith (you say he also wanted to buy it from you), you could have gone back to St. Louis with welcome and much-needed funds for your darling college, plus written evidence of your Psalter trick. You didn't do any of that: you clung to your unreadable book and took it back to England with you. But why didn't you exploit it there? It was your Exhibit A, your only exhibit, in fact; why was it never put on public display? Why did you never use it in illustrating any of your books? The anti-Mormon world would have prized this treasure almost as greatly as the Mormons, if only as a rather sensational museum-piece. Yet to the end you kept it by you, and it has never been heard of since. I think the explanation of this *may* be that any real scrutiny of the book would betray the trick.

Caswall: But I said from the first that it was an old parchment manuscript.

Reporter 2: And you also said it was easy to read for

anyone knowing a little Greek. There are such manu-
scripts, but this plainly was not one of them. As long as
the book was in your possession, Mr. Caswall, you could
tell your story, but if it ever got out of your hands the
thing could easily backfire. I can think of no other reason
why you should have guarded it so carefully.

Moderator: You seem to know a great deal about this,
Mr. Wye. What do you think actually did happen?

Reporter 2: Ah, there we are on dubious ground. The
first thing to remember is that Mr. Caswall, in the retirement of his rural English deanery, makes happen what *he*
wants to happen, as his evolving history shows. In that
case we are not bound to accept any claim of his as a
statement of what actually did happen.

Moderator: Do you even doubt that he was in Nauvoo?

Reporter 2: Of course not. But what he did there is
another thing. He may have seen Smith driving out in a
wagon, for on 19 April 1842, he did drive out in a wagon
to inspect some lands—but he was not running away from
Caswall! The fact that Mr. Caswall himself omits that part
of the story in all versions after 1843 admits that: it is much
too good to leave out *if it is true.* Again, Smith actually was
in Carthage on April 18, so that Mr. Caswall was very
probably told as much, and very probably did not meet
him on that day. In fact, what is clearest from all his accounts is what did *not* happen. I doubt very much that he
ever met Smith, in view of his professed inability to see
his eyes, the fantastic conversation and *lack* of conversation
that took place between the two men, and his comments
on Smith's oversized hands—deleted from later versions.
Such deletions were counter-balanced by the picturesque
introduction in 1851 of the Old White Hat—another suspicious circumstance.

Reporter 1: So all we have is negatives?

Reporter 2: Not at all. The negatives belong only to the
third day. Now, it is an interesting and very significant

thing that Mr. Caswall, in all his various accounts, leaves the story of his first two days in Nauvoo, if we can call them that, unchanged — if variety interests him, why does he not play around freely with those days as he does with the third day? All his manipulations, deletions, additions, and alterations have to do with the story of the third day, his world-famous meeting with Joseph Smith. Here he is not satisfied with the original and carefully works it over through the years to make it hold water. The *whole account* of the meeting with Smith, from the landing to the departure on that third day, must be put on the dubious list, because Mr. Caswall gives conflicting versions of every episode and speech. And if he was willing to indulge in creative writing *after* 1842, I see no reason why he should not have done the same in the 1842 version itself. See what damage you have done, Mr. Caswall!

Caswall: Damage? It is not damage to make this monstrous perversion hateful in the eyes of the world. "The reader of the preceding history," as I said in conclusion, "can have distinguished little in his [Smith's] character besides unscrupulous audacity, reckless falsehood, low cunning, grovelling vulgarity, daring blasphemy, and grasping selfishness, combined with a genius eccentric in its aims, fertile in its expedients, and mad in its ambition."[142]

Mrs. B. carries on

Reporter 2: No, no. I don't mean that. I mean your own cause. You have exposed to view not only your own eager mendacity, but that of some of our most esteemed writers. Listen to one of the latest repetitions of your story:

> One visitor, Henry Caswall, an Episcopalian preacher from a St. Louis college, armed himself with an ancient manuscript psalter written in Greek and, pretending to be ignorant of its contents, offered it to Joseph for scrutiny. Under the prophet's questioning he finally

admitted that he believed the language to be Greek, but this Joseph contradicted. Caswall, exaggerating the imperfections of Joseph's grammar, later related the story as follows.

At this point the author we are quoting, instead of relating the story, gives the grotesque quotation beginning, "No, it ain't Greek at all," etc., followed immediately by the conclusion:

> When the prophet left the room, Caswall turned triumphantly to the men present and exposed the trick. "They appeared confounded for a while," he wrote, "but at length the Mormon doctor said: "Sometimes Mr. Smith speaks as a prophet, and sometimes as a mere man," etc.[143]

Now look how you have led this poor soul astray, Mr. Caswall. She gives as her only authority for all this your 1842 *City of the Mormons, or Three Days at Nauvoo,* yet obviously it is the later version she is following. Take her story point by point. First, she says you "tricked Joseph Smith" with a Greek Psalter. But in your 1842 account, which she gives as her only source, no trick of any kind was mentioned or implied. She says the trick consisted of arming yourself with an ancient manuscript Psalter written in Greek and "pretending to be ignorant of its contents." This is a direct contradiction of your own specific declaration of 1842, that far from pretending to be ignorant of the book's contents, you protested loudly and repeatedly to Smith's followers that you knew exactly what the book was—you told *them* what it was, and you also told Smith what it is. He does *not* have to squeeze this information out of you; you did *not* "finally admit" the language was Greek "under the prophet's questioning": you volunteered the information promptly and immediately—there was no cross-examination. There was no "scrutiny" of the text by Smith before he got your explanation out of you; in fact, there was no scrutiny at all—Smith had hardly looked at the thing before you took it away from him and wrapped it up, to the great chagrin of the Mormons. You did *not* then "turn triumphantly to the men present." To make your trick effective, Mrs. Brodie must have it all happen there on the spot; and so she carefully omits the telling details of how you later went down to the street, saw Smith dash by in his wagon, and then got into a long hassle with the Mormons, toward the end of which you mentioned the Psalter without exploiting your "triumph." Of course there was in 1842 no "triumph," since it was the Mormons who claimed the victory; and you definitely did not "expose the trick," you simply repeated what you had been saying all along. Then comes the payoff: you have won— the Mormons are suddenly confounded, and the doctor frankly admits that Smith was wrong. But if it happened that way, why do you always leave that part out after 1843? And why, incidentally, do you never name the doctor who conducted you around Nauvoo? Of course, Mrs. Brodie, whose monument of primary research we have been quoting, conveniently forgets to mention that there is not just one, but at least six primary and contradictory documents all written by you; and such disturbing details as the fact that in your 1842 report it is not the Greek Psalter at all, but a hieroglyphic text that trips up the prophet, are passed by in silence.

Moderator: After all, Mr. Wye, you can hardly blame Mr. Caswall for liberties that others have taken with his writings. Mrs. Brodie has taken it upon herself to improve on the Caswall story: nowhere does Mr. Caswall say that he ever pretended to be ignorant of the contents of his book; at no time does he say or imply that he only admitted that the book was Greek "under the prophet's questioning"; even in his 1865 version the trick is not anything as neat and foolproof as Mrs. Brodie makes it out to be by having the professor press his advantage on the spot, "turn

triumphantly to the men present and expose the trick" —
there was no such exposure described by him. Mr. Caswall
may have stretched things a good deal, but Mrs. Brodie is
responsible for her own performances.

Reporter 2: And this is just one of them, I admit. But
the mischief began with Mr. Caswall — others have caught
his spirit and carried on in the tradition.

Recapitulation and finale?

Moderator: I think it is about time to sum things up
now. It is customary on these programs to ask our guest
to leave the studio during the final appraisal. Mr. Caswall,
have you anything you would like to tell or ask us before
you leave? It has been very instructive and helpful having
you here with us, and if our investigators have been a bit
brusque at times, we want to ask your forgiveness. Is there
anything you would like to say in closing?

Caswall: It has been a privilege and a pleasure to meet
with you, gentlemen, though "the task of delineating the
prophet's infernal character has been certainly far from
agreeable to the author; . . . Joseph Smith, without his
blasphemy and vulgarity, would be a very different being
from the 'Prophet of the Nineteenth Century.' "[144] That is
all I have to say. Good day, gentlemen. (*Exit Caswall*)

Moderator: Now that our guest has been escorted from
the studio and taken to lunch in the Byzantine Room of
Barchester Towers, we shall ask our panel of experts for
their frank appraisal of the Greek Psalter story. It is claimed
that Joseph Smith once declared in the presence of witnesses that a Greek Psalter was a dictionary of hieroglyphics. Did he or didn't he?

Reporter 2: The first thing to notice is that only one
witness to the tale has ever been found — and that just
happens to be the man who invented the Psalter trick; isn't
it just possible that this ingenious and imaginative soul
also invented the Psalter *story?*

Reporter 1: That is what we want to determine if we can. It is certain that deception has been practiced, either by Smith or by Caswall. Which is it?

Reporter 3: First step: look for the motive! Let's compare Smith's possible motives with Caswall's. What could Smith have gained by declaring a Greek Psalter, which he couldn't read, to be a dictionary of hieroglyphics — which he knew it was not?

Reporter 1: Maybe he really thought it was — self-deception, you know.

Reporter 3: Really thought it was a mixture of Greek, hieroglyphic, and reformed Egyptian that looked just like the characters on the golden plates? Hardly! He would certainly be making that up if he said it. So what would that get him?

Reporter 1: A chance to show off before his followers.

Reporter 2: But as far as his followers were concerned, Smith was already tops — he didn't have to impress *them!* And he knew that he could not impress the owner of the book, who had already told everybody what *he* thought it was. Moreover, far more than a gesture of omniscience is involved here, for Smith actually offered to buy the book for a great sum of money, knowing that it was not worth it and that once he had bought it before all those witnesses he would be stuck with it and called upon for an exhaustive demonstration — which he could not give! In the capacity of Caswall's favorite idiot, Smith might have hailed a bundle of illegible parchment as an Egyptian treasure and offered to purchase it on the spot for a fabulous sum, but no rational, let alone cunning, human being would have done it. Notice that everything Smith does in the presence of Caswall is not only foolish but utterly suicidal — he invariably does the worst possible thing from his point of view and the best possible thing from Caswall's. No, gentlemen, we are more or less stuck for motives where Smith is concerned. But how about Caswall?

Reporter 3: The poor man has spilled the beans all over the place. Even without our *Methodist Quarterly Review*, my notes scream prejudice on every page. Caswall went to Nauvoo with the fixed idea that Joseph Smith was totally depraved — he preached it on the journey. We do not have to assume a professional jealousy of Smith, since Caswall is good enough to tell us about it himself, specifying that Smith has succeeded where he had failed, and describing him as an unscrupulous competitor but for whose "delusive attractions to the rising generation" his own church and school might have had better success. He declares a policy of no mercy and no quarter to Joseph Smith, to think or speak well of whom could only indicate "great want of charity." His host and principal informant in Montrose was the bitterest enemy of the Mormons in all the region. In a revealing preface he has shouted his prejudice from the housetops, declaring that the whole purpose of his activity is to make Mormonism hateful in the eyes of the world. He has announced that the purpose of his visit to Nauvoo was to "help destroy the very foundations on which the Latter-day doctrine is built," and that his lethal weapon is to be the "Psalter trick." Here Caswall says, "I have given my own testimony as to what I myself saw of the false prophet, and heard from his own lips, within his own house. And *this* testimony helps to destroy the very foundation on which the 'Latter-day' doctrine is built."[145] That is Caswall's last statement on the subject, and, as Mr. Zee has said, it supplies us with both the motive — Mr. Caswall's single-minded dedication to one objective — and the means by which he meant to encompass it. Now the question is, did those means include the outright invention of the Psalter story? What do you think, Mr. Ecks?

Reporter 1: Well, first of all I ask myself, would he have gone so far? Would Mr. Caswall actually lie?

Reporter 3: He is certainly willing to exaggerate. Even Mrs. Brodie admits that.

Reporter 1: But Caswall tones things down progressively in his books.

Reporter 3: Which means that he goes beyond exaggeration — which can be an impulsive and emotional thing without intent to deceive — to cool and deliberate invention and manipulation, or, if you will, fabrication.

Reporter 2: And along with the toning down and deletion of certain things we have the equally conspicuous tendency to add and embellish, which, in the nature of anything as brief, direct, and simple as the Psalter story, bears the mark of fabrication. Also, through the years Caswall shows a marked tendency to move from the specific to the general — to shift his ground — a plain indication that he was not standing on sure ground in the beginning. From the point of view of veracity it might not be so bad to omit from all subsequent editions the nice things he said about the Mormons in 1842 — that is a mark of prejudice rather than deceit; but it is another matter when he goes on through the years adding long and elaborate speeches which are supposed to be given verbatim but which grow like snowballs: here we are manifestly faced with inventions of the author.

Moderator: Can't we just call them embellishments?

Reporter 2: We can. But no plea of pardonable exaggeration or embellishment can excuse the complete revamping of the story that takes place in 1851, when everything shifts from a test of scholarship to a test of inspiration, and a whole new introductory speech by Caswall is invented as a prelude to the exhibit. What Caswall wanted was the opportunity to discredit Joseph Smith once and for all, and he determined that his trip to Nauvoo should furnish him with a perfect opportunity.

Reporter 1: How could he count on that?

Reporter 3: By producing the whole thing in retrospect. All Mrs. Eaton needed was a reputation of having actually lived in Palmyra to make her an authority on everything

Joseph Smith said and did. All the Reverend Caswall needed was to be able to say truthfully that he had actually spent three days at Nauvoo: from there he was on his own, an unchallenged authority free to invent at will and at leisure. If the Mormons questioned what he said, of course he would brush that aside as prejudiced. He was on pretty safe ground, but still he was taking no chances. It is wonderful to see the precautions the man took against being found out or even questioned.

Reporter 2: Exactly. And if his story were true, he would want to be questioned about it: he would fall all over himself to supply corroborating evidence. Look how eager he is to imply the presence of many witnesses for every episode he reports, yet he never supplies their names or any other information that might be used to check up on his story. Instead of inviting the public to confirm and follow up his adventures, he takes the greatest pains to prevent any possible inquiry about them. He is always careful that he and only he shall tell the story—not even Gentile witnesses are allowed to be present! This man *wants* no witnesses. You may have noticed that I emphasized the point of his disguise.

Reporter 1: And you always pointed out that it must have been a very flimsy disguise. Why?

Reporter 2: The disguise is an important clue. With all his talk of sacred duty, clerical vows, and the like, Caswall nonetheless lays off the clerical garb that would have got him a warm reception in Nauvoo and in no way interfered with his Psalter trick. I doubt if even his natural timidity would induce the reverend to go about his missionary labors without his cloth unless he had a very special reason—that of making it as hard as possible to check up on him.

Reporter 1: But all along you insisted that the disguise was a very flimsy one; that it wouldn't fool anybody.

Reporter 2: And I insist again. The "disguise" is a remarkably poor one, and Caswall could not for an hour have concealed his profession from the Mormons. Note the absurdity of having the Mormons completely baffled and wildly curious as to his identity, while at the same time he went around town being formally introduced to everyone: by what name? Most everyone in Nauvoo had been in St. Louis, some of them many times—did he suppose for a moment that none of the Mormon leaders who were always on hand would recall the name of the man who had headed the college there for years? Remember, Caswall complained that some of his own students had been wooed away to Nauvoo.

Reporter 1: So the disguise was no good. Then why did he bother with it?

Reporter 2: Because the disguise is purely for the benefit of the reader. Caswall wants his *readers* to *think* that he was successfully disguised. Just as he will never have to name or identify any of those witnesses of whom he is constantly speaking, so no Mormon can ever claim to remember, recognize, or refute the man who so brilliantly tricked Smith—for he was in disguise! A minister in his robes would be easily recalled, but a common traveler could be anybody.

Moderator: But this common traveler is supposed to have created an immense sensation.

Reporter 2: Another reason for believing that it didn't happen that way. For *nobody in Nauvoo, official or unofficial,* reports the earth-shaking event. I am not referring to the Psalter, but simply to Mr. Caswall's sensational visit and street-sermons. Remember how the "perfect crowd" that followed him up the street in the 1842 account dwindles to nothing at all by 1865? So much for the immense sensation. Now, consider Caswall's reluctance to sell the book.

Moderator: We already have. He refused to sell it for $900 in gold.

Reporter 1: Did he really think it was worth all that? He

had recently acquired it, he says, for the specific purpose of testing Smith, but *after* the test he refuses to sell it. This is another step in covering up his traces: by rejecting every offer for the book he is removing it from the category of evidence. Henceforth its only value is the value *he* chooses to put upon it "as a memento of his visit to Joseph Smith."

Reporter 2: If his story is true, his behavior is unaccountable, and so is Smith's—begging to buy a book that is worthless to him and will only put him in a tight spot. But if he is making the story up, then it all makes perfect sense, for then he would have to produce the certificate or the money and, worse still, there would be a damaging witness to his trickery at large. The Psalter would show at the very least that he had loaded the dice when he went "to test the prophet's scholarship." But Caswall is always careful that there shall be no witness and no evidence to testify to his activities in Nauvoo.

Reporter 3: I find the behavior of the Mormons even stranger than that of Caswall.

Moderator: What do you mean?

Reporter 3: Caswall may have had a good reason for not wanting things to go on too long, but consider the amazing apathy of the multitude. Here were all these people who by Mr. Caswall's clever tactics had been worked up to a fever pitch of excitement about the book. Curiosity has reached the point of hysteria when, to crown everything, the prophet announces not only that the book is in very deed a wonderful one—far more wonderful than its owner had supposed—but that *he knows what is in it.* Yet no one asks him a single question! No report of this marvel ever spreads abroad, even as gossip. No Mormon or Gentile reports it. No one, including Smith, protests when Caswall brings the examination to an abrupt halt before it has even got started. Caswall favors with italics Smith's declaration that the characters in the book are like those on the golden plates. What a sensation such an announcement would have created in Nauvoo—the news would spread like wildfire! Why didn't it? Where is it mentioned anywhere? There in the upper room a hundred questions immediately spring to mind. But there was no questioning period there; Caswall himself must keep up the conversation by asking to see the papyri. Smith is all the things Caswall thought he would be: "Even more wicked than I could have supposed him to be," is his expression. His unbelievable speech is completely out of keeping with the known manner of Smith at the time, but perfectly in character with the idiotic slob of the Caswall stereotype. The false prophet immediately starts swaggering and boasting, rudely contradicting his distinguished guest—he and he only knows the answers; he uses the three or four minutes at his disposal with devastating economy as he prates of Egyptian hieroglyphics and golden plates and characters in reformed Egyptian and the angel, all in the most preposterously crude language. Of course he must identify the book as "Reformed Egyptian," though that was a *New World invention, not to be found in any Old World document.* This is another fatal slip, but Caswall, who had not read the Book of Mormon, didn't know it: everything must be true to *his* idea of what the boob Joseph Smith would say.

Reporter 2: Not only is Caswall the sole witness to what is supposed to have happened in Nauvoo—never mentioned in any other writings than his—but what is more, he *knows* he is!

Reporter 1: What makes you so sure of that?

Reporter 2: The great freedom with which he improvises. He could only take the liberties he does if he were quite sure that no one *else* would ever tell the story. And why is he so absolutely certain that no one else ever will tell that story or any part of it? Why is he perfectly free to tell it as he chooses? Simply because it is a product of his own imagination. To close the door to inquiry, he has fixed it so that no one will ever identify his Mormons, and they will never identify him.

Moderator: So what is your final opinion, Mr. Wye?

Reporter 2: That the Greek Psalter story is the end product of a long process of revising and reediting in an attempt to provide a story of fraud that would stick. The original plot called for a frame-up and a trap: there was to be an interview with Smith at which he was to fail to recognize a Greek Bible. To make sure that he would fail, a doctored text was used, a text that no scholar in America could read, though Caswall was to announce publicly that the test would be a very simple and elementary one. The moment Smith had admitted or in any way displayed his incapacity to read the book, it was to be taken from him, tied up in many wrappings, and scrupulously kept out of the hands of the Mormons, no matter how much they offered for it. Only then, after the book had been sealed, would Caswall announce that Smith "had effectively demonstrated his ignorance," since the bearer of the book "knew it positively to be a Greek Psalter." Then the professor would be free to "make known to the world" how the prophet had exhibited his gross ignorance.

Only the interview never took place, as is clear (a) from the fact that it is nowhere mentioned save in Caswall's own writings, though Nauvoo was an open city and the interview was supposed to have caused a great sensation; (b) from the intrinsic absurdities with which Mr. Caswall's account of it abound, e.g., his inability to see Smith's eyes; (c) from Caswall's willingness to change his story to suit any later convenience; it is absolutely certain that he composed and altered various episodes in retrospect. That would not be so bad if we had, in the key episode (the identification of the Psalter by Smith), an unchanging nucleus. But (d) that is the very part of the story which has been doctored the most.

Since the interview did not take place, Caswall was

free to follow Cicero's method of reporting "in his leisure time" fully and lovingly all the things that should have happened, had the plan been tried, with Smith the perfect clown and Caswall the Christian hero. It is an old and familiar device. It is clearly and repeatedly stated in the earlier versions that the purpose of the interview was to expose Smith's ignorance by putting his scholarship to the test. An afterthought or minor embellishment of the original version — that since Smith had declared the Psalter to be what was tantamount to another Book of Mormon, he could not be an honest man, and since he was not honest he could not be a true prophet — is later adopted as the leitmotif of the story, and after 1851 it is pretended that the purpose of the test from the first was not to test Smith's scholarship but the divinity of his calling. Accordingly, the story is thoroughly revamped to fit the new thesis.

Reporter 3 (with a start): How long have we been off the air? Do you realize what time it is?

Reporter 1: We must have wasted hours with that old fellow.

Reporter 2: Hardly wasted. Here is the most respected, the most scholarly, the most unassailable witness who ever testified to the villainy of Joseph Smith, and it has been our privilege not only to test his veracity but actually to see what makes him tick. A rewarding experience, gentlemen — "another page," as Mr. Caswall would say, "in the great book of human nature."

Notes for Part 3

1. W. S. Parrott, *The Veil Uplifted, or the Religious Conspirators of the Latter-Day Saints Exposed* (Bristol: Taylor and Sons, 1865), 14.

2. Ibid., 14–15.

3. Henry Caswall, *Mormonism and Its Author: Or, a Statement of the Doctrines of the 'Latter-Day Saints'* (London: SPCK, 1851), 2.

4. W. H. G. Armytage, "Liverpool, Gateway to Zion," *Pacific Northwest Quarterly* 48 (April 1957): 39.

5. Henry Caswall, *The Prophet of the 19th Century; or, the Rise,*

Progress, and Present State of Mormons or Latter-Day Saints (London: Rivingtons, 1843), vi.

6. Parrott, *Veil Uplifted,* 19.

7. Caswall, *Prophet of the 19th Century,* 222.

8. Ibid., vii.

9. Daniel P. Kidder, "Mormonism and the Mormons," *Methodist Quarterly Review* 25 (January 1843): 127.

10. Ibid., 124.

11. Ibid., 125, 127.

12. Henry Caswall, *City of the Mormons, or Three Days at Nauvoo, in 1842,* 2nd ed. (London: Rivingtons, 1843), 59.

13. Caswall, *Prophet of the 19th Century,* 223.

14. Caswall, *City of the Mormons,* 57.

15. Ibid., 44.

16. Henry Caswall, *America, and the American Church,* 2nd ed. (London: Mozleys, 1851), 307–10.

17. Caswall, *City of the Mormons,* 60.

18. Parrott, *Veil Uplifted,* 26.

19. Caswall, *Prophet of the 19th Century,* 222.

20. Caswall, *Mormonism and Its Author,* 24–25.

21. Anonymous, *Is Mormonism True or Not?* (London: Religious Tract Society, 1855), 9.

22. Ibid.

23. Parrott, *Veil Uplifted,* 19–20.

24. Ibid., 23.

25. Caswall, *Mormonism and Its Author,* 2.

26. Parrott, *Veil Uplifted,* 15 (emphasis added).

27. Caswall, *City of the Mormons,* 49.

28. Parrott, *Veil Uplifted,* 23.

29. Ibid., 25.

30. Caswall, *City of the Mormons,* 57.

31. Parrott, *Veil Uplifted,* 23.

32. Ibid., 24.

33. Caswall, *Prophet of the 19th Century,* 222.

34. Caswall, *City of the Mormons,* 85–86.

35. Ibid., 84–85.

36. Caswall, *America, and the American Church,* 351.

37. Caswall, *City of the Mormons,* 85–86.

38. Parrott, *Veil Uplifted,* 21.

39. Ibid., 20–21.

40. Ibid.

41. Caswall, *Prophet of the 19th Century,* 222.

42. Parrott, *Veil Uplifted*, 22.

43. Ibid., 21 (emphasis added).

44. Caswall, *City of the Mormons*, 50.

45. Robert Richards, *The Californian Crusoe* (London: Parker, 1854), 84.

46. Ibid.

47. Caswall, *City of the Mormons*, 87.

48. Ibid., preface.

49. Ibid., 49.

50. Ibid.

51. Caswall, *Prophet of the 19th Century*, 224.

52. Caswall, *City of the Mormons*, 22.

53. Ibid., 4–5.

54. Ibid., 5.

55. Henry Caswall, *The City of the Mormons*, 1st ed. (London: Rivington, 1942), 20–21. Religious Tract Society, *The Visitor: or Monthly Instructor for 1842* (London: Religious Tract Society, 1842), 405–6.

56. Ibid., 21.

57. Ibid.

58. Ibid.

59. Religious Tract Society, *Visitor*, 406–7.

60. Caswall, *City of the Mormons* (1st ed.), 27. Religious Tract Society, *Visitor*, 408.

61. Eber D. Howe, *Mormonism Unvailed; Or, a Faithful Account of That Singular Imposition and Delusion* (Painesville, OH: the author, 1834), 253–54; Religious Tract Society, *Visitor*, 406–7.

62. Religious Tract Society, *Visitor*, 408.

63. Ibid.

64. Ibid.

65. Ibid., 406.

66. Caswall, *City of the Mormons* (1st ed.), 21. Religious Tract Society, *Visitor*, 406.

67. Ibid., 22.

68. Caswall, *City of the Mormons* (1st ed.), 33–34. Religious Tract Society, *Visitor*, 408.

69. Caswall, *City of the Mormons* (1st ed.), 35. Religious Tract Society, *Visitor*, 408.

70. Josiah Quincy, *Figures of the Past from the Leaves of Old Journals* (Boston: Roberts Brothers, 1888), 380–81.

71. John Quincy Adams, *The Birth of Mormonism* (Boston: Gorham, 1916), 101.

72. Richards, *Californian Crusoe*, 61.

73. Caswall, *City of the Mormons* (1st ed.), 35–36. Religious Tract Society, *Visitor*, 408–9.

74. Caswall, *City of the Mormons*, 50.

75. Fawn M. Brodie, *No Man Knows My History* (New York: Knopf, 1947), 290.

76. *Missouri Republican*, Daily, 3 May 1839.

77. Henry Brown, *History of Illinois* (New York: New World, 1844), 403.

78. Caswall, *City of the Mormons* (1st ed.), 36. Religious Tract Society, *Visitor*, 409.

79. Caswall, *City of the Mormons*, 37.

80. Ibid., 41.

81. Ibid.

82. Ibid., 43.

83. Ibid.

84. Charles Kelly and Hoffman Birney, *Holy Murder: The Story of Porter Rockwell* (New York: Minton, Balch, 1934), 7.

85. Caswall, *City of the Mormons* (1st ed.), 42–49.

86. Ibid., 43–44.

87. Caswall, *City of the Mormons* (1843 ed.), 5.

88. Ibid.

89. Ibid., 9, 16, 18; Caswall, *Prophet of the 19th Century*, 224.

90. Caswall, *City of the Mormons,*18.

91. Ibid.

92. Ibid., 19

93. Ibid., 15.

94. Ibid., 19.

95. Ibid.

96. Ibid., 23.

97. Ibid., 30.

98. Ibid., 31.

99. Ibid., 35.

100. Ibid.

101. Caswall, *Prophet of the 19th Century*, 223.

102. Caswall, *City of the Mormons*, 36.

103. Ibid., 37.

104. Ibid., 36–37.

105. Caswall, *Prophet of the 19th Century*, 223–24.

106. Caswall, *City of the Mormons*, 43.

107. Ibid., 38.

108. Ibid., 44–45.

109. Caswall, *Prophet of the 19th Century,* 224.

110. Ibid.

111. Caswall, *City of the Mormons,* 46.

112. Ibid., 49.

113. Ibid., 47.

114. Ibid.

115. Ibid.

116. Ibid., 43–44.

117. Caswall, *America, and the American Church,* 357–58; Caswall, *Mormonism and Its Author,* 4–5.

118. Caswall, *America, and the American Church,* 358.

119. Ibid., 356.

120. Caswall, *Mormonism and Its Author,* 5.

121. Ibid.

122. Ibid.

123. Caswall, *America, and the American Church,* 358.

124. Ibid., 358–59.

125. Ibid., 359.

126. Ibid.

127. Caswall, *City of the Mormons,* 46–47.

128. Ibid., 49.

129. Parrott, *Veil Uplifted,* 19.

130. Ibid.

131. Ibid., 17.

132. Ibid., 18.

133. Ibid.

134. Ibid.

135. Caswall, *City of the Mormons* (1st ed.), 44.

136. Parrott, *Veil Uplifted,* 18–19.

137. Ibid., 25.

138. Caswall, *Prophet of the 19th Century,* 223.

139. Parrott, *Veil Uplifted,* 17–18, 25.

140. Henry Caswall, *America and the American Church* (London: Mozley, 1839), 323.

141. Francis Kirkham, *A New Witness for Christ in America: The Book of Mormon,* 2 vols. (Salt Lake City: Utah Printing, 1942–51), 2:114.

142. Caswall, *Prophet of the 19th Century,* 222.

143. Brodie, *No Man Knows My History,* 290.

144. Caswall, *Prophet of the Nineteenth Century,* vii–viii.

145. Parrott, *Veil Uplifted,* 19 (emphasis added).

Sounding Brass

Introduction

A generation ago, the older and dingier parts of our big cities contained, along with Chinese laundries, Greek restaurants, flophouses, pawnshops, and fifteen-cent movie barns, a fair sprinkling—sometimes a solid row—of huge, dirty, dusky, wonderful secondhand bookstores, where the bemused and besmudged investigator with a week's allowance in his pocket, prowling in dark cellars and rickety galleries, would not be surprised to run across a little library in Burmese or Tagalog or a fair collection of well-marked Classics, or a shelf of Icelandic or Persian—sold for a song by the wives and spinster daughters of defunct missionaries and professors. In those days this little globe of earth seemed as vast and mysterious as outer space does today, and here in these grimy literary *douanes* lay unclaimed baggage from distant times and places, to be had for little more than the pains of carrying it away.

In most of these gloomy *suqs* a large and conspicuous area of wall space on the main floor was set aside and designated as the *Mormon* reservation—meaning, of course, anti-Mormon. These books are all gone today—they are now collectors' items fetching ridiculous prices. But in their day they made up a formidable corpus and unique genre of American letters. The pretentious bindings, screaming double titles, lurid engravings, hysterical

---

Sounding Brass *was originally published in Salt Lake City by Bookcraft in 1963. It carried the subtitle, "Informal Studies in the Lucrative Art of Telling Stories about Brigham Young and the Mormons."*

italics, and rampant exclamation points invited the reader into a world of horror, mystery, and human perversity that put the imaginations of Jules Verne and Sir Rider Haggard to shame. The literary style was as stilted, artificial, and extravagant as the illustrations, both being produced by and for a naive and uncritical generation.

Read today, these books seem as dated as gas-lighting. But don't be fooled—they are still being produced! The same books which a hundred years ago were nothing but rehashes of earlier rehashes are being warmed over at this very hour. Nothing new has been added to the Mormological library (*Mormo* being Greek for *monster*); all the long years of zealous research have failed to produce a single significant item to add to the wild tales of the busy gossips of Palmyra and Montrose; nothing has been found to confirm, but a great deal to discredit, their stories and those of their imaginative successors. For over a hundred years specialists in Mormon atrocities have done nothing but borrow from each other.

As the three mirrors of a kaleidoscope, by reflecting only a few bits of broken glass or scraps of paper, produce endless but strangely monotonous and tiring varieties of design, so the producers of anti-Mormon epics (to say nothing of American literature in general) seem incapable of anything but endlessly repeating each other. "A" picks up a story from "B" and hands it on to "C," from whom it progresses through the hands of "D," "E," "F," etc., whose combined authority ultimately convinces "I," "J," and "K" that they must be telling the truth. So one of these last becomes assigned reading for the students or even the congregation of Drs. "O" and "P," and so on. Thus Mr. Irving Wallace will take some grisly tale from the pages of Mrs. Ann Eliza Webb Dee Young Denning, who has got the story from her friend Mrs. Stenhouse, who got it from the terrible Bill Hickman, whose book was written by a rather sordid hack writer named Beadle, who confirms his frightful charges by appealing to Judge Harding, who got *his* best Mormon stories from his cousin Pomeroy Tucker, who is beholden to J. C. Bennett for his insights. And every one of these people steps before the public as a firsthand authority on the Mormons, bandying the old threadbare tales about with the skill and assurance of one who really knows.

In such a Sea of Story the thing the student misses most is a genuine original source. Where are the pristine and primary documents that will liberate us from the old vicious cycle of repetition and speculation? Mrs. Brodie and her cohorts thought they had discovered such, but their Tuttles, A. W. Bentons, and the Purples will not stand investigation. And now comes Mr. Irving Wallace who thinks he has a firsthand informant in Ann Eliza Young. In this he has been beguiled apparently by the recent work of Mrs. Woodward, through whose efforts it would seem Ann Eliza has achieved new fame and glory as one of the Representative Women of the West on the pages of *Life Magazine*. That such a person should at this late date be brought from fields Elysian and groomed for the witness stand is a good indication of how desperately bankrupt the anti-Mormon fraternity really is. It is our intention to examine the case of Ann Eliza Young as a guide to what really goes on in the half-world of anti-Mormon studies. Our attention will accordingly be confined to that lady and her intimate circle of supporters. A full-scale study of the whole field is indicated, but such a quantification of the obvious is properly the function of computing machines and not of human beings. Mr. Wallace is as representative a writer of our times as Mrs. Young was of hers. "The harm Ann Eliza did to the cause of Mormonism is beyond calculation," the editors of *Life* assure us,[1] and since Mr. Wallace is determined that the work of this "remarkable woman" shall not go unrecognized in this generation, we cannot do better than to select the works of this scholarly pair as a sampling of the more dignified and sophisticated school of Mormology.

Notes to Introduction

1. Robert Wallace, "The Frontier's Fabulous Women," *Life Magazine* 46/19 (11 May 1959): 84.

Part 1

"In My Mind's Eye, Horatio . . ."

Personalized History

"The story which I propose to tell in these pages is a plain, unexaggerated record of facts which have come immediately under my own notice, or which I have myself personally experienced. Much that to the reader may seem altogether incredible, would to a Mormon mind appear simply a matter of ordinary every-day occurrence."[1]

Thus Mrs. Stenhouse begins a book whose title, *Tell It All: The Story of a Life's Experience in Mormonism,* promises everything. But the student who searches through it in hopes of discovering a single episode of her personal experience which could be called "altogether incredible" or even improbable is doomed to disappointment. Whatever is strange and marvelous in the Stenhouse story is always taken from the stories of *other* people. How can she claim it all for her own? Very easily, on the principle that whatever I am aware of comes "*immediately* under my *own* notice"—who else's? and how else but "immediately?" Now let us notice how Ann Eliza Young paraphrases Stenhouse: "All the events which I shall relate will be some of my own personal experiences, or the experience of those so closely connected with me that they have fallen directly [immediately] under my observation [notice], and for whose truth I can vouch without hesitation."[2] Plainly the reader is in for a feast of gossip. If both ladies are prepared to chalk up as personal experience whatever is brought to their personal attention, to what limits may they not go? Both devote considerable space to atrocity stories that took place long before their time, and Ann Eliza can give verbatim reports of highly secret conversations between Joseph Smith and Brigham Young and "vouch without hesitation for their truth" because forsooth it is all part of her own simple story—it is "closely connected" with her because she actually *was* a Mormon.

"I spoke truths of which I was a living witness—truths which had been burned into my soul through suffering that words can never tell." Thus Ann Eliza begins her second (1908) book as "a living witness": but to what? Not to events but to "truths," not necessarily to things seen and heard but "suffered," or, better still, "burned into my soul through suffering"[3]—her experience consists in what she has suffered: "I am not imagining situations. . . . There is not a pang, not a throb of anguish which I have depicted that I have not felt myself."[4]

Here the lady defines a "situation" as anything she has felt, and since only she is the judge of her feelings, she feels free to tell other women's stories as her own—for all their pangs and throbs of anguish are hers: "The voices of twenty thousand women speak in mine."[5] "I knew every pang which *she* was suffering, for I have passed through it all myself."[6] Nothing could be more convenient to the author of a book of atrocity stories than to have his own feelings pass as evidence in the case, allowing him to substitute other people's exciting experiences for his own very drab ones as long as he feels morally certain that both he and they have suffered the same "pangs."

Excuse It, Please

Writers of anti-Mormon studies have a pretty way of excusing themselves first for the awful things they are about to tell, then for the awful things they cannot tell.

Mrs. Stenhouse assures us that "much that to the reader may seem altogether incredible" is simply routine "to a Mormon mind,"[7] and Mr. Wallace opens his book by disclaiming responsibility for whatever absurdities he may perpetrate in words that apply to Richard Burton but certainly not to him: "I am conscious that my narrative savours of incredibility: the fault is in the subject, not in the narrator."[8] But Burton was reporting his own experience. Wallace is simply parroting Mrs. Ann Eliza Webb Dee Young Denning. Now Mrs. Young in her first book promised "A COMPLETE Exposé of Mormonism." When it was shown her that it was her *duty* to expose the Mormon Monster, she "adopted it without hesitation" and pulled out all the stops.[9] Yet she insists that what she has told is nothing compared with what she could tell: "I am compelled to silence on points that would make what I have already said seem tame in comparison."[10] "Another volume, as large as this, would not contain all I could write on this subject."[11] The stuff sold well, but the sensation-hungry public must have novelty, and when "it became a matter of life and death that this commodity be kept marketable and attractive,"[12] one might expect Ann Eliza to dip into her vast reserve of untold stories. Yet though in her second book (the 1908 edition) — written after thirty-three years of thinking it over — she promises to "exhibit still more fully the whole career of Brigham Young," the best she can come up with is "a handful of anecdotes" — the same anecdotes she told in her first book, only fewer — "far too little of life with the Prophet and too few facts of her own physical existence," says the exasperated Mr. Wallace.[13]

What is wrong? What makes the lady so strangely reticent? Out of thousands of personal experiences whose "horror" is beyond belief,[14] isn't it odd that she has not a *single one* to add to her first story, especially since the avowed purpose of the 1908 opus is "to expose that accursed system with its polygamic, murderous and other

criminal practices, . . . arouse the . . . people of America,"[15] "above all, to awaken still deeper interest . . . that
shall at length swell into indignation"?[16] The way to do
that is not to hold back on unpleasant details, as none
knew better than Eliza Young. "For almost half a century,"
Mr. Wallace assures us, " . . . she paraded publicly, over
and over again, every intimate detail of the old existence."[17]
The "unremitting hysteria" of her language is more savage
than ever in her last book, and she is perfectly willing to
tell more horror-stories — but they are all the stories of other
women; she has nothing to add to her own. Why not? If
we examine the *actual events* of her life as she describes
them, they all turn out to be quite humdrum and ordinary;
ah, but the pangs, the anguish — that is another thing! Here
again we meet a peculiar situation, for every time Ann
Eliza suffers Promethean pangs, she is careful to conceal
her sufferings from all the world — even "her [dear] mother
to whom," as Mrs. Woodward observes, "she was almost
morbidly attached,"[18] is never allowed for a moment to
suspect what is going on in little Ann Eliza's seething
interior. The fact that *nobody at the time* is ever aware of
the sufferings of this "imaginative, excitable child," as she
calls herself,[19] is a pretty good indication that those sufferings were invented in retrospect. There is not a scrap
of external evidence for any of the horror that surrounds
our informant; the outrage never lies in what actually happens, but only in Ann Eliza's very private and very secret
reaction to it.

Such is the stuff of her — and Mr. Wallace's — dramatic
history. With Stenhouse it is the same. Take one moving
instance: "What a shock this was to me; for that sum
. . . was gone at one sweep! 'Can it be possible,' I said,
'that he [Brigham Young] can be so mean as that? Where
can his conscience be? or has he any; to deprive me of my
hard earnings in this way. He shall not do it — I will *make*
him pay me.' "[20] Here, plainly, the lady is reporting a

harrowing experience—firsthand. Brigham Young, it is clear to all, has done something monstrous, something particularly cruel and evil and greedy. What is the event that triggers this agonized reaction? Simply this; that Mrs. Stenhouse's husband (Mr. Stenhouse) had suggested that the family make a try at paying tithing, receiving tithing credit in return for work done for the Church, like other Mormon families—this is the full extent of the atrocity Mrs. S. so vividly describes. No tithing was paid, but the emotional damage was done and the world has another atrocity to chalk up against Brother Brigham. But it is Ann Eliza we are going to tell about. Here is her story.

The Two or Three Lives of Ann Eliza Webb Dee Young Denning

First, behold Ann Eliza the infant, "consecrated to sorrow by the baptism of my mother's tears upon my baby brow."[21] "Many a time she has knelt with me clasped fast in her arms, the tears falling on my wondering face, and prayed frantically that we both might die."[22] Of course she was too young to remember any of this, but what a production she makes of it! Actually it comes right out of Stenhouse: "My only comfort was in my children; no revelation, I felt, could change *their* relationship to me. But over my little daughter Clara [Ann Eliza's friend] I mourned, for I thought . . . she would some day be called upon to suffer as I did."[23] Both ladies put full blame for this infant damnation on Brigham Young. From the age of two Ann Eliza has a "distinct remembrance" of a very happy time at Winter Quarters.[24] At the age of three as the "little dancin' missy" she was "petted by everybody" and thoroughly enjoyed herself.[25] Then came the great trek, with Ann Eliza, "a little blue-eyed girl, dancing merrily under the trees," or "running along by the side of a covered emigrant-wagon."[26] "I . . . was petted almost as much by my fellow-travellers as I had been . . . in Missouri. It is a wonder that I was not completely spoiled; I daresay I should have been, had it not been for my mother's sensible and judicious training. I was her idol, the one object for which she cared the most in the world."[27] To idolize Ann Eliza is the one "sensible and judicious" course for anyone to take; anything less than that she considers persecution.

At last an element of real horror: at the usual age of eight she is baptized—a pleasant and edifying experience to which most Mormon children eagerly look forward. But not Ann Eliza! "So great was the nervous shock that I could not think of it without a shudder for years after."[28] Little did the witnesses of this perfectly ordinary, familiar, and interesting ordinance realize that they were actually beholding a grisly episode right out of Edgar Allan Poe. To show that there is no mistake, let us here interrupt our chronological sequence to mention Ann Eliza's third baptism, in her thirtieth year. By her own free will and choice she had elected to have herself baptized again—by now she should have known what she was up against; but again she was thoroughly brutalized: "I was led into the water by a great strapping fellow," and emerged "gasping for breath," some "words were spoken over me, and the farce ended."[29]

Of growing up in a polygamous household, she reports, "In our own family it was very smooth sailing,"[30] and so she must resort to seeking her harrowing tales in *other* people's houses. But then comes the indescribable horror of the "Reformation," during which people had to answer "a list of singular questions, many of which I distinctly remember."[31] This is out of Stenhouse, who says that all trace of such a catechism had completely disappeared.[32] Fortunately Ann Eliza remembers it, but discreetly clams up: "I *dare* only mention a few [she mentions none]. . . . Many were grossly indelicate, others laughably absurd."[33] How does it happen that this sheltered child comprehended and remembered both the obscenity and the absurdity of these forbidden questions, none of which she cares to repeat as an adult? She remembers how one man confessed to stealing a sheep, and sure enough, right there in the meeting little Ann Eliza saw some sheep's wool clinging to the lapel of his Sunday suit, in which no doubt he did his sheep-stealing.[34] Well no, she won't go that far, but she is absolutely sure of one thing: "I *know* I wondered if that was from the sheep he had stolen."[35] And that is good enough for evidence. But no, she promises more: "I tell the incidents from actual knowledge, and not from mere hearsay."[36] So what follows? A long letter written by the wife of "a merchant of Salt Lake City," telling of events that had nothing to do with Ann Eliza's little world; none of the characters in the story is named, "at the special request of the writer of the letter."[37] Even so it wasn't a very good atrocity, "somewhat remarkable, because it was unattended by bloodshed";[38] then why does our author bother with a mild atrocity which does not concern her? Because, she explains, it is "the best description" of many "similar scenes" she *might* report.[39] She retells the same story, incidentally, in 1908, not in the form of a letter but as a personal experience.[40]

"I Wants to Make Their Flesh Creep"

But now comes a genuine atrocity, eagerly exploited by Mr. Wallace as Ann Eliza's firsthand experience of Mormon brutality at its worst.[41] It seems that when Ann Eliza was a small child, the daughter of her uncle married a Gentile named Hatten, who shortly after was killed by Indians on the way to California. It is significant that in Mr. Wallace's book nobody is ever killed by Indians, even in the wild 1850s—but always by "Indians"—alias you-know-who. Only little Ann Eliza knew who the real murderers were—namely, Brigham Young and Heber C. Kimball, who wanted to marry Hatten's bride. Since she can give us the very words that passed between the two in planning the murder and the very words in which Brigham Young ordered it, Ann Eliza should have told the bride what she knew, for though Mrs. Hatten dearly loved her late husband, she "became a Mrs. Kimball without a protest";[42] she should at least have told her own parents years later, for then they would not have insisted on *her* marrying the murderer, Brigham Young. It was only "after many years," she says, that Mrs. Kimball "learned the bitter truth"—the bride herself never suspected anything.[43] In that case, how could it have been such a harrowing experience for her little cousin? What she actually experienced was hearing that a man she hardly knew, a distant relative by marriage, had been killed by Indians: and this she and Mr. Wallace parlay into her one personal experience of a "victim of Blood-Atonement," though what the death of a Gentile can have to do with Blood Atonement remains a mystery.

Next comes Ann Eliza's prize exhibit, "the murder of a woman named Jones, and her son," because "they were suspected of falling away in the faith."[44] It was in Payson where she was living, at the age of ten, with her mother: "I did not see the bodies, nor did my mother, although they were driven past our door; we both shunned the fearful sight."[45] But the rest of the town was whooping it up, including "plenty of women . . . who gloried in their death as a deed of service to the Lord."[46] The bodies, "shockingly mutilated, were placed in a wagon, and exposed to the crowd by being driven through the streets, attended by a jeering, taunting mob, who could not cease their insults though their victims were still in death."[47]

The impressive engraving of the vast crowd lining the streets as the wagon moves through the town is enough to justify Mr. Wallace's enthusiastic retelling of the tale. Only he overlooks one significant detail: "Concerning the murders," says Mrs. Young, "the majority of the people

This is a faithful representation, from Mrs. A. E. Young's book (1876), of the Payson murders. Unfortunately most of the people in Payson, according to Mrs. Young, missed the parade and never heard about it. Payson must have been a very large city.

knew nothing, and supposed that the Indians were the assassins, as they were always told."[48] The huge ticker-tape parade, the taunting, howling mob, the bodies on public display in the small village of Payson not only failed to make an object-lesson of the widow Jones and her son, but never even came to the attention of "the majority of the people." Where could they all have been before, during, and after the monster celebration to have heard nothing of it? This is simply another example of the two worlds of Ann Eliza—a well-known public event, a typical Indian atrocity, is veiled by a shadow world of easily imagined horror.

Hardly less intimate is Ann Eliza's experience of the Mountain Meadows massacre. "I was but a child at the time, but I recollect, perfectly, hearing that an emigrant-train had been attacked by the Indians, and all members . . . with the exception of a few of the smaller children killed; and I remember, also, *seeing* these children, who . . . were to be cared for by the Mormon people."[49] She puts *seeing* in italics to establish herself as a witness. But to what? The report of another Indian massacre in the worst year of Indian depredations, that was all. But that will never do: "Young as I was, I *felt* the mystery . . . and I knew *instinctively* . . . that something was being hidden from the mass of the people, by their leaders."[50] Is that the way the child Eliza had been taught to think about "the leaders"? "The very mystery which veiled it made it more awful to me, an imaginative, excitable child; and though I followed the example of my elders, and never spoke of the subject, even to my mother, it haunted me perpetually, and I grew absolutely terrified at the constantly recurring fancies which I drew of it."[51] This is a revealing illustration of how Wallace's informant operates: the outward experience was hearing of another Indian massacre and seeing the survivors, but that is merely incidental to her story, which is that she *experienced* the real thing inwardly, secretly, "instinctively," so that even her mother never suspected that she knew a thing, which is not surprising, since nobody else suspected anything either. Yet at that time the child Eliza not only suspected but knew exactly what had happened and who was behind the whole thing—John D. Lee! "I had never even seen the man; but knowing the record of his crimes, and always hearing of him in connection with some deed of bloody brutality, my horror and fear of him never diminished, and he remained, what he had always been, the ogre of my childish fancies."[52] Now this is interesting. How well known was Lee before the Mountain Meadows tragedy? Who but Ann Eliza knew "the record of his crimes"? Scouting and settling distant places had been his calling, and we shall examine his career later on. What bothers us now is how a sheltered child in "the strictest of Mormon households" could have heard all about the unnamed crimes of an obscure minor

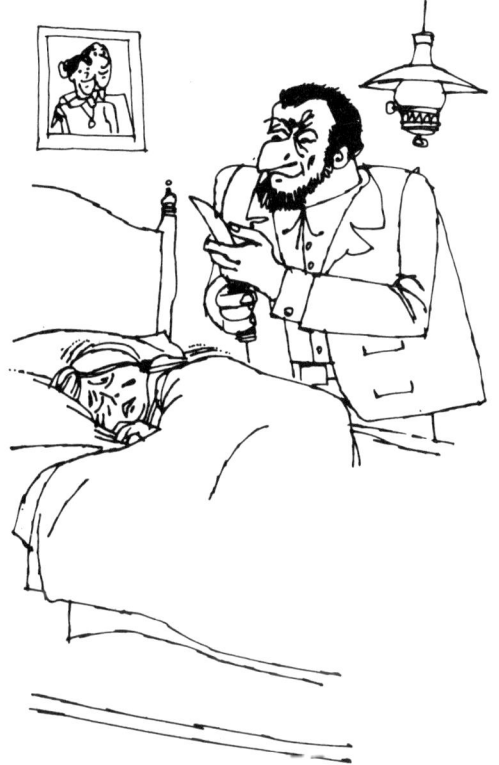

official three hundred miles away, and not only that but immediately surmise that *he* had been the author of the Mountain Meadows atrocity. Here we have an excellent indication of the reliability of Mrs. Ann Eliza Young as a historian. Yet it is her version of Mountain Meadows that Mr. Wallace follows meticulously.

Even more than baptism, the rite of the "Endowment," as they call it, is, as Ann Eliza points out, the most cherished experience of all good Mormons. But for her it was just more cruel abuse, and we find her suffocated, strangled, nauseated, on the point of collapse and hysterics before it is over, and along with that "quite dissatisfied" and "as hopeless and apathetic as I had before been eager and buoyant."[53] She had been expecting a show, and when it failed to come up to expectations, her vaunted religious fervor collapsed at a touch: "It was so different from what I expected that I was saddened and disappointed by it all."[54] But whose fault is that?

Private and Confidential

A chapter entitled "Troubles in Our Own Family" promises at long last something specific involving Ann Eliza, but alas, that chapter begins: "I know a first wife who was driven to such utter desperation."[55] And so on and on until the lady catches herself: "I could cite hundreds of such cases . . . but I will, instead, tell a little what the 'Reformation,' and the subsequent 'Celestial Ordinance' fever, did for our own family."[56] Why only a *little* when she knows so much? What follows is little enough, to be sure — the amusing story of how one of the "Hand-Cart Girls" snagged her father.[57] Here Ann Eliza, the doughty champion of suppressed Morman womanhood, actually describes one of these victims of tyranny as a shameless hussy on the make. How can that be? Well, in this case the husband happens to be her own father — all *other* Mormon men are brutes below the level of beasts; he alone is the victim of a wily female.

But all the time Ann Eliza is not suffering at all; she is a gay carefree girl, laughing and joking with her friends about polygamy, as they sympathize with her and resent Brigham Young's jealous interference with her boyfriends, "and a more rebellious set of mortals was never seen."[58] Unaware that even the slightest hint of criticism of the priesthood can mean only quick and certain death, and that Brigham Young "holds them so completely, body and soul, that they shrink before his displeasure in absolute terror,"[59] the foolish girls go right on with their suicidal talk: "We indulged in the most incendiary talk, and turned the torrent of our wrath especially against polygamy."[60] Next, undamaged, she is sponsored by Brigham Young in her stage career, working in highly edifying surroundings: "It was almost like a family; and I do not believe there was ever a theatre where there was less of envyings, and jealousies, and strifes, than there was among us."[61] But where Ann Eliza herself has no inner anguish to report, Mr. Wallace comes to the rescue: Brigham Young cracks the whip and *commands* her to become an actress, for he secretly lusts after her.[62]

This is apparent from the episode of the buggy, in which Woodward and Wallace take understandable delight, it being the only indication that Brigham Young thought of marrying Ann Eliza as early as she thought of marrying him. Her girlfriends, she says, suggested that President Young might be after her, and sure enough, a few days later he picked her up in his buggy and gave her a lecture on marriage. In spite of her girlfriends' insistence and Young's bluntness and clumsiness, our heroine completely missed his drift, and insisted *forever after* that he was not in love with her but just wanted to cut her down to size. Yet in telling her story she does her best to help the willing reader to the opposite conclusion. Why this wild ambivalence? Because it must be her story that Brigham Young desires her, though she insists that such a thing never occurred to her during *any* of her talks with Young.

Against the united protests of parents and friends, Ann Eliza married the dashing and handsome Dee, whom all the girls were after. He did his best to come up to her romantic expectations—"There is such a sweet humility about a woman's love!"[63] is her comment on this—but within a month she was completely disillusioned and suffering beyond all imagination. He even knocked her out once "in his fury at what he termed my stubbornness," but "I very quickly forgave him: it was so sweet to feel the old tenderness again."[64] Nevertheless this typical family spat with the very monogamous Dee (why does she omit the episode from her *expanded* autobiography of 1908?) serves as the text for one of Mrs. Young's most impassioned discourses on the evils of polygamy. They had two children, and Dee with rough good humor[65] used to play with them. But what a reaction! "He used to either take no notice of them at all, which I infinitely preferred, or he would handle them so roughly that the little things would shriek with pain and terror, and I would be almost frantic with fear lest he should kill them in his mad frolics."[66] Such is the Mormon father, either contemptuously indifferent or madly sadistic, threatening the lives of his babes as he gloats over their pain and terror. Is it any wonder that he finally attacked Ann Eliza herself? He "seized me by the throat, and threw me back into the chair. The screams of the terrified child brought my mother into the room at once. She snatched the baby from my arms, . . . called my father, and he came and rescued me from the infuriated man who held me."[67] Again it was the reaction that made the drama: "I was dizzy with pain, and almost suffocated from the grip; but my maternal instinct was stronger than the pain, and I never relaxed my hold on my child."[68] Ann Eliza's stock demonstration of nobility and anguish was brief, however, since mama and papa came "at once" from the next room. Dee never got a chance to tell his side and didn't even appear in court when Ann Eliza got her divorce with the greatest of ease. Two days later, she said, she celebrated the merriest Christmas she had known in years; she was, as she put it, "supremely, selfishly happy"[69] — which may suggest to some that the whole thing was staged. Indeed, in the 1908 version she omits the whole dramatic episode and confines herself to stating, "At last my parents were eyewitnesses of my husband's brutal violence towards myself. . . . Until that time they had known

nothing of the treatment which I received from my husband."[70] They had all been living in the same house for
two years, with papa and mama watching Dee like a hawk,
yet with all this "brutal violence" going on under their
noses the doting parents detected no marks or bruises, no
suspicious noises, no betraying tears—"they had known
nothing" of Ann Eliza's sufferings. Again, only she is the
witness to what she had gone through—Dee always denied
it and nobody else ever noticed a thing.

After the divorce Ann Eliza moved to Cottonwood,
where "I was royally happy,—happier than I ever was in
my life before,"[71] with mama babying her darling as ever
and waiting on her hand and foot. "Here, I think, I was
happier than I had ever before been in my life. My health
was much improved."[72] It is hard to believe after that, that
her life had been ruined forever, yet "for the rest of her
days Ann Eliza would always refer to James Dee as the
man who 'blighted' her life."[73] She describes herself as a
real beauty and "very fond of gay society,"[74] though of
course "I had suffered too much" ever to be as she was
"in the old frolicsome days."[75] Yet she frolicked merrily
with her children, until one summer evening as she sat
cradled in her mother's arms thinking (so she says) how
little the goings and comings of one Brigham Young concerned her, the man himself set out for Cottonwood to get
her! The very next day he proposed marriage to Ann Eliza
through her parents. The courtship we have treated under
a separate head, as its supreme significance deserves; let
us skip now to the married life with Brigham.

It is precisely here, where she promises so much, that
Ann Eliza Young, to Mr. Wallace's annoyance, serves history so poorly with her measly "handful of anecdotes."
The first is how Clara Decker, "sadly in want of some
furs,"[76] gave Brigham Young a lecture on his own viciousness and the depravity of the Mormon religion—and
promptly got the furs. Next Ann Eliza "preferred a similar

request, and was met by a similar torrent of abuse,"[77] whereupon she "burst into tears, . . . puzzled and astonished at this new revelation of my Prophet-husband's meanness and coarseness. The next time he came to see me he brought me my furs."[78] If this is indeed one of her few authentic revelations of domestic life with Brigham, why does Ann Eliza omit it in her expanded life story of 1908? Why does Woodward completely distort it by reporting that the lady did *not* get the furs? Is it because it makes Brigham Young look rather good and her not so good?[79]

Next she asks for some silk to reline the muff—and gets it. This is worked into an epic battle of wills: "When he had finished he cut off *a quarter of a yard* of narrow silk from an entire piece, . . . and gave it to me with as many airs and as much flourish as though he were presenting me with a whole dress pattern. It is needless to say that my muff was not lined with *that* piece of silk."[80] Needless to say, that is, if you know our Ann Eliza. Next she reports that Brigham once denounced the foolish and unhygienic fashion of long trains on ladies' dresses by announcing, "The very next time that I see one of my wives with a dress on sweeping the ground, I will take the scissors and cut it off."[81]

"The very next day," Ann Eliza reports, "I was passing through a door in front of him, when he accidentally stepped upon my train, which was a very long one. . . . To my great surprise, he not only refrained from the threatened application of the scissors, but from any comment, even so much as an apology for his awkwardness."

This little act, staged by Ann Eliza herself, failed to get a rise out of her husband: he neither assailed her with scissors nor with the usual "torrent of abuse." Deliberately challenged, he displayed perfect self-control—or indifference. Her reaction? Disgust with the brute who didn't offer "even so much as an apology for his awkwardness."[82] Ann

Eliza is again the victim. Then she had to endure the humiliation of being driven to the polls and instructed "how to vote" (not for whom, but how) by of all things her husband's *coachman!* (The italics and the howl are hers.)[83] The "outrageous absurdity"[84] of receiving instructions from a mere *coachman* was more than she could stand, and never again did she soil her lovely hands with a Utah ballot.[85]

Next we read how Amelia Folsom banged a garden gate in Ann Eliza's girlish face and shouted at her: "There, madam! I'd like to see you get in now."[86] Since all Ann Eliza had to do was open the gate and walk in, one would fail to see the point of this story, did not Ann Eliza entitle it "Amelia Tries to Shut Me Out."[87] The second encounter with Amelia was even more intimate and harrowing: "During the dessert she reached the cake-basket to me, and with as freezing a tone and manner as she could assume, asked,—'Will you have some cake?' I declined, and that ended our conversation—the last and indeed *the only one I ever had* with her."[88] The passage is worth the italics we have given it, for Ann Eliza claims to be the intimate, personal, firsthand authority on the most personal details of the life of Amelia Folsom Young. This may all be interesting, but is it really a tale of horror such as no words can describe?[89] That comes next in the episode on the farm.

The Work Farm

Ann Eliza "dreaded the ceaseless hours of manual labor that awaited her"[90] at the farm, says Wallace, and yet to all *appearances* she had no objections. How do you explain that? Since the lady has overlooked the slip, Mr. Wallace shows that he knows the formula by coming to the rescue with his own insight into the secret mind of his subject: "Her first instinct was to protest," but she didn't because "she wanted no fight."[91] That is *not* the way she tells it: "As it was my husband's will, I went, without a word of

protest."[92] She could wail like a banshee for a muff and fight like a tigress for the silk to line it with—but not one word of protest about going to the farm. Why not? Because the farmhouse was a very grand place, "had a lovely appearance" and was "one of the pleasantest looking places that one would care to see,"[93] and "I knew I should be obliged to perform as mistress of the farm-house."[94] There was a lot of work to be done: "There were butter and cheese to make from forty cows, all the *other* dairy work to attend to, besides cooking for twenty-five or thirty men."[95] Besides "I . . . took care of the house, did the washing and ironing, and was allowed the extreme pleasure of carrying the farm supplies to the other wives every week."[96]

With all that to do on a five-day week—and she definitely implies, and Wallace apparently believes, that she *did* do it—one is surprised to learn what her real grievances were at the farm. One was that in order to reach her bedroom she had "to pass through a dining-room thirty feet, and a parlor forty feet in length" —which gives you an idea of the layout; but even worse was that "hired men, family, and visitors were all compelled to use the same staircase."[97] What humiliation—the same staircase as the hired help! Most of all she suffered from boredom "long, uneventful years,—and how I hated my life! . . . Even the love I bore my children was changed."[98] The picture of the fastidious lady pining away the uneventful years hardly suits with the moving engraving in the book that shows Ann Eliza toiling heroically over enormous washtubs. Where must the correction be made? In the washtubs. When one starts to figure out the minimum staff required to perform the tasks enumerated above, it quickly becomes apparent that Ann Eliza did not do it all herself. (1) She actually mentions hired help—a lot of it, e.g., cooking for twenty-five or thirty men; only (2) *she* didn't do the cooking: "My mother . . . took charge of the cooking. I assisted in the latter."[99] (3) And what does she mean by "take charge?" Not doing the actual work, certainly. She was "mistress of the farm-house," with absolutely nobody over her to make her do anything. John W. Young was right when he said: "She did not have to raise her hand" at the farm,[100] for Brigham Young rarely visited the farm and never went into the house. In view of her quick and efficient reaction to whatever she considered abuse, the fact that she stuck it out three and a half years and left it in high spirits[101] shows how little she suffered; when shortly after, she tried to run a small boarding-house, the project collapsed almost immediately—which shows plainly enough that she had neither the strength nor the skill to carry on as she *says* she did at the farm.

Here is how Mrs. Young itemized her sufferings at the farm in a neat deposition for the Court: "During the year 1869 he sent me, (1) against my wishes, to a farm . . . where . . . I (2) was compelled to (3) labor until I was (4) completely broken down in health; . . . (5) my only companion was my mother; . . . (6) except the limited fare which the defendant allowed me, he (7) appropriated all the proceeds of the farm; . . . (8) on the few occasions when he visited the farm he (9) treated me with studied contempt, (10) objecting even to my aged mother remaining with me, (11) after her health was destroyed by overwork on his farm."[102]

Questions on the above points:

(1) Didn't you say you went "without a word of protest?"[103] How was anyone to know it was against your wishes?

(2) Who compelled you to labor? You were "mistress of the farm-house,"[104] and Brigham Young, you say, never bothered you there. Oh, but he was "addicted to fault-finding, and so easily displeased, that we took no pleasure in his visits. . . . I dreaded them, and grew ill with nervousness and apprehension every time he came to us."[105]

(3) From that it is clear that you managed things badly. It is also clear that you had recourse to your usual "out" of becoming, as you put it, "ill with nervousness . . . *every time* he came." Now how could one so delicate be forced, as Mr. Wallace so movingly puts it, to "ceaseless hours of manual labor?"[106] You had only to dislike a thing to "grow ill with nervousness" and take to your bed and your novels.

(4) Mr. Wallace notes that you were happy and gay, your "satisfaction was complete" as you returned from the farm to your new home in Salt Lake.[107] Granted some of your pleasure sprang from feelings of relief, how could any "*completely* broken down" person be as blithe as you were?

(5) The farm was, as you say "within pleasant driving distance"[108] of the city, where you were free to go anytime; it was in the midst of a thriving rural community where you had many near neighbors, while the farm itself was a bustling hive of activity; then there were all sorts of church and family activities; you had your doting mother and your children with you, and you often insisted that

your whole life was completely wrapped up in them: how then can you or Mr. Wallace say that you were starved for companionship? Whose fault was it? You would not associate with hired help—even to use the same stairs was an indignity; there was old Mrs. Lewis the housekeeper, a pitiful victim of Brigham Young's rapacity as you report it; and yet you say there was not room enough for you and her even in that enormous house.[109] Wallace insists that you yearned for Brigham Young's stimulating companionship, and you complain that (8) he visited you rarely and (9) then treated you "with studied contempt." But you also say that you "took no pleasure in his visits and dreaded them." Under those circumstances how can you complain of his leaving you alone?

(6) Now as to that "limited fare," your own mother, you say, "took charge of the cooking," and in one stirring episode you tell how she forced Brigham Young to allow her to set the kind of ample table she felt the farmhands should have;[110] you also say you "assisted" in the cooking, and yet you want us to believe that you were "allowed" only "limited fare"—that your mother let her daughter starve while she fed the field hands sumptuously?

(7) Since the farm was Brigham Young's, who else *should* "appropriate all the proceeds" of it?

(10–11) "*After* her health was destroyed by overwork on his farm," Brigham Young tried to get your mother to return to her own home at Cottonwood. Wasn't that the humane thing to do when he saw she was working herself to death? Brigham hardly ever visited the farm; it was *you* who saw your mother slaving away day after day; it was *you* who insisted on her coming to the farm and staying there for years—carried on hysterically and said you couldn't live without her. Who made her work so? Who was in charge? Who kept her from returning to her own home and family at happy Cottonwood, wildly protesting against her retirement from the farm even after her health was ruined? Who but Ann Eliza?

But the clue to the whole story of the farm is Ann Eliza's summary of her life there: "I lived here for three years and a half, — long, uneventful years, — and how I hated my life! It was dull, joyless, oppressed, and I looked longingly back to the dear old days at Cottonwood, the restful days that never could come again. Even the love I bore my children was changed."[111]

Three and a half years is more than half of her life with Brigham Young! And of all that time she remembers only two brief anecdotes — not about herself, but about how her mother rebuked Brigham Young for his meanness towards the farmhands. Of her six-hundred-page book devoted to a "COMPLETE Exposé" of life in Mormonism, this woman of the flawless memory who never overlooks a chance to get in a dig at Brigham Young, devotes *less than two pages*[112] to her three and one-half years of heroic suffering and Herculean labors at the farm! Ann Eliza is not the one to overlook any affront to her rank, or minimize any privation. The fact that she has nothing to say about life at the farm aside from the above generalities is conclusive evidence that her life there was indeed dull and uneventful — because she had nothing to do.

The Exodus

During her last days at the farm we find Ann Eliza merry again, for soon she would be back in town "performing once more as a genteel lady. She was happy."[113] Brigham Young was building her a house strictly to her specifications. Again the shock: as she stepped through the front door of her "exceedingly pretty cottage,"[114] her world collapsed: "nothing seemed attractive";[115] she was stunned, shocked, hurt; ignoring all the good features of the house, which were substantial and expensive, she could only see that it was "very inconvenient, and badly arranged."[116] She soon converted it into a boarding house to make some extra money, which she expected Brigham Young to supply: "My family had increased,"[117] as she puts it, and it was her husband's duty to support her "family." She depicts herself not as taking in boarders but "obliged to rely upon the charity of friends."[118] Wallace paraphrases this grimly to read, "She survived only through the good offices of her boarders and neighbors,"[119] which is true of most people who run hotels for a living.

Mrs. Woodward here slips in a particularly effective touch: "It was her Gentile boarders who nursed her."[120] Ann Eliza says nothing about being nursed. What W. and W. generously fail to mention is that the boarders who "nursed" her so touchingly—for almost three weeks!— were at that very time planning to collect a vast sum of money ($100,000!) from her; she was their gold mine.[121]

Next Brigham Young cruelly withholds medical supplies from Ann Eliza—until he learns that she needs them, whereupon they are promptly supplied. Again it is the reaction that counts: "No medical supplies on earth," sobs Mr. Wallace, "could repair the emotional damage done to her."[122] Then we come to the climax of the story, Ann Eliza's point of no return—the episode of the stove: "Damn him! Damn him!" shrieks Mrs. Woodward; he would learn "how much that stove he wouldn't buy for Ann Eliza was going to cost him."[123] Wallace eagerly takes up the cry: this refusal to get his wife a larger stove was his crowning act of selfishness and cruelty.[124] After such heroics it is an anticlimax to learn from a letter she wrote to Fanny Stenhouse just two weeks after the event that Ann Eliza *did* get "a stove out of him" without any fuss.[125] Badly needing some real act of villainy to make their stories plausible, our biographers have not hesitated to ignore Ann Eliza's own original version.

In Salt Lake City, she met the Rev. Stratton and his wife, who became friends and listened to her woes. At the

same time she read the pamphlet written by Mrs. Stenhouse. Though even the Rev. Stratton protests that her
husband has provided a comfortable home for her which
she would be foolish to give up (where would he get *that*
idea if the woman was actually starving?), Ann Eliza hear-
kens to the voices of her Gentile boarders and resolves to
leave Brigham Young and sue him for $200,000. The three
blackguard lawyers insisted on fifty percent of the take,
but the lady stuck by her guns, and the seasoned and
unscrupulous conspirators "bent to her will."[126] This was
after she had retired to the Walker House, "a poor, de-
fen[s]eless, outraged woman," the victim of Brigham
Young's brutality.[127] But first, acting with such great speed
"that no one had time even to suspect my intention," she
whisked all her furniture to a public auction, where her
enthusiastic friends converted it to cash "at large prices."[128]
The reason for such speed was not, as implied, to elude
Brigham's spies — the auction was a public one, and even
they might wonder why the furniture vans? — but to pull
a fast one, as the neglected Stenhouse letter makes clear:
"I . . . instructed an auctioneer two weeks ago to take
away the furniture and sell it, as a part of it was my own,
and *I thought I was entitled to the rest.*"[129] She had to work
fast because the stuff she was selling wasn't hers. She
pulled the same sort of trick on her next husband.[130]

Fleeing to the Walker House, she is "fairly bewildered . . . to find that my name had gone the length and
breadth of the country."[131] "It had never occurred to me
that it would be made a public matter, and I shrank from
the very thought."[132] How was she going to help all those
other women by her example (that, she insists, was her
sole aim in asking for $200,000 instead of taking the $15,000
that was offered) if the thing was never to be made public?[133] At the hotel, "ladies and gentlemen called on me
with offers of sympathy. All the persons connected with
the hotel were kindness itself."[134] Her father came and

stayed with her constantly. Brigham Young's daughter and the ward teachers visited her. Surrounded by eager reporters, she told her stories. And what is the reaction? "She treated her rooms as a fortress and spoke constantly of being kidnapped or murdered."[135] When reporters asked embarrassing questions, she quickly changed the subject, "glanced nervously at the windows and door," and *whispered*, "Would you think that they could abduct me from here? . . . Ah, you don't know them. . . . I dare not let my little boy leave the room, and I eat all my meals here."[136]

She was putting on an act. To stay with friends, she says, would be to "endanger their lives and their home."[137] Yet on the night of her "perilous escape" from Salt Lake she went to the house of those friends, and they all came out of the house together, "and started, ostensibly to walk home,"[138] showing that she was perfectly free not only to visit her friends "ostensibly," but to leave her hotel. Another check: "I could not leave my room, nor did I dare to do so, nor to allow my children out of my sight for nearly two months."[139] Well, she did leave her room during that time, to give an anti-Mormon lecture in the lobby.[140] But more important is her report that just before going to the hotel, "I had sent the elder of my boys to his grandmother" in Cottonwood.[141] It is simply not true that she dared not allow her children out of her sight: the one was living in Cottonwood in perfect safety, where the other soon joined him—but it is a necessary fiction if her story of imminent danger is to hold up. So far was the lady from hiding out from the Mormons that she "complained bitterly" that her Mormon friends did not visit her, as indeed some of them did—including the ward teachers![142]

After the great siege episode comes the great escape. Leaving the Walker House by the back door (a way undiscovered by the Danites), Ann Eliza openly parades on the street, visits her friends the Strattons, with whom she is seen "ostensibly" going back to her hotel.[143] Suddenly

she mounts a carriage and dashes off to catch a train at a distant and unspecified place in the mountains—it would never do to let the reader know that the place was really Ogden; what could be tamer? The excitement of her "providential escape" lies entirely in what she *imagines* during the ride; there is not the slightest indication of any attempt to stop or overtake her, which would have been the easiest thing in the world if anybody had wanted to do it. She got to the station with only two minutes to spare: if *that* is not a hairbreadth escape from Mormonism, what is? This remained forever after the melodramatic climax of her life story. "Ahead lay Wyoming and freedom," writes Mr. Wallace, unable to resist such a perfect Hollywood cliché.[144]

Freedom had been hers any time she wanted it: she had been publicly offered $15,000 cash and safe conduct out of the territory.[145]

Out in the World

After her "providential escape" Mrs. Young traveled around the country giving "racy" lectures on life with Brigham, accompanied by her manager, a dashing, handsome fellow who knew his way around. Now it happens that sex sells newspapers as well as lecture tickets, and the ever-cynical gentlemen of the press were not slow in making inevitable comments about Mrs. Young and her interesting partner.[146] Again the reaction is everything. "After reading the scurrilous piece," writes the sympathetic Mr. Wallace, "Ann Eliza sat stunned. Her first words, when she could find words, to Major Pond were 'Brigham Young's money is at the bottom of this.' "[147] Of course it was; Mr. Young is at the bottom of all her sufferings. What gives it away is the reaction of the gallant Major; though a man of the world and professional purveyor of scandal, he too is shocked and wounded. *His* chaste mind simply can't conceive of such a thing: "I cannot imagine its object," he wrote, lost and bemused, "unless its source comes through Mormon influence."[148] That, of course, is the answer: "I have long been looking for a stab in the back from Brigham."[149] What treachery—a stab in the back, after all he had done for Brigham! For Mr. Wallace this was Brigham Young's fiendish way of attacking Ann Eliza "through her best friends," though throughout the history any specific friends strangely fail to materialize.[150]

Finally "Ann Eliza had attained every goal,"[151] celebrating "the victory of national monogamy toward which she had contributed so great a part."[152] Again the reaction: she had no "peace of mind." While "her public face, except for the past suffering she exploited professionally, . . . was the face of success and contentment, her secret second face, the one behind the lyceum mask, remained disturbed and distraught."[153] Free from the horrors of Mormon bondage, she still suffers, and as always the suffering is of her own making.

In the quiet Michigan town of Manistee, the Moses E. Dennings, hailed as the town's model couple, had just celebrated twenty-three years of happily married life. Woodward says it was their *golden* wedding anniversary, and that Denning "had children older than Ann Eliza."[154] According to Wallace he was at most fifty-three years old.[155] Ann Eliza (who a year later was to lecture in Ohio on "Utah's Curse and the Nation's Shame") was staying at the home of the wealthy and hospitable Dennings. Time passes, but not very much. We return within two years to find the model marriage broken up and the elderly Mr. Denning married to the charming houseguest. What is Ann Eliza's reaction to that? Total silence. In her complete autobiography of 1908 she makes no mention of Denning. But what a production she could have made of it if she had been in the first Mrs. Denning's shoes! Even Mrs. Woodward raises an eyebrow, for Ann Eliza can hardly have been madly in love with the "rich old logger with one arm."[156] In no time at all Ann Eliza was playing her accustomed role of the abused and neglected wife. Like Dee and Young, Denning was a brute, "so that by living with him, the health of your oratrix became weak and impaired and broken."[157] But though she "refused to sustain the relation of wife to him any longer,"[158] she stubbornly refused to divorce him—which Wallace finds most noble of her. Denning begged her to leave him, "offered to give me all he had if I would leave Manistee, which I refused to do."[159] Why? Because, Wallace explains, "she was not ready now to separate herself" from the advantages of "a permanent marriage in monogamy."[160] But what are the advantages of living with a monogamous husband who "called his wife 'bitch' and 'whore' and accused her of wanton behavior with half the male population of Manistee"?[161] What could she see in the loathsome Denning, who hated the sight of her? The answer to that question (as if you didn't already know the answer) is simple — Denning was loaded. Now it is worthy of note that from the moment Ann Eliza became the rich Mrs. Denning she ceased entirely from her great Mormon crusade. "Does any one think," she had cried, "that, for the sake of emolument, I could thus open my heart? . . . Never. My womanhood revolts at the idea. As a means of support, I would never have undertaken it."[162] Yet when she finally had the means and the time to carry on her great crusade in style she suddenly lost all interest in it: the lecture she gave the week she married Denning was the last one she ever gave,[163] which is strange indeed if she *never* lectured for money. "Driven by the demons of duty and money,"[164] she strangely forgot about the duty as soon as she got the money.

As soon as Denning left her for the last time, Ann Eliza went on a great spending spree, buying up the town and charging everything to Denning on the advice of her attorney. "She bought about a thousand dollars worth of groceries and provisions, dry goods, shoes, slippers, furniture and hardware in a couple of days."[165] The reader may recall how on the advice of her lawyers, moving with great speed "so as to escape detection," she auctioned off Brigham Young's furniture just before leaving *him*,[166] converting everything to cash at a handsome rate. Again, however, she is the frail martyr, noble to the end: "Nothing shall be set down in malice,"[167] she tells the reporters as she sets about to portray the monster Denning, who in the end tried to starve her — just like Brigham!

Wallace has gone to no end of trouble to search out the last days of this "remarkable woman." We find her happy at last with her son Edward, whose marriage with a Southern Socialite had broken up, leaving him free to devote his full time to mama as they settled down in a bungalow in Denver. But then "perhaps from lack of money," Wallace explains, "she sold her Denver property and was forced to dispossess her son."[168] Still disdaining money, she next turns up in Utah to claim a $2,000 legacy left her by the generous and forgiving Dee. It was pretty decent of him, since she never had one generous thing to say about Dee,[169] whom for fifty years she had been describing as the blight of her life. Then she moved in on her brother Gilbert in El Paso, where she "occupied four different residences in five years."[170] "During these years," says Wallace, "Ann Eliza's neighbors knew her only as 'Mrs. Anna E. Denning, widow of Moses R.,' " though Moses R. was still "very much alive."[171] Here is the same old Ann Eliza, passing herself off in her last days as something fine and noble, a sweet retiring widow, instead of the much-divorced wife of a man who had done everything he could to get rid of her.

In 1908, painting a heroic picture of herself as a lone warrior against the powerful hierarchy, who "have found huge enjoyment in their own guile and cunning in evading punishment for their crimes,"[172] she can speak with the same intimate inside knowledge of Utah and the Mormon leaders that she had displayed in 1876, though she has been away from Utah for thirty-five years. She shows us here what she has been doing all along, i.e., converting old atrocity stories into firsthand experience by merely tagging her name to them.

The last we hear of the living Ann Eliza is a statement attributed to her older grandson in 1930: "I hope to hell I never see her again."[173]

Such briefly but without major omissions is the heart-rending story of Ann Eliza Young, the story which she has parlayed into a six-hundred-page book of suffering and horror such as no words can describe. But we should not pass by in silence one particularly harrowing experience

that occurred to Ann Eliza in the East some time after she had escaped from Mormon Bondage:

When once, in a car, I saw a manly little fellow, about twelve or thirteen years of age, rise with a rare grace, and give his seat to an old lady, the tears sprang to my eyes, such an unaccustomed sight was it. I contrasted that boy with the youth of Utah, and I felt with a new indignation flashing through all my veins, and a new sorrow tugging at my heart, the curse that polygamy was to the young men, as well as to the young girls, who are growing up under the teachings of that baneful system. It is horrible! It fouls and poisons the stream at its very source (and it adds mud and filth as it crawls along its slimy way), sending up its noxious vapors, etc., etc.[174]

Even if all this comes by way of comment on her marriage with the exceedingly monogamous James Dee, it just gives you an idea of how the woman suffered.

Notes to Part 1

1. Mrs. T. B. H. (Fanny) Stenhouse, *Tell It All: The Story of a Life's Experience in Mormonism* (Hartford, CT: Worthington, 1874), 31.

2. Ann Eliza Webb Young, *Wife No. 19; Or, The Story of a Life of Bondage, Being a Complete Exposé of Mormonism, and Revealing the Sorrows, Sacrifices and Sufferings of Women in Polygamy* (Hartford, CT: Dustin, Gilman, 1875), 32–33.

3. Ann Eliza Young, *Life in Mormon Bondage* (Philadelphia: Aldine, 1908), 1.

4. Young, *Wife No. 19*, 401.

5. Ibid., 601.

6. Ibid., 576 (emphasis added).

7. Stenhouse, *Tell It All*, 31.

8. Irving Wallace, *The Twenty-Seventh Wife* (New York: Simon and Schuster, 1961), 9.

9. Young, *Wife No. 19*, 568.

10. Ibid., 591.

11. Ibid., 601.

12. Wallace, *Twenty-Seventh Wife*, 278.

13. Ibid., 431.

14. Young, *Wife No. 19*, 279.

15. Young, *Life in Mormon Bondage*, 1.

16. Ibid., 26.

17. Wallace, *Twenty-Seventh Wife*, 278.

18. Helen B. Woodward, *The Bold Women* (New York: Farrar, Straus and Young, 1953), 330.

19. Young, *Wife No. 19*, 230.

20. Stenhouse, *Tell It All*, 351.

21. Young, *Wife No. 19*, 99.

22. Ibid., 106.

23. Stenhouse, *Tell It All*, 143.

24. Young, *Wife No. 19*, 111.

25. Ibid., 112–13.

26. Ibid., 118.

27. Ibid., 114.

28. Ibid., 180.

29. Ibid., 545.

30. Ibid., 142.
31. Ibid., 186.
32. Stenhouse, *Tell It All,* 314–15.
33. Young, *Wife No. 19,* 186.
34. Ibid., 183.
35. Ibid. (emphasis added).
36. Ibid., 190.
37. Ibid.
38. Ibid., 194–95.
39. Ibid., 190.
40. Young, *Life in Mormon Bondage,* 149–50.
41. Ibid., 197.
42. Ibid., 195.
43. Ibid.
44. Ibid., 197.
45. Ibid., 198.
46. Ibid.
47. Ibid.
48. Ibid.
49. Ibid., 229.
50. Ibid. (emphasis added).
51. Ibid., 230.
52. Ibid., 231–32.
53. Ibid., 370.
54. Ibid.
55. Ibid., 292–93.
56. Ibid., 296.
57. Ibid., 296–97.
58. Ibid., 375.
59. Ibid., 374.
60. Ibid., 375.
61. Ibid., 382.
62. Wallace, *Twenty-Seventh Wife,* 128.
63. Young, *Wife No. 19,* 385.
64. Ibid., 402.
65. Ibid., 405.
66. Ibid.
67. Ibid., 407–8.
68. Ibid., 408.
69. Ibid., 411.
70. Young, *Life in Mormon Bondage,* 305; cf. Young, *Wife No., 19,* 408.

71. Ibid., 411.
72. Ibid., 412.
73. Wallace, *Twenty-Seventh Wife,* 150.
74. Young, *Wife No. 19,* 373.
75. Ibid., 423.
76. Ibid., 132.
77. Ibid.
78. Ibid., 132–33.
79. Woodward, *Bold Women,* 322.
80. Ibid., 134.
81. Ibid., 134–35.
82. Ibid., 135.
83. Wallace, *Twenty-Seventh Wife,* 388.
84. Ibid.
85. Ibid.; Young, *Wife No. 19,* 94–95.
86. Young, *Wife No. 19,* 461.
87. Ibid., 455.
88. Ibid., 462.
89. Ibid., 591.
90. Wallace, *Twenty-Seventh Wife,* 224.
91. Ibid.
92. Young, *Wife No. 19,* 533.
93. Ibid.
94. Ibid., 532–33.
95. Ibid., 534 (emphasis added).
96. Ibid.
97. Ibid., 533–34.
98. Ibid., 536.
99. Ibid., 534.
100. Wallace, *Twenty-Seventh Wife,* 229.
101. Young, *Wife No. 19,* 536; Wallace, *Twenty-Seventh Wife,* 229.
102. Young, *Wife No. 19,* 554.
103. Ibid., 533.
104. Ibid.
105. Ibid., 534.
106. Wallace, *Twenty-Seventh Wife,* 224.
107. Ibid., 230.
108. Young, *Wife No. 19,* 532.
109. Wallace, *Twenty-Seventh Wife,* 228.
110. Young, *Wife No. 19,* 534–35.
111. Ibid., 536.
112. Ibid., 534–36.

113. Wallace, *Twenty-Seventh Wife,* 229.

114. Young, *Wife No. 19,* 537.

115. Wallace, *Twenty-Seventh Wife,* 232.

116. Young, *Wife No. 19,* 537.

117. Ibid., 542.

118. Ibid., 537, 555.

119. Wallace, *Twenty-Seventh Wife,* 19.

120. Woodward, *Bold Women,* 325.

121. Young, *Wife No. 19,* 555; she sued Brigham for $20,000 for legal fees, plus $1,000 per month, plus $200,000 for the care of herself and children. Cf. Wallace, *Twenty-Seventh Wife,* 244–46; the lawyers were expecting to get 50 percent of the suit, but she insisted on a flat rate of $20,000.

122. Wallace, *Twenty-Seventh Wife,* 237.

123. Woodward, *Bold Women,* 325–26.

124. Wallace, *Twenty-Seventh Wife,* 22, 238.

125. Stenhouse, *Tell It All,* 288.

126. Wallace, *Twenty-Seventh Wife,* 244.

127. Young, *Wife No. 19,* 549.

128. Ibid., 546.

129. Stenhouse, *Tell It All,* 288 (emphasis added).

130. Wallace, *Twenty-Seventh Wife,* 412–13.

131. Young, *Wife No. 19,* 549.

132. Ibid., 548.

133. Ibid., 551–52.

134. Ibid., 551.

135. Wallace, *Twenty-Seventh Wife,* 257.

136. Ibid., 256.

137. Young, *Wife No. 19,* 548.

138. Ibid., 569.

139. Ibid., 549.

140. Ibid., 567.

141. Ibid., 547.

142. Wallace, *Twenty-Seventh Wife,* 247.

143. Young, *Wife No. 19,* 569.

144. Wallace, *Twenty-Seventh Wife,* 277.

145. Young, *Wife No. 19,* 551.

146. Wallace, *Twenty-Seventh Wife,* 310–11.

147. Ibid., 311.

148. Ibid., 317.

149. Ibid.

150. Ibid., 250.

151. Ibid., 333.
152. Ibid., 409.
153. Ibid., 333.
154. Woodward, *Bold Women,* 330.
155. Wallace, *Twenty-Seventh Wife,* 396.
156. Woodward, *Bold Women,* 330.
157. Wallace, *Twenty-Seventh Wife,* 410.
158. Ibid., 414.
159. Ibid.
160. Ibid., 411.
161. Ibid.
162. Young, *Wife No. 19,* 568.
163. Wallace, *Twenty-Seventh Wife,* 396.
164. Ibid., 278.
165. Ibid., 413.
166. Young, *Wife No. 19,* 546.
167. Ibid.
168. Ibid., 415.
169. Wallace, *Twenty-Seventh Wife,* 420.
170. Ibid., 416.
171. Ibid., 417.
172. Young, *Life in Mormon Bondage,* 4.
173. Wallace, *Twenty-Seventh Wife,* 427.
174. Young, *Wife No. 19,* 400–401.

Part 2

The Two-Faced Monster

If the double image of Ann Eliza is disturbing, her two Brigham Youngs are nothing short of eerie. For the most part of her life Ann Eliza's mother, a woman given to secret fantasies and morbid brooding, carried about with her (according to her daughter) a perfectly false image of her hero, Brigham Young, "a creature of her imagination, and utterly unlike his real self."[1] Along with that, Mrs. Webb had another idol, her adored and pampered daughter. And the dream of her life was to bring her two idols together in marriage. The daughter, who describes herself as a neurotic and overimaginative child, shared and surpassed her mother's talent for cloud piling, revelling in the vision of wonderful things to come and weeping bitterly when reality failed to match her expectations, as it always did.

But if one can dream of heroes such as never were, cannot one also imagine a corresponding breed of villain? The girl was sure she had heaven on a platter when she got James Dee; but when he failed to deliver he forthwith became no melted chocolate soldier but a walking horror, a swashbuckling hetman, a gloating sadist; henceforth she always spoke of Dee as "the man who 'blighted' her life."[2] Since she admits that the premarital Dee was the simon-pure native product of her own wishful thinking, are we to accept the picture as sober reality when she turns the image neatly inside out? Ann Eliza's third husband was, according to all reports, *before* she met him just such a model father and mate as Dee became *after* she left him; but the moment she married Denning he underwent a hideous transmogrification into an elemental brute. That Ann Eliza certainly did things to men.

Well, between the two D's comes Mr. Big himself, the man from whom mama expected everything—and mama did have a way of letting Ann Eliza in on her little secrets. For him to let our Annie down was to invite a denunciation commensurate with his stature and his crime; only a full-scale epic could do justice to the theme, and that epic, the studied after-thoughts of a woman whose rage and frustration knew no bounds, is the subject of Mr. Wallace's great American novel. But just as Wallace is hard put to keep the real face of Ann Eliza from peeping out at us through his carefully censored pages, so all his piety and wit fail to make his portrait of Brigham Young come to life. The trouble is not that the Prophet is falsely portrayed, but that he is not portrayed at all. This is no living thing; such a creature never moved upon this earth nor in the waters or under the earth. This golem who does Mr. Wallace's bidding, trembling with rage or staring with fascination as he is told to, has nothing in common with the man whose life is as fully documented as that of any figure in our history; to his self-revealing letters, sermons, and deeds, Mr. Wallace prefers the Ann Eliza-Stenhouse image every time. And what is that image?

First, *Brigham the Cad,* either fawning or bullying, "arrogant to his inferiors, and unpleasantly familiar to the very few whom he desires for any reason to conciliate."[3] Mean and ignoble he was: "I do not believe there is anywhere a man so suspicious of his workmen, . . . so anxious to cut their wages."[4] "It don't make any difference whether they are satisfied or not" was the policy.[5] If his assistants slipped up "he cursed them 'in the name of Israel's God'; he ridiculed them in public. . . . Their sole fault was, they had been too faithful to him."[6] He cannot give the most casual instructions without being "sharp and abusive" about it.[7] The only reason his closest friends put up with him is that "their interest and associations bind them to the church."[8] *Heartless* is the word for Brigham: "I believe that, if every friend he had in the world lay before him, cold and still and with frozen pulse, he would look on unmoved and indifferent, and never shed a tear, so utterly heartless is he."[9] Through the years the "faithful friendship" of Ann Eliza's mother was "met, *as a matter of course,* by unkindness and treachery on his side."[10] His children "know nothing of fatherly affection, and . . . they feel, personally, only a dread and fear of him. He never invites their confidences, nor shows himself interested in their affairs." And why not? Because "all this would be quite incompatible with his ideas of prophetic dignity."[11] That means he can't be decent to *any* of his children. When his little granddaughter was poisoned, "Brigham . . . rudely turned him [the doctor] out of doors. . . . The agonized parents dared not interfere, and in a few moments their child died before their very eyes, . . . an innocent victim to the Prophet's egotism and bigotry."[12] Of course it was a different story when *he* took sick: "a doctor is summoned at once; . . . he employed at least half a dozen, . . . so great was his terror, and so absolute his horror of fatal consequences."[13] For like all bullies he is a great coward, who "cringes . . . as a whipped cur" at "any adverse criticism."[14]

His specialty was mistreating the gentle sex, for "he had . . . no conception of feminine delicacy or sensitiveness."[15] He was especially "fond of sneering" at his more "sickly wives," and the fact that one is an invalid "is sufficient to preclude her from receiving care or sympathy from her husband."[16] Many a bride, "unused to toil and hardship, nurtured in luxury, reared in tenderness and love," had wakened up one morning to find herself "ruled over by a grasping, lecherous, heartless tyrant, who laughed at a woman's sorrows and flouted at her wrongs."[17] When wives are discontented "he whines . . .

and mimics them, until they are fairly outraged by his heartless treatment, and their indignation or grief gets the supremacy over their other trouble," and so tranquility reigns again in the household.[18] Only by the spectacle of his own discomfiture did the brute supply his afflicted family with a few moments of emotional release: "As deeply hurt as Emmeline was by his rude boorishness of manner, . . . she could not help being pleased at seeing the punishment he was receiving at the hands of the outraged favorite."[19]

With the image of Brigham the Cad in mind, we are prepared for *Brigham the Criminal,* nothing less, in fact, than "the greatest criminal of the 19th century";[20] "in crafty cunning and malicious shrewdness he is far in advance of any of his associates,"[21] and this has made it possible for him to manage "a great many murders, of which he would probably avow himself entirely guiltless, since his hand did not perform the deed."[22] Mr. Wallace is willing to buy this,[23] though evidence for these thousands of murders on the plains comes from Hickman, who "claims that he did them all at Young's instigation."[24] "What do you suppose I care for the law?" cries the crafty, cunning Brigham. "My word is law here. I wish you distinctly to understand that."[25] In Ann Eliza's book this arch criminal sinks to the lowest depths when he even refuses to pay his hired assassins.[26]

For we must not forget *Brigham the Miser.* As his first counselor and dearest friends said, "Brigham's God is gold. . . . He has become a selfish, cold-hearted tyrant."[27] More than one aged crone "supports herself entirely, independently of the man who has swindled her out of her home and her property,"[28] for "he will do anything for money, or to have his wives get it for him"[29] — a bizarre way of acquiring wealth for an empire-builder, it must be admitted; but that just goes to show. "His avarice is so inordinate that no amount of suffering stands in the way

of his self-enrichment";[30] Indian wars were simply an opportunity "in some mysterious manner to make large sums
of money";[31] the Mormon Battalion was really Brigham's
scheme for getting rich by pocketing every penny of the
soldier's pay, "and if a soldier's wife ventured to ask him
for anything, no matter how trifling it might be, she was
rudely repulsed."[32] "Men who have been in his employ
for years . . . have never received the least remunera-
tion";[33] the Hand-Cart scheme was another "heartless and
mercenary experiment . . . merely to help fill the purses
of a false prophet and his corrupt followers";[34] "indeed,
the entire Hand-Cart expedition was a good speculation
for the President, and helped replenish the prophetic
pocket."[35] No wonder he "rubbed his hands and smiled
with overflowing complacency" as he thought about it.[36]
When missionaries asked for travel money from the huge
missionary fund, "they were coolly told by Brother
Brigham that there was no money for them—'not one
cent'!" On the contrary, the Presiding Bishop *took* forty
dollars from each of them for travel, and promptly trotted
over to Brigham with the loot.[37] When unscrupulous missionaries were able to pick up a sizeable bundle in the
mission field, that was all right with Brigham as long as
he got half the take. " 'Brother Calkins' not only visited
him, but divided the spoils with him, his own share
amounting to several thousand dollars."[38] Another source
of income was the theater: "built by money extorted from
the people for the avowed purpose of erecting a Temple
to God, it, of course, was no expense to him."[39] But the
big bonanza was "the 'church fund,' which virtually means
'Brigham's private purse.' . . . None of it has ever been
appropriated to the cause for which it was supposed to be
intended."[40] While his wives toil at various menial tasks
to support him, "he has $7,000,000 in the Bank of Eng-
land," owns a third of all the property in Utah, and has
an income of "probably much more" than $40,000 per

month.[41] "The story of his sordid avarice and his contemptible meanness in the accumulation of money would fill a volume," writes Mrs. Stenhouse,[42] and though she gives no specific information, you get the sketch from Ann Eliza: "to covet his neighbors' goods is to possess them in some way or other, either honestly or otherwise [go on—finish the sentence!],—generally otherwise."[43] Many were sent on missions and "thus heartlessly ruined and unjustly exiled . . . to gratify the covetousness and grasping of an avaricious tyrant."[44] Three men who "absolutely refused to give up their stock" for one of his projects were chained together in a schoolhouse in Parowan, while Brigham Young took the herd and "sold every one of them to pay a large debt which he owed."[45] He enjoyed this sort of thing, since "he could not endure to see a dollar go into another man's pocket. I believe the sight was positive pain to him."[46] "The Prophet," writes Ann Eliza, "has a most decided objection to seeing any of his followers becoming independent. . . . He always finds some way to put a stop to their growing prosperity."[47] Thus instead of being a great leader and colonizer when he had a chance to, "one of the benefactors of the human race, he has set the *worst example* which despot or false prophet ever presented to the world."[48]

He was able to get away with all this only because he was *Brigham the Tyrant*. The forms of democracy are meaningless "in polygamous Utah, ruled over by a treacherous tyrant."[49] "There is no despotic monarchy in the world where the word of the sovereign is so absolute as in Utah."[50] "The right of suffrage had been not granted, but commanded."[51] "Every person of the female sex, from the babe in the arms to the oldest, bedridden, imbecile crone, has the right of elective franchise, and is compelled to use it."[52] While babes in arms and aged crones were being driven to the polls, "young men, and even boys, were forced, not only into marriage, but even Polygamy, and

none dared resist. . . . Everyone *must* marry."[53] The slightest show of independence brought an instant charge of apostasy or excommunication, "the way in which persons are served even now who venture to disagree with Brigham Young,"[54] and such a charge could mean only one thing — quick and certain death.[55]

But we must not let the enormity of his crimes blind us to the more endearing qualities of Brigham Young as the plain garden variety of *Ignoramus and Boor*. "Brigham

Young is an uneducated man," Stenhouse reports; " . . . his opposition to education in others and to all that is intellectual and elevating does him little credit."[56] Like all Mormon leaders, he "discouraged every attempt at self-improvement" in his followers.[57] The ladies put Young in his place intellectually with a charge so crushing that we hesitate to repeat it: "He was, by trade, a painter and glazier, and has frequently said *in public* that in those times he was glad to work for 'six bits' a day."[58] Of course his manners are atrocious and his vanity ridiculous, "more finical than an old beau, and vainer and more anxious than a young belle, concerning his *personnel*."[59] Having no taste or self-control, "he indulges in the coarsest witticisms, and is not above positive vulgarity and profanity, both in language and manner."[60] He was disgustingly pompous, and "royalty itself could assume no more the manner of receiving only what it is entitled to, than this ex-glazier, who used to work for 'six bits' a day."[61] His gross ignorance and appalling boorishness were not redeemed by any practical good sense, for in his affairs Young was no less than "the Prince of Blunderers."[62] Along with that he was the laziest man alive; indeed, Ann Eliza's only recollection of her grandparents is that her grandfather "used to assert that Brigham was the laziest man that ever lived,"[63] and believe, me, friends, that is something.

But what we are all waiting to hear about is *Brigham Young the Sex Fiend*. Here the ladies let us down badly—but not Mr. Wallace! True, Ann Eliza can testify that her husband, "the monstrous polygamist,"[64] "is filled with moral rottenness to the very core,"[65] and Mrs. Stenhouse cries out, "What decent person could refrain from loathing such a man!"[66] But for specific details we must go to Wallace: "*Fifty-two wives*," he screams in italics.[67] During the last-minute crisis of the exodus from Nauvoo, Wallace's Brigham chose to retire like Paris to the harem and spend his days and nights in abandoned orgies. Wallace ticks off the list of women with a zest and relish rivaling that which he attributes to Brigham Young himself. In one day, in the final climactic crisis of Nauvoo, Brigham married four women. Why, we ask, since Mr. Wallace reports that he never had any progeny by any of the four?[68] Plainly to take them under his protection in the dreadful time ahead— Wallace admits this two hundred pages later, but this is not the time to spoil the fun. On the very next day, he reports wittily, the man married again "almost as an after-thought," and then after just eleven days of "recuperating from his marathon of celestial marriages, Brigham vigorously returned to the altar."[69] Those loaded words "recuperating" and "vigorously" should bring the reader to his senses in case he begins to suspect that this marathon of marriages was dictated by something more than lust.

So we have, summarizing all too briefly, even flippantly, what impassioned writers have devoted whole books to: Brigham Young the beast without a spark of honor, decency, humanity, or charity—mean, unspeakably cruel, resentful, suspicious of all, without a friend in the world; the miser, the murderer, the thief, the absolute tyrant, the oaf, the fop, the Prince of Bunglers, and the laziest man alive; and of course the lecherous degenerate. Wallace labors to make Brigham Young not less a villain but only a more plausible one: his man is just as tricky, greedy, tyrannical, cruel and bloody, and far more lecherous than the earlier and more spectacular Brigham. Yet without seeking beyond these same lurid pages we can discover a Brigham Young totally at variance with the one they have so dramatically described.

Brigham, the Good Guy

First of all it appears between the lines that this Brigham Young was a man of considerable achievement. Wallace minimizes this for all he is worth, passing by in silence Young's own valuable and revealing commentary on events as they occurred and discreetly omitting mention of what the man was really up against and how brilliantly he overcame incredible obstacles. His Brigham Young is simply a heavy-handed, oversexed, rather pompous robber-baron. By admitting that Young did achieve something, the ladies, on the other hand, are hard put to explain how he did it. It was simply by giving the *appearance* of being busy, if we would believe Ann Eliza,[70] that "the laziest man that ever lived," parlayed his "six-bits a day" into "enormous riches."[71] That was possible only because he was lucky, says Stenhouse: the man "whose narrow soul could never look beyond the little circle in which he lived; whose selfishness and heartlessness have been only equalled by his cruelty and degrading avarice, has, by force of circumstance alone, obtained a place in the recognition of the world, to which by nature or by grace he had not the shadow of a claim."[72] It was just the purest luck that he found himself in one nightmare circumstance after another: that marauding bands burned the farms and villages in Illinois and Missouri; that Nauvoo was destroyed in midwinter; that fevers and epidemics swept the camp; that there was a desperate food shortage and totally inadequate supply of animals and vehicles; that the government drafted the five hundred, most able-bodied men at the crucial moment for a march to Mexico; that the saints arrived in the valley completely out of food and supplies in late July of one of the hottest and driest years on record; that mountain fever became general; that restless Indians threatened depredations on all sides; that there were plagues of crickets and grasshoppers; that a swarm of hostile and crooked spies and officials was followed up by the might of the U.S. Army; that calls for extermination of the Mormons in Congress and from the pulpit grew steadily louder, with Ann Eliza's shriek rising above the din.

Even if these were just lucky breaks for Brigham, shouldn't he be given some credit for knowing how to use them? Not a bit of it; it was all *forced* on him: "Experience, and a careful study of his life and doings, have convinced me that he is certainly not a great man or a man of genius in *any* sense of the word."[73] It is not surprising that Mr. Wallace, faced with the thesis that B. Y. did what he did accidentally and quite in spite of himself, chooses to look the other way and forget that the fellow achieved anything at all.

Then there is a little matter of appearances. "To look at the man, rosy and smiling, comfortable in every particular, you would never take him to be the hard, cruel despot he is. He looks clean enough outwardly, but within he is filled with moral rottenness to the very core."[74] We grant that appearances are not everything, but when after a long life of "moral rottenness" a man at the age of seventy-three appears "rosy, smiling, comfortable in every particular," we begin to wonder. "I was much pleased with the manner and appearance of Brigham Young," writes Stenhouse, "and felt greatly reassured; for he did not seem to me like a man who would preach and practice such things. . . . The Prophet made himself very affable. . . . His wives, too, . . . I found, as far as I could judge from such a casual acquaintance, to be amiable and kind-hearted ladies."[75] But that will never do: "I, of course, regarded him from a woman's stand-point; but there were others who were accustomed to study physiognomy, and they detected — or thought they detected — in the cold expression of his eye and the stern, hard lines of his lips, evidences of cruelty, selfishness, and dogged determination which, it is only fair to say, I myself never saw."[76]

But none of those expert physiognomists were in a class with the great Richard Burton, a world traveler and linguist, a master in the art of dealing with pious rogues and religious impostors, who himself had played dangerous masquerades in the East and knew every trick in the book:

I had expected to see a venerable-looking old man.

. . . Scarcely a grey thread appears in his hair. . . . The Prophet's dress was neat and plain as a Quaker's. . . . Altogether the Prophet's appearance was that of a gentleman farmer in New England—in fact, such as he is. . . . He is a well-preserved man, a fact which some attribute to his habit of sleeping . . . in solitude. His manner is at once affable and impressive, simple and courteous: his want of pretention contrasts favorably with certain pseudo-prophets that I have seen. . . . He assumes no airs of extra sanctimoniousness, and has the plain, simple manners of honesty. . . . He has been called hypocrite, swindler, forger, murderer. No one looks it less.[77]

Another and very different man of the world was Horace Greeley, who earlier found Brigham Young "very plainly dressed," with "no air of sanctimony or fanaticism. . . . He is a portly, frank, good-natured, rather thickset man of fifty-five, seeming to enjoy life."[78] Now we can understand why the ladies were so generous in their description of the outer man: because others could see Brigham Young too—here there is a check on their creative powers, which only come into play in situations where they are the only witnesses. The exterior fooled everybody but Ann Eliza. Greeley describes Brigham at fifty-five, Burton at fifty-seven, Stenhouse at seventy-three, Ann Eliza at seventy-four, and to all he is the same placid, cheerful, "frank, good-natured" man. Is that the triumph of hair dye, pancake make-up, or lighting? What human system could survive the "matrimonial spree" that Wallace knows all about[79] and, while "filled with moral rottenness to the very core," present for decade after decade an appearance "comfortable in every particular?"[80] That just proves to Ann Eliza what a total hypocrite he is: "The cunning of his device is shown in the religious mask which he puts upon its frightful face, and the Christian robes with which he hides its horrible deformity."[81] So perfect is the disguise, fooling even a Richard Burton, that the only way one can detect it is to know the man's *motives*. Mrs. Brodie's classic libel of Joseph Smith is based entirely on her intuitive capacity to interpret his motives. According to Trevelyan,[82] Macaulay "had a disastrous habit of attributing motives: he was never content to say that a man did this or that, and leave his motives to conjecture; he must always needs analyze what has passed through the mind of his *dramatis personae* ("actors in the drama"), as if he were the God who had created them."[83] Deny this privilege to your Ann Elizas, Brodies, and Wallaces and what becomes of their stories? Thus Mr. Wallace can assure us that "Brigham *instinctively* understood what most military leaders learn from experience,"[84] when, at the time he is describing, Brigham had had more experience in leadership than any ten generals since Washington.

In order to bring their double images of Brigham Young into focus, mesdames Stenhouse and Young want us to think that the two different men were the same Brigham at different *periods*. "When I first knew him," writes Stenhouse, "he dressed in plain, homespun, homemade and every article about his person and his houses, was as plain and unostentatious as could possibly be."[85] Was that perhaps in Vermont? New York? Kirtland? Nauvoo? No, that was in the 1860s, when Brigham, the total fop, as Woodward describes him, first tried to woo Ann Eliza. For the times when he was a good guy, Ann Eliza herself must go back much farther: "I . . . look back almost to my very babyhood, and contrast Brigham Young as he then was with the Brigham Young of to-day. . . . [His manner] had nothing of the assumption and intolerance which characterize it now. Indeed there was, at that time, a semblance of humility."[86] The lady seems to forget that it is this earlier tolerant Brigham who is the real monster of her story—it is to him she must go for all her atrocity stories up to the horrors of the "Reformation time," it is only the later

Brigham who must watch his step and pine for the days long-passed when the simple drawing of his bowie knife from its sheath meant the immediate demise of a recalcitrant.[87] Well, which was the devil, the young Brigham or the old one? What makes the problem more difficult is that both men seemed to have enjoyed enormous popularity. Which brings us to the problem of—

The Beloved Bogey

Without a single redeeming feature—hard, cruel, vicious, cowardly, treacherous, uncompromising—Brigham Young was still greatly loved and revered by the people. Stranger still, the nearer people were to him the more they loved him. "Most of his daughters worshiped him,"[88] and "strange as it may seem," the wives he treated most savagely revered him as much as any.[89] Ann Eliza has an explanation for that—the women were simply crazy: "What a lapse of memory. . . . Oh, what folly, what inconsistency, what madness!"[90] No one ever catches *her* in such lapses of memory. "New indignation thrilled me as I told my story of bondage, such as my hearers never dreamed of."[91] But even in her account the monster looks suspiciously like a papier-mâché dragon. The man who kept everyone in abject and terrified submission still "never dared to do anything which should advance 'Joe' [his darling son] in the church, for he knew very well that the people would not tolerate it for an instant."[92] He ruled in the most absolute sovereignty on the face of the earth;[93] "whatever he may say or do, no one dares resent his interference."[94] Now turn the page and read along with Annie: "He does not seem to make a very decided impression on his listeners, however; even his wives and daughters following their own inclinations rather than his teachings."[95] If another wife feels disaffected as Ann Eliza does, Brigham lets "her abuse religion and him as much as she pleases behind his back," exactly as Ann Eliza herself did,

while her son "openly expresses his disgust at his hypocrisy and meanness, which he sees through very clearly."[96]

But if Brigham Young is a lax and inefficient tyrant, his suffering victims are even more oblivious to the role they should be playing. They always seem to enjoy their anguish. For two long years the Mormon Battalion "sent all their pay to their families, to the care of Brigham Young," who pocketed every penny of it and "rudely repulsed" any soldier's wife who "ventured to ask him for anything."[97] One would expect some sort of complaint or investigation, or at least that some sly corporal would send his federal pay directly to his wife instead of to John D. Lee (wouldn't you know it?), who, according to Ann Eliza, was the party who always got the money and took it to Brigham. It is all so delightfully frank and brutal—John D. Lee is the crowning touch—that one wonders what need President Young had for his infinite powers of dissemblance. He doesn't even have to try to fool people: "Ignorant as he is, coarse and vulgar as he is, he has at least succeeded in winning women of refinement, of delicate sensibilities, as wives; and in many cases it has been done without the slightest attempt at coercion on his part."[98] When a reporter asked Ann Eliza, "Has Brigham ever used profane language to you?" she replied, "I can't say that he has, but he has used shockingly insulting and grossly vulgar language to me. Oh, sir, he is a vile old creature. I have heard him swear in the pulpit when talking of the Gentiles."[99] The *only* knowledge she has of his vice is what she hears in *public meetings*—a significant admission indeed from the woman who is supposed to have known the man, oh so intimately.

While the people groaned under "the cold-blooded, scheming, blasphemous policy of Young," they rejoiced in his leadership, for "their faith was sublime in its exaltation."[100] "He is met outside of every settlement which he visits" by a full-scale parade, marching under banners and cheering like mad,[101] and none cheered louder than Eliza's own family, though Brigham had kept the family impoverished, separated, discouraged, and toiling in his interests ever since Nauvoo. Through the years Mr. Webb "had no time, of course, to devote to his family, or to labor for its support; he must give his strength, and his time, and his labor to Brigham Young."[102] At the same time Mrs. Webb's "faithful friendship" for Brigham was "met, as a matter of course, by unkindness and treachery on his side."[103] Yet these were the parents who were determined that their daughter, the apple of their eye, should marry

Brigham Young. From the first, however, they made it clear that the girl would not have to marry the man if she really didn't want to, and here is a strange thing. For one year, she says, she fought by every means in her power[104] to avoid having to marry Brigham Young; with what weapons did she fight? She could only think of one argument — the President was too *old* for her.[105]

If Ann Eliza *had known just one really bad thing* about Brigham Young, her parents would never have pressed her to marry him, or even permitted it. Along with that we have her own emphatic and repeated assurance that she knew of nothing wrong with Mr. Young until *after* she married him.[106] True, he was a "monstrous polygamist," but as wife No. 19 she should at least have suspected that. Polygamous yes, monster, no: on the day he proposed (not to her but to her parents) Brigham Young talked long and earnestly with her on the subject of marriage, she says, yet even then she could not even remotely conceive of his having any but a fatherly interest in her. She had lived at the Lion House and knew all about the home life of Brigham Young, whom she and her family had known intimately all her life, and yet nothing was farther from her mind, she says, than the idea that President Young should lust after her — she simply couldn't believe it. And that gives you an idea of the high opinion she had of Brigham Young at the time: she was pleased and delighted, she says, to walk with him; she knew nothing bad about him whatever. Yet by this time his great crimes, including those against her own family, those crimes for which Ann Eliza is our chief informant, were already behind him. Something is badly out of focus.

It Must Have Been Two Other People

But if our portrait of Brigham Young is all awry we can always blame *him* for it. The man is so inconsistent. "In business matters," for example, ". . . his word is as good

as his bond, but in the accumulation of wealth he has
evinced an amount of dishonesty which can scarcely be
credited."[107] It is indeed hard to accept the total dishonesty
of a man whose word is the soul of honor. He "always
meets his obligations, and pays his debts," according to
Stenhouse, ". . . but the way in which he has obtained his
wealth would put to the blush the most dishonest member
of any 'ring' in New York, or elsewhere."[108] This is the
more remarkable since Ann Eliza insists that the man *never*
meets his obligations or pays his debts, but is always legally
correct in his acquisition of wealth. The two ladies tell
diametrically opposed stories. Another inconsistency was
the way the ignorant Brigham would appear "a simple,
easy-talking, courteous gentleman before strangers
but . . . harsh and uncouth with those who are dependent
upon him"[109] — a real Jekyll and Hyde, since nothing short
of a miracle could make an *uncouth* man polished and urbane simply by stepping into the next room.

If Brigham Young the avowed foe of education insists
on having his children study hard, that for Mrs. Stenhouse
is simply another example of "his usual inconsistency"
(not hers but *his*).[110] Ann Eliza in her paraphrase of the
Stenhouse passage tries to remove the inconsistency without success: "Unlettered and uncultured as he is, he recognizes the power of education, and that is why he is such
a bitter opponent to general culture, and why, at the same
time, he takes special care that his own children shall lack
no advantages."[111] Bearing in mind, of course, that he took
no interest whatever in his children, even though he took
time off from his busy schedule to come to Ann Eliza's
fourth birthday party. His children, inheriting this wild
inconsistency, adored their father who, too proud to notice
them, nevertheless gave them earnest lectures and wrote
them long letters. With equal consistency this man who
"detested secrecy in general,"[112] chose to operate all his
days through a secret society — the mysterious Danites; and

though "ill-cast for the role of model polygamist,"[113] he played that role with "surprising (or understandable) zest."[114] Of course the useful word "understandable" makes everything perfectly clear. To show you just how contrary the man can be, "he is . . . as sensitive to public opinion as though he were not constantly defying it."[115] That is, he pays no attention to that public opinion to which he is so keenly sensitive. In short, he was a "turbulent, passionate, shrewd, illiterate, strangely powerful man,"[116] who was at the same time cold, self-possessed, clumsy, bungling, remarkably well-informed, but withal weak and cowardly ("he cringes and crouches in as servile a manner as a whipped cur, when any adverse criticism is passed"),[117] fawning, fickle, mean, vain and vulgar, "the great deceiver," "a remarkable union of compelling power over men and women and repulsive fraud and meanness."[118] Seeing him in action, "you would *never* take him to be the hard, cruel despot he is."[119] Neither would you take Pavlova to be a clumsy ox or Niels Bohr to be feeble-minded. Brigham Young is like the fruit that grows on the apple tree, looks like an apple, tastes like an apple, bears authentic apple seeds — and yet is a lemon. It is no wonder everybody thinks it is an apple, since it passes all known tests for apples — but for those who really know it is a lemon, that only makes its applelike qualities the more repulsive and fraudulent. Ann Eliza Young tells how seasoned journalists come from the East "brimming over with disgust and indignation,"[120] eager to learn the worst about Brigham Young, and how the better they get to know him the more they come to admire him, until soon they are writing the most glowing reports about the man and his work; how Brigham does this Ann Eliza does not know — "I suppose his manner of influencing them differs, but I think it will be readily understood."[121] Will it? Why must she be so evasive if it is so obvious? *At any rate* they call

Brigham an apple, and to that she has only one reply: "It is not true, not one word of it[!]"[122]

The most remarkable treatise on the ambivalence of Brigham Young is Mr. Wallace's account of his marriages. The scene is, to use Mr. Wallace's favorite word, Fabulous. It is the picture of Brigham Young whiling away the hours in Byzantine dalliance while directing almost single-hand-edly the exodus from Nauvoo. Mr. Wallace never bothers to inform himself or his readers as to just what "sealing" and "celestial marriage" are; later on in the book he casually notes that "almost half of the women mentioned were Brigham's spouses in name only,"[123] that in some cases "it is doubtful if their marriage was more than platonic"; he tells of one widow "salvaged by Brigham," and another woman who married him only for the duration of the trek, who at the end of it "had not yet cohabited with Brigham, asked him for an annulment . . . and it was granted."[124] Even a professor of history might find it a little bit odd that all the marrying was done just before the departure from Nauvoo, and that "once established in Salt Lake City, Brigham refrained from further marital acquisitions and temporarily concentrated his energies on organizing a se-cure and civilized community";[125] or as Mrs. Woodward puts it, he was too busy to think about petticoats. But not half so busy as he had been in Nauvoo! At last safe from his enemies, Brigham is free to indulge his lusts and ap-petites in Lucullan leisure—but prefers city-building in-stead. It was only during the Nauvoo crisis that the man chose to go on a sex binge without parallel in the history of the world—trust us to know all about the history of the world.

Here the Mormons are being driven from Illinois in the dead of winter; those mounted marauding mobs that were to become infamous in later years were already at work in cahoots with military and civil officials, inflicting maximum damage; the danger was increasing hourly, and on the

shoulders of one man rested the responsibility for making and carrying out life-and-death decisions. So this man, who proved himself the ablest of leaders in this as in a hundred other dire emergencies, chose this time of all times for his "matrimonial spree."[126] In Nauvoo as at Winter Quarters, "amid chaos Brigham maintained iron discipline and organization,"[127] while he himself was sunk in riotous bouts of debauchery. Even Wallace should wonder just a little bit when he reports that "in the twenty-three days preceding the exodus . . . Brigham married eleven women ranging in age from seventeen to forty-two,"[128] actually marrying seven in seven days running and another four on four successive days. Is that the way of libertines? Must they give their name to the women they carouse with? Must they be equally impartial to young and old? Those acquainted with the arcana of erotic literature tell me that such planned and imaginative debauchery requires before all else time, luxury, relaxation, and privacy — a few things that Brigham Young had less of at this juncture than any man in America. Yet this was the time and place he chose for his great "matrimonial spree," "recuperating" from one bout to "vigorously return" to the next.[129] This is the satyr who is to lust after the fair Ann Eliza a generation later to make a plot for Mr. Wallace.

Notes to Part 2

1. Ann Eliza (Webb) Young, *Wife No. 19; Or, The Story of a Life of Bondage, Being a Complete Exposé of Mormonism, and Revealing the Sorrows, Sacrifices and Sufferings of Women in Polygamy* (Hartford, CT: Dustin, Gilman, 1875), 39.

2. Irving Wallace, *The Twenty-Seventh Wife* (New York: Simon and Schuster, 1961), 150.

3. Young, *Wife No. 19*, 519–20.

4. Ibid., 526.

5. Ibid., 535.

6. Ibid., 226.

7. Ibid., 345.

8. Ibid., 588.

9. Ibid., 516.

10. Ibid., 39 (emphasis added).

11. Ibid., 530.

12. Ibid., 350.

13. Ibid., 351.

14. Ibid., 212.

15. Ibid., 441.

16. Ibid., 491

17. Ibid., 224.

18. Ibid., 392.

19. Ibid., 328.

20. Ann Eliza Young, *Life in Mormon Bondage* (Philadelphia: Aldine, 1908), 197.

21. Young, *Wife No. 19*, 519.

22. Ibid., 269.

23. Wallace, *Twenty-Seventh Wife*, 30.

24. Young, *Wife No. 19*, 270.

25. Ibid., 176.

26. Ibid., 278–79.

27. Ibid., 519.

28. Ibid., 286.

29. Wallace, *Twenty-Seventh Wife*, 308.

30. Young, *Wife No. 19*, 514.

31. Ibid., 162.

32. Ibid., 165.

33. Ibid., 526.

34. Ibid., 214.

35. Ibid., 225.

36. Ibid., 214.

37. Ibid., 169–70.

38. Ibid., 596.

39. Ibid., 381.

40. Ibid., 521.

41. Wallace, *Twenty-Seventh Wife*, 308.

42. Mrs. T. B. H. (Fanny) Stenhouse, *Tell It All: The Story of a Life's Experience in Mormonism* (Hartford, CT: Worthington, 1874), 272.

43. Young, *Wife No. 19*, 234.

44. Ibid., 175.

45. Ibid., 162–64.

46. Ibid., 344.

47. Ibid., 174.

48. Stenhouse, *Tell It All*, 274 (emphasis added).

49. Young, *Wife No. 19*, 93.

50. Ibid., 308.

51. Ibid., 94.

52. Ibid.

53. Stenhouse, *Tell It All*, 321.

54. Young, *Wife No. 19*, 92.

55. For general tone, see ibid., 277–78.

56. Stenhouse, *Tell It All*, 269.

57. Ibid., 270.

58. Ibid., 265 (emphasis added).

59. Young, *Wife No. 19*, 520.

60. Ibid., 135.

61. Ibid., 428.

62. Ibid., 221.

63. Ibid., 469.

64. Young, *Life in Mormon Bondage*, 477.

65. Young, *Wife No. 19*, 269.

66. Stenhouse, *Tell It All*, 281.

67. Wallace, *Twenty-Seventh Wife*, 356.

68. Ibid., 85.

69. Ibid.

70. Young, *Wife No. 19*, 285.

71. Stenhouse, *Tell It All*, 274.

72. Ibid., 266.

73. Ibid.

74. Young, *Wife No. 19*, 269.

75. Stenhouse, *Tell It All*, 263–64.

76. Ibid., 264.

77. Wallace, *Twenty-Seventh Wife*, 92–93.

78. Ibid., 88.

79. Ibid., 84–87.

80. Young, *Wife No. 19*, 269.

81. Ibid., 329.

82. George M. Trevelyan, *Clio, A Muse, and Other Essays* (London: Longmans, Green, 1930).

83. Ibid., 45–46.

84. Wallace, *Twenty-Seventh Wife*, 191 (emphasis added).

85. Stenhouse, *Tell It All*, 291.

86. Young, *Wife No. 19*, 517.

87. Ibid., 520.

88. Wallace, *Twenty-Seventh Wife*, 265.

89. Young, *Wife No. 19*, 124–25.

90. Ibid.

91. Ibid., 572.

92. Ibid., 471.

93. Ibid., 308.

94. Ibid., 129.

95. Ibid., 131–32.

96. Ibid., 488.

97. Ibid., 164–65.

98. Ibid., 464.

99. Wallace, *Twenty-Seventh Wife*, 257.

100. Young, *Wife No. 19,* 204.
101. Ibid., 427.
102. Ibid., 336.
103. Ibid., 39.
104. Ibid., 444.
105. Ibid., 443.
106. Ibid., 441.
107. Stenhouse, *Tell It All,* 271.
108. Ibid.
109. Wallace, *Twenty-Seventh Wife,* 254.
110. Ibid., 271.
111. Young, *Wife No. 19,* 527.
112. Wallace, *Twenty-Seventh Wife,* 80.
113. Ibid., 81.
114. Ibid., 83.
115. Young, *Wife No. 19,* 520.
116. Ibid., 456.
117. Ibid., 212.
118. Wallace, *Twenty-Seventh Wife,* 371.
119. Young, *Wife No. 19,* 269 (emphasis added).
120. Ibid., 394.
121. Ibid.
122. Ibid.
123. Wallace, *Twenty-Seventh Wife,* 356.
124. Ibid., 86–87.
125. Ibid., 87.
126. Ibid., 84.
127. Ibid., 65.
128. Ibid., 84.
129. Ibid., 85.

Part 3

How to Write an
Anti-Mormon Book
(A Handbook for Beginners)

Having read thus far, the student is now prepared to give serious thought to a few *general rules* observed by all successful writers in this fascinating and lucrative field. The rules are best exemplified in the works we have been studying. They are as follows.

RULE 1: *Don't be modest!* Your first concern should be to make it clear that *You are the man for the job,* that amidst a "mass of lies and contradictions" you are uniquely fitted to pass judgment: "I emerged from my researches . . . with my objectivity unblurred," writes Mr. Wallace. "If I enjoyed or suffered any deviations from neutral observer, they were slight." "During close to three years of intensive research on Ann Eliza, and on her Church, I became neither anti-Mormon nor pro-Mormon."[1] The ingenuous reader might suppose that the only way to avoid either accepting *or* rejecting the claim to modern-day revelation is to leave it strictly alone, not to write a book about it. That is all the more reason for you to get in there and stake your claim; make it clear that here at last is one capable of preserving perfect objectivity where all others have failed. That is high tribute indeed to be paying to one's self, but don't hesitate to bestow it; to leave it to others to judge of *your* qualification is sheer suicide. No successful anti-Mormon writer could be guilty of such negligence.

RULE 2: *A benign criticism of your predecessors* will go far

towards confirming your own preeminence in the field.
Refer gently but firmly to the bias, prejudice, and inadequate research, however unconscious or understandable,
of other books on the subject. The student would do well
to study Mr. Wallace's technique here; how skillfully he
reprimands Ann Eliza Young without jeopardizing her
value as a source when he chides: "The prose was marred
by unremitting hysteria"![2] The ordinary reader might get
the impression that a work of unremitting hysteria is hardly
to be recommended as an unimpeachable historical source,
but since Mr. Wallace depends on Ann Eliza for nearly all

of his history, he sagely limits the damage of her unremitting hysteria to its effect on the lady's *prose*—a secondary consideration by all counts.

RULE 3: *Curtsies and bouquets to everyone* can be delivered in a profuse and unctuous appendix or introduction and go a long way toward establishing the image of the writer as a really good fellow who admires and respects everybody and is therefore the last man in the world to distort or exaggerate. What could be more magnanimous and disarming than Mr. Wallace's master stroke, a favorite device of anti-Mormon writers: "I want to acknowledge, also, my thanks to a number of high-ranking Mormon Church officials whose objective cooperation might be misunderstood and whose names I am not at present at liberty to reveal."[3] A master stroke because it has the manifold advantage of resting the author's case on the highest possible authority while insuring him against the risk of ever having to produce evidence; at the same time it makes him appear not only conscientious and well informed, but a very noble fellow to the bargain. If he is challenged to give specific information, the writer merely enhances his prestige by refusing to name anybody.

A Word of Caution! Don't overdo your own buildup! The worst mistake J. C. Bennett ever made was to preface his book against Joseph Smith (an invaluable gold mine of information for all anti-Mormon writers) with a large number of character references and a portrait of himself in the attitude of Napoleon. Does an honest man need fifteen pages of testimonial to his honesty? One might well wonder if Mr. Wallace's appendix with its fervid protestations of goodness, truth, and nobility might not raise a few eyebrows, or whether the portrait of the great-man-in-repose on the back dust cover of his book, surpassing even that of Bennett for sheer grandeur, might not inspire more wonder than awe in irreverent breasts.

RULE 4: *Proclaim the purity of your motives,* especially

GEN. JOHN C. BENNETT,
Doctor of Medicine.

your freedom from mercenary considerations. But again, don't overdo it! Mrs. Ann Eliza Webb Dee Young Denning has only shocked incredulity for those who could even hint that she should write for money.[4] But is it a crime to write for money? Does Mr. Wallace need to go so far as to assure us that he gave three years of his life and a sizeable outlay of cash in the disinterested cause of "preser[ving] a remarkable woman for history"? It is hard to keep a dry eye as we read of how a large staff "gave so selflessly of

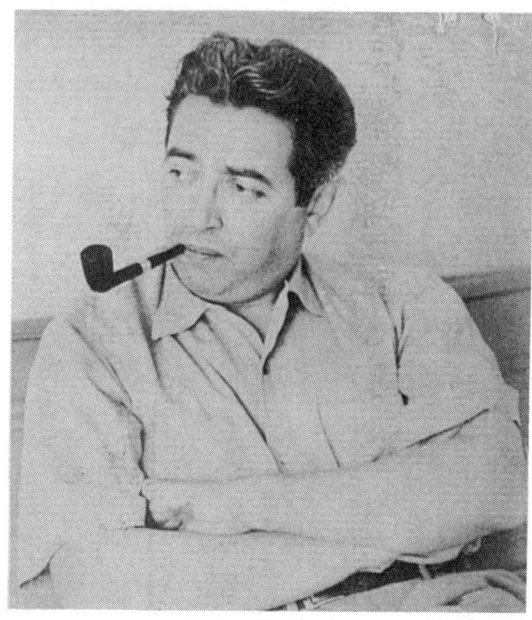

Irving Wallace

their time and energies to collaborate with me"[5] in the cause of truth. Granted that Wallace was "fascinated by the woman herself,"[6] the captious reader might nonetheless ask: Was the woman really *that* remarkable? Is there anything in her book that is not in Mrs. Stenhouse's book? Does she ever display the slightest sign of originality or the feeblest spark of humor? And as for heroism, did she ever take a step or say a word without having first assured herself of perfect immunity? Is there a sentence in her whole book that is not trite, hackneyed, and stereotyped? True, the lady is not without an element of interest—a more gaudy case for the psychiatrist would be hard to imagine—but Wallace will not touch that part of the story. Is he really so very interested in the woman? The student should avoid such a Simon-pure posture; the merchant who keeps reminding us what a wonderful bargain we are getting can arouse our suspicions.

Still, within bounds, a gracious and appealing protestation of pure goodness can be effective. "I . . . have tried to adhere to the two-sided facts as I found them. I tried to interpret these facts and recounted her story, with all its contradictions, as truly as I could tell it."[7] Doesn't that sound good? What does it mean? one may ask. Read it again. It means nothing. What is a two-sided fact? What fact cannot be interpreted two ways? This simple, open-hearted avowal of integrity would be equally valid if applied to the writer's rendering of a Sogdian text: "I have *tried*," he could write with perfect truth, "to interpret this text, with all its obscurity and mystery, as well as I possibly could." What more could any reader ask? Mr. Wallace will now entertain us with a cello solo, and no laughs, please, in case he has never handled a cello in his life — after all, he is doing the best he honestly can under the circumstances. Where is the evidence that Joseph Smith "swore, . . . drank, and whored"?[8] Never mind; Mr. Wallace, detached and impartial, is doing his best for all of us.

RULE 5: *Proclaim your love for the Mormon people.* Even Ann Eliza does this touchingly and often: "I feel that I must pay this tribute to the Mormon people. Naturally, they were a law-abiding, peace loving, intensely religious people";[9] "humble, spiritual-minded, God-fearing, law-abiding";[10] "their faith was sublime in its exaltation,"[11] etc. All this is very well, but even the beginner should see the impasse into which this can lead us, as when Mrs. Young says that Joseph Smith never "ceased his injunctions" to these good people to commit rape and rapine — and that they always obeyed him without hesitation![12] On the same page on which she declares her undying love for the Mormon people, Mrs. Young issues the call: "Mormonism is entitled to no mercy; it invites fire and the sword. The American people must therefore continue their holy crusade against this antichristian system."[13] But who could possibly be the victims of the fire and sword if not her beloved Mormon people? Mr. Wallace avoids this glaring inconsistency by dimming the glare: his praises and damnings are both fainter: on the bad side he makes the Mormons appear more ridiculous than monstrous, and on the good side he sees far less to admire in them than even Ann Eliza or Stenhouse do. The student will recognize here the touch of *Life-Time-Fortune* journalism, enhancing the writer's own superiority at the expense of all he describes. If you can't love the Mormons, at least (and this is our next rule):

RULE 6: *Allow the Mormons a few normal human failings.* That will make your story more plausible, establish you as a fair-minded and tolerant reporter, and so render your verdict all the more damning when you choose to lower the beam. Observe how candid Mr. Wallace can be when he writes, "I am certain that polygamy had its good points, too—but then I am a male."[14] That is both cute and disarming, and at the same time a very effective bit of slander, branding polygamy as nothing but a form of sexual indulgence.

The image of yourself as a person of boundless charity and perfect integrity will be wasted, however, unless you also establish your scholarly qualifications.

RULE 7: *Furnish documents!* "Nowadays," writes H. R. Trevor-Roper, "to carry conviction, a historian must document, or appear to document, his formal narrative."[15] In former times documentation was largely the work of imaginative engravings: thus in Mrs. Young's book we behold serried ranks of finely uniformed dragoons in flawless drill formation, their banners proudly flying, advancing on the huddled victims of the Mountain Meadows massacre; or we see the huge victory parade celebrating the murder of the widow Jones in Payson; Mr. Beadle shows us actual drawings of "Hickman killing Yates, by order of Brigham Young,—Hosea Stout holding the lantern,"[16] of "Hickman delivering the murdered man Yates' money to Brigham

Though this picture of the Mountain Meadows Massacre may excite skeptical comments from some, it is nonetheless an exact reproduction of the artists' original drawing, and it is taken right from A. E. Young's book.

HICKMAN KILLING YATES, BY ORDER OF BRIGHAM YOUNG,—HOSEA STOUT HOLDING THE LANTERN.

HICKMAN DELIVERING THE MURDERED MAN YATES' MONEY TO BRIGHAM YOUNG TO BE TURNED
OVER TO THE CHURCH.

Young,"[17] etc. These drawings are, however, no longer acceptable as evidence. In fact, viewed with a critical eye, they tend rather to discredit than corroborate the tales they illustrate. Therefore modern scholars like Wallace, while telling the identical *stories,* consciously or otherwise omit illustrations that show only too plainly how little the original tellers bothered themselves about the truth.

In their place *photographs* are a must. An actual photograph of Brigham Young, of the Lion House, of the Beehive House, "a reproduction of the title page of Ann Eliza's sensational exposé of polygamy"[18] — Wallace has them all, and what could get nearer to the source than that? It makes no difference that the librarian in any public library could come up with a number of such photographs in ten minutes — nobody is going to ask where you got them as long as they are the real thing. The subject of your reproductions is not important: cartoons lampooning Brigham Young,

Mysteries of Mormonism — This is a documentary study of Mormonism. It is illustrated by actual pictures.

portraits of anybody connected in any way with the history or even with the place or time of its occurrence, scenic views, locomotives, patented machines, famous catastrophes, theater placards, menus, photographs of buildings — anything will do to show that you, so to speak, were there. Anti-Mormon writers long ago discovered the wisdom of inserting neutral, stuffy little items amid all the lurid engravings — dull picture-postcard views of the Great Salt Lake, the Tabernacle, Main Street, Salt Lake City, the Wasatch Mountains, etc., reassure the reader that all this is very sober and correct, giving substance to what would

MORMON LIFE.

Note the caption to these valuable engravings. This is Mormon life. The man on the left is about to interrupt a private discussion: Mormon men have bad manners. How many women are hoeing in the field? What would happen if the man turned his back?

otherwise appear much too imaginative. The student will notice that nearly all of Mr. Wallace's illustrations are of this dull, factual sort — showing that Mr. Wallace is leaning over backwards to be plain, matter-of-fact, and unsensational. No one can accuse *him* of embellishing a story!

RULE 8: *Avoid footnotes!* This is not only the easiest but also the safest rule to follow. The student who compares Mrs. Brodie's footnotes with the actual sources indicated by them will quickly appreciate the wisdom of Wallace in simply lumping his sources together in an appendix. Seeing them in that form, the reader assumes that the author has read with equal care all the books and articles named and made proper and proportionate use of each, never suspecting that in reality, roughly ninety percent of Mr. Wallace's information comes right from Ann Eliza her-

A MORMON HOME RULER.

After the honeymoon depicted in the upper picture, the family settles down to ordinary domestic life as shown below. Whose skull is on the door? How many weapons do you see?

self. So remember — an appendix instead of footnotes! And here is the primary rule for that:

RULE 9: *Be lavish in your appendix!* Pour it on! Name everybody and everything: Mr. Wallace speaks his gratitude to people who are quite unaware of having been accessory to his performance and by no means pleased at finding themselves among his valued informants. Never mind: nobody is going to protest having nice things said about him — who but a heel *would* protest? Thank one and

The man in the upper picture is without his whip, but he keeps a firm grip on his knife. If the man in the lower picture dozes he may drop his whip, and then what will happen?

MAKING THEM USEFUL.

all for valuable assistance and express regrets at having to pass hundreds more by in silence. Name every library at which you or your assistants have thumbed through a card catalogue or inquired at the desk as having rendered eager and invaluable assistance. Make it appear that your project was something of a national crusade in which not only your assistants "gave so selflessly of their time and energies to collaborate with me," but even "several hundred organizations of every description co-operated in answering inquiries."[19] Who would not accept such a book at face value if only to show a decent respect for those *hundreds* of high-minded organizations?

WAITING FOR THE OLD MAN.

Study this picture carefully. It is a typical scene in a Mormon household. The bottles on the bed should not be misinterpreted. If you look carefully you will notice that they are used to hold candles. Mormon women do not drink.

RULE 10: *Be a name dropper!* The average reviewer is the last person in the world to be seriously critical of sources (why should he seek for trouble?) and will be only too glad to go along with a writer who is good enough to include real names from time to time among the usual harvest of "it is said," "it was reported," "it was believed," etc. These handy devices are employed as eagerly and as effectively by Mr. Wallace (usually to conceal the fact that his source is just more Ann Eliza) as by the ladies he follows. Note how impressively Mr. Wallace refers to the "magnificent Ann Eliza, Major Pond, and James Redpath correspondence"[20] — without ever bothering to quote from it. When he tells us that he learned about Ann Eliza's elder brother from a living witness, "Joe T. Place, of Duncan, Arizona," who had known Gilbert well, what reader is going to ask how well Mr. Place would have known the middle-aged Gilbert seventy years before? When he assures us that he

"CHURCH" STORE—*MUST* BE RIGHT!

There is a slight flaw in this scene of normal life among the Mormons (supplied by Mrs. Stenhouse). One of the men seems to be holding a cigar. Mormon men do not smoke.

has learned about Ann Eliza's world from "old settlers" in Salt Lake City,[21] who is going to stop and ask how well they could have known the lady who had left town *eighty-five* years before? As A. E. Housman reminds us, the public is only too eager not to ask such questions if a writer will only follow its rules.

RULE 11: *Control your sources!* When, for example, Ann Eliza brings a particularly damning and patently false charge of murder against Brigham Young, Mr. Wallace dismisses it with a good-natured chuckle: "But it must be remembered that at this time Ann Eliza was an angry wife."[22] With even greater skill he brushes off a very serious matter of ghostwriters. After parading Bill Hickman as his star witness against the Danites, he casually mentions, two hundred pages later, that Hickman's story was ghostwritten by J. R. Beadle, "a frequently impoverished editor and hack,"[23] and of course makes no mention of Beadle's state-

This is not a picture of St. Peter's Square during a Jubilee Year but of an ordinary visit of Brigham Young to a tiny Mormon village. How many people can you count? Well try, stupid! Then guess! Ha, that is approximately 4 1/3 times the population of Utah (from *Wife No. 19*).

ment that he was given a free hand to "fix up" the Hickman story—well, did anybody ask? Even more gingerly does he mention in a single sentence the extremely significant fact that Beadle was Ann Eliza's own ghostwriter. Just how far does this go? Mr. Wallace spares us such irksome details. What does it mean when he tells us, "Almost all of the material supporting Ann Eliza's point of view against Brigham Young or the church was obtained from non-church sources"?[24] Examine that statement. Until the day she fled the Mormons, Ann Eliza (so she emphatically insists) knew nothing whatever about Gentiles, and they knew even less about her—what "non-church sources" then could there possibly be for her history? Ah, that is just the point! Look again. It is not her history, but her *"point of view"* that Mr. Wallace is able to document, and come to think of it—*any* anti-Mormon book ever writ-

The authenticity of this damning document (furnished by Mrs. Sten-house) is as obvious as its originality. Describe the scene. Is the woman in the picture cool? Is she detached? That proves that her story is scientifically accurate.

ten will "support" Ann Eliza's *point of view* "against the church."

RULE 12: *Wave your credentials!* Remind the reader from time to time of your "years of intensive research." If you need high authorities you can always promote your helpers to meet the demand. Note with what easy dominion Mr. Wallace not only bestows the doctorate on one Wilford Poulson, M.A., for his welcome gossip, but with it the title of "Foremost living authority on Mormonism," heading the parade of the "host of scholars" (unnamed) who instructed Mr. Wallace "on various aspects of the Mormon past." Only a cavilling pedant and relative of Mr. Poulson, such as the writer, would ask how one who had never contributed a page to the immense scholarly and pseudoscholarly literature of Mormonism could be classed as the foremost authority in the field.

DRIVEN FROM HOME.

A moving incident reproduced in Mrs. Young's book. It is highly authentic and of course has no connection with a similar scene in Mrs. Stenhouse's book. Or do you think it has? That is impossible because this woman is wearing shoes.

RULE 13: *Establish immediate intellectual ascendancy* by opening your book, as is the fashion, with a tremendous blast of meticulous erudition to intimidate the reader and discourage any smart-aleck questions. Set the scene by telling about the century in which your characters lived: "This was the time when stout, stuffy little Victoria might be seen bustling with fifty trunks [have assistant look up exact number—it was usually reported in the newspapers] between Balmoral [be sure to spell it right!] and wherever it was, . . . when the lights would be burning late in whatever street it was on which Pasteur had his laboratory [don't mention Paris—flatter the reader's erudition],

. . . when Daniel Home the wizard was electrifying whatever crowned heads he was electrifying with his magic feats, . . . when Walter Pater with a white rose was discoursing to, . . . " etc., etc. There is no end to this sort of thing; you can look up all the details or have somebody else do it; and when you have gathered a fat handful of note cards, throw them smartly in the reader's face before he gets to page twenty: that will cut him down to size if he is the kind who asks questions. Beat the critical reader to the punch; show him that you are up to his tricks and will thank him to trust your scholarship from here out. Mr. Wallace informs us by page two that "almost all Americans knew" that "a similar polygamy" to that of the Court of Siam was practiced in Utah, and "that the Vermont-born leader of this colony had twenty-seven wives and fifty-six children."[25] Dear me, did "almost *all* Americans" really know that? But before we can even ask, Mr. Wallace in the next sentence has changed the subject: " 'Modern Mohammedanism,' Francis E. Willard, the temperance crusader, would write in Chicago, 'has its Mecca at Salt Lake.' "[26] When "would" he write it? Why Willard? What has Chicago to do with it? Never mind, the next sentence changes the subject as we are swept along breathless, exhilarated, and somewhat abashed by the man's sheer erudition.

RULE 14: *Have something new to sell.* Every anti-Mormon writer is selling what has already been sold again and again, like Mr. Wallace, peddling old clothes in a shiny new pushcart. See to it that your pushcart looks shiny and new! To do this you must add some ingredient of your own. Mr. Wallace begins his book by noting that "it is a curious fact of history" that in the year 1873 Ann Eliza Young divorced Brigham Young and in the *same* year Mrs. Anna H. Leonowens published her book on life in a Siamese harem.[27] It is true that Mr. Wallace, having pointed out this amazing coincidence, never refers to it again, but

it has served its purpose—his book can now be recommended as an original contribution and he can proceed to sell *Wife No. 19* all over again with a free conscience.

RULE 15: *Get an inside track!* Aside from your personal qualifications and zeal, you must enjoy the position of a privileged observer. No one, but no one, according to Mrs. Stenhouse, has any business writing on Mormonism except a "woman who *really* was a Mormon and lived in Polygamy," i.e., Mrs. Stenhouse. Mrs. A.E.W.D.Y. Denning agrees. But where does that leave us? All the other anti-Mormon books, according to Stenhouse, "with but one exception," were books whose fraudulence could "in a moment be detected by any intelligent Saint who took the trouble to peruse them."[28] But how can one become intimate with the Mormons and still avoid the dangerous proximity of any intelligent Saint? The answer is simple and obvious: follow Mr. Wallace's example and take as your informant one "who had once been an orthodox Mormon and had then become a bitter anti-Mormon"![29] The whole corpus of anti-Mormon literature rests foursquare on the testimony of people who claim they were *once* good Mormons. To get an inside track you have simply to latch on to one of these, and they are not hard to find. The fact that any intelligent Saint would recognize in a moment that Ann Eliza Young was never anything remotely resembling an orthodox Mormon should be a warning to keep one's distance from informants who are still Mormons.

RULE 16: *Don't answer questions!* Remember the useful phrase "But as this comes from a Mormon source it must be discounted." When skilled and experienced newspapermen put some of Ann Eliza's claims to the test and found Brigham Young and the Mormons very different from the way she described them, she simply replied, "It is not true, not one word of it!"[30] If the Mormons "deny all Bennett's statements," made before she was born, the lady can still counter directly: "They knew perfectly well that the greater portion of them was true."[31] Which portion? How does she know? Well, Mr. Smarty, if you must know, she was *born* a Mormon. Being a Lutheran or Catholic or Episcopalian has never been held to mark one an authority on those religions, but from the days of Nancy Towle to those of Irving Wallace, merely to have talked to a Mormon face to face somehow qualifies one as an expert on the subject.

Actually nothing is easier than to avoid questions. Remember the words of A. E. Housman:

> The average reader knows hardly anything about textual criticism, and therefore cannot exercise vigilant control over the writer: the addle-pate is at liberty to maunder and the impostor is at liberty to lie. And, what

is worse, the reader often shares the writer's prejudices
and is far too well pleased with his conclusions to examine either his premises or his reasoning.[32]

Bear in mind that you are in complete control: that the
Mormons can say only what *you* choose to let them say.
Who would guess from a perusal of Mr. Wallace's or Mrs.
Brodie's pages that Joseph Smith or Brigham Young ever
had anything significant to say for themselves, let alone
that they were the most articulate and lucid of men?

RULE 17: *In place of evidence use Rhetoric!* When one is
making grave criminal charges, either directly or by broad
implication as all anti-Mormon writers do, questions of
evidence can be very bothersome unless one has the wisdom and foresight to avoid all such questions. Surprisingly
enough, this can be done rather easily. As Housman has
just reminded us, the writer who is telling the public what
it wants to hear will never have to answer embarrassing
questions about evidence. The ancients discovered that any
public prefers rhetoric to evidence, and the modern historian will soon learn the truth of the time-tested and
timeworn maxim of the Doctors of old, that rhetoric and
not truth is the key to success in this world. The basic
principles of the classical rhetorical method are two: (1)
eikos, that is, the building up of a case not on facts but on
probabilities, and (2) the use of *loci communes,* standard
responses to standard situations (hence our word "com-
monplace"), the appeal to familiar stock phrases to avoid
thought and the use of emotive words of tested reliability
to avoid evidence. We can illustrate how these two principles work together in a situation which we shall call "The
House That Jack Built":

1. It is common knowledge that Jack built a house. It
is that house which we are now discussing.

2. There are rumors that a good deal of malt—very
probably stolen—was stored in the house. What lends

plausibility to the report is the building of the house itself — by Jack. Why a house, if not to store the stolen malt?

3. It is said that the malt was eaten by rats, and in view of the high nutriment content of malt (see Appendix A for references to scholarly and scientific studies proving beyond a doubt that malt is nutritious), there is no good reason for doubting this report.

4. The rats may very possibly have been killed by a cat, as some believe, and there is certainly nothing intrinsically improbable in the event. On the contrary, studies made at the Rodent Institute of the University of So and So, etc. . . . The report that only *one* rat ate the malt is of course erroneous, since the consumption of such a large quantity of malt would require many years and probably a large number of rats.

5. That the cat was chased by a dog is only to be expected. Only a fanatic would question it.

6. The same applies to the dog's being tossed by a cow, though that is admittedly a less common event.

7. *"At any rate"* (a very useful expression) we can be reasonably certain that the cow was milked by a milk-maid — what other kind of maid could it have been? — and also (since there is no good reason to doubt it) that the milkmaid, whose name may have been Bertha, was wooed by a man all tattered and torn. There are unmistakable references in the newspapers of the time (or at most a generation later) to poorly dressed men known as "tramps" roaming parts of the country. There can therefore be little doubt that Bertha was engaged in a passionate public wooing.

8. The exact date of Bertha's marriage to her tatter-demalion lover is not known, though it *may* have been some time late in January 1858. Certainly the court records of the time are silent on any earlier or later marriage.

9. Though there is no direct evidence that Bertha was mistreated by the man who wooed her so passionately, there is every evidence of cruel neglect both in the proven fact that Bertha apparently had no house to live in (at least there is no record of her having a house in the county archives) and in the character of the man who married and abused her.

It will hardly be necessary to point out to the student the solid advantage of such little touches as "the *exact* date . . . " in No. 8. Since no date at all is known, it is perfectly true to say that the exact date is not known, implying that an approximate date is known: "it *may* have been in January 1858" — true again, perfectly true — it may also have been in September 1902 or May 1320. Again, if there is no evidence whatever that Bertha was mistreated (or even that she existed), it is both shrewd and correct to say that there is no *direct* evidence, implying, while not saying, that there is plenty of indirect evidence. Let the student check the above ten points for evidence. There is none! We have given the world a suffering Bertha and her brutal spouse without having to prove a thing; it is all *eikos* — we have created a little world of our own, and got the reader so emotionally involved that he is ready to lynch the man-all-tattered-and-torn or any of his followers without bothering to ask whether he even existed or not.

This brings up another important point: if one can only show that the man *did* exist, that he was a real flesh-and-blood person, then *everything* we have said about him is somehow proven true. Joseph Smith and Brigham Young really lived — who then can doubt the truth of Mrs. A.E.W.D.Y. Denning's history or of Mr. Wallace's repetition of it? Let us see how Mr. Wallace reconstructs the sex lives of Joseph Smith and Brigham Young to make the cornerstone of his whole history. First Smith:

> The Prophet had been *intrigued* by the polygamic practices of Abraham, Jacob, Solomon, and David. *There is little doubt* that he sincerely believed that the plural-wife system . . . was the God-favored system of marriage. *Beyond* this *there may have been* decisive *personal factors* that *influenced* him. *Quite possibly* his juiceless and forbidding wife. . . . *Evidently* Smith had a roving eye. . . . *Yet* his stern puritanical upbringing did not give him the easy conscience of a rake. He could not allow himself mistresses. And so, *possibly,* to have his cake and eat it, too, he allowed himself a plurality of wives. *However* . . . Smith *realized* that he could only make it acceptable for himself if he made it acceptable to his wide following. . . . *Or perhaps,* as the Mormons insist, none of this elaborate intrigue was necessary, for Smith *did* receive an order from on high. *At any rate* . . . Smith began to devote himself to premature polygamy.[33]

Note that every sentence here is speculative, every word which we have put into italics is an escape hatch in case one should ask Mr. Wallace for evidence; notice how the artist constantly shifts his ground, appearing by the use of the right transitional word to be adding evidence when he is really changing the subject: thus his final "however" turns a whopping contradiction into an apparent confirmation, and his closing "at any rate," which simply admits that none of the above is proven, seems to be summing up a rigorous presentation of evidence. But the master stroke is the sentence in which Wallace himself employs the italics: "Or perhaps, as the Mormons insist . . . Smith *did* receive an order from on high." This is the well-known rhetorical trick of generously presenting one's hearers with an alternative, but an alternative so ridiculous and fantastic that they have no choice but to accept one's own explanation and stop asking questions: "So what if there isn't any evidence? Just look at the alternative!"

Mr. Wallace employs the same technique on Brigham Young:

> Because Chauncey [Ann Eliza's father] had risen in the community, Brigham Young considered him a valuable Mormon. As such, Chauncey was ordered to serve a tour of duty as a missionary in Sheffield, England. Tied closer to the Church than ever by polygamy, . . . Chauncey was forced to comply. [On his mission, he] decided (without too much pain, it may be assumed) [that an English wife] might be more decorative than the home-grown product.[34]

The whole story is built up on the simple fact that Webb went on a mission: all the motives and the mind reading are supplied by Wallace himself with his busy word shuffling—"Because . . . considered . . . as such . . . ordered . . . tied closer . . . forced to comply . . . decided . . . it may be assumed . . . " It is all the purest House-That-Jack-Built.

RULE 18: *Use lack of evidence as evidence!* No knack is more useful than that of turning one's lack of information into a definite asset in dealing with the Mormons. For example, the involvement of the Church in the Mountain

Meadows massacre raises a number of quite unanswerable questions; note, then, how cleverly Mrs. Stenhouse admits that fact while turning it to a new incrimination against the Mormons: "No answer can be returned to these questions without disclosing secret scenes of sin and shameful iniquity at the mention of which even the souls of fiends might stand aghast."[35] Does that answer your question? Remember, the worst crimes are those for which there is *no* evidence even that a crime was committed: "There were crimes then perpetrated in secret which will never be known until the Day of Doom."[36] "I say *nothing* of those of whose fate *nothing*—not even a whisper—was ever heard."[37] Two nothings make a wonderful story. What can be safer or more convenient than to rest one's case on charges of which one admittedly knows nothing and is determined to say nothing? The argument of silence is useful, as when Ann Eliza demonstrates Brigham Young's culpability in one crime by the "significant fact that no one has preserved more utter silence on the subject than the 'Revelator,' Brigham Young."[38] The argument of absence is even more significant: So-and-so must have been murdered by Brigham Young, "All sorts of rumors were afloat respecting his disappearance. . . . At all events, he has never appeared to interfere."[39] Baptiste the grave-robber belongs to the floating riff-raff of the frontier: "Some said that he was put on a little island in the lake, and left to perish. Others said that Porter Rockwell looked after his interests. But *certain* it is that he 'disappeared,' and was never seen again."[40] Baptiste didn't just disappear, he "disappeared," just as nobody is killed by Indians but only by "Indians" in Mr. Wallace's book. We should point out that Mr. Wallace himself spent a good deal of time and money trying to find out whatever became of his heroine Ann Eliza, a figure of national importance—well, if you must know, she disappeared. People sometimes do, but when they disappear from the Mormon scene it is silly to waste such valuable and incriminating evidence.

Take the case of the missing $3,000 a year. Brigham Young, "a year before her marriage," verbally and privately promised Ann Eliza an allowance of three thousand a year, "but at no time," says Wallace, "did she see a penny of this money."[41] Let us pass by the fact that there were no witnesses to the offer and that Ann Eliza flatly *turned it down* and (according to her) continued fiercely repelling the man's advances for another year—i.e., that there was no contract or agreement whatever. To consider a parallel case: I dreamed that Mr. Wallace promised to give me $100,000, but look how the man has tricked me: I can *prove* that "at no time have I seen so much as a penny of this money!" Of what money? Why, the money Wallace has failed to pay me—*this* money! Thus Mr. Wallace accepts the mythical contract so that the unscrupulous Brigham can break it, and the money he offered and she indignantly refused becomes "*this money*" which he basely denies her.[42]

RULE 19: *Use the unfulfilled condition* to make out a case against the Mormons where there is neither evidence *nor* absence of evidence, i.e., where *nothing at all* has happened. "The spirit of assassination still remains," writes Ann Eliza, "and were it unchecked hundreds *would be* . . . sent into eternity without a moment's warning, for no crime at all except daring to differ, if ever so slightly, from those in authority."[43] A parallel statement will reveal the anatomy of this argument to the student: "Were it not that something restrained him, Mr. Wallace would by now have murdered thousands of people by stabbing them in the back with a long, silver, velvet-handled ice pick for no crime at all except chewing gum in public." That sentence, with all its embroidery, is strictly true—and it does Mr. Wallace no good at all. Mr. Wallace employs this device with skill and experience: "Her enemies might abuse her in print, curse her in the Tabernacle, consign her to hell, but they would not dare to murder her."[44] Another illustrative parallel: "Mr. Wallace *might* kick and abuse his wife at home, but he would not dare strangle her at a cocktail party." Again the statement is quite true and quite damning. "If he had not been afraid of final vengeance," says Judge Brocchus of Brigham Young, "he *would* have pointed his finger at me, and I should *in an instant* have been a dead man."[45] In the next sentence we read that Brigham Young did point his finger at the Judge, who did not become a dead man; which proves, of course, that Young *was* afraid of final vengeance. When official investigation fails to bear out Ann Eliza's charges against Brigham Young she has only to say, "there is little doubt that the confession *would* have . . . implicated the whole of the First Presidency" if the same had not "worked upon Lee's feelings to such an extent that they evidently induced him to withhold his original statement. . . . I am certain that this is the case."[46] With such license to interpret, the student can pretty well write his own ticket.

RULE 20: *Be generous with hints*—they are very effective and you never have to prove anything. When Ann Eliza writes, "It is no wonder that suicides have been so common among the Mormon women,"[47] who is going to stop the train to ask for an explanation: *are* suicides common? They must be because it is no wonder. Be virtuous about your hinting as you announce the things you refuse to talk about: "There are events of daily occurrence which decency and womanly modesty forbid my even hinting at."[48] Isn't that a clever bit of hinting? Isn't that nicer than trying to tell a story which cannot possibly be as bad as the story you don't have to tell, running the risk of disappointing your reader and getting yourself involved in that nasty business of evidence? When Mrs. Stenhouse announces, "I have nothing to say of those of whose fate nothing— not even a whisper—was ever heard,"[49] she has already said plenty, whereas if she had tried to be specific instead of dropping hints, she could, by her own confession, have said nothing. "If such words were spoken in the pulpit and published *by the Church*, what may we not suspect to have been said and done in secret?"[50] This is Mr. Beadle's blank check on the Mormons — and he is Ann Eliza's ghost-writer: if we know one thing really bad about the Mormons, that leaves us free to suspect and to publish anything else we please. Mr. Wallace has his own blank check and does not hesitate to cash it; here is his proof for the existence of Ann Eliza's "Danites" in the hotel: "nothing was utterly impossible on that still rough and paranoiac frontier."[51] If *nothing* was impossible, that leaves Mr. Wallace in the clear. But let us be charitable; let us say nothing, not one word, of those crimes of Mr. Wallace of which, great as they may be, we know nothing; suffice it to say that but for certain restraining influences those crimes *would* be even greater, for nothing is impossible in paranoiac New York.

RULE 21: *Use quotation marks without sources* — the most effective hinting device, and the most popular with anti-Mormon writers. "From an ignorant, superstitious farmer's boy, he became 'Prophet, Seer, and Revelator,' founder of a new religion . . . made by 'Divine appointment' 'God's Viceregent upon the earth, and Religious Dictator to the whole world.' "[52] Having put the familiar title "Prophet, Seer, and Revelator" in quotes, Mrs. A. E. Young follows it up with purely fictitious titles, and the two quotations appearing in conjunction look equally valid. "The stern old Mosaic law . . . is . . . insisted upon by them. Indeed, they have added to its severity, until now it stands, 'A life for an offen[s]e, real or suspected, of any kind.' "[53] From what source can the woman possibly be quoting? Herself, but the uninformed reader has no means of knowing that, and if taken to task the lady can look with wide-eyed innocence and exclaim with perfect truth, "But I never *said* that was a Mormon quotation!" The implication of these sourceless tags, which all anti-

Mormon writers favor, is that they are either such well-known Mormon expressions as to need no documentation or so intimately a part of the writer's vocabulary as to come out quite spontaneously.

RULE 22: *Discuss motives; read minds!* This is a must in dealing with Mormon history. Here we have people claiming divine revelation and as a result doing all sorts of unusual things; since there is no such thing as divine revelation, how do we explain the unusual doings? Only by reading the minds of the actors. The anti-Mormon writer cannot afford to share D. S. Freeman's contempt "for the popular, novelized biography full of glib insights into the inner man."[54] Without such insights where would Brodie and Wallace be? They both know just why Smith changed the name of Commerce, Illinois, to Nauvoo. Mrs. Brodie says "the name sprang fresh out of his fancy," and "had the melancholy music of a mourning dove's call";[55] while Wallace, faithfully following Ann Eliza, tells us that "the appelation Commerce had distressed the Mormon leader."[56] Both our philologists take delight in announcing that there is no such Hebrew word as Nauvoo; but Eduard Meyer thought there was,[57] and in M. Jastrow's new dictionary[58] we learn that the root means both "pleasing, handsome," and "marked-off place, . . . dwelling," and that in the one instance in which it is used as a place name it is spelled with a double *waw,* with the sound of *aw* or *oo.*

When Ann Eliza's brother was acquitted by an Arizona court on a charge of highway robbery but excommunicated by the Church, Mr. Wallace can assure us that the acquittal came because "the jury was predominantly Mormon," and the excommunication because the accused gave financial assistance to Ann Eliza[59]—in both cases a dirty Mormon trick. What a convenient tool this is! All the apparently wise and generous things Brigham Young ever did are nothing but cheap villainy once you know the man's *mo-*

tives for doing them, as Ann Eliza does. If he displayed miraculous skill and energy in the rescue of the stranded handcart company, it was only because "he was nearly beside himself with fear of the consequence . . . when this crowning act of selfish cupidity and egotistical vanity and presumption should be known."[60] We have seen how Wallace's penetration into the mind of Joseph Smith discovered the motive for introducing the disastrous practice of polygamy—"perhaps he had a roving eye," explains everything; but well might he ask, "What on earth had impelled Brigham Young to make the sensational announcement?"[61] Four solid pages of mind reading follow, without one reference to Brigham Young's own full explicit statements on the subject. Wallace bestows his clairvoyant talent on all, attributing motives right and left as he tells us of "Male reformers, perhaps jealous of the 'sexual variationism afforded' " by polygamy, and of "Clergymen [who] saw the appeal of the practice as a threat to the older, established religions."[62] Did they? Did they really think polygamy would prove popular instead of being the perfect club to beat the Mormons with? Even the devious and elusive mind of Richard Burton is Wallace's oyster: "He believed in polygamy, perhaps because it was bizarre and exotic."[63] Observe, however, the cautious authentication of statements by noncommittal quotation marks and that *very* useful little "perhaps." That permits you to say anything you please without being responsible for it.

RULE 23: *Be cute!* Lytton Strachey has amusingly described the quixotic General Gordon with "his fatalism, his brandy-bottle and his Bible." The brandy bottle, Trevor-Roper informs us, is Strachey's own invention: "The real object had been not a brandy-bottle but a prayerbook. Unfortunately, 'brandy-bottle' is funnier than 'prayer book'; Strachey could not resist that final touch of absurdity."[64] In the same spirit Wallace has Joseph Smith squinting through the Urim and Thummim,[65] and the Nauvoo Legion parading "comic-opera uniforms."[66] Morally obligated to justify the title of his book, he evades the responsibility with appealing cuteness: "Actually Ann Eliza was Brigham Young's twenty-seventh wife, give or take a few";[67] and a hundred pages later, still unable to come up with an accurate count, he proceeds to "support the elusiveness of a correct count" by telling one of many versions of the old story of how Brigham Young (a man with a fabulous memory for names and faces) failed to recognize a member of his family.[68] Wallace does not maintain that the story is true, but it settles the vexing problem once and for all with a merry laugh.

Anti-Mormon humor is especially effective when it is the gentle irony of a man of the world. Of a full and detailed account of a top secret affair in the family of Joseph Smith of which Ann Eliza could know nothing but for which she is our only informant, Mr. Wallace shrewdly observes, "The forest of exclamation marks did not hide the trees."[69] What does that mean? Exclamation marks are not meant to hide anything, but to call attention to "the trees"; still Wallace's gently ironic comment sounds both significant and sinister. What in all the eloquence of Stenhouse and Young is half so devastating as the copydesk urbanity of Wallace's remark: "Leaving the Meadows, the Mormons enjoyed a hearty breakfast, then returned to the scene of the crime"? Heber C. Kimball in the eyes of "a young visiting author," we are told, resembled "an Italian mountebank-physician of the seventeenth century."[70] We are not told the name of the young author or how well he knew either mountebank; it is just one of those things that is too good to leave out—like General Gordon's whiskey bottle. Wallace's account of Joseph Smith can teach the pupil how a superior and detached amusement can take the place of no end of research: It was "on a summer's day" (actually it was in May) that Smith "was wandering out into the grove" (he didn't wander but went with a purpose); there "perhaps he was not surprised when a brilliant light appeared before him. . . . With remarkable aplomb, young Smith asked which religious sect he might best join. He was advised firmly and at length, to join none, since none were worthy of him."[71] There is only one source for all this, Joseph Smith's own story, which has been available to the public free of charge in pamphlet form for many years. But to this day no anti-Mormon writer has let Smith tell the story his way; there is always the gentle irony, the knowing wink, the nudge in the ribs: "Perhaps he was not surprised . . . with remarkable aplomb . . . firmly and at length . . . none were worthy of him," —those are Mr. Wallace's original contributions, to which he adds as he continues to tell how Smith "began to recount his adventure to one and all."[72] This is a direct refutation of Mrs. Brodie's momentous thesis that nobody heard a peep about the vision for at least eighteen years; and yet Mr. Wallace has just pronounced "Fawn M. Brodie, his [Smith's] best biographer."[73] Which illustrates the literary rule that all things, including evidence, must give way to a good story.

RULE 24: *Make atmosphere your objective.* "Nowadays," writes Trevor-Roper, "to carry conviction, a historian must document, or appear to document, his formal narrative, but his background, his generalizations, allusions, comparisons remain happily free from this inconvenience. This freedom is very useful: against an imaginary background even correctly stated facts can be wonderfully transformed."[74] It is this all-important background to which we would now call the student's attention. Once we can establish in a reader's mind the suspicion that Lincoln or Columbus was a mountebank, anything we say about him will weigh against him. The whole life history of one merely accused of being subversive takes on sinister colors—and nothing is easier than to plant such a suspicion: all you have to do is mention it! So get in there and fix that first impression – after that everything will be smooth sailing. Study how Mr. Wallace goes about it.

First the paper cover of the book, on which an artist has painted an imaginary scene that fairly throbs with a mood of evil brooding. Then at the head of the second chapter the first words that catch the eye in sharp italics: *"Whenever I see a pretty woman I have to pray for grace."*[75] Never mind who invented that one, the accusing finger points without pause to "Joseph Smith, first Prophet and founder of the Mormon Church." Then the inner covers of the book proper, in deep ochre, displaying solemn and dingy photographs of twenty-one wives with a particularly sour portrait of Brigham Young himself; then a quotation from Mrs. Leonowen's book describing the harem of the King of Siam; then a quotation from Richard Burton: "I am conscious that my narrative savours of incredibility; the fault is in the subject, not in the narrator"; then a shotgun blast of promiscuous erudition: "It is a curious fact of history [is it?] that 1873 – the year during which Ulysses S. Grant began his second term as President of the United States, financial panic bankrupted five thousand businesses, yellow fever decimated the South, William 'Boss' Tweed was convicted of fraud, and the cable car was introduced to San Francisco"; then a scholarly discourse on Anna and the King of Siam, an epochal historical parallel which is never referred to again. It is all atmosphere.[76] Note how the engravings in the older books run to moonlight scenes: "Brigham 'Takes Care' of the People's Cattle!" (moonlight cattle raid), "The First Plural Marriage" (moonlight rites), "Scene after the Massacre" (moonlight). Since Ann Eliza, who lived in the Lion House, has nothing to report of mysterious hidden passages beneath the building, one wonders why Wallace should bother to discuss the "lurid rumor," as he calls it. Well, to prove there is something to it, he pointedly notes that the rumor was being *denied* "as late as 1940."[77] That brings it up to date

BRIGHAM "TAKES CARE" OF THE PEOPLE'S CATTLE!

THE FIRST PLURAL MARRIAGE.

This remarkable reproduction of "The First Plural Marriage" is taken right from Mrs. A.E.W.D.Y. Denning's own book and certainly proves that she and Mr. Wallace write about all this. Note the moon. Note the people in the picture. Note the shrubbery where the artist was concealed.

SCENE AFTER THE MASSACRE.

and somehow confirms it—another of those hints that go far toward building up an atmosphere. Feel free to admit that dirty stories about your subject are baseless, *but be sure to tell them!* Remember, what you are doing is not proving anything—you are simply establishing an atmosphere that will be all the proof you ever need against the Mormons. Mr. Wallace is frank to admit that John Hyde's picture of temple ordinances is quite false, but he is careful to report it just the same and to designate his informant as "Elder John Hyde," though Hyde when he told his lies was anything but an Elder.

RULE 25: *Attack not the thing but the Image!* For your readers Mormonism is what *you* say it is: it is to establish that thesis that you have been at such pains with your personal buildup. Once entrenched as an official guide, you can take your readers where you please; it is not the *thing* you are showing them from then on, but your *inter-*

pretation of the thing. It has been the practice of religious polemic in every age to attack not what the opposition practice and preach but our impression of what they practice and preach. "Blasphemy!" was the heading of the first published report on the Book of Mormon, and Alexander Campbell sincerely believed it *was* blasphemy. The early anti-Christian writers were just as sincere: Blasphemy had been from the beginning the stock charge against Jesus and the Apostles, just as it is the favorite word of anti-Mormon writers. Didn't Jesus recommend publicly that those who "offended" should be glad to have a millstone hung about their necks and be cast into the sea? Blood Atonement! Didn't he instruct his followers to hate — yes, hate — their own mothers and fathers and children? Horrible, horrible! To hate even their own lives? A cult of suicide, no less! And then to have innocent babes and venerable ancients damned eternally for no other sin than not having had the ridiculous dunking that so shocked

Ann Eliza; and to proclaim that an offender should cut off his own hand or pluck out his own eye—a cult of self-mutilation! And didn't the founder spend his time in private "conversations" with women, including women of ill-repute? And weren't his followers the dregs of society, who admitted that respectable people avoided them? Didn't they preach the shocking doctrine of a physical resurrection?—even Doctors of the Church like Origen and Jerome squirm uncomfortably. Their notorious "love-feasts"—too indecent to write about—show that they meant it literally when they called each other "brother" and "sister" and then proceeded to intermarry in a cult of incest.

Just as our ladies can react volcanically to whatever the Mormons *do,* no matter how tame and ordinary, there is no limit to the interpretations they can put on what they *teach. Never mind the externals:* "Joseph Smith, whatever he said and did in private, always denied it in public, and after his death the leaders of the Church followed his example."[78] Hence anything you might learn about the Mormons from the record must be discounted—the record means nothing. Joseph Smith, for Ann Eliza—who never saw him—"either must have been a polygamist or something infinitely worse,"[79] so that it doesn't make any difference *what you* say about him, just so it is bad. For Mr. Wallace and the rest of the world, Ann Eliza's zany ideas about the Mormon doctrines of deity, atonement, marriage, and the rest are the real thing. Brigham Young, the zealous throat-cutter, preached "a 'blood-atonement'—in other words, the *duty* of assassination,"[80] as he openly and emphatically urged from the stand "the cutting of every Gentile and apostate throat" as "a public expression of the mysteries of the Endowment oaths."[81] That's how it looks to the ladies, and Mr. Wallace is more than willing to have us believe that Brigham had a real, not a figurative, broadsword for the "cutting-off of members" — not the Church's member but *theirs!*

The key to Mrs. Stenhouse's atrocity story above is the useful phrase "in other words"; i.e., that is how *she* chooses to interpret it. When Brigham Young says, "Five minutes of revelation would teach me more than all . . . that I should have packed in my unlucky brains from books," he is simply making a statement of fact to which any Christian scholar will enthusiastically agree, yet there are many professors of our acquaintance who would interpret the passage exactly as Ann Eliza and Fanny Stenhouse do, as a slashing attack on all education, and sure proof that Brigham Young loathed learning.[82] Again, in the days before every church and synagogue had its Social Hall attached, the Mormon association of recreation and religion was uniformly and sincerely held up as evidence of total depravity.[83] By putting one's own interpretation on Brigham Young's concept of revelation, one can point to every failure, every exploration, every experiment of this practical man as proof of fraud: "Most of Brigham's 'revelations' [such as the] wild scheme of producing sugar from beet-roots, were gigantic failures, although he will not acknowledge it."[84] *Real* prophets don't need to explore or experiment — and they never fail. Why didn't he simply make bread from stones? Why didn't Jesus?

RULE 26: *Enjoy the prerogatives of "unequal scholarship,"* i.e., "the scrupulous straining at small historical gnats which diverts attention from the silent digestion of large and inconvenient camels. How choosily," Trevor-Roper continues, the historians of unequal scholarship "nibble when the matter is of no great significance [thus winning tributes to their scholarship from lay reviewers], and yet what enormous gulps they take when no one — they think — is looking!"[85] Note with what exquisite accuracy Mr. Wallace reminds his readers more than once that the train on which Ann Eliza made her thrilling escape went at a top speed of exactly twenty-two — not twenty-three or twenty-one, but twenty-*two* — miles an hour.[86] In the face of such meticulous and exhaustive attention to detail, who would not overlook the fact that Mr. Wallace has here mistaken the average speed of the train for its top speed (in 1830 trains were doing better than that!), or excuse the long chain of absurdities that make up the rest of the story of the great escape?

The nice thing about the principle of unequal scholarship is that it allows you, when you have no evidence for your main theme, to talk about something else for which you do have evidence. Such a dodge needs no apology, for as any writer knows, it takes very little skill to establish some sort of connection between any two subjects on earth. When Mr. Wallace says of his heroine that "the life path she trod lay trackless, almost untouched by other literary spades,"[87] he is simply reporting that she is his only source; this he calls a "challenge" which he meets easily enough — by writing about something *else,* specializing in those "non-Church sources" which "[support] Ann Eliza's *point of view* against Brigham Young or the Church."[88] So he proceeds to fill whole pages with stuff that Artemus Ward has already sold at top prices, and which Ward never expected to be taken as anything but the broadest ribbing of the Mormons, and he converts it to sound evidence by the scholarly observation that "Artemus Ward was only partially accurate."[89] Which is no help at all unless we know which part is accurate and which is not; but who cares? The impression is what counts, and that is what you get from Artemus Ward. Unable to produce any good inside information on polygamy, after promising a lot of it, Mr. Irving Wallace pacifies us with a rather obscene remark by the Bey of Morocco, which, though it has nothing whatever to do with the Mormons, becomes significant by the impressive assurance that the story comes from "Dr. Edward Westermarck, a scholar on marital evolution."[90] Let the student note in passing that Wallace is at pains to name his eminent informants when his material is safely irrelevant, but omits mentioning sources to the atrocity stories and the murder charges.

A stunning example of unequal scholarship is the way in which Mr. Wallace shifts his nearly "three years of intensive research"[91] from his subject, Ann Eliza Young, to far more imposing and enigmatic fields and figures of study. As the man who knows just how fast Ann Eliza's train went he is surely qualified to toss off an authoritative study of Joseph Smith without leaving his typewriter. Joseph Smith, Brigham Young, the Mormons, "the great globe itself, and all that it inherit[s]," are but appendages to the epic history of Ann Eliza. Merely by knowing a few facts about that little lady, we place ourselves in the unfathomable mines of recondite research. For it should be obvious to anybody that the scholar who can tell us about even the most trivial things must be the master of great ones.

RULE 27: *Be literary!* As a creative writer you should feel free to say whatever you please without having to answer to anybody. No one can call you to account for what is put down as pure fiction. Consider the opening words of Mr. Richard Wormser's prefatory note to his recent book: *"Battalion of Saints* follows history fairly closely, but it is a novel."[92] What could be neater? Mr. Wormser is now in the clear—he can write what he jolly well pleases about the Mormons, and forget about the evidence. And the beauty of it all is that whatever he may say about his *imaginary* Mormons is going to stick, more or less, to the real ones. For where can you draw the line between them? How close is "fairly closely"? By designating make-believe Mormons and real Mormons with the same labels, the literary gentry have always managed not so much to confuse as to identify the two species of being in their own and their readers' minds. The Mormon image is very largely a literary production.

Here is one of Zane Grey's great works, revived in paperback as of 1961; on the front cover in bold yellow letters the publisher promises a tale of "How a determined tenderfoot risks his life to save a woman from a Mormon village of 'sealed' wives!"; and on the back in bright red capitals the caption "I won't be a Mormon's extra wife any longer!" The book first came out in 1915, and is as phony as any western Mr. Grey ever spawned; but today it is available in drugstores and bus depots as an authentic contribution to American letters—and a nice dig at the Mormons, who have no comeback, of course, since this is only fiction after all.

The *Saturday Review* hit the nail on the head when it praised Mrs. Brodie's now classic libel of Joseph Smith for the "originality of its research" and the "suppleness of its prose" (the review is quoted in a blurb on the jacket of the present edition of Mrs. B's book). Originality and suppleness, highly desirable in a work of literature, can make a travesty of history. Mrs. Brodie is nothing if not supple: she always has the adroit phrase or loaded word to implicate the Mormons and extricate herself, interweaving fact and fancy, insinuation and documentation, until her pages squirm like a nest of garter snakes. But it is Mr. Bernard De Voto's verdict, appearing on the same cover, that is most revealing. Ecstatically he hails the author as "a detached, modern intelligence, grounded in naturalism, rejecting the supernatural," and hence peculiarly fitted to write "the best book about the Mormons so far published."

Had Mr. De Voto been Mrs. Brodie's worst enemy he could not have proclaimed more clearly or succinctly that lady's total incapacity for dealing with her subject. What he is telling us is that she is supremely qualified to write about a religion because she rejects all religion! By the same token a "practical, modern mechanic, grounded in the solid

realities of running a garage, rejecting everything artistic,"
would be preeminently suited to write a detached and
impartial book on music or art. Mr. De Voto tells us in no
uncertain terms that we have here a woman whose mind
is made up, whose viewpoint is settled, and whose opinions are fixed for all time so far as religion is concerned.
Before she ever touches a key of her typewriter, Mrs. Brodie
has rejected out of hand the whole premise on which the
words and actions of Smith and his followers are predicated. For a "modern intelligence, grounded in naturalism,
rejecting the supernatural" even to consider the proposition that Joseph Smith *might* have been telling the truth is
simply unthinkable; to take such a position would be to
abdicate the throne of reason, betray the foundations of
mind itself, renounce the faith, stamp on the altar, and
wreck one's own career. Mrs. Brodie knows that. How,
then, can her critics applaud her rocklike and unflinching
dedication to the party line and in the same breath hail
her objectivity and detachment? For the literary mind this
presents no problem at all. All things are possible for those
who know how to use the right clichés.

Actually, for anyone who is not a Mormon the question
of whether the "Mormon version" of things is to be taken
seriously never arises, and Mr. Wallace's unctuous assurance that he emerged from his researches "neither anti-
Mormon nor pro-Mormon"[93] would be exquisite nonsense
were it not just another cliché. There is no neutral ground
between Smith and Young as impostors and Smith and
Young as honest men. That is why we must refer to the
whole corpus of writings about the Mormons as either
Mormon or anti-Mormon. The proposition that Mormonism is fraudulent is the cornerstone of all anti-Mormon
studies, and the question of Joseph Smith's veracity never
becomes an issue at all. Hence, your business as a writer
is not to consider whether or not Smith and Young deceived, but only to show the world how they did it. If you

can give any explanation except the Mormon explanation, even if it be as feeble as Mrs. Brodie's "plastic" and "magnetic" Joseph, the world will hail you as "a detached, modern intelligence" and a light to the Gentiles.

It is your prerogative as a creative writer to *claim your poetic license.* Literature should be superior to the mean quibbling and meticulous hairsplitting of philology or history — does a great painting have to have the accuracy of a photograph? Anti-Mormon literature is the creation of a society of scalds who share a common material and a common goal, who freely borrow from each other and freely refashion what they borrow. The facts of the Mormon story are as well known to these bards as the corpus of classic mythology once was to the poets — since the main tales and images are never in doubt, the individual artist is free to do with any one of them pretty much what he will. If Mrs. Brodie wishes to deflate a supernatural experience by inserting a roguish, earthy detail of her own — "somewhere a bird chirped" — who is going to object? They were in the woods, and birds *do* chirp. Who is going to take Mr. Wallace to task for having Moroni announce himself as "a messenger from the Maker," or having the gold plates engraved in "Egyptian hieroglyphics," containing a history of migrants "from Babylon and Jerusalem to America"?[94] What if it is all incorrect? — you get the general idea.

Let us illustrate how an artistic brotherhood can create and cherish its own values. Mrs. Brodie had written: "Many in the church shared the attitude of Brigham Young who had a healthy understanding of human frailty." Then she quotes Young as saying: "If he [Joseph Smith] acts like a devil, he has brought forth a doctrine that will save us, if we abide by it. He may get drunk every day of his life, sleep with his neighbor's wife every night, run horses and gamble. . . . But the doctrine he has produced will save you and me and the whole world." This passage, quoted by *Time Magazine* (wouldn't you know it?), was quoted neatly out of context by Mrs. Brodie, who in the process converted a hypothetical condition into a damning statement of fact.[95] Actually the charges were made against Joseph Smith not by Brigham Young but by a sectarian minister; Young at the time had never met Smith, but replied that even if Smith was as bad as you could imagine him, his doctrine was still wonderful. But Wallace takes up Brodie's chorus and improves on it: "Mormon colleagues did not deny Smith's prophetless habits and manners. In fact, Brigham Young was once said to have remarked, 'That the Prophet was of mean birth, that he was wild, intemperate, even dishonest and tricky in his youth, is nothing against his mission.' "[96] Vaguer and nastier, you will notice; Brodie has been paraphrased as Wallace's contribution to original research, and the rest is what Young was *once said* to have remarked. Such a charge screams for complete and accurate documentation, and the student will readily appreciate Mr. Wallace's wisdom in avoiding footnotes. In their place he has cunningly inserted that telling little "in fact." Go back and read it again. What is the *fact* reported? That somebody is said to have said at some time that Brigham Young once said, . . . Never mind that, the point is that Mr. Wallace is speaking *facts!*

RULE 28: *Develop a special vocabulary of loaded and emotive words.* As a literary artist, you have this prerogative. Mrs. Brodie does wonders with such sure-fire psychic terms as *plastic, intuitive,* and *magnetic,* which sound important enough but can't be pinned down. Mr. Wallace favors a more popular jargon: Brigham Young never asks — he commands; his family is always the "harem," even though Mr. Wallace admits that nothing less like an Oriental harem could be imagined;[97] instead of being told how the Church is organized or operates, we are referred darkly and vaguely to a mysterious "hierarchy," whose officers are of course "Brigham's underlings." Wallace does not even bother to paraphrase Ann Eliza's description of Amelia "forcing the out-of-town wives . . . to serve her."[98] *Forcing* them — how? To *serve* her — how? It turns out that these ladies helped serve their guests when they gave dinner parties — as hostesses usually do — instead of letting the guests prepare the meal. But doesn't it sound simply too thrilling the way Annie and Wallace put it? When we read that Brigham Young painted a picture of "a Mormon heaven as brilliant as the Mohammedan heaven,"[99] we are not supposed to reflect that Dante did the same, that all people who believe in heaven think of it as a brilliant place, and that the Moslem and sectarian ideas of heaven and hell are far closer to each other than either is to the Mormon concept; Mr. Wallace's phrase was not designed to promote theological speculation but merely to bring those two loaded words "Mormon" and "Mohammedan" together in the same context. When he says, "Smith made himself the lieutenant general of this legion,"[100] who would not assume that Smith bestowed the rank on himself? He did not; Congress did. When he says, "As Nauvoo grew, Joseph Smith looked for foreign conquests,"[101] who would not think of a little Caesar or Alexander, instead of a church sending out missionaries to new fields of labor?

RULE 29: *Study the techniques of gossip.* To the discerning reader of the Sisterhood of Mormon Bondage the word that comes most often to mind is bound to be "gossip." For that very reason the student should follow Mr. Wallace's example and scrupulously avoid ever using the word, which would be sure to let the cat out of the bag. Let us admit that our anti-Mormon classics are clearinghouses of gossip. What else are those swarming quotations without sources, or the constantly recurring "it is said," "it was reported," "I know one woman who . . . "? Take the story about Brigham Young failing to recognize this or that member of his family: "A very amusing story was told me of Brigham, by a lady who vouches for its truth; and although I cannot, of course, corroborate it, I am quite ready to give it credence enough to publish it."[102] A related story is told of Joseph Smith: "Some of these women have since said they did not know who was the father of their children: this is not to be wondered at, for after Joseph's declaration annulling all Gentile marriages, the greatest promiscuity was practiced."[103] Note in this last instance how the first proposition leans on the second for support, while the second receives all its corroboration from the first. Take another example: "I have been informed that Joseph taught his followers that it was right . . . to take anything they could find which belonged to their enemies. . . . I can the more easily believe this to be true, because the spirit of the Mormon Church has always been that of retaliation. The stern old Mosaic law . . . stands, 'A life for an offence, real or suspected, of any kind.' "[104]

Note also in these examples how careful the gossip has been to protect herself: she won't vouch for anything, but she *will* tell it. Mr. Wallace displays unequalled skill and caution in this direction; his unfailing "perhaps," and "possibly," and "it may be assumed" are models for the student who wants to have his cake and eat it: "I am conscious that my narrative savours of incredibility; the fault is in the subject, not in the narrator."[105] How clever of Mr. Wallace! He cannot even be held responsible for the remark that frees him of all other responsibility, for it is Richard Burton speaking; and he is really not a narrator narrating a narrative at all, but a gossip purveying gossip. According to his informant, it "is always the case when two Mormon women meet, and are together for any length of time, the talk turn[s] onto polygamy";[106] "when any two women meet, it is the chief topic of their conversation."[107] Always? *Any* two women? Well, if one of them is Ann Eliza—and away she goes, with little Mr. Wallace tightly clutching her skirts: At Nauvoo, Joseph Smith had a " 'Revelation,' giving the most unbridled license to all the worst passions of their nature."[108] That should be some revelation, if we only knew where to find it. Then "when the church was located in Utah . . . every man was compelled to enter it [polygamy], under pain of Brigham's displeasure,"[109] i.e., swift and certain death. "It soon became very unpopular for a man to have but one wife, and he [every man] quickly found himself looking out for another."[110] Of course "the pecuniary condition of a man is never taken into consideration,"[111] and so "if a man attended a party with only one wife, he felt ashamed and humiliated, and would instantly select some unappropriated young woman, and . . . talk matrimony."[112] And so on. Ann Eliza's real talent is gossip, the one art that requires no originality, no creativity, no imagination, no discipline, no restraint, no integrity. This eager communication of minds demands of the hearer, as of the speaker, only the pleasant surrender of the critical faculty, which is a killjoy anyway.

Conscience is satisfied in this sordid business by that air of modest reserve which every practiced gossip assumes with unpremeditated art: "Modesty and decency forbid my throwing too strong a light" — on Mormon domestic life, that is — and so the lady writes a book about it.[113] "I feel myself utterly inadequate to tell the story of the Mountain Meadows Massacre," says Mrs. Stenhouse " — it is so shocking, so fiendish. And yet [sigh] it must be told."[114] Mrs. Ann Eliza Young goes her one better; she too hates to tell it, "but it cannot be told too often."[115] Brigham Young is responsible for "such disgusting atrocities and such impure statements that for the sake of decency and propriety I dared not even mention them."[116]

Inspired by the example of these Victorian ladies who protest themselves much too proper to mention the things they mention, Mr. Wallace with downcast eyes and maidenly reserve excuses himself for something Brigham Young once said "in almost unprintable language," and then proceeds to print it — the only lengthy quotation from Brigham Young in his whole book.[117] In the same spirit Horace Greeley protests: "I deeply regret the necessity of believing this; but the facts are incontestable."[118] It turns out that the "facts" he reports have no substantiation whatever, but Mr. Greeley's becoming hesitation almost convinces us. The history of Emmeline Young "I cannot give again to the world. I think the dead eyes would haunt me forever,"[119] says Ann Eliza who, of course, proceeds to tell the story of Emmeline. "There was also one wife who . . . was said to have 'run away to California' . . . but it was whispered among wicked Gentiles that she paid the full penalty of the Endowment-Oaths. . . . I simply give it in common with much else for what it is worth."[120] What is it worth? — the whispering, the quotation marks, the sarcasm, the disavowal? Cold cash to a publisher, but Mrs. Stenhouse will not be responsible for it. "I simply mention these facts without any comment of my own. Let the reader form his own conclusion."[121] Isn't that disarming? Actually the lady, instead of supplying facts without comment, has done just the opposite. What are we to think when she tells us that every man, woman, *and* child in the Tabernacle knew that Brigham Young was lying when he said that soldiers or gamblers had killed Dr. Robinson: "which statements, however, were known by everyone present to be utterly false."[122] That's the fact, and now you can draw your own conclusions — I wouldn't influence you for the world!

Of the child survivors of Mountain Meadows, "Mrs. Cooke says they used often, in their childish prattle, to tell events of the massacre, which showed that *they knew perfectly* what part Lee and his confederates had in the affair." One of these babes "said one day, very quietly, but very determinedly, . . . I will kill Lee myself. I saw him shoot my sister, and I shall not die happy unless I kill him."[123] Never mind how the kids recognized Lee in disguise or knew him by sight and name — their ghoulish prattle makes wonderful gossip. But just listen to Ann Eliza: "To this day [1876], jewelry is worn in Salt Lake City, and teams are seen in the streets, that are known to have belonged to the fatal immigrant train."[124] It was the very jewelry "torn from the mangled bodies." Doesn't that do things to you? Only a schlemiel would ask who would recognize the jewelry or why the women would be wearing it during a three-day Indian battle, or stoop so low as to point out that fifteen years is an unusually long working life for a horse and ask how come that teams that were fully grown, had traveled thousands of miles, and were so exhausted at the time of the massacre that (according to Mrs. Stenhouse) they could barely make ten miles a day, could escape a three-day hail of bullets and artillery to turn up

parading about the streets of Salt Lake City *twenty years* later.

Memory plays strange tricks with gossips. Ann Eliza reports that "one of the bright spots in my childhood, to which I am especially fond of looking back," was her home life of the winter of 1846–47, which she describes in intimate detail — though at the time she had just turned two.[125] Or take a sampling of a conversation which the lady overheard *at the age of four:* " 'Oh, I don't know,' said Ann Eliza's mother miserably, 'but I can't endure this life.' 'And yet you entered it voluntarily,' said Chauncey relentlessly. 'I don't understand you. You are strangely inconsistent.' "[126]

If that sort of thing sounds a bit steep, it is only fair to point out that the "relentlessly" and "miserably" were

supplied by Mr. Wallace. And why not? He has just as
much right to report how it *must have been* as Ann Eliza
herself does, and once a gossip has this basic premise, the
rest is easy. *Imagined conversations* such as the above are a
specialty with anti-Mormon writers; Ann Eliza can report
verbatim conversations that took place between Joseph
Smith and his wife in their most secret sessions;[127] between
Smith and Brigham Young; between Young and Kimball,
cooking up a murder; Young and his son Joseph (secret),[128]
Young and Hyde (supersecret);[129] she can tell us the very
words with which Smith proposed to various young ladies,[130] and with which Young proposed to Amelia Folsom
or wheedled a future wife out of her property. She even
reports that many of Smith's fair victims "made affidavits . . . and their statements were published in many of
the leading newspapers all over the country."[131] True, no
such affidavits have been found in any newspaper, but we
must remember that the public of 1876 had not been educated by the modern crime novel, and never thought of
questioning such obvious and forthright statements. Mr.
Wallace wisely forbears to repeat the lady's indiscretions,
while unhesitatingly accepting her picture of Mormon she-
nanigans. Because of Ann Eliza, according to him, the Lion
House was shaken to its foundations, all its members
seized by a panic of insecurity. The evidence for that? Mr.
Wallace's knowledge of human nature. Again, Brigham
Young meets daughter Alice on the street: " 'Good heavens, Alice! What are you rigged out in that style for? You
look like a prostitute.' She faced him with an expression
so like his own that it was absolutely startling, and, with
terrible intensity, replied, —'Well, what else am I? And
whose teachings have made me so?' "[132] Absolutely startling to whom? The graphic illustration in the book shows
that the two met alone—no other person present. Did Alice
know how startling her expression was, or was it Brigham
Young himself who told the story? We also fail to see how

Insulted by her father

Brigham Young's fanatical insistence that everybody get married and have children would make his daughter a prostitute, or cause her to dress like one. In Mr. Wallace's book we find: "Whenever I see a pretty woman I have to pray for grace."[133] What reader would ever guess that that quotation can be traced back no further than one W. Wyl, published in 1886 in a rabidly anti-Mormon newspaper? And where did Wyl get it? From a woman; at least he said that "someone had told him that someone had said that Joseph Smith had made that remark to an *unnamed* friend."[134] That is enough for Mrs. Brodie, *Time Magazine,* and Irving Wallace. In the same way Ann Eliza tells a tale of fiendish murder about Bishop Wells, admits it is apocryphal, but makes it stick by appending a full and lengthy list of all the man's titles and offices. And when Wallace brings equally terrible charges against Porter Rockwell, he is always careful to refer to the man by the full name of

Orrin Porter Rockwell to show that even if Hickman and Beadle were thundering liars, our scholar has done his homework.

RULE 30: *Preserve a gap* between your readers and the Mormons. At a passage where even the most obtuse reader might boggle at the sheer excess and enormity of your tale, do not hesitate to remind him that he is in no position to know about things happening in the far away Tibet of the Rockies. "No one outside of Utah and Mormonism can understand it in the least," says Ann Eliza, "because no-where else is there a possibility of such wretchedness to exist."[135] The Reverend Henry Caswall, by publishing only in England, was able to build a career on the single fact that he had actually been in Nauvoo; even the most rabid anti-Mormon reviewers in America were disgusted by the absurdities of his account, but he was on safe ground, speaking to a public thousands of miles removed from the scene he described.

When the Mormons moved to Utah they obligingly widened the gap between themselves and the nation—at the present time there are still unexplored areas in the state. An almost complete geographical gap between the Mormons and the world has made possible a booming traffic in atrocity stories of the Zane Grey variety. When-ever the gap has been closed, the atrocity stories have disappeared, so that we can follow the retreat of the pulps from Salt Lake City to San Pete to the Four Corners to Short Creek. A number of recent magazine articles on the Short Creek "Mormons" are careful to describe with the mystery and drama of a science fiction thriller the utter inaccessibility of that community in its desert fastness, which happens to be just six miles by a good road (I have walked it) from the highway between Salt Lake City and Los Angeles.

Ann Eliza herself led the retreat into the wilderness to preserve that all-important gap; when increasing numbers of Gentiles visited Salt Lake City and liked what they saw, she fell back on the hinterland, explaining that since "the Gentiles do not go into our country places much, only Salt Lake City," they are of course not aware of what the Mormons are really up to.[136] Today when the curious can follow six-lane freeways from the Gate of the Angels right into the Mormon lair, it is necessary to look for other gaps — the social gap and the time gap.

Recall Mrs. Young's statement that "No one outside of Utah *and* Mormonism can understand it in the least."[137] Mrs. Stenhouse is furiously insistent that being in Utah is not enough; one must also be or have been a Mormon. But even that is not enough — one must know the inner circle. Remember, whatever the Mormon leaders said and did privately they denied publicly,[138] so that only an Ann Eliza or a Stenhouse can possibly have the remotest inkling of the real thing, and they, of course, are beyond question or criticism. "Newspaper correspondents visit Salt Lake City, and when they arrive they are brimming over with disgust," writes Ann Eliza Young, "but, by-and-by a change comes over them," and they send back glowing reports to their papers. It is Brigham who closes the gap; he "manages to get hold of them . . . [and] they soon see things as he intends they shall see them. I suppose his manner of influencing them differs, but I think it will be readily understood."[139] This passage deserves repetition if only because it is a foundation stone of Mr. Wallace's book that Brigham Young attacked Ann Eliza through the Gentile press, and she is his authority for saying so; here we can see just how much she knows about it — she is "supposing" everything, and as to Young's methods being "readily understood," it would be hard to imagine anything less readily understandable than how tough, seasoned correspondents brimming with disgust and on their guard from the first should be so easily taken in by a cheap trickster. But the gap must be preserved at any cost: "The

truth is simply this: the Mormon people are absolutely afraid to have the outside world come too close to them; they let them see just so much, but not one bit more."[140] Hence even a Richard Burton is completely fooled: "The mass of the people are but a cunningly manipulated lot of marionettes, who perform certain antics for a curious public, while the shrewd wire-puller sits behind, and orders every movement, and makes every speech."[141] If you think the little lady's pen might be running away with her to describe the man who is always up front, stealing the show and making every speech, as the mysterious plotter who "sits behind," shrewdly and cunningly concealing his operations, you have failed to reckon with the public's unlimited vulnerability to dramatic clichés and the thrill of unknown evil.

As the geographical gap between the Mormons and the world has narrowed, the *time* gap has been steadily widening to take its place. If a trip to Utah in the early days could change one's mind about everything, few enough people were ever in a position to take such a trip; and if today a brief journey into the records of a hundred years ago will convince anyone how flimsy are the charges against Joseph Smith and Brigham Young, who is going to take the trouble to make such a tedious time-journey? The Wallaces and Brodies are on as safe grounds as the Ann Eliza Youngs and Fanny Stenhouses—they know there is a broad and safe gap between them and the vast inertia of the public. But the time gap is not new; Ann Eliza herself must always go back to a vague and distant time for her atrocity tales: "It *was* a terrible time, indeed, and one fairly shudders to recall the blood-curdling atrocities that were committed at that period."[142] But though she tells us that " 'Altars of sacrifice' were loudly recommended," and that whenever victims "would not become willing sacrifices . . . 'somebody' took the matter in hand," she remains splendidly impersonal and lets those sinister quotation marks carry the whole burden of proof. Though at one place she narrows the time gap to ten years, it is always there; "even ten years ago, an Apostate's or Gentile's life was worth absolutely nothing. . . . It was enough that he should be merely suspected, and his fate was just as certain, coming swift and sure."[143] This reaching back into the bad old times of the Reformation and beyond ("the time is forever past when the 'unsheathing of his bowie-knife,' or the 'crooking of his little finger,' pronounced sentence upon offenders")[144] entails a minor contradiction which the student should avoid, since both Stenhouse and Ann Eliza insist that back in those old times the Mormons "were then simply an earnest religious people,"[145] and that (as we have seen) Brigham Young was honest and upright, and even Joseph Smith "an earnest but ignorant Christian preacher."[146]

The greater the distance in time (as in space) from his subject, the freer the anti-Mormon writer is to invent. Thus the story of the Jarviss family, told in 1876 by simply quoting a letter written by a woman Mrs. Young had never seen, is retold thirty-five years later as a personal experience of Ann Eliza, without any mention of the letter.[147] The Mormons were charged, as a matter of course, with the murders of Governor Boggs and President Garfield, and though there is no evidence whatever for either charge, Mr. Wallace can only dismiss the Garfield libel as "significant" (whatever that means, it's bad for the Mormons), while he makes a stab at making the Boggs' accusation stick (though even Ann Eliza denies it) because it is fifty years older.

RULE 31: *Learn when to be silent.* Nothing you say about the Mormons can be more damning than what you fail to say. The really competent anti-Mormon writer does not only exploit gaps—he creates them, by omitting relevant information. Note how daintily Mr. Wallace picks his way through the evidence: Joseph Smith and Brigham Young are never invited to take the witness stand, while J. C. Bennett, J. H. Beadle, the *Police Gazette*, the mysterious Fanny Brewer, the writer of an anonymous letter to a newspaper, to say nothing of Ann Eliza and Mary Burton, etc., are given close and sympathetic hearing; the Book of Mormon is brushed aside with a glib Menckenism of the youthful Bernard De Voto about "the cheap story of the golden plates"—why should Mr. Wallace jeopardize such chaste economy by bothering to mention that the mature De Voto recanted and admitted that he was "brash" and "irresponsible" when he wrote those things?[148] Having quoted Josiah Quincy as reporting that Joseph Smith was wearing a "linen jacket, which had not lately seen the washtub," when he met him, Wallace shrewdly leaves it at that, discreetly omitting Quincy's glowing tribute to the prophet.[149] It is also wisdom in Mr. Wallace to omit from his heavily padded bibliography the name of Mr. Sam Taylor, the one writer who really knows something about Mormon polygamy. Following Ann Eliza's example, Wallace tells of the three witnesses to the Book of Mormon leaving the Church, but omits the really remarkable ending of the story—how two of them came back into the Church and none of the three ever denied his testimony of seeing the plates: why should he spoil the effect? In the same spirit Ann Eliza glories to report that her father and mother have at last seen the light and left the Mormons[150]—without, of course, bothering to mention that her father returned to the Church and her mother threw the Bible into the stove along with her Mormon faith and declared Gentile marriage to be as bad as polygamy.

It is not only by skillful addition but no less discreet subtraction that Mr. Wallace is able to improve on some of Ann Eliza's own stories. When she reports the rumored implication of the Mormons in the murder of Boggs, she is honest or careless enough to report also that Porter Rockwell was proven to be elsewhere at the time of the crime, and Joseph Smith "escaped by a legal technicality" (i.e., no evidence), but even this grudging concession of innocence is too much for Wallace, who is content to mention the Mormons and the crime together, clinch the implication by casually referring to Orrin Porter Rockwell (what precision!) as "a paid assassin," and let it go at that. He takes pains to mention Brigham Young's private opinion of the character of the defunct Zachary Taylor as proof of treason[151]—though there are plenty of good Americans who have identical opinions of other former presidents, living and dead—but nowhere in his book does he mention the great patriotic sacrifice of the Mormon Battalion, even though Ann Eliza counts it among her personal experiences. Nothing could be more trivial than the Zachary

Taylor story or more fundamental than the history of the Battalion, but by going out of his way to dramatize the one and suppress the other, Mr. Wallace is making history. On the other hand he does mention that Parley P. Pratt was acquitted by a hostile and reluctant court in Arkansas, a point that Stenhouse and Young omit: for them Pratt is simply "the guilty wretch" and that settles it.[152] But having made this dangerous concession, Wallace snatches victory from defeat by a simple House-That-Jack-Built maneuver: "Stung by this lechery, Hector McClean once pulled a pistol in court."[153] What lechery? Why, the lechery that McClean imagined, the lechery that the court packed with "an unruly Arkansas mob," could not prove — *this* lechery — Pratt's, of course. He "was honorably discharged" by the reluctant court,[154] but not by Mr. Wallace. Admittedly that was a close call — the student is not advised to take such chances; a safe rule to follow is simply to overlook anything that might give aid or comfort to the Mormons or discredit their enemies. The student who compares Mrs. Ann Eliza's 1876 book with her 1908 rewrite will readily recognize that every good thing said about the Mormons in the early work is carefully deleted in the later one. Thus while the part about Brigham Young once being a good and honest man[155] is deleted in 1908 so that Brigham can be all bad,[156] the part about van Buren's being a stuffed shirt with his "impressiveness which expressed so much and meant so little"[157] is politely omitted in 1908[158] to make him a Christian hero.

But the most effective use of the discreet omission is that by which Wallace builds up his story of what he calls the "handcart fiasco." The mere title as he puts it effectively screens the fact that there were eleven handcart crossings, all but one highly successful — Wallace never mentions that fact or even hints that there were other handcart expeditions; for him and for us it is simply the handcart migration scheme. He begins by telescoping a helpfully explanatory letter from Brigham Young into a short, cynical, and brutal note, *omitting* the little dots which indicate that one is making deletions in a quotation, so that the reader assumes that he has Brigham Young's own statement before his eyes.[159] This, we should warn the student, is a bit drastic; it is in fact libelous—but what are the chances of its being discovered? Never does Wallace indicate that Ann Eliza's supposed intimate firsthand knowledge of the handcart fiasco comes right out of Stenhouse, who in turn gets it all from Mary Burton's letter. Didn't Ann Eliza's father actually help to make the carts? Yes, and *he* thought the company had a good chance of getting through, as he passed them by on the road "with the other elders, . . . intending to return, *if* they found it necessary."[160] Just one thing made trouble—an early "more than ordinary winter" that caught everyone by surprise: "In fact," writes Mary Burton, "it came on earlier and more severely last year *than at any time* before."[161] So what if there was a freak storm—doesn't that show that Brigham Young was a false prophet? As a prophet he should have known, according to Mary Burton.[162] Well, he did give emphatic orders against traveling that late in the year, but his orders were not heeded. And right here is where our principle of silence proves so useful—our Wallaces, Stenhouses, and Ann Elizas simply leave such disturbing details out. But having proven Brigham a false prophet through his drastic lack of foresight, Mrs. Stenhouse is free to turn right around and prove him a criminal because he knew all along what would happen! The Church leaders, she says, "must have *fully* known the dangers and difficulties of the way."[163] Therefore the whole thing was deliberately set up, a criminal conspiracy, with John Taylor promoting himself in New York even "if all the poor Saints . . . should die of starvation and exposure,"[164] which Ann Eliza converts into Daniel Spencer having fun at the expense of untold sufferings: "What were a thousand or more human lives in comparison to his enjoyment? Less than nothing, it would seem, in his estimation."[165] Thus Ann Eliza picks up the story from Stenhouse, and substituting her own father for Levi Savage, the one man who "dared tell the truth,"[166] lights into Brigham, who planned the whole "heartless and mercenary" scheme just to make money. It was he who after the arrival of the second company walked about among the miserable wrecks of humanity, ruined for life, gleefully rubbing his hands "with overflowing complacency."[167]

Even Ann Eliza has some admiration for the phenomenal speed and efficiency with which Young got relief to the stranded party, and though she explains it as an act of cowardice, Brigham being "beside himself with fear" lest his crime be discovered, still it may have been better to have passed that impressive episode by in silence, as Wallace does. For remember, if you say anything good about Brigham Young you place yourself in the awkward position of having to explain it away. For example, Captain Hunt, overtaking the ill-fated company with his wagon train, "had been expressly forbidden to pass the handcarts," thereby being on hand with needed assistance — a wise precaution to say the least. Ann Eliza is able to convert this into evidence of criminality, it is true, but not without straining a point: "which shows conclusively enough that those very persons who sent the emigrants off at that unfavorable season feared for the results."[168] Do parents who pack their children off to summer camp with first-aid kits "show conclusively" thereby that they know what the little nippers are in for? Now if Hunt had been ordered to drive on, that would *really* be something to pin on the leaders. Either way the Mormons can't win if you know your business; but it is better to avoid too elaborate sophistries by omitting such details altogether, as Mr. Wallace does. See how he builds up his handcart fiasco by a series of skillful omissions: he makes no mention of the success or even the existence of the other handcart companies; of Brigham Young's warnings and orders; of the insistence of the party itself on starting out against orders; of the unprecedented nature of the storm; of the unparalleled skill and speed with which the party was rescued, of the general confidence, well justified by all previous experience, that the party could get through. It is only by omitting such far from minor details that the handcart fiasco becomes what Mr. Wallace makes it, a clumsy, foolish, ill-advised, criminal, and tragic and thoroughly typical example of Mormon insanity.

RULE 32: *Be bloody, bold, and resolute!* What the public wants in an atrocity story is straight horror, not namby-pamby explanations: the propaganda artists of World War I proved that once for all. As the murder mystery demonstrates so often, the emotionally involved reader is a functionally blind reader who will not see the evidence that is staring him in the face. Wallace's most vivid, factual, and convincing atrocity story is Ann Eliza's firsthand account of the Payson murders; yet even as she tells it the evidence screams the absurdity of her interpretation. Wallace's solution, of course, is to ignore the evidence.

Wherever you can, paint your picture in black and white. Ann Eliza does not shilly-shally: During the "Reformation" time, "bloodshed and murder were the order of the day. If *any* person or family were *supposed* to be lacking in the faith . . . that person or family was sure to be visited by some disaster."[169] All Mormons "have been taught that the Lord commanded them to hate *all* persons not of their belief, and that it was an act pleasing to Him whenever a Gentile was put out of the way. Without being murderers at heart, they have been taught that murder is a part of their religion, a *vital portion* of their *worship*."[170] "Its leaders always have been . . . disloyal to the government under which they live, treacherous to their friends, . . . believing *nothing* which they teach, and tyrannical and grasping in the extreme."[171] "The Saints were taught openly that it was their duty to 'destroy in the flesh' *all* upon whom the leaders of the church *frowned*."[172] For the leaders "believe most implicitly in vicarious suffering, and it is with them *always* the innocent and helpless who are punished."[173] D. Wells "has ever been Brigham's right-hand man in iniquity, fearlessly disposing of life and property in the name of the Lord, counselling his superior to *deeds of blood without number*."[174] "A strict surveillance was kept over the movements of *any* stranger in the city, and if his words or actions displeased the Mormon spies, he *never* got far beyond city limits."[175] Among the Mormons themselves, "if no other charge could be brought against a person, he was called a 'spy,' and this, of course, gave sufficient reason for putting him out of the way very summarily."[176] "Everything, even the most trifling, that a person did, which was at all offensive to *any* member of the priesthood, was accounted apostasy, and punishment administered as speedily as possible. . . . Some of the most revolting and heartsickening crimes were committed. . . . So common were they that . . . *nothing* was thought of them."[177] "If anyone became tired of Mormonism, or impatient of the increasing despotism of the leader, and returned to the East, or started to do so, he *invariably* was met by the Indians and killed before he had gone very far. The effect was to discourage apostasy."[178]

Is it necessary for us to go on and on like this? Yes, it is, to show the student that the more incredible an atrocity story is, the less proof it requires: all this is but a tiny sampling of the writing of Ann Eliza Young which Mr. Irving Wallace in 1961 embraced as the most reliable single handbook on Mormonism. If a scholar like Wallace doesn't boggle at these outrageous absurdities, why should anyone else?

But if a good atrocity story paralyzes the critical faculties, it would certainly be a waste of talent were it not spiced by a delicious sense of possibility. As a mere novel, the wildest anti-Mormon classics would fall flat; what sold *A Study in Scarlet* was the grizzly awareness that there actually were people called Mormons and a place called Utah. Therefore instead of talking sense or supplying evidence, let the writer satisfy the public by an occasional reminder that the reality is infinitely worse than anything he might describe: "Exaggeration . . . is simply impossible, I could not exaggerate. Not a word of all my story is exaggerated or embellished. The difficulty has been rather to suppress and tone down. Language is inadequate to even half unveil the horrors."[179] So Wallace: "I am conscious that my narrative savours of incredibility,"[180] etc. Once we have firmly established the principle that *one cannot exaggerate,* then it becomes a mere quibble whether what we say is true or not — it is all sober understatement: Smith "either must have been a polygamist or something infinitely worse."[181]

RULE 33: *Uphold the tradition! Correct and improve the legends!* By the time Joseph Smith was twenty-five years old, everything bad that could be said about a man had been said about him, publicly, loudly, and often. This left his critics with no new heights to scale in the art of vituperation and small room for advancement in the invention of new atrocities. From Bennett to Brodie a century of pawing over the old trash pile produced astonishingly little that was new: the anti-Mormon researcher must be content to retell and resell the old horrors all over again.

The problem is not therefore to find out what really happened but to devise ways of making the old stories believable; progress in anti-Mormon studies is necessarily in the fields of *technique* — the very techniques we have been discussing. It is the business of each new generation to improve upon the stories of the preceding one while retelling them — plugging up old loopholes, correcting or expunging disastrous boo-boos, deleting absurdities that can no longer stand examination, touching up the stories where they are weak, toning them down where they are overdone, quietly removing contradictory statements, and above all casting about for anything that might be taken for new evidence. The discovery of one new document, or even a new slant given to an old familiar document, is enough to justify the reprinting of six hundred pages of old stuff. Let us view a few examples of progressive cooperation among practitioners in this vital field.

Mrs. Stenhouse sees in Joseph Smith "a man of ten times the intellect" of Brigham Young: "a man ignorant and deluded, it is true, but at the same time, a man in whom was the material for one of those natural giants."[182] Mrs. Young, however dependent on Stenhouse for everything else, can correct her astigmatism to present Smith as nothing but a "singular combination of the pretentious demagogue and the lecherous hypocrite, persistent violator of the laws of God and man," whose "wicked, blasphemous spirit abides in the community he organized . . . and threatens . . . to destroy the peace and prosperity of the American people."[183] In her turn she has gone too far over on the other side, so it is Mr. Wallace's prerogative to salvage not Joseph Smith's reputation but Mrs. Young's credibility by toning down her overdrawn portrait to the more believable dimensions of J. Smith the frontier bully-boy who "wrestled, gambled, swore, . . . drank, and whored."[184] Not proven, indeed, but plausible.

The Mountain Meadows story has been subject to constant revision. Take this, for example:

> There is legal proof [Mrs. Stenhouse talks a lot about legal proof and "conclusive evidence" without ever supplying any] that the clothing stripped from the corpses was placed in the cellar of the tithing office, where it lay about three weeks, when it was privately sold. The cellar is said to have smelt of it for years. Long after this time, jewelry torn from the mangled bodies of the unfortunate

women was publicly worn in Salt Lake City, and every one knew whence it came.[185]

Now see what Ann Eliza does with this:

> It is told by a man, who then was a mere boy, that . . . the cellars were filled with everything that had been taken from the emigrants, and the bloody garments, stripped from the dead bodies, were thrown down on the floor. . . . Suddenly . . . the cellar . . . resounded with cries, groans, sobs, and the most piercing, agonized shrieks. It is not the first time, by any means, nor the last, that a Mormon public building has been haunted. The property of the emigrants was sold at public auction. To this day, jewelry is worn in Salt Lake City, and teams are seen in the streets, that are known to have belonged to the fatal emigrant train. A lady in Salt Lake City was one day showing a silk dress and some jewelry to some friends, in the presence of one of the children who had been saved from the massacre. The little one, on catching sight of the dress, burst out into a frantic fit of weeping, and between the sobs cried out, "O, my dear mama! That is her dress; she used to wear it." It is said that other children identified clothing and trinkets which they had seen worn by members of the party.[186]

Observe that Ann Eliza treats the items in the same order as Mrs. Stenhouse, but what a production! The lingering odor (for *years*?) becomes a more romantic haunting by spirits; the private sale becomes a public auction; the statement that everyone in Salt Lake City recognized the jewelry "torn from the mangled bodies" being patently absurd (did the women wear their jewelry during the trek across the plains and a three-day Indian battle? Had everyone in Salt Lake City seen the jewels worn?), it is changed to recognition by the children of the slain, with a fine touch of melodrama. As usual, however, Ann Eliza goes overboard in having the teams of the victims parading the streets of

Salt Lake City — twenty years after. Yet she introduces that item less as a touch of drama than a piece of evidence — the horses can be seen to this very day, if you must know! And how does Mr. Wallace treat this? While accepting Ann Eliza's story of Mountain Meadows implicitly, he gallantly forbears making an issue of these irrelevant details, especially when they show his informant to be a free-wheeling liar.

Concerning the child survivors of Mountain Meadows, Mrs. Stenhouse reports that "two of them are said to have uttered some words from which it was presumed that their intelligence was in advance of their years. They were taken quietly and — *buried!*"[187] That is grizzly enough, but Ann Eliza cannot leave it there: "It is said — on how good authority I do not know — that Daniel H. Wells, mayor of Salt Lake City, one of the First Presidency, Second Counsellor to Brigham, Lieutenant-General of the Nauvoo Legion, killed one of these babes with his own official hand. As I said before, I cannot vouch for the authenticity of this rumor, but those who know the man best are the most ready to believe it. He is certainly capable of an act like this."[188] It is a question of which is the more remarkable in this statement, the gossipy virtue with which the accuser clears herself of any responsibility for the ghastly indictment or the crushing weight of official protocol with which she tries to make it stick. Just so Wallace on the cover of his book appends to a banal and disgusting quotation for whose authenticity *he* cannot vouch, the resounding and accusing words, "Joseph Smith, first Prophet and Founder of the Mormon Church." Mrs. Young does not repeat the charge against Wells in her 1908 book, nor does Wallace mention it.

But if the 1908 opus, out for Mormon blood as never before, contains far less specific information than the earlier work, it makes up for the defect by an impressive wealth of text and editorial comment.

For example, in 1875 Ann Eliza tells of a case in which sisters married the same man and concludes: "All this is sanctioned by the President."[189] In 1908 the passage is improved to read: "All this incest and consanguineous intermarriage was sanctioned by President Young."[190] Of course the marriage of sisters to one man is not consanguineous marriage nor incest, but Mr. Wallace is good enough to take Ann Eliza's word for it and even touch it up a little, leaving his readers properly stunned: Brigham Young "believed that incest was not a crime."[191] To the name Utah in her 1876 text,[192] she appends the 1908 comment, "or Deseret as it was then called by the Mormons. The word 'Deseret' was said to mean 'the Land of the honey-bee.' Yet strange to say, there were no native bees in that desert region."[193] Though the Mormons never said there were native bees in the valley, or gave that definition to the word, it does make them look rather ridiculous. Plain Devil's Gate in the early book[194] becomes "Devil's Gate" (ominous name!) in 1908,[195] and "The Apostle Orson Pratt"[196] becomes "The Apostle Orson Pratt, grim-bearded monster."[197] In 1876 we read, "The Indians have become convenient scapegoats,"[198] but in 1908 the same passage has become "The Indians were *always* convenient scapegoats,"[199] a proposition to which Mr. Wallace loyally adheres. The "hand-cart fiasco" was bad enough in 1876, but in 1908 we are told, "Never in the history of any civilized people has there been a recorded case of such gross mismanagement."[200]

And this is the emotional padding by which Mrs. Young keeps her promise to tell us more and worse than ever. Many of her best stories are missing from the later work, and no new ones are added, so that Mr. Wallace is obliged to draw almost exclusively on the earlier, discredited volume. Discredited? Of course. Would she have omitted her best stories, including almost *all* of her personal life with Brigham Young, if there was not something wrong with them? Wallace does his best to make her look good: "Now," he cries, "she was able to tell the whole story of the Mountain Meadows massacre and of Lee's eventual execution."[201] Because anybody could tell it in 1908; but what has that to do with *her* story? Actually she simply repeats the old 1876 version with her own priceless personal touches of intuition and anguish *deleted;* she makes no mention of the childish instincts on which her whole original story is based; the masked batteries of the original version[202] have disappeared;[203] the crucial letter that tells the whole story has vanished;[204] the homey and convincing but utterly preposterous story of how Lee, "like the Ancient Mariner, . . . went up and down compelling every person whom he met to listen to his story" is of course deleted in 1908;[205] the assurance that "the value of their wagons, horses, and stock alone was said to be $300,000"[206] is discreetly cut down to $30,000 in 1908,[207] etc. In 1876 Brigham Young's evil plot against the emigrants is proven by his absolute ban on the sale of any food to them—it was death to sell them a loaf of bread;[208] in 1908 the sure proof of Mormon guilt is their sale of grain to the emigrants, showing only too clearly that they knew they would get it all back again.[209]

On the positive side, Ann Eliza by 1908 has become quite an authority on strategy and tactics and knows all about Brigham Young's military policies and operations;[210] she can now even explain the great mystery of Mountain Meadows as part of a Mormon War against the States. In 1908 she can tell us all about the Bank of Kirtland,[211] or exactly what went on between Brigham Young and John D. Lee,[212] because by then anybody could buy Lee's book. In her big autobiography of 1876, the Mormon Battalion is mentioned only as "another illustration" of Brigham Young's "cruelty and greed"; but in 1908, after the Battalion had a secure place in American history, its departure is numbered among Ann Eliza's personal reminiscenses of

Winter Quarters;[213] Wallace, as we have seen, never mentions it at all.

As Ann Eliza improves first on Stenhouse and then on herself, so Wallace improves on both. When Mrs. Young quietly drops a discredited story, Wallace, at the safe distance of time, can revive it. She has her reasons and they are good ones for dropping the stories of Amelia at the ball,[214] the "very amusing story" of how Brigham failed to recognize his own wife,[215] the Badley and Moon Story,[216] the tales of Baptiste the grave-robber,[217] etc. But Wallace has equally good reason for resurrecting them, for without them, his image of Brigham and the Mormons would bear no conviction. The Baptiste story, for all its grizzly atmosphere, is irrelevant, but Wallace salvages it boldly by converting the clothing and jewels which the grave-robber understandably coveted into Mormon temple clothing, which nobody could possibly want. Note how neatly he converts the well-known Gentile superstition that Mormons have horns into a *Mormon* superstition that *Gentiles* have horns: "At a social gathering . . . she met an infidel named Howard Sawyer, and she was pleasantly surprised to find that he did not have horns."[218] Thus he preserves Gentile nonsense by transmuting it with disarming tolerance and good humor into Mormon nonsense. On those rare occasions on which Ann Eliza corrects and tones down Stenhouse, Wallace defers to the older and more lurid version. Thus where Ann Eliza admits with reluctance that she has never heard Brigham Young use profanity (a thing he abhorred above all else), Mr. Wallace calls upon Stenhouse to correct her: he did swear, and in the Tabernacle. Ann Eliza hedges on Stenhouse's story of "one terrible meeting" at which four-fifths of the congregation confessed to adultery — an inconceivable oversight if the story had any foundation whatever — so Wallace must tell it as the fruit of his own valuable researches,[219] though it comes right out of Stenhouse.[220] Ann Eliza describes the crossing

of the plains as a jolly adventure (and so my own grandfather always described it); but that is *not* the proper atmosphere for an anti-Mormon book: Stenhouse quotes Mary
Burton: "What weary days we spent!"[221]—and this, apparently, is enough to authorize Mr. Wallace to describe
not Burton's but Ann Eliza's *own* journey as "a nightmare
of monotony."[222] Ann Eliza is content to report that the
members of the Tobin party were ambushed at the Santa
Clara River, a favorite ground for Indian attacks; but Wallace cannot let it go at that: "It *may* have been a coincidence"
is his biting editorial comment.[223]

An easy and pleasant way of contributing to the anti-
Mormon corpus is to supply the gestures where others
have supplied the conversation. As we have seen, Mrs.
Young's history is full of imagined, stilted, and artificial
conversations; by a few deft touches Wallace makes them
come to life. Ann Eliza herself shows how this is done,
i.e, in her own retelling of a conversation in which Brigham
Young secretly instructs an aged wife not to blab about his
dirty business deals: " 'They would not understand, you
know,' murmured he in his most drivellingly sweet accents."[224] Since it is hard to believe that Mrs. Lewis, who
loved Brigham Young and hated Ann Eliza, actually told
her about those drivellingly sweet accents, it is safe to
attribute them to Ann Eliza herself. But how they bring
the story to life! Thus speaks Joseph Smith: " 'It is your
privilege to have all the wives you want,' he said coolly."
It is inconceivable that he ever said anything of the sort,
but if he had it would have been cool, all right, and so we
have caught him red-handed. Again, "Smith smiled
wanly." Who said he smiled? Who said wanly? Mr. Wallace
both times,[225] with telling effect. "Brigham did not so much
as blink,"[226] he stared with fascination at Ann Eliza,[227] he
stared hard with a "steady, unflinching gaze,"[228] his "face
flushed with rage"[229]—it is little touches like this that make

a story real and convincing, and if you, like Mr. Wallace, are convinced of the story — well, go ahead and make them!

But in so doing seek not to scale the heights that Wallace ascends in his story of the cow! Here surely is a rewriting feat of heroic proportions. In 1876 Ann Eliza told how Mary Angell, Brigham Young's first wife, lives in "the old school-house behind the Bee-Hive, a dilapidated, cheerless place, not nearly so good as the house she has left."[230] Using the commonest of all expressions to describe big houses, the fastidious Ann Eliza continues, "It is indeed, little better than a barn, and is furnished very scantily."[231] With those key words, *barn* and old *school-house*, Wallace performs a minor miracle:

> Mary Ann Angell . . . had the right to claim one-third of his enormous estate under the law. Instead, a constant invalid, she kept to the privacy of her own quarters, the abandoned school-house behind the Lion House, which she shared with a cow who lived in a partitioned stall. On June 27, 1882, at the age of seventy-nine, she died.[232]

Could anything be more withering than that ominous procession of loaded words — right, enormous estate, law, invalid, abandoned schoolhouse, cow, stall, died? Is there a word in the grim passage that is *not* loaded? It is all there, the dirt, the cold (for cow stalls were unheated in those days), the smells, the loneliness, and the sad patient animal, old age, cruel poverty, sickness and pain, rights meanly denied by a cynical libertine, property basely stolen, and then finally death and merciful deliverance! And all that, apparently, out of Ann Eliza's gossipy "school-house" and "big-as-a-barn." Who is going to remember amidst choking indignation at such injustice that Mr. Wallace has noted that "Actually Mary Ann Angell, widely respected in Utah, had become a recluse in The White House on the hill."[233]

And what was "The White House on the hill"? One of the finest mansions in the Territory, which Brigham Young had built just for Mary Ann Angell. It served many years as a headquarters of the Elks Lodge, and was not torn down (for the inevitable parking lot) until 1958. While it was being built, Mrs. Young shared the even more magnificent Gardo House with Amelia. Actually there was a large barn right behind the Lion House. It was never used as a school, Preston Nibley informs me, and nobody ever lived in it. Directly across the street to the east of the Lion House and the barn was Brigham Young's schoolhouse, now immortalized by a bronze plaque, an elegant little building which never served as anything but a schoolhouse. A block further east stood the splendid "White House on the hill," where Mrs. Young spent the last years of her life, known to all "as 'Mother Young' and was much esteemed as the 'Mother' of the family,"[234] and there she died.[235] A member of the First Presidency "had visited the deceased during her illness," and spoke at her funeral, which was attended by a "large body of mourners."[236] Her two eldest sons were Joseph A. and Brigham Jr., the very Brigham Jr. who, according to Wallace, took his father to task more than once for his neglect of Ann Eliza.[237] And these, Brigham Young's most influential offspring, would allow their adored mother to suffer the refined tortures of Brigham's criminal neglect?

Slips and oversights are inevitable in any historical writing and cannot be held as major crimes. But since Mr. Wallace has found in the last years of Mrs. Young a demonstration of the depths of depravity to which Brigham Young descends, one wonders if he has not gone a bit too far.

RULE 34: *Be patriotic.* Anti-Mormon classics tend to be of a strong patriotic tone. Ann Eliza's 1908 volume is a perfect demonstration of how patriotism can be exploited to make Mormon-baiting pay. In her earlier writing she had expressed a fastidious and ladylike disdain for voting and all that goes with it; but she had learned in the meantime that to be a champion of the downtrodden womanhood, she would have to wrap herself in the flag. Her message of 1875 is that the Government is criminally soft on Mormonism: "When it was shown me that I might . . . open people's eyes to the enormity of the religious system which was tolerated by the Government, I hesitated no longer."[238] "People of America," she shouts, "are these incarnate fiends . . . still to be objects of worship and reverence to thousands of our countrymen? . . . I warn my fellow-countrymen against their false pretenses, their adulterous practices, their murderous oaths, their uncharitable animosity towards the American Government and People."[239] The desire of Utah for statehood certainly proved treasonable intent: "The Mormons . . . sought to be freed from Federal restrictions by securing the full rights of Statehood, so that they could make their own laws without interference. After years of wily political manoeuvering they gained their objective in 1896. . . . Calmly and carelessly Congress conferred independent Statehood upon an unorganized band of unscrupulous traitors."[240] Whatever the Mormons were, they could hardly be accused of being unorganized; but traitors? Well, didn't Brigham Young say Zachary Taylor was in hell? If you don't think that is treason, just ask Mr. Wallace.[241] Ann Eliza has even better proof: "The foundation of Americanism is absolute security for the life and honor of women. . . . That man is a traitor to his country who makes light of the honor of women. Mormonism is . . . horrible treason to the fundamental ideal of American institutions."[242] Why does the Constitution allow it? Only because the Founding Fathers "could not conceive of a deranged, visionary mountebank, calling himself a prophet, seer and revelator, and counseling his followers to debauch young women under the pretense of religion."[243] Such fervid syllogisms spring as readily to the mind as the big resounding adjectives do to the mouth of the practicing patriot. The reader will readily appreciate the advantage of placing himself in the position where to question him is to be against the America he stands for. It is an old and favorite trick of professional patriots.

RULE 35: *Join the ladies.* Any anti-Mormon writer does well to follow Mr. Wallace's example and take his stand with the ladies or behind their skirts. All the most effective anti-Mormon books have been written by women—Nancy Towle, Orvilla Belisle, Ettie V. Smith, Maria Ward, Fanny Stenhouse, Ann Eliza Webb Dee Young Denning, Mrs. Dr. Horace Eaton, Emily Austin, Ellen Dickinson, Lily Dougal, Winifred Graham, Fawn M. Brodie—to name a few, because we can think of no others just now. Women have always worked with the clergy, who through the years have been the principal promoters of anti-Mormon literature; women are the fragile and helpless victims of male brutality, commanding sympathy and attention; women cannot be questioned too closely in delicate matters; the natural modesty of the sex exonerates them from the task of telling shocking stories or giving any proof for them while at the same time the humanity and idealism of the same sex requires them to be sure to mention the stories and tell *about* them; to be emotional rather than explicit is woman's prerogative, which no one with a spark of chivalry would question. Small wonder, then, that the *feminine touch* is the hallmark of anti-Mormon creativity. Naturally any of the above authoresses can supply us with abundant illustrations, but we remain true as ever to Ann Eliza (especially since that saves us a lot of work) and glory in her femininity.

Being a woman enables her, in the first place, to speak for all other women. It is like being a Jew — "Does he know Hebrew?" cried my friend with passion. "Does he know Hebrew!? Man, he *is* a Jew!" The wives of Brigham Young don't need to speak for themselves; Ann Eliza can speak for them: "I have no hesitation in saying, from my own experience with and knowledge of them, that more unhappy and wretched women do not exist in the world, than the more cultured and delicate wives of Brigham Young."[244] If one of them should venture a word of protest, Ann Eliza can slap her down as no man would dare: "what blindness, what madness, what folly!" "There is nothing for *any* Mormon woman to do but to submit, and let her heart break in the meanwhile."[245] "In her heart of hearts, no woman of them all believes it to be right."[246] "What Mormon mother ever gets the tender care . . . that other happier mothers get?"[247] "I often wonder if there is a child in Mormondom, born under the blight of polygamy, who knows what it is to have a happy, joyous childhood."[248] " 'You are mine, body and soul, but you have no right to claim anything from me more than what I choose to give you,' is the attitude of every man in polygamy towards his wives."[249]

And what men! "Their . . . spiritual natures deadened; their animal natures quickened; they lose manliness and descend to the level of brutes; and these dull-witted, intellectually-dwarfed moral corpses, the women are told, are their only saviors,"[250] so they "discuss women, with reference to their 'points,' as jockeys would talk of horses, or importers of fine stock."[251] "Happiness and contentment are utterly unknown to Mormon women."[252] "Who wonders at the immovable mouths, expressionless eyes, and gray, hopeless faces, which tourists mark *always* as the characteristics of the Mormon women?"[253] Mormonism had "made the faces grow repulsive and grim, and taken from them all the softness, and the tenderness, and grace which glorify a happy woman's face. . . . It is no wonder that the women of Utah are not beautiful."[254] Worst of all, the hymn-singing, bigoted women of Utah *had no children*: childlessness was the universal curse, and when a child was born, "maternity brings no such joy, and added love, and tender care" as it does to women outside of Utah.[255] It is almost more than a reader can stand: "I have felt my heart throb and ache with jealous anguish for the little ones in Utah, and above all for their weary-hearted mothers."[256] Those not born in polygamy are born "under the *blight* of polygamy," and long after leaving Utah, Ann Eliza would shed hot tears and palpitate with explosive rage at the thought of how her own two little ones had been denied a father's love "by a fiendish system,"[257] in which their father never had any part. So don't think that Ann Eliza didn't suffer.

As a brave little woman, Ann Eliza doesn't have to put up with any nonsense from great strapping men who question her story. When the official findings of the Mountain Meadows failed to match her own, she had only to declare them "a sarcasm upon justice, a gross, hideous burlesque from beginning to end," which merely showed "the utter futility of expecting anything like justice in a court where this man's followers are allowed to sit on a jury."[258] She has no patience with a government and a constitution that allow religious liberty to such people; isn't the first object of government "absolute security for the life and honor of woman"? If a president of the United States failed to respond as U. S. Grant did (he was a pushover) to her heroics, she roundly berates him in public press and reminds him of his duty.[259]

Well instructed, Mr. Wallace gives the "last word" on polygamy to a woman, "a daughter-in-law of Brigham Young."[260] Why the last word? the reader may wonder. Does being a daughter-in-law of a man with many daughters-in-law make one an authority on anything? Well, "as Edith Young Booth, a granddaughter of Brigham Young, informed this writer: 'Men had a wonderful time under polygamy.' "[261] What particularly qualifies this woman to speak for the other sex of a generation she never knew is that she said it directly to Wallace. What more could you want in the way of proof. Would you question a lady?

RULE 36: *Your target is Mormonism!* Anti-Mormon books are not written to describe or discuss the human foibles of any group or individual but to discredit a doctrine. Every episode, however trivial, irrelevant, or fictitious must be made to serve as the text for a single sermon—the monstrousness of believing in revelation. The bad thing about the "heartless and mercenary" handcart fiasco is "that all this should be done 'in the name of the Lord.' . . . Take this home to yourself, and you will be able to appreciate as never before the horrors of Mormonism." Therein resides the horror: "A better people—aside from their religion . . . it would be difficult to find. Their fault was in their *faith*."[262] "To have deceived a credulous people by wanton misrepresentation is wicked enough, but to do it 'in the name of the Lord' is a sin that can never be atoned for to God or man. It is the height of blasphemy, and I fairly shudder as I endeavor to comprehend, in some slight degree, the magnitude of such an offence."[263] Every anti-Mormon book is a sermon, and the most effective of sermons is the one, as Augustine long ago observed, that excites to action by running away with the emotions and leaving reason and judgment far behind. Here is how Ann Eliza sums up her *Thousand and One Nights*: "Yet all these incredible distortions of reckless fancy have become veritable facts. They have been crystallized into a monstrous system of wickedness, guarded by a band of loathsome ogres, who feast upon the spoils of their victims and . . . take delight in their misery. . . . The American people therefore must continue their holy crusade against this antichristian system."[264]

Mr. Wallace is not so direct and forthright, but he is just as determined and dedicated; for old-fashioned, editorial rhetoric he substitutes modern sophisticated techniques of news-slanting. Particularly effective is the insertion of numerous little asides, mendacious tidbits too trivial to challenge, fleeting subliminal impressions that build up the same cumulative force as the repetitious old breast-thumping. It is not true that the passing of the Fifteenth Amendment "still did not open the Mormon Church to Negroes,"[265] or that the Archives Room of the Genealogical Society is "open only to Mormons,"[266] but who is going to quibble about it? But whether you choose the hysterical or the suave treatment, it all adds up to the same thing—the miasmic atmosphere of Mormonism, stifling, foul, and always at least a little bit disgusting. The real villain of every anti-Mormon book is Mormonism. And this is as true today as in 1830. Not human greed and viciousness but Mormonism was responsible for Mountain Meadows; Smith, Young, Kimball, "the hierarchy" and "the underlings" go through their grotesque paces for Mr. Wallace not as human beings but as Mormons; nobody ever commits a crime *in spite* of being a Mormon, but always because of it—that should have a familiar ring to any perceptive Jew. The concluding sentence of Ann Eliza's first book proclaims, "It is my life-mission . . . to see the foul curse removed, and Utah—my beloved Utah—free from the unholy rule of the religious tyrant,—Brigham Young."[267] But when Young was dead and gone she easily transferred all her loathing to his successor, "a tall, benevolent-looking man . . . the smooth-tongued hypocrite . . . a cold, heartless, unfeeling master and a reckless falsifier of facts";[268] and then to *his* successor, "the hoary criminal," Lorenzo Snow;[269] and then to *his*—Joseph F. Smith, "a thorough-paced despotic Mormon . . . glorying in his shame. . . . He lives in regal splendor, . . . a monarch among his subjects, . . . an autocrat equal in power . . . to Brigham Young in his palmiest days. . . . His rapacity is felt in the manufactures and other industries of Utah, which are all compelled to pay tithes to his storehouse."[270] Obviously, the Mormons can't win.

It is helpful to remember that the Mormons have only themselves to thank for this sort of treatment, which they invite when they accept the supernatural. How can a "detached, modern intelligence, grounded in naturalism, rejecting the supernatural,"[271] make any compromise with gold plates and angels? What C. S. Lewis says about Jesus Christ applies to any prophet: you cannot simply write him off as a well-meaning oaf; he was not just a good-hearted ignoramus who went about claiming to be the Son of God—good-hearted ignoramuses do not go about making such claims. That is why Mr. Wallace has no choice but to damn Brigham Young, and why his claim to be neither for nor against the Mormon position is patently absurd. To say "I became neither anti-Mormon nor pro-Mormon"[272] is to say that one neither accepts *nor* rejects modern-day revelation, the impossibility of which proposition would, to quote Stenhouse, "in a moment be detected by any intelligent Saint."[273]

Special Bulletin: They Were All Such Good Mormons

It is understandable that nearly all the standard exposés of Mormonism have been written by women. The Mormon woman, quietly standing on the sidelines or moving inconspicuously through the community on her round of simple duties, is in a uniquely advantageous position to see and hear all. But only if she is a *good* Mormon. Until Mrs. Stenhouse came along, according to Mrs. Stenhouse, "with but one exception — that of a lady who . . . so mixed up fiction with what was true, that it was difficult to determine where the one ended and the other began — no woman who *really* was a Mormon . . . ever wrote the history of her own personal experience."[274] It is she who underlines that *really*, recognizing it as the key to the whole problem. Though the extensive literature "purporting to be written by Mormon wives," Mrs. Stenhouse continues, ". . . may be imposed upon the Gentile world as genuine, that they were written by persons outside the Mormon faith would in a moment be detected by any intelligent Saint who took the trouble to peruse them."[275]

It is to establish their unique ascendency in a competitive market that our female Mormonologists must insist that they were not only Mormons but very *good* Mormons, and through family ties directly or indirectly connected with the highest authorities. Granted that such connections are a misleading standard, since it is no great thing in such a small community to be related to everybody, and since the higher brackets in the Church have always furnished the highest percentage of apostates, still it goes over with the general public and many Mormons. The only ones who are not fooled are, as Mrs. Stenhouse rightly observes, any intelligent Saints if such there be.

And the first thing any intelligent Saint notices about our tale-tellers is that one and all they never were the good Mormons they claim to have been. As Milton R. Hunter points out, any ten-year-old Mormon who went to Sunday School could correct Mrs. Brodie on a number of things.[276] No one who had been a good Mormon could possibly make the slips she does, barring, of course, the feebleminded. It is the reviewers in the journals who give Mrs. Brodie her authority—but what do they know about Joseph Smith? Only what she tells them. So they hail her as their licensed guide while she proudly waves their reviews as her license, and everybody is happy.

What justifies Mr. Wallace in placing his hand trustingly in Ann Eliza's and bidding her lead the way is the profession that his guide "had once been an orthodox Mormon and had then become a bitter anti-Mormon." Her greatest affliction was the "trauma of having abandoned, within herself, her lifelong faith."[277] "I dared not question," she tells us. "The system must be right, and my doubts, when doubts arose, must be wrong."[278] She begins her book by telling how people always ask one question before all others—"Why I ever became a Mormon?" How did a lady of her lofty moral standards ever come to marry Brigham Young? The answer had to be good. Ann Eliza herself has no sympathy for "an Eastern born and educated girl," who "entered polygamy with her eyes open," but only for "those poor girls who are educated in Mormonism, and know nothing else"—including, of course, herself.[279] It was, she insisted, her deep religious convictions that drove her to it: "I did not know but that I was fighting the will of the Lord as well as the will of the Prophet. . . . The thought struck me, in a sudden terror, 'What if God should take my children, to punish my rebellious spirit?' It was agony. 'Not my will, but thine,' was my heart-broken cry. . . . I would become the wife of Brigham Young!"[280]

Bible? What Bible?

That is her story, and "any intelligent Saint" can see that it is a fraud. If only her absurd protestations of extreme ignorance and naiveté are considered, they are enough to discredit it. At thirty she still believes that Gentiles have horns, if we trust Mr. Wallace; or if we believe her, at that same age she "could not understand this religion [non-Mormon] which regarded woman as an independent soul, with a free will, and capability of judgment."[281] Yet years before this she had been scandalized and amused at the Mormon idea of letting women vote. When after leaving Utah she saw an aged couple walking side by side, "I could scarcely believe my own senses. . . . I could only wonder and weep."[282] With Mrs. Stenhouse she bleeds for the women of Utah, "those hymn-singing, devotional women, who childless and husbandless here, dream of the glories of the world to come, while they never knew the duties, the obligations, the sweet and hallowed sympathies of the world in which they live."[283] We submit that the picture of the women of Utah in general doomed to a state of *childlessness* is overdoing it a bit. Ann Eliza was amazed to learn from a minister's wife that "her husband's God was her God as well."[284]

Some time after leaving the Mormons, Mrs. Young confessed to a preacher as follows, quote: "No, I never read a Gospel in my life. . . . I know nothing about Jesus Christ; I am a perfect child."[285] That is quite enough to show what kind of a Mormon she had been, and what kind of an upbringing she had received. No minister ever quoted the Bible more frequently or more aptly than Brigham Young or urged the reading of it more importunately on one and all. The Bible was his book. If Ann Eliza had even so much as peeked into the Book of Mormon she should know that its whole substance is the mission of Jesus Christ. She continues her confession to the reverend:

"nor have I heard more than two sermons since my escape from that false religion."[286] A professional lecturer on the evils of false religion, making "blasphemy" her stock in trade, this little lady evinces not the slightest interest in any *other* religion. Her religious interest stops with Mormonism, and her program is simple: "I . . . expect to loathe it more and more while I live."[287]

But since the ministry are her agents and the churches her auditoriums, Mrs. Young cannot well continue as an infidel: "I had drifted blindly on, with no belief in anything, no faith in any system; sometimes, even, doubting the existence of God."[288] And is this the reaction to her "providential escape" from torture and enslavement? She duly joins the largest and most respectable and most reliable of her customers, and her "conversion to the Methodist Episcopal faith was printed far and wide."[289] "Tossed all my life on a stormy sea of superstition," she announced, "I was at last anchored in the sheltered haven of Christian belief."[290] Which sheltered haven she presently deserted, true to form, to find another in Christian Science.

It is only her indifference to religion in general that explains Ann Eliza's remarkable ignorance of Mormonism. When did the Mormons ever teach that confirmation places one "beyond the possibility of falling from grace or missing the celestial gate"?[291] When had Joseph Smith ever "announced himself as another Messiah"?[292] Since when were marriages "performed in the Gentile form . . . not binding"?[293] When did any Mormon ever preach that "the 'First Presidency' . . . is supposed to be the earthly representative of the Trinity, 'the Eternal Godhead, Three in One' "? To this last she adds, "It is needless to say, which rank Brigham assigns himself"[294] (laughter). For such obvious things proof is needless. Since practicing physicians were among the first leaders of the Church, it is enlightening to read that "no Mormon in good standing would ever entertain the suggestion [of consulting a doctor] for a moment."[295] When did Brigham Young declare in the Tabernacle "that they [doctors] should never enter heaven, but that he would himself close the doors against them"?[296]

According to Ann Eliza, "the God of the Mormon belief was . . . a jealous God, a cruel, avenging Spirit. . . . Retribution, and justice untempered by mercy, were all He had for His subjects, not children."[297] Yet it was to *that* God that Ann Eliza's own good, Christian parents became converts? In the Endowment House, she says, "We swore also to entertain an everlasting enmity to the United States Government, and to disregard its laws so far as possible, . . . and to teach our children to foster this spirit of revenge also." That explains why "the cutting of every Gentile and apostate throat . . . so openly and emphatically urged from the stand by Brigham Young and others, is only a public expression of the mysteries of the Endowment oaths."[298] "*We* swore" to all that? Ann Eliza and her "strictest of Mormon households" went along with it all, though they knew that "the whole system of Mormon religion was a mass of revolting crime and wickedness. . . . The very thought of it brings a shudder. The most horrible things were taught from the pulpit, and decency was outraged every time a Mormon leader opened his mouth to speak."[299] Sunday after Sunday the intelligent and independently minded Webb family sat drinking in the words of the leaders (nay, if we believe Mr. Wallace, Ann Eliza knew many of them by heart!): "There was not a pure character in all the Bible history which their dirty hands did not besmear, and their foul tongues blacken."[300] What sermons! And the good *Familie Webb* were converts, remember, who knew very well what was preached in good Christian churches: she cannot claim for her parents as she does for herself, the innocence of never having known any better. So to save their reputation, she develops the thesis that Mama and Papa, like herself, never really believed in Mormonism, but had certain reservations.

The Skeptical Fanatics

But in that case, what happens to her fervid claims of orthodoxy? Here Mrs. A.E.W.D.Y.D. has to walk a tightrope; she must have us believe that she was the most devout and unquestioning of believers, but at the same time was much too smart and noble to be taken in by all that nonsense. Thus she brands as either liars or fools those women who speak well of the endowment ceremony and assures us that "such absurdities may have weight with some women, but they did not affect my mother."[301] Then she goes on to tell how that same mother "was overjoyed" at the prospect of her daughter's endowments, while "as a matter of course, I shared her feelings *most fully.*"[302] With respect to polygamy, when we read of Mrs. Webb's cool appraisal and damning indictment of the whole "ridiculous farce," it is something of a surprise to learn that "it *never* occurred to her that the system was false and horrible in the extreme; she only felt that *she* was lacking in grace."[303] Mrs. Stenhouse shows what we are up against when she reports: "To face opposition or to give my *all* for my religion, I was willing indeed; but to depend upon others for my daily bread was utterly repugnant to my feelings, although, of course . . . it was only right that the members of that Church should undertake the responsibility," i.e., to support her while her husband was away on a mission.[304] So having professed her willingness to suffer and give all for the Church, she bitterly complains that the Church is not giving her enough. To "any intelligent Saint," to quote the same lady, this is a dead giveaway; it means that she can never have been the good Mormon she says she was. Always she wants to have it both ways; she is both a Mormon and not a Mormon: "Let him [the reader] remember that, although my faith was shaken, it was not wholly destroyed."[305] Like her friend Mary Burton, she criticized everything right from the first, eagerly grasping at anything that looked like a contradiction in doctrine or inconsistency in practice, always alert for any gossip that might discredit the authorities, ever nursing a sense of personal offense. As for Ann Eliza, it was during those deliriously happy days at South Cottonwood in the bosom of her devoted mother that she was "getting all these peeps into the inside experiences of polygamy."[306] She may never have looked into the Bible or the Book of Mormon, but *these* stories she learned literally at her mother's knee.

As a child, Ann Eliza saw through the Mormon fraud and suspected the worst when even her elders did not. At the age of twelve she knew the story of Pratt not in the "Mormon version" but "as the anti-Mormon press featured it."[307] She knew all about the crimes of John D. Lee long before Mountain Meadows, and she "sensed" long before anybody else in the family that he was the real instigator of the atrocity. Before her marriage to Brigham Young she knew of all his crimes, including those against her own family, and "had lost," as she puts it, "at that time, much of my faith in my religion."[308] And then just after marrying Brigham Young she roundly seconds a speech of Emmeline: "Well, I've lost faith in the whole thing. I consider Mormonism a stupendous humbug, and all the people who have been made to believe it terrible dupes," etc.[309] Though Emmeline was long dead when Ann Eliza reported this stirring peroration, she can say of herself at the time, "I had begun to think things out for myself, and I had arrived at very much the same conclusion that Emmeline had."

This is the lady whose separation from her "lifelong faith" was to inflict such a spiritual trauma. As a child, "though I was duly advised by teachers and catechists to marry into polygamy, . . . I gave very little heed to the advice, and set about making my own romance . . . in my imagination."[310] This is our good, obedient, trusting Eliza, giving "very little heed" to her Mormon teachers and full rein to her romantic imagination. For her, baptism meant "so great was the nervous shock that I could not think of it without a shudder for years after."[311] Her girlhood was spent eagerly gossiping about the horrid old man. The endowments brutalized her as cruelly as baptism.[312] She was saddened and "disappointed" when the ordinances did not come up to her expectations of "something solemn and awful."[313] Her sublime faith collapses at a touch, just as her hopes and dreams do every time she opens the box: Nothing is ever good enough for our Eliza.

Towards all the teachings of the Church she is heedless, resentful, openly contemptuous; everything nauseates, hurts, offends, abuses, disappoints, frightens, sickens, and shocks her and Mr. Wallace. All she ever got from the teachings of Brigham Young was a headache; she reports "with exaggerated disgust," as Mr. Wallace puts it: "The only good counsel I ever received from him was to practice the strictest economy."[314] When the President tells her that it is her duty to marry, she replies: "It can't be, I should not recognize a duty of that kind. I consider myself old enough . . . to judge of my duties without any assistance."[315] Yet it was nothing less than her religious sense of duty, she insists, that later drove her to marry that same much-married man! We have seen how she behaved toward him, wearing the longest possible train because he spoke his strong disapproval of the silly fashion. Brigham Young laid great stress upon the basic Mormon institution of family prayer, but Ann Eliza "used to go whenever I felt inclined, which was very seldom; and the longer I was a member of the family, the more infrequent became my attendance."[316] Talking with the wives who would listen to her, she never tired of railing against polygamy, and "expressed myself strongly and bitterly against it."[317] Nobody forced her to go to prayers or to suppress her opinions; while still married to Brigham Young she intrigued busily against him with his enemies, with whom she "spoke very freely on the subject of Mormonism,"[318] nay

"I talked to them unreservedly. . . . I told them . . . all the occurrences of my marriage to Brigham Young."[319]

But what gives Ann Eliza away most completely to any intelligent or unintelligent Saint is the very obvious fact that she was never active in the Church in any capacity. Now this is a singular circumstance, not only because the Mormons have always called upon all to do their share, and in those days were terribly short-handed, but because the lady herself insists that she is a born *slave to duty*, the guiding star of her life.[320] Why then during her thirty years of iron orthodoxy were the Mormons at no time able to appeal to that exquisite sense of duty? Why is she with her energy and her crusading spirit completely passive during those great years on the frontier? Is it for the same reason that her great crusade in the East came to an abrupt end the moment she married the rich Mr. Denning? But we are being unfair. Ann Eliza did carry on her own little crusade from her first childish denunciations of the priest-hood—*against* the Church. This can be best understood if we consider the wonderful ways of her devoted mother.

The Burning Faith of Mrs. Webb

It is mother who carries the family along by her faith and her strength. It is also mother who supplies Ann Eliza with her arsenal of anti-Mormon atrocity stories during the long happy days at Cottonwood. It is through Mama's eyes that Ann Eliza views the horrors of polygamy. And there was that mission call for her son. While other mothers rejoiced in such an event, "an added sorrow to my mother came, when . . . my eldest brother was sent on a mission to the Sandwich Islands. She mourned his departure deeply, and even I could not comfort her."[321] What kind of a Mormon mother was that? On the subject of polygamy she pulled out all the stops: "My mother has often said that the 'Revelation' was the most hateful thing in the world to her, and she dreaded and abhorred it."[322] She would protest "with unutterable anguish against the life that she felt was false and in direct contradiction to every law of moral right."[323] As to arguments in its favor, religious or not, "such absurdities may have weight with some women, but they did not affect my mother."[324]

Why did she accept it then? Because "she was afraid to oppose it, lest she should be found 'fighting against the Lord.' "[325] This false and hateful thing, opposed to "every law of moral right," nevertheless came from God. She knew that Brigham Young was a criminal: "my mother and other Mormons . . . would have disapproved of the proceedings, and even called them dishonest, had they dared."[326] Why didn't she dare? Didn't she roundly denounce him as a crook in her own kitchen? Well, she wasn't afraid of *him*, it was her *conscience* that kept her in line: "It never occurred to her that the system was false and horrible in the extreme: she only felt that she was lacking in grace."[327] "Conscience . . . made her cling to her religion long after reason taught her that it was a delusion, and made her accept as a sole means of salvation a practice which her whole soul revolted against."[328] Read that over again: While her *whole soul* revolted, the *conscience* part of her soul told her it was the only means of *salvation*. And this even though "her religion . . . brought her not one ray of comfort, but in after years blighted her domestic life."[329] So we have Mama sticking to a religion that offered not one ray of comfort, and which she knew was false and utterly immoral, because her conscience told her—what?

In a pioneer community where everyone did his share, Mrs. Webb, "considered a person of superior attainments by the Saints," was naturally asked to help out as a teacher, her sons being grown and her husband away on a mission. As her daughter puts it, "In Utah she had often been solicited to resume her profession. She had *always* hitherto *refused*," but finally "she decided to accept the situation, which was fairly *thrust* upon her."[330] When under Ann

Eliza's constant prodding, both her parents left the Church, her mother, now married to a good non-Mormon, promptly divorced him. Not a word of this in Ann Eliza, who reports that Mama is now "happy in a home safe from the intrusion of polygamy, every shade of bigotry blotted out, her reason unfettered, her will free, I am happier than I ever can say."[331] At the same time Mrs. Webb says of her daughter: "I do not see much of Ann Eliza; she comes about once in six weeks and stays not more than two days." Then she lowers the beam: "There is quite as much bigotry, superstition, and fanaticism in the east as in the west, and more trouble in monogamic marriage than I had supposed."[332] Well, well, "every shade of bigotry blotted out"! Now she was free to read the Bible without Brigham Young looking over her shoulder, and when someone recommends the Old Testament and the New to her, "I told him I was in favor of both going into the stove together."[333] Such was her burning faith.

Mrs. Webb holds the key to Ann Eliza's story. Through the years, mother and daughter were as close together as two human beings could be. Nothing escaped Mama's keen eye, an eye single to the glory of her idolized daughter, who *could* not have experienced and suffered what she did without her mother's awareness of it. Yet her mother *was* unaware of the true history of Ann Eliza! Not until it was all over did our heroine let her mother know of her childhood insights into the true nature of Mormon atrocities; not until she had suffered the brutal assaults of Dee for two years did Mama suspect anything was wrong — and she living right in the same house with them all that time! The titanic two-year struggle against the crude and unfeeling advances of Brigham Young was carefully concealed from her mother — who had no reason to guess that all was not well; and then finally all those years of married life, with Mama never suspecting a thing, but crushed and bereaved only when she learned to her immense surprise

that Ann Eliza had left her husband—and she had been living right with her daughter all those years, too. Why was Mama never let in on any of Ann Eliza's real life? It was because, we are told, the considerate daughter kept her devoted mother in the dark in order to spare her religious sensibilities.

Even to save herself from "the contaminating clutches of Brigham Young" she would not point out the falseness of his position to her mother: "I dared not enter into religious discussion with her, for I felt so bitterly that I should be sure to say something to shock her."[334] After all she had heard from Mama about Brigham! And then as the wife of Young, "I could not tell my feelings to my mother, for . . . she could never separate him from her religion."[335] Even after the old lady had worked herself to death on the farm, "although she was losing confidence in Brigham Young, she still clung to her religion."[336] Thus Mrs. Webb's religious fanaticism is a conveniently flexible covering for the glaring inconsistencies in Ann Eliza's history. Which makes one more inconsistency, since Mrs. Webb was anything but a fanatical Mormon. Fanatic she was, on that one theme which rivals religion alone as the commonest object of fanaticism—the quest for position and status. And if she had religious feelings, they were certainly divided between her Church and that other object of her worship, Ann Eliza.

Papa was a good Mormon too. From the earliest days of the Church, according to his daughter, he had almost completely distrusted Joseph Smith: "My father . . . distrusted [him] almost entirely."[337] And after Brigham Young took over, and especially since 1857, he "had no faith" at all in Mormonism.[338] The only reason he joined the Church was to satisfy Mrs. Webb, and he firmly believed that Joseph Smith was responsible for all the misfortune of his family and of the Church in general "by his, to say the least, unwise teachings."[339] When Ann Eliza convinced the old man that Brigham Young was to blame for all the newspaper gossip about her and her handsome agent, he denounced Young publicly as "a corrupt leader," and was cut off from the Church—a cruel blow, as Ann Eliza describes it. But why a cruel blow? He had always known Brigham for what he was and yet insisted on making his darling daughter marry the monster. Ann Eliza's brothers and sons likewise ended up as apostates, and none of the family ever seems to have held any office in the Church. Since it is virtually impossible to be an "orthodox Mormon" for long, let alone a Mormon in intimate contact with the leaders of the Church as the Webbs were, without being called to some position of responsibility,

Ann Eliza's claim to have been raised in "the strictest of Mormon households" calls for drastic amendment.

In nothing are the marks of distortion, conscious or unconscious, more apparent than in the study of the time scale of anti-Mormon works. Mr. Wallace labors idealistically to construct a scheme by which his heroine in a long series of agonized and convulsive fits tears herself away by degrees from a deeply rooted faith. There was, as we have seen, no such faith—it is a necessary fiction to explain her playing the game with Brigham Young for all those years. She may have detested the man, but if she really believed in his religion, as she perpetually protests, her behavior would have been totally different: at the very least she would have gone to prayers, kept the Word of Wisdom, and paid tithing—none of which she did.

Likewise, the dramatic series of crises—unknown even to her mother—is another invention in retrospect. Consider, at seventeen she puts the horrid old man in his place; at twenty-one she gives him a lecture on authority, telling him that she can do very nicely without any of his brand, thank you; at twenty-two she seconds Emmeline in denouncing her husband and his religion as total frauds; on the farm she says, "I had not *one spark* of faith in it remaining."[340] Soon after, she told the Strattons "that she had not been a Mormon in heart for a number of years."[341] Yet at the end of her life of total disillusionment as the wife of Brigham Young, she (and Wallace) can announce with full tremolo, "In addition to the dread and dislike which had grown up [!] in my heart toward my husband, I was *beginning* [!] to lose faith in the religion which he represented."[342] So what does she do? She has herself baptized again, though she assures us that the whole thing was a "farce," that her attempts to take it seriously were "I assure you" entirely unavailing, and that she "was thoroughly disgusted, and made no further effort to believe in Mormonism."[343] This episode is an enlightening one; she describes the business as the last effort on her part to believe, and is at great pains to assure us that of course she had not the slightest intention of believing. To such a clumsy device she must resort by way of explaining why she got herself baptized again—obviously in a last desperate bid for Brigham's favor. She says she didn't believe and couldn't—and then makes great parade of her religious motivation, while Mr. Wallace is inspired by this to turn out some of his finest cliché-work: "a time of doubt and vacillation, of struggle and agony, and finally of triumph."[344] It was four and a half years after Brigham Young had perpetrated his last and cruellest swindle on the Webb family that Ann Eliza decided that she "could no longer look upon him as a spiritual guide and director."[345] Yet six years before, she had given him that stirring lecture in which she told him that she was quite able to do her own spiritual guiding. Spiritual director, indeed!

But enough of this. By now the reader should have a pretty fair idea of the quality of Ann Eliza's personal belief. We have her word for it that her own romantic imaginings took precedence over the teachings of the prophets. Well, that's her business. Even in the Lion House she didn't have to go to prayers if she didn't want to, and we are not going to make her. Her literary sisters have been as free as she was, and in some cases we know just as rebellious against the Church, just as spoiled by their mamas, just as invincibly snobbish as she was. It is an old Mormon heritage, and one against which Brigham Young fought almost single-handedly and in vain. The Mormons have paid a heavy price for indulging in that acquisitiveness and snobbery which so appalled Brigham Young. It is still with them, and one of its results is to make rebels of some who feel robbed of their full meed of glory.

Notes to Part 3

1. Irving Wallace, *The Twenty-Seventh Wife* (New York: Simon and Schuster, 1961), 429.

2. Ibid., 358.

3. Ibid., 433.

4. Ann Eliza (Webb) Young, *Wife No. 19; Or, The Story of a Life of Bondage, Being a Complete Exposé of Mormonism, and Revealing the Sorrows, Sacrifices and Sufferings of Women in Polygamy* (Hartford, CT: Dustin, Gilman, 1875), 568; Wallace, *Twenty-Seventh Wife*, 307, 278, etc.

5. Wallace, *Twenty-Seventh Wife*, 432.

6. Ibid., 429.

7. Ibid., 430.

8. Wallace, *Twenty-Seventh Wife*, 38.

9. Young, *Wife No. 19*, 58.

10. Ibid., 34.

11. Ibid., 204.

12. Ibid., 54–55.

13. Young, *Life in Mormon Bondage*, 512.

14. Wallace, *Twenty-Seventh Wife*, 430.

15. H. R. Trevor-Roper, *Men and Events* (New York: Harper and Brothers, 1957), 116.

16. John H. Beadle, *Brigham's Destroying Angel: Being the Life, Confessions, and Startling Disclosures of the Notorious Bill Hickman, the Danite Chief of Utah. Written by Himself, with explanatory notes by J. H. Beadle* (New York: Crafott, 1872), 109.

17. Ibid., 119.

18. Photos in Wallace, *Twenty-Seventh Wife*, 32–33.

19. Ibid., 432.

20. Ibid., 433.

21. Ibid., 432, 434.

22. Ibid., 30.

23. Ibid., 360.

24. Ibid., 433.

25. Ibid., 12.

26. Ibid.

27. Ibid., 11.

28. Mrs. T. B. H. (Fanny) Stenhouse, *Tell It All: The Story of a Life's Experience in Mormonism* (Hartford, CT: Worthington, 1874), 618.

29. Wallace, *Twenty-Seventh Wife*, 429.

30. Ibid., 394.

31. Ibid., 74.

32. A. E. Housman, *Selected Prose* (Cambridge: Cambridge University Press, 1961), 136.

33. Wallace, *Twenty-Seventh Wife,* 51–52 (emphasis added).

34. Ibid., 98–99.

35. Stenhouse, *Tell It All,* 329.

36. Ibid., 337–38.

37. Ibid., 320 (emphasis added).

38. Young, *Wife No. 19,* 227.

39. Ibid., 485.

40. Ibid., 372 (emphasis added).

41. Wallace, *Twenty-Seventh Wife,* 179.

42. Ibid.

43. Young, *Wife No. 19,* 263 (emphasis added).

44. Wallace, *Twenty-Seventh Wife,* 336.

45. Ibid., 79 (emphasis added).

46. Young, *Wife No. 19,* 257 (emphasis added).

47. Ibid., 310.

48. Ibid., 591.

49. Stenhouse, *Tell It All,* 320.

50. Beadle, *Brigham's Destroying Angel,* 15.

51. Wallace, *Twenty-Seventh Wife,* 28.

52. Young, *Wife No. 19,* 63–64.

53. Ibid., 46–47.

54. "The Virginians," *Time Magazine* 52 (1948): 108.

55. Fawn M. Brodie, *No Man Knows My History* (New York: Knopf, 1946), 256.

56. Wallace, *Twenty-Seventh Wife,* 46.

57. Eduard Meyer, *Ursprung und Geschichte der Mormonen* (Halle: Neimeyer, 1912), 142, n. 2; English translation by Heinz F. Rahde and Eugene Seaich, in *The Origin and History of the Mormons* (Salt Lake City: University of Utah, 1961), 102, n. 3.

58. Marcus Jastrow, *A Dictionary of the Targumim, the Talmud Babli and Yerushalmi, and the Midrash Literature,* 2 vols. (New York: Pardes, 1950), 2:334, 887.

59. Wallace, *Twenty-Seventh Wife,* 410.

60. Young, *Wife No. 19,* 212.

61. Wallace, *Twenty-Seventh Wife,* 77.

62. Ibid., 14.

63. Ibid., 91.

64. Trevor-Roper, *Men and Events,* 283.

65. Wallace, *Twenty-Seventh Wife,* 35.

66. Ibid., 47.

67. Ibid., 240.

68. Ibid., 356.

69. Ibid., 52.

70. Ibid., 13.

71. Ibid., 33.

72. Ibid., 34.

73. Ibid., 52.

74. Trevor-Roper, *Men and Events,* 116.

75. Wallace, *Twenty-Seventh Wife,* 32.

76. Ibid., 11–12.

77. Ibid., 182.

78. Stenhouse, *Tell It All,* 103.

79. Young, *Wife No. 19,* 140.

80. Stenhouse, *Tell It All,* 273.

81. Young, *Wife No. 19,* 368–69.

82. Stenhouse, *Tell It All,* 387.

83. Young, *Wife No. 19,* 378–81.

84. Ibid., 586.

85. Trevor-Roper, *Men and Events,* 117.

86. Wallace, *Twenty-Seventh Wife,* 279.

87. Ibid., 430.

88. Ibid., 433 (emphasis added).

89. Ibid., 131–38 (especially 138).

90. Ibid., 13–14.

91. Ibid., 429.

92. Richard Wormser, *Battalion of Saints* (New York: McKay, 1961), [iii].

93. Wallace, *Twenty-Seventh Wife,* 429.

94. Ibid., 34–35.

95. Milton R. Hunter, Review of Fawn M. Brodie's, *No Man Knows My History,* in *Pacific Historical Review* 15 (June 1946): 227.

96. Wallace, *Twenty-Seventh Wife,* 39.

97. Ibid., 180–81.

98. Ibid., 207.

99. Ibid., 47–48.

100. Ibid., 47.

101. Ibid.

102. Young, *Wife No. 19,* 155.

103. Ibid., 71.

104. Ibid., 46–47.

105. Wallace, *Twenty-Seventh Wife,* n.p. (quote by Richard F. Burton in the front pages).

106. Young, *Wife No. 19,* 156.

107. Ibid., 413.

108. Ibid., 62.

109. Ibid., 138.

110. Ibid., 136.

111. Ibid., 150.

112. Ibid., 136.

113. Ibid., 137.

114. Stenhouse, *Tell It All*, 324.

115. Young, *Wife No. 19*, 232.

116. Stenhouse, *Tell It All*, 620.

117. Wallace, *Twenty-Seventh Wife*, 156.

118. Ibid., 30.

119. Young, *Wife No. 19*, 509.

120. Ibid., 515.

121. Stenhouse, *Tell It All*, 339.

122. Ibid.

123. Young, *Wife No. 19*, 251 (emphasis added).

124. Ibid., 250.

125. Ibid., 113.

126. Young, *Wife No. 19*, 106.

127. Ibid., 68–69.

128. Ibid., 153–54.

129. Ibid., 326.

130. Ibid., 153–54.

131. Ibid., 70.

132. Ibid., 482.

133. Wallace, *Twenty Seventh Wife*, 32.

134. W. Wyl, *Mormon Portraits: Or the Truth about the Mormon Leaders from 1830 to 1886* (Salt Lake City: Tribune, 1886), 55.

135. Young, *Wife No. 19*, 308.

136. Wallace, *Twenty-Seventh Wife*, 325.

137. Ibid., 308 (emphasis added).

138. Stenhouse, *Tell It All*, 103.

139. Young, *Wife No. 19*, 394.

140. Ibid.

141. Ibid.

142. Ibid., 267–68.

143. Ibid., 268; cf. 264.

144. Ibid., 520.

145. Stenhouse, *Tell It All*, 47; cf. Young, *Wife No. 19*, 34.

146. Ann Eliza Young, *Life in Mormon Bondage* (Philadelphia: Aldine, 1908), 4.

147. Young, *Wife No. 19*, 190–94.

148. Bernard De Voto, "A Revaluation," *Improvement Era* 49 (March 1946): 154.

149. Wallace, *Twenty-Seventh Wife,* 38–39.

150. Young, *Life in Mormon Bondage,* 453.

151. Ibid., 78–79.

152. Young, *Wife No. 19,* 236.

153. Wallace, *Twenty-Seventh Wife,* 112.

154. Young, *Wife No. 19,* 236.

155. Ibid., 166–67.

156. Young, *Life in Mormon Bondage,* 132.

157. Young, *Wife No. 19,* 55.

158. Young, *Life in Mormon Bondage,* 49.

159. Wallace, *Twenty-Seventh Wife,* 104–7; Gustive O. Larson, *Prelude to the Kingdom* (Francestown, NH: Jones, 1947), 194–215; also printed in Gustive O. Larson, "The Handcarts of '56," *Improvement Era* 59 (1956): 500–502, 525–27, 569–70, 589–91; the same in LeRoy R. Hafen and Ann W. Hafen, *Handcarts to Zion* (Glendale, CA: Clark, 1960).

160. Young, *Wife No. 19,* 209 (emphasis added).

161. Stenhouse, *Tell It All,* 221 (emphasis added).

162. Ibid.

163. Ibid., 212.

164. Young, *Wife No. 19,* 206.

165. Ibid., 204.

166. Stenhouse, *Tell It All,* 212.

167. Young, *Wife No. 19,* 214.

168. Ibid., 219.

169. Ibid., 189–90 (emphasis added).

170. Ibid., 59 (emphasis added).

171. Ibid., 59–60 (emphasis added).

172. Ibid., 81 (emphasis added).

173. Ibid., 75 (emphasis added).

174. Ibid., 578 (emphasis added).

175. Ibid., 264 (emphasis added).

176. Ibid., 278.

177. Ibid., 279 (emphasis added).

178. Ibid., 161 (emphasis added).

179. Ibid., 591.

180. Wallace, *Twenty-Seventh Wife,* n.p. (quoting Richard F. Burton on the front pages).

181. Ibid., 140.

182. Stenhouse, *Tell It All,* 265.

183. Young, *Life in Mormon Bondage,* 56.

184. Wallace, *Twenty-Seventh Wife,* 38.

185. Stenhouse, *Tell It All,* 337.

186. Young, *Wife No. 19,* 249–51.

187. Stenhouse, *Tell It All,* 337.

188. Young, *Wife No. 19,* 248.

189. Ibid., 311.

190. Young, *Life in Mormon Bondage,* 242.

191. Wallace, *Twenty-Seventh Wife,* 218.

192. Young, *Life in Mormon Bondage,* 102.

193. Ibid.

194. Young, *Wife No. 19,* 227.

195. Young, *Life in Mormon Bondage,* 173.

196. Young, *Wife No. 19,* 150.

197. Young, *Life in Mormon Bondage,* 120.

198. Young, *Wife No. 19,* 161.

199. Young, *Life in Mormon Bondage,* 129.

200. Ibid., 154.

201. Wallace, *Twenty-Seventh Wife,* 419.

202. Young, *Wife No. 19,* 240.

203. Young, *Life in Mormon Bondage,* 182.

204. Cf. Young, *Wife No. 19,* 243; Young, *Life in Mormon Bondage,* 184.

205. Young, *Wife No. 19,* 251; Young, *Life in Mormon Bondage,* 189–90.

206. Young, *Wife No. 19,* 234.

207. Young, *Life in Mormon Bondage,* 176.

208. Young, *Wife No. 19,* 232–33.

209. Young, *Life in Mormon Bondage,* 175–76.

210. Cf. Young, *Wife No. 19,* 341 with Young, *Life in Mormon Bondage,* 261–64, 267.

211. Young, *Life in Mormon Bondage,* 34–35.

212. Ibid., 189.

213. Young, *Wife No. 19,* 113; Young, *Life in Mormon Bondage,* 92–94.

214. Young, *Wife No. 19,* 326–27; Young, *Life in Mormon Bondage,* 251–52.

215. Young, *Wife No. 19,* 155; Young, *Life in Mormon Bondage,* 124.

216. Young, *Wife No. 19,* 174–75; Young, *Life in Mormon Bondage,* 136–37.

217. Young, *Wife No. 19,* 372.

218. Wallace, *Twenty-Seventh Wife,* 18.

219. Ibid., 387.

220. Stenhouse, *Tell It All,* 315.

221. Ibid., 208.

222. Wallace, *Twenty-Seventh Wife,* 68.

223. Young, *Wife No. 19,* 481; Wallace, *Twenty-Seventh Wife,* 249 (emphasis added).

224. Young, *Wife No. 19,* 283.

225. Ibid., 53–54.

226. Ibid., 89.

227. Ibid., 157.

228. Ibid. 433.

229. Ibid., 267.

230. Young, *Wife No. 19,* 470.

231. Ibid.

232. Wallace, *Twenty-Seventh Wife,* 372.

233. Ibid., 189.

234. Susa Young Gates and Mabel Young Sanborn, "Brigham Young Geneology," *Utah Genealogical Magazine* 11 (April 1920): 52; Wallace, *Twenty-Seventh Wife,* 189.

235. "In Memoriam: Death of Mary Ann Angell Young," *Deseret News,* 5 July 1882, 369.

236. "Funeral Services: The Last Rites over the Remains of Mrs. Mary Angell Young," *Deseret News,* 5 July 1882, 380.

237. Wallace, *Twenty-Seventh Wife,* 237.

238. Young, *Wife No. 19,* 567.

239. Young, *Life in Mormon Bondage,* 5.

240. Ibid., 2.

241. Wallace, *Twenty-Seventh Wife,* 78–79.

242. Young, *Life in Mormon Bondage,* 510.

243. Ibid.

244. Young, *Wife No. 19,* 464.

245. Ibid., 505 (emphasis added).

246. Ibid., 597.

247. Ibid., 404.

248. Ibid., 98.

249. Ibid., 393.

250. Ibid., 591.

251. Ibid., 400.

252. Ibid., 592.

253. Ibid., 591 (emphasis added).

254. Ibid., 395.

255. Young *Wife No. 19*, 99; Wallace, *Twenty-Seventh Wife*, 236.

256. Wallace, *Twenty-Seventh Wife*, 99.

257. Young, *Wife No. 19*, 406.

258. Ibid., 253.

259. Wallace, *Twenty-Seventh Wife*, 385–88.

260. Ibid., 15.

261. Ibid., 124.

262. Stenhouse, *Tell It All*, 274 (emphasis added).

263. Young, *Wife No. 19*, 204–5.

264. Young, *Life in Mormon Bondage*, 511–12.

265. Wallace, *Twenty-Seventh Wife*, 198.

266. Ibid., 356.

267. Young, *Wife No. 19*, 605.

268. Young, *Life in Mormon Bondage*, 479–80.

269. Ibid., 491.

270. Ibid., 493–95.

271. Bernard De Voto, New York *Herald Tribune* (see the dust cover of Fawn M. Brodie, *No Man Knows My History* [New York: Knopf, 1983]).

272. Wallace, *Twenty-Seventh Wife*, 429.

273. Stenhouse, *Tell It All*, 618.

274. Ibid.

275. Ibid.

276. Hunter, "Review of Brodie," 228.

277. Wallace, *Twenty-Seventh Wife*, 22.

278. Ibid., 323.

279. Young, *Wife No. 19*, 476.

280. Ibid., 453–54.

281. Ibid., 541.

282. Ibid., 323.

283. Wallace, *Twenty-Seventh Wife*, 236.

284. Young, *Wife No. 19*, 590.

285. Wallace, *Twenty-Seventh Wife*, 334.

286. Ibid.

287. Ibid., 324.

288. Young, *Wife No. 19*, 575.

289. Wallace, *Twenty-Seventh Wife*, 335.

290. Young, *Wife No. 19*, 576.

291. Ibid., 354.

292. Ibid., 33.

293. Ibid., 103.

294. Ibid., 577.

295. Ibid., 350.
296. Ibid.
297. Ibid., 101–2.
298. Ibid., 368–69.
299. Ibid., 306–7.
300. Ibid.
301. Ibid., 104.
302. Ibid., 351 (emphasis added).
303. Ibid., 145–46 (lifted from Stenhouse; emphasis added).
304. Stenhouse, *Tell It All,* 101 (emphasis added).
305. Ibid., 159.
306. Young, *Wife No. 19,* 422.
307. Wallace, *Twenty-Seventh Wife,* 111.
308. Young, *Wife No. 19,* 405.
309. Ibid., 507.
310. Ibid., 323.
311. Ibid., 180.
312. Ibid., 359–61.
313. Ibid., 356.
314. Wallace, *Twenty-Seventh Wife,* 288.
315. Young, *Wife No. 19,* 436.
316. Ibid., 529.
317. Ibid., 503.
318. Ibid., 539.
319. Ibid., 540.
320. Ibid., 568.
321. Ibid., 337.
322. Ibid., 101.
323. Ibid., 106.
324. Ibid., 104.
325. Ibid., 101.
326. Ibid., 162.
327. Ibid., 145–46.
328. Ibid., 396.
329. Ibid., 41.
330. Ibid., 181–82 (emphasis added).
331. Ibid., 601.
332. Wallace, *Twenty-Seventh Wife,* 346–47.
333. Ibid.
334. Young, *Wife No. 19,* 443.
335. Ibid., 535.
336. Ibid., 544.

337. Ibid., 41–42.
338. Young, *Wife No. 19*, 211.
339. Ibid., 52.
340. Ibid., 544 (emphasis added).
341. Wallace, *Twenty-Seventh Wife*, 251.
342. Young, *Wife No. 19*, 538 (emphasis added).
343. Ibid., 545.
344. Wallace, *Twenty-Seventh Wife*, 32.
345. Young, *Wife No. 19*, 538.

Part 4

It Fairly Sears the Screen—
A Romance You
Will Never Forget!!

Here We Go Again

The commonest objection to this writer's mystery thriller, *The Myth Makers,* is that the book is a waste of paper—less in a literary sense than as a laboring of the over-obvious, the beating of a dead horse. Would that were so! When friends and enemies protest that the charges against Joseph Smith are brought by witnesses so obviously prejudiced and unprincipled that only an idiot would make an issue of their accusations, it is the writer's painful duty to point out that those accusations are to this day the soul and substance of a large and flourishing school of anti-Mormon literature, most of it going under the banner of serious scholarship. If the investigator really wants to know how far supposedly intelligent and serious-minded people can go in their myth making, we would recommend a calm appraisal of Mr. Wallace's story of Ann Eliza's wondrous romance with Brigham Young. As a piece of sheer effrontery it is unsurpassed in the annals of literature, or at least in the literature that this writer has got through in forty years of grimly systematic reading.

Let it be clearly understood, then, that but for one peculiar circumstance, the discussion that follows is a total waste of time and paper. The peculiar circumstance is that the drivel we are to survey is taken seriously by large numbers of our fellow citizens and were it to go unchallenged would pass in time as a correct and accurate history, a true portrait of Brigham Young and a true measure of his religion. It already passes for that today with a large portion of the population, and Mr. Wallace is seeing to it that the numbers of such believers shall increase.

The Ann Eliza Version

There are, Mr. Wallace admits, two versions of the great romance of Ann Eliza and Brigham Young — hers and his ("the Mormon version"). According to the first, he chased her: "I did not seek the position of wife to him; it was forced upon me."[1] "I never loved him and never said to him that I loved him. I looked upon him as a heartless despot."[2] According to the second, she chased him.[3] In most romances both parties do some of the chasing, but Ann Eliza's position is uncompromising. "Whose version can one believe?" asks the sapient Wallace, and after the inevitable pompous cliché — "*Probably* the truth lies *somewhere* in between" — he goes all out for his Ann Eliza: "There is no reason to doubt Ann Eliza's account of the Prophet's love and pursuit of her."[4]

The evidence for the Ann Eliza version rests on three stirring conversations — all fictitious. The first was between her and Brigham Young when she was seventeen, the second ditto when she was twenty-two, and the third was a brisk altercation with the Webb family just before the marriage.

The pursuit motif runs through Ann Eliza's story from beginning to end. It starts out with Brigham Young lusting after the three-year-old Annie — not in so many words but unmistakably: "I attracted a great deal of his attention," which was indeed significant, "since he is not noted for fondness for children, even his own."[5] "He had watched me from my infancy," Brigham Young is supposed to have told Ann Eliza's father; he "had always loved me and intended to marry me."[6] Then when she was sixteen "he seemed suddenly to realize that I had grown to be a young lady, and the first intimation he gave of it was by interfering with my beaux."[7] This he did "out of some inexplicable impulse," according to Wallace, who proceeds to explain the inexplicable by reporting Ann Eliza's reaction: "The very thought was outrageous to Ann Eliza. . . . 'I wouldn't have him if he asked me a thousand times—hateful old thing.' "[8] Do you still not know what this is all about? Well, "Inevitably," Mr. Wallace assures us in his best House-That-Jack-Built style, "a report of Ann Eliza's declaration got back to the Prophet. Perhaps he was annoyed."[9] Ann Eliza herself is more emphatic: when her spirited speech was reported to Brigham, "his vanity was sorely hurt,"[10] and the great duel was on between the empire builder and the sixteen-year-old Ann Eliza. He soon contrived to pick her up in "the presidential carriage" of which he was "the sole occupant" (for there is never a witness to any of Ann Eliza's crucial meetings with Brigham), and with infinite subtlety played his opening card: "I heard you said you wouldn't marry me if I wanted you to ever so much."[11] But only a short while after, President Young presided at Ann Eliza's marriage to James Dee—with a breaking heart, to be sure, for he "always hoped that the time would come when he would have me."[12]

When she was again free, he accordingly laid Homeric siege to her heart. First "he tried in every way to win me, a willing bride,"[13] but she shrank with aversion from "a man older than my father . . . the father of children older, by many years, than myself."[14] She did more than shrink, however: "Thus began a year of anguish and torture. I fought against my fate in every possible way." With him trying "in every way" to catch her, and her trying "in every possible way" to escape, it was indeed a battle of the giants. "For almost two years," as Wallace puts it,

"Brigham wooed Ann Eliza, and for two years she resisted him." Only after the great man's infinite resource and experience were exhausted in vain attempts "to win me, a willing bride," he "attempted to coerce me."[15] His hot campaign of "ardent" wooing,[16] based on intimidation, bribery, and trickery,[17] culminated in a Machiavellian business maneuver of imperial proportions, designed to force the lady to yield in order to save her brother's position in the Church. Gilbert's embarrassment gave Young the whip-handle he needed — "with his departure the black threat hung over the household";[18] and so they were married — "my doom was fixed. My religion, my parents — everything was urging me on to my unhappy fate."[19] But lo, from the wedding day Young treated the apple of his eye with "studied contempt" and cruel neglect,[20] while she on her part was always the model wife, by Brigham Young's own admission (according to her) "the least troublesome of any wife he had ever had,"[21] until, alas, his selfishness and cruelty finally forced her to abandon him.[22]

Such briefly is the Ann Eliza–Wallace version of the great romance. What evidence is there to support it? We know that Ann Eliza married Brigham Young, but was that how it happened? Mr. Wallace says it was. The proof? That Ann Eliza actually married Brigham Young! For a generation and more, Ann Eliza herself held that lone fact up as full and sufficient evidence for whatever she chose to say about Brigham Young and the Mormons. The powerful clincher to this argument for Mr. Wallace is the undeniable fact that he was a man and she was a woman — need one look farther? "There is *no* reason to doubt Ann Eliza's account of the Prophet's love and pursuit of her" is his thesis, and the proof is that she was "young, pretty, and available,"[23] while "neither his potency nor his fecundity was impaired by his great age."[24]

Brigham's lust for Eliza — that is Wallace's *mēnin aeide*

Thea,[25] the grandiose theme trumpeted forth on the very cover of his book. Yet he must establish his thesis by laborious indirection and devious sophistry, prodding the reader by degree along a path that never once offers him the firm foothold of solid evidence. He begins with a subtle innuendo: "Sometimes, it was said, Brigham's interest in young actresses — as in the case of Ann Eliza Webb — was less fatherly."[26] Of course "it was said," but by whom? Wallace gives satisfaction by following up with a report of how Heber C. Kimball once remarked during family prayers, "The greater the strumpet, the more brother Brigham is after her." A more utterly impossible story could not be imagined, but Mr. Wallace assures us that it has the high authority of "Dr. Wilhelm Wyle, the German researcher." All the world possesses of this great scholar is a thin volume of unauthenticated and lurid stories published in Salt Lake in 1886 "by Dr. W. Wyl, A German Author." What he was a Doctor of, nobody knows, but by turning him into Dr. Wilhelm Wyle, *the* German researcher, Wallace calls the impressive credentials of nineteenth-century Teutonic *Wissenschaft* to his aid, and though conceding in the next sentence that "the story, from an anti-Mormon source, is likely apocryphal," he has left us properly impressed — for who has not heard of *the* famous Dr. Wyle?

Before we can pause to wonder about this, Mr. Wallace rushes us on with an admonition that the story may be true, since "as a matter of recorded fact, Brigham Young did have one protracted and public love affair with an actress."[27] Who can challenge a recorded fact? And where is the record? Well, in 1905 an anti-Mormon by the name of John S. Lindsay recollected that back in those days, some half-century before, "speculation was rife, and much surprise and wonder was excited in certain quarters" about Young's interest in a certain actress visiting the city. Since there was never any shortage of speculation about Brigham Young in many quarters, we need something better than this, and so Wallace hurries us on: "There seems every evidence that Brigham, at sixty-four, had a deeply romantic involvement." *Every* evidence is pretty strong, and it is too bad to have to spoil it with that poor little "seems"; let us have the evidence. Well, Brigham Young gave two receptions for the actress and actually sent *his own sleigh* to bring the guest of honor to the party! Some unimaginative and uncooperative readers might think that this was simply the normal way an ardent patron of the theater would pay his respects to a great actress and ask impatiently for the proof of anything like a red-hot love affair. Here it is at last: "It is said that Brigham tried to convert the actress to the Mormon faith and even proposed marriage. But Julia Dean Hayne would have her patron neither as Prophet nor as polygamist."[28] It would sort of spoil things to let the deliciously mystified reader know that the provocative "it is said" here refers to our good friend A.E.W.D.Y.D. and to Mrs. S., and that neither of them will vouch for the story. But it is a *known fact* that Julia Dean Hayne (always give the full name in case like this, to show you've got the goods) *never did* marry Brigham Young—which gives Mr. Wallace full authority for saying that she would have him neither as a Prophet nor as a polygamist.

So far where are we? We have learned that people gossiped about Brigham Young. But that is hardly news; it is time for Wallace's bombshell: Ann Eliza heard a rumor that President Young had Miss Hayne's "temple work" done for her after she was dead; Wallace followed up the lead and struck pay dirt—"long-forgotten Church records" show that the lady was "sealed" to Brigham Young.[29] So were many, many others. It is as characteristic of any good Latter-day Saint to want temple work done for a dead Gentile friend as it is for him to try to convert a living one. Marrying here and sealing beyond are by no means the same thing—after all, the party concerned was dead, and the sealing, however sentimental may have been the motive behind it, was an extremely common, almost routine affair, albeit confidential. The point is that this is Mr. Wallace's prize evidence for a "*protracted* and *public* love affair with an actress." What was protracted and public was the speculation, and that is all our authority has to go on. We need something better than a leer and a snicker when so much is being claimed. One does not have to go to very private records to prove the reality of a protracted *public* event.

Wallace labors heroically on the youth-and-beauty angle — his Ann Eliza is, as she depicts herself, always very young and very beautiful. Only others did not see it that way: To the reporters who studied her, she was "no 'Spring chicken,' "[30] and at the time she left Brigham Young they guessed her age at thirty-five rather than thirty;[31] experienced newspaper reporters, willing enough to play up the lady's glamour, would go no further than to concede that "her face is attractive rather than handsome."[32] Wallace and Ann Eliza, on the other hand, have given us an image of youth and beauty that Brigham Young "found . . . irresistible."[33] Yet at the time of the marriage, Ann Eliza was by no means the prize package that she and Wallace present for our inspection; she was a twenty-four-year-old divorcee with two children, still unmarried after four years of living at home. On the face of it, her case was desperate — by the standards of her society she was far beyond the ideal age for marriage. To cover this up, she insists on describing herself as a veritable babe: "I was a child with my children, and it would be difficult to tell which of us got the most scoldings and pettings from the fond grandmamma."[34] As to Mr. Young lurking and slavering in the wings, "What was that to me? How did it affect me when he came or went? . . . So I thought, as I lay cradled in my mother's arms that summer evening."[35] But the very next day the man proposed — to Ann Eliza's parents: "Had I known it, I should by no means have . . . frolicked so gaily with my children."[36] Brigham at the time "looked upon my assertions as girlish affectation that a good offer would speedily overcome."[37] And so on and on—Ann Eliza is the perpetual ingenue, the frolicking girl-child, a contemporary not of Brigham Young's other wives (of whom she was *not* the youngest) but of his *younger* children. The wives "I had known from my childhood, and they were old and intimate friends of my mother's,"[38] while "I . . . enjoyed myself very much with some of the *younger* members of the family."[39]

Flaws in the Diamond

Even if Ann Eliza's youth and beauty were not desperately exaggerated, they prove nothing. Actually her story collapses at a touch; a fabric of moonshine. The great proposal scene is a phony. It takes place on the way home from a meeting at which Brigham Young had never taken his eyes from her; "I am sure he saw my discomfort; but he was pitiless."[40] Also he was apparently unaware that everybody's gaze was on *him*. Yet nobody—not even all-perceptive mama—suspected a thing. When Ann Eliza gave her a verbatim account of the President's clumsy proposal of marriage immediately after the meeting, the good woman "seemed amused by it, but did not give it any more serious thought . . . than I had done."[41] And this was the woman who, according to Ann Eliza herself, desired nothing in the world so much as to see her daughter married to Brigham Young. Is any further evidence necessary to show that Eliza is making this all up? Here she tells mama that Brigham Young has within the hour told her that "now I was free, and he was at liberty to tell me, what he had wanted to tell me long before, that he loved me."[42] Yet neither she *nor* her mother suspected for a moment what the man had in mind, so that when Young proposed to her, the girl was absolutely thunderstruck, stunned, incredulous—she thought it was a joke, she says, for during that long and amorous conversation, "I had *no idea at all* of Brigham's real object in thus sounding me, and drawing me out. It *never occurred* to me that he could want me for himself."[43]

There can be only one explanation for such obtuseness: the conversation never took place. Indeed it is a very different story she tells in the Stenhouse letter, as we shall see. The long, romantic conversation of the book is a free composition, a sumptuous afterthought. Go back to the meeting. All the time he was totally absorbed in staring tactlessly at Ann Eliza while everybody else stared at him, President Young was engaged in a lively exchange of vituperation with members of the congregation, who openly accused him of skulduggery. The key to the situation is one Van Etten, who, according to Ann Eliza, endeared himself to the Prophet on the occasion by tossing his tormentor, Howard, out of the meeting. After that, Brigham endorsed Van Etten so enthusiastically that the latter could take to a life of crime with complete immunity to prosecution. He began by stealing a hundred sheep from Ann Eliza's own brother Gilbert, and then disappeared with "several thousand" stolen beasties into parts unknown.[44] Meanwhile Howard, the man who attacked the President, according to Ann Eliza, voluntarily went off on a mission for the Church to England.

Here we have rich scandal in the very bosom of Ann Eliza's family, with Brigham Young at the center of it. Why not a word of all this in Mr. Wallace's book? Why does he never mention Van Etten? Is it because Ann Eliza, *nee* Webb, is lying? But Van Etten is the key to her whole story of the meeting. To make up for the vivid and dramatic story he passes by in such peculiar silence, Mr. Wallace on his own authority reports how Young stares with tactless fascination at Ann Eliza from the stand, how he trembles with rage when a member of the congregation hurls charges against him, and how he takes off like an alley cat after the meeting in pursuit of our heroine, while the Church dignitaries stand about "casting knowing glances at one another."[45] All this is pure invention, and what Wallace calls "their long walk and secret conversation" on the way home[46] is no less so.

For it was a short walk and a very unsecret conversation. Ann Eliza reports the latter in half-a-dozen lines in her Stenhouse letter, where Brigham Young gives her exactly the same advice that he gave all young ladies. "I thanked him for his counsel," she concludes, "and as my home was so near to the place of meeting, the conversation abruptly terminated."[47] So much for the long walk, and the conversation which in her later book is developed into a four-page melodrama. In the latter, the protagonists exchange in stilted and artificial language remarks that are both absurd and impossible. Brigham explains that it "was a great shock to him" when she married Dee, but "now I was free, and he was at liberty to tell me . . . that he loved me."[48] Since Young himself had performed the ceremony, to which Ann Eliza's family (his close personal friends) strenuously objected "as a duty,"[49] why hadn't Brigham protested too? The answer is a killer: "I knew you was doing the wrong thing when I saw the man. I could have told you so, *but you didn't ask my advice.*"[50] Both as the General Authority performing the ceremony and as a personal friend, Brigham Young would be obliged and expected to give counsel and advice in a routine interview. Brigham, like everybody else, says Ann Eliza, deplored the move she was taking; yet though his heart was breaking, and he saw his beloved Eliza going to ruin, he uttered not a word of protest—"you didn't ask my advice." Since when did Brigham Young, of all people, wait to be asked before giving advice to sixteen-year-olds? And then when she got her divorce, who granted it? Brigham Young did: so at last she was free. And so *two years* later he proposes.

In the four-page conversation which is the cornerstone

of the great romance, Ann Eliza is as exquisitely noble and literate as Young is clumsy and boorish. To the Prophet's discourse on marriage and his "tenacious inquiries into her love life,"[51] she replies that she is a mature woman of hard and bitter experience who had put all thought of marriage from her mind forever. If not marriage, what then? She tells us: "I pictured myself growing old in this quiet spot, with my strong, brave boys near me."[52] She describes herself on the same page as a real beauty — healthy, vivacious, and "frolicsome" — yet her only thought is to look forward to a quiet old age in Cottonwood. Actually this is exactly what she did have to look forward to — but do you really believe she relished the prospect? She has Brigham protest: "Women of your age, and your looks, don't stay single all their lives; not a bit of it,"[53] while she pointedly refers to the army of suitors that constantly besiege her.[54]

Again the buzzer and the red light: Who were these suitors? They are necessary to make it appear that Ann Eliza was eminently desirable, but why is none of them ever named? Why is no episode of her many Mormon wooings ever mentioned by a woman who gives us verbatim accounts of so many *other* women's wooings? For two years, she says, she employed every possible means of avoiding a mating with Young. Yet if she is telling the truth, the door of escape was wide and beckoning. For on the evening of the great walk, she instructed her father to convey to Brigham the answer she gave "to all my *other* suitors,"[55] and reminded her mother of her "aversion to another union, *above all*, to him."[56] Brigham Young, then, was but one suitor among many, and by far the least desirable. Among "every possible means" of avoiding him, the most obvious and convenient would certainly be that of marrying any of the other men "who with each other vie to do her menial duty." Her parents left the decision entirely up to her;[57] why didn't she simply choose somebody else? Is it for the same reason that she never *names* anybody else? Because there *was* nobody else?

Ann Eliza says her parents, though they wished her to marry Mr. Young, would not force her to,[58] yet in two years she cannot think of a single good reason for not marrying him except his age—which means that all the brutal mistreatment and cynical plundering of the Webb family are also Ann Eliza's invention. And what about that two-year "ardent wooing" that is the theme of Mr. Wallace's book?[59] The woman who can recall every syllable of her long private conversation on the way home from meeting remembers *nothing* of the long and ardent wooing that followed. She recalls *not a single episode,* revealing or otherwise, of that hectic campaign by a master wooer—what a book she could have made of *that,* if it had only occurred! She trims and hedges, telling how *after* Brigham was unable to move her by kindness, he "tried another tack. He asked my father if a house and a thousand dollars a year would make me comfortable."[60] But in her letter to Stenhouse, this proposal is made on the very day he walked her home from church; that is, there was no romantic preliminary whatever.[61] Even the famous conversation is ruled out by the Stenhouse account.

And how did the master-wooer woo? By visiting the family from time to time, when "he manifested all the growling propensities of an old 'cur.' "[62] When her father reported her reluctance to the great lover (who never bothered to propose to *her*), "he only laughed," and told the family that he expected them to get results. "The last remark was made with a peculiar emphasis and a sinister smile, which every Saint who had had dealings with him knew very well, and whose meaning they also knew."[63] This too took place on the day of the walk from the church—Brigham starts out putting on the pressure in the nastiest way—which makes it perfectly clear that there was no romantic approach: it was business from the first. To get Ann Eliza into his power, Brigham threatens the family with ruin—why? The family was already enthusiastically on his side—why ruin *them*? "With his departure the black threat hung over the household," says Mr. Wallace, surpassing even the *Police Gazette* for sheer banality. But the household continued to love Brigham. What was the threat, incidentally? Not anything so trite as financial ruin—Ann Eliza insists that money plays no part in all this; no, the threat is "the Prophet's curse!"[64]

Then, when he finally won her consent, "he was triumphant, *although he did not show it*";[65] while she "still fought against it, but the conflict now was *all internal*."[66] The family of course was elated, "and everything 'went merry as a marriage-bell.' "[67] At the moment of decision *she* was successful in concealing her sorrow from the world—"I did not dare admit anyone to my confidence, not even my mother"[68]—while he was just as successful in concealing his joy. This is a preposterous situation, but it is necessary to explain why there were *never any witnesses* to the Ann Eliza version.

But how about that passionate soul-baring on the way home from church? That is a fabrication: in the Stenhouse letter it is made not to Ann Eliza at all, but to her father, and when in the book it is shifted to her, it is freely adorned and expanded. It is quite inconceivable that she and her mother should have missed the point of such a speech, if it had been given. The lady herself insists that she never had the remotest suspicion that Young was being romantic, in any of those dramatic conversations *before* the marriage.

And *after* the marriage? From the hour the ceremony was performed, he overwhelmed her with abuse and treated her with studied contempt—that is her story. So where does that leave the great Romance? Can you blame those who accept the "Mormon version" in view of Ann Eliza's own admission that there was *no overt evidence whatever* either for Brigham Young's pursuit of her or of her avoidance of him? "He was triumphant although he did not show it," while no one—not even her mother—was aware of Ann Eliza's reluctance. The truth is not that "there is no reason for doubting Ann Eliza's version of Brigham's pursuit of her," but that by her own confession there is no reason for believing it beyond the ready rhetoric of her secret history.

The Real Ann Eliza?

If the Ann Eliza–Wallace version leaks like a sieve, what about "the Mormon version," i.e., that it was Mrs. Webb and her daughter who sought the marriage—while Brigham Young "protested that he was an old man" (which he was) "and wanted no more wives"? His First Counselor told how the ladies used to come to Brigham Young's office, where mama would plead, "Let her have the joy of being called by your name"—she will be satisfied with that—"while the daughter sat weeping into her carefully arranged pocket handkerchief."[69] And indeed Ann Eliza herself tells how she studied before her marriage to move the great man with her tears and actually sat cooling her heels in the waiting room of his office only, as she puts it, she was intending to plead not for herself but for Gilbert.[70] So, unwittingly, she supplies us with all the elements of the "Mormon version"; it is only the *motives* that need adjusting. If Brigham Young was chasing her, why did she have to wait—in vain—for an interview at the office? Again, that belongs to her secret history, never revealed even to her mother—the *public* history is that she sat in the waiting room. There was nothing highly irregular in being married in name only: Brigham Young, as we have seen, had already given his name and protection to many women; "very many more," says Ann Eliza, ". . . have been married to him 'for eternity.' I should be sorry even to guess their numbers."[71] Sorriest of all is that she is among that number, for she insisted *publicly and often* that she had never had marital relations with Brigham Young.[72] Mr. Wallace cannot accept that mortal blow to his whole thesis. Though Ann Eliza solemnly makes that claim in an official biographical register, he dismisses it out of hand: "Undoubtedly it was false."[73] Having called his informant a liar in a crucial matter to which she is the only possible witness, our guide then gallantly explains that she is merely trying to "disassociate herself from Mormonism."[74] Yet in the same lectures in which she confesses, "It was impossible for me to ever interest my husband,"[75] she tells how very, very hard she *tried* to gain his attention and affection, making it only too clear that the disassociation was all on his side, not on hers.

Kimball Young says "the mother of Ann Eliza 'engineered the match with Brigham—for the sake of prestige and money' ";[76] and according to Dee's descendants, Mrs. Webb "was aggressive and wanted her daughter in society."[77] A wicked Mormon fiction? Then why does Mr. Wallace admit that "Ann Eliza's mother . . . *desperately* wanted the marriage for the standing it would give her daughter and the entire family"?[78] And why does Ann Eliza herself report, "My mother and father both favored his suit, and labored with me . . . to view it in the same light"?[79] Before we consider Brigham Young's deep-freeze treatment of Ann Eliza, there is one item that cannot be overlooked in evaluating her story, and that is her own character.

Even to the casual reader it is apparent that we have to do with a spoiled and pampered creature. "It is a wonder that I was not completely spoiled," she reports with evident pleasure. "I daresay I should have been, had it not been for my mother's sensible and judicious training. I was her idol, the one object for which she cared the most in the world."[80] To idolize Ann Eliza is merely being sensible and judicious. "A spoiled child, eh?" says the Squire, "continu[ing] to stare" (the stare is Mr. Wallace's contribution to history), and the damsel replies, "My will seems to be everybody's way at home."[81] Is it her fault if everyone is insanely jealous of her? In the spirit of "sweet humility," albeit against the advice of parents and friends, she stole Dee from all the other girls and immediately began to compete with him for the affections of a girl friend: "In order to win *me* from her," she says, and "to break up our friendship, he pretended very great interest in her."[82] When she discovered that her friend was quite innocent of competing for her husband's attention, i.e., that the sordid triangle was of her own making, she still would never forgive her: "To this day I cannot see my old friend that a feeling of the most intense bitterness does not rise up in my heart against her."[83] Ann Eliza never forgives anyone, and why should she, since they are to blame? "But some persons never forget, and my husband was one of those; . . . he was revenging himself for the opposition shown to him by my friends."[84] Then when she has a child, Dee is insanely jealous of *it:* "He did not care for my baby, seeming to consider it a rival, and my love for it seemed to anger him."[85] So she proceeded to rub it in: "All the tide of my affection, that had been so rudely repelled, turned towards it [the baby]. . . . I should live in and for my child."[86] Then she has another child, and the two infants become rivals for her love: "I had been at first jealous of the little new-comer for the other baby's sake. . . . The measure of my love seemed to be the measure of their father's indifference, and even hate. He used to either take no notice of them at all, which I infinitely preferred, or he would handle them so roughly that the little things would shriek with pain and terror, and I would be almost frantic with fear lest he should kill them in his mad frolics."[87]

Can you imagine trying to live with that woman? The poor kids were in for it: "I can have no room for other love while I have them to care for," she told Brigham Young. "They fill my heart exclusively, and . . . I should be jealous if I saw the least hint of regard for *anyone* creeping in. I couldn't love anybody else; I wouldn't. . . . I am a woman . . . with hard, bitter experiences; . . . a mother, too, who will not give her children a rival."[88] Is it too much to call such a woman possessive? When President Young suggested, she says, that she "might give them a protector," she answered (she says), "They don't need it; my love is sufficient protection. Besides, they . . . will be my protectors in a few years."[89] "No one would dispute with me for their affection," she cries — as if anybody wanted to — "no one claim their love. I was supremely, selfishly happy. . . . I dreamed for them, I planned for them, lived in them."[90] "My romance had died; my idol, with its feet of clay, was broken; . . . but the little souls . . . were more beautiful than any idol."[91] "I dreaded the days . . . when my clinging arms could no longer infold them, when my love alone would cease to satisfy."[92] And so forth. It is not surprising to learn that when Ann Eliza's sole surviving son's marriage with a Southern Socialite (non-Mormon) was broken up, he moved into a cottage with mama, only to have her "sell the house over his head" when she needed money.

Naturally one expects all of Young's wives to be insanely jealous of Ann Eliza, and Wallace tells us that her "youth and beauty" were actually a threat to "the economic comfort and security of the other wives."[93] But it won't wash. Aside from the fact, noted even by Stenhouse, that she was his least loved and worst-treated wife, we have her own unguarded admission: "*Others* were cared for, and it was more than a woman's nature could stand, to see them thus petted."[94] Where is our noble Ann Eliza, who thinks only of the happiness of other women? Where is the darling of the harem, the dread and envy of them all?

In Ann Eliza's code of chivalry there is no halfway: either a man makes stars in a woman's eyes or he is an

utter cad. "I made an ideal; then I set myself to find some
living person to invest with all the virtues and graces,
mental, moral, and physical, of my imaginary hero. I found
the person, and straightway set myself to worship. . . . There is such a sweet humility about a woman's
love"![95] And she never forgave James Dee for falling short
of her ideal—he "blighted her life" forever: within "a
month . . . I learned that I had made a fatal mistake in my
marriage,"[96] as Dee's "*desire* to torment me made life almost
unbearable."[97] He *wanted* to hurt her. The same fatal flaw
was discovered with the same promptness in her next two
husbands, guilty, like Dee, of "treating me in the indifferent, matter-of-fact manner . . . which most Mormon
men assume towards their helpless wives."[98] Woe to the
man who treats Ann Eliza in a matter-of-fact manner! All
her husbands are cads. Brigham Young "refused to care
for me when it was his duty to do so";[99] and Denning sent
her "messages . . . entirely unbecoming a man—such as,
'Now she can starve, and see how she likes that.' "[100] Yet
all three men were model husbands with their other wives.

The program she had planned for her sons, "to help
my faltering footsteps over the stony places," precluded
any happy married life for them.[101] She repeatedly puts
her male relatives on the spot—they must rescue her from
Dee (who never got a word in edgewise).[102] Poor little
Edward Milo must interfere with the President's private
affairs and get bounced from his office because Ann Eliza
put him up to it with the news "that his sister was being
ill-treated by the Prophet";[103] her father, she told the reporters, would take care of the terrible Danites if they laid
a hand on her—we wonder how father felt about that?
When Brigham Young asked for her in marriage, she again
put papa on the spot: "Why, I belong to you, father. Tell
him so, and that you can't give me away to anybody."[104]
But father was on Brigham's side. Even Presidents of the
United States are disowned and denounced by Mrs. Young

for their lack of chivalry in failing to comply with all her instructions.[105]

Ann Eliza is always having to be rescued — beauty in distress is her specialty, frail loveliness brutally assaulted — the infant drenched with the frantic tears of a mother who prayed for merciful death — "every hour of her life her heart was torn by some new agony";[106] the babe innocently unaware of the lurking Squire, the child shocked and brutalized simply by being baptized — a sacrificial lamb "consecrated . . . to . . . the Mormon faith";[107] the sensitive innocent terrified by the image of J. D. Lee leaning over her bed; when she was twelve, had her father not prevented "making his little girl a victim," she would have been snapped up by one of the competing "church dignitaries";[108] the girl all but swooning from the brutality of the endowment rites; the adolescent pursued by the panting Squire. At sixteen she paints a picture of herself as "quite a martyr to the Mormon priestly rule."[109] Wallace is titillated by the idea of Mormon men discussing women "with reference to their 'points,' as jockeys would talk of horses, or importers of fine stock"[110] — it gives you an idea of how Dee treated Ann Eliza. Then the dazzling beauty, helpless beneath Brigham's basilisk stare: "I am sure he saw my discomfort; but was pitiless."[111] And then the way her own family dragooned her into marrying Brigham Young — only Mr. Wallace can describe the scene with lovely Eliza at bay, tortured by her own parents. And then she enters Brigham Young's home and finds there one of the wives who "had been a servant [ugh!] in my mother's family. . . . She used to take care of me when I was a baby, and . . . wished with all her heart that she had choked me when she had a good chance."[112] Not a very pretty picture — but that is how people treated our Eliza. Of course she must be rescued from "the contaminating clutches of Brigham Young" under the most harrowing and breathtaking circumstances — all of her own invention. But when she had made good her "escape," she turned to Mrs. Cooke, and when she spoke her voice was weak and helpless. " 'What shall I do?' she asked."[113] She is always getting herself into these situations and then appealing to the chivalry of bystanders to rescue her. After her liberation from the Mormons, "her own bouts with nervous illness and fatigue were more frequent. . . . She feared the loneliness and obscurity of retirement."[114] People just aren't nice enough to Ann Eliza.

Incidentally, part of Mr. Wallace's Ann Eliza image is the host of loyal friends she has, friends through whom Brigham Young is able to hurt her after she leaves him. Who were they? If Mr. Wallace in his vast researches ever ran across the trace of any real friend of Mrs. Young, he has failed to mention it. The gallant Major, the Judge, the Gentile Boarders who magnanimously paid their rent for three weeks, the Clergy, the people at the Hotel—all were kindness itself, as they carefully calculated just how much they were going to get out of Mrs. Young. Even the devoted Mrs. Cooke, who was paid to go with her, presently left her and returned to Salt Lake. Correction, "bravely returned," says Mr. Wallace,[115] since just to go back there would obviously be suicide if Ann Eliza's story of the Danites is true.

Ann Eliza is not a little proud of her skill at weeping. Of her first husband she says, "I presume I annoyed him greatly by my tears and reproaches. A woman in Mormonism has need enough for tears, but it is little use for her to shed them."[116] But she went on shedding them just the same and notes as a remarkable phenomenon that when she had her first baby, "I *even* forgot to cry under the sweet restful influence."[117] But she didn't forget when Brigham proposed: "Oh! the horrible hours that I spent in crying and moaning, no tongue can picture."[118] And as the gentlest and quietest of all Brigham Young's wives, she always got what she wanted by crying. At the farm, she

says, she never ceased weeping. When Young wanted to relieve Mrs. Webb of the drudgery of the farm which, according to Ann Eliza, was ruining her health, her daughter's reaction was prompt and effective: "I cried bitterly. . . . I could not live without her. I leaned on her in piteous dependence, . . . the child from whom she had never been separated."[119] And this in her thirtieth year: still the weeping, piteous child.

Of Ann Eliza as the "gimme girl," little needs to be said—she has told that story herself. One passage will suffice: "I could not get anything else out of him, except by the hardest labor [Now we know what she means by the "hard, unceasing labor" to which she was forced], and the little that I got was given so grudgingly that I hated myself for accepting it; and many a time I would have thrown the pitiful amount back in his face, but stern necessity would compel me to accept the money and overlook the insult. . . . The hot blood tingles to the very ends of

my fingers as I recall the insults I received from that man
while I was his wife."[120] Insult consists in not giving Ann
Eliza all she wants: "I would not now be bought," she says
of her refusal of a generous cash settlement of $15,000, "by
the man who refused to care for me when it was his duty
to do so."[121] The trouble was that the cash settlement was
not *enough*. She asked for double rations and got them.
Her reaction? Scathing sarcasm: "Unheard-of liberality!—
I was allowed to draw sugar twice a month."[122] "I never
learned to hate anything in my life as I did the word 'economy,' while I was Brigham Young's wife."[123] Not *polygamy*,
but *economy* is the naughty word. In marrying Brigham
Young she "undoubtedly expected to be rewarded with
the luxuries of regal living. Her disenchantment was immediate and enduring."[124] Thus Mr. Wallace; well, at least
we know now that she had a very good motive for marrying
Brigham—the luxuries of regal living, which she confidently expected.

    And which she demanded—for she was a terrible snob.
The Webb house, she says, was "regarded with admiration, and ourselves with envy, since no one else had so
fine a place."[125] What makes Brigham Young's clutches
"contaminating clutches"[126] is that "this glazier . . . once
worked for two-bits a day." In Ann Eliza's code a lady
does not work; hence any wife who helps around the house
is really supporting herself, and hence her husband—
Brigham Young's wives toiled all the day to support him.
Lucy Bigelow's charge of the fine house at St. George
means for Ann Eliza that her "position as housekeeper"
is "that of servitor, entirely";[127] Lucy Decker in managing
the Beehive House "was not only obliged to cook for them,
but to wait upon them at the table, in the capacity of a
servant."[128] Her family and friends objected to Dee because
"they saw that he was in no way my equal,"[129] and indeed
when she gave him "the truest love a woman can give a

man . . . he repaid it as *men of his class* . . . usually repay it—in neglect and abuse when once I was in his power."[130]

The Amelia Story

A useful clue to the motives of Ann Eliza is her obsession with Amelia Folsom. She can't get Amelia out of her system; Amelia is all the things that Ann Eliza wants to be. Both Wallace and Ann Eliza work hard to make it appear that Amelia and Ann Eliza were rivals, as they must have been if Ann Eliza's story is true. Amelia was Ann Eliza's "main competition,"[131] Wallace assures us, "Ann Eliza's principal rival,"[132] the only other woman "so difficult to conquer"[133] in all of Young's vast experience. No wonder Amelia must hate her with a "deadly hatred."[134] With Emmeline safely dead, Ann Eliza uses her as her foil in the great dual with Amelia; it is Emmeline, not Ann Eliza who cries out, "Can I never go any where without having her thrust in my face?"[135] "Seems to me you're taking Emmeline's part pretty strong—ain't you?" says the Squire, to which Ann Eliza, gallant as ever, replies, "Yes, I am, for I think you've treated her badly." "Guess a little of the mad is on your own account—isn't it?" says the Squire, correcting his grammar; but Ann Eliza is equal to him: "Not a particle of it. Amelia doesn't interfere with me."[136] Ann Eliza jealous? Ha!

It is Ann Eliza who furnishes Mr. Wallace with the intimate portrait of her closest rival, her own inverted mirror-image. But how well did she know Amelia? She tells us in a most revealing sentence, which has been the object of some of Wallace's deft and drastic surgery. We have already quoted the sentence: "During the dessert she reached the cake-basket to me, and with as freezing a tone and manner as she could assume, asked—'Will you have some cake?' I declined, and that ended our conversation—the last, and indeed *the only one I ever had with her.*"[137] And now the Codex Wallace: "Suddenly, said Ann Eliza [did she?], Amelia shoved the cake basket at her 'and with as freezing a tone and manner as she could assume, asked, "Will you have some cake?" I declined, and that ended our conversation.' "[138] Period. Does the reader perhaps wonder why our emender cut off Ann Eliza's sentence in the middle? Let him not feel cheated, for in return for what he has removed from the text, Mr. Wallace has adorned it with a generous addition, telling us on the word of Ann Eliza—who said nothing of the sort—how Amelia *"suddenly . . . shoved* the cake basket at her."[139] It is only fair to point out that if Mr. Wallace often omits essential material, he just as often supplies it out of his own magnanimous mind.

Though Amelia never spoke to Ann Eliza, she chose to act out her most disgraceful private scenes with her husband in that lady's presence: "I was once present when she wanted her husband to do something for her; he objected, and she repeated her demand, threatening to 'thrash him,' if he did not comply"—that was the one sure way to control Brigham Young. "It is, perhaps, unnecessary to say [see? we told you so!] that she was not obliged to ask him again."[140] Because Brigham Young was a meticulous tidy housekeeper, Amelia loved to eat peanuts and throw the shells all over the house; because he abhorred bad language above all else, she made it a point to use the vilest. Screaming, bullying, smashing furniture, splitting the ears of all and sundry with the voice of a banshee and the language of a stevedore, a singularly repulsive combination of a pig, monkey, and water buffalo, Amelia had her way in everything. When Mary Van Cott had a child, Amelia forbade Brigham Young ever to see the mother again, and "for several months Brigham sheepishly obeyed."[141] That is Wallace speaking—where does he get such stuff? Well, *"apparently* Mary told Ann Eliza what happened, and Ann Eliza repeated it."[142] The alternative, that Ann Eliza is making it up, never occurs to our scholar—

his only source for all this is Ann Eliza, and "apparently" is good enough evidence for Wallace, when a story is as nasty as this one.

And speaking of nasty stories, the worst of all is the harrowing tale told by Mrs. Lewis, for which Ann Eliza is our only informant. Mrs. Lewis's son had walked home with a girl who had caught the eye of a Mormon bishop:

> Lewis's doom was sealed at once; the bewitched Bishop was mad with jealous rage, and he had only to give a hint of his feelings . . . and the sequel was sure. . . . An injury so brutal and barbarous that no woman's pen may write the words that describe it. . . . Whether this victim of priestly rule is dead or living must for ever remain a mystery. [Why forever?] . . . Yet during the whole of this affair the bishop was sustained by Brigham Young, who knew all about it.[143]

Ann Eliza finds it a "great marvel," which by 1908 has become "the almost incredible marvel,"[144] that the victim's poor distracted mother, who nursed him with a breaking heart, "still retained her faith in Mormonism," and since has been "sealed to Brigham Young as one of his wives."[145]

What was Young's object in marrying the old lady? To get her property, for when she held out, "the agents . . . rushed in breathless haste to the Prophet, and told him of Mrs. Lewis's rebellion. He instantly formed a plan of inducing her to surrender."[146] The plan was simple: since according to the Mormons, "no woman can enter heaven except some man go through the ordinances with her," he had the widow where he wanted her—she would have to marry him to be saved. There are two things wrong with this: (1) there is no such Mormon doctrine, and (2) Ann Eliza forgets that Mrs. Lewis, "an old lady, with children all grown,"[147] had long since "attended to all the important matters" with her husband Mr. Lewis. Anyway, he told her to keep things to herself: " 'They would not understand, you know,' murmured he in his most drivellingly sweet accents."[148] And that is how it came about that she told *only* Ann Eliza, whom she hated. We leave it to the reader to detect the flaws in the story, which Mr. Wallace now gives to the world as a public service.

As a widow, Amelia lived a long, busy public life, but Wallace discounts the testimony of those who saw her every day to give priority to one lone anonymous telegram to a New York newspaper saying she married a railroad man,[149] to which dubious report, innocuous enough even if it were true, Mr. Wallace manages to impart a flavor of scandal.[150] In her lectures Ann Eliza made it clear that in Amelia she had met her equal: "Almost everyone agreed that she possessed enough 'spirit' to have been Amelia Folsom's match," said the review.[151] And what on earth could all those Gentiles have known about Amelia Folsom? Only what Ann Eliza chose to tell them about her, of course; it was she who went around the country telling of the rivalry between the two beauties—she *wanted* to be thought of as "Amelia Folsom's match." Ann Eliza can repeat the very speech with which Brigham Young proposed to Amelia and announce, "This is the same argument he used to win me."[152] Isn't it odd that she tells the story of Brigham's proposal to Amelia, but except for this casual reference, tells no story of any proposal made to *her?* Plainly Amelia is another of those dream-creations in which Ann Eliza specialized, the grand lady in whom she saw the wish-image—the deadly rival—of herself.

In Amelia we have an interesting control for our speculations. Ann Eliza and Wallace want us very much to think that she was Amelia's match and counterpart. The conjunction is unfortunate, for the contrast speaks volumes. If Brigham had felt toward Ann Eliza as he did toward Amelia and as Wallace assures us he did,[153] why does Amelia live in a palace while Ann Eliza lives in a "tiny, ancient house"?[154] If it was passion for Eliza that

finally overpowered passion for Amelia, why did he desert
Ann Eliza on her wedding night for "fear of Amelia," who
knew nothing about the marriage?[155] If Ann Eliza was his
engrossing love, why was he "paying his addresses while
he was wooing me" to Mary Van Cott, whom Amelia
considered a more serious rival?[156]

While Ann Eliza is the best and sweetest wife Brigham
Young ever had, Amelia wears ever "a querulous, discontented expression,"[157] and "hates Brigham," and "uses the
vilest language in her common conversation."[158] "She is a
perfect virago, and carries everything by storm,"[159] which
she is able to do because the President lives in mortal dread
"that she might expose his personal business,"[160] even
though he "never discussed Church or personal business
with his mates."[161] Now Ann Eliza through her family
knew more about Young's personal business in a minute
than Amelia did in a month—why didn't he lick *her* boots?
The point is that Amelia, the *worst* wife, has everything
that Ann Eliza wants, including influence with the great
man, while Ann Eliza, the *best* wife, "never could influence
him in the slightest."[162]

Wallace assures us that it was the "love and physical
attraction" of Ann Eliza that broke "Amelia's power over
him."[163] Amelia too had resisted Brigham's wooing, but
he was "a most arduous and enthusiastic lover, and during
all the time that his suit was in progress, his carriage might
be seen standing before the door . . . several hours at a
time every day. . . . He promised her anything that she
might desire."[164] What a contrast to the "old cur" who
molested the Webb family! At least we know that Brigham
Young knew how to go about winning a difficult lady—
why didn't he employ these techniques on Ann Eliza? She
is not one to leave it unrecorded if the Presidential carriage
had stood daily in front of *her* house. Far from promising
her everything, the man drove a hard bargain with her
parents—and got what he wanted. The picture of Ann

Eliza, the superbeauty, the dread and envy of them all, having to beg "two bits worth of fresh meat"[165] while the other wives get mansions and carriages, is, to say the least, incongruous. Amelia is a useful control to show us how Brigham Young *would* have treated Ann Eliza before and after marriage had he felt toward her as she and Mr. Wallace insist that he did.

If Amelia gives us a pretty good idea of the grand lady that Ann Eliza would like to have been, Louise, a plural wife of Ann Eliza's father, gives an even better one of the woman she was. As Ann Eliza tells it, Louise married Mr. Webb on the recommendation of the authorities, but he "received her proposition somewhat coolly and cautiously, for, to tell the truth, he would much have preferred to make his own selection." Yet Mr. Webb had to go through with it because "he would have been . . . held up to derision in the Tabernacle, had he ventured to refuse."[166] We search the *Journal of Discourses* in vain for any such sort of derision, but Ann Eliza must clear her father and put all the blame on this defenseless girl.

Well, immediately there was trouble. Louise "did not love work, and she would not do it. She said she was a milliner, and had once been an actress, and declined 'to soil her hands with menial labor.' "[167] So "the new wife was unhappy, and . . . all the rest were disgusted with her selfishness and indolence." She insisted "that she was my father's wife, and her rights in the house were equal to any other person's."[168] Accordingly, Mr. Webb treated Louise "with such a marked coolness that she demanded the cause," and when he told her that she showed "lack of respect for herself, him, or his family, . . . she was very penitent, and promised all sorts of things if he would only allow her to remain in his family; she went about the house the very personification of grief and humility."[169] Next "she determined to create a sensation in the family" and took to her bed with a broken heart and "a great display of grief in the shape of a pocket-handkerchief." She resorted to the "trickery" of "trying to win Eliza [one of the other wives] over to her."[170]

When the thirteen-year-old Ann Eliza visited her, "she was very pathetic in her conversation with me, and made me quite miserable by the recital of her wrongs."[171] Then she said she was going to die: "my husband does not love me, and I cannot live; all I desire is death," and announced that she had taken poison.[172] "We had all considered before this that Louise was giving us a taste of her dramatic powers," says Ann Eliza;[173] and when after a touching farewell "she tried her hand at acting a kind of stupor," Mrs. Webb, "losing all patience," called her bluff, whereupon "Louise answered, her eyes flashing suddenly, and a great deal of the old-fashioned spirit in her will," accusing her of spoiling everything by administering an antidote.[174] When the hired men came to inquire about Louise's condition, "the men thought . . . very heartless" the answer that Mrs. Webb gave them, but she was in a rage at the way Louise "had turned the house topsy-turvy."[175]

When Mr. Webb arrived, he recommended some cayenne tea for the sufferer; and his wife, with "a little malice in her heart," gladly fixed it. "I fancy," says Ann Eliza, "there never was a stronger decoction mixed than the one my mother prepared for the imposter."[176] The drink threw Louise into "paroxysms of pain," and she was told by Mr. Webb "that she must no longer consider herself a member of his family,"[177] and "in spite of tears, entreaties, and protestations, she was taken to Salt Lake City, and we none of us ever saw her again."[178] However, "she married again in a very short time, and in three weeks was divorced from her second husband, . . . went to the southern part of the Territory, and married another man, whom she persuaded to take her to St. Louis. While there she suddenly went away one day, taking her husband's money and leaving him behind."[179] He "made no attempt to follow her" or to get his money back, being only too pleased to be rid of her.

It would be hard to imagine a closer parallel in real life to Ann Eliza's own behavior. What she has told us in joyfully recounting the story of Louise is that there really are such women; and if she has not a kind word for the lone and friendless girl, we can hardly be accused of cruelty in pointing out the resemblance of the two stories.

For Mother, Just for Mother

Ann Eliza was as close to her mother as paper to the wall. "I was her idol, the one object for which she cared the most in the world."[180] And "Ann Eliza's mother [Wallace speaking] . . . desperately wanted the marriage for the standing it would give her daughter and the entire family."[181] Ann Eliza knew what mama wanted, all right, for mama "labored with me . . . to view it in the same light."[182] Did she oppose her mother's plans? She did *not* — when he asked to walk home with her she said she would be very pleased; "I was pleased, too, for I knew that in bringing him home with me I should be conferring the greatest happiness on my mother."[183] Why great happiness? Wouldn't Mrs. Webb have been just as happy if President Young had come to the house with any other member of the family?

From the Stenhouse letter it would appear that Mama had arranged that little walk which so delighted both her and her daughter; for here we learn (it is omitted from the book, although implied)[184] that President Young and the other dignitaries had all been invited to dinner at the Webb house, which was very near the church. So it was *not* lust but a perfectly normal procedure for Brigham Young to accompany a member of the family to the home. But the point is that we find Ann Eliza here playing the game right along with mother and enjoying it; and when she was heroically fighting off Young's advances, she would never let mother know it: "I could not tell my feelings to my mother, for . . . she could never separate him from her religion."[185] "I dared not enter into religious discussion with her, for . . . I should be sure to say something to shock her."[186] This by way of explaining why Ann Eliza appears always to be accessory to the act; why she never really *seemed* to oppose marriage with Brigham, but always went along with Mama.

Here Mrs. Woodward's thesis[187] deserves mention: she notes that Ann Eliza only married Dee when it became evident that Brigham Young was not to be had, but when two years later Young married again and was therefore in the market, Ann Eliza with lightning speed divorced Dee and went after the President. Remember that her "friends did not approve of my lover [Dee] at all." Why not? "They saw that he was in no way my equal."[188] Who *was* her equal? She has Brigham Young resenting the interest shown in her by even the young blue-bloods — some his own relatives; who then *was* fit for Ann Eliza? Who but the man her mother "desperately wanted" her to marry? That the showdown with Dee was rigged and timed is apparent from a number of things. First, Dee was a very decent sort: the fact was that in two years of watching, the perceptive and resentful mama ("she had opposed my marriage as a *duty*")[189] living under the same roof with Dee (who had a perfectly good house of his own) found nothing to accuse him of, even though "her motherly eyes were too keen, her maternal instinct too unerring, to be deceived by my [noble] silence."[190] But the giveaway is Ann Eliza's announcement that, thanks to the divorce, "my children were better off, and stood far better chances of becoming the men that *both she and I* wished them to become, under *my* guidance *alone*."[191] Both Mrs. Webb and her daughter had plans, then, to which Dee was an obstacle.

Brigham Young's treatment of the Webb ladies is significant: he always deals with them as a team. It was not

with her but with her parents that all proposals and arrangements of marriage were made. "After the ceremony
was over, Brigham took me back to my mother's house"[192];
and the first month of the marriage she spent at home with
Mama, during which time, she writes, "I was happy indeed" — she was happy because she was with Mama and
could "almost forget that *he* had any claim upon me." Her
alarm was groundless: "At last he came to me and told
me that he was ready for me to move into the city, and
invited my mother to come and live with me."[193] The same
invitation was tendered when Ann Eliza moved to the farm
and back again to a new house in the city. Brigham Young
always takes it for granted that Mama is going to provide
companionship for Ann Eliza. All of which, if practical, is
anything but romantic and certainly gives strong support
to the "Mormon version." It was Mama who was so terribly
shocked, so heartbroken, when Ann Eliza left her husband.
"The idol is rudely broken that I have worshiped so
long."[194] But Ann Eliza was alive and well — what *was* the
idol? Specifically, Ann Eliza married to Brigham Young:
that was the idol that was broken.

Nobody else would do; indeed, Ann Eliza reports that
her parents "were no more anxious for me to marry than
I myself" — where anyone *else* was concerned "if I did not
wish to marry, that was quite enough."[195] But when President Young was the suitor, what a different story! They
drove the poor girl to distraction, though she bravely concealed her emotions and gave every appearance of being
as pleased as they. And then the terrible shock of the
divorce: why a shock? Hadn't Mama known all along just
how Ann Eliza felt about the man? Of course she did, and
that just shows what a wild story Eliza has cooked up: is
it conceivable that her parents, knowing all those awful
things about Brigham Young who had perpetrated crime
after crime against their own family — the father disbeliev-
ing Mormonism from the first, the mother loathing polyg-

amy and all connected with it — would force their darling
daughter to marry the monster, the superpolygamist? Is
it conceivable that when the beast began from the day of
the marriage treating their child with every form of abuse
and contempt and kept it up without intermission for seven
years, the entire family should be not only surprised but
heartbroken — utterly desolated — when she left him, not
for the way he treated her, but for what she was doing to
them? "My fault has been in loving you too well, and
having too great anxiety for your welfare," her mother
moaned, while she "longed to fly to her; but even to make
her happy I could not violate my conscience."[196] Has
mother no conscience, then? Have the family no principles
whatever? Why didn't Ann Eliza appeal to their conscience
before and after marrying Brigham Young? Why didn't she
simply tell them that she could not marry a practicing
criminal? None knew the man's evil ways better than the
high-minded Webb family who had so often been his victims. Yet she can only protest lamely that he is too old for
her. Why had she so carefully concealed her true feelings
from everybody before and during her marriage to Young?
To spare their feelings? But she spared nobody's feelings
in the terrible denunciation scene:

> Oh, Mother, Mother! Have you turned against me
> too? Am I to fight you all, singlehanded, alone? Won't
> you, at least, stand by me? . . . Do you think it would
> not be wrong to stifle all natural feelings, all aversion to
> another union, above all, to him? . . . She glared at her
> mother, and then, thrusting her words at her mother
> like a spear, she demanded, "Do you want to get rid of
> me?"[197]

Here the perceptive reader can discern the crude con-
triving of the great romance. For what Ann Eliza is objecting to is not just marriage with Brigham Young but
marriage with anybody. *Any* other union is repugnant to
her: "I belong to you, father. . . . You can't give me away

to *anybody*."[198] How true! The cruelty of the family consists not in wanting to "get rid" of her to Brigham Young in particular, but to anybody else in general. She must insist on her "aversion to another union," Brigham or no Brigham, to explain why she does not marry someone else. But having done that, she is faced with her own emphatic declarations that her parents made not the slightest effort to influence her, except where Brigham Young was concerned, and always gave her her own way.[199] For in the great denunciation scene with which Mr. Wallace wrings our hearts, Ann Eliza has created an issue which by her own accounting could not possibly have arisen.

As if to clinch the absurdity of the scene, we find no mention by Ann Eliza of Brigham's crimes, so well known to her family. The only specific objection she can give to marrying Young is that he is too old. Why no mention of his horrendous past? Because that might offend her mother's religious sensibilities or, as Mr. Wallace so carefully puts it, she was "determined not to become mired down in a religious discussion."[200] But when shortly after Brigham "delivered a terrible threat to the first Mrs. Webb," promising to excommunicate her son Gilbert unless she forestalled him "by 'counselling' her daughter to become his wife,"[201] the religious issue could not be avoided. Since the marriage was Mrs. Webb's dearest desire, and since she had never counseled anything else, the threat is of course as absurd as it is melodramatic. But when Mrs. Webb replies, "I know enough to know when my children are ill-used and cheated, Brigham Young,"[202] she has taken a moral stand and given Ann Eliza her reprieve; henceforth it was not her parents' wishes that force her to marry the monster, but only her concern for Gilbert's salvation, which of course depended on the pleasure of this holy man. But then once Ann Eliza capitulated, all "went merry as a marriage-bell."[203] What a story!

We need not waste time analyzing the silliness of all

this—comparison with Ann Eliza's letter to Stenhouse shows that she is making it all up. But even without that evidence, the lady's descriptions of her own emotions and reactions are sufficient to give her away completely.

Don't Touch Me, but Hold Me Tight

On the morning of the day he proposed, Brigham Young, in a long and intimate conversation, had inquired into Ann Eliza's love life, told her how beautiful and marriageable she was, how shocked he was when she married Dee, that he had always loved her and meant to have her himself, that now she was free he could tell her so, etc., while she told him just why she would never marry again and eloquently declared her independence in matters of the heart. As soon as she got home she recounted the whole thing to her mother—who was amused by it, but gave it no further thought; Ann Eliza, who of course dismissed the whole thing from her mind, could recall it— letter perfect—years later. But that very evening Brigham did an amazing thing. He proposed marriage, of all things—not to Ann Eliza herself, but to her parents. "I cannot describe my feelings; I was frightened. The thought of it was a perfect horror. I thought Father had gone crazy, and *I would not believe his statement for hours*."[204] Do you really believe she—or her mother!—was *that* naive? Raise your right hand. At noon she told Brigham Young, "I am a woman . . . with hard, bitter experiences; a woman who has lost faith in mankind, and hasn't much faith in matrimony,"[205] and he had spoken of nothing but marriage and his feelings towards her—and all the time she never *dreamed* what he was getting at.

If the lady's innocence and incredulity are awfully overdone, her protestations of disinterestedness are no less so. When a reporter asked the perfectly normal question, whether she "thought it would be better to marry the highest man in the Church, and be well cared for, than to marry some one in an inferior station?" she spilled the beans with the lofty declaration, "I had *no* such thoughts."[206] Granted that wealth and position were not even important in considering a marriage, what woman on earth would fail to consider them if only as a minor factor? Only Ann Eliza, apparently. Yet in protesting too much, she is caught in another fib, for she *must* have had such thoughts if, as she says, her parents and friends and girlish associates were constantly forcing them on her; she could not have been without them either in her social-minded environment or as a human being. Had she expected and wanted *nothing,* as she insists, she would hardly have rent the air with her banshee wail of poverty and neglect at never getting enough. What does she object to in Brigham Young page after page? His cheapness. From the first, the noble and disinterested Ann Eliza starts raising hell—she isn't getting *enough.*

ACT II, Scene iii. *The Garden. Enter Melissa right.*

Melissa: "No, as I have said it to all my other suitors, . . . I do not even thank him for the position he intended to confer upon me, for he knew I did not want it. Does he think I have escaped one misery to wish to enter another? 'Position!' I wonder what he thinks there is particularly fine about being a plural wife even to Brigham Young?"[207]

Well, the Squire took her at her word—"the position he intended to confer" on her was not very exalted after all, and so Item One in the divorce bill is that Brigham Young did not support her "in a manner proportionate to his means nor to her *station* in life."[208] Position indeed! "To support myself and children suitably" would require, she insisted, "the sum of two hundred thousand dollars" and a thousand a month pending settlement.[209] Not bad for the little lady who *never* gave a thought to money.

But back to our thesis that it was Ann Eliza who pursued Brigham Young before the marriage, and not the other way around. Time and again she assayed to appeal to him: "I was sure that I could move him. I would make myself so humble, so pathetic, before him." Only her courage failed her, and she never went through with it: "Two or three times I started to call to see him, but I would only . . . turn back faint and trembling."[210] She saw her chance one day when she met him in the street, but again it flopped: "All my eloquence was frozen under the chilling glance of the steely-blue eyes, which had not a ray of sympathetic warmth in them."[211] And this was the man who would give anything for a smile from Ann Eliza? All he gives her is the brush-off, so we have her word for it that even "at the last, he was influenced *entirely* by pique and wilfulness"—he didn't love her at all.[212] Why did he go through with it then? "Well," Ann Eliza explained to reporters, "we think it is vanity. They like to show that if they are old men, they can marry young women."[213] She tries to prove this, as she does her claim that Brigham Young threatened her father and had a special revelation for her, by elevating it to the level of an indisputable General Principle—that was the way Brigham Young *always* operated: he always threatened, he always has revelations as a last resort, and always marries only "because he is conceited, vain, and fond of showing his power and increasing his importance in this way."[214] But if number of marriages was the measure of prestige, why did he keep the number of his marriages a secret that even Wallace could not crack?

Anyway, we have Ann Eliza's admission that she did seek out the President and that he avoided her, which is simply the "Mormon version" so far as overt behavior is concerned. What converts the story into the Ann Eliza–Wallace version is that insight into the motives of the actors which may be derived only from Ann Eliza's telling of the story. If Brigham Young's behavior suggests anything but a man who has lost his head over a girl, and Ann Eliza's suggests anything but a woman who felt nothing but aversion for the man she was pursuing, and if the Webb family's reaction suggests anything but that of people losing their dearest treasure to the man they had most reason to hate, all these apparent absurdities can be explained if we realize that Brigham Young was simply being sadistic, Ann Eliza utterly self-sacrificing — throwing her life away just to spare the feelings of poor, superstitious Gilbert — and the family deeply religious, worshipping the prophet they all despised.

Once married to the man from whom she "cringed with aversion," Ann Eliza's constant complaint was neglect. From the first, he left her strictly alone while she hungered for "companionship and stimulation," and "looked forward to seeing Brigham as often as possible."[215] Why? She had her doting mother, her darling boys for whose affection she would tolerate no rival, a huge and bustling household, the society of Salt Lake City a "lovely four miles" away,[216] a constant round of church and social activities — why did it have to be Brigham? Never mind: the fact is that she sought his society after the marriage as much as he avoided hers. She invited him to social functions and was furious when other wives came along — by his special invitation. What is more, she was as sweet as pie to him all the time, while he treated her like an old cur. On the same page where she announces, "I never loved him," she can also report: "He had said I was the best wife he had, . . . for I had never given him a cross word or look."[217] And while she treated him "with the utmost tenderness,"[218] he treated *her* "with studied contempt."[219]

And then there is that little matter of rebaptism after she had fully made up her mind to leave her husband. *After* her final disillusionment, *after* weeks of plotting with Young's enemies against him, *after* having poured her whole story into eager Gentile ears and having discussed divorce procedures with Judge Hagen, *after* discovering the wonderful free outside world and the way leading to it, Ann Eliza lets loose with a blast at the Ward Teachers that leaves them "stunned"; but when the teachers begged the lady ("pleaded" is Wallace's invention) to get herself rebaptized, what does she do? She consents! Mr. Wallace's explanation for that is deliciously absurd: she yields because she is "wearied by evangelism."[220] What a way to escape the ennui of evangelism — to follow its advice and become recommitted to its ways just as one is in the act of kissing it all good-bye! Wallace attributes this astounding gesture to Ann Eliza's lingering religious sensibilities, but she herself makes it clear enough that she had none, when at the baptism "I was trying to feel solemn and to exercise faith, — a signal failure, I assure you."[221] Yet it would have taken a *great deal* of faith to induce the fugitive from bondage to place herself again in the hands of the Mormons if faith had anything to do with it. With so little faith, why would she submit to "the farce," as she calls it, at such a late date? Wallace comes up with the answer when he has the ward teachers suggest that Ann Eliza, by getting baptized, might improve her standing with Brigham and even become the Favorite Wife.[222] To the very end she is pursuing him.

According to both Wallace and A. E. Young, Brigham Young lusted after Ann Eliza longer than any other of his victims, and tried longer and harder to win her. "He would not give me up," she told the family, confessing that he "had intended to propose for me so soon as I was old enough" — he had been waiting for her since childhood.[223] Hence "he tried in every way to win me, a willing bride, before he attempted to coerce me."[224] Her conquest was the most difficult and hence the most glorious of Young's amatory attainments.[225] At the time of the great wooing, "It is likely," Wallace reports, that "he would have found

Ann Eliza irresistible."[226] Here surely are the makings of a great romance. But what do we find? The strangest courtship in the history of the world. Ann Eliza is good enough to tell us by what tried and true procedures Brigham won *other* willing brides—lavish gifts, delightful surprise, constant attentions, a gay progress of plays and balls. Why were there no such goodies for Ann Eliza during two years of "ardent wooing?" The woman who can recall every syllable of that four-page conversation on the way from Church reports not a single episode, revealing or otherwise, of the long and arduous wooing that followed. The woman who can recite Brigham's amorous speeches to other victims recalls none addressed to herself. Indeed she explicitly points out in recounting *both* of her personal conversations with Young—the one when she was seventeen and the other when she was twenty-two—that she never had the remotest inkling of a suspicion either time that Brigham Young was being romantic, and in each case states her firm conviction that he did *not* love her either time, but was speaking purely from vanity and from a desire to show who was the stronger.[227]

It was only after the marriage was arranged that Young gave his bride "some very pretty dresses, and a small sum of money, as a wedding-gift; but I never got such a present again afterwards."[228] That's funny; *other* wives of Brigham Young got such presents afterwards—lots of them. Ann Eliza quotes the speech with which Brigham Young, very privately, proposed to Amelia, and casually remarks in passing that that was the same one used on her, and *all* the more difficult victims.[229] But that is the only hint we get of any such proposal being made to her. It is perfectly clear throughout that Mr. Young settled everything not with Ann Eliza but with her family. If he actually proposed to her, why must she put amorous speeches in his mouth and at the same time specify that he did *not* love her and that those speeches never suggested to her the slightest hint of amorous intent? She is trying her best to make out that Brigham Young made *some* sort of proposal, but this insinuation, denial, and fabrication is the best she can do.

So Brigham wooed the family, and in his visits to the house "he manifested all the growling propensities of an old 'cur.' "[230] And they, though they "desperately" wanted the match, barked right back at him: "After a still more spirited contest with my mother, the Prophet took his departure in a great rage."[231] Curiouser and curiouser! Is that the way to get them on his side, or to get him on theirs? No, that was hardly necessary, since they were already so firmly on his side that two years of pleading by Ann Eliza could not pry them loose; while he was so wild about Ann Eliza that he was one hundred percent with the family. Actually when he acts like an old cur it can only mean that they are wooing him and he is being difficult. Sweet Eliza's thesis, however, is that he wanted to get the family into such a jam that Ann Eliza would have to marry him to save them. But since he was mad about Ann Eliza who was devoted to her family, why did she let him put the screws on the family — and do nothing to relieve them? If Brigham was really her ardent suitor, he would have done anything — or at least *something* — for Gilbert or Papa, just to please her. But he makes no effort to please her; she has no power over him at all — this clever and heroic girl has no bargaining power whatever. His attempt "to win me a willing bride" is supposed to have preceded a later effort at bribery when all blandishment failed, yet there were no blandishments; the bribe of a house and money, which Ann Eliza in her book insists came later, was made according to the Stenhouse letter on the very night on which Brigham *first* proposed — to the family. Why didn't he propose to *her*? She had told him that morning that she was of age and quite able to make up her own mind and that her parents gave way to her in everything — why, then, didn't Brigham ask *her* to marry him before appealing to them? Is this the romantic way to go about it—to play his opening gambit by accosting the father with the veiled threat and sinister smile with which he always gave orders?

In the end Ann Eliza marries Brigham Young entirely on *his* terms; during two years of "ardent wooing" *she won not a single concession from him,* received not a single gift; according to her he promised to make her a queen—but what substantial earnest did he offer? Consider the wedding and the honeymoon.

"After the ceremony was over, Brigham took me back to my mother's house, where I was to remain for the present, until he should deem it prudent to let Amelia and the United States government know that I was his wife."[232] Wallace gratefully—desperately—accepts this feeble effort to explain why the great lover stood up his greatest conquest on the wedding night: "Because he was not yet ready to face Amelia's outrage and the harem's disapproval, Brigham returned his twenty-seventh wife to her father's home outside the city and then retired alone to his bedroom in the Lion House."[233] But please note—Amelia and the government as yet know nothing of what our lovebirds have been up to—they will not know in fact until Brigham finds it "prudent" to *let* them know. What is to stop them from going on with the show? Nothing but Mr. Young's free choice. He did not hesitate to marry sweet Eliza in the first place in spite of Amelia and the government; he had made her his lawful wife, whether Amelia liked it or not— the damage was done and as yet no one the wiser; it remained only for the victor to claim the spoils. What a time to back out! Immediately after the marriage ceremony, according to the Stenhouse letter, President Young accompanied Ann Eliza to the Tabernacle in the most public meeting of the year, for the wedding day was April 6, *the* day of General Conference. A less secret time could not have been chosen: everything the President did on that day would be noted. But all the time he is worried about what Amelia and the U.S. Government will think when they find out; and so he leaves his bride with her mother and for three weeks does not see her again.

This puts her in a silly position too: "I didn't feel specially complimented," she says in the understatement of the year.[234] To rescue her from a desperate case, Mr. Wallace quotes a letter of Ann Eliza to a personal friend (without telling us that it is simply the Stenhouse letter). "I had considerable of his attention; his visits were frequent"[235] — a vague, noncommittal attempt at face-saving, for we can be sure that Ann Eliza would not have told a story so shockingly unflattering to herself if she had a better one. Here was one time she could not invent a lurid tale about the lustful Squire—for April 6, her wedding day, was a day on which every move of President Young could be strictly accounted for. But finally he did get her alone. Shortly after the wedding day he came to take his bride for a drive (would Amelia tolerate that?). "He did not enjoy the drive one bit, for he was in constant terror lest he should be discovered."[236] Then why not go into the house—couldn't better arrangements be made than that? Must the poor man put himself into a state of "constant terror" just to be with Ann Eliza? "He took me round all the by-ways." Alone at last! And his reaction after twenty-odd years of hungering for Ann Eliza? "He was anxious and *distrait*; while I, on the contrary, was in the highest spirits. I laughed and chatted . . . and was jubilant in proportion to his misery."[237]

No wonder even Wallace omits these precious lines — they have it all backwards. Instead of the triumphant Squire yielding to his great passion in the seclusion of the by-ways, we have a courteous and preoccupied gentleman taking a lady for a ride because it is the decent thing to do; instead of a cowering and terrified victim, we have the lady at last "jubilant," triumphant, laughing and chatting in her glory. As if to prove that this is not a mistake, "he repeated the drive, which was no more comfortable for him than the first one had been. . . . With the exception of those drives, *I never went anywhere with him alone.*"[238] Another bad slip: Brigham was terrified of being seen with Ann Eliza, yet he made sure wherever they went that they *would* be seen, and never be alone together. Far from being terrified of being seen with Ann Eliza, he chose the one way of making sure of it. But then who said he was terrified? That is Ann Eliza's own mind reading. The one thing that is really apparent from all this is that Brigham Young dutifully and reluctantly took his bride for drives, though he did not enjoy her company in the least—while she thoroughly enjoyed herself. Chalk up another for the "Mormon version."

Ann Eliza confirms our suspicions when she complains of his unromantic behavior: "I didn't feel especially complimented, to be sure; but, as I did not desire his attentions, and was happier without them, I did not allow my pride to receive a very severe wound, but was exceedingly gracious to him, the more nervous and absorbed he got."[239] More of the same: while she is "exceedingly gracious, . . . jubilant" and "laughed and chatted" in his company, he is in "misery, . . . anxious and *distrait* . . . nervous and absorbed," that is, paying as little attention as possible to her. What a miraculous reversal of role that strange wedding has accomplished! Or is it? When had it been otherwise? Next *she* invited *him* to a ball: "He was my husband, and whom else should I invite?"[240] Well, since she *preferred* to have him leave her strictly alone, how about that army of warm friends, admirers, and old flames? "I was very much annoyed, . . . and really a little hurt that he could not take me somewhere just once without someone else along."[241] Again she's got it all wrong: *he* is supposed to be the monster from whose contaminating clutches she "did shrink with aversion"[242] (the expressions are hers); and *she* is supposed to be the one object for which he has

lusted most through the years — yet he treats her to a strict hands-off policy — and she resents it like mad.

The leit-motiv of Ann Eliza's life with Brigham Young is clear and unmistakable — neglect. She was "mortified" that he did not pay more attention to her.[243] By a courtship in which he treated her with the most icy aloofness and threatened to ruin a family which was ardently supporting his suit, marriage "was forced upon me; and I was now compelled to endure the indignities which he chose to heap upon me."[244] How queer can you get? She had been unmoved by "the position he *intended* to confer upon me,"[245] but no sooner were they married than he "chose" to heap on indignities instead. "I never asked for the smallest necessary of life that I was not accused of extravagance and a desire to ruin my husband."[246] Is that the way to treat the best wife one ever had — to deny her even the *smallest necessary* of life? "The hot blood tingles to the very ends of my fingers as I recall the insults I received from that

man while I was his wife."[247] Insults, neglect, indignity—
what next? He refused her the "companionship and stimulation" which she "desperately wanted,"[248] and was totally immune to her enticements: Wallace tells the story,
"possibly apocryphal," of how Ann Eliza bought thirteen
roosters and one hen so that the hen wouldn't suffer neglect "the way your wives do!"[249]

If "her disenchantment was immediate and endur-
ing,"[250] it is only fair to note that the same immediate and
enduring disenchantment marked both her other marriages. She expected moonlight and magnolias from Dee
and quickly learned about the "indifferent, matter-of-fact
manner . . . which most Mormon men assume towards
their helpless wives";[251] and she had hardly married Denning when he took to staying just as far away from her as
he could get, telling her how infinitely preferable the
charms of other women were to hers, and finally announcing his intention to let her starve to death.[252] Isn't it an
interesting coincidence that all three of these men were
model husbands to their *other* wives? Stenhouse, sympathetic as she is to Ann Eliza, cannot resist a couple of little
digs as to her unique unenviable position among the wives
of Brigham Young: she was, she pointedly writes, "his last
but yet not his best-beloved,"[253] and observes that "she is
the only wife whom Brigham has not supported"[254]—an
enlightening statement in view of Ann Eliza's insistence
that the other wives had to work to support not only themselves but their husband, and Mr. Wallace's moving description of the savagely cruel neglect of Mary Ann Angell.
It will never do to have Ann Eliza the *least* loved of all the
wives, when Wallace's whole story rests on the thesis that
she was the *best*-loved! Her complaint is that "*others* were
cared for, and it was more than a woman's nature could
stand, to see them thus petted."[255] He forced her children
to wear homespun, she says, "and yet I noticed that none
of his own children were compelled to do so."[256] The stin-

giness towards her, the memory of which sends the hot blood tingling to her fingertips, was never turned against the other wives: She insists that she was "the least expensive" of all the wives, "for he spent but very little money for me."[257]

And all the time he neglects and insults her, Ann Eliza is being sweetness itself to Brigham, treating him "with the utmost tenderness," in return for his "systematic course of neglect."[258] What is more, he recognized and acknowledged the noble effort she was making: "He had said I was the best wife he had, . . . for I had never given him a cross word or look."[259] "I was, in fact, a perfect Griselda; and my husband had got so used to such unquestioning obedience and submission from me that I think he was never so surprised in his life as he was when I rebelled."[260] "He would have looked for rebellion from almost any other wife sooner than from me, I had been so quiet and acquiescent during all my married life with him."[261] "He said, up to the very last of my living with him, that I was the least troublesome of any wife he had ever had."[262] But instead of being grateful to the woman who finally consented to marry him after years of hungering for her and who went all out to be agreeable once married, he merely "took advantage of my quiet tongue, and imposed upon me fearfully."[263] "I was neglected, insulted and humiliated in every way imaginable,"[264] or, as Wallace puts it, "deprived of material necessities and affection."[265] So do you blame us for asking: Why did Ann Eliza, who "*never* loved" Brigham Young and always "looked upon him as a heartless despot"[266] *always* behave towards him in the most acquiescent and ingratiating manner, while he, whose grand passion she had been lo, these many years, who had greatly loved, hotly pursued, and always admired her, treat her not with the cruelty of a Liliom but with "studied contempt"[267] and "a systematic course of neglect,"[268] rejoining to heap humiliation and

insults on her? Others were not treated so by him. "Clara,"
by no means the favorite, "had everything that she could
desire. . . . Not a wish that she expressed but was instantly
granted."[269] Even A. Cobb, who "for several years past"
had been "grossly neglected by the Prophet," was "still a
very stylish, elegant woman," though merely sealed to
Brigham Young.[270] Why does everybody have it so much
better than Ann Eliza?

And why, treating her as he did, was Brigham so sure
of her that (according to her) the greatest surprise of his
life was when she rebelled? What could he expect after
inflicting such abuse on the woman? Why was he so surprised when she finally turned against him? There can be
only one reason: the marriage had been her idea in the
first place. Her final decision to have herself rebaptized
(Brigham didn't ask her to) is quite enough to show that.
If he had really pursued her with passion, he had every
right to expect fireworks for giving her the deep-freeze
after the marriage, and she had every right to set them
off — reminding him of the crooked way in which she had
been forced into the marriage and the vile way he had
treated her ever since. If her story is true, she had plenty
of bargaining power — first with the great man "who wooed
her so ardently"[271] and then with the husband whose secrets she knew. *Why did she never use any of that bargaining
power,* even to alleviate her own terrible sufferings as her
husband year after year heaped studied insults and abuse
upon her? Why did this fiery little lady make no gesture
of self-defense? The woman deserves no sympathy who
will take such vicious and unjust treatment meekly and
cheerfully: "I had been so quiet and acquiescent during *all*
my married life with him."[272] For heaven's sake, why? It
is conceivable that if Brigham had made an effort even to
meet her halfway, she might, in spite of her spoiled and
jealous nature, have done the same towards him, but this
total and absolute surrender — in going *all* the way to please

him, while he thinks up new insults and abuses — what is behind it?

The pursuit after as before the marriage is all on her side. Why can't the man make any concession to her at all? Why should he accuse his *best* wife of ruinous extravagance *every* time she asked for the mere necessities of life? "I saw that it was impossible for me to ever interest my husband."[273] Do you get that? — he simply wasn't interested in her — not even for old time's sake! "Indeed, of so little importance was I, or my actions, that he never troubled himself to come near me after he had given his consent (to run a boarding house)."[274] "Speaking to him concerning these matters was worse than useless, for I never could influence him in the slightest, while *every* suggestion which I ventured to make irritated him extremely."[275] If she couldn't interest the man, she did irritate him extremely, but even so she couldn't get a rise out of him; he refused even to quarrel with her — which is why she says *she* never quarreled with him; she tried indeed to stir him up, as in the affair of the train, but he refused to give her the satisfaction. Either her technique was the worst in history, or else Brigham Young felt not only no affection for her but what is more significant, no obligation beyond supporting her and showing her common courtesy. She knew that the one way to influence him would be to have children by him,[276] and her explanation for her failure to do that is as good as any — that she had never had marital relations with him. She had no hold over him at all.

Ann Eliza, whose only accomplishment was acting, aspired to play the lead opposite Brigham Young, and Mr. Wallace is now determined to give her her wish. But who will deny that the keynote of her life with Brigham is total frustration? She tells us how as a girl she lived in a world of romantic make-believe and glorious expectations, and shows how she and her mother could give substance to

their dreams through their unique talent for self-drama-
tization.

As a child, the mother had known insecurity and starvation as a homeless servant girl in England. Marrying
Webb had liberated her from bondage and set her up for
life. His second marriage, according to Ann Eliza, took it
all away again; from then on, "every hour of her life her
heart was torn by some new agony,"[277] as she passed her
days in "unutterable anguish."[278] The thought of having
to share anything with anybody was the one thing that
drove Mrs. Webb perfectly wild.[279] She spoiled Christmas
dinner for her own family just to have the pleasure of
keeping the other wives from getting any turkey—though
those other wives were, by Ann Eliza's admission, splendid and self-sacrificing women.[280] She would gladly have
seen her husband die rather than permit another wife to
assist in nursing him to health.[281] And she imbued her only
daughter with her own passion for absolute possession.
Ann Eliza was "her idol, the one object for which she cared
the most in the world."[282] For Ann Eliza it had to be top
billing or none; for her to marry a commoner like Dee was
a catastrophe; for her to desert Brigham Young was even
worse, for regardless of everything else he was still top
man.

No one will deny that Mrs. Webb had plans for her
daughter, and that those plans all centered on marriage to
Brigham Young. And only a fool would deny that Ann
Eliza herself was privy to those plans, and fancied herself
in the stellar role of an Amelia. But the play flopped—
Brigham Young was not available for the lead opposite
Eliza. He had other things to do. What next? If the show
is to go on, we must find a substitute for the role of Brigham
and move the production back East, where nobody will
know the difference. The man chosen to play Brigham
Young was a palpable ham who stamped and roared and
leered and snarled and glared in a way to delight the hearts

of the matinee crowd seeking escape from anything resembling real life. To this animated dummy, Ann Eliza
makes her stirring and gallant speeches, going through her
stereotyped gestures of sweet appeal, screaming despair,
and exquisite scorn. It is all her own production—she plays
the lead and directs the rest, and you can be sure that
everything goes off the way she wants it to.

In reviving the flimsy melodrama, Mr. Wallace has
sought to give it substance by playing up that religious
fervor which the real Ann Eliza never felt and by placing
her stilted and impossible heroics against a pseudohistor-
ical background which he thinks can be made plausible by
well-known production gimmicks, using skillful sound and
lighting effects to evoke a grim and somber atmosphere,
as we have seen, that disarms and intimidates any who
might feel inclined to snicker at that gallant little lady or
to scoff at a tale of human suffering or treat lightly the
most horrible crimes of the century. Whether these things
are true or even distantly plausible becomes a mere quibble
when our skilled producer begins to work his magic. Criticism is awed and silenced in the presence of such artistry
and zeal.

To get to the heart of the great love drama, we present
herewith some random questions for Mrs. Young or her
doughty champion to answer. There are an even fifty of
them, just to keep things under control.

1. Why would your doting parents want or even permit you to marry the man who had done so many evil
things to them?

2. Why do you and Wallace claim not to know
Young's reason for interfering in your love life, if he was
always so blunt and tactless about it?

3. Why did he wait for two years after your divorce
before proposing?

4. Since you were the object of his affections, why

did he never propose to you personally, as he did to other women?

5. Why do you say that offers of money and grim threats were employed only as a last desperate device to win you if, as you say in the Stenhouse letter, those offers and threats were made on the very first night of the negotiations?

6. Why did you always fail to guess Young's real interest in you or to interpret his crude advances? Why did you never suspect anything but a fatherly interest in you?

7. Why did your mother, who dreamed of the match, utterly fail to see the significance of his glaringly obvious remarks to you — if those remarks were actually made?

8. Why do you and Mr. Wallace suppress the fact that Young walked home with you not of his own devising but because your mother invited him to the house while you knew that by walking with him "I should be conferring the greatest happiness on my mother"?[283] Doesn't that put you two on the offensive?

9. Why, if Brigham Young stared at you hypnotically from the stand throughout the meeting, did nobody, including your mother, notice his significant behavior?

10. Why does Mr. Wallace never mention Van Etten, the key to the meeting story? Why did the man who assailed Young so viciously in the meeting willingly accept a missionary call soon after?

11. Why didn't you counter Brigham Young's attack on you by accepting any of your other and less obnoxious suitors?

12. Why in a book on Mormon marriage customs do you never name any of your army of suitors — including the "high church officials" that sought your hand when you were only twelve? Why do you not recount a single episode of those many courtships?

13. First you tell of a gigantic economic enterprise and

swindle: "All this was for the purpose of influencing me";[284] and then you say it was not money but fear of "the Prophet's curse"[285] that did the trick. Did your family really place such store on the "curse" of a Prophet they had so often denounced as a fraud?

14. Then you say you did it all to save *Gilbert's* faith and position in the Church. What faith? What position? Were you willing to throw your life away to appease what you describe as Gilbert's foolish superstitions?

15. Then you say that for the sake of your *friends*,[286] you were willing to marry even Brigham Young. Then why did you resist the pleas of those same friends for two years?

16. Then you say it was your *children* that decided you: "What if God should take my children, to punish my rebellious spirit?"[287] Did it take you two years to realize that you were being rebellious?

17. Why during the courtship did Brigham Young make no concessions out of his love of you? Why, if he loved you so, were you never able to influence him in the least?[288]

18. Why did he never shower you with gifts and attention as he did other ladies whom he wooed and wives whom he favored? With his vast experience, why didn't he try the Amelia approach on you?

19. If he "succumbed to love and physical attraction,"[289] why did he rebuff you coldly whenever you approached him during the courtship?

20. If he desired you so passionately, why did he subject you to "a systematic course of neglect"[290] during your whole married life?

23. Why does the knowledgeable Mrs. Stenhouse call you "his last but yet not his best-beloved,"[291] and say that you were the only wife he did not support,[292] if he had really worked harder to win you than to win any other wife?

24. Why did he begin his suit by proposing not to you

but to your father, and that "with a peculiar emphasis and a sinister smile"?[293] Is such the way of the great lover?

25. You say, "He tried in *every way* to win me, a willing bride."[294] In what ways? You report no romantic courtship and no presents—aren't those some of the things he might have tried?

26. Why were your heart-rending appeals to the parents who worshipped you completely unavailing? Why did you bother to appeal anyway, since your parents were determined *not* to make you marry against your will? You say you fought the marriage with every resource at your command: Whom did you fight, since your parents would not force you, and Brigham Young never proposed to you?

27. Why were you "surprised" when Brigham Young spoke to you after the meeting, even though he had stared at you the whole time and you knew he was supposed to walk home with you to dinner?

28. The *only* objection you mention to your parents is Brigham Young's age; but you were free to marry a younger man—why didn't you?

29. If "it is likely he would have found [you] irresistible,"[295] why did Brigham Young resist you so effectively? You say, "If a man wants to marry a woman, the woman must marry him. They dare not refuse."[296] Where was the top man's unlimited power when, with your parents' aid, he besieged you for two years? Why with all his power did he have to resort to such an elaborate subterfuge?

30. Why, though you were a "woman . . . with hard, bitter experiences,"[297] does Brigham Young make his proposals and arrangements only with your family—in your absence? Doesn't that show that they were approaching him, since it would have been improper for you to do so? If he was the aggressor, why did he never propose to you personally?

31. If he did propose to you, as you imply in comparing

your case with Amelia's, why do you report nothing of that dramatic event?

32. If Brigham Young accosted you in your youth "not, I think, from any particular affection, . . . but . . . to show me that his will was stronger than mine,"[298] how can you say that he had always loved you and meant to have you?

33. You say that as a member of Brigham Young's household you put on a gay exterior for the sake of others: "I was very happy to see her happy, and enjoyed myself very much."[299] How then was Brigham Young or anyone else to know of your sufferings?

34. At seventeen, you say, "I considered myself quite a martyr to the Mormon priestly rule."[300] Why? "I expressed my opinion of the Prophet very freely," you continue, ". . . [and] fairly horrified my mother."[301] And yet it was your religious feelings that drove you to marry the same prophet? And when the time came to save yourself from his "contaminating clutches," you did not "dare admit anyone to my confidence, not even my mother."[302] For fear of "shocking" her, you say. After all, *she* had told *you* about Brigham and polygamy.

35. You always got what you asked for from Young, but you say it was never enough: how much would it take to satisfy you? (Answer: $200,000).

36. If you "got a stove out of him,"[303] as you wrote to Mrs. Stenhouse, why do Wallace and Woodward insist that you did not?[304]

37. If you were, as you say, the least demanding and most easily pleased of the wives, how does it happen that you moved around more and had more houses than any of them?

38. If Brigham Young alone is responsible for your sufferings, how does it happen that you suffered the same pangs with Dee and Denning? How does it happen that all three got along famously with their other wives, but only had trouble with you?

39. If Brigham Young really said you were "the best wife he had," why were you treated so much worse than the others—"neglected, insulted and humiliated in every way imaginable?"[305]

40. If you despised his offer of social standing, why was your chief complaint against him that he did not support you as his position and station in life demanded? If you spurned all the luxuries he offered, why did you complain so loudly when those luxuries were denied you?

41. With your sweet disposition, why were you so unpopular with the other wives? Why are the wives with which you were intimate always dead ones?

42. How did you, a gentle and uncomplaining soul, suddenly become a master of vitriolic prose when you took up the pen? Did you really write the book, by the way? If it is your own story, why does so much of it come right out of Stenhouse, and why is it in the style of Beadle?

43. Since you had fought Brigham Young so long and so fiercely, and since you never lived with him after the marriage, why was Brigham Young so sure that you, of all the wives, would be the last to leave him? Why was he so sure of you after treating you like dirt, if the marriage was not *your* idea?

44. Brigham Young never hesitated to grant a divorce if a wife asked for it. Why didn't you ever ask him? Why didn't you ask for the freedom for which you yearned? Why? If there was anything Brigham Young would not do it was to lure anybody back into the fold, as Wallace suggests.[306] Why did you ask for rebaptism when you were about to leave him? He never suggested such a thing— weren't you making a last bid for him?

45. You and Wallace say you had to escape because "death, incarceration in a madhouse and many other terrible things had been threatened."[307] And that at a time when Brigham Young still thought you were his meekest and safest wife! Threatened by whom? When? Where?

How? Why? Why should Brigham Young threaten "the best wife he had" with such things?

46. Why do you make out that Brigham Young wanted desperately to keep you from leaving Utah, after he had offered you $15,000 cash to clear out?[308] You were already free and had already told your story to the press. Why keep you in Utah? Couldn't he have stopped you any time? Isn't that an elaboration of the foolish pursuit motif? Why should Brigham Young ever pursue you?

47. Why should the invisible Danites be a mortal threat to you in Utah, but helpless the moment you crossed an invisible line into Wyoming?

48. To save your life you had to barricade yourself in your hotel room for two months. But how about the next three months — didn't you stay on in Salt Lake?

49. With Brigham's spies everywhere, how were you able to move out all your furniture and sell it at a public auction without being discovered?

50. If you always viewed Brigham Young as "a heartless despot" whom you had "never loved,"[309] why do you complain so bitterly of his not loving you? And if you were "happy indeed," when you could "forget that he had any claim upon [you],"[310] why did you resent his absence?

51. Wallace says Brigham Young used the press to attack you through your "best friends and family."[311] That is your version, but what have articles in the *San Francisco Chronicle* to do with your friends and family? Who were the friends in question? If Brigham Young controlled the press, why did no man in America ever have a worse press?

This sort of thing can go on indefinitely, but let us get to more meaty matters.

Notes to Part 4

1. Ann Eliza (Webb) Young, *Wife No. 19; Or, the Story of a Life of Bondage, Being a Complete Exposé of Mormonism, and Revealing the Sorrows, Sacrifices and Sufferings of Women in Polygamy* (Hartford, CT: Dustin, Gilman, 1875), 543.

2. Mrs. T. B. H. (Fanny) Stenhouse, *Tell It All: The Story of a Life's Experience in Mormonism* (Hartford, CT: Worthington, 1874), 287.

3. Irving Wallace, *The Twenty-Seventh Wife* (New York: Simon and Schuster, 1961), 168.

4. Ibid. (emphasis added).

5. Young, *Wife No. 19*, 115–16.

6. Stenhouse, *Tell It All*, 286 (emphasis added).

7. Young, *Wife No. 19*, 373.

8. Wallace, *Twenty-Seventh Wife*, 122–23.

9. Ibid., 123 (emphasis added).

10. Young, *Wife No. 19*, 375.

11. Young, *Wife No. 19*, 376–77.

12. Stenhouse, *Tell It All*, 286; cf. Young, *Wife No. 19*, 444–45.

13. Young, *Wife No. 19*, 444.

14. Ibid., 443.

15. Ibid., 444; Wallace, *Twenty-Seventh Wife*, 168.

16. Wallace, *Twenty-Seventh Wife*, 220.

17. Young, *Wife No. 19*, 445.

18. Wallace, *Twenty-Seventh Wife*, 172.

19. Young, *Wife No. 19*, 453.

20. Ibid., 554.

21. Ibid., 458.

22. Ibid., 543.

23. Wallace, *Twenty-Seventh Wife*, 168 (emphasis added).

24. Ibid., 220.

25. "Sing of the wrath, O Goddess," are the opening words of Homer, *Iliad* I, 1. The preamble explains how Achilles' wrath sent thousands of men to their deaths and fulfilled the will of Zeus. It is a statement of the cause of the catastrophe whose story follows.

26. Wallace, *Twenty-Seventh Wife*, 134.

27. Ibid.

28. Ibid., 136.

29. Ibid., 137–38.

30. Ibid., 367.

31. Ibid., 254.

32. Ibid., 282.

33. Ibid., 168.

34. Young, *Wife No. 19*, 423.

35. Ibid., 425.

36. Ibid., 438–39.

37. Ibid., 441.

38. Ibid., 465.
39. Ibid., 508 (emphasis added).
40. Ibid., 433.
41. Ibid., 438.
42. Ibid., 445.
43. Ibid., 437 (emphasis added).
44. Ibid., 432–33.
45. Wallace, *Twenty-Seventh Wife,* 158.
46. Ibid., 162.
47. Stenhouse, *Tell It All,* 286.
48. Young, *Wife No. 19,* 445.
49. Ibid., 399.
50. Ibid., 437 (emphasis added).
51. Wallace, *Twenty-Seventh Wife,* 159.
52. Young, *Wife No. 19,* 423.
53. Ibid., 437.
54. Ibid., 423–24.
55. Wallace, *Twenty-Seventh Wife,* 164 (emphasis added).
56. Ibid., 165 (emphasis added).
57. Stenhouse, *Tell It All,* 286.
58. Ibid.
59. Wallace, *Twenty-Seventh Wife,* 220.
60. Young, *Wife No. 19,* 445.
61. Stenhouse, *Tell It All,* 286.
62. Young, *Wife No. 19,* 451.
63. Ibid., 444.
64. Ibid., 453; Wallace, *Twenty-Seventh Wife,* 172.
65. Young, *Wife No. 19,* 455 (emphasis added).
66. Ibid. (emphasis added).
67. Ibid.
68. Ibid., 455–56.
69. Wallace, *Twenty-Seventh Wife,* 167.
70. Young, *Wife No. 19,* 453.
71. Ibid., 515.
72. Wallace, *Twenty-Seventh Wife,* 219.
73. Ibid., 220.
74. Ibid., 219.
75. Ibid., 314.
76. Ibid., 167.
77. Ibid., 152.
78. Ibid., 165 (emphasis added).
79. Young, *Wife No. 19,* 445.

80. Ibid., 114.
81. Wallace, *Twenty-Seventh Wife*, 160.
82. Young, *Wife No. 19*, 391 (emphasis added).
83. Ibid.
84. Ibid., 399.
85. Ibid., 403.
86. Ibid.
87. Ibid., 405.
88. Ibid., 435–36 (emphasis added).
89. Ibid., 436.
90. Ibid., 411.
91. Ibid.
92. Ibid., 536.
93. Wallace, *Twenty-Seventh Wife*, 180.
94. Ibid., 234 (emphasis added).
95. Young, *Wife No. 19*, 385.
96. Ibid., 390.
97. Ibid., 399 (emphasis added).
98. Ibid., 390.
99. Ibid., 552.
100. Wallace, *Twenty-Seventh Wife*, 414.
101. Young, *Wife No. 19*, 423.
102. Ibid., 408.
103. Wallace, *Twenty-Seventh Wife*, 423.
104. Young, *Wife No. 19*, 443.
105. Wallace, *Twenty-Seventh Wife*, 381, 385–89.
106. Young, *Wife No. 19*, 105.
107. Ibid., 180.
108. Ibid., 323.
109. Ibid., 374.
110. Wallace, *Twenty-Seventh Wife*, 148.
111. Young, *Wife No. 19*, 433.
112. Ibid., 460.
113. Wallace, *Twenty-Seventh Wife*, 277.
114. Ibid., 395.
115. Ibid., 297.
116. Young, *Wife No. 19*, 391.
117. Ibid., 404 (emphasis added).
118. Stenhouse, *Tell It All*, 286.
119. Young, *Wife No. 19*, 538.
120. Ibid., 459–60.
121. Ibid., 552.

122. Ibid., 459.

123. Ibid., 465.

124. Wallace, *Twenty-Seventh Wife*, 179.

125. Young, *Wife No. 19*, 124.

126. Ann Eliza Young, *Life in Mormon Bondage* (Philadelphia: Aldine, 1908), 454.

127. Young, *Wife No. 19*, 489.

128. Ibid., 485–86.

129. Ibid., 384.

130. Ibid., 386 (emphasis added).

131. Wallace, *Twenty-Seventh Wife*, 204.

132. Ibid., 205.

133. Ibid., 206.

134. Young, *Wife No. 19*, 461.

135. Ibid., 509.

136. Ibid., 510.

137. Ibid., 462 (emphasis added).

138. Wallace, *Twenty-Seventh Wife*, 211.

139. Ibid., (emphasis added); cf. Ann Eliza's story in Young, *Wife No. 19*, 462.

140. Ibid., 499.

141. Wallace, *Twenty-Seventh Wife*, 209–10.

142. Ibid., 210 (emphasis added).

143. Young, *Wife No. 19*, 280–81.

144. Young, *Life in Mormon Bondage*, 213.

145. Ibid.

146. Young, *Wife No. 19*, 282.

147. Ibid.

148. Ibid., 283.

149. Wallace, *Twenty-Seventh Wife*, 375.

150. Ibid., 375–76.

151. Ibid., 295.

152. Young, *Wife No. 19*, 498.

153. Wallace, *Twenty-Seventh Wife*, 206.

154. Ibid., 190.

155. Young, *Wife No. 19*, 456.

156. Ibid.

157. Ibid., 497.

158. Wallace, *Twenty-Seventh Wife*, 211.

159. Ibid., 256.

160. Ibid., 212.

161. Wallace, *Twenty-Seventh Wife*, 198.

162. Young, *Wife No. 19*, 537.
163. Wallace, *Twenty-Seventh Wife*, 209.
164. Young, *Wife No. 19*, 498.
165. Stenhouse, *Tell It All*, 288.
166. Young, *Wife No. 19*, 297.
167. Ibid., 298.
168. Ibid.
169. Ibid.
170. Ibid.
171. Ibid., 300.
172. Ibid.
173. Ibid., 301.
174. Ibid., 302.
175. Ibid., 303.
176. Ibid.
177. Ibid., 304.
178. Ibid.
179. Ibid., 304–5.
180. Ibid., 114.
181. Wallace, *Twenty-Seventh Wife*, 165.
182. Young, *Wife No. 19*, 445.
183. Ibid., 434.
184. Stenhouse, *Tell It All*, 286.
185. Young, *Wife No. 19*, 536.
186. Ibid., 443.
187. Helen B. Woodward, *The Bold Women* (New York: Farrar, Straus and Young, 1953), 320.
188. Young, *Wife No. 19*, 384.
189. Ibid., 399 (emphasis added).
190. Ibid.
191. Ibid., 423 (emphasis added).
192. Ibid., 456.
193. Ibid., 457 (emphasis added).
194. Ibid., 550.
195. Ibid., 424.
196. Ibid., 550.
197. Wallace, *Twenty-Seventh Wife*, 165.
198. Young, *Wife No. 19*, 443 (emphasis added).
199. Ibid., 385.
200. Wallace, *Twenty-Seventh Wife*, 165.
201. Ibid., 171.
202. Ibid.

203. Young, *Wife No. 19*, 455.
204. Wallace, *Twenty-Seventh Wife*, 163 (emphasis added).
205. Young, *Wife No. 19*, 436.
206. Wallace, *Twenty-Seventh Wife*, 257–58 (emphasis added).
207. Young, *Wife No. 19*, 442.
208. Wallace, *Twenty-Seventh Wife*, 244 (emphasis added).
209. Young, *Wife No. 19*, 555.
210. Ibid., 453.
211. Ibid.
212. Ibid., 457 (emphasis added).
213. Wallace, *Twenty-Seventh Wife*, 256.
214. Ibid., 295.
215. Ibid., 226.
216. Ibid., 224.
217. Ibid., 228.
218. Ibid., 244.
219. Young, *Wife No. 19*, 554.
220. Wallace, *Twenty-Seventh Wife*, 21.
221. Young, *Wife No. 19*, 545.
222. Wallace, *Twenty-Seventh Wife*, 247.
223. Young, *Wife No. 19*, 444; Wallace, *Twenty-Seventh Wife*, 163, 168.
224. Ibid.
225. Wallace, *Twenty-Seventh Wife*, 206.
226. Ibid., 168.
227. Young, *Wife No. 19*, 376–77.
228. Ibid., 456.
229. Ibid., 498.
230. Ibid., 451.
231. Ibid., 452.
232. Ibid., 456.
233. Wallace, *Twenty-Seventh Wife*, 175.
234. Young, *Wife No. 19*, 457.
235. Wallace, *Twenty-Seventh Wife*, 175; Stenhouse, *Tell It All*, 287.
236. Young, *Wife No. 19*, 457.
237. Ibid.
238. Ibid., 465 (emphasis added).
239. Ibid., 457.
240. Ibid., 465.
241. Ibid.
242. Young, *Wife No. 19*, 443.
243. Wallace, *Twenty-Seventh Wife*, 314.

244. Young, *Wife No. 19,* 543.
245. Ibid., 442 (emphasis added).
246. Ibid., 466.
247. Ibid., 459–60.
248. Wallace, *Twenty-Seventh Wife,* 226.
249. Ibid., 228.
250. Ibid., 179.
251. Young, *Wife No. 19,* 390.
252. Wallace, *Twenty-Seventh Wife,* 410–14.
253. Stenhouse, *Tell It All,* 282.
254. Ibid., 288.
255. Wallace, *Twenty-Seventh Wife,* 234 (emphasis added).
256. Young, *Wife No. 19,* 466.
257. Ibid., 458.
258. Wallace, *Twenty-Seventh Wife,* 244.
259. Ibid., 228.
260. Young, *Wife No. 19,* 466.
261. Ibid., 551.
262. Ibid., 458.
263. Ibid.
264. Wallace, *Twenty-Seventh Wife,* 314.
265. Ibid., 233.
266. Ibid., 228 (emphasis added).
267. Young, *Wife No. 19,* 554.
268. Wallace, *Twenty-Seventh Wife,* 244.
269. Young, *Wife No. 19,* 473.
270. Ibid., 504.
271. Wallace, *Twenty-Seventh Wife,* 220.
272. Young, *Wife No. 19,* 551 (emphasis added).
273. Wallace, *Twenty-Seventh Wife,* 314.
274. Young, *Wife No. 19,* 539.
275. Ibid., 537–38 (emphasis added).
276. Ibid., 513.
277. Ibid., 105.
278. Ibid., 106.
279. Ibid., 100.
280. Ibid., 420–22.
281. Ibid., 339–40.
282. Ibid., 114.
283. Ibid., 434.
284. Ibid., 452.
285. Ibid., 453.

286. Wallace, *Twenty-Seventh Wife*, 255.

287. Young, *Wife No. 19*, 454.

288. Ibid., 537.

289. Wallace, *Twenty-Seventh Wife*, 209.

290. Ibid., 244.

291. Stenhouse, *Tell It All*, 282.

292. Ibid., 288.

293. Young, *Wife No. 19*, 444.

294. Ibid. (emphasis added).

295. Wallace, *Twenty-Seventh Wife*, 168.

296. Ibid., 255.

297. Young, *Wife No. 19*, 436.

298. Ibid., 377.

299. Ibid., 508.

300. Ibid., 374.

301. Ibid.

302. Ibid., 455–56.

303. Stenhouse, *Tell It All*, 288.

304. Wallace, *Twenty-Seventh Wife*, 238: "She saw Brigham once more, for the last time, it would turn out, and his rejection of her request for a new stove finally hardened her growing resolve." Helen Woodward, *Bold Women*, 326: "Brigham Young must have realized . . . how much that stove he wouldn't buy for Ann Eliza was going to cost him. By his frugality, he had delivered into the hands of his enemies such a mouthpiece as they could not have hoped for: a certified wife of the Prophet who happened to be also a trained actress."

305. Ibid, *Twenty-Seventh Wife*, 228, 314.

306. Ibid., 248.

307. Ibid., 275.

308. Ibid., 250.

309. Ibid., 228.

310. Young, *Wife No. 19*, 457.

311. Wallace, *Twenty-Seventh Wife*, 250.

Part 5

Is There a Danite in the House?
You Never Know.

The Danites a "Must"

One cannot long explore the dark half-world of the anti-Mormon classics without finding oneself in the lair of the terrible Danites. It is more than a racy seasoning that the Danite brotherhood brings to the seething cauldron of the myth makers—they are nothing less than the prime ingredient of the stew.

"Fear of Porter Rockwell and his Destroying Angels was the most powerful influence within the Mormon church," Messrs. Kelly and Birney solemnly assure us in their classic study of the Danites, ". . . but for the fear of Rockwell and his Danites, Mormonism would not have long survived its enforced hegira to the savage deserts of the Great Basin."[1] "What is now the news circulated throughout the United States?" said Brigham Young in 1857, the year of Johnston's Army, "That Captain Gunnison was killed by Brigham Young, and that Babbitt was killed on the Plains by Brigham Young and his Danite band. What more? That Brigham Young has killed all the men who have died between the Missouri river and California. . . . Such are the newspaper stories."[2] In that same year, according to our Ann Eliza, " 'Altars of sacrifice' were loudly recommended [the quotation marks prove that], and the victims were advised to place themselves thereon voluntarily; if they would not become willing sacrifices, they became involuntary ones, for 'somebody' took the matter in hand, and saw that the 'atonement' was made. Usually this mysterious 'somebody' was one of the 'Danites,' or 'Destroying-Angels.' . . . It is said that the band had its origin in Missouri. . . . But they never became so very notorious until the 'Reformation' times, when their peculiar talents were called into play, and their services into constant requisition."[3] Mr. Wallace can appreciate Ann Eliza's own terror of "fantasied strangulation at the hands of one of Brigham's fanatical Danites,"[4] for though the strangulation might be fantasied, "nothing was utterly impossible on that . . . paranoiac frontier"[5] (i.e., there *might* have been Danites after all).

In the four passages just quoted, the appeal to the Danites is neither casual nor playful — those Danites are an absolute necessity. They are necessary to supply by inference the evidence against Brigham Young and the Mormons that is so sorely needed and so conspicuously absent. We have learned from our *dames savantes* that ordinary Mormons, like Ann Eliza's friends and neighbors, were just plain folks, the unsuspecting dupes of a depraved hierarchy; they never suspected what was really going on and were simple enough to believe that Indians killed people. On the other hand, said depraved hierarchy carefully abstained from criminal acts: "As loudly as the Mormon leaders talked to the people about doing their 'dirty work' themselves, they, nevertheless, shrank from soiling their own fingers," so that even Brigham Young "would probably avow himself entirely guiltless, since his hand did not perform the deed."[6] With the common people "humble, spiritual-minded, God-fearing, law-abiding,"[7] and somehow managing to ignore the clarion call of their leaders to "dirty work," and with the leaders themselves fastidiously refraining from "soiling their own fingers," what evidence have we got against the Mormons? Who was carrying on the efficient and brazen system of mass murder that for years filled all the Utah valleys with altars and graves — none of which has ever been discovered? Who but the Danites, who, as Kelly and Birney observe, operated so very secretly that one can hardly be asked to produce evidence of *their* activities.[8]

The Danites thus supply the anti-Mormon fraternity with a blank check backed by unlimited reserves of horror. Any unexplained death is automatically their doing; accidents don't just happen on the frontier — they are Danite manipulations; we need not bother with the extensive evidence that the Indians were numerous and deadly in the West and along the routes,[9] for we know that people just talk about Indians because "they dare not say boldly who they believe those 'Indians' are."[10] Even when an official non-Mormon investigation supported the obvious explanation of a disaster, as in the case of Captain Gunnison, the whole thing was just a cover-up for the Danites. Well, why not? — any calamity *might* be a Danite doing. "Even then," says Ann Eliza of her unimpeded escape to Ogden in 1874, "the 'Danites,' those terrible ministers of Mormon vengeance, might be upon our track."[11] And Mr. Wallace nods vigorous assent: they might indeed, for, evidence or no evidence, *"nothing* was *utterly* impossible on that still rough and paranoiac frontier."[12]

The "Mormon Version"

It is significant that those who have written on the Danites, from Bennett to Brooks, have not bothered to mention that the earliest and fullest discussion of the subject is by Joseph Smith himself. Is it not odd that they will not consider this account — coming four years earlier than Bennett's lurid exposé — even as a point of departure? Where evidence is so extremely scarce, one would think a word from any source would be welcome; but unfortunately the early Mormon accounts of the Danites are so perfectly plausible and consistent that the creative writer is denied the perfect liberty he enjoys where hints and whispers are his only control.

In October 1838, Joseph Smith recounted the history and background of the Danites as it had been brought to his attention. "Doctor Sampson Avard," he says, "who had been in the Church but a short time, . . . was secretly aspiring to be the greatest of the great, and become the leader of the people."[13] He began by holding secret meetings, the room being "well guarded by some of his followers," where he claimed "that he had the sanction of the heads of the Church . . . and proceeded to administer to the few under his control, an oath, binding them to everlasting secrecy."[14] Speaking as a true religious enthusiast, he "would often affirm to his company that the principal men of the Church had put him forward as a spokesman, and a leader of this band, which *he* named *Danites*."[15] After daily preliminary meetings, "he held meetings to organize his men into companies of tens and fifties. . . . He then called his captains together and taught them" as basic doctrine, " 'the riches of the Gentiles shall be consecrated to my people, the house of Israel; and thus you will waste away the Gentiles by robbing and plundering them, . . . and in this way we will build up the kingdom of God.' " This he followed up with dire threats against any who should jeopardize the secrecy of the society. "At this lecture all of the officers revolted," and when Avard protested that a new dispensation called for a new moral code, he was unanimously voted down and gave way. Avard suggested "that they had better drop the subject, although he had received his authority from Sidney Rigdon the evening before. The meeting then broke up; the eyes of those present were opened," and henceforth "very little confidence was placed in him, even by the warmest of the members of his Danite scheme."[16] "When a knowledge of Avard's rascality came to the Presidency of the Church, he was cut off from the Church, and every measure proper used to destroy his influence, at which he was highly incensed, and went about whispering his evil insinuations, but finding every effort unavailing, he again turned conspirator, and sought to make friends with the mob."[17]

For a firsthand story of these events—which were only reported to Joseph Smith by others—we are beholden to Lorenzo Dow Young, whose confidential and unpublished remarks to his nephew on the evening of February 5, 1890, were made with no thought of the market or the public in mind.[18] They can be trusted. The old man began by remarking that he had been reading Bancroft's story of the Danites in which their founding was erroneously attributed to David W. Patten. Even the anti-Mormon writer, T. B. H. Stenhouse, incidentally, notes that Patten was the victim of deliberately cultivated falsehoods about the Danites.[19] As Mr. Young tells it, "he first heard of Dr. Avard" when "he was sent by the Prophet Joseph on a mission" to "the South-east corner of the State of Ohio," where Avard was presiding over a branch of the Church. In his tour of inspection, Brother Young was disturbed by what he found at Avard's church: "He . . . did not like the spirit or teachings of the man." Later he found "that the Dr. and Elder S. Rigdon were on quite intimate terms, and that the latter was considerably tinctured with the ideas and spirits of the former." When Lorenzo Young reported on his mission to the First Presidency, and came to report on Avard's doings, "Elder Rigdon manifested his displeasure," he says, "by animadverting rather sharply on my remarks"; but Joseph Smith encouraged him to go on and make a full report "without fear or favor." Whereupon he declared that Avard impressed him as being a rascal, and assured Rigdon, "Give Dr. Avard time and he will prove that he is a consummate hypocrite and a wicked man."[20]

Later in the summer of the same year (1838), Brother Young went with other Saints to Far West, Missouri, where he learned that Dr. Avard had already arrived on the scene and was "holding secret meetings attended by a few who were especially invited. I was one of the favored few."[21] Avard had very winning ways with what Joseph Smith calls "his smooth, flattering, and winning speeches, which he frequently made to his associates."[22] So Lorenzo Young sat in and learned that Avard's group was "a secret organization of which, so far as I know, he was the originator and over which he presided. At one of these meetings he stated that the title by which the members of the society were known, 'Danites' interpreted meant 'Destroying Angels.' He also stated that the organization was to take vengeance on their enemies. . . . The teachings and proceedings appeared to be wicked, bloodthirsty, and in direct antagonism to the principles taught by the leaders of the Church, and the Elders generally." Here then were the wicked Danites in embryo. Then came the showdown:

> The culmination finally arrived. At one of the meetings Dr. Avard particularly required that all present who had been attending the meetings should at once join the society by making the required covenants, and I was especially designated. I asked the privilege of speaking which was granted. I began to state my reasons to joining the society, and was proceeding to state my reasons and in them expose its wickedness, when Dr. Avard peremptorily ordered me to be seated. I objected to sitting down until I had fully expressed my views. He threatened to put the law of the organization in force there and then. I stood directly in front of him and was well prepared for the occasion. I told him with all the emphasis of my nature, in voice and manner [i.e., he lost his temper], that I had as many friends in the house as he had, and if he made a motion to carry out his threat he should not live to get out of the house for I would instantly kill him. He did not try to put his threat in execution, but the meeting broke up. From the meeting I went directly to Brother Brigham and related the whole history of the affair. He said he had long suspicioned

that something wrong was going on, but had seen no direct development. He added we will go at once to brother Joseph who has suspicioned that some secret wickedness was being carried on by Dr. Avard. Dr. Avard was at once cited before the authorities of the Church and cut off for his wickedness. He turned a bitter enemy of the saints.[23]

The ex- and anti-Mormon T. B. H. Stenhouse, Fanny's husband, confirms the important part of the affair when he writes, "Joseph and the Church withdrew fellowship from Avard, his Danite organizations were broken up, his teachings were disavowed; he shook hands with the mob, and asserted that Danitism in the Church was a fact."[24] Even Ann Eliza admits that "Joseph Smith . . . repeatedly repudiated both them and their deeds of violence,"[25] a detail which Wallace overlooks. Faced with a complete lack of evidence to incriminate the leaders of the Church, Mr. Stenhouse falls back on the argument that "the strict surveillance which 'the authorities' exercise over the actions of individuals" makes it hard to believe "that Dr. Avard was alone in the organization of the Danite Band."[26] But we have already seen from the "Mormon version" that he had the support of Rigdon; the question is whether he received official recognition. Actually the Avard situation is a familiar one to many who have lived in distant branches of the Church. To say that the "surveillance of 'the authorities' " extends to checking the actions of individuals in hundreds of widely scattered branches is simply ridiculous. Any surveillance of the members of a ward or branch must be exercised through the bishop or president of the organization—and Avard happened to be the president of a branch in an outlying district: and many a branch president has abused his splendid isolation exactly as Avard did.

Avard's behavior from first to last is thoroughly typical. His aspirations "to be the greatest of the great, and become the leader of the people," are still to be found among a certain class of Mormons, and, as Brigham Young recalls, in the time of Joseph Smith the Church was fairly swarming with half-baked converts and dangerous crackpots. The members of the Church today are far more responsive to the General Authorities than they were in the days of Joseph Smith and Brigham Young, when only a small minority paid any heed to such principles as tithing or the Word of Wisdom, and yet grandiose schemes and exotic doctrines still have a way of springing up almost anywhere. If Avard had, as he claimed, "the sanction of the heads of the Church," why did he hold his meetings secretly, barring Church members in good standing? The Mormons did have a very necessary military organization—for "border ruffianism" of the Bushwhacker and Jayhawker variety was a reality, reaching its most deadly excesses in the two decades *after* the Mormons left the area—but they made no secret of it. If there was anything in the world that Joseph Smith would not tolerate, it was a private army, organized and led by an untried newcomer to the Church. Also, it is not true that "by robbing and plundering . . . we will build up the kingdom of God,"[27] for that is not the way anything is built up, and nobody knew that better than Joseph Smith and Brigham Young, for no two men in history have given more convincing proof of knowing what *does* build a society.

When Ann Eliza and Mrs. Stenhouse failed to realize their personal ambitions in the Church, they went about "whispering evil insinuations," as is perfectly clear from their own writings; and when that got them nowhere they both turned against the Church and "made friends with the mob." We cite their case to show how typical Avard's behavior was. The entire corpus of anti-Mormon literature draws its substance largely from such people. The process is still going on. There are various groups in the Rocky Mountains today under the leadership of ambitious and disgruntled men and women who have turned against the Church exactly like Avard. To the outsider, these groups — some of them emphasizing polygamy, others communal living, others the supremacy of self-appointed leaders — are all simply Mormons, and indeed some of them deliberately seek to give that impression. The Church in modern as in ancient times has always moved amidst a swarm of such satellites, and while nine out of ten Latter-day Saints know nothing of their existence, it is easy for those on the outside to identify them with the Church. And it was an easy thing for Avard to stir up the Missourians by insisting that the Danites *were* a part of the Church. That is the crux of the matter. The story as the Mormons give it is strictly true to form.

The Church did organize bands of tens and fifties, as Joseph Smith points out, but "let it be distinctly understood, that these companies of tens and fifties got up by Avard, were altogether separate and distinct from those companies of tens and fifties organized by the brethren for self defense. . . . One company would be engaged in drawing wood, another in cutting it, another in gathering corn, another in grinding, another in butchering, another in distributing meat, etc., etc. . . . Therefore, let no one hereafter, by mistake or design, confound this organization of the Church . . . with the organization of the 'Danites,' of the apostate Avard, which died almost before it had existed."[28] This warning has gone unheeded by Juanita Brooks, who would prove the existence of Mormon Danites by a statement of Joseph A. Stout: "The Church organized under captains Tens, Fifties, One Hundreds, and One Thousands. . . . They [the Missourians] called our organization the DANITE BAND."[29] Of course they did, and Joseph Smith has just explained why — because the frustrated Avard had gone about *telling* the Missourians that the Mormon organization was the Danites.

Against her admission (ignored by Wallace) that "Joseph Smith . . . repeatedly repudiated both them and their deeds of violence," Mrs. A.E.W.D.Y. Denning places the testimonies of the apostates Marsh and Hyde (hailed with glee by Wallace). Yet all she can make of them is that two men swore affidavits "against Joseph and the Mormons in general, accusing them of the grossest crimes and outrages, as well as of abetting the Danites and their deeds."[30] "Abetting" is pretty weak; no one claims that Joseph and the Mormons in general *were* Danites or even that they organized the Danites, but only that they "abetted" them and their deeds — just as anyone who is not to the Right of everybody else in politics is accused of "abetting" Communism.

Even weaker is the affidavit itself (Hyde merely confirmed Marsh's report in a single sentence: "The most of the statements in the foregoing disclosure I know to be true; the remainder I believe to be true")[31] — which, far from confirming Ann Eliza's charge of "grossest crimes and outrages," speaks only of the Danites' dire capabilities, with never a word about their deeds:

> They have among them a company, considered true Mormons, called the Danites, who have taken an oath to support the heads of the Church in all things that they say or do, *whether right or wrong*. Many, however, of this band are much dissatisfied with this oath, as being against moral and religious principles. On Saturday last, I am informed by the Mormons, that they had a meeting at Far West, at which they appointed a company of twelve, by the name of the 'Destruction Company,' for the purpose of burning and destroying, and that if the people of Buncombe came to do mischief upon the people of Caldwell, and committed depredations upon the Mormons, they were to burn Buncombe.[32]

This is followed by a report that Joseph Smith had earlier said that he would bear down on his enemies, Moslem fashion, with the sword. This has nothing to do with the

Danites, and Marsh and Hyde both retracted their "confessions" later and returned to the Church. But even at its worst, what could be more vague and hedging? "They have among them a company, considered true Mormons, called the Danites." That agrees perfectly with Joseph Smith's own statement: There was such a society, they did consider themselves true Mormons, and Avard did give them the name of Danites. The trick of Marsh's testimony is to make it appear that the Latter-day Saints themselves considered the group true Mormons and called them Danites—though the affidavit is careful *not* to say so. Next, the resolution of the Danites to support the heads of the Church is meant to signify that the heads of the Church are supporting *them*—again, without saying so. Even within "this band," however, there are many who do not go along. Note that at no time is it claimed that any authority of the Church was actually a member, or even approved of the society, let alone that the Church organized it officially—a thing which Marsh, as ex-President of the Twelve Apostles, was in a better position to know than anyone else.

Next Mr. Marsh reports: "On Saturday last, I am *informed* by the Mormons, that they had a meeting at Far West." He has been talking about the Danites, and "I am *informed* by the Mormons" is inserted parenthetically: the "they" who hold the meeting must be the Danites, not the Mormons. But by bringing in the Mormons as his informants, he makes it look as if *they* had engineered the meeting—though again he is careful not to say so. This impression he backs up by threats of military might once breathed forth, he claims, by Joseph Smith, which, whether truly reported or not, have no demonstrable connection with the Danites. And that's the story. What Thomas B. Marsh's testimony amounts to is that there was a Danite society among the members of the Church—a proposition which Joseph Smith himself has clearly stated.

The one thing we need and expect from Marsh and Hyde, and which they are singularly willing and able to supply *if it exists,* is irrefutable proof that this group was organized or even sanctioned by the heads of the Church. But for such a statement we look in vain. The two men had rushed off to Richmond Courthouse in high dudgeon to pour forth "all the vilest slanders, aspersions, lies and calumnies" they could think of into willing ears.[33] Willing to go the limit in insinuating the worst, they still had nothing specific to report. The direct association of the Danites with the Church authorities, which they merely had to mention to make it stick for all time, is conspicuously absent.

The Other Versions

The most remarkable thing about the Danites is that though they operated openly and insolently for many years, cutting throats right and left in a prolonged orgy of bloodshed, not a single scrap of evidence for their vast and prolonged operations has ever been discovered.[34] Let us see what the experts have to offer.

That great classic *Holy Murder, the Story of Porter Rockwell,* by Charles Kelly and Hoffman Birney, first deserves our consideration if only for its suspicious resemblance to Mr. Wallace's book. From the damning quotations on the flyleaf to the ingratiating acknowledgments at the back, these gentlemen have somehow anticipated the latter epic in every detail of organization, form, and method. First of all a high-minded dedication to the Cause of Truth; then, on the next page, three devastating quotations, one by a scholar who is supposed to have known Rockwell intimately — and who *always* refers to him as *Peter* Rockwell; the second by a certain Milo M. Quaife, whose candid opinion is that "the most damning picture of Mormonism . . . is that supplied by the testimony of the leaders of the Church themselves"; the third confirms this doctrine by coming right from Brigham Young himself: "I have many a time, on this stand, dared the world to produce as mean devils as we can. We can beat them at anything." Which, taken out of context, says as plain as day that the Mormons are wicked people who glory in their wickedness.

We soon learn that Porter Rockwell is not the real subject of the book, but a convenient peg for hanging up libels of Joseph Smith and the Mormons in general. Since every direct attack on Smith leads nowhere (see *The Myth Makers*), it has been found advisable to resort to the indirect attack:

> The biography of a servant is inseparably bound with that of his master, and the life story of Orrin Porter Rockwell parallels those of Joseph Smith, Jr., translator of the Book of Mormon, founder of the Church of Jesus Christ of Latter Day Saints, Prophet and Martyr; and of Brigham Young, who appropriated and draped about his own paunchy figure the blood-stained mantle. . . . Filled with an holy zeal, he slew only in cold blood and for the glory of the Mormon God and the exaltation of that God's viceregents, the Mormon Prophets.[35]

This is the Wallace technique: the resounding titles, the sinister opening chord, the inevitable return to the *leitmotif* of the depravity of Mormon prophets. Joseph Smith is a thousand times harder to explain than any Porter Rockwell or Ann Eliza; but see how clearly our authors avoid the dangers and pitfalls that confound Smith's biographers by treating his career simply as a side issue, throwing out all the old charges and incriminations in an easy off-handed way, while sparing the reader the trouble of considering the evidence and themselves the burden of producing it. For Wallace, as for Kelly and Birney, it is enough to give us a quick look at Joseph Smith by way of leading up to the main subject, painting with quick, deft strokes the portrait of the lecturer, swindler, and drunkard, and then passing on to the main theme.

But don't be fooled—Joseph Smith *is* the main theme. The conscientious anti-Mormon writer rarely forgets to remind us after every grizzly episode that the true horror of it all is that everything can be traced back to false prophets claiming revelation from God. Kelly and Birney's Porter Rockwell is little more than a front man for "Holy Joe"—even after the Prophet had been dead for years. They begin by describing Smith in exactly the gay, carefree manner of Mr. Wallace, the knowing man-to-man locker-room style that needs no verification: "The original Seer and Revelator was a lusty laddie. He . . . could out-run, out-jump, out-wrestle, and out-cuss any of his contemporaries; was a judge of good liquor; and had a keen and appreciative eye for such mundane things as the points of a good horse or the curves of a feminine ankle."[36] His portrait in Kelly and Birney's book bears only the simple and austere caption: "I've got to get drunk now and then to keep the people from worshipping me."[37] How did Mr. Wallace happen to miss that one? It is from that same Dr. Wyl who supplied him with the leading caption for *his* book: "Every time I see a pretty woman I have to pray for grace." Apparently while a touch of Dr. Wyl goes a long way, too much of him would give away the game.

Naturally a book with the title *Holy Murder* is going to be about the Danites, and we have every right to expect something special in the way of evidence from Messrs. Kelly and Birney. But we don't get it. Their *Hauptquelle* is a source that other anti-Mormon writers avoid, the anonymous "Achilles," privately printed in San Francisco in 1878. The general neglect of this heroic work is hard to understand in view of the high credentials that Kelly and Birney discover for it, for "the unknown author states that . . . 'Rockwell admits every word to be true' "[38]— though every word of it damns Rockwell to hell. Now if the unknown author *himself* says that Rockwell *himself* says that *every* word is true, who are we to question it? When

Kelly and Birney note of the long and fantastic "Danite oath," found only in "Achilles," that "certain of its features are quite obviously interpolations," that proves to them that the Mormons have been corrupting the text, with never a suspicion of "the anonymous but fully cognizant 'Achilles.' "[39] With such a knowing informant to hand, why do other writers on the Danites refuse the helping hand which has enabled Mr. Kelly and Mr. Birney to write a full-length book about them? The answer is simple: if they accept "Achilles" they will have to throw away their other sources, for "Achilles' " version of such well-known horror epics as the Payson murders and the son of the widow Lewis, though full and specific, have hardly the remotest resemblance to the same stories as told by Ann Eliza and her friends. If "Achilles" knows anything, then all the others are hopelessly wrong, and since all are claiming intimate personal knowledge, well, you see what that does.

Kelly and Birney's No. 2 Informant is a Mr. Fitzhugh Ludlow, who in 1870 claimed to have had an intimate personal interview with Porter Rockwell, whom he insists on designating throughout his story as *Peter* Rockwell — which makes one wonder. Kelly and Birney have done a brilliant job of covering up by an ingenious compromise: instead of quoting Ludlow as writing of *Porter* Rockwell, which he plainly did not, or of *Peter* Rockwell, which he did, our authors settle for *Poter* Rockwell, a brand-new name, but one that is bound to be passed over by the casual reader as an obvious printer's error. By such cunning devisings do Messrs. Kelly and Birney compound their epic of Holy Murder. As, for example, when they have Sampson Avard tell his Danite story not after he left the Church but before[40] — which makes all the difference in the world, though the reader, of course, does not suspect what is going on. For them, J. C. Bennett, the world's prize liar, is a fountain of truth when he speaks of the Danites because

"Bennett . . . is positive upon the point."[41] Liar he may be, but if he is positive, that settles it. Kelly and Birney also place high value on the "carefully kept diary" of one William Swartzell,[42] which, as we shall see, was *not* a diary and was *not* carefully kept but was carefully rewritten as an anti-Mormon pamphlet. No copy of the diary is known to exist.

Such, plus Mrs. Stenhouse, are Kelly and Birney's basic sources for a whole book on the Danites. It is not surprising that they must shore up such feeble supports with a special kind of evidence, which on the first page of their book they claim to have found in "the testimony of the leaders of the Church themselves." Which testimony they find ready to hand in the *Journal of Discourses:* All Mormons, they assure us, are "docile, ignorant, and blind, . . . but blindest of all were those who permitted the publication of the *Journal of Discourses.*"[43] Our astute author assures us that the Mormons would of course never keep any Danite records, even secret ones[44] — yet it never occurs to them that the leaders of the Church, who sanctioned the publication of their speeches year after year as the *Journal of Discourses,* never would have done so had those speeches contained anything in the least incriminating. It is all a matter of selection and interpretation, which can, without too much effort, make the Bible itself a catalogue of depraved doctrines and deeds. Let us run through the list of Mormon testimony, including "Brigham's acknowledgment that the Danites existed and were a weapon ever ready to his hand."[45]

First there is a long quotation from J. M. Grant, who argues that the putting to death of transgressors under certain conditions would be consistent with the practice of ancient Israel, and makes it clear that though he personally would like to see such practices in force, such a thing is out of the question under present conditions. By omitting all mention of biblical parallels and all admission by Grant that he is speaking only for himself, one can make this sound pretty bad; but as far as historical evidence is concerned, the man might just as well have been telling the story of David and Goliath. The sermon, according to Kelly and Birney, "was favorably received and the sermons delivered in the Tabernacle became more and more sanguinary."[46] Here is a fatal flaw that all writers on the Danites seek to hide behind — a screen of rhetoric. For if there is one aspect of Danite operations that transcends and conditions all else, it is their observance of total secrecy. The simple Saints and the general public, we are constantly reminded, knew nothing of what was going on and were scrupulously kept in the dark — they really believed that Indians killed people![47] Yet the only evidence our authorities can produce for the doings of their Danites is in the form of remarks made by Church leaders at large meetings open to the general public. What a time and place to choose for divulging the secrets of Danitism! When we are told that "the sermons in the Tabernacle became *more* and *more* sanguinary," we hold on to the edge of our seats for what comes next.

And this is it: next that terrible Mr. Grant went to Kaysville, where he preached on kindness to animals and "flayed the Saints of that hamlet for their sins and called upon them, one and all, to renew their covenants with the church, to confess their faults, and to present themselves for re-baptism."[48] Except for the re-baptism (hardly a "sanguinary" rite), we detect nothing here that ten thousand ministers do not dish out to their congregations every Sunday. But now we come to the solid core of evidence "that Blood Atonement was openly advocated by the Mormon leaders during the Reformation period."[49]

The prize quotation is another by Grant: "I say there are men and women here that I would advise to go to the President immediately and ask him to appoint a committee to attend to their case, and then let a place be selected and let that committee shed their blood."[50] That sounds ghastly, but if we take the passage in its context it becomes immediately apparent that fire-eating Mr. Grant is simply advocating capital punishment for capital crimes. In the sentences preceding and following the quotation (they are omitted, of course, by our researchers), Grant makes it perfectly clear that the parties he refers to are those who have committed capital crimes, crimes so great "that cannot be forgiven through baptism."[51] "They are the old hardened sinners, and are almost—if not altogether—past improvement, and are full of hell."[52] There were such characters on the frontier, pathological types past rehabilitation and a serious menace to society. What was to be done with them? The idealistic George Bernard Shaw earnestly recommended euthanasia for such, but Mr. Grant is more humane—he merely advises the rascals to do something which he knows perfectly well they will *not* do. He is not advocating bloodshed but merely trying, as he says at the beginning of his sermon, to shock the people out of their complacency by "giving them hell."

The one peculiar aspect of the thing, that people who have done wrong should actually *ask* to be punished, was seriously taught by Plato: "The criminal and the dishonest man," he says, "are completely wretched, indeed, but they are even more miserable if they are not punished . . . and less miserable if they are punished and chastened by gods and man."[53] And so he goes on to argue that since what is just is beautiful, a person who is being justly punished suffers beautiful acts, while the one doing the punishing performs them.[54] It follows that a wrong-doer "should hurry to the judge, as though to a physician," and ask to be punished, "so that the disease of injustice may not became chronic and make his soul ulcerous and incurable."[55] This will be readily recognized as akin to the well-known Christian teaching that it is better that the body should suffer than that the soul should be lost in hell—an undeniably biblical teaching, whatever one may think of it. In practice it has led to such outrages as Salem witch burnings and autos-da-fé, but there is no evidence that it ever led to acts of overt violence among the Mormons. The best our critics can hope to do is to show that it was "advocated by the Mormon leaders," and assume from that that one has discovered the clue to every crime and outrage committed between the Mississippi and the Pacific in the midnineteenth century. The next damning statement by a Mormon leader is from Brigham Young.

Brigham Young had held the people rigidly in check during the affair with Johnston's Army, but on October 25, 1857, he told the Saints that if another army should ever march against them, "I shall never again say to a man, 'Stay your rifle ball,' when our enemies assail us, but will say, 'Slay them where you find them.' "[56] This is simply the command "Fire at will," given to an armed host: in terms of an airborne operation, "Slay them where you find them" expresses the order of the day pretty well. Brigham Young is here speaking not only of a strictly military operation, and a defensive one at that ("when our enemies assail *us*"), but of a hypothetical one only, an operation which he was personally convinced would never take place. But what can defense against an enemy in arms possibly have to do with "Blood Atonement," of all things? Never mind: by entitling their chapter "Slay Them Where You Find Them," Kelly and Birney make it perfectly obvious that Brigham Young ordered all Mormons to kill everybody else whenever and wherever they could.

The next quotation, from Heber C. Kimball, is an even better example of what can be done by *beginning* and *ending* a quotation just at the right moment to destroy its context entirely, while removing from the *middle* of the passage whatever might still give some hint of that context. Here is the passage as Kelly and Birney give it:

When it is necessary that blood should be shed, we

should be as ready to do that as to eat an apple. That is my religion, and I feel that our platter is pretty near clean of some things, and we calculate to keep it clean from this time henceforth and forever. . . . And if men and women will not live their religion, but take a course to pervert the hearts of the righteous, we will "lay judgment to the line and righteousness to the plummet," and we will let you know that the earth can swallow you up as it did Koran [sic] with his hosts; as Brother Taylor says, you may dig your graves and we will slay you and you may crawl into them.[57]

What emerges from that is the clear images of Mormons suspected of unorthodoxy being forced to dig their own graves by relentless cold-eyed fanatics. Here is the Mormon horror beyond description which Ann Eliza and Mrs. Stenhouse and the rest proclaim from the housetops, and this is the authority for it. But if we restore the passage to its context, we also restore the reader to a sane and humane world. It becomes immediately apparent that Kimball, like Young, is speaking strictly of a *military* operation. "Well," he says, "there are those troops over yonder [speaking of Johnston's Army]. . . . Some of you thought they were coming here, and several ran away." He notes that "Brother Brigham has fulfilled his word" in giving safe conduct to the army camp to "any man or woman that wanted to go," including Mrs. Mogo, a local Madame, to whom he wishes well. Then he expresses his satisfaction that Brother Groesbeck's company was able to evade the Army: "God gave him wisdom, and he is here, and he escaped those troops." Next he gives a sympathetic picture of poor Mr. Johnston himself, suffering from "fever all the way," with nothing now but the dismal prospect of a long march through difficult terrain: "By the time he goes up and down Ham's Fork [on the Green River] a few times, it will take away his strength. . . . I had as lieve sit on a bayonet as a fork."

It is all good-natured banter, and then President Kimball gets serious: "I feel the Lord designs the thing should move along and *no blood be shed,* because I do not consider God is so anxious that we should be bloodthirsty men as some may be. God designs we should be pure men, holding the oracles of God in holy and pure vessels; but . . . "[58] At this very point, Kelly and Birney interrupt to begin their quotation, omitting all that has gone before, including even that small but very important *but.* "But," says Kimball, "when it is necessary that blood should be shed, we should be as ready to do that as to eat an apple." Note that he does not want *any* bloodshed in this *war,* and is glad that it has been avoided so far, but if it does come to shooting, Kimball reminds his people, that will not be the time to be squeamish. There are few Christians who would not agree to that proposition, bearing in mind its military setting and the humane expressions that accompany it, both of which are scrupulously suppressed by our authors. From the middle and ending of their quotation the same omit the words explaining that this is simply a fair warning to particular parties, namely "all such scoundrels" as go over and join the enemy who have come to fight the Mormons; such persons as identify themselves with the enemy cannot expect immunity when the fighting begins. That is what President Kimball is talking about; they are digging their own graves and can expect the worst when and if the shooting starts, though he hopes it won't. In making it perfectly clear that this refers specifically to "those corrupt scoundrels" who have become hangers-on of the enemy camp, the speaker reminds his hearers of the need to resist military conquest and occupation: "Well, they would come from Dan to Beersheba, and from California to France, — that is, wicked and abominable spirits would have come into this valley when those troops came, do you not see? The blacklegs, and highway robbers, and whore mongers, and whores would have gathered into this place, if those troops could have come into this place to have slain our leaders."[59] This could have happened before, and it must not happen now, even if the army must be resisted with force. And what has this all to do with "Blood Atonement"? Nothing whatever. There is only one way to make Heber C. Kimball look worse than to quote his words out of context, and that is to follow Mr. Wallace's example and not read them at all, simply dismissing the man as Wallace does, without further ado, as a brutal and depraved "mountebank."

Brigham Young observes that it would have been better for many to have died than to have fallen from grace and become "angels to the devil." Jesus Christ put it even more strongly: It would have been better, he said, to have a millstone tied to one's neck and be cast into the sea; it would be better never to have been born; it would be better to cut off one's own right hand than to have it commit offense, etc. True, Jesus did not actually expect such sentences to be carried out, but then neither did Brigham Young or even J. M. Grant: they were, as they explain, simply stirring the people up. Note that all this "evidence" is supposed to prove not that the Mormons ever practiced "Blood Atonement," for which there is no evidence, but that it was *advocated* by the Mormon leaders." We knew people who are convinced that anybody who accepts the XVI Amendment of the Constitution is advocating communism. Who advocates what is a matter of interpretation, and the minister who describes hell-fire as a vital part of God's economy is simply advocating the burning of the opposition: it's Holy Murder, that's what it is!

But so far we have had no mention of the Danites, and with only one quotation to go it must be a good one. Indeed it is, according to our guides, nothing less than "Brigham's acknowledgment that the Danites existed and were a weapon ever ready to his hand."[60] This statement by Brigham Young has been exploited a good deal by anti-

Mormon writers, and here it is: "If men come here and do not behave themselves, they will not only find the Danites, whom they talk so much about, biting the horse's heels, but the scoundrels will find something biting their heels. In my plain remarks I merely call things by their own name."[61] The plain remarks do not refer to heel-biting, which is a biblical figure of speech, but to calling scoundrels scoundrels. Brigham Young is here referring to organized gangs of highway robbers, and is expressing his determination to make Utah safe for the *Gentiles*. But what about the Danites? "The Danites, whom *they* talk about" are the only Danites mentioned, and that with a characteristic touch of irony that only Kelly and Birney could miss. Brigham is not "acknowledging that the Danites exist," but declaring as he had a month earlier[62] that they are a Gentile myth. And what are these mythical Danites doing? "Biting the horse's heels." *Ich werde dich beaureumbullum!* ("I'll *aureum bullum* you!") shouted the Great Elector of Saxony at his son, whose studious ways enraged him. For Kelly and Birney this could only mean that the monarch intended to golden-bull the Crown Prince.

The Danite hocum is here treated with the broad sarcasm it deserves. But if we must go along with our authorities and interpret the passage literally, then we must admit on Young's testimony that the Danites do *not* pursue the scoundrels in question: the Danite activities are limited to "biting the *horse's* heels," while "*their* heels" are not bitten by Danites but by "something." Whatever that something is — and it must be pretty terrible — it is *not* Danites.

And this, if you please, is the evidence that "the Danites were an institution." The culmination of these devastating admissions by Mormon leaders is "given by John Doyle Lee, himself a Danite, an elder, and an adopted son of Brigham Young." Of course he was none of those things at the time the statement was written, but still he is quoted as a Mormon leader. And this is what Kelly and Birney have him say:

> It was at that time [1857] a common thing to see Danites going out of Cedar City and Harmony with suspected Gentiles, to send them "over the rim of the basin," and the Gentiles were always sent. This practice was supported by the people, and everything of that kind was done by orders from the Council, or by orders from some of the Priesthood. When a Danite or a Destroying Angel was placed on a man's track, that man died.[63]

When, however, we go to the source to which our authors refer us (as vaguely as possible, simply as "Lee, op. cit."), i.e., Lee's "Confessions" of 1877, this is what we read:

> At that time it was a common thing for small bands of people on their way from California to pass through by way of Cedar City on their journey. Many of these people were killed simply because they were Gentiles. When a Gentile came into a town he was looked upon with suspicion, and most of the people considered every stranger a spy from the United States army. The killing of Gentiles was considered a means of grace.[64]

That is bad enough, the second one, but no mention of Danites or Destroying Angels. If the reader wonders where they come from or finds it hard to believe that any author would take such liberties with a quotation, let him compare the 1877 edition of *Mormonism Unveiled: or the Life and Confessions of the Late Mormon Bishop John D. Lee,* with the 1905 printing of the same book as *The Mormon Menace, Being the Confession of John Doyle Lee, DANITE, Official Assassin of the Mormon Church under the Late Brigham Young.* Let him turn to Chapter XVIII of the latter work, entitled "The Danite and His Duty,"[65] and compare it with the text of the 1877 edition which it is supposed to be reproducing.[66] The 1905 opus, under the inspired editorship of Mr. Alfred

Henry Lewis, swarms with Danites on every page (mentioned twenty-one times in the chapter—twelve times in the first six pages), yet after a diligent search we find only *one* occurrence of the word in the corresponding original text of 1877—Mr. Lewis has inserted it every other time! In the particular passage (chapter 18) we have quoted above he blithely changes "brethren" to "Danites"—but even so he does not go as far as Kelly and Birney, who in the end can only bring the Danites to life by diligently rewriting their sources.

The man responsible for bringing out Lee's original "confessions" in 1877 was his attorney, William W. Bishop, whose introduction to the book is remarkable because it labors mightily to prove just one point—that Brigham Young "favored the shedding of blood as an atonement for sin"[67]—and seeks to do so only by quoting from the sermons we have just mentioned. What Christian would deny the theory, so prominent in the Old Testament? Why is Mr. Bishop so exercised about an abstract doctrine? Why does he wave the menu before us for twenty pages instead of serving us the dinner? Because there is no dinner! Even the bitter apostate Lee makes out no case for the Danites that departs a hair's breadth from the "Mormon version." He tells us that he *was* a Danite in 1838, but he never mentions being a Danite after that, let alone being the Danite Chieftain; indeed in all the rest of his book there is only *one* mention of Danites, a parenthetical reference that may well be an interpolation.

Mrs. Brooks seems to establish an official status in the Church for the Danites by using Lee's account of the Gallatin election riot, where the Mormons responded to a Danite sign of distress by coming to the rescue of a hard-pressed fellow.[68] She supports this by citing Swartzell, who does tell of the riot but makes no mention whatever of Danites. Mrs. Brooks not only fails to mention that Swartzell is silent on the subject of Danites at Gallatin, but she also overlooks the significant fact that according to Lee, of the thirty Mormons at the polls, only eight participated in the melee, though all Danites were bound to respond when they saw "the *sign*."[69] This shows the Danites as a small minority operating independently of the rest of the Mormons, who refused to support them even as hard-pressed Mormons; and there is nothing anywhere in Lee's book to indicate the contrary. The situation is depicted by Lee himself in his description of the two organizations.

In August 1838, the same month in which the election riot took place, according to Lee, "all the males over eighteen years of age, were organized into a military body, according to the law of the priesthood, and called 'The Host of Israel.' "[70] He then describes the organization of tens, fifties, and hundreds under captains—exactly as Joseph Smith describes it, concluding that "the entire membership of the Mormon Church was then organized in the same way." At the very same time, he tells us, "*another* organization was perfected, or then first formed—it was called the 'Danites.' "[71] This organization is then described with no mention of who organized it or who comprised it. The former organization, formed "by command of God, as revealed through the Lord's Prophet, Joseph Smith,"[72] was placed completely under his control. But what of the other organization which, as Joseph Smith explains, imitated and duplicated it? (Though many preliminary meetings had been held in Ohio, it was not until this time, as Lee observes, that the Danites were formally organized along the biblical pattern.) What could justify its running competition with the rest of the Church if not its supersecrecy? As a secret arm of the Church it would necessarily be tied closer to the leaders, and especially to Joseph Smith than any other, and yet by all accounts it was under the direction of a new convert, an ambitious "doctor," who had performed no services for the Church and held no offices save that of branch president: he it was who called the meetings, presided at them, and laid down the law. Even had he preached perfect loyalty to the Prophet and the authorities, such a situation would have been intolerable, nay, unthinkable, to them. The Church was nothing if not centralized, and the peculiar dominance of Avard over the Danites is enough in itself to prove that they were not sanctioned by the Church. There were indeed Danites in the Battle of Crooked River, but even Lee reports that it was "the *Gentiles* [who] said afterwards that Captain Patton," gave the cry "Charge, Danites, charge!"[73] By that time Avard had diligently spread the fiction that all Mormons in arms were Danites, and the Missourians believed it.

Then there is Lee's famous journal, which contained, according to him, "many things not intended for the public eye," including "an account of many dark deeds, . . . especially very much concerning the crimes of Mormon leaders."[74] So he wrote in 1877, convinced that his journals had fallen into Mormon hands and would never come to light. "John D. Lee was an indomitable and persistent diarist," write his editors, Cleland and Brooks. "Day after day . . . he kept a faithful record of his experiences, activities, thoughts, feelings, and opinions."[75] He even tells of the mysterious "Council of Fifty" "and on occasion gave more than a suggestion of its grim discussions and decisions."[76] "For sheer horror and repulsive detail," Lee's account of a dream ". . . has few parallels in the macabre literature of this or any other time."[77] It is reassuring to know that our authorities are so thoroughly steeped in the arcane literature of all nations, but why do we go on like this? To make it perfectly clear that Lee is holding nothing back in his diary. Because we are going to ask the reader, how does it happen that in the twenty years of his diary that have survived (1848–67), covering the very time when Lee is supposed to have been the kingpin of the Danite system, *not a single mention* of the Danites occurs? Even in his *Mormonism Unveiled* he never mentions the Danites after 1838. That must all be supplied by Alfred Henry Lewis, Kelly and Birney, Stenhouse, Wallace, and the like.

As one of the standard anti-Mormon classics and sources, Lee's book deserves more attention than we can give it here. But some things should be noted. For one, the techniques employed are exactly those of Stenhouse and Ann Eliza, whose works had already appeared and caused a great sensation—bear in mind that this book was compiled and published by W. W. Bishop *after* Lee's death. There are the same basic contradictions. Lee, the perfect Mormon, animated only by a sublime faith and a perfect trust in the leaders—especially Brigham Young—is nonetheless entirely aware from 1847 of all the crimes and treachery of those leaders, of which he is often the victim. This by way of explaining how the author can know so much and still be so innocent. As he explains it, he got his information about Brigham's "destroying angels" (no mention of Danites) secondhand, "they let me into the secret of all they did,"[78] though he never witnessed any of it himself, and of course never participated. But why did "they"—meaning the Chief of Police of Nauvoo and his assistants—bother to confess all their crimes to the innocent Lee? Because "they looked to me to speak a good word for them with Brigham, as they were ambitious to please him and obtain his blessing."[79] Then why didn't they report directly to President Young, as was their duty? And how could they expect a *good* word from the idealistic Lee by reporting only their *crimes* to him? And such crimes! The man who could *imagine* and write down in his journal things which "for sheer horror and repulsive detail" appall his editors could certainly impute such things to the Mormon leaders when he suddenly decided in the last days of his life that they were a lot of "low, deceitful, treacherous, cowardly, dastardly sycophants and serfs . . . combined to fasten the rope around my neck."[80] That gives an inkling of the man's state of mind when he wrote his "confession," which, except for the Mountain Meadow episode, consists entirely of the confession of *other* people's sins—especially Brigham Young's. Still the work is unintentionally very self-revealing.

"I once thought," he writes, "that I never could be induced to . . . expose the wickedness and corruption of the man whom I once looked upon as my spiritual guide."[81] Just like Ann Eliza, he knows Brigham Young for the wicked and corrupt man he is, and yet accepts him for his spiritual guide. Only at the very end of his life does he turn against Young, and only then because he has been "driven to the wall . . . and [has] been forced to resort to the first law of nature, self-protection."[82] Surely this is an enlightening admission from this man who would, according to himself, condone any crime in Brigham Young, and will do *anything* when he is forced to by the law of self-preservation, i.e., to save his own skin. And in such a desperate crisis will he draw the line at prevaricating— with an imagination like his? And a character like his?

A word as to character—Lee's runs true to form. As he tells it, he always was terribly put upon by Brigham Young; he never got his fair share of anything; the actual grievances as he describes them are unspeakably petty— he dwells at length, for example, on the imposition of having to arrange for a dinner whenever the President visits him in Southern Utah. The dinner was a modest affair and everybody enjoyed it, but the fact that he had to provide it rankled horribly. He constantly goes to Brigham with complaints against the others and protestations of ill treatment; but when others do the same he denounces them as "Brigham's pets." He was occasionally hailed before the high council on the charge of grabbing more than his share, and it is plain from his own writing that he was a very unpopular man. He was one of those whom Brigham sent to the most out-of-the-way places (such being the fate of habitual troublemakers), not as a leader but as clerk and recorder.

And yet, resolved to "tell it all," Lee, the author of this last major eyewitness classic, has nothing to tell! That's right, he is just like the ladies. All he can do is report the gossip of other people, larded with his own hysterical editorial comments. Search his pages for what actually happened, and his sufferings and the crimes of the Mormon leaders both turn out to be of his own making. The one atrocity he reports firsthand is of course the Mountain Meadows Massacre, the sort of debacle in which he is just the sort of man to let himself go, and then, in all sincerity, shift his guilt to others. For throughout his book he is never guilty of anything, and he is never understood and never gets what is coming to him, because it all goes to Brigham Young's "pets." Lee's main concern in telling the story is "the first law of nature, self-protection," and that meant exonerating himself by shifting the whole blame to others, particularly to Brigham Young.

In attempting to do this he falls into the usual error of overlooking the wide discrepancy between his accusations and what actually happened as he describes it. Since this discrepancy characterizes his book from its first page—as it also does Ann Eliza's—it is not surprising it gets by in the supreme episode. Here, far from discovering anything apart from Lee's editorial rantings to implicate any General Authority, we find frequent indications to the contrary. Consider the conversation between the two leaders on the morning after the massacre:

Col. Dame: "I must report this matter to the authorities."

Haight: "How will you report it?"

Dame: "I will report it just as it is."

Haight: "Yes, I suppose so, and implicate yourself with the rest?"

Dame: "No, I will not implicate myself, for I had nothing to do with it."

A heated discussion ensues as to who is to blame, and then a general council is held where it is agreed with "exhortations and commands to keep the whole matter secret from every one but Brigham Young."[83]

There is great local concern lest the authorities learn of what has happened; Brigham Young must of course be told, but it is perfectly clear that neither he nor any other of the "authorities" knew anything about the tragedy. Since this is supposed to have been a Danite job, though Lee makes no mention whatever of Danites, Kelly and Birney sagely observe that though Porter Rockwell was in Salt Lake City at the time, still he *could* have arranged it.[84] But if a historian is allowed to present as history anything that *could* have happened, there is no limit to his license. There are some common-sense questions, however, which every historian should ask himself. Kelly and Birney, while generally avoiding these questions, do ask themselves one at the end of their book, but leave it unanswered with a bewildered shaking of the head: "When one considers Rockwell's record it is strange indeed that he was never in a gun fight. . . . The friends and relatives of his victims were legion, but no man took it upon himself to exterminate the exterminator. . . . It is difficult to understand why some professional bad-man from California or Missouri . . . did not take a pot shot at the Danite chieftain just for luck."[85]

This impossible discrepancy between "Rockwell's record," as Kelly and Birney see it, and the facts is not just strange, it is preposterous. The real record must be brought into line with the Porter Rockwell myth at all cost: Does the keenly observant Jules Remy find Rockwell a paragon of men, nature's nobleman in a deluxe edition?[86] In that case "historical accuracy makes it necessary to amend that charming pen-portrait"[87] — how? By appeal to "Achilles"!

Is Mr. Fitz Hugh Ludlow equally impressed? He must remind himself that this fine man cannot possibly be the real Rockwell: "No one ignorant of his character would take him on sight for a man of bad disposition in any sense. . . . It seemed strange to be riding in the carriage and by the side of a man, who, if universal report among the Gentiles were correct, would not hesitate to cut my throat at the Church's orders."[88] So Ludlow's invaluable firsthand report turns out to be nothing but a report on prevailing Gentile rumor. Was Rockwell shown to be in Nauvoo when somebody shot at Boggs? Well, put it this way: "In an incredibly short time Porter Rockwell was back in Nauvoo (assisted by a relay of horses provided by the Prophet) bringing the glorious tidings of the death of Boggs."[89] Incredible it may be—but we've got to have a story. Was Rockwell in Salt Lake during the Mountain Meadows Massacre? Well, he "*could* have told Ginn . . . that orders had been issued and awaited only execution by the chief of the Danites and his subordinates."[90] Couldn't he? Couldn't Ann Eliza? Where Rockwell is clearly exonerated in a shooting, "one must read between the lines in order to understand the facts."[91] With Kelly and Birney's permission to do that, we are free to accept their verdict no matter what.

Everywhere we look these damning discrepancies stare us in the face and shower us with questions. If the Danites operated with complete insolence and immunity, why is no clear case known of a Danite operation? If their activities were meant as a warning and a lesson to the people, why were the people always made to believe that there were no such activities, but only Indian atrocities? If it has always been "the fundamental conviction entertained by every Latter Day Saint that to rob or cheat a Gentile was to perform an holy deed,"[92] why have the Mormons never been aware of this or sought to gain merit by complying with the doctrine? Why does Lee *never* refer to himself as a leader of the Danites if that is what he was? Why does he never mention Danite activities after 1838, if he was the arch-Danite and greatly given to telling wild stories? When Joseph Smith was being assailed by mobs, imprisoned in dungeons, and in dire risk of his life, surviving one deadly peril after another, where were the Danites? Why were Marsh and Hyde not liquidated the very day they betrayed the Danites? How could they go about unscathed for years before returning to the Mormons? The Nauvoo Legion was present in a crisis — why no sign of the Danites? Why did Lee, a morbidly conscientious diary keeper and lifelong clerk and recorder in the Church, not write his last intimate confession with his own hand? He prided himself on his penmanship and spent his days in prison teaching the other inmates to write. Why was it "written at his dictation and delivered to William W. Bishop, attorney for Lee, with a request that the same be published"?[93] We are not even told to whom he dictated his confession, but we do know that additions and alterations are easily effected in a document of unknown provenance, while an autographic document is much harder to tamper with. As it is, the lawyer is free to do pretty much what he pleases with a hundred-page manuscript by an unidentified hand, only one page of which is signed. Why does Lee devote so much of his "confessions" to telling other people's stories, to which he was not a witness?

The questions go on and on, but there are points at which Lee can be definitely "controlled." His own passion and prejudice cannot escape the casual reader. But then another question: If the man is so bound and determined to incriminate Brigham Young, both to save his own skin and to get even, why must he always resort to rhetoric instead of producing a single concrete instance of Young's criminality? Like all the others, he seeks to prove the President's guilt by citing his sermons, knowing that the public did not have access to the *Journal of Discourses*. But the teachings he attributes to Brigham Young are the exact opposite to what fills those pages. Was there ever a preacher or leader more willing to admit his fallibility or more emphatic in exhorting his followers *not* to follow him blindly or believe a thing was so because he said it? If there was one teaching that Brigham Young emphasized more than any others, it was the importance of the individual's getting a testimony for himself independently of all human guidance, and putting his trust not in the words of any leader but in the Holy Ghost. Lee is not merely ranting, he is lying when he says: "Brigham Young, *is God*. . . . To disobey the will of Brigham Young is, in his mind, a sin against the Holy Ghost, and is an unpardonable sin to be wiped out only by blood atonement. The followers of Brigham Young are serfs, slaves, and willing instruments to carry out the selfish designs of the man."[94] Such statements as that furnish helpful indication of the man's general reliability.

We get the same sort of thing in Kelly and Birney:

> "Blood" was the word uppermost in every man's thoughts; "Blood Atonement" was on every tongue, blood stained the hands of many. There can be found no parallel in history for the bloody frenzy.[95]
> Such words as zealotry, fanaticism, and bigotry are meaningless in the contemplation of an entire people gone rabid with blood-lust. One reads the published addresses of the First Presidency of the Mormon Church . . . and staggers before the thought that nineteenth century America could produce men who would preach a doctrine of human sacrifice.[96]

And the whole evidence for this "entire people gone rabid with blood-lust" is to be found in the passages we cited above; though people gone rabid are neither cautious nor discreet, they have left not a trace of their bloodlust, of which their children and grandchildren are totally unaware.

Having hurled their monstrous charges, these scholars hasten to confirm them: "As a single example . . . there may be cited the case of the third wife of Milo Andrews."[97] And they are off, telling with zest on the authority of Mrs. Stenhouse (!) the fate of Mrs. Andrews: "The public was informed that she had died in childbirth," but her husband and Porter Rockwell knew better, being the only witnesses to what happened, though of course *they* "kept the secret."[98] How Mrs. Stenhouse found out about it under those circumstances we will never know. But enough: "*a single example*" taken from a professional gossip, of an occurrence whose only witnesses never breathed a word to anyone, suffices to illustrate and attest the greatest mass bloodbath in history. Surely our authors, if they had *anything to go on at all*, would not have to fall back on such feeble stuff.

A favorite trick of the anti-Mormon teratologists, desperately casting about them for something in the way of evidence, is to appeal to general principles to support their grim particulars. How can you doubt that "throats were slit right and left" if it was "the belief of *all* good Mormons" that they should be when the leaders spoke?[99] Need you ask for evidence where "the fundamental conviction entertained by *every Latter Day Saint*" sanctifies criminal acts against Gentiles?[100] Is Rockwell a paradox? There is a simple explanation: "He was a Mormon — and any attempt to analyze the man must be predicated upon that statement. . . . He was a Mormon. He was a good Mormon. That is equivalent to saying that he was ignorant, illiterate, superstitious, and as easily led as a mongrel dog."[101] Granted the general principle, all particulars are readily explained. But how do we prove the general principles? By the grizzly particulars, of course. All Mormons are wicked; Rockwell was a Mormon, *ergo*, Rockwell was a wicked man. If you ask for further proof that all Mormons *are* wicked, a single example will suffice, the case of the notorious Porter Rockwell—was there ever a bloodier villain? You ask the particulars? Well, "the newspapers of that day were full of complaints of Mormon thefts and raids and Porter Rockwell's name appears early. . . . Witness an item from the *Burlington Hawkeye and Iowa Patriot.*"[102] Again the lone item from the bursting archives, and it turns out to be a story in which Porter Rockwell is not mentioned, the story of how when some goods were stolen someone suggested looking for them in the skiff of a certain Mormon; the skiff was searched and the stolen goods were *not* there. End of story. And this is what they dish up as evidence of the early depredations of Porter Rockwell. Never mind that Rockwell isn't in the story, and that the Mormon didn't steal the stuff—you get the idea.

Since Kelly and Birney lean heavily on Mrs. Stenhouse for their Danite revelations, as do Ann Eliza and her doughty disciple, Stenhouse is the one to call on next. To find her in top form we must call on her in London, where we find her sitting over the teacups with a young English girl. This is away back in 1855, and the young girl, who is introduced to us as Mary Burton, turns out to be Mrs. Stenhouse's informant on the Danites. Our curiosity is aroused. Who is this girl? A convert. Has she ever been in America? No. Then where did *she* find out about the Danites? Oh, here in London—from hearing people talk. And *she* is Mrs. Stenhouse's informant about the Danites? I can't believe it! Well, let us listen to them talk.

Mary says:

> Well, I hardly like to tell you, if you have heard nothing about the matter, for I'm not quite sure whether it all is true; but we have had some strange reports floating about here. . . . It is said that in the time of Joseph Smith a band of men was organized who put to death any one who was troublesome to the Church or offended the Elders. Some people say that it was one or perhaps more of this band who fired at Governor Boggs, of Mis-

souri. . . . Dr. Avard and Sidney Rigdon are said to have
been mixed up in the matter, and that wretched man,
John C. Bennett, tells a frightful story about it. But that
is not the worst, for Elder Shrewsbury himself told me
long ago that Thomas B. Marsh, the then President of
the Twelve, when he apostatised, took oath that the
Saints had formed a "Destruction Company," as he
called it, for the purpose of avenging themselves, and
Orson Hyde, in a solemn affidavit swore that all that
Marsh had said was true.[103]

The little English girl rattles on like an encyclopedia,
accurately ticking off all the key names with intimate fa-
miliarity in the stilted and anything but conversational
manner of Stenhouse herself. This is how the lady gets it
all in without taking any responsibility. On the contrary,
she piously refuses to believe a word of it: "Well dear,"
she says, "I've heard all that before, but no doubt it is all
scandal." So Mary Burton puts her right:

> I'm afraid not, . . . for I have heard from people who
> ought to know, that since the Saints have been in Salt
> Lake Valley the same things have been done; only now
> they speak of those men as "Danites" and "Avenging
> Angels." People say that those who are dissatisfied and
> want to leave Zion, almost always are killed after they
> set out, *by the Indians,* and they dare not say boldly who
> they believe those "Indians" are. Then, too, one lady
> told me that she had heard from her sister that not only
> were apostates killed in a mysterious way by Indians or
> some one else, but that many people were "missing,"
> or else found murdered, who were only *suspected* of being
> very weak in the faith. These things are horrible, and
> sometimes I think I will never go out to Zion.[104]

Still the familiar strains from Beadle, with Stenhouse
still protesting that the tales are "without foundation." She
has chosen a safe, noncommittal, roundabout way to present her Danite material, but it is all there. Ann Eliza lifts

the passage with but minor alterations, and satisfies the devoted Wallace that she knows all about Danites. Yet Stenhouse must go back twenty years to a conversation in London with a native girl who is not too sure of herself: "I'm not quite sure"; "we have had some strange reports floating about [who are we?]"; "it is said"; "some people say." When Stenhouse demurs, Mary Burton becomes more emphatic: "I have heard from people who ought to know"; "people say"; "one lady told me that she had heard from her sister." We are not told who the lady was, or who her sister was, or who told her sister; but little Mary Burton takes it up from there, and the others have seen to it that this priceless proof of the Danite horror shall not be lost, but be properly processed and handsomely packaged for delivery to your convenient corner drugstore.

To show that Mary Burton was right after all, Ann Eliza tells the story of the Aiken party, as reported by Beadle on the authority of Hickman.[105] Kelly and Birney have since confirmed these authorities by reproducing an *actual photograph* of the hotel in Salt Lake where the Aiken brothers stayed "before being murdered on the Sevier River in 1857" (it couldn't very well have been after).[106] This is followed in Ann Eliza by the Yates murder, taken "from his [Hickman's] own account."[107] Then to prove that all this is possible she quotes the "blood atonement" sermons since used by Kelly and Birney, with the specification "It is no secret that all this was understood *literally*."[108] If it is no secret, that clears us, of course, from having to prove any of it, though one can only wonder why if it is no secret, nobody has been able to find out about it. Oh, but they have! "There is good reason to think that Lieutenant Gunnison and his party were also victims, although it was said that they were shot by 'Indians.' "[109] The "good reason" is Hickman again, though a thorough government investigation, which would have been willing and eager to discover Mormon villainy, found only the Goshutes to blame. And isn't

that a long way to go for evidence of "blood atonement"?
Were the Aiken, Yates, and Gunnison parties apostates?
What, then, can "blood atonement" possibly have to do
with them? Here for seven years and more murder was
the order of the day, reaching the point, says Ann Eliza,
where nobody thought anything of it; it was practiced
constantly, insolently, and openly; all the fair valleys of
Utah ran with blood; the word "blood" was uppermost in
everybody's thoughts as all participated in an orgy of mass
bloodlust unparalleled in history or imagination. That is
what they say; yet whenever the accusers are asked for
evidence, where must they go for it? To Indian attacks
away back in the early days on non-Mormon parties in
obscure and distant parts of the wilderness, where, by the
way, the Indians really were dangerous right up to our
own generation.

In her treatment of the Danites, our Ann Eliza simply
follows Stenhouse except for two valuable contributions
of her own. The first of these opens her chapter on "Danites
and Their Deeds": "It is only a very few weeks since two
prominent officers of the Mormon Church were overheard
in the street, in Salt Lake City, angrily discussing some
person who had 'broken his covenants.' Said one,—'He
ought to have his throat cut.' 'It wouldn't do,' replied the
other; 'there are too many Gentiles about.' "[110] One wonders who could have overheard this tactful conversation;
it must have been a Mormon, but in that case one wonders
even more how and why it was so fully reported to Mrs.
Young, who at the time was lecturing against the Mormons
in the East. She pursues her theme: "Ten years ago, an
apostate's or Gentile's life was worth absolutely nothing. . . . The doom of either was irrevocably fixed. . . . It
was enough that he should be merely suspected, and his
fate was . . . swift and sure, before he had even an opportunity of defending himself."[111]

There was a time in Utah, then, when every apostate

and Gentile was assassinated without compunction or de-
lay—and that as recently as ten years back, when our informant was a grown woman and intimately familiar with
the doings of the Mormons high and low. Yet whenever
she wants to report something specific, she must needs
go way back to the "Reformation" time of the middle fifties,
when she was a very sheltered little girl. The nearest she
gets to the Danites personally is the claim, "I have been
told this by a person who heard the oaths administered at
a meeting of the band in Daviess County."[112] But the Mormons have never denied that there were Danites in Daviess
County, why must Ann Eliza go clear back there to discover
the devilish doings which she claims are going on all
around her all the time? She admits that "Joseph Smith
always denied that he had in any way authorized the formation of the Danite bands; and, in fact, in public he
repeatedly repudiated both them and their deeds of violence."[113] "However," she hastens to add, "Thomas B.
Marsh . . . apostatized" and accused Joseph Smith "of
abetting the Danites and their deeds."[114] That, as we have
seen, is as well as she can do to tie Smith up with the
Danites—and it leaves everything to be desired in the way
of evidence. Where were the Danites and their unbreakable
oaths when Marsh and Hyde betrayed them?

To prove that the Mountain Meadows Massacre was
the work of the Danites, Ann Eliza makes much of the fact
that Brigham Young's secretary, i.e., the only man who
knew of his complicity in the crime, "was found . . .
'drowned' in three inches of water."[115] Since nobody drowns
in three inches of water, this is obviously another Danite
horror. According to the news report, the man was found
dead at 6 a.m. with his head downstream in the irrigation
ditch on North Temple street, the face was swollen, and
"the Jury failed to find any marks of violence on the body,
except a slight bruise near one of the eyes. . . . Verdict . . . [was] death by drowning."[116] It does not occur to

our little detective that one does not wait twelve years to erase a party from whom one is in mortal danger, that one does not put one's private secretary out of the way most secretly on a downtown main street, or that people who want to make a drowning look accidental do not choose to submerge their victim in three inches of water. The Danites, those masters of supersecrecy, seem capable of concealing nothing on earth but their own existence—and that's a waste of time, because *everybody* knows about that. It is not until 1908 that Ann Eliza volunteers the helpful information that her husband's title was "Chief Archer of the Danites."[117] A strange little oversight.

Mrs. Young's one terrifying personal contribution to Danite history comes from her last hours in Utah. Though she is able to announce the gratifying news that "an apostate nowadays is comparatively safe from any deeds of violence"[118] and describes Brigham Young as the helpless dragon who longs for the day, forever past, when the crook of his finger meant lights out for anybody he didn't like, still you never know: "Even then, the 'Danites,' those terrible monsters of Mormon vengeance, might be on our track."[119] Mr. Wallace makes great capital of this, but can we seriously call it firsthand proof that the Danites were still operating? Or that they ever operated? "The outrages committed by these Danites . . . caused the expulsion of the Saints from Missouri," she writes.[120] Yet Stenhouse says they really did not get going or take the name of Danites until they got to Utah.[121] Even Mrs. Brodie declares that "there is no reliable evidence that the Danite organization was continued in Illinois except among Joseph's personal body-guard."[122] In this, her only mention of the Danites, Mrs. Brodie, running true to form, cites only the worthless Bennett as her informant, and says just enough to incriminate Joseph Smith and no more. What the reliable evidence for the bodyguard is she does not say, but tells us in a footnote: "White uniforms [not robes] were part of their military attire. John D. Lee, one of Joseph's body-guards, proudly wore his red sash in later years when he went to dances in southern Utah." No source is given for this information, and no effort is made to establish the relevance or significance of the red sash—but it all sounds beguiling, significant, and sinister.

Nothing has given as much body and substance to all the dark hints and whisperings about the Danites as the story of the Aiken party. "It was fourteen years before the truth of this affair was known," writes Ann Eliza. " . . . Now their fate is known beyond a doubt, and foremost in the list of assassins stands the name of Brigham Young."[123] Nobody had been able to pin anything on the Mormons until fourteen years later, when Bill Hickman came to the rescue with his thrice-welcome "confessions" (even Ann Eliza puts it in quotes), a long and lurid catalogue of blood in which every major crime committed in Utah is mechanically and unimaginatively pinned on Brigham Young. This work established once and for all the useful and simple formula of attributing to the Mormons every crime committed in the West, and leaving it to *them* to prove their innocence; lack of evidence is simply proof of Mormon secrecy—for in view of their doctrine of Blood Atonement,[124] every Mormon must be considered guilty before the law until proven innocent.

Stenhouse and Ann Eliza take their Danites from Hickman. But Hickman himself had a ghostwriter, "a frequently impoverished editor and hack," as Wallace so nicely puts it,[125] who was struggling to make a living and whose stock in trade was the Mormon Monster. His book, *Life in Utah*, by J. H. Beadle, editor of the *Salt Lake Reporter*, and *Utah Correspondent* of the *Cincinnati Commercial*, printed in 1870, was reprinted in 1882 under the title "*Polygamy*, by J. H. Beadle, late editor of the Salt Lake Reporter; . . . and Clerk of the Supreme Court for Utah."[126] Here was a man who knew the value of sensationalism. And now the plot thickens. "Since Beadle was short of funds in 1874 and 1875," writes Mr. Wallace, "it is possible that he had assumed the task of serving as Ann Eliza's shade," i.e., her ghost-writer. Wallace hastens to assure us, however, that Ann Eliza "undoubtedly wrote or dictated *Wife No. 19*," since "the tone of Ann Eliza's private letters and impromptu interviews . . . indicates" as much, "although she may have retained a professional writer to correct and polish it."[127] Why does Wallace concede so much, since his whole story depends on the reliability of his star witness? Is something wrong? We are asked to take Wallace's word for it that "the *tone* of Ann Eliza's private letters and impromptu interviews with the press" proves "undoubtedly" that she wrote her book—yet it doesn't rule out a ghostwriter. If "tone" is all we have to go on, "tone" should be amply, nay exhaustively, documented. Let the reader compare the "tone" of Beadle's long introduction to Hickman's book (by Beadle) with *Wife No. 19* and he will discover a very likely source of those key tags and phrases that Stenhouse and Ann Eliza Young later claimed for their own. Here are a few characteristic Beadlisms: "Against the pure principle of 'Peace on earth and good will to men' [they] . . . wrest the mild precepts of the Gospel, and deduce therefrom license for themselves, and a sanction for vengeance on their enemies."[128] "Mormonism is sanctified selfishness: a system which teaches practically, that very little restraint need be put upon the baser passions. . . . On its members such doctrines must produce a terrible effect."[129] "Fortunately most of the common Mormons have not quite entered into the spirit of, or 'lived up to,' their faith."[130] "Slavery and polygamy—'twin relics'—may well be put beside each other in a brief parallel."[131] "Love, forgiveness, kindly charity, must wither in such an air."[132] This is followed by the favorite passage about Brigham Young's bowie-knife,[133] etc.

Here the student will recognize the characteristic sentiments and the ironic undertone of our moralizing ladies, couched in the familiar jargon. If "tone" is to be our criterion, then Beadle must be given far more credit than Wallace is willing to concede. It is Beadle who first goes all the way in applying the lucrative formula "M is for Mormon and Murder"—Hickman, as we shall see, never dreamed of such a thing until Beadle put him up to it; and it is Beadle who perfects the standard tricks and clichés that Stenhouse, Young, and Wallace find so helpful. As for the "tone" of Ann Eliza's personal letters and interviews, Mr. Wallace never lets his readers see a single one of those letters or sit through one of the interviews. Her long letter to Stenhouse *is* available, however, in Fanny's book, and the most remarkable thing about it is the tameness of its "tone" as compared with *Wife No. 19,* which is definitely in the Beadle vein.

Now about this Beadle. It seems that Hickman brought his life story to Beadle for his expert advice and assistance. What was the understanding between the two? "Our conversation need not be recorded," writes Beadle, thereby arousing suspicions which are not allayed when he continues: "I then agreed to take charge of his manuscript, and, to use his own language, 'Fix it up in shape, so people would understand it.' "[134] That is a pretty broad commission. That the spelling and punctuation were to be corrected would be taken for granted anyway—even the printer would do that—fixing the thing up went definitely beyond that—Brother Beadle had a free hand, and he used it, as we shall soon see. But first his own story of how he came into possession of the awful facts is too good to miss.

"For years," he begins, "I had heard of 'Bill Hickman, Chief of the Destroying Angels, Head Danite,' &c., &c., *ad nauseam* but like most persons unacquainted with Mormon history, I regarded such matters as the creations of a fertile fancy."[135] Let us stop the film there for a moment: He and everybody else living back East always kept hearing (*ad nauseam*) for years and years about this Bill Hickman. But how could that be if the *first* knowledge the public had of Hickman and his deeds, according to Ann Eliza, came with the startling revelations of his book—first edited *by Beadle himself* in 1870? What could those earlier stories of Hickman and his Danites possibly have been? Who gave them out? Why are they not found in his autobiography? If they are, why no reference to earlier publications? *Only* Hickman knew those stories, and it was to Beadle that he first told them.

And then that business about Beadle and the rest of the general public, "unacquainted with Mormon history," refusing to credit such atrocity stories. Was that really the reaction of the public to the Mormon horror tales from the beginning? Did people actually take the side of the Mormons when these tales were handed out to them from the high authority of the pulpit and the press? They did not: the public is neither prone to spurn sensationalism nor to take a cool and detached view of Mormonism. Beadle is making all this up. Disillusionment came, he says, only when he was "convinced by a longer residence in Utah that there was and had long been *some* kind of a secret organization dangerous to Gentiles and recusant Mormons."[136] Stop the camera again: these were the very years when, according to Ann Eliza, "a Gentile's life was worth *absolutely nothing*"[137] in Utah. Granting that Mr. Beadle's *was* worth just that, still he, a snooping Gentile, lived and labored for a long time in Utah before he became "convinced . . . that there was . . . *some* kind of a secret organization" at work. It took long and intense investigation even to make him suspicious: this cannot possibly have been Ann Eliza's Utah of the bloody valleys.

But what *did* convince the astute Beadle that something was wrong? Not shots in the dark, knives in the door, or notes on the table—no, during all his time in Utah there was no indication that he was ever in the slightest danger.

The light dawned when "I began to examine the history of the Church more carefully; and . . . was struck by two curious and then unexplainable facts."[138] Fact one was that the notorious Hickman, openly denounced by the leaders of the Church as a bad and dangerous man, was never prosecuted. Fact two was that said Hickman *"was on terms of personal intimacy with Brigham Young."*[139] Stop the film again: He got all that out of the history of the Church? Whose history of the Church? He had read *anti*-Mormon histories and not believed a word of them, because they offered not a scrap of proof. So now he turns to the Mormon history, where the figure of Hickman commands his attention. But where does Hickman's name appear in the history of the Church? Where do we read of his intimacy with Brigham Young? To Beadle's mind the significant thing about Hickman was that the Mormons knew he was bad and yet did not prosecute him. Prosecute him for what? The West was full of bad and dangerous men who couldn't be prosecuted until they were caught in a crime. Hickman's early crimes were all most secret, known only to himself, until he confessed to Beadle. Why *then,* when all became known, was he never prosecuted? Were the Mormons protecting him then? If Hickman's only business with Brigham Young was, as he avers, the execution of secret, black, and midnight acts, O, most damnable, the dangerous association would of course be kept scrupulously out of the history of the Church — yet that is where Beadle says he found all about it.

With such clumsy artifice Beadle sets his stage. Why, if he has a direct and authentic tale to unfold, must he protest over and over again in his introduction that the Mormons as a whole are so very, very wicked that it makes no difference *what* you say about them, it can't be bad enough. Why does he seek to make his history plausible by appealing lamely to "*late* developments in Utah," which "have poured a flood of light on many dark and bloody mysteries,"[140] and then leave us completely in the dark as to what those developments might be or to what dark and bloody mysteries he is so darkly referring? His Hickman behaves like a moron, and his Brigham Young like an idiot, as they unimaginatively and repeatedly go through the same routine: the henchmen go forth on the hour every hour to commit their monotonous murders and return with their routine reports to receive the Prophet's routine blessing along with some such ingenious remark as "Dead Men Tell No Tales"!—inevitably paraphrased by the ladies as "Dead *women* tell no tales"! In order to work at all, the crude Beadle formula requires a cooperative and confiding public, but when has such ever been wanting where the Mormons are concerned? When you come right down to it, our contemporary experts, though more devious, are almost as crude.

To adorn and confirm the Hickman book, Mr. Beadle solicited the aid of Judge Stephen S. Harding, and got it. And in Harding we have just the control we need. First, a word about the good Judge. He was born in Palmyra in 1808, and because of that was able to give to the world a priceless description of the boy Joseph Smith: "He had hardly ever been known to laugh in his childhood; and would never work or labor like other boys; and was noted as never having had a fight or quarrel with any other person. . . . He was hard on birds' nests, and . . . it was a common saying in the neighborhood: 'That is as big a lie as young Joe ever told.' "[141] Now it happens that the Harding family moved to Indiana in 1820, when little Stephen was only twelve years old; and when in 1827 he saw a newspaper report of the "Golden Bible" sensation in Palmyra, the name of the place caught his eye, he says, but "I had at the time no certain recollection as to who this "Joe Smith" was; but remembered having seen a long-legged, tow-headed boy of that name, who was generally fishing in the mill-pond at Durfee's grist-mill."[142] It turned out later that that was sure enough Joe Smith, but that was *all* that Harding remembered of him. Then in 1829 he visited Palmyra and spent a good deal of time at the printing office, where they made a present to *him*[143] of "the first title page of the *Book of Mormon* that was ever printed";[144] but in spite of his persistent efforts he failed to get any response from Joseph Smith himself. He did learn all about him, though, from his cousin, Pomeroy Tucker. We have shown how irresponsible Tucker was when it came to inventing stories about Joseph Smith,[145] and it is interesting that Harding ends his long letter with a Tucker story, to which he adds his own contribution:

> The best part of the story, however [i.e., that J. Smith insisted on a large black sheep instead of a small white one as a sacrifice when he dug for treasure], had been forgotten by Mr. T. . . . "The reason why it must be a *black* sheep," said the young deceiver, "is because I have found the treasure by means of the *black* art." This, of course, was unanswerable, and the *black* wether was given up.
>
> With malice toward none, and charity for all, I subscribe myself,
>
> Respectfully yours,
Stephen S. Harding.[146]

Such was a good Judge Harding, a well of truth. But he hated Brigham Young with a consuming hatred. When on July 7, 1862, he became Governor of Utah, he "joined hands with Colonel Connor in assuming for Utah a military police supervision," cracking down on the Mormons, but withholding military aid to them even "when they were harassed by Indian raids."[147] Harding's undisguised hatred of the Mormons burst out in a furious attack on their patriotism and morals in a speech to the Utah legislature in December 1862. Within six months he was removed from office by President Lincoln and transferred to a judgeship in Colorado. He continued to work steadily against state-

hood for Utah. And to this man Bill Hickman confessed
six years before he came to Beadle. So it was a natural
thing for Beadle to write to the Judge for confirmation and
more dirt for his book. But what have we here?

This is the situation: Here is Governor Harding, who
has been in office less than a year and is already on his
way out "on account of continuous struggles between himself and the Mormon church,"[148] whose career has been
wrecked by Brigham Young. To his door in the middle of
the night of March 3, 1863, comes one Bill Hickman, "a
born killer," as Kelly and Birney put it, who "enjoyed his
profession. He was cold-blooded, crafty, and heartless, . . . a huge man, as strong as a bull. . . . His eyes
were a steel-grey, the whites always bloodshot, and no

.

man who looked into them ever craved a repetition of the experience."[149] If any man hated Brigham Young more than Harding did, it was Hickman. On that momentous night he "stood up (I often think now of the man and his manner), and said, 'Governor, . . . I *know* Brigham Young and his rabbit-tracks! Rabbit-tracks! . . . Brigham Young has more reason to be afraid o' Bill Hickman than Bill Hickman has to be afraid o' Brigham Young.' I never looked on a face with more of a scowl of defiance."[150] Well, you get the pitch: Hickman is *not* the man to hold anything back from timidity or modesty, and Harding is not the man to let such information go to waste. The two met often after that; they were "confederates," as Kelly and Birney put it, the one Brigham Young's arch-Danite and chief assassin, now turned against Brigham with insane fury, and the other the frustrated Governor who would give anything to pin something on Young. "All the army," said Brigham Young in 1860, "with its teamsters, hangers-on, and followers, with the judges, and nearly all the rest of the civil officers, amounting to some seventeen thousand men, have been searching diligently for three years to bring one act to light that would criminate me; but they have not been able to trace out one thread or one particle of evidence that would criminate me."[151]

What a feather in Harding's cap to be able to pin something on Brigham Young! He badly needed such a feather — the one thing that would save his career. And here was Hickman right in his own office in secret session — the one man who knew all the crimes of Brigham Young inside out! Why didn't Harding bring charges against Brigham Young the very next morning, as duty, pleasure, and desperate self-interest prescribed? There were other sessions with Hickman after this one: why didn't Harding *ever* bring charges? Why was Hickman, though he lived until 1883, never prosecuted? Plainly he was safe enough. As *chief* Danite he would know about plenty of crimes that would not directly incriminate himself, or by the learned judge's advice he could at least turn state's witness and save his skin. Yet never a peep out of Harding! He went off to Colorado demoted, and hence to retirement in Indiana with not a word of Brigham's Danite operations. In 1890 he contributed two lengthy chapters on the Mormons to Thomas Gregg's anti-Mormon classic with not so much as a hint of his own dealings with those terrible people in Utah. Of course he asked Hickman about the Danites on their very first interview, but, would you believe it, Hickman had nothing to report!

Here they are, Young's two deadliest enemies, cheek by jowl—"thoughts black, hands apt, drugs fit, and time agreeing"—in a top-secret session that had just one object in the world. Hickman is reporting to the Governor: "He gave me a short sketch of his life," the latter reports, "and did not seem very proud of his title as 'Danite Captain.' On this subject, however, he was reticent."[152] *That* man ashamed? Under *those* circumstances? He didn't have to incriminate himself, as we have said—what a time to be "reticent" on that theme!

One thing emerges clearly from this. Neither in that or in any of their subsequent sessions did Harding learn anything he could use against Brigham Young. It was only when Hickman came to Beadle six years later that Hickman suddenly remembered and revealed for the first time all the now familiar tales of the Danites. Beadle was a professional purveyor of scandal, "a frequently impoverished hack," says Mr. Wallace, a sometime editor, court clerk (only in later years when he is safely back East, does he become clerk of the Supreme Court for Utah), Utah correspondent for a Cincinnati paper, professional anti-Mormon, and ghostwriter for our own Ann Eliza. Hickman handed this man his story with a free hand to "fix it up."

That is why we believe that those tales are Beadle's invention, for the celebrated "Confessions" that suddenly sprang to life in 1870 can in no wise have resembled Hickman's long and intimate communications to Harding—if they had, Harding would have had Brigham trapped in no time. Harding's attempts to attribute his own lack of information on the Danites to Hickman's tender conscience and maidenly reserve is worthy of Gilbert and Sullivan.

It was not until Beadle got to work that every solved *and* unsolved crime of the century was traced directly and simply to Brigham Young through the helpful Hickman, who receives his orders, liquidates his Aikens, Yates, et al., and reports to Brigham with the regularity of clockwork. If he and Beadle were singularly weak in inventive skill, must we attribute the same total lack of resource to the crafty Brigham Young? No wonder Hickman was never prosecuted. The patent absurdity of the "Confessions" becomes apparent on the most superficial investigation and grows with every monotonous episode.

Hickman raises a lot of questions: To sum them up, how could Beadle and everybody else back East know all about Hickman and his Danites for years before Hickman ever divulged his deep secrets? In what history of the Church did Beadle read about Hickman's intimacy with Brigham Young? Why did Hickman hold back his evidence against Brigham Young in his talks with Harding? Harding's explanation—because he was not "very proud" of his own association with the Danites—raises yet more questions. Was Hickman the squeamish type? As Top Danite, couldn't he implicate Young in particular crimes of which he himself was not guilty? Was Harding so indifferent or devoid of ingenuity as to overlook an opportunity like this to throw the book at Brigham Young? As a lawyer, couldn't he have made some use of such incriminating evidence? Why did he make no use at all of the material Hickman gave him? It is Beadle who asks, Why was Hickman never prosecuted by the Mormons before he confessed to anything, if the Mormons were not condoning his crimes? But that raises much more serious questions: Why was he never prosecuted at all? Why was he, living on an isolated ranch alone for years, never liquidated by the Danites he betrayed? The questions pile up, and they all have the same answer: The Hickman stories were not true.

Only desperation could lead Mr. Wallace and his army of trained researchers to bring so pitiful a witness into court as Horace Greeley, to give "some credence to the continuing rumors of threat and violence." "Some credence" isn't very good, but it is far better than what Greeley gives us. He reports that "there is some basis of truth for the current Gentile conviction that the Mormons have robbed, maimed, and even killed persons in this territory. . . . I deeply regret the necessity of believing this; but the facts are incontestable." What begins a sentence as "some basis of truth" turns up at the end as "incontestable facts." And where does he get his incontestable facts? From "United State soldiers encamped near Salt Lake City," who told him that " 'not less than seventy-five distinct instances of murder by Mormons because of apostasy . . . are known to the authorities here.' "[153] Why didn't he consult the "authorities"? What could bored and resentful G.I.'s, robbed of an easy victory and condemned to the confinement of a dusty camp, find better to do than to propagate rumors in the grand old army manner? Greeley and Wallace, by locating their informants "near Salt Lake City," have them enjoying a ringside view, as it were, of all that went on in the Mormon community, never hinting that they were actually isolated in a camp forty-five miles away and forbidden to fraternize with the Mormons. That the camp should be a hothouse of barrack-room and mess-hall rumors, and that the poor soldiers should be pitifully grateful for a chance to show off to a famous newspaper man is understandable; but Mr. Greeley could have spared himself great mental anguish if he had only asked himself how soldiers stationed far from any Mormon settlement and objects of suspicion to the civilian population could possibly know about the inner workings of the Mormon system in dealing with "apostates."

When Richard Burton later went to the same source for enlightenment, he discovered that the soldiers could furnish no evidence whatever for the stories they told so well. Of this singular lack of confirmation Burton observes, "They attribute the phenomenon to the impossibility of obtaining testimony, and the undue white-washing action of juries."[154] Of course they do — thus adding Mormon rascality to Mormon criminality. But whatever the reason the proof was not forthcoming, the rumor-loving G.I.'s refer confidently and characteristically to "the authorities" and to Mormon cover-up tactics as their franchise for unlimited invention, and their eager gossip is the whole substance of Mr. Greeley's "incontestable facts."

After his appeal to Greeley, Mr. Wallace is content to quote Ann Eliza: "Brigham Young had 'managed' a great many murders, of which he would probably avow himself entirely guiltless, since his hands did not perform the deed."[155] Lacking all support for this terrible charge, Wallace clinches it with a rhetorical trick, commenting with withering irony: "But, of course, by this time Ann Eliza was an angry wife."[156] Of course we can't believe an angry wife, even if our whole book is nothing but the gossip of an angry wife.

The most valued witness, perhaps, for those who write about the Danites is "the diary of William Swartzell, another convert."[157] In designating it thus, Mrs. Brooks fails to note that Swartzell was not a convert but an *ex*-convert (what Mormon was not a convert in 1838?), and that the document in question is *not* the man's diary, but a careful reworking of it into an anti-Mormon pamphlet. The revamped diary of an apostate is, we insist, *not* the same thing as the diary of a convert. Consider the preface to

Mormonism Exposed . . . by William Swartzell, Sometime a Deacon in the Church of "Latter-Day-Saints": "The darkest page of history can furnish no parallel to the wicked and damnable deeds, the high handed impostures, the mad fanaticism, and the violent outrages against morality, decency, and regular law, etc., etc. . . . And all this under the sacred name of religion"! Here in 1840 we have the formula full-blown—the terrible indictment, the appeal to all history, the crowning horror of perverting "the sacred name of religion."[158] And then, already true to form, the perfectly tame and innocuous story that follows—ordinary enough except when the author uses it as a frame to hang his polemic on. What makes Swartzell interesting is his frequent resort to clumsy and obvious interpolation and fabrication.

Take Swartzell's first entry, for example. Here Swartzell, brand-new in the Church, has joined the Saints just three days before; he has just met Joseph Smith, who has been very kind and helpful. And to the day's entry he adds:

> The most prominent and influential members of the fraternity were generally the only ones upon which donations of land were conferred. I particularly observed that the *least* among the brethren were the *least noticed*, and *got the least*. . . . I took note of a great many things, while I superintended the cooking department, that did not *savor* very strongly of piety, or honesty. The boss cook was not asleep.[159]

Does that reminiscence of the past read like a journal entry of specific events on the day they happened? Does this little sermon of wise disillusionment, critical scorn, and vague generalities, written in the past historical tense, suggest the starry-eyed youth who has been just three days with the Saints? He is already talking like Ann Eliza; he is being editorial and retrospective, displaying a frankly hostile spirit right at the time when he is supposed to be an ardent follower of the Prophet. The next day he reports: "This day Joseph Smith says to me, 'We are getting along, brother Swartzell; be a faithful steward, and we will remember you well.' Thinks I to myself, 'So much for that.' "[160]

Wasn't it a bit early for the young enthusiast to be scoffing at the Prophet? Why had he cast his lot with the persecuted Mormons if he only came to sneer and mutter caustic asides? Ten days later he describes himself as a thorough-going enthusiast for the cause: "As the Lord has blessed and prospered the proceedings of the last week, I bless his holy name for his many tender mercies."[161] Can this be the same person who has been commenting on events with such withering sarcasm? No, that is the apostate Swartzell of later days.

This can be clearly demonstrated from the entry for June 27, 1838:

> The god of the Mormons, I begin to perceive [he had perceived it on the first day in camp], is the god of Mammon. . . . It seems that in order to induce many of the dupes of Mormonism to emigrate to Missouri, some of the leaders take advantage . . . by representing . . . that they have thousands of acres in wheat. This bait many of the poor half-starved creatures readily swallowed, and emigrated to Missouri; but they found no wheat there, or any thing else to live upon.[162]

Note here how our diary writer slips into the past narrative tense, and then goes on to describe developments that could only have taken place much later. For on June 27, 1838, the oldest Mormon settlement in Missouri was less than six weeks old — which gives the saints back East and abroad less than six weeks to receive news of the settlements, be duped into believing that at that season of the year thousands of acres of wheat awaited them in Missouri, and upon hearing the report to sell out, pack up, and "emigrate to Missouri," only to find no rich harvests awaiting them. Swartzell is plainly putting this stuff into his "diary" in retrospect.

Two days after this, Swartzell reports the fulfillment of a personal revelation: "went to the place to which my vision pointed, and found it precisely as I had anticipated."[163] Yet scarcely a week has passed before he announces, "From this day, I concluded to make my escape from this *blessed* land, and as soon as possible."[164] Another bad slip: He is writing about something he did on a certain day in the *past*. He does not say "From this day on I resolve" or the equivalent, but can already report a resolution to which he has remained firm.

Now comes the important part, the entry of July 14, 1838, quoted as the one firsthand description of a Danite meeting: "It was held in a grove, in the woods, adjoining brother White's house, where a number of benches were made out of trees split in two. Sentinels, armed with pistols, swords, and guns, were posted on the outskirts of the grove, while the Daranites, as they were called, occupied the centre."[165] All very damning and very specific. The trouble is that Swartzell wasn't there. All he can report is: "Some talk of a meeting—for what purpose I do not know—it is called a Daranite meeting." And then the description of the grove. After the meeting, he says, Brother Thayer said to him, "Ah! brother Swartzell, you should have been at the meeting; you should have heard all about the Daranite business, for brother Joseph preached, and brother Hiram, and brother Rigdon."[166] And did brother Joseph preach for the "Daranites" or against them? That is important to know, since this is the only direct association of Joseph Smith with the Danites.

What Danites? Swartzell refers to them always and only as "Daranites": If everyone was going about talking about Daranites, how is that only Swartzell knows that peculiar name? The indication is that he heard the name incorrectly, which is quite possible; but in that case he could have heard it from only one person—not repeated by many different persons in a form which occurs only in his "diary." He is extending things as usual. Why should Thayer come right from the meeting from which Swartzell had been excluded, "deprived," he says, ". . . of being then let into the secret, or being admitted to the meeting"[167]—to report to him what happened in it? Extending, did we say? Suddenly, now that he has mentioned the "Daranites," Swartzell's diary takes on epic proportions with entries ten times the normal length. Why is that? Is it because he found the "Daranites" of particular significance? Not at all: he tells us that at the time, being a good Mormon (has he already forgotten his resolution to "escape"?), he did *not* realize the importance or significance of all this, which occurred to him only later. Yet suddenly his "diary" becomes minutely discursive and accompanied by parenthetical comments and footnotes not found elsewhere in the book, to attest its working-over. If the Danites meant no more to him than any of the other Mormon activities, as he insists, why does he give them five times as much space as anything else?

The long and sensational entry of July 19, 1838, is introduced by a statement in brackets meant to anticipate obvious objections, but actually putting the critical reader on his guard:

> It may not be improper here to state, that when I wished to make an entry in my Journal, while stationed among the Mormons I was under the necessity of retiring some distance from the camp, to a large tree, under whose boughs they believed I was offering up my daily prayers; where I wrote without being disturbed, as none were aware that I kept a record of their transactions—nor did I at that time have the most distant idea, that at some future period these notes would be laid before the public in the form of an exposition of the corruptions of a band of religious fanatics.[168]

This raises a number of questions, such as: Since the Mormons have always encouraged the keeping of journals by their members, and since at that time, as you explain, you were a good Mormon with nothing to hide, why the elaborate subterfuge? Most of your entries are very short and innocuous—did you have to go through a masquerade to jot them down? Where did you keep your diary during the day? You tell of a number of little expeditions you made by yourself away from the camp, and as chief cook you were obviously trusted and let alone a good deal of the time—do you expect us to believe that you could only be by yourself when you were pretending to pray? And that you chose a conspicuous spot for your prayers, where you would be observed? Were you expected to "retire" to a place where the Mormons could watch you at prayer— you and your diary? Why do you wait until the "Daranite" story to explain how you kept your secret journal, since you insist that at the time you had not "the most distant idea" of using it against the Mormons? Why should they think there was anything wrong with your journal if you didn't? If you never dreamed that your jottings might someday be used to expose the "corruptions" of the Mormons, how do you explain the bitter anti-Mormon polemic that begins with your very first entry? Where is the "record of their transactions" that the Mormons never suspected you of keeping? We search the diary in vain for anything but ordinary glimpses of camp-life relieved by frequent insights into Mr. Swartzell's passionate and peevish character. If there is any record of Mormon transactions, it is the account of what happened after Swartzell was actually admitted to the Danites. What does he say about that?

At the initiation "the High Priest performed the ceremonies, and commented upon the order of things with his head uncovered, and hair cut in a peculiar manner."[169] Since we know of nothing either to corroborate this statement or to invest it with a sinister allure, we pass to the next: "I was initiated into the mysteries of Daraniteism,"[170] followed by the horrible oath: "Now I do solemnly swear, by the eternal Jehovah, that I will decree to hear and conceal, and never reveal this secret, at the peril of committing perjury, and the pains of death, and my body be given to be shot, and laid in the dust. Amen."[171] The gist of this strange wording is "cross-my-heart-and-hope-to-die"; it was explained by a speaker thus: "If any of you should run away and betray this trust which is committed to you, though he should be five thousand miles distant, the Destroying Angels will pursue him, and take his life." To which Swartzell adds his comment after a dash, "—have him shot privately, so that it may not be found out or known to men."[172] This is the only part of Swartzell's diary that is supplied with footnotes, and at the end of the entry the author adds, "I have not stated every thing accurately, perhaps, as my memory does not always serve me fully."[173]

Granted all that, we are still waiting for the hair-raising disclosures, and Swartzell finally obliges with italics and exclamation point to mark the high-water mark in his tale of terror: The Daranites were told that if they ran away in battle "You will be *shot down by your own officers!*"[174] This is where he gets that business about being shot if you run away; but that has always been the fate meted out by the laws of war (theoretically at least) to deserters in *any* army, and Swartzell insists that the Danites were a strictly military organization.

After this culmination of terror, the rest of the little book is an anticlimax, albeit a lucid commentary on the personality of the author. The very next day he has a run-in with Sidney Rigdon, who maintains that any single man in the camp should be willing to do his own washing "or get a nigger to do it," since "the fair daughters of Zion should not touch a dirty rag!" He was referring to Swartzell's shirt, but our hero replied with spirit, "For my part, I will go with a dirty shirt before I will be my own washerman" — not a very helpful addition to a camp of religious refugees.[175] The next day he discovers that Hiram Smith is a dirty swindler (no particulars),[176] and on July 28 attends a "Daranite meeting," where there was "a vast expenditure of breath in expounding to the dupes," but nothing worse.[177] Of a speaker who suggested on August 5, 1838, "it may be that we will have to flee beyond the Rocky Mountains," Swartzell comments, "He seemed to talk unreasonably, but many of the innocent dupes did not see the destruction that *was* coming, and I dared not give them any warning."[178] We have underlined the "was" to show that this entry was put down not on the day indicated but in retrospect, after the Missouri disaster.

On August 13 Swartzell writes, "I have got the *horrors* — thinking about home."[179] And then a week later, August 20: "This morning I left the Mormon camp. When I had got four or five miles from the city of Adam-on-Diammon, I shouted so loud for joy that the blood came out of my mouth."[180] An enlightening passage. Not one word of planning for a getaway or of hair-breadth escape or pursuit — he simply walked away from the Mormon camp, as he could have done any time he felt like it, and nobody made the slightest effort to stop him. Then having relieved his feelings and revealed his state of mind in a hair-raising scream, he went on to the Clay County Courthouse, and there "I told them something about the band of warriors, and charged them never to tell on me, as every Daranite was sworn to take my life, if they could find out *that I had seceded* from their ranks."[181] Would the Gentiles have to "tell on" Swartzell before it dawned on the Daranites that he was no longer with them? Would the Mormons never guess that their chief cook had seceded unless the outsiders told them so? Either Swartzell was free to go his way unmolested, as he did, or else the Mormons had no way of knowing he had left the camp, as he implies. In either case it is clear that the man is fabricating about the danger he was in. He concludes his history with an appendix taken from the writings of E. D. Howe.

T. B. H. Stenhouse, an apostate and anti-Mormon writer, has told how the confessions of Marsh and Hyde were exploited in the manufacture of rumors to rally the people against the Mormons, and how those false rumors resulted in the death of Patten at Crooked River.[182] Having recognized the extent and influence of false rumors about the Danites, Mr. Stenhouse then seeks to nullify the effect of his pronouncement by the neatly rhetorical proposition that whether "Danitism was taught . . . by the authority of Joseph Smith or without, it matters not—the terrible dread of vengeance was all the same."[183] Which is the equivalent of saying, "Whether John Wilkes Booth or Louisa May Alcott shot Lincoln matters not—it was a terrible crime all the same." When it is Joseph Smith who is on trial for these crimes, does it make no difference whether he had anything to do with them or not? Not with Mr. Stenhouse, just so you can get them into the same sentence. He goes even farther: "The intelligent Mormon knows to-day that though there may be no *bona fide* organization called the Danites, there have been in church fellowship, from the days of Avard up to the present, men who have done the deeds charged to the Danites."[184] This is the same argument in an even more brazen form: Stenhouse is doing his best to make out a case against the Mormons, even though he knows there is no evidence for the Danite myth. After all, there have been in *every* church men who have done the very "deeds *charged* to the Danites," whether there were any Danites or not. And out of that Stenhouse would forge his subtle verbal link between the Mormons and the Danite image. Kelly and Birney rejoice in a further disclosure of Stenhouse, namely that there was a man who failed to deliver a message from Joseph Smith in the Carthage jail and that years later in the West "by odd coincidence, he died '*it is said of dysentery.*' "[185]

Can you think of a single cause of death in any time or place that would *not* be "an odd coincidence" to these gentlemen?

What we are trying to point out is that all these writers on the Danites have no foothold after 1838 and know it. The most effective exploitation of the Danite myth has in fact been through works of pure fiction: It was Joaquin Miller's Broadway hit *The Danites, or the Heart of the Sierra* that established the tradition that Zane Grey and some early movies ("The Mormon Maid") continued. In 1881 Miller changed the name of his play to *The Danites in the Sierras*,[186] because the book treats chiefly of that once dreaded and bloody order—in the Sierras yet.The Kauffmans in their work of high scholarly pretense prove that "the Danites, or 'Destroying Angels,' pillaged often and sometimes slew the argonauts,"[187] by citing as their source the novel *The Viper's Trail*, by Alfred Henry Lewis, the same man who converted Lee's autobiography into a Danite epic by the simple and effective device of inserting the word "Danite" into the text every few sentences.

Well, what else can you expect? "The very nature of the Danite organization precluded the keeping of records," Kelly and Birney remind us. "The Danite oath, together with the Book of Mormon, Doctrine and Covenants, and all of Joseph Smith's revelations from Yahveh, has suffered many changes, deletions, and additions from time to time."[188] That leaves our authorities free to announce, "There is no mention of Porter Rockwell in the many accounts of the dark days that preceded the great migration. We may assume, with entire safety, that he was not idle."[189] Having assumed so much, they take their next step with the same entire safety: "there are indications [not given] that Porter was in Nauvoo when General J. J. Hardin . . . entered the Holy City and searched it for evidence of the hasty burials of Danite victims."[190] Doesn't that make your blood run cold? The General found no evidence, but

A. W. Babbit practically confessed everything when he caustically pointed out to the General that it would be silly to bury victims right on the banks of the Mississippi with the river right next door. Which of course proves that Rockwell threw his victims into the river.[191]

"Porter's first murder in Utah" is another creation *ex nihilo*, Kelly and Birney basing their case on two points, (1) that the victim was "supposed by the Mormons" to have been once a member of the Illinois mob at Carthage, and that "even to be suspected of such complicity was sufficient to seal any man's death warrant," and (2) to this useful General Principle is joined the *concrete evidence*, that many later emigrants to Utah have actually seen the place where the murder took place! If that is not enough, Slater and Nelson (our authors' informants), claim that some of those emigrants actually *told them personally* of having seen the place![192]

How can you doubt after that? The Gunnison atrocity "was charged to the Indians," and indeed proven against them, "but to this day," Kelly and Birney remind us, "gossip in Utah alleges that Rockwell and the Danites participated in the slaughter."[193] Mormon gossip? What were Gentiles doing on the lower Sevier? To prove that the gossip is well founded, Kelly and Birney note that the killers "carried away all the maps, instruments, and written records of the survey party—articles which were absolutely of no value to savages." But the fact that "all of the stolen material was afterwards recovered"[194] fails to suggest to our sleuths that the stuff was obviously of no use to the men who took it—they made no effort to divide it up, hide it, sell it, or use it, as white men would have done.

The most revealing commentary on the art of creating Danites out of nothing is Kelly and Birney's last chapter. A few examples: "More than thirty years ago the Society of Friends spent several hundred thousand dollars on a large irrigation project on the Sevier River. Nothing re-

mains of that endeavor but an abandoned schoolhouse.
. . . The gentle Quakers were taken 'over the rim' by Porter
Rockwell's ghost."[195] Just what is the charge here—that
Porter Rockwell, dead for over twenty years, attacked the
Quakers? That they were assassinated? That the Mormons
wrecked their project? Here the critics show their hand—
this is the quality of their vaunted historical objectivity.
Writing as of the year 1934, they say,

> Constant vigilance has made of the Gentile residents
> of Utah a tribe of congenital hypocrites. . . . Throats are
> no longer slit, but the very few who do not tremble in
> the Shadow of the Sword can be counted upon the fin-
> gers of a one-armed man. . . . With but one notable ex-
> ception no Gentile cleric dares speak of the Mormon
> hierarchy in any but the most cordial terms; the Shadow
> of the Sword lies athwart their pulpits.[196]

Here the line of reasoning is simple and direct: If even the
Gentiles will not sustain their awful charges against the
Mormons, then the Gentiles one and all, "with but one
notable exception," are simply liars and hypocrites.

"In the good old days," our guides assure us, "the Salt
Lake City daily *Tribune* was frankly, rabidly, courageously,
and joyously anti-Mormon, . . . but it received the surgical
attentions of the ghost of Porter Rockwell." Next the *Telegram* "sold out to the ghost of the Danite chieftain."[197]
What is all this talk about ghosts? This free play between
unbridled imagination and positive assertion is the trick
behind every successful anti-Mormon book. It is Ann Eliza's trump card in dealing with the Danites:

> Yet the *spirit* of assassination still remains; and *were*
> it unchecked, hundreds *would* be . . . sent into eternity
> without a moment's warning, for no crime at all except
> for daring to differ, if ever so slightly, from those in
> authority.[198]
> He . . . *longs for a return of the days when one word of
> his would* have put a summary and permanent end to

the existence of this sheet, by the utter annihilation of everything and everybody connected with it. But the time is forever past when the "unsheathing of his bowie-knife," or the "crooking of his little finger," pronounced sentence upon offenders.[199]

The technique is always the same; the protasis is discreetly contrary-to-fact, but the apodosis is so vivid and horrible that the reader easily forgets that detail in his emotional involvement. The classic example of this is Ann Eliza's great Danite sermon:

> If *anyone* became tired of Mormonism, or impatient of the increasing despotism of the leader, and returned to the East, or started to do so, he *inevitably* was met by the Indians and killed before he had gone very far. The effect was to discourage apostasy, and there was *no one* but knew that the *moment* he announced his intention of leaving Zion . . . he pronounced his death sentence.

There was admittedly *no evidence* for any of this:

> The faces were as friendly that he met every day, the voices just as kind; his hand was shaken at parting, and there was *not a touch* of warning or sarcasm in the "God speed" and *bon voyage*. But HE KNEW he was a lucky man if in less than twenty-four hours after leaving Salt Lake City, he was not lying face downward on the cold earth, shot to death by an unerring rifle ball, while the stars looked sorrowfully down [etc.], . . . and a man rode swiftly cityward, carrying the news of the midnight murder to his master. . . . "Ah, poor fellow; killed by the Indians," said all his friends; but Brigham Young and Bill Hickman or 'Port' Rockwell KNEW better.[200]

We don't need the mention of Hickman to tell us where this comes from. Notice that the purpose of this system is "to discourage apostasy," while the potential apostates were all told—and believed—that it was the doing of Indians, thereby defeating the purpose of the whole operation. Notice also that the proof rests on the leading verb, which is always what somebody *thought*: There is no evidence whatever for the doings of the Danites except what the victim knows and what Brigham and Hickman know. The murder she talks about is the murder that the victim knew he would be lucky to escape if he ever became tired of Mormonism. So with the Mountain Meadows Massacre: "Young as I was, I *felt* the mystery that shrouded the whole transaction, I *knew instinctively*" what even her parents did not suspect — and she thirteen years old.

If "any stranger in the city" by "his words or actions displeased the Mormon spies," according to Ann Eliza, "he never got far beyond the city limits."[201] Her witness for this is a visiting intellectual, Mr. Langford, who *"felt sure* that if one word in disparagement, or criticism, of the Mormon people, or their religion, had crossed his lips, he would have been a dead man."[202] Again the inner voice. But what if somebody in Salt Lake was a well-behaved visitor or a member in good standing, wouldn't he be safe then? Not a bit of it! "If no other charge could be brought against a person, he was called a 'spy'; and this, of course, gave sufficient reason for putting him out of the way very summarily."[203]

As we review the charges (they are too long to repeat here),[204] we are forced to the astonishing conclusion that, according to Mr. Wallace's guide, for many years in Utah (seven at the very least), if a person was a Gentile he was immediately killed; if he was an apostate he was immediately killed; if he was weak in the faith, he was immediately killed; if he was merely suspected of being weak in the faith, he was immediately killed; if he "dared to neglect the counsel of the Priesthood," he "was at once charged with apostasy" and immediately killed; if he "committed even the most trifling offense to *any* member of the priesthood [including each and every male in the church above the age of eleven], he was immediately killed; if no charge of apostasy or deviation could be brought, he would still be accused of being a spy and instantly killed; if he was a casual visitor or transient and let slip one uncomplimentary word, he was immediately killed. Joseph Smith taught his people "openly that it was their duty to 'destroy in the flesh' all upon whom the leaders of the church frowned."[205] Her proof of this is Doctrine and Covenants 132:26, which has nothing to do with the case. Brigham Young, in turn, "set at nought all morality with his horrible and debasing teachings . . . the *duty* of assassination."[206]

Insanity is no word for it. Are these people telling the truth or aren't they? Is this a likely situation? Do you find it appealing, or convincing? For people living on the narrowest margin of survival, as the Mormons were in the 1850s and 1860s, this doctrine seems singularly weak in survival value; what would such a policy do to any society? It seems even weaker in its human appeal. Murder the order of the day year after year? People think nothing of it? We wonder. The vast majority of these people in Utah were recent emigrants from Northern Europe, where the too frequent assassination of one's neighbors was frowned on, at least in the straight-laced nineteenth century. Why no protest from them? Why were the Mormons, to whom the liquidation of Gentiles and apostates was a sacred duty, never proud of their Danites? Why are none of their exploits known or praised by the Saints? Surely such a dedicated and efficient band must have at sometime performed some useful service *besides* murder during the years when there was so much else to be done. The fact that they never appear, either in times of crisis or in those parades of which the Mormons were so fond, is, to say the least, a suspicious one.

Finally our own Mr. Wallace has caught the Danite spirit and carried on the fine old tradition. If Ann Eliza is weak enough to admit that Joseph Smith always denounced the Danites or that Porter Rockwell did not shoot

Boggs, Wallace charitably and quietly overlooks such slips; and if she fails to detect Danites where Danites might have been, he obligingly corrects the oversight. We refer the reader to Ann Eliza's account of the vivid terror of her first night in the Walker House, where she expected every moment to be murdered in her bed by the *Gentiles* because she was a Mormon.[207] Since she had been running a boarding-house for Gentiles only and had been intimately closeted with some of the leading Gentiles of the territory for some time as they worked out their plots against Brigham Young, the lady's naiveté, though touching, is preposterous—she is prevaricating. As if that were not enough, however, Mr. Wallace improves on her story. As he tells it, she starts out fearing the Gentiles, but then, sometime during the night, shifts her ground to "fantasied strangulation at the hands of one of Brigham's fanatical Danites."[208] "Her image of death . . . shifted from faceless Gentile to familiar Mormon. No Danite, she decided in terror, would allow her to remain alive in this hostile hotel or to escape Utah Territory."[209] All this is strictly Wallace's invention; how the Danites become a reality and acquire familiar Mormon faces only in the mind of Ann Eliza is mirrored in the eery depths of his own.

This clever devising is promptly underpinned by another slick invention: "Ann Eliza knew by heart many of the public threats Brigham Young had thundered forth from the Tabernacle pulpit against apostates, those who had forsaken the faith." And to his erudite definition of an apostate he appends one threat which "she particularly recollected" (though how he knows that he does not tell us): "The time is coming when justice will be laid to the line and righteousness to the plummet: when we shall take the old broadsword, and ask, 'Are you for God?' and if you are not heartily on the Lord's side, you will be hewn down."[210] Did Brigham Young actually own a line, plummet, and broadsword? Even the Destroying Angels are strictly biblical, and that broadsword which suggests such horrendous cuttings-off to our authors is entirely figurative, like Heber C. Kimball's sieve. Christians, Jews, and Moslems have always promised a dismal fate to apostates — what religion does not? It remains for Mr. Wallace to demonstrate that Brigham Young's warnings had anything to do with threats of physical violence. The policy in dealing with apostates is stated clearly and often in Brigham Young's sermons: there were to be no hard feelings (even Ann Eliza makes that clear),[211] and, if requested, substantial assistance in getting back home or out to California was forthcoming.

But to show that he is being fair and noble, Wallace next concedes that "it was unlikely that Brigham Young would have dared, or even desired, to send an assassin into a bedroom of Walker House to garrote or knife his twenty-seventh wife." Which gives the reader a pretty fair idea of how the man would operate if he had a free hand. Having made this dangerous concession, however, our author retrieves the situation by the neatest coup of all: "Yet nothing was utterly impossible on that still rough and paranoiac frontier."[212] If nothing was impossible, or rather, to make a double hedge, if nothing was *utterly* impossible, then the question of evidence becomes a mere quibble — there *could* be Danites after all! "Moreover," our eager informant hastens on, "there was every evidence that the Mormons had maintained, in their earlier days . . . and perhaps still in Utah . . . a special secret-service force to frighten off or even dispose of dangerous enemies of the Church."[213] The feeble "perhaps" pulls the props out from under "every evidence," but every evidence is pretty strong; let us by all means have a look at every evidence, which is conveniently contained in the very next paragraph, taken from J. C. Bennett and John Hyde: "Certainly, in 1838 . . . the Mormons had formed a 'death society,' as Elder John Hyde labeled it."[214] John Hyde was not an elder but a bitter apostate, and the "death society" was indeed his invention. Nothing more clearly betrays the fraudulence of reports about Wallace's "special service" than the bewildering variety of fantastic names attributed to it by their authors, among whom there is no agreement. Mr. Wallace, magisterially discoursing on a number of these, can tell us how they chose first one name and then another, until "the Sons of Dan, soon shortened to Danites, was permanently adopted."[215] How does he know all this? Well, how do the others come by *their* information? Never mind, there is "every evidence . . . *perhaps*" for Danites in the halls of the Walker House. Is anything utterly impossible?

With the reader thus dazed and off-balance, Wallace follows through with elan. How glibly he next describes Porter Rockwell as a paid assassin, "a long-haired man who was said to have shot the governor of Missouri"![216] He does not even have the fairness of Ann Eliza to mention that Rockwell was proven to have been far from the scene of the *attempted* assassination of an *ex*-governor—but mentions just enough of the affair to justify without evidence the title of paid assassin. The next step is obvious, as Wallace reports that under Rockwell and Hickman, "who published his confessions of mayhem in a paperback book in 1870, the Danite idea seemed to survive the exodus west."[217] The Danite *idea*? *Seemed* to survive? How conveniently vague and noncommittal—and yet how shivery! Next the appeal to Horace Greeley and his G.I.'s to give "some credence to the continuing rumors of threat and violence."[218] But Greeley, as we have seen, was reporting army-camp rumors of the 1850s—does that put the Danites on the trail of Ann Eliza in 1873?

To keep the Danite image alive, Mr. Wallace tells how the ward teachers were admitted to Ann Eliza's hotel room, "after being properly screened, no doubt, and it being ascertained that they were not Danites."[219] That canny "no doubt" pretty well takes care of the evidence. No one ever mentions the fact that while Ann Eliza Young barricaded herself in the hotel for two months, she spent more than *five* months in the city after moving to the Walker House — from July 15 to November 27. Where were the ever-vigilant Danites during those other three months? Why were they so easily eluded on the night of the Great Escape? Well, they weren't — aren't we reminded that "even then, the 'Danites' . . . might be upon our track"?[220] Still no Danite materialized or any sign of a Danite — an inefficient crowd to say the least. But Mr. Wallace, for all the rampant absurdities that surround him, still clings loyally and tenaciously to his precious Danites, reminding us that his heroine *"considered* her peril real," and that *"possibly* it *may* have been."[221] What can one say in the face of such dedication?

But then we are puzzled by this. Why do Ann Eliza and her spiritual Eckermann, Mr. Wallace, heave such a sigh of relief once the lady has chugged across the boundary at 22 m.p.h.? "Ahead lay Wyoming and freedom." Freedom from the Danites? Wasn't Wyoming a pretty "rough and paranoiac frontier" too? Weren't there Mormons even there? What on earth was there to hinder the Danites, those past masters in the art of "Indian" attacks and "accidents," from operating as freely beyond the Utah Territory as within it? The world had lent a willing ear when William Smith, the brother of Joseph Smith, no less, had reported,

> They are in every town and city throughout the whole of the United States, and . . . their object is not known by the people; . . . they are all over the world; . . . there are thousands of them; and . . . the life of every officer that comes here [to Utah] is in the hands of the Danites; . . . even the President of the United States is not safe; for, at one wink from Brigham, the Danites will be upon him and kill him.[222]

In all their thousands of murders, moreover, they were

never caught red-handed — not once! They were that clever and efficient.

With a record like that, and granting Mr. Wallace's useful thesis that "*nothing* was utterly impossible," and Mrs. Young's announcement that the Danites *could* be anywhere, our heroine wouldn't have had one chance in a million if things were as she and Wallace say they were. Unless the Danites were a myth, Ann Eliza never could have gotten out of Utah or spent long years unguarded on the road and all over the country. When she visited Utah to lecture against the Mormons, then of course Brigham would not dare let anything happen to her (Wallace generously concedes that); but what about the rest of the time? She was as safe as anybody else, and she knew it.

Was Brigham Young a shrewd operator, or wasn't he? If we would believe honest Judge Harding, "Brigham Young is no fanatic; it is nonsense to say that a man of his coldness, executive ability, and acuteness, can be fooled by such stuff as makes his system. When they talk to me about a man like Brigham believing such fooleries, I can only adopt the saying of Bill Hickman, 'All rabbit-tracks! All rabbit-tracks!' "[223] The ladies would agree that Brigham Young was not the true believer but the complete opportunist. Now it takes no administrative genius to foresee, what H. H. Bancroft has pointed out,[224] that the Mormons had nothing whatever to gain and everything to lose by the Mountain Meadows Massacre, which, occurring when it did, would give the people of the United States the very thing they had been looking for so long — a real case against the Mormons. Nothing could be more obvious than that.

Nothing could be more idiotic, therefore, than the thesis that Brigham Young himself worked out the whole suicidal operation, unless it is Mr. Wallace's announcement that Brigham Young "infected his underlings with fighting fever," and by keeping his people in a state of perpetual hysteria he "made possible Mountain Meadows."[225] What would be gained by such a policy? In 1857 Brigham Young was playing fearful odds and knew it: he won the game by iron self-control. It was the year of the crickets, the drought, and the worst Indian wars of all, and, to top it off, a full-scale invasion by the U.S. Army. And this was the time, according to Mr. Wallace, that Brigham Young chose for his senseless swashbuckling, his insane and pointless ranting, driving his overburdened people to follow a course of crime and sure self-destruction. Such historic insight is only matched by Wallace himself in his production of the Great Nauvoo Bacchanalia.

One wonders at times if all this nonsense might not have suggested some interesting parallels to Mr. Wallace. There is far more and better evidence for the killing of the Holy Child of La Guardia by the Jews in 1428 than there is for the doings of the Danites; yet what does examination of the evidence show? That "the child of La Guardia never existed."[226] High officials of church and state accused the Jews of the Damascus ritual murders of 1841 — which were completely fictitious. Volumes of impressive testimony to numerous other ritual murders carried out by the Jews in various countries have been published,[227] and the belief that "Jews require the blood of human beings for ritual purposes persists to this day."[228] The scandalous trial of Mendel Beilliss in 1913 should have exposed the fraudulence of charges once and for all, but the Poles and then the Nazis revived the issue, bringing out long and important-looking legal reports to prove their case. When evidence is lacking, resort is readily had to the teachings of the Jews to prove the worst. What of the Protocols of the Elders of Zion? What about the dreaded Stern gang? Didn't the Jews teach openly the "Expiation of the Polluted Land"?[229] There's blood atonement for you! Wasn't there a warning inscription in the Temple at Jerusalem threatening death to all non-Jews?[230] Haven't the Jews been known to pray openly for vengeance on their enemies? Horrible! Horrible!

And against all that—and we have not even scratched the surface—Mr. Wallace waves excitedly one dingy little paperback of 1870, written by an impoverished hack for an old drunk who had been nursing a deadly hatred of Brigham Young for years, but hadn't enough solid information even to help out poor Governor Harding.

Such is the baseless fabric of the Danite vision which has served so long as the solid bedrock of the Mormon atrocity stories. This writer cannot claim Mr. Wallace's Olympian aloofness and majestic impartiality where Brigham Young is concerned, for he accepts the man as a prophet and his religion as divine. He feels accordingly that such stories as are being circulated abroad today should not go unchallenged and submits that the foregoing inquiry, however inadequate and unworthy of the theme, justifies the suspicion that those stories do not always rest on a foundation of truth.

Notes to Part 5

1. Charles Kelly and Hoffman Birney, *Holy Murder: The Story of Porter Rockwell* (New York: Minton, Balch, 1934), 287–88.

2. *JD* 5:77.

3. Ann Eliza (Webb) Young, *Wife No. 19; Or, The Story of a Life of Bondage, Being a Complete Exposé of Mormonism, and Revealing the Sorrows, Sacrifices and Sufferings of Women in Polygamy* (Hartford, CT: Dustin, Gilman, 1875), 268.

4. Irving Wallace, *The Twenty-Seventh Wife* (New York: Simon & Schuster, 1961), 238.

5. Ibid., 28.

6. Young, *Wife No. 19*, 268–69.

7. Ibid., 34.

8. Kelly and Birney, *Holy Murder*, 23.

9. Nels Anderson, *Desert Saints: The Mormon Frontier in Utah* (Chicago: University of Chicago, 1942), 117–31.

10. Mrs. T. B. H. (Fanny) Stenhouse, *Tell It All: The Story of a Life's Experience in Mormonism* (Hartford, CT: Worthington, 1874), 169.

11. Young, *Wife No. 19,* 569.

12. Wallace, *The Twenty-Seventh Wife,* 28 (emphasis added).

13. *HC* 3:178–79.

14. Ibid., 3:179.

15. Ibid., 3:179–80.

16. Ibid., 3:180–81.

17. Ibid., 3:181.

18. Lorenzo Dow Young, *Diary and Reminiscences,* Manuscript in Church Historian's Office.

19. T. B. H. Stenhouse, *The Rocky Mountain Saints: A Full and Complete History of the Mormons, from the First Vision of Joseph Smith to the Last Courtship of Brigham Young* (New York: Appleton, 1873), 93–95.

20. Young, *Diary and Reminiscences.*

21. Ibid.

22. *HC* 3:179.

23. Young, *Diary and Reminiscences.*

24. Stenhouse, *The Rocky Mountain Saints,* 93.

25. Young, *Wife No. 19,* 48.

26. Stenhouse, *The Rocky Mountain Saints,* 91.

27. *HC* 3:180.

28. Ibid., 3:181–82.

29. Juanita Brooks, *John Doyle Lee, Zealot-Pioneer-Builder-Scapegoat* (Glendale: Clark, 1972), 32.

30. Young, *Wife No. 19,* 48.

31. *HC* 3:167.

32. Ibid.

33. Ibid.

34. Joseph Fielding Smith, Jr., *Blood Atonement and the Origin of Plural Marriage* (Salt Lake City: Deseret News, 1905), 15.

35. Kelly and Birney, *Holy Murder,* 3.

36. Ibid., 7.

37. Ibid., facing p. 46.

38. Ibid., 301.

39. Ibid., 24.

40. Ibid., 33.

41. Ibid., 48.

42. Ibid., 27.

43. Ibid., 130.

44. Ibid., 23.

45. Ibid., 130.

46. Ibid., 133.

47. Young, *Wife No. 19*, 198.

48. Kelly and Birney, *Holy Murder*, 133.

49. Ibid., 133–34.

50. Ibid., 134; Not only are Kelly and Birney imprecise with their quotation (cf. *JD* 4:49), but they also cite the wrong date!

51. *JD* 4:51.

52. *JD* 4:49.

53. Plato, *Gorgias* 509b.

54. Ibid.

55. Ibid., 480a-b.

56. Kelly and Birney, *Holy Murder*, 134; cf. *JD* 5:353.

57. Kelly and Birney, *Holy Murder*, 134.

58. *JD* 6:34.

59. Ibid., 6:35.

60. Kelly and Birney, *Holy Murder*, 130.

61. Ibid., 135.

62. *JD* 4:345.

63. Kelly and Birney, *Holy Murder*, 135–36.

64. John D. Lee, *Mormonism Unveiled: or the Life and Confessions of the Late Mormon Bishop John D. Lee, Written by Himself* (St. Louis: Mason, 1877), 273.

65. John D. Lee, *The Mormon Menace* (New York: Home Protection, 1905), 277–97.

66. Lee, *Mormonism Unveiled*, 269–86.

67. Ibid., 16.

68. Brooks, *John Doyle Lee*, 32–33.

69. Lee, *Mormonism Unveiled*, 59–60.

70. Ibid., 57.

71. Ibid.

72. Ibid.

73. Ibid., 73 (emphasis added).

74. Ibid., 74.

75. Robert G. Cleland and Juanita A. Brooks, *A Mormon Chronicle: The Diaries of John D. Lee, 1848–1876*, 2 vols. (San Marino, CA: Huntington Library, 1955), 1:XX.

76. Ibid., 1:XXIII.

77. Ibid., 1:XXVI.

78. Lee, *Mormonism Unveiled*, 159.

79. Ibid.

80. Ibid., 268.

81. Ibid., 161.

82. Ibid.

83. Ibid., 246–47.
84. Kelly and Birney, *Holy Murder,* 152–53.
85. Ibid., 246.
86. Ibid., 120–22.
87. Ibid., 122.
88. Ibid., 224–25.
89. Ibid., 49.
90. Ibid., 153 (emphasis added).
91. Ibid., 195.
92. Ibid., 37.
93. Lee, *Mormonism Unveiled,* 213.
94. Ibid., 101–2.
95. Kelly and Birney, *Holy Murder,* 137.
96. Ibid., 129.
97. Ibid., 137.
98. Ibid.
99. Ibid., 136 (emphasis added).
100. Ibid., 37 (emphasis added).
101. Ibid., 280–81.
102. Ibid., 43.
103. Stenhouse, *Tell It All,* 169.
104. Ibid., 169–70.
105. Young, *Wife No. 19,* 270–76.
106. Kelly and Birney, *Holy Murder,* facing p. 272.
107. Young, *Wife No. 19,* 277.
108. Stenhouse, *Tell It All,* 318.
109. Ibid., 319.
110. Young, *Wife No. 19,* 262.
111. Ibid., 264.
112. Ibid., 47.
113. Ibid., 48.
114. Ibid.
115. Ibid., 289.
116. *Deseret News,* 21 April 1869, 18:132.
117. Ann Eliza Young, *Life in Mormon Bondage* (Philadelphia: Aldine, 1908), 42.
118. Young, *Wife No. 19,* 263.
119. Ibid., 569.
120. Ibid., 48.
121. Stenhouse, *Tell It All,* 169.
122. Fawn M. Brodie, *No Man Knows My History* (New York: Knopf, 1946), 315.

123. Young, *Wife No. 19,* 276.

124. Ibid.

125. Wallace, *The Twenty-Seventh Wife,* 360.

126. John H. Beadle, *Life in Utah; or, the Mysteries and Crimes of Mormonism. Being an exposé of the Secret Rites and Ceremonies of the Latter-Day Saints, with a full and authentic history of Polygamy and the Mormon sect from its origin to the present time* (USA: National, 1870); reprinted as John H. Beadle, *Polygamy, or the Mysteries and Crimes of Mormonism. Being a full and authentic history of Polygamy and the Mormon sect from its origin to the present time. With a complete analysis of Mormon society and theocracy, and an exposé of the secret rites and ceremonies of the Latter-day Saints* (USA: National, 1882).

127. Ibid.

128. William Hickman, *Brigham's Destroying Angel: Being the Life, Confession, and Startling Disclosures of the Notorious Bill Hickman, the Danite Chief of Utah. Written by Himself, with explanatory notes by J. H. Beadle* (New York: Crofutt, 1872), 9.

129. Ibid., 10–11.

130. Ibid., 13.

131. Ibid.

132. Ibid., 14.

133. Ibid., 15.

134. Ibid., vii.

135. Ibid., v.

136. Ibid.

137. Young, *Wife No. 19,* 264 (emphasis added).

138. Hickman, *Brigham's Destroying Angel,* v.

139. Ibid., v–vi.

140. Ibid., vii (emphasis added).

141. Thomas Gregg, *The Prophet of Palmyra* (New York: Alden, 1890), 39.

142. Ibid., 36.

143. Ibid., 48.

144. Ibid., 52.

145. Hugh Nibley, *The Myth Makers* (Salt Lake City: Bookcraft, 1961), 57–74; reprinted in this volume, pages 103–406.

146. Gregg, *The Prophet of Palmyra,* 56.

147. Anderson, *Desert Saints,* 222.

148. *The National Cyclopaedia of American Biography,* 63 vols. (New York: White, 1907), 5:515.

149. Kelly and Birney, *Holy Murder,* 113–14.

150. Hickman, *Brigham's Destroying Angel,* 215.

151. *JD* 8:143.

152. Hickman, *Brigham's Destroying Angel*, 214.

153. Wallace, *The Twenty-Seventh Wife*, 29–30.

154. Ibid., 30.

155. Ibid.

156. Ibid.

157. Brooks, *John Doyle Lee*, 30.

158. William Swartzell, *Mormonism Exposed, Being a Journal of a Residence in Missouri from the 28th of May to the 20th of August, 1838* (Pekin: Swartzell, 1840), iii.

159. Ibid., 9–10.

160. Ibid., 10.

161. Ibid., 11.

162. Ibid., 15.

163. Ibid.

164. Ibid., 17.

165. Ibid.

166. Ibid., 18.

167. Ibid., 17.

168. Ibid., 19–20.

169. Ibid., 21.

170. Ibid.

171. Ibid., 22.

172. Ibid.

173. Ibid., 23.

174. Ibid., 22.

175. Ibid., 24–25.

176. Ibid., 25.

177. Ibid., 25–26.

178. Ibid., 28 (emphasis added).

179. Ibid., 33.

180. Ibid., 35.

181. Ibid., 36 (emphasis added).

182. Stenhouse, *The Rocky Mountain Saints*, 88–95.

183. Ibid., 78–79 (see footnotes).

184. Ibid., 93.

185. Kelly and Birney, *Holy Murder*, 63.

186. Cassie H. Hock, "The Mormons in Fiction," Ph.D. diss., University of Colorado, 1941, 38.

187. Ruth Kauffman and Reginald W. Kauffman, *The Latter Day Saints* (London: Williams and Norgate, 1912), 76.

188. Kelly and Birney, *Holy Murder*, 23.

189. Ibid., 77.
190. Ibid.
191. Ibid., 77–78.
192. Ibid., 101.
193. Ibid., 109.
194. Ibid.
195. Ibid., 289.
196. Ibid., 290–91.
197. Ibid., 291–92.
198. Young, *Wife No. 19,* 263 (emphasis added).
199. Ibid., 520 (emphasis added).
200. Ibid., 161 (emphasis added).
201. Ibid., 264.
202. Ibid., 266 (emphasis added).
203. Ibid., 278.
204. The reader can find some representative examples in ibid., 75, 264, 273, 278.
205. Ibid., 81.
206. Stenhouse, *Tell It All,* 273.
207. Young, *Wife No. 19,* 547–48.
208. Wallace, *The Twenty-Seventh Wife,* 238.
209. Ibid., 28.
210. Ibid.
211. Young, *Wife No. 19,* 161.
212. Wallace, *The Twenty-Seventh Wife,* 28.
213. Ibid.
214. Ibid., 28–29.
215. Ibid., 29.
216. Ibid.
217. Ibid.
218. Ibid.
219. Ibid., 247.
220. Young, *Wife No. 19,* 569.
221. Wallace, *The Twenty-Seventh Wife,* 274 (emphasis added).
222. *JD* 4:345.
223. Hickman, *Brigham's Destroying Angel,* 217.
224. H. H. Bancroft, *Works,* 26 vols. (San Francisco: The History Company, 1889), 26:544.
225. Wallace, *The Twenty-Seventh Wife,* 117.
226. Isidore Loeb, "Le Saint Enfant de la Guardia," *Revue des Etudes Juives* 15 (1887): 232.
227. Salomon Reinach, "Des Persécutions des Juifs," *Revue des*

Etudes 25 (1892): 161–80; Isidore Loeb, "A Calomnie du Meurtre Rituel," *Revue des Etudes* 18 (1889): 179–211; Harry Schneiderman, "The Ritual Murder Libel," *Jewish Quarterly Review* 27 (1936–37): 179–87.

228. Schneiderman, "The Ritual Murder Libel," 179.

229. Raphael Patai, "The ʿEgla ʿArufa or the Expiation of the Polluted Land," *Jewish Quarterly Review* 30 (1939–40): 59–60.

230. Elias J. Bickerman, "The Warning Inscriptions of Herod's Temple," *Jewish Quarterly Review* 37 (1946–47): 387–88.

Index of Passages

Index

Abbott, John S. C., 70, 201, 237
"Achilles" (anti-Mormon book),
  659–60
Adams, Charles Francis, 180
Adams, John Quincy, Reverend,
  59, 73, 140, 199, 237
Adultery, Joseph Smith accused
  of, 318–19
Affidavits against Joseph Smith,
  107
Aiken party, murder of, 683, 687
American Whig Review, 67
Andrews, Mrs. Milo, 680
Angell, Mary Ann, 547–49, 626
Angels: power of reaping
  committed to, 91; dictionary
  definition of, 93; Jehovah and
  Elohim categorized as, 93
Animal sacrifice connected to
  money-digging, 211–14
Anti-Mormon book writers, rules
  for: avoiding modesty, 474;
  criticizing predecessors, 474–
  76; acknowledging helpers,
  476; proclaiming purity of
  motives, 476–79; proclaiming
  love for Mormons, 479–80;
  furnishing documents, 480–84;
  avoiding footnotes in favor of
  appendix, 484–86; dropping
  names, 487–88; controlling
  sources, 488–90; waiving
  credentials, 490; establishing

intellectual ascendancy, 491–
  92; selling something new,
  492–93; having an inside
  track, 493–94; avoiding
  questions, 494–95; replacing
  evidence with rhetoric, 495–
  99; using lack of evidence,
  499–501; using unfulfilled
  condition, 501–2; using hints,
  502–3; using quotation marks
  without sources, 503–4;
  reading minds, 504–5; being
  cute, 505–7; creating
  atmosphere, 507–10; attacking
  image rather than reality, 510–
  13; using "unequal
  scholarship," 513–15; using
  literary license, 515–20; using
  loaded and emotive words,
  520–21; citing gossip as fact,
  521–28; preserving gap
  between subject and
  audience, 528–32; employing
  discreet omissions, 532–37;
  relating atrocities, 537–39;
  revising old stories, 539–49;
  being patriotic, 549–50;
  aligning with women, 550–53;
  targeting Mormonism itself,
  553–56; being former "good
  Mormons," 556–57
Anti-Mormonism: Joseph Smith's
  "firsthand acquaintance